BELIEVING and CONFESSING

365 Meditations on the Belgic Confession

REFORMED
FREE PUBLISHING
ASSOCIATION
Jenison, Michigan

©2023 Reformed Free Publishing Association

Meditations: Covenant Evangelical Reformed Church

11, Jalan Mesin #04-00
Standard Industrial Building
Singapore 368813
https://www.cerc.org.sg/clm_dm.php

All rights reserved.

Adapted for publication and printed with permission.

Printed in the United States of America.

No part of this publication may be reproduced, stored in a retrieval system, or transmitted in any form or by any means—electronic, mechanical, photocopying, recording, or otherwise—without the prior written permission of the publisher. The only exception is brief quotations in printed reviews.

Scripture cited is taken from the King James (Authorized) Version. Italics in Scripture quotations reflect the authors' emphasis.

Cover design: Amy Zevenbergen
Interior design: Katherine Lloyd, The DESK

Reformed Free Publishing Association
1894 Georgetown Center Drive
Jenison, Michigan 49428
616-457-5970
mail@rfpa.org
www.rfpa.org

ISBN 9781944555696
Ebook ISBN 9781944555702
LCCN 2023941000

BELIEVING and CONFESSING

January 1 — **Introduction to the Belgic Confession**

The Belgic Confession is one of the four best-known Reformation-inspired confessions: the Belgic Confession, the Heidelberg Catechism, the Canons of Dordrecht, and the Westminster Confession of Faith. It is part of the creedal basis for Reformed Churches around the world.

The Belgic Confession was written by an itinerant preacher named Guido de Brès. He left Roman Catholicism and preached the truths of the Reformation with great courage in the Lowlands, comprised of what is now Holland, Belgium, and Luxemburg. The date of the Confession is 1561, a date that places this confession as the first of the four mentioned above.

The occasion for the Confession was the bitter persecution of Protestants in the Lowlands by the cruel Roman Catholic Church. The Spaniards especially, under whose rule the people in the Lowlands lived, were the agents of persecution. The excuse for persecution was that the Protestants were rebels in the kingdom and enemies of the authority of their rulers. The confession was written to prove this charge to be false: the Protestants were no rebels guilty of treason but were lowly people of God who would obey their rulers in all things except what was contrary to the will of God revealed in the Scriptures.

They were determined to be faithful to their God and were ready to "offer their backs to stripes, their tongues to knives, their mouths to gags, and their whole bodies to the fire, well knowing that those who follow Christ must take his cross and deny themselves"* rather than deny the truth of God's word, expressed in this confession. The confession breathes the spirit of martyrdom.

Guido de Brès wrote the confession to show that those who opposed the doctrines of the Roman Catholic Church were not guilty of treason but were only being faithful to Scripture, and therefore their persecution was unjust. In 1562, a copy was sent to the Spanish king with the hope and prayer that persecution would be eased. But King Philip II paid no attention to the plea. Guido de Brès himself was a martyr; he was publicly hanged when he was forty-seven years old.

The Confession treats the truths of Scripture systematically, following the order in the six loci of Dogmatics: Theology, Anthropology, Christology, Soteriology, Ecclesiology, Eschatology.

It is a living testimony of the power of faith in the lives of the people of God and a living record of the truth for which they died. May that same courage of faith be ours.

Herman Hanko

---

* Quoted in Philip Schaff, ed., *The Creeds of Christendom with a History and Critical Notes*, 6th ed., 3 vols. (New York: Harper and Row, 1931; repr., Grand Rapids, MI: Baker Books, 2007), 1:505. Unless otherwise specified, all the quotations of the Belgic Confession that appear in this book are from Schaff, *Creeds of Christendom*, 3:383-436.

Article 1

THERE IS ONE ONLY GOD

We all believe with the heart, and confess with the mouth, that there is one only simple and spiritual Being, which we call God; and that he is eternal, incomprehensible, invisible, immutable, infinite, almighty, perfectly wise, just, good, and the overflowing fountain of all good.

January 2 — Our Faith in the One True God

Read: Isaiah 40:21–28

The Belgic Confession properly and importantly begins with the truth concerning God. All the faith of believers begins with God and ends with God. It begins with God because all the truth is only what God himself has said about himself: his divine being, his attributes, his works that he performs. And all the truth ends with God, because all the truth is revealed by God so that God may receive all the glory that is due to himself alone.

The world is full of theologies, but they are theologies that are about many things other than God. Arminianism is man-centered and talks only about what man can do to save himself, thus robbing God of his glory. A social theology is concerned with making this world a better place to live, a sort of heaven here on earth. A prosperity gospel is interested only in telling people how to become rich in this world's goods. And so the list goes on. The truth that is confessed, if it is based on Scripture, is God-centered. It is about God.

Calvin was accused of being drunk with God. He never considered that remark to be an insult, but readily acknowledged that he was interested only in God and his glory. *Soli Deo Gloria* was his motto.

Only if we begin and end with God will we also be guarded from error. If one has the doctrine of God correct, as that doctrine is taught in the holy Scriptures, he will never stray from the path of truth. But the opposite is also true: if one strays in any doctrine of Scripture, one says something wrong about God as well.

Although the Confession deals with many different doctrines—in fact, with all the doctrines of Scripture—all these doctrines are only different aspects of the truth concerning God. The Bible is, after all, the infallibly inspired record of the revelation of God who seeks always and only the glory of his great and holy name.

Let us also seek the glory of God in our thoughts as we contemplate the wonders of what God has done and as we seek to understand the truth revealed in the Scriptures. Many, not understanding well the central truth concerning God, plead for less doctrine and more practical teaching. This is wrong. The knowledge of God is eternal life and therefore everlasting blessedness. The Belgic Confession is intended to say to all the world: "These truths are the truths of Scripture and of our salvation. For them we are ready to die."

Herman Hanko

January 3 — Confessing and Believing the Truth of God

Read: Romans 10

What the church confesses to be the truth of God, the church also believes with its heart and confesses with its mouth. The reference here is to Romans 10:9. The truth of God is what "we all believe in the heart, and confess with the mouth."

We believe this truth, not as we believe a history book—that is, that the facts in the book actually happened—but we believe in our hearts. We believe that we know the God revealed in the Scriptures to be our God and covenant friend.

We know God through Jesus Christ, for God has given us an infallible record of his revelation in Jesus Christ. God is revealed, therefore, as the God of our salvation in his own Son.

But when we know Christ through the Scriptures, the infallible record of God's revelation in Christ, then it is not as if we know about him as we would know about a famous person from a biography of him; but we know Jesus Christ personally and experientially so that we have fellowship with him, and, through him, with God.

Believing the truth of God's word, we confess it with our mouths. We cannot be silent about that which we believe with our hearts, for such a belief is more important to us than anything else, and we want all the world to know about it.

It is true that the Belgic Confession was written to prove to the Roman Catholic persecutors of the churches in the Lowlands that what they believed was Biblical doctrine and not treasonous propaganda. But the fact remains that the believer cannot help but bear witness of his faith. He is excited about it, moved by the wonder of it, thankful that God has, through Christ, saved him, an undeserving sinner. We may very well ask ourselves the question whether this excitement and wonder are true of us, for frequently we take what we believe for granted.

But the believer also knows that he is called by God to be a witness to the world of the faith he holds dear. So he confesses that truth. He confesses it with his mouth and with his life. Even when he knows that the consequences of his confession will be persecution, he does not waver in his confession.

May God give us all the grace to be faithful witnesses.

Herman Hanko

January 4 — God Is One God

Read: Deuteronomy 6:1–6

Article 1 of the Belgic Confession speaks of all of God's attributes. The first attribute is found in the words: "there is one only simple and spiritual Being, which we call God."

God is, first of all, a spiritual being. He is not material as is this world in which we live, nor is he spiritual in the sense that heaven and all the creatures in heaven are spiritual. Heaven is not made up of material substance nor filled with material creatures. We cannot see heaven, nor can we see angels. We could not see heaven even if we were in heaven, unless we were changed. Angels can be seen only when they appear, that is, take on a form that makes them visible to us men.

But God is not even spiritual in the sense of heavenly things. While this is totally beyond our understanding, God is pure spirit. Even those in heaven cannot see God, though they are spirits, too. God is seen in heaven only when he reveals himself in Jesus Christ. "Now unto the King eternal, immortal, invisible, the only wise God, be honour and glory for ever and ever. Amen" (1 Tim. 1:17).

John 4:24 teaches us how we must worship in such a way that the greatness of God is preserved in our worship: "God is a Spirit [better translated, "God is Spirit"]: and they that worship him must worship him in spirit and in truth." We are able to know him because we are created with a spirit (1 Thess. 5:23).

The article also mentions God's attribute of simplicity: "There is only one simple and spiritual Being." God's simplicity means, first, that he is the only God. This was written against all polytheism, which teaches that there are many gods or that there is one god who becomes many different gods.

But if God is all-powerful, there cannot be two gods, for there cannot be two all-powerful beings.

Further, God's simplicity means that God is not composed of parts and he cannot be divided into parts. God must not be defined as being three in person with each person possessing one third of the divine being. Nor are God's attributes characteristics of different parts of God. God's attributes are one. His mercy is his justice. His love is his grace. He is one simple being.

No wonder when we pray to such a great God, we bow in reverence and fear before him.

Herman Hanko

January 5 — God Is Eternal

Read: Isaiah 40:12–31

When I attended grammar school, my teacher tried to teach us the difference between time and eternity. She drew a circle on the blackboard and said that the circle represented eternity because the line that composed the circle was without beginning and without end. But when she explained time, she drew two lines through the line that made a circle and said: "This is time, for the arc has a beginning and an end."

I didn't like the illustration very much when she used it, and I like it still less now. Time is not a segment of eternity. Eternity is fundamentally different from time. It is true that eternity is without beginning and without end, while time has a beginning and an end. But God is the creator of time and is not bound by time. We are creatures of time who cannot escape from it.

God, the Eternal One, is changeless, while we, creatures of time, change. "Time, like an ever-rolling stream, bears all its sons away,"* we sing in Psalm 90. Or, to quote an old poet: "Change and decay in all around I see; O Thou who changest not, abide with me."**

We cannot comprehend eternity, for we are too bound by the chains of time. We cannot conceive of someone who has no beginning and no end. But the wonder of salvation for us is that we shall be given an inheritance in heaven that is truly everlasting; it has no end—although it does have a beginning.

We tend to confuse eternal and everlasting, but this is a mistake. Only God is eternal; our life in heaven is everlasting.

God created time, and God is the sovereign ruler of time. God controls time sovereignly and so controls all that happens in time. Although the Scriptures say that in heaven time shall be no more, this does not mean that we become eternal. "Eternal" is an attribute of God that we shall never possess.

God's eternity makes him so much different from the creature that he is worthy of all our praise. We serve and love a God who is not made with human hands, as the idols of the heathen are, but is the only Eternal One. He alone must be worshipped and served.

Herman Hanko

---

* No. 247:5, in *The Psalter with Doctrinal Standards, Liturgy, Church Order, and added Chorale Section*, reprinted and revised edition of the 1912 United Presbyterian Psalter (Grand Rapids, MI: Wm. B. Eerdmans Publishing Co., 1927; rev. ed. 1995).

** From the hymn "Abide With Me," by Henry Francis Lyte (1793–1847).

January 6 — God Is Incomprehensible

Read: Romans 11:33–36

Although the sacred Scriptures are the infallible record of God's revelation to us, given so that we may know him, the Scriptures also constantly remind us that what we know of God is very little, for he is infinitely greater than his own revelation in the Scriptures.

Job says: "Behold, God is great, and we know him not, neither can the number of his years be searched out" (Job 36:26).

Isaiah proclaims in wonder at God's own word concerning himself: "Hast thou not known? hast thou not heard, that the everlasting God, the Lord, the Creator of the ends of the earth, fainteth not, neither is weary? there is no searching of his understanding" (Isa. 40:28).

God's word through Jeremiah is: "Am I a God at hand, saith the Lord, and not a God afar off? Can any hide himself in secret places that I shall not see him? saith the Lord. Do not I fill heaven and earth? saith the Lord" (Jer. 23:23–24). And Solomon prayed at the dedication of the temple: "The heaven and heaven of heavens cannot contain thee; how much less this house that I have builded?" (1 Kings 8:27).

God is so great that he is in all things, above all things, around all things, beneath all things. He is present with the whole of his being in every atom of the universe, and yet he is infinitely extending beyond his creation.

I recall the pastor of my youth frequently praying after a sermon: "Lord, we have tried to say a few things about thee. But we have only mumbled and stuttered a bit, for thou art far, far greater than our understanding of thee."

Though we shall grow in the knowledge of God into all eternity, we shall never reach an end of our search for the riches of God's blessed being. Everlasting life is not long enough to exhaust the riches of the knowledge of God. Though we know what the Scriptures say of God, our knowledge of God is less than a thimbleful of water in comparison with all the oceans and seas on the earth.

Yet, we know him—know him as our Friend, our Redeemer, our covenant God! What a wonder, for he shows us enough of himself for us to live in warm, covenant fellowship with him.

Let us exalt his holy name.

Herman Hanko

January 7 — **God Is Invisible**

Read: 1 Kings 8:22–30

In an earlier article, we touched briefly on God's invisibility. The key text for this attribute of God is 1 Timothy 1:17, "Now unto the King eternal, immortal, invisible, the only wise God, be honour and glory for ever and ever. Amen."

God's invisibility follows from his other attributes. Because God is unique in his being, he is also invisible. He is like no other creature. There is no being like his being. He is "the wholly other one." He is in a class by himself. He cannot be compared with anything. And so, he is also invisible.

We cannot see him; the angels cannot see him; the saints in heaven cannot see him. His greatness is of such a kind that no one can see him. The only way he can be seen is by his revelation of himself. He speaks about himself. He speaks about who he is, what he is like, what great works he does. And he speaks of himself in a way that we can understand him.

Calvin spoke of God's revelation as "baby-talk,"* for he is so much greater than we are that he has to come down to us and adapt his speech to our feeble and imperfect understanding.

It is common today and characteristic of the shallow and superficial religion so many people have that even ministers speak of God and to God as if they were chatting over the backyard fence with a neighbor of equal importance with themselves. They open worship services with, "Good morning, God" (or worse, "Hello, Daddy"). They throw mud on God's great majesty.

The believer is over and over again deeply impressed with God's greatness. He comes to God with fear, trembling, humility, awe, wonder, and a deep sense of God's greatness.

God reveals himself in Scripture and speaks of himself in such a simple way that we can understand what he says. But Scripture is the record of all that God does through Jesus Christ. When we read the Scriptures, we meet Jesus Christ. We come to know him as our Savior and Lord. And when we know him, we know God.

So it will be in heaven. Though God is invisible, we shall see him. But we shall see him in the face of Jesus Christ, for our Savior is both God and man in one divine person. "He that hath seen me hath seen the Father" (John 14:9).

Herman Hanko

---

* John Calvin, *Institutes of the Christian Religion*, trans. Henry Beveridge (Peabody, MA: Hendrickson Publishers, 2008), 1.13.1.

January 8 — God Is Immutable

Read: Hebrews 6:11–20

The confession that we are discussing tells us that Scripture teaches the immutability of God. That is, one of God's incommunicable attributes is his unchangeableness. The classic text in the Bible to prove this is Malachi 3:6, "For I am the Lord, I change not; therefore ye sons of Jacob are not consumed."

It is important that we confess this attribute of God, for many in our day deny it. These false teachers teach that God is changeable, and that, in fact, his attitude towards people in the world changes because he reacts to their faith or unbelief. This blasphemy of God arises out of Arminianism, an error that teaches that the final decision on the question of salvation rests with man's will. God reacts with happiness and approval or with anger depending on what man's choice is.

God is unchangeable in his own being. All his attributes also are unchangeable. It is not true that although God is just, his mercy and love override his justice and cancel it out.

Because God is unchangeable in his own divine being and attributes, he is unchangeable in his counsel. This is clearly taught in Isaiah 46:9–10, "Remember the former things of old: for I am God, and there is none else; I am God, and there is none like me, declaring the end from the beginning, and from ancient times the things that are not yet done, saying, My counsel shall stand, and I will do all my pleasure."

Because God is unchangeable in his counsel, he is unchangeable in his works of grace and love which he shows to us. Because our Lord Jesus Christ is divine as well as human, "Jesus Christ the same yesterday, and to day, and for ever" (Heb. 13:8). He is unchangeable also in his promises which he has made to establish his covenant with us and our children. And because God is unchangeable, and his promise is unchangeable, we "have a strong consolation, who have fled [to Christ] for refuge" (Heb. 6:18).

What a comfort this is, for we are fickle and changeable. Today, we pray earnestly; tomorrow, we do not pray at all. Today, we confess our sins; tomorrow, we return to them. Sometimes we are fervent, and sometimes we are cold as ice. Sometimes our love is strong, and sometimes it turns weak and hardly noticeable. But our God in Jesus Christ is the unchangeable one in all his promises to us.

Herman Hanko

January 9 — God Is Infinite

Read: Isaiah 44

God's infinity is very closely related to his other incommunicable attributes. Infinity is best understood in contrast to our finiteness.

We are, in all respects, finite. We are finite because we are creatures and completely dependent on God for everything.

To be finite means to be limited. We are limited to this creation and cannot be in heaven as well as on earth. We are limited in being in only one place at a time; we cannot be both in Singapore and in the States at the same time, nor even in Jurong and in Woodlands. We are bound by time. It takes twenty to twenty-four hours to travel by plane from Grand Rapids to Singapore. We can do only so much work within a given time, and we often say, "I ran out of time."

We are more than ever limited with the entrance of sin into the world. We are limited in what we can do because our strength is limited. We are limited in what we can see because our eyes cannot see very far and cannot penetrate objects in the way. We are limited by sickness and disease. We are limited by old age, and our limitations become very great when we are past eighty years old.

But God is not limited in any way. He is not limited by space, for he is, with the whole of his essence, present in every particle of the creation, but he is still infinitely extended beyond the entire universe. His being knows no boundaries. He is not limited by time, for he is without beginning and without end. He is the Eternal One. His counsel is eternal. In his counsel and plan, Cain eternally killed Abel. In his changeless purpose, Christ eternally died and rose again. All history is eternal and without limitation before the mind of God.

We cannot even begin to imagine God's infinity. If we could imagine what God's infinity is, then it would not be infinity anymore, for it would be limited by the limitations of our minds.

There are truths concerning God that we must not even try to understand, for in doing so with our finite minds, we destroy the infinite. We can only bow in worship and adoration before such a great God as we have. And our adoration turns to praise and thanksgiving when we believe that this God is our God.

Herman Hanko

January 10 — God Is Almighty

Read: Job 38

When we pray the Lord's prayer, we conclude the prayer with the words: "For thine is the kingdom, and the power, and the glory, for ever. Amen" (Matt. 6:13). We confess that God possesses "the power." That means that all power belongs to God. There can be no power anywhere except it be the power of God.

God's power belongs to his infinity. If God's power is infinite, so that all power is his, then God is also the only God. It is impossible that there be two powers, both infinite, both possessing all power. Therefore, God is almighty: all-mighty.

What a great God we have!

God showed his power in the work of creation. He spoke, and it came to pass. All things were formed by the word of his mouth. His power is manifested not only in the creation of this universe, but also in the creation of heaven.

God's power is everywhere present in the world every moment, for he continues to give each creature its existence. He not only created an oak tree by the word of his power, but he continues to speak that word, and that is the only reason the oak tree continues to exist.

God's absolute sovereignty is the exercise of his power, and he is sovereign over all, including wicked men and devils. The devils had to ask Christ's permission to go from the man who was devil-possessed into the pigs (Mark 5:11–13). God is sovereign, although he exercises his sovereignty over the wicked in such a way that they remain responsible for their sins.

God is almighty in his work of salvation. Our Canons of Dordt say that God's power is revealed in the work of salvation just as much as in the work of creation (Canons 3–4.12). It takes a mighty power of God to make a depraved and blaspheming sinner a praying saint. It takes a power greater than anything man possesses to change a totally depraved enemy of God to a glorious child of God. It takes a great power of God in Jesus Christ to perform the work of atonement, resurrection, and ascension by which we are saved.

God can do all things. He can do all things for you and me. He can and will do all that is necessary to make us his people.

Praise be to God!

Herman Hanko

January 11 — God Is Perfectly Wise

Read: 1 Timothy 1:17, Proverbs 8

The Belgic Confession speaks of God's wisdom as the first communicable attribute. Historically, the attributes of God have been divided between his incommunicable attributes and his communicable attributes. The former are attributes that belong to God alone; the latter are attributes that are found in man created after the image of God.

But the Confession speaks of God as being "all-wise." The meaning is that all wisdom is God's wisdom, and all wisdom possessed by man is God's wisdom.

Wisdom, if we would define it, is God's determination to seek the best possible goal for all his works, and the best possible way to attain that goal. The best possible goal for God to seek is the glory of his own name. And the best possible way to attain that goal is to reveal himself through Jesus Christ. That is why Jesus Christ is called in 1 Corinthians 1:24, "the wisdom of God."

In medieval times, Roman Catholic scholastics would argue about very strange and wrong things. They would argue about how many angels can dance on the point of a pin. They would debate whether the fact that God is almighty means that God could create two mountains without a valley in-between. They would debate whether God's wisdom means that there are an infinite number of ways in which God could have realized his own glory. Foolish questions.

The answer to all these questions is simply that God's wisdom is revealed in the highest and best possible way, and that is the way of salvation in God's own eternal Son. None of God's attributes can be exercised in such a way that their exercise is contrary to his own infinitely perfect being.

God's wisdom is an attribute of God's counsel. Therefore, as that counsel is worked out in the history of God's creation, all that happens in history is wise, the wise works of God, best suited to manifest God's great glory.

Only God's people have wisdom. The wicked are fools, and all that they do is foolish. But God gives his people wisdom so that they may be wise as they walk in the world. They are able to choose the best possible goal for their lives—the glory of God. And by the wisdom God gives, they are able to choose the best possible way to attain that goal: obedience to God.

And "if any of you lack wisdom, let him ask of God" (James 1:5).

Herman Hanko

January 12 — God Is Just

Read: Job 34

Justice is also a communicable attribute of God.

That God is just means that all God does is in perfect harmony with his goodness. From the viewpoint of its manifestation in creation, God's justice means that God blesses the one who is good as he is but punishes the one who is wicked and breaks God's commandments.

And so, because God is just, the one who sins against God is punished in this life and eternally in hell.

The Arminians argue that indeed God is just, but that God's grace and goodness overcome his justice. That is, although God could justly put every sinner in hell, he does not do this because he is also a gracious and loving God.

But this heresy is answered by the Heidelberg Catechism in Lord's Day 4, in which three objections are raised against God's justice. The last one reads: "Is, then, God not also merciful? God is indeed merciful, but he is likewise just; wherefore his justice requires that sin, which is committed against the most high majesty of God, be also punished with extreme, that is, with everlasting punishment both of body and soul."[*] Read the entire Lord's Day, for it says much about the justice of God.

God is also just in saving his people—in spite of the fact that they are just as wicked as the worst sinners in the world. But because his justice demands that sin be punished, God has punished the sin of his people in his own Son, our Lord Jesus Christ. So, the suffering and death of Christ reveal both God's justice and his mercy and grace. Justice and mercy kiss each other at the cross of Christ.

God is just in all that he does. He is just when he sends sickness upon men, when he sends catastrophes in the creation that kill thousands, when he sends trouble and grief upon people which disrupts their lives and makes their experiences bitter. His justice towards the wicked is revealed in all these things because they are the evidence of God's just fury against man for his sins.

But God is also just and merciful to his people when he makes all the trials of this present time work for their eternal salvation.

Herman Hanko

---

[*] Heidelberg Catechism 11, in Schaff, *Creeds of Christendom*, 311.

January 13 — God Is Good

Read: Psalm 145

Many years ago, when my father was a minister in a small and very poor congregation, a terrible hailstorm swept over the area where he and most of the members of his congregation lived. One man in particular was devastated by the storm. He had a family of ten or eleven children; his wife was in the hospital for many months; and he earned his living by growing vegetables, which were difficult to sell, because it was the Great Depression of the 1930s.

My father thought it good to visit this man whose entire crop was destroyed. He found that man standing at the side of his field. My father came and stood alongside him but said nothing. The man turned to my father with tears streaming down his cheeks and said: "Pastor, the Lord is good."

Such is the confession of the child of God in the sorrows of life.

God's goodness is closely related to his holiness. He is supremely good in himself and in all his divine being. He has no moral fault or stain, but is transcendently good as Father, Son, and Holy Spirit.

Because God is good in all his being, he is good in all that he does. He is good in the work of creation and providence. He is good to his creation when he makes the earth produce an abundance of good things. He is good when natural disasters come by his hand, for he defends the holiness of his own name when he punishes sin. He is good and manifests his goodness when he gives the wicked health, food, drink, riches, and a long life in the world.

This does not mean that he is gracious towards them. But his gifts are always good; he never gives evil gifts. The very goodness of his gifts increases the sin of the wicked, for they abuse his good gifts and use them for their own pleasure rather than for the glory of him who gave them.

God is always good to his people in all that he does, even when he destroys the means of their livelihood, for "all things work together for good to them that love God, to them who are the called according to his purpose" (Rom. 8:28).

Let us confess together his goodness towards us in all he does.

Herman Hanko

January 14 — God Is the Overflowing Fountain of All Good

Read: Psalm 147, Psalm 116

There are many more communicable attributes of which the Belgic Confession could have spoken: mercy, truth, grace, lovingkindness, compassion, love, etc. But finally, overwhelmed by the many virtues of the infinite God, the article sums them all up with the words, "He is the overflowing fountain of all good" (Article 1). God's goodness is the one attribute that sums up all the others.

In Psalm 116, the inspired singer of Israel tells us that he was drowning in very severe troubles and sorrows. He does not tell us what his troubles were, but they were grave dangers to his faith and to his fellowship with God. They were "sorrows of death" and "pains of hell" (v. 3). And all he knew was "trouble and sorrow" (v. 3).

But he called upon the name of the Lord and made supplication to God, beseeching him for deliverance. The Lord heard his cry and helped him (v. 6); and so he could speak to his soul: "Return unto thy rest, O my soul; for the Lord hath dealt bountifully with thee" (v. 7).

The Psalmist, most likely David, was so filled with gratitude to God for his mercy that he contemplates the possibility of bringing to God some gift to express his thankfulness. "What shall I render unto the Lord for all his benefits toward me?" (v. 12).

His answer to that question indicates that, upon consideration of the matter, he could bring nothing at all to the Lord, for all things were already his. "The cattle upon a thousand hills" are his (Psalm 50:10). He cannot give himself or anything he has, for even he himself belongs to God, and all he possesses remains the possession of God. It was like a man taking a cool and delicious cup of water out of a mountain stream and, after drinking part of it, expressing his thanks to the stream by pouring half of the cup back into the river.

But there are two things he can do. The first is to say "Thanks" for what he has received. That is the meaning of the cup of thanksgiving: the last cup of wine in the Passover feast, by which Israel expressed thanks to God for the salvation symbolized in the Passover.

The second thing he can and will do is "call upon the name of the Lord" (116:17). That is, he will go to God to ask for more.

That is all he can do, for God is the "overflowing fountain of all good."

Herman Hanko

Article 2

BY WHAT MEANS GOD IS MADE KNOWN UNTO US

We know him by two means: first, by the creation, preservation, and government of the universe; which is before our eyes as a most elegant book, wherein all creatures, great and small, are as so many characters leading us to contemplate the *invisible things of God*, namely, *his eternal power and Godhead*, as the Apostle Paul saith (Rom. 1:20). All which things are sufficient to convince men, and leave them without excuse.

Secondly, he makes himself more clearly and fully known to us by his holy and divine Word; that is to say, as far as is necessary for us to know in this life, to his glory and our salvation..

January 15 — We Can Know God!

And this is life eternal, that they might know thee the only true God, and Jesus Christ, whom thou hast sent. —John 17:3

The Christian church rests on the truth that God has made himself known to us in a manner that we are able to understand and comprehend. We make the distinction between knowing God and being able fully to comprehend God. We cannot begin to fully comprehend the mysteries of the Divine. God is so great and so far removed from us as finite beings that we can only scratch the surface of his glory. But what a wonder that God has made himself known in a manner that we are able to understand!

Throughout history, saints have at times despaired in the midst of their troubles, questioning whether they could know God and experience his grace and mercy. David in Psalm 88:14 cries: "Lord, why castest thou off my soul? why hidest thou thy face from me?" Job, in the midst of his intense pain and sorrow, despaired in Job 23:8, "Behold, I go forward, but he is not there; and backward, but I cannot perceive him." There are times when we feel that the heavens are closed up like iron and stone. We do not seem to be able to hear God's word to us. But the child of God by God's grace overcomes those doubts and fears and rests in the blessed assurance that God makes himself known through revelation as the God of our salvation.

Revelation means simply that God, as a personal being, actively communicates knowledge to his people in such a way that they are able to understand. God uncovers or makes manifest that which he desires men to know. God created man in his image and therefore capable of understanding God's speech to man. All knowledge of God is dependent on his self-revelation to us. Apart from God's work of making himself known to us and working in us the understanding of that revelation, we would not be able to know God. Natural man knows about God but lacks the intimate knowledge that God provides by revelation.

Consider today that God has given you to know him. Our calling is to hold high his revelation to us and to search the Scriptures in order to grow in that which gives us the knowledge of Jesus Christ and the hope of everlasting life!

Allen J. Brummel

January 16 — **God's Revelation**

For the invisible things of him from the creation of the world are clearly seen,
being understood by the things that are made,
even his eternal power and Godhead; so that they are without excuse.
—Romans 1:20

The fact that the Almighty God of Heaven and Earth, the one so great and marvelous that no man hath seen nor can behold him, the spiritual and invisible one, makes himself known to us is remarkable. That he who is so great would come to us and speak our language in a manner which we can understand is a wonder of grace. God did not leave Adam and Eve hiding in the garden after the fall, as he well could have. God searched them out and came to them and made himself known to them.

This is the greatest wonder! God makes himself known to sinners, to those who are his enemies! The miracle and wonder of God's revelation is closely connected with the wonder of God's grace in realizing the salvation of his people.

God determined the precise manner in which he would reveal himself to man. God could have worked in man some inborn knowledge of himself, but God did not do so. God could have made it so that in some mystical manner, man would be able to know God through personal meditation. Again, God did not do so. God ordained two main means by which he makes himself known: by means of creation and by means of the Scriptures. There are other ways in which God makes himself known, such as in history, in the consciences of men and women, and through dreams, visions, and angels in the Old Testament. But the two main ways in which God's revelation comes to us is by means of the creation and the word.

The creation is set forth as a "most elegant book" (Article 2) revealing to us the being and majesty of God as an artist reveals something of himself through his paintings.

It is the revelation of God through the Scriptures that allows us to understand and see Jesus Christ as Savior. The Scriptures serve as the means by which we are able to see Christ in the creation and in history. The Belgic Confession not only guides us to see the important place of the creation, but most importantly, not to neglect that love letter from God, the Bible, in which we read of his revelation to us through Jesus Christ unto our salvation.

Allen J. Brummel

January 17 — **God's Revelation in Creation**

The heavens declare the glory of God;
and the firmament sheweth his handywork.—Psalm 19:1

God is the creator of the heavens, the earth, and the entire universe. By his work, he, the Creator, is revealed and known. The course of history reveals his power and government, as Psalm 33:10–11 teaches: "The LORD bringeth the counsel of the heathen to nought: he maketh the devices of the people of none effect. The counsel of the LORD standeth for ever, the thoughts of his heart to all generations."

God makes himself so clearly known through the creation that all men everywhere know that there is a God and that he must be worshipped.

19. Because that which may be known of God is manifest in them; for God hath shewed it unto them.
20. For the invisible things of him from the creation of the world are clearly seen, being understood by the things that are made, even his eternal power and Godhead; so that they are without excuse;
21. Because that, when they knew God, they glorified him not as God. (Rom. 1:19–21)

In everything found on earth and in the heavens, God makes himself known. None can deny his matchless wisdom, his great goodness, or his marvelous power, except by denying and rejecting the witness that is daily set before their eyes.

There is the witness of God through history by which he governs all things and demonstrates that everything is being operated in an orderly way and with a defined plan. The revelation of God in creation reveals that he is orderly and that all things serve his divine plan.

This revelation in creation can only be understood properly through the testimony of the Scriptures which reveal God's purpose and plan for all things. For this reason, when we think of revelation, we think most fully of the revelation of God in the word.

For the child of God, the Scriptures open our eyes to creation as the most elegant book. We read of the sunrises, the lilies, the mountains, and the trees. We read of the roots, the branches, and all the wild beasts, as well as the lamb, and we see Christ in all of creation. God reveals his love and grace through all the word-pictures that he incorporates in the creation.

Thank God who has opened your eyes to see today not only evidences of his judgment and power in the creation but also of his marvelous love and grace in Jesus Christ. Pray for grace more and more to see Christ and his glory in the creation around you.

Allen J. Brummel

January 18 — Revealed by His Word

Search the scriptures; for in them ye think ye have eternal life: and they are they which testify of me. —John 5:39

The chief form of revelation that God has given to his church is that of the Scriptures, which reveal everything necessary to know and believe concerning God and the way of salvation.

We must treasure the Scriptures through which God has revealed himself to us. It is so easy to say that we treasure them but to then give little attention to the Bible throughout the week. The Belgic Confession begins almost every article with a "We believe" or a "We confess." That believing and confessing is on the basis of the word that God has given to us. So precious this word of God was to the persecuted believers during the time in which the confession was written, that they were willing to "offer their backs to stripes, their tongues to knives, their mouths to gags, and their whole bodies to the fire,"[*] rather than deny the truth of God's word. The saints knew and loved the word and lived out of it.

So that the word will never be doubted or forgotten by God's children, we have it preserved for us in written form by God; we can read it regularly and grow in our knowledge and love of God, living in obedience to his commandments.

It is easy to try to twist and distort the teachings of the Bible. We find that despicable behavior taking place in churches throughout the world. And tragically, it is easy for us to fall prey to the temptation to try to justify our own sins by twisting the word to allow us to live according to our own pleasure.

The Bible reminds us that we are liars, and we need to submit to the word that has been preserved in written form. In God's great wisdom he clearly makes known his will so that no man can contest it or claim to have heard it incorrectly. We must have the highest regard for the written word so that we don't need to look anywhere else to know God's will for our lives.

Allen J. Brummel

---

[*] Quoted in Schaff, *Creeds of Christendom*, 1:505.

January 19 — A Knowledge for Believers

I have manifested thy name unto the men which thou gavest me out of the world: thine they were, and thou gavest them me; and they have kept thy word. —John 17:6

Specifically, this second article of the Belgic Confession is talking about how believers, God's people, are able to know God. By faith, we know God through the Bible, and that word has priority and explains more fully the revelation of God to us in the creation. Without the glasses of the word, no one can read the book of creation and understand God as Jehovah, the covenant-keeping God. The unbeliever is not capable of knowing God simply by means of the revelation of God in creation. Even though that revelation of God in his works is clear and unmistakable, natural man is blind, hates God's evidence, and refuses to confess or know God. His depravity prevents him from knowing God by means of his works.

God made use of dreams, visions, appearances, and direct speech in order to reveal his will to mankind. Through miracles and wonders, God displayed his power and his glory, but the most marvelous wonder is that of his word. The Bible is a miracle from God because it makes known the living and unseen God to us through Jesus Christ, the Word made flesh. That written word reveals all that is necessary for us to know in this life to God's glory and our salvation. This written word confronts the believer with the message of his sinfulness and depravity and the wonder of God's grace.

It is only through the written word that we are able to know the Word who became flesh, who is the living Word.

We confess the accuracy of the written word. Although the translations that we have are subject to error and mistranslation, we confess that God preserved his word so that we have the word of God, and that word as to its original autograph is inspired, infallible, authoritative, and necessary.

We read and meditate on that word. It is easy to take for granted the treasure that God has given us in the word. It is easy for us to become lax in our reading of it. May God stir us up not only to a confession of the wonder of his revelation to us but also to the joy of reading, studying, and growing in our knowledge of that glorious revelation in his word so that we can know more fully the glory of God and the confidence of our salvation.

Allen J. Brummel

January 20 — Unbelievers Left Without Excuse

Because that, when they knew God, they glorified him not as God, neither were thankful; but became vain in their imaginations, and their foolish heart was darkened. —Romans 1:21

Can a person be saved through the testimony of the creation? The answer is clearly no. The significance of the revelation of God through the creation is that it leaves the unbelievers without an excuse for their rebellion. The testimony of Romans 1:18–31 is clear. Every person who is summoned before the tribunal of God will know that there is a God and that God required of him worship. No one will be able to say he or she did not know there was a God.

This revelation, then, has no saving power. We may not speak of it as a kind of grace. Instead, the Belgic Confession, quoting from Romans 1, makes very clear that this revelation is a revelation of God's wrath and serves only to leave the wicked without excuse. It is not the case that there are different ways of salvation—some apart from the Scriptures. It is not the case that men can be saved with the word and apart from faithful preaching of that word. Romans 10:14 requires not only the word, but the faithful proclamation of that word through servants who are called and sent by the church.

There are important implications of this truth. The revelation of God through creation is the reason why no one will ever be able to claim that he or she did not know there was a God. There are no atheists as far as the Bible is concerned. God will judge the wicked on judgment day because they knew God but refused to glorify him, continued to walk in an unthankful manner, and worshipped the creature instead of the Creator.

This knowledge of God is not capable of bringing a man to salvation, but is "sufficient to convince men, and leave them without excuse" (Article 2) for their wickedness and rebellion. There are no atheists according to Psalm 14:1. The fool says in his heart that "there is no God." The fool is one who denies reality; he knows better and yet in his wickedness suppresses the knowledge in unbelief. This means that all who turn away from God and the gospel do so out of rebellion against the true God whom they do know.

We thank God for his grace in rescuing us from that bondage and giving us the mercy to see Jesus Christ as the power and wisdom of God unto salvation revealed through the preaching of the gospel. Pray that God will open the eyes of those with whom you have contact who remain in that bondage.

Allen J. Brummel

January 21 — No Other Revelation

The scripture cannot be broken. —John 10:35

There are many in our day who insist that the Scripture is broken. They say that the Bible is not able to help us understand what took place in the beginning with the wonder of creation, and the Bible does not give us direction in the realm of the roles of husbands and wives in marriage. Further, they believe that the Bible is time-bound and culturally conditioned, and that in many areas it is broken. More important in their estimation are the subjective ways in which God reveals himself to individuals personally. By denying the Scripture and making God's revelation relative, they not only despise the word of God, but also lose the assurance of eternal life as Revelation 22:18–19 teaches.

All that man needs to know for salvation is found in the Bible. Every human opinion, tradition, and law must be judged in the light of the divine Scripture. The antichristian spirit is among us, and therefore the calling of believers is to "believe not every spirit, but try the spirits whether they are of God: because many false prophets are gone out into the world" (1 John 4:1). This warning we need to hear today.

The Bible is the way by which our path in the midst of the darkness of this world is illumined. The Bible is the way in which we are able to be assured of the salvation that has been earned for us by Jesus Christ. The Bible is the means by which we are able to know Jesus Christ, and, therefore, we must "give the more earnest heed to" this Scripture (Heb. 2:1)!

The light of the Bible will not be seen if you are not reading its pages. You need to use and wear out your Bibles! Read the Bible every day. Study it, praying that God will cause its light to shine brightly in your heart. And follow that light as God directs and guides your pathway to the glory of his name and for your salvation!

Allen J. Brummel

 *Article 3*

OF THE WRITTEN WORD OF GOD

We confess that this word of God was not sent nor delivered by the will of man, but that *holy men of God spake as they were moved by the Holy Ghost*, as the apostle Peter saith. And that afterwards God, from a special care which he has for us and our salvation, commanded his servants, the prophets and apostles, to commit his revealed word to writing; and he himself wrote with his own finger the two tables of the law. Therefore we call such writings holy and divine Scriptures.

January 22 — God's Special Revelation to Us

Read: Hebrews 1:1–8

The one true, living, and glorious God can only be known to man through his own self-revelation. He cannot be known by man's philosophical speculation or scientific investigation. God can only be rightly known when he makes himself known to us by his wonderful grace and Spirit. According to Romans 1:20, God reveals himself in his creation. He shows his "power and Godhead" in all the world. "The heavens declare the glory of God; and the firmament sheweth his handiwork" (Ps. 19:1). God reveals himself in his creation as the sovereign and almighty creator of all, who must be worshipped and glorified. But fallen sinful man denies God's revelation in his creation. Knowing God, he glorifies him not as God (Rom. 1:21). Man's foolish heart is darkened (v. 21). He professes himself to be wise (v. 22). He rejects the true and living God and creates a god after his own imagination. The god of man's foolish imagination is a mere creature, a helpless and dumb idol, that cannot help or save man from the fall and misery into which he plunged himself. The idol god of man's imagination is a lie, even when it is made of gold or other precious materials. The revelation of the true God in creation leaves man without excuse. He is condemned for his foolishness.

In the darkness of this sinful world, God has made known the glorious light of his truth and salvation to his people. The Bible is the written record of the word of God whereby he makes himself fully known as the true and blessed God of salvation through his Son Jesus Christ. The truth of God revealed in the Bible can only be understood by the Christian through God-given faith and by the Spirit and grace of God in his heart.

How the Bible is regarded by Christians is of greatest importance. If the Bible is not in every part true, then we must forever remain in doubt as to who God is and how we can be saved by him. Through the Bible, we come to know the true, living, and blessed God of our salvation. The Bible teaches us all that is necessary for life and godliness.

Today, there are many who no longer believe that the Bible is absolutely the word of God. In the past, these people were mostly outside the church. But today, there are those right in the church world who maintain that the Bible is full of errors. Christians must be on their guard against these false teachers and all their vain attempts to try to cast doubt on God's revelation of himself in his word.

The question of the absolute truth of the Scriptures is of utmost importance. The Protestant Reformation taught that the whole of the Christian religion must be based on the Bible. One of the great watchwords of the Reformation was *sola Scriptura*. All that we believe about who and what God is must be derived from the Bible. Every doctrine we confess, every truth we maintain in the church, must be derived from the Bible. False doctrine must be condemned and rejected on the basis of the Bible. The whole of the Christian life is set forth in the Bible. We may not add or subtract anything from what the Bible says about God.

What a great treasure the Bible is when we consider it to be the revelation of God and of his Son Jesus Christ! What a blessing to find in the Bible the glorious and blessed God of our salvation! This God we must worship and serve with godly fear, thanksgiving, and praise. To know this God and his Son Jesus Christ is to have eternal life.

Arie den Hartog

January 23 — The Bible is the Word of God

Read: 2 Peter 1:16–21

We cannot prove what we said so far by mere human reason. Sinful man exalts his own reason above the Bible and becomes a critic of the Bible. Through his supposed historical research and scientific investigation, unbelieving man claims that the Bible is full of errors.

We believe that the Bible is the word of God, through the testimony of his Spirit in our hearts and through God-given faith. This reasoning might not satisfy the world, but it is sufficient for us. We are silent before God's word, not contradicting it with our own mere human reason.

We believe that the Bible is the word of God on the basis of its own testimony of itself. There are many passages which speak of the fact that the Bible is the word of God. In many places in the Bible, we find absolutely authoritative statements that God speaks to us in his word, such as, "Thus saith the Lord" and "the Word of the Lord came unto me saying." The Belgic Confession quotes a very important passage from the Bible. It is taken from 2 Peter 1:20–21, "Knowing this first, that no prophecy of the scripture is of any private interpretation. For the prophecy came not in old time by the will of man: but holy men of God spake as they were moved by the Holy Ghost." Notice the contrast. The prophecies of Scripture came not by the will of man, but by the Holy Spirit.

A second classic passage which contains Scripture's own testimony of itself is found in 2 Timothy 3:16–17. There we read: "All scripture is given by inspiration of God, and is profitable for doctrine, for reproof, for correction, for instruction in righteousness: That the man of God may be perfect, throughly furnished unto all good works." This passage does not merely mean that the human authors of the Bible wrote with great feeling or on moving subjects, as might be said of the authors of some mere human piece of literature or poetry. What Paul means in 2 Timothy 3:16 is that the Scriptures were breathed forth from the mouth of God himself. The Scriptures were produced by the wonderful work of God himself. Therefore, the Scriptures are true, as true as God is true.

In the passage quoted above from 2 Peter, the inspired apostle of the Lord tells us earlier in the same chapter: "For we have not followed cunningly devised fables, when we made known unto you the power and coming of our Lord Jesus Christ" (2 Pet. 1:16). After this, Peter says: "We have also a more sure word of prophecy; whereunto ye do well that ye take heed, as unto a light that shineth in a dark place, until the day dawn, and the day star arise in your hearts" (v. 19). Jesus Christ is the day star. When he comes, the dark night of sin will be over, and the great light of God will shine. The prophecies of Scripture all concentrate on the blessed and glorious hope of the coming of Christ for our salvation.

The Christian religion is in no part based on human fables and myths. It is based on the absolute truth of God. In this, we have confidence before God and a certain hope of the coming again of Christ for the final salvation of his people.

One of the great proofs that the Bible is true is evident in the fact that prophecies made thousands of years before the birth of Christ were all fulfilled in him. What an amazing and wonderful thing!

Arie den Hartog

January 24 — Holy Men Spake as They Were Moved by the Holy Spirit

Read: Revelation 1:1–11

How do we know that the Bible is truly the word of God? The Belgic Confession answers this important question by quoting 2 Peter 1:21. This passage does not address the question of how we can come to the right interpretation. How we interpret the Bible is, of course, very important. But Peter is speaking of how holy men of God received revelation from God and how writers of the Bible themselves understood the word of God. They did not each have their own private interpretation of the prophecies which God by special revelation gave to them. Rather, "holy men of God spake as they were moved by the Holy Ghost." Literally, they were carried along by the Holy Spirit. This was a wonderful work of God. A work that produced an infallible Bible.

God used men to write the Bible. The Bible did not fall down from heaven, as is claimed by other religions concerning their sacred books. The Bible was given through the instrumentality of men, who were in themselves sinners, but who were holy men of God.

Many would argue that since God used men to give us the Bible, it must follow that the Bible is in part the word of God and in part the word of men. Since God used fallible men, their human limitations and errors inevitably entered into the Bible. Therefore, not every part of the Bible is the word of God. Since the men through whom we received the word of God lived long before the age of scientific investigation and historical research, these men were limited. There were many things that they could not have known in the times in which they lived. Many of these things were discovered centuries later. It is even claimed that the ancient men who wrote the Bible often confused mythology with reality and fact.

In our modern times of the amazing knowledge of scientific investigation and historical research, it has been claimed that the Bible contains many errors. It is said that we must change our thinking about the Bible. It is said that the word of God is *in* the Bible, but not all of the Bible is the word of God. It is said that the Bible is infallible only in matters that speak of salvation, but not in all matters of which it speaks. Thus, the work of the church and of the believer when reading the Bible is to discern what belongs to the truth of salvation and what belongs to science and history.

As a result, the Christian is left with hopeless uncertainty and confusion regarding which part of the Bible is to be received as the word of God and which part reflects ancient, limited, and undeveloped knowledge. The Bible becomes a collection of ancient mythology. Many of these so-called "myths" were part of a body of mythology which found its way into many other religions besides the Christian religion. While these myths contain spiritual lessons, they do not convey absolute truth. We adamantly reject such a view of the Bible. Our religion is not based on myths, but on the absolute truth of God.

The Belgic Confession denies this false teaching that is troubling and confusing so much of the church today. God directed the hearts and minds of the men of God who were used to bring God's word to his people. They themselves received the very word of God. They spoke the absolute truth. As God is true, so also the Bible is true and without error. For this reason, we have "a more sure word of prophecy" (2 Pet. 1:19) upon which we as Christians base our undoubted faith in the hope of the coming of the Lord Jesus Christ.

Arie den Hartog

January 25 — The Word of God was Written Down

Read: 2 Timothy 3:14–17

There was a time when there was no Bible. The word of God was given to his people before the Bible was written. God spoke to the patriarchs Abraham, Isaac, and Jacob, sometimes directly out of heaven. For many years, the word of God was kept alive among God's people through oral tradition. Parents told their children about the word of God. For example, the history of creation, the fall, and the works of God among his people were told and retold from generation to generation over hundreds of years.

In order to have the word of God preserved for all ages and for us also, God had his word written down. The term "the Scriptures" literally means "the writings." The writing of the Scriptures took place over 1500 years of time, from Moses to the apostle John. Many different men were engaged in the work, men in vastly different times and cultures. The word of God was progressively revealed to man in more and more rich fullness, unfolding God's glorious purposes of salvation. In spite of this, all the men that God used for the writing down of his word agreed with each other. They did not contradict each other. This alone is one of the greatest proofs for the infallibility of the Bible.

God used men to record his word for all ages. These men were not mere secretaries to whom God dictated his words to be recorded in a very mechanical way. Rather, God used their whole person, the gifts of the human writers and their life circumstances, including the problems and difficulties they faced in the world at that time. The human authors of the Bible were convicted in their own hearts concerning their own writings. They knew and loved God and were devoted to him and the declaring of his truth. God ordained and prepared each of the writers of the Bible in the totality of who they were and the circumstances in which they wrote the Bible.

A careful study of this matter will reveal that Jesus quoted from all the major sections of the Scriptures. He set his seal of authority as the Son of God on the whole of the Old Testament. At the time that Jesus lived on the earth, the thirty-nine books of the Old Testament were already collected together and distinguished from all other books. Together, they were referred to as "the Scriptures." Jesus, during his earthly ministry, appealed with finality to the Scriptures. He often used the phrase, "it is written." This he considered to be the end of all argument and debate. Jesus considered what was written to be the absolutely authoritative and true word of God. He said that the Scriptures could not be broken. In the Sermon on the Mount, recorded in the gospel of Matthew, Jesus declared that not one jot or tittle would pass from the law of God until all was fulfilled (Matt. 5:18). If Jesus is true, and he is because he is the Son of God, his word is absolutely true.

Later, the apostles of the Lord referred to the word which they preached as being absolutely authoritative. It must not be doubted nor questioned. That word was the foundation on which the church was to be built. Paul boldly declares in 1 Corinthians 2:4–5, "And my speech and my preaching was not with enticing words of man's wisdom, but in demonstration of the Spirit and of power: that your faith should not stand in the wisdom of men, but in the power of God" (see also 1 Cor. 3:10–11).

How blessed we are that God has so preserved his word for us, that we might know him and the truth that is in him so that we might believe in him for our salvation without any doubt.

Arie den Hartog

Article 4

CANONICAL BOOKS
OF THE HOLY SCRIPTURE

We believe that the holy scriptures are contained in two books, namely, the Old and New Testaments, which are canonical, against which nothing can be alleged. These are thus named in the church of God.

The books of the Old Testament are, the five books of Moses, namely: Genesis, Exodus, Leviticus, Numbers, Deuteronomy; the books of Joshua, Judges, Ruth, the two books of Samuel, the two of the Kings, two books of the Chronicles, commonly called Paralipomenon, the first of Ezra, Nehemiah, Esther; Job, the Psalms of David, the three books of Solomon, namely, the Proverbs, Ecclesiastes, and the Song of Songs; the four great prophets: Isaiah, Jeremiah, Ezekiel and Daniel; and the twelve lesser prophets, namely, Hosea, Joel, Amos, Obadiah, Jonah, Micah, Nahum, Habakkuk, Zephaniah, Haggai, Zechariah, and Malachi.

Those of the New Testament are the four evangelists, namely: Matthew, Mark, Luke, and John; the Acts of the Apostles; the fourteen epistles of the apostle Paul, namely: one to the Romans, two to the Corinthians, one to the Galatians, one to the Ephesians, one to the Philippians, one to the Colossians, two to the Thessalonians, two to Timothy, one to Titus, one to Philemon, and one to the Hebrews; the seven epistles of the other apostles, namely, one of James, two of Peter, three of John, one of Jude; and the Revelation of the apostle John.

January 26 — All Scripture is Given by Inspiration of God

Read: John 15:26; 16:13–14

Article 4 of the Belgic Confession gives a list of the books which the church historically has considered to be included in the "canon." The word *canon* means, literally, *standard* or *measure*. The idea is that, according to a specific measure or criteria, certain sacred books were received to be inspired while others were not. This is, of course, a very important question. Many sacred books have been written over the centuries. Almost every pagan religion has its sacred book or books. Even in the days of ancient Israel, sacred books were written. Some of these were included in the canon of Scripture, others were not. The Old Testament mentions sacred books, books even of true prophets of God, which did not become part of the thirty-nine books of the Old Testament later referred to as the Scriptures.

At the time of the Reformation there were sacred books called the Apocrypha, which the Reformers did not consider part of the sacred Scriptures. The Roman Catholic Bible wrongly, we believe, contains these books. Today, the Protestant Bible does not contain them.

At the time of Jesus, the writings of "Moses and the prophets" were already received as canonical. Jesus, with his authority as the Son of God, declared these and these only to be the Scriptures. He quoted with authority from these books and said concerning them that "the scriptures cannot be broken" (John 10:35).

The New Testament contains twenty-seven books. The early church councils listed these books as the complete canon. No other books were determined to have the same authority. It is possible that some of the other apostles of the Lord wrote sacred books. They were not included in the canon. It is possible that the apostle Paul wrote a third letter to the church of Corinth, which was lost and not made part of the canon, though written by Paul.

How did all of this happen? It was not because the church as such has authority over the Scriptures. In fact, the truth is the opposite. The church is founded on the absolute authority of the Scriptures. Jesus promised that after his ascension, he would give his apostles—and later, the church founded by them—"the Spirit of truth" (John 16:13). He would lead and guide the church into all truth (v. 13; see also 14:26).

When the apostles preached, they were aware of the fact that they had the Spirit of Christ in their office. Therefore, they believed that the word they brought had absolute authority. Paul states in 1 Corinthians 2:4–5, "And my speech and my preaching was not with enticing words of man's wisdom, but in demonstration of the Spirit and of power: that your faith should not stand in the wisdom of men, but in the power of God."

Over time, various criteria were used to determine which sacred books were intended to be recognized as the sacred word of God. Sometimes, it was due to the office which human authors received from God. Moses was the mediator of the old covenant. He wrote the first five books of the Old Testament. The prophets of the Old Testament stood in a special office in which God spoke to them directly, and later they wrote down the word of God. The apostles in the New Testament time also had a unique office given by the church, to lay the foundation of the word of God for the whole church. After the so-called Apostolic Age, there was no need of new revelation. Rather, the church must be founded on the foundation already laid, Jesus Christ being the chief cornerstone (1 Cor. 3:10–11).

Arie den Hartog

January 27 — The Old and the New Testament

Read: Hebrews 1:1–3

Article 4 of the Belgic Confession speaks of the two books of the Bible. They are the Old and New Testament. The word *testament* is another word for covenant. The Old Testament contains the history of the covenant promises of God as they were revealed to the ancient nation of Israel. The New Testament records the fulfillment of all of God's covenant promises in the incarnation, cross, resurrection, and exaltation of the Lord Jesus Christ.

The fact that the Bible has these two books on the covenant is amazing. It teaches us that the central purpose of God's revelation to us is to make known his beloved Son Jesus Christ as our Savior. Jesus said concerning the Old Testament: "Search the scriptures; for in them ye think ye have eternal life: and they are they which testify of me" (John 5:39).

As soon as man fell into sin and rebelled against God, God in mercy revealed the promise of the coming of the Messiah to save his people from their sins. This promise was first made known in Genesis 3:15.

Throughout the whole Old Testament given over a period of thousands of years, there are hundreds and hundreds of passages repeating this promise, and many types picturing the coming of the Savior. His birth from a virgin is revealed (Isa. 7:14). His wonderful person was made known hundreds of years before his birth (Isa. 9:6). The mighty and glorious work he would perform to realize his everlasting kingdom of glory is made known everywhere in the Scriptures. The thousands of sacrifices and ceremonies of the tabernacle and the temple of God pointed beforehand to the work of Christ. All the prophets, priests, and kings were types of the great prophet, priest, and king that was to come, who alone could do the great work of God (see John 1:18 and Heb. 1:1–3). Jesus was the fulfillment of all the priests of the Old Testament, being made the great high priest of our salvation. The book of Hebrews speaks extensively of this. Jesus came as the great king from the line of David. He is the almighty and glorious king, "the King of kings, and Lord of lords" (1 Tim. 6:15), who has and will finally conquer all of God's and our enemies and establish his glorious everlasting kingdom of righteousness in the new earth and the new heavens.

There is much to be gained through the study of the prophecies and types of the Old Testament. The Old Testament should never be considered as mere interesting ancient Jewish history. From beginning to end, the Old Testament speaks of Christ. We should never end our study of a passage in the Old Testament until we have through prayer and the Spirit found Christ therein.

The New Testament shows that Christ is the fulfillment of all of God's covenant promises. We know that Jesus is truly the Christ when we learn how he is the fulfillment of the Scriptures.

The blessed truth of God and of his salvation, already taught in wonderful ways in the Old Testament, is fully and completely revealed in the New Testament. So, we know by reading the New Testament that Jesus is truly the Christ whom God sent into the world for our salvation. And we must believe in him for our salvation, finding our all in him and glorying in him alone.

Arie den Hartog

January 28 — The Complete Revelation of God

Read: Revelation 22:16–21

After God gave his final word to the apostle John and commanded him to write it down in the book called "The Revelation," the Scriptures were complete. "Blessed is he that readeth, and they that hear the words of this prophecy, and keep those things which are written therein: for the time is at hand" (Rev. 1:3). No more revelation is necessary now. We have, recorded in the Scriptures, all that is necessary for us to know God truly and to have faith unto salvation in him. John warned at the end of the book of Revelation: "If any man shall add unto these things, God shall add unto him the plagues that are written in this book: and if any man shall take away from the words of the book of this prophecy, God shall take away his part out of the book of life, and out of the holy city, and from the things which are written in this book" (Rev. 22:18–19).

Attempts have often been made to add to the Scriptures. The Roman Catholic Church in the Middle Ages raised the so-called apocryphal books to the same authority in the church as the sixty-six books of the canon. Throughout history, so-called Christian sects, such as Jehovah's Witnesses, Christian Science, and many others, have claimed new revelation received in strange ways. These have added books containing this supposed revelation. Modern-day charismatics claim they have received new revelations and prophecies besides the Bible. Some private persons claiming to be leaders in Christendom have claimed to have received some new and private revelation which gave them greater knowledge than anyone who went before. Many have been led astray by false teachers who say "here is Christ; or, lo, he is there;" (Mark 13:21). Believe them not, no matter how high-sounding and dramatic their claims.

Based on the passage from Revelation 22, the Belgic Confession declares that only the sixty-six canonical books contain the special revelation of God to his people. We are not in need of any new or additional revelation. The word of God is perfect and complete for the church throughout the New Testament Age, until the Lord returns at the end of the world.

This is both wonderful and perfect. God has spoken his word. This word is absolutely final. In his word, he has revealed to us everything we need to know him, and to have a life of faith and godliness. The written word cannot be added to or subtracted from. Neither need we anything more. In God's word, there are final warnings to men to repent and sure and blessed promises of everlasting salvation and glory for those who believe.

The treasures of the wisdom and knowledge of our salvation, as they are in Jesus Christ alone, are given to us in the holy Scriptures. What we need to do today is carefully and prayerfully search the Scriptures daily so that we might more and more know the one only true God and his Son Jesus Christ, whom to know is everlasting life. The Lord Jesus promised that he will continually give to his church the Spirit of truth, who will lead and guide us into all truth. Every doctrine that we hold of Christ must be derived from the Scriptures alone. If this is true, we will not be led astray, but will be in his truth. We will not walk in darkness, but in the light of life. We say with Peter that "we have…a more sure word of prophecy" on which we can rely and never doubt unto the day of the coming of our glorious and blessed Lord (2 Pet.1:19). In that day, he will give us perfect understanding of all things.

Arie den Hartog

Article 5

WHENCE DO THE HOLY SCRIPTURES DERIVE THEIR DIGNITY AND AUTHORITY

We receive all these books, and these only, as holy and canonical, for the regulation, foundation, and confirmation of our faith; believing, without any doubt, all things contained in them, not so much because the church receives and approves them as such, but more especially because the Holy Ghost witnesseth in our hearts that they are from God, whereof they carry the evidence in themselves. For the very blind are able to perceive that the things foretold in them are fulfilling.

Article 6

THE DIFFERENCE BETWEEN THE CANONICAL AND APOCRYPHAL BOOKS

We distinguish those sacred books from the apocryphal, namely: the third book of Esdras, the books of Tobias, Judith, Wisdom, Jesus Syrach, Baruch, the appendix to the book of Esther, the Song of the Three Children in the Furnace, the history of Susannah, of Bell and the Dragon, the Prayer of Manasses, and the two books of the Maccabees. All of which the church may read and take instruction from so far as they agree with the canonical books; but they are far from having such power and efficacy as that we may from their testimony confirm any point of faith or of the Christian religion; much less detract from the authority of the other sacred books.

January 29 — We Receive the Bible as Canon

When ye received the word of God which ye heard of us,
ye received it not as the word of men, but as it is in truth, the word of God,
which effectually worketh also in you that believe. —1 Thessalonians 2:13

The Bible, that is, the sixty-six books of the Bible listed in Article 4, constitutes the *canon* of Scripture. By this, we mean that these books form the "rule of faith," for *canon* means *rule*. The idea of rule is the measure of faith, much like a ruler measures out the length of an object. The books of the Bible form for us the measure of our faith. What we believe is expressed in the teachings of the books of the Bible. What we hold for truth is set forth in the Bible. We use the Bible for this purpose.

We draw two conclusions from this fact.

First, the canon is limited to the sixty-six books of the Bible. There are no other books than these which we receive as inspired of God and which, therefore, can function as a canon, a measure of faith.

Second, we do receive these *as inspired* of God. This is the rock and foundation of our faith. We accept the Bible as the authoritative word of God without question.

Now, this article instructs us how to respond to this beautiful fact: "We receive all these books, and these only, as holy and canonical, for the regulation, foundation, and confirmation of our faith" (Article 5).

We follow the example of the Thessalonians mentioned above. Because the Bible was not completely written at that time, the child-like faith expressed by the church at Thessalonica was their acceptance of the word preached by the apostles. But now, at this date in history, we have the written word of God.

When we speak of a proper response to the fact that God has given to us his word in written form, we receive that word. We don't require someone to "prove to me" the Bible is God's word. We do not require the church to hold a meeting to decide which books of the Bible are a proper "rule of faith." No, we receive these books as a proper rule of our faith.

This is faith's response. I ask you, do you have that faith? Do you receive the Bible this way?

Jason Kortering

January 30 — We Receive The Entire Bible as Canon

All scripture is given by inspiration of God. —2 Timothy 3:16

Perhaps you are a young Christian who reads these words. By young, I mean young in age, or I may also mean young in faith, in that you only recently became a Christian. Either way, your faith will be soon challenged by what I have to say in this brief meditation.

If you have not encountered a person who questions the teaching of the *whole* Bible, you will encounter such a person very soon. You may have heard someone mock the teaching of the Bible concerning the creation of the world. Others mock the teaching of the Bible concerning miracles, laughing at anyone who would be so naïve as to accept that the water of the Nile River turned into blood. Still others focus on the teachings of Christian living, mocking the Bible's teachings on marriage, the Christian home, and family.

Some of these people are secular (reject all religion), some hold to other religions (Buddhist, Hindu, etc.), and some claim to be Christian and hold to the Bible but interpret the Bible differently.

Obviously, these last do not "receive all these books, and these only, as holy and canonical" (Article 5). If they did, they would bow humbly in faith and accept the teachings of the Bible.

The historical Christian faith (and also, what is designated as the Reformed faith because of the teaching of the Sixteenth Century Reformation, which includes our Belgic Confession) says clearly and boldly, "We receive all these books…believing, without any doubt, all things contained in them" (Article 5). We do that because of what Paul led young Timothy to express: "All Scripture is given by inspiration of God, and is profitable for doctrine, for reproof, for correction, for instruction in righteousness" (2 Tim. 3:16).

Ah, that God may give to all of us such child-like faith.

As we go along, we will see that this article gives us two reasons why we have such faith.

But for now, I want you to focus on your response to the Bible.

Don't ask for scientific proof, for historical confirmation, for ecclesiastical agreement, as necessary before you can accept the teaching of the Bible. The approach of unbelief is "show me and I will believe," rather than "I believe because God has taught me."

This is critical for your young faith.

May God show to you that what he says is true.

Jason Kortering

January 31 — **Role of the Church and the Canon of Scripture**

Therefore, brethren, stand fast, and hold the traditions which ye have been taught, whether by word, or our epistle. —2 Thessalonians 2:15

The language of Article 5 of our Belgic Confession is interesting: "We receive all these books, and these only, as holy and canonical...not so much because the church receives and approves them as such, but more especially because the Holy Ghost witnesseth in our hearts, that they are from God, whereof they carry the evidence in themselves."

There is some history behind the wording of this article. You may recall that the Roman Catholic Church takes the position that the church determines what the Bible teaches to be truth; they apply the same thing to the canon of Scripture. The church made a judgment on the canon of Scripture and insists that this makes the difference between the books of the Bible and secular literature.

Our Reformed forefathers do not deny the importance of the church selecting and forming a judgment as to which books of the Bible were inspired and therefore part of the canon, part of the sixty-six books of the Bible. This was done at Councils, such as Carthage in A.D. 397. Notice, then, the article's careful wording: we accept the sixty-six books of the Bible listed in Article 4 as canonical "not so much because the church receives and approves them." Rome places all the emphasis on this because this is determinative for them. For us of Reformed persuasion, we recognize the role of the church as significant, but something is far more important to us. That is, we accept the canon of Scripture for two important reasons: first, because the Holy Spirit testifies in our hearts that they are the inspired and authoritative Scripture, and second, because the books verify that they are inspired by their own testimony, by the contents themselves.

For now, we want to focus on the role of the church in this process.

As in 2 Thessalonians 2:15, we follow the example of the early church which accepted Scripture's teaching (traditions), whether by word or epistle. The written content (epistle) was determinative, as was the word (spoken by the apostles).

We do not accept the Bible because the church tells us to do this. The moment these books were written, they were the word of God, and the church accepted them as such.

How precious that we and believers of all ages recognize the Bible as God's word.

Jason Kortering

February 1 — The Holy Ghost Convicts Us That the Bible Is God's Word

But ye are not in the flesh, but in the Spirit,
if so be that the Spirit of God dwell in you...and if Christ be in you...
the Spirit is life because of righteousness. —Romans 8:9–10

In our brief review of Article 5 of the Belgic Confession, we have come to focus on this point: we accept the sixty-six books of the Bible not so much because the church has concluded this (and they have), but because the Holy Spirit testifies to us that the Bible is the authoritative word of God.

It is expressed this way in the article: "The Holy Ghost witnesseth in our hearts that they are from God" (Article 5). What follows is evidence of how the Spirit does this witnessing, by the evidence in the Bible itself. For now, let's just meditate on this amazing fact: I believe all that the Bible says and teaches because the Holy Spirit of God gives me this conviction.

This is important both for understanding our own faith and as we deal with others who do not have this conviction.

First, we look at ourselves. We are spiritually blind and dead as much as anyone else. We are born this way into this world. Nothing we do in personal study or research in the world can open our eyes to see the truth of God's word. Romans 8, quoted above, explains what it takes. We do not remain in the flesh, but we are renewed in the Holy Spirit. That Spirit is the Holy Spirit of God who is also given to Jesus Christ to open our eyes so we can see spiritual things spiritually. He testifies to us through the word, the Bible, that it is indeed the complete and inspired word of God. Isn't it amazing that we should be so blessed?

Second, we look at others. We understand that without the Spirit working in them, they are blind to accept the Bible as God's word. Besides that, we also know that all the argumentation and reasoning in the world will not convict them. It takes the Holy Spirit to testify in their hearts. If you really want this to happen, you know you must pray to God and ask the Holy Spirit to do so. Only God by his Spirit can do this for them.

Let no one take this conviction away from you. Pray daily for the Holy Spirit's guidance.

Jason Kortering

February 2 — The Bible Itself Demonstrates It Is the Word of God

I am Alpha and Omega, the first and the last: and,
What thou seest, write in a book,
and send it unto the seven churches. —Revelation 1:11

We learned so far that no man comes to the conviction that the Bible is God's word without the testimony of the Holy Spirit in his heart.

Now, we learn that the Holy Spirit works this faith in our hearts by means of the word of God itself. This is a fundamental truth regarding the Holy Spirit: he limits his revelation to the written word, and he binds that word to the hearts of his own. This is important today when many claim they hear the voice of God directly.

Article 5 expresses it this way: "The Holy Ghost witnesseth in our hearts, that they [canonical books of the Bible] are from God, whereof they carry the evidence in themselves" (Article 5).

This evidence comes in two ways.

First, the Bible claims this for itself as indicated in the quote of Revelation 1:11 above. John received a vision and was instructed to write it down in a book and send that book to the churches of Asia Minor. The churches received these letters as sent to them from the exalted Christ. We have them to this day, and we read them as the very word of God.

Second, there is evidence in the Bible that the prophecies were fulfilled. This is mentioned in Article 5: "For the very blind are able to perceive that the things foretold in them are fulfilling." Think of Isaiah 7:14, which says that Jesus would be born of a virgin mother. Isaiah 53 gives such accurate description of the suffering and death of Jesus that we stand amazed. Isaiah 45:1 mentioned that a Persian king (even named him as Cyrus) would allow the captives to return to Jerusalem. Anyone who reads these beautiful passages without prejudice is convicted that the Holy Spirit of God gave revelation to the prophets and fulfilled them in the appointed day.

Such testimony recorded in the Bible itself is used by the Holy Spirit to convince every child of God that the truths contained in the sixty-six books of the Bible are reliable and are the very words of God.

Are you so convinced? The importance of this is the gospel itself; it is from God and comes to you with divine authority. Christ Jesus stands at the heart of that gospel.

Jason Kortering

February 3 — What Are the Apocryphal Books?

We have also a more sure word of prophecy...
for the prophecy came not in old time by the will of man: but holy men of God
spake as they were moved by the Holy Ghost. —2 Peter 1:19, 21

In contrast to the inspired books of the canon of the Bible, this article lists fourteen other books which are called "apocryphal." This designation refers to the fact that these books are unknown as to their authors. They were written sometime between 300 B.C. and A.D. 100.

As you may know, controversy over the legitimacy of these books took place almost from the time they were written. Jerome, one of the early church fathers, directed attention to their being called apocryphal because of their uncertain authority. The Council of Laodicea (A.D. 364) rejected them, finding them non-canonical. The Church of Rome accepted them as inspired and part of the Bible, influenced as they were by the inclusion of the books in the Septuagint Bible (Greek translation of the Hebrew Old Testament). They subsequently were included in the Latin translation and eventually accepted by Rome at the Council of Florence and Trent (A.D. 1546).

Daniel R. Hyde, in his excellent commentary of the Belgic Confession entitled *With Heart and Mouth* (I gleaned much of the above information from this book as well), gives us several reasons why we as Reformed Churches reject the apocryphal books as canonical.* I will list them here:

1. "The Jewish church never received them as canonical."
2. "Neither Jesus nor the apostles quoted from them."
3. "They were not received as canonical by the ancient church." This goes beyond our purpose with this brief meditation, but for the interested reader, much evidence is given to prove this point.
4. "They contain historical inaccuracies and fanciful tales." For example, Judith calls Nebuchadnezzar the king of Nineveh, which was destroyed years before; Bell and the Dragon has Daniel proving that the king's god was not eating the food offered, but that a fierce dragon was the culprit.
5. "They contain teachings in direct conflict with the biblical faith." For example, the doctrine of purgatory is supposedly proven by 2 Maccabees 12:43–45, which mentions prayer for the dead.
6. "At least one apocryphal book admits that it was not divinely inspired." See 2 Maccabees 15:38, "If it is well told and to the point, that is what I myself desired; if poorly done and mediocre, that was the best I could do."

Jason Kortering

---

* Daniel R. Hyde, *With Heart and Mouth: An Exposition of the Belgic Confession* (Grandville, MI: Reformed Fellowship Inc., 2008), 91-99.

February 4 — Limited Use of the Apocryphal Books?

We have also a more sure word of prophecy…for the prophecy came not in old time by the will of man: but holy men of God spake as they were moved by the Holy Ghost. —2 Peter 1:19, 21

Article 6 not only distinguishes the sacred books from the apocryphal, but also does much more. It adds these words: "All which the church may read and take instruction from, so far as they agree with the canonical books; but they are far from having such power and efficacy as that we may from their testimony confirm any point of faith or of the Christian religion; much less to detract from the authority of the other sacred books."

The big difference between the apocryphal and canonical books of the Bible is divine inspiration. Without that, the apocryphal lack authority. The above quotation from 2 Peter 1:19–21 summarizes this nicely for us. The prophecy which came "in old time" was not "by the will of man" but by the will of God as the Holy Spirit moved them to write. Hence, they are a more sure word of prophecy. The apocryphal books lack this entirely.

Rome differs with us on this. This is a bit understandable because Rome has a more open mind on the traditions of men. Still, this is an important issue, especially when Rome quotes from the apocryphal books in support of their errors. This puts them on shaky ground.

Our Reformed fathers did not want to throw the apocryphal books away as of no value. They may have historical value in so far as they agree with the canonical books. Notice, the rule, the measure for faith and life, is found in the holy, inspired canonical books. The apocryphal books must be viewed as written by men, much like any history book or historical novel. They do not stand by themselves with any authority; they must be evaluated in light of the holy Scriptures.

Let's be practical for a moment.

You probably do not even know of the existence of these fourteen apocryphal books. You probably have never read any of them. Now that you learn about them, you may ask yourself, ought I to read them? Are they important to me?

My answer is that they are not important for your faith. If you have curiosity, satisfy it, but read with discretion. More than anything, thank God that your faith is focused upon the more sure word of prophecy: the canonical books of the Bible.

Jason Kortering

Article 7

THE SUFFICIENCY OF THE HOLY SCRIPTURES TO BE THE ONLY RULE OF FAITH

We believe that these Holy Scriptures fully contain the will of God, and that whatsoever man ought to believe unto salvation, is sufficiently taught therein. For since the whole manner of worship which God requires of us is written in them at large, it is unlawful for any one, though an apostle, to teach otherwise than we are now taught in the Holy Scriptures: *nay, though it were an angel from heaven*, as the apostle Paul saith. For since it is forbidden *to add unto or take away any thing from the Word of God*, it doth thereby evidently appear that the doctrine thereof is most perfect and complete in all respects. Neither may we compare any writings of men, though ever so holy, with those divine Scriptures; nor ought we to compare custom, or the great multitude, or antiquity, or succession of times or persons, or councils, decrees, or statutes, with the truth of God, for the truth is above all: for all men are of themselves liars, and more vain than vanity itself. Therefore we reject with all our hearts whatsoever doth not agree with this infallible rule, which the apostles have taught us, saying, *Try the spirits whether they are of God;* likewise, *If there come any unto you, and bring not this doctrine, receive him not into your house.*

February 5   **The Sufficiency of the Bible as a Rule of Faith**

From a child thou hast known the holy scriptures,
which are able to make thee wise unto salvation. —2 Timothy 3:15

We now focus our attention on a new article of this confession, Article 7. It is one of the most detailed descriptions of the value and usefulness of the Bible in our daily life of faith. Because of this, we will devote fourteen meditations to exploring its depth.

As we read the entire article, we notice that one word stands out in bold relief: it is the word *sufficient*, as "whatsoever man ought to believe unto salvation is sufficiently taught therein" (Article 7).

Paul expressed to Timothy that the value of the holy Scriptures was that from childhood on, they were able to make him "wise unto salvation" (2 Tim. 3:15). This is something every one of us desires. We desire not only salvation, but we also desire the wisdom that is necessary to save us.

To express this differently, the Bible functions as a rule of our faith. We considered this before; it functions as the ruler whereby we can know what is true and what is false.

Now, this article adds that the Bible alone is sufficient to function as such a ruler for what we believe and how we are to live.

Think on that for a moment.

Where do you turn for instruction? You have questions about doctrines or teachings of the church. You wonder out loud how you are to conduct yourself as a young Christian.

Your resource is the word of God, the Bible.

Do you need other books or helps? They are available and useful. Yet, if all you had were your Bible, it is sufficient alone to make you wise unto salvation. The reason for this is obvious: God is the God of our salvation. God is the one who has written the Bible. He gives us all that is necessary for us to know in order to be saved in the Bible. That makes the Bible so special and different from every other book.

Treasure your Bible and read it regularly. Meditate upon it. Turn to it for answers to your questions. It is able to "make [you] wise unto salvation."

Jason Kortering

February 6 — The Bible and the Will of God

Because thou wilt not leave my soul in hell, neither wilt thou suffer thine Holy One to see corruption. —Acts 2:27

The opening sentence of this article of faith reads: "We believe that those holy Scriptures fully contain the will of God."

We want to focus on those words, "will of God."

The quotation above from Acts 2 gives us a clue. Peter quotes David, who prophetically states that Jesus will not remain in the corruption of the grave but will arise from the dead. He uses the word *will*, which refers to God's sovereign will, for, when God acts according to his eternal will and good pleasure, it is established as certain and true. God planned for Jesus to enter the grave and arise from the dead as his will for Jesus, and hence, it is recorded that Jesus will not remain in the grave but will arise from the dead.

The Bible is the revelation of God's will and fully reveals to us what God wants us to know.

The idea of God's will is used in two ways.

First, it is God's eternal good pleasure, which includes all his decrees that form the basis of his program for history. It includes whom he wills to save (election); what is the basis for our salvation (the cross and resurrection of Jesus); the method of salvation (faith through the preaching of the gospel); and the purpose of salvation (godly living and thankful worship). The Bible spells this out in detail.

Second, God's will is that that pleasure of God be communicated to us with authority and compassion. The Bible does not come to us as a dogmatic book of information. It comes to us as a boundary within which we obtain favor with God and outside of which is judgment and wrath.

To be in the will of God is important for us, as regards both our belief and our life of service.

We learn this will of God in the Bible. Isn't this wonderful? As we said, God doesn't tell us every detail of his will for us, only what he deems necessary for our faith and life of obedience. That is sufficient to guide us daily so that we may be certain we walk with God.

Do you read your Bible with this in mind? It is a treasure!

Jason Kortering

February 7 — The Bible Tells Us What to Believe

*And that from a child thou hast known the holy scriptures,
which are able to make thee wise unto salvation through faith
which is in Christ Jesus.* —2 Timothy 3:15

"Whatsoever man ought to believe unto salvation is sufficiently taught therein" (Article 7). Here, our attention is directed to those few words, "ought to believe." Brief as they may be, they contain the most important words imaginable. What must I believe to be saved? Where do I turn? How can I learn about salvation?

Paul approached young Timothy as a spiritual father and reminded him that being "wise unto salvation" was the most important thing for him (2 Tim. 3:15). Salvation can be viewed in different ways. One of my favorites is the figure of God reaching down into hell, graciously picking me up, taking me out of that abyss, and lifting me powerfully into his presence in heaven. The knowledge and experience of that salvation is the most blessed event a person can enjoy. I trust that, as you read this brief meditation, you can say in your heart: "Thank God, I am saved."

This confession and the writings of Paul to Timothy tell us certain things are necessary for us to believe in order to be saved. These things are written upon the pages of the Holy Bible. That is not a surprise, for the Bible is God's written word, and in his writing, he tells us what salvation is, including how it began in eternity past, how it is confirmed upon the cross of Jesus, and how it is made alive in our hearts by faith. It is important for us to know the way of salvation in order to be certain that we have walked that way. It is important for us in order to guide others to become saved.

Now, the point of this meditation is this: we can be sure we are saved, and we can be sure that we lead other people in the way of salvation, when we follow the Bible as our guide. Nothing can take the place of our open Bibles.

Is it any wonder then that we must take advantage of every opportunity to learn more from the Bible? The word is explained for us in our Sunday worship, the word is discussed at our Bible studies, we meditate upon the word in our own devotions. Treasure that word.

Jason Kortering

February 8 — The Bible Fully Contains the Will of God

*All things that I have heard of my Father
I have made known unto you.* —John 15:15

We now begin to consider why the Bible is sufficient for our faith and practice. The opening sentence of this article states: "We believe that those holy Scriptures fully contain the will of God" (Article 7).

Notice that the article does not say that all there is to know about God is comprehended in the Bible. God has chosen to manifest himself also in the realm of creation and history. The point that is important for us to remember is that the Bible is the sufficient source for our belief. It is the inspired source, and on that basis, what we learn of God from his creation is not on par with what the Bible teaches. Creation may never be used to contradict the Bible. Rather, it amplifies and verifies what God says in his word. We do not need creation or history to verify our faith. Our faith is firmly founded on the word of God because that word fully contains God's will for our belief and life of service. Jesus said: "All things that I have heard of my Father, I have made known unto you" (John 15:15).

The reason for this is that the Bible is not an accident of history. Rather, God planned everything written in the Bible and providentially arranged for its inclusion by inspiring the authors to write what they did and when they did it. This explains how the Bible could be written over a period of nine hundred years by some forty authors and never contradict itself. There is really one author, the Holy Spirit. This was not a surprise that resulted in the quirks of time, but rather, the God who predestinated a people unto himself determined before the foundation of the world that his Son would be the redeemer of these people, and, gathering this same people unto himself, has provided for us at this date in history a record that is sufficient for our faith.

What an amazing thought!

You see how important it is to believe the Bible is God's inspired word.

God planned it, arranged its writing, and made sure it includes all that is necessary for our faith.

The Bible is an amazing gift of God and source of our surety of faith.

Jason Kortering

February 9 — Men Ought to Believe what the Bible Teaches

Every word of God is pure: he is a shield
unto them that put their trust in him. —Proverbs 30:5

Men ought to believe what the Bible teaches. This is a compelling conclusion from what the article has said so far. If it is true, as we believe it is, that the holy Scriptures fully contain the will of God and that salvation is sufficiently taught therein, then man ought to believe it.

We live in an age in which a person's faith is considered personal, and he has a right to believe whatever he wants. This has become the postmodern gospel, both in the church and in the world. No one has the right to impose on anyone a faith that is not acceptable to him. This is due to the absence of all authority. Modern man treats parents this way, government this way, and the church this same way. Who are you to tell me what I ought to do?

This article differs from such an approach. Men ought to believe what the Bible teaches.

This seems to be an imposition from without—someone making me believe what I ought to believe. If we approach faith this way, we naturally resent it, we harden ourselves against it. So, how ought we to approach the Bible? It must be from hearts that have been touched by the Holy Spirit. The author of the Bible is our heavenly Father, whom we love and trust. We are willing to put our future into his hands. Since he wrote the Bible, yes, we do feel a certain obligation to believe it, but, most of all, we delight to know his way.

Proverbs 30:5 expresses it well: "every word of God is pure: he is a shield unto them that put their trust in him." That is a conclusion that is taken from the Bible: because the word of God bears the mark of the Author, it is *pure*. Such purity functions as a shield in this wicked and abominable world of sin.

The Bible does not allow you to have a "take it or leave it" attitude towards its teachings. God's love in dealing with his children is deeper than that. It is our rule of faith, and when we have this faith, we understand.

Our response is, yes, I must believe all that the Bible teaches. I do so from a heart that loves God.

Jason Kortering

February 10 — The Manner of Worship

*Not forsaking the assembling of ourselves together,
as the manner of some is.* —Hebrews 10:25

This article now adds that the Bible also is sufficient to instruct us in the "whole manner of worship which God requires of us" (Article 7).

What is meant by worship?

As we focus on the idea of worship, we must be careful not to make that too general.

It is true that our whole lives are lives of thankful praise and service of God. We can even say that we worship God in our entire lives of reverence and obedience. We do pray without ceasing. We worship God with our personal devotions and family worship. This is a beautiful thought.

Yet we must not take this statement of Article 7 out of its historical context. The Reformers directed their attention to the corruption of the Roman Catholic Church. The Reformers taught that the written word of God was the only source of truth. They applied this truth to both the teaching of the church and the worship of the church.

The worship addressed in this article is mainly corporate worship of the church on the Lord's Day. The text above refers to this as "the assembling of ourselves together" (Heb. 10:25). By this, it is meant that every Christian ought to participate in the worship of God as part of the body of Christ. It is terrible to worship alone; God has provided for us a way to worship him by being part of the church, that church which is the local assembly of believers of like precious faith. By belonging to such a congregation as members, we express our delight in God providing us such a church and making worship a delight.

We are told here that the manner of this worship is clearly given in the Bible and that God requires it of us. Pause a moment to reflect on the manner of your worship of God in church on Sunday. Is it man-centered, determined by what man wants? Do you church-hop to try to find a church that meets your man-centered standard?

Here, we are told that this is wrong. The important question we face is, do we worship God as he instructs us in his word? The God we worship cares about how we worship him, and he gives clear direction in his word. True faith reverences this God in worship.

Jason Kortering

February 11 — **The Manner of Worship Includes the Elements**

*For I delivered unto you first of all that which I also received,
how that Christ died for our sins according to the scriptures.*
—1 Corinthians 15:3

Let's expand a bit on what is included in the manner of worship mentioned in Article 7: "For since the whole manner of worship which God requires of us is written in them [books of the Bible]." We believe that "the whole manner of worship" includes what we call the "elements of worship." These are enumerated in the Bible as follows:

1. Reading of the word of God and preaching. Jesus did this in the synagogue, when he read from Isaiah and expounded what he read (Luke 4:16–21). As Reformed churches, we include in our public worship on the Lord's day the reading of the Bible and preaching of the gospel.
2. Prayer and singing. Ephesians 5:18–19 says: "Be filled with the Spirit; speaking to yourselves in psalms and hymns and spiritual songs, singing and making melody in your heart to the Lord." Also in 1 Timothy 2:1, the exhortation is given by Paul to Timothy to offer prayers for "all men," that is, for all classes of men, for God will have all kinds of men saved. Hence, we also have congregational prayers in our worship.
3. Receiving offerings. 1 Corinthians 16:1–2 says: "Now concerning the collection for the saints…Upon the first day of the week let every one of you lay by him in store, as God hath prospered him." During every service, the deacons receive the offerings, with special emphasis on the poor.
4. Sacraments. In Acts 10:48, we read: "And he commanded them to be baptized in the name of the Lord." We do this with both infants and adults during our worship. And 1 Corinthians 11:26, "For as often as ye eat this bread, and drink this cup, ye do shew the Lord's death till he come." We follow this instruction because we read in 1 Corinthians 15:3, "For I delivered unto you first of all that which I also received." We read this during the Lord's supper.

All these elements of worship are clearly taught in the Bible and must be viewed as a manner of worship which is required. God tells us to practice this.

Is this true of your worship? Each element is given us by divine instruction. As we make use of them, we may rest assured God will bless them to us.

Jason Kortering

February 12 — The Manner of Worship Is from the Heart

> *Every man according as he purposeth in his heart,*
> *so let him give; not grudgingly, or of necessity:*
> *for God loveth a cheerful giver.* —2 Corinthians 9:7

We now focus on another aspect of the manner of worship. Not only must our worship include all the elements given to us in the Bible, but we must worship God in a spiritually correct way. This article speaks of "the whole manner of worship" that is required of us in the Bible. God is not pleased simply with formal worship, something we all must admit is the greatest threat to our spiritual life. You know how that goes: we read the Bible, listen to preaching, sing and pray, take collection, and observe the sacraments, and do that so mechanically that we leave church as empty as when we came. The answer to this is to worship in a spiritually correct manner. The text above is an illustration of when we contribute to the Sunday offering. If anything can be done wrongfully, it is our giving money during worship. Putting money into the offering bag seems no big deal. Yet, you note from the above text, it is our attitude and heartfelt response that matter; it must be done cheerfully and not grudgingly.

Let's direct our attention to three such attitudes.

First, we must be reverent in our worship. Hebrews 12:28 says: "Wherefore we receiving a kingdom which cannot be moved, let us have grace, whereby we may serve God acceptably with reverence and godly fear." Our hearts must be so overwhelmed with the majesty and holiness of God that from the heart we bow humbly and obediently before him.

Second, we must appear before God in confession and repentance of sin. Ezekiel 33:11 says: "I have no pleasure in the death of the wicked; but that the wicked turn from his way and live: turn ye, turn ye from your evil ways; for why will ye die, O house of Israel?" This is a call to deal with our sins by confessing them before God and forsaking them.

Third, we come with joy, as in Psalm 98:4, "Make a joyful noise unto the Lord, all the earth: make a loud noise, and rejoice, and sing praise."

Wonderful qualities, and so often absent. Heartfelt worship is so desirable, and it comes in the way of spiritual preparation, prayer, and meditation at home and at church.

Jason Kortering

February 13 — Unlawful to Teach Anything Contrary to the Scripture

But though we, or an angel from heaven, preach any other gospel unto you than that which we have preached unto you, let him be accursed. —Galatians 1:8

Here, we are taught carefulness as we assess our worship. Since both what we believe and how we are to worship God are dictated to us in the Bible, we must use the Bible as our rule. This is emphasized in Article 7 in this way: "it is unlawful for anyone, though an apostle, to teach otherwise than we are now taught in the holy Scriptures." Then, the words quoted above from Galatians 1:8 follow.

Think on these words: "For since it is forbidden *to add unto or take away any thing from the Word of God*, it doth thereby evidently appear that the doctrine thereof is most perfect and complete in all respects" (Article 7). This is a direct quote from Revelation 22:18–19, "For I testify unto every man that heareth the words of the prophecy of this book. If any man shall add unto these things, God shall add unto him the plagues that are written in this book: and if any man shall take away from the words of the book of this prophecy, God shall take away his part out of the book of life." These are sobering words.

The Belgic Confession takes the positive approach, that "the doctrine thereof is most perfect and complete in all respects." This is heartwarming for any Christian, whether young or old.

We face many challenges in our faith and practice. There are those who believe and practice things very different from us, and that forces us to ask, who is right? In addition, many attack us for what we believe and practice; they ridicule it and openly charge us with being unchristian in our belief and practice.

Are you shaken by this? Do you begin to doubt?

The rock and foundation of our belief and worship is upon the Bible. This is what God instructs us, and as long as we are obedient and faithful to God's word, we are right and in God's favor.

Along with our forefathers, we say it is unlawful to contradict or replace the teaching of God's word.

This is not our opinion. It was the conviction of the church leaders at the time of the Reformation. It is our conviction of faith as well.

Jason Kortering

February 14 — **The Doctrine of the Bible Is Most Perfect and Complete**

If any man speak, let him speak as the oracles of God; if any man minister, let him do it as of the ability which God giveth: that God in all things may be glorified through Jesus Christ, to whom be praise and dominion for ever and ever. Amen. —1 Peter 4:11

There are two ways to deal with error.

First, we are to expose the lie and see it for what it really is.

Second, we are to meditate upon the truth and extol the God who revealed to us that truth.

We want to briefly meditate upon this second aspect now.

When we use the Bible as a rule of faith and believe that it is sufficient to determine our doctrine and our practice, it is more than a way to expose error. The positive side is that it defines for us the content of our faith and assures us that our practices are in truth the will of God. We have explored this in the areas of both teaching and worship. Let's give a bit more attention to the use of the Bible to enhance our faith positively.

According to the quotation above, when we worship on the Lord's day and the pastor speaks, we may conclude that he speaks "as the oracles of God" (1 Pet. 4:11). When the pastor, elders, or deacons minister to us the word of God to help us personally and individually, we may receive them as from God and glorify God through their actions. I ask you whether you actually do this. Are you tempted to argue with them? Do you resent it that they come with authority that compels you to listen and conform your way to their teaching? There is only one right way, and that is to receive them as speaking the "oracles of God." That is pretty clear. It is good that the above quote warns the church leaders that they don't let this get out of hand. "If any man minister, let him do it as of the ability which God giveth."

We refuse to compare the Bible to any other "holy book." It is the only revelation from the true God which is most complete and perfect. It is true, reliable, and all-sufficient.

Just think, you hold that book in your own hand. Pray that its truths may be in your heart.

Jason Kortering

February 15 — **The Bible and Other Writings**

And my speech and my preaching was not with enticing words of man's wisdom, but in demonstration of the Spirit and of power. —1 Corinthians 2:4

We come to the part of Article 7 which makes a comparison between the Bible and other human writings: "Neither do we consider of equal value any writing of men, however holy these men may have been, with those divine Scriptures."*

These human writings are listed: "councils [church meetings which consider issues], decrees [doctrinal conclusions arrived at by these councils], or statutes [conduct regarding our behavior, arrived at by these councils]".

The values considered by these human writings are also listed: "custom [behavior which has become commonplace], or the great multitude [majority of people believe and practice these things], or antiquity [faith and practice which goes back a long time in the history of the church], or succession of times [been embraced for many years] or persons [oftentimes, leaders of great learning and fame]."

All these things may not influence us in comparing these writings with the Bible, and may not be considered "of equal value with the truth of God."**

The difference between the Bible and these writings is the authorship. Even though church fathers and councils were often guided in their writing by the Holy Spirit, yet the Holy Spirit's influence in writing the Bible is different. None of these writings may be called inspired in the sense the Bible is inspired. The Bible was inspired in such a way that the product was without sin and perfect. Other writings were inspired but yet the product of sinners. Hence, the article says, "for all men are of themselves liars, and more vain than vanity itself." This referred to many claims by the Roman Catholic Church of the infallibility of theologians and church councils.

In no way does this article make disparaging remarks towards the writings of godly men and church councils. We all grow spiritually through their maturity of faith and ability to explain the Bible clearly. This is on two levels: through individual men of God who contribute their skills towards the explanation of truth and church councils who have contributed creeds.

Yet, they must never be placed on a level with the Bible. Even Paul knew that his preaching was not done with enticing words of men, but its value was in its conformity to the Bible, "a demonstration of the Spirit and of power" (1 Cor. 2:4).

The Bible stands apart from all human writings.

Jason Kortering

---

* Belgic Confession 7, in *The Psalter.*
** Belgic Confession 7, in *The Psalter.*

February 16 — Try the Spirits

Beloved, believe not every spirit,
but try the spirits whether they are of God:
because many false prophets are gone out into the world. —1 John 4:1

Because the human heart is "desperately wicked" (Jer. 17:9), also in the realm of spiritual writings, Article 7 of the Belgic Confession states: "Therefore we reject with all our hearts whatsoever doth not agree with this infallible rule, which the apostles have taught us, saying, *Try the spirits whether they are of God.*"

Because all men are liars by nature and more vain than vanity itself, it is little wonder that even men who claim to be Christians can write some bad things. Some of them are not motivated by the one holy desire that we ought to have, and that is to write in agreement with all the Bible teaches for our belief and worship. They have many wrong motives; such could be the desire to have their writings accepted by the populace (fame); or it may be money, to profit from their writings (greed); or, as in the history of the Christian Church, to avoid rejection and persecution (conformity to the crowd). This was true at the time of the Reformation; it is also true today. These wrong motives are not far from any of us. So, our opposition is not only from the world of unbelief and ungodliness, it is also from the church. We are literally surrounded by evil spirits, and we can easily become involved in "fellowship with devils...and the table of devils" (1 Cor. 10:20, 21).

There is only one good response to this: "try the spirits" (1 John 4:1).

You are called upon by God not to be naïve, gullible, and trusting everyone who poses as a Christian. Your goal is to mature and be discerning. We know all about the truth of human depravity because we know our own. I know the cunning of the human heart because my nature is the same. The evil one uses this.

You have the most important weapon in this spiritual battle: "take...the sword of the Spirit, which is the word of God" (Eph. 6:17). Use your Bible as the standard of right and wrong. Seek good instruction and counsel from church leaders you know to be people of God. Measure all human writing, reject the lie, and extol the truth.

The Holy Spirit uses the Bible to convict you; it also convicts others.

Jason Kortering

February 17 — Receive Him Not into Your House

If there come any unto you, and bring not this doctrine,
receive him not into your house, neither bid him God speed. —2 John 10

Not only are we to try the spirits, we are also to know how to handle those who bring the lie: "If there come any unto you, and bring not this doctrine, receive him not into your house, neither bid him God speed" (2 John 10).

We ought to remind ourselves that not all Christians agree on what this doctrine is. Here, we have to make a careful distinction between erring brothers and sisters in Christ and heretics. The distinction is important because we must not treat them all alike.

There are Christians who err in doctrine and practice but who do not contradict the gospel, doing so with the conviction that their teaching is faithful to the Bible, and they must be viewed as erring brothers and sisters. They still believe that salvation is through the blood of the atonement and that salvation is God's wonderful work but may differ in other areas. You find such in Bible-believing churches all over the world.

In distinction, there are many who pose as Christians but deny the gospel, and their error is a blatant disregard for the teaching of the Bible (even if they claim otherwise). Such must be viewed as heretics and enemies of the faith. These are found in liberal churches who have abandoned the gospel. They may appear at your doorstep in the form of a cult—Jehovah's Witnesses come to mind.

To the latter group, the words quoted above and in the article of the Belgic Confession apply. We must not associate with them, nor pretend that they are our Christian friends. There must be a rejection of their persons because their teaching and practice contradicts what a Christian may believe or how he is to live. They reject the word of God.

Some of you may know the pain of separation over false religion. If you stop to think of it, your Christian forefathers had to do this over against the followers of the Chinese religion.[*] The same is true for you today regarding your peers who may claim to be Christians, but are not.

Be careful in making this distinction and exercise love to all your enemies. The goal is to gain them for Christ.

Jason Kortering

---

[*] These meditations were originally written for believers in Singapore.

February 18 — Embrace the Truth

But the hour cometh, and now is, when the true worshippers shall worship the Father in spirit and in truth: for the Father seeketh such to worship him. —John 4:23

This is a good summary of what we have been considering in Article 7 of our Belgic Confession.

We have focused on God as our Father. We have looked at the holy Scriptures, which is his gift of the Spirit to us. We have concluded with this confession that the Bible contains everything necessary for our faith and worship. We have been instructed to reject all that contradicts the Bible's teaching and those who bring such teaching. The writings and practices of men may never be considered of equal value to the Bible.

What better way to conclude this article than to say: "The hour now is when true worshippers shall worship the Father in spirit and in truth" (John 4:23)?

I sincerely pray that this may be your portion.

A true worshipper is one who has a heart for God, is drawn into his holy presence in contrition and confession of sin, desires to praise God in song and prayer, rejoices to be with the congregation to contribute to the needs of the poor, and is blessed by the sacraments as they confirm his faith by water, bread, and wine.

How wonderful it is that we can still do this at this late date in history with the conviction that our faith and worship is acceptable to God because we do it in the manner God wants.

Our conviction is founded upon our knowledge of the word of God. Objectively, the Bible is the most comprehensive standard for everything we believe and all our behavior as Christians. We have the Bible, which includes everything necessary for our salvation. God has graciously provided that by his Holy Spirit. We must hasten to add, we also have subjectively the application of all of this by the Holy Spirit who works grace in our hearts to accept the Bible as the word of God and all its teachings.

This amazing grace is truly amazing. Never take grace for granted. Always humbly pray to God that he will give to you this amazing grace to be the Christian he wants you to be.

Thank God, for all these blessings come from him. To him alone be the glory.

Jason Kortering

Article 8

GOD IS ONE IN ESSENCE, YET DISTINGUISHED IN THREE PERSONS

According to this truth and this word of God, we believe in one only God, who is one single essence, in which are three persons, really, truly, and eternally distinct, according to their incommunicable properties; namely, the Father, and the Son, and the Holy Ghost. The Father is the cause, origin, and beginning of all things, visible and invisible; the Son is the Word, Wisdom, and Image of the Father; the Holy Ghost is the eternal Power and Might, proceeding from the Father and the Son. Nevertheless God is not by this distinction divided into three, since the Holy Scriptures teach us that the Father, and the Son, and the Holy Ghost have each his personality, distinguished by their properties; but in such wise that these three persons are but one only God. Hence, then, it is evident that the Father is not the Son, nor the Son the Father, and likewise the Holy Ghost is neither the Father nor the Son. Nevertheless these persons thus distinguished are not divided nor intermixed; for the Father hath not assumed the flesh, nor hath the Holy Ghost, but the Son only. The Father hath never been without his Son, or without his Holy Ghost. For they are all three co-eternal and co-essential. There is neither first nor last; for they are all three one, in truth, in power, in goodness, and in mercy.

February 19 — God Is One and Not Three

For there are three that bear record in heaven, the Father, the Word, and the Holy Ghost: and these three are one. —1 John 5:7

The Belgic Confession has set forth that our knowledge of God is acquired by means of his creative work and written word. We have considered the unique character of the Bible as God's word.

As we now turn to the content of the Bible, the Confession indicates that the Bible's central message is the knowledge of God himself. Of the many truths God reveals about himself, the first and most significant is that of the Trinity: God is one being and three in persons.

We begin by stating briefly that on the basis of God's self-revelation, we believe there is *one* God, not three.

There are many religions, such as Hinduism, that hold to many gods, and others, like Islam, which hold to only one. We use the terms polytheists (many gods) and monotheists (one god).

Often, the Christian church is accused of being polytheistic because of the Trinity; some claim that if God is three persons, there are three Gods. Even the cults accuse us of this. We can appreciate the problem they raise, because a person is connected with a being, and nowhere else do we encounter one being in three persons. This defies even our wildest imaginations. The only claim to such a trinity of persons is in Jehovah, the Christian God.

The answer to this is that God has revealed himself as only one being; if we hold to three beings, then we could rightly be accused of trusting in three gods.

The text quoted above makes this clear: there are three persons, and those three are one: "There are three that bear record in heaven, the Father, the Word, and the Holy Ghost; and these three are one" (1 John 5:7). God is three persons in one divine being.

Article 8 states: "We believe in one only God, who is one single essence, in which are three persons."

What a blessing for us to know this one God. He is all that is necessary for our faith, for beside him, there is no other. All our salvation is in him alone.

May God help us to keep our eyes of faith upon him.

Jason Kortering

February 20 — **God Is the Only God**

But to us there is but one God, the Father, of whom are all things, and we in him; and one Lord Jesus Christ, by whom are all things, and we by him. —1 Corinthians 8:6

We must make a distinction between the fact that God is *one* and that he is the *only* God.

We have explained that when we say God is one, we say that he possesses one being, not three. This is important, for we must be clear in our minds that the God of the Bible is one in his nature. An example of this is that God possesses a mind, and with it the ability to think and reason. God does not have three minds, but only one.

Now we must add, this one God is the only God.

Article 8 expresses it this way: "According to this truth and this word of God, we believe in one only God." Later in the same article, we read: "God is not by this distinction divided into three, since the holy Scriptures teach us that the Father, and the Son, and the Holy Ghost have each his personality, distinguished by their properties; but in such wise that these three persons are but one only God" (Article 8).

To put it simply, we believe that our God is the only God there is.

Because we believe this, we Christians are hated and accused of being egotists and non-conformists. In our post-modern world, there is no standard for truth, so everyone claims the right to believe and understand anything of religion, including who God is. The emergent church openly teaches this in the name of Christianity. No one, neither pastors nor members, can claim they have the exclusive understanding of anything religious. It does not impress such people at all if we claim the authority of the Bible because they reject this as well.

Yet, in obedience to Christ and his word, we say the only true God is the God of the Bible, and the only way of salvation is in Jesus Christ, his Son. 1 Corinthians 8:6 says: "But to us there is but one God," and he is the only God.

Be careful that your knowledge of the only God does not make you proud. Humbly bow before him and thank him for revealing himself to you.

Do you have these convictions? Are you already suffering for them?

Jason Kortering

February 21 — God Possesses One Single Essence

> *Hear, O Israel: the LORD our God is one LORD."*
> —Deuteronomy 6:4

What will be said in this devotional has been stated briefly before in our consideration of Article 8 of the Belgic Confession, but now we can expand on it a bit more.

We use the word *essence* interchangeably with *being* as it relates to God. They are the same and describe something of the nature of who God is.

We speak of "human nature" when we refer to ourselves. It is our make-up as we came forth from the creator. Our human nature was subsequently changed as the consequence of God's sentence of death. Even still, our human nature distinguishes us from the plants and animals and from the angel world. We are "soul creatures" drawn from the dust of the earth, we have the capacity to think and reason, we have desires and can project them into the future, we show emotions, and we are spiritual creatures in the sense that we have the capacity to love and hate.

Similarly, we can speak of God's "divine nature" or "being" or "essence." If we remember that man was made in the image of God, then certainly God possesses the ability to think, to reason, and this he does as God in the divine mind. He expresses his will and good pleasure because he possesses the ultimate will: his will is sovereign over all creatures. He expresses deep emotions of joy and displeasure. His heart is perfect love, and from it flows forth the divine good pleasure to save in contrast to his hatred, which burns towards the wicked.

The point of Article 8 is that God possesses one mind, one will, one emotion, one heart, and we know this because he has revealed himself in this manner throughout all history. Though there are three persons, yet God is one being, and all three persons express themselves in the one nature of God. Three persons think in one mind, three persons will in one will, three persons express divine emotions, and three persons love from the one heart of God.

"Hear, O Israel: the LORD our God is one LORD" (Deut. 6:4). God is one single essence. The heathen that surrounded Israel had many gods. Paul faced a multitude of gods on Mars' Hill as he stood before the Athenians. So also today, we are surrounded by polytheists.

Yet, we have one God, powerful, loving, and mighty to save. Meditate on this and marvel.

Jason Kortering

February 22 — **The Three Divine Persons**

Go ye therefore, and teach all nations, baptizing them in the name of the Father, and of the Son, and of the Holy Ghost. —Matthew 28:19

We said last time that there are three persons who think in the one divine mind. A person is one who has the capacity to think, to desire, to love. A person is one who can say *I* and be the subject of the action. Hence, an animal is not a person, because it acts on instinct. Angels are persons, humans are persons, and now, God is personal. He possesses three persons, each with the capacity to reason, to will, to love, to express emotions.

What Article 8 does for us, and we focus briefly on this, is that it tells us that these three persons are equal in everything as they function in the divine nature. Later, we will focus on the individual personality and activity.

Article 8 states that the three persons have their own personality, distinguished by their properties: "but in such wise that these three persons are but one only God…For they are all three coeternal and coessential. There is neither first nor last; for they are all three one, in truth, in power, in goodness, and in mercy" (Article 8).

There is no ranking, as if the Father is more important or takes priority over the Son, or the Son is more important than the Holy Spirit. If that were true, then the three persons would be superior or inferior one to the other. They are all equal. They all possess the attributes of God: eternal, omnipresent, holy, and loving. Each of the persons of the Trinity possesses these attributes of God equally; there is no superiority of one over the other. We must quickly add as well that neither are God's virtues split up into three parts, as if one third of his power or love is in the Father, another third in the Son, and still another third in the Holy Spirit. Even though we cannot understand this, yet it is important because each of the persons functions in a special way in the work of God.

Baptism is an example. It places us into fellowship with God, as each of these three persons has a role: the Father in nurturing us, the Son in redeeming us, and the Holy Spirit in our sanctification. Thus, baptism is the sign and seal of God's work of salvation.

Each person is almighty God.

Jason Kortering

February 23 — The Person of the Father

But to us there is but one God, the Father, of whom
are all things, and we in him; and one Lord Jesus Christ,
by whom are all things, and we by him. —1 Corinthians 8:6

It is humanly impossible for us to comprehend the Trinity. For example, how can one person be called Father and not exist before Son and Holy Spirit? All our ideas of father have to do with conceiving that which was not yet born. Here, Article 8 says: "The Father is the cause, origin, and beginning of all things visible and invisible." By distinction, the Son is "the word, wisdom, and image of the Father." The Holy Ghost is the "eternal power and might, proceeding from the Father and the Son" (Article 8). We get into serious trouble if we think here in terms of time with historical events and a succession of moments. If we think this way, we have to conclude that the Father existed, even in eternity, before the existence of the Son. This is not true. All the persons are eternal, none existed without the other, and yet, each person has its own property and activity.

The Father is said to be "the cause, origin, and beginning of all things visible and invisible." The passage quoted above states this. He is called Father, because in the divine being, outside of time, he is the source of all things.

I trust that the mere mention of father arouses in you a deep sense of love and understanding. Some of you may not have had a father even close to the biblical description, especially if your father was not a Christian. Even if such is true, you can understand the role of a Christian father given in the Bible. It is beautiful and precious. For a father is not only the author of life, but the provider and protector of his family. In an earthly way, we see a little something of God the Father.

This helps us to understand a little how the triune God is a covenant God. God the Father speaks to God the Son: he is the originator of those thoughts, and the Son receives these thoughts as the word of God. The role of the Holy Spirit is to breathe forth these words to both Father and Son. In summary, God holds conversation within himself, and talking together is what the covenant is all about.

God's covenant with us originates in himself.

Jason Kortering

February 24 — The Person of the Son

In the beginning was the Word, and the Word was with God, and the Word was God. The same was in the beginning with God.
—John 1:1–2

There is a very close relationship between God the Son (the second person of the Holy Trinity) and the Son of God (Jesus). Sometimes in Scripture, it is hard to distinguish, yet it is important to keep this in mind.

The text from John 1:1 illustrates this: Is the Word referred to here Jesus or the second person of the Trinity? Actually, they are both included: the Word is a name for Jesus, but notice, the Word was God. How was Jesus God? He was the second person of the Trinity.

Article 8 describes God the Son this way: "the Son is the word, wisdom, and image of the Father." All three have their own "personality, distinguished by their properties; but in such wise that these three persons are but one only God." It adds: "Hence then, it is evident, that the Father is not the Son, nor the Son the Father…the Father hath not assumed the flesh, nor hath the Holy Ghost, but the Son only" (Article 8).

God the Son is the second person of the Holy Trinity. In eternity, he enjoyed fellowship with the Father and the Holy Spirit. We are told in John 1:3, "All things were made by him; and without him was not anything made that was made." He is called the Word because already in the creation, God the Father called out to the Son, and through the Son the call echoed forth in the heavens and the earth which the Holy Spirit used to bring creation into existence. Genesis 1:3 indicates, "And God said…"; and John 1:3 reflects: "All things were made by him [the Word]; and without him was not anything made that was made." Turning back to Genesis 1:2, we read: "And the Spirit of God moved upon the face of the waters." You see how the three persons of the Trinity were involved in creation, each in his own personal way.

Even more significant for us lost sinners is the truth that God the Son took on flesh to redeem the lost creation. As the second person of the Trinity, being God and divine, he was qualified to accomplish the redemption necessary through his descent into hell and resurrection from the dead.

All this is sealed in that God the Son became the Son of God.

Jason Kortering

February 25 — The Person of the Holy Spirit

But if I cast out devils by the Spirit of God,
then the kingdom of God is come unto you. —Matthew 12:28

Even as we made a distinction between God the Father and the fatherhood of God, God the Son and the Son of God, we must make a distinction between God the Holy Spirit and the Spirit of Jesus Christ. God the Holy Spirit is the third person of the Holy Trinity, while the Spirit of Jesus is the third person of the Trinity given to Jesus upon the completion of his earthly ministry, as a reward for the atonement accomplished. Even though we make this distinction, we must keep in mind that the Holy Spirit given to Jesus, and in turn given to the church on earth at Pentecost, is in truth the third person of the Trinity.

The Holy Spirit is a divine person. Article 8 states: "the Holy Ghost is the eternal power and might, proceeding from the Father and the Son." The Holy Ghost has his personality, distinguished by his properties. "The Father hath never been without his Son, or without his Holy Ghost. For they are all three coeternal and coessential. There is neither first nor last; for they are all three one, in truth, in power, in goodness, and in mercy" (Article 8).

Spirit means breath, energy, and that describes the work of the third person. He brings to pass all that the Father wills, whether creation, incarnation, or salvation. Though he is involved in all three areas of divine work, it is in the latter, our sanctification and salvation, that he plays his key role. As the Father in creation, and the Son in redemption, so the Holy Spirit is in sanctification.

He possesses all the power and majesty of the triune God.

In the quote above, Jesus asserts: "If I cast out devils by the Spirit of God, then the kingdom of God is come unto you" (Matt. 12:28). Jesus demonstrated this by his miraculous power over demons. As is true with all the miracles which Jesus performed, the miracles over demons are object lessons of salvation. Jesus made the blind to see, the dead to arise, the sick and lame to walk. The devil represents our ultimate enemy and hindrance to salvation. With him defeated, our salvation is sure.

The Holy Spirit is abundantly qualified to perform his role in our salvation. All our salvation is from above.

Jason Kortering

Article 9

THE PROOF OF THE FOREGOING ARTICLE OF THE TRINITY OF PERSONS IN ONE GOD

All this we know, as well from the testimonies of Holy Writ as from their operations, and chiefly by those we feel in ourselves. The testimonies of the holy Scriptures, that teach us to believe this Holy Trinity are written in many places of the Old Testament, which are not so necessary to enumerate as to choose them out with discretion and judgment.

In Genesis 1:26-27, God saith: *Let us make man in our image, after our likeness,* etc. *So God created man in his own image, male and female created he them.* And Genesis 3:22, *Behold, the man is become as one of us.* From this saying, *Let us make man in our image,* it appears that there are more persons than one in the Godhead; and when he saith *God created,* he signifies the unity. It is true he doth not say how many persons there are, but that which appears to us somewhat obscure in the Old Testament is very plain in the New. For when our Lord was baptized in Jordan, the voice of the Father was heard, saying, *This is my beloved Son;* the Son was seen in the water; and the Holy Ghost appeared in the shape of a dove. This form is also instituted by Christ in the baptism of all believers. *Baptize all nations in the name of the Father, and of the Son, and of the Holy Ghost.* In the Gospel of Luke, the angel Gabriel thus addressed Mary, the mother of our Lord: *The Holy Ghost shall come upon thee, and the power of the Highest shall overshadow thee, therefore also that holy thing which shall be born of thee shall be called the Son of God.* Likewise, *The grace of our Lord Jesus Christ, and the love of God, and the communion of the Holy Ghost be with you.* And: *There are three that bear record in heaven, the Father, the Word, and the Holy Ghost, and these three are one.*

In all which places we are fully taught that there are three persons in one only divine essence. And although this doctrine far surpasses all human understanding, nevertheless, we now believe it by means of the Word of God, but expect hereafter to enjoy the perfect knowledge and benefit thereof in Heaven.

Moreover, we must observe the particular offices and operations of these three persons toward us. The Father is called our Creator, by his power; the Son is our Savior and Redeemer, by his blood; the Holy Ghost is our Sanctifier, by his dwelling in our hearts.

This doctrine of the Holy Trinity hath always been defended and maintained by the true Church, since the times of the apostles to this very day, against the Jews, Mohammedans, and some false Christians and heretics, as Marcion, Manes, Praxeas, Sabellius, Samosatenus, Arius, and such like, who have been justly condemned by the orthodox fathers.

Therefore, in this point we do willingly receive the three creeds, namely, that of the Apostles, of Nicea, and of Athanasius: likewise that which, conformable thereunto, is agreed upon by the ancient fathers.

February 26 — God Has Revealed Himself as Triune

*I am the Almighty God; walk before me,
and be thou perfect.* —Genesis 17:1

If you are like most people, your faith in God as three persons in one being is vexing. It is vexing because we cannot fathom it, cannot explain it, and for most people, cannot convincingly prove it. The one great relief is that we conclude with personal conviction, I know God is triune because he has revealed himself as such in his holy word. That is it! We need no more nor less.

This is significant because faith in God is beyond reason. That is not to say that there are no elements of our faith which can be explained and about which we can talk reasonably with people. We console ourselves when we stand before this amazing truth about God that we do not have to be able to understand nor explain in human reasoning to convince everyone. Our belief in God is exactly that, *faith*, which is based upon divine revelation.

This is how God stood before Abraham: "I am the Almighty God; walk before me and be thou perfect" (Gen. 17:1). Notice, how simple: I am the Almighty God! I identify myself, I reveal myself, I tell you who I am. And our response must be: "Speak, Lord, for thy servant heareth" (1 Sam. 3:9).

Are you ready to listen to God?

We have struggled our way through the articles of faith which describe for us how God is three persons in one being. We learned that as Father, he is precious to us, for all things have their origin in him. As Son, he comes to us as our savior and Lord, and as Holy Spirit, he assures us that he is not dependent upon human strength to accomplish his purposes. Remember, "not by might, nor by power, but by my spirit" (Zech. 4:6). Now, we must reflect a bit more on one additional aspect: all of this is true because God has told us that this is true about him.

This calms our hearts.

For my personal faith, for my answer to all doubters, and for those who want to argue in resistance to the great truth that God is triune, my one reply is, God has so revealed himself to me in his word.

Article 9 expresses this: "All this we know…from the testimony of holy Writ." May God show that to each of us.

Jason Kortering

February 27 — Old Testament Evidence of the Trinity

And God said, Let us make man in our image,
after our likeness…So God created man in his own image,
in the image of God created he him; male and female created he them.
—Genesis 1:26–27

We have come to the part of the Belgic Confession where the author sets out to demonstrate that God has revealed himself as three persons in one being. Article 9 states:

> All this we know, as well from the testimonies of Holy Writ as from their operations, and chiefly by those we feel in ourselves. The testimonies of the holy Scriptures that teach us to believe this Holy Trinity are written in many places of the Old Testament, which are not so necessary to enumerate as to choose them out with discretion and judgment.

The two passages they refer to are the one quoted above and, in addition, Genesis 3:22, "Behold, the man is become as one of us."

You might ask, how does this prove the Trinity? The reference to which we point regards the plural pronouns used: "Let *us* make man," and "Behold, the man is become as one of *us*."

There is only one convincing explanation for these pronouns. God is speaking to himself. People who talk to themselves have problems, because they are one person—we are meant to speak to others. With God it is different; he is three persons in one, so when he speaks to himself, there are three persons involved in the conversation. Thus, God could say, "Let us make man." The Father, Son, and Holy Spirit are involved in the creative process.

As Article 9 says: "From this saying…it appears that there are more persons than one in the Godhead" (Article 9). If you meditate on this thought: the plurality of persons, it says something about God that is wonderful. From all eternity, God was never lonely, never silenced; rather, he experienced friendship in the highest and most perfect sense of the word. Theologically, this means that God is a covenant God, a God of friendship. His decrees are not a dead blueprint for history but living thought and purpose within the Godhead. We were in the eternal mind of God in his good pleasure of election. All things are in the eternal presence of God, the living God of personal friendship.

From the very beginning of revelation, God said: "I am a triune God."

Jason Kortering

February 28 — New Testament Evidence of the Trinity

The grace of the Lord Jesus Christ, and the love of God, and the communion of the Holy Ghost, be with you all. Amen.
—2 Corinthians 13:14

The Confession now turns to the New Testament for proof of the Trinity.

It refers to the baptism of Jesus: "the voice of the Father was heard, saying, *This is my beloved Son*; the Son was seen in the water; and the Holy Ghost appeared in the shape of a dove."

This was incorporated into the baptism formula of Matthew 28:19, "Go ye therefore, and teach all nations, baptizing them in the name of the Father, and of the Son, and of the Holy Ghost."

In connection with the conception and birth of Jesus, the "power of the Highest" is the Holy Spirit sent of the Father. He would overshadow the virgin, and therefore, "that holy thing which shall be born of thee shall be called the Son of God" (Luke 1:35).

A reference is also made to the apostolic blessing: "The grace of the Lord Jesus Christ, and the love of God, and the communion of the Holy Ghost, be with you" (2 Cor. 13:14).

Finally, we look to the summary given in 1 John 5:7, "For there are three that bear record in heaven, the Father, the Word, and the Holy Ghost, and these three are one."

The grand summary is given:

> In all which places we are fully taught that there are three persons in one only divine essence. And although this doctrine far surpasses all human understanding, nevertheless we now believe it by means of the Word of God, but expect hereafter to enjoy the perfect knowledge and benefit thereof in heaven.

I like that last statement; it demonstrates the humility of faith. I cannot rationally explain the meaning of the Trinity, and I cannot demonstrate it from nature. Some try—for example, water, vapor, and ice, which are all forms of one chemical—yet that is wholly inadequate. It comes down to our accepting the Bible as God's revelation. If God tells us he is three persons in one being, by faith my response is to bow before this God. I may not adequately understand it now, but there is a future life in glory where I will have a greater capacity for understanding. In heaven, I will see more of the revelation of the triune God when I look into the face of my Savior.

Faith relies upon God. Keep doing this.

Jason Kortering

March 1 — We Experience the Operations of the Trinity in Ourselves

*And because ye are sons, God hath sent forth the Spirit of his Son
into your hearts, crying, Abba, Father.* —Galatians 4:6

You recall that we said awhile back that the Belgic Confession states that we know of God triune through the Bible and from "their operations, and chiefly by those we feel in ourselves" (Article 9).

From this, we recognize that feelings of faith are of value. We need not go to the extremes of the Pentecostals or Charismatics, nor ought we to deny our Christian experience. How, we then ask, do we experience or "feel" the triune God?

Let's first look at the person of the Father. Article 9 states: "The Father is called our Creator, by his power." He is the originator of our life. We could not even be born into this world without him. Even more so, we could never become Christians without our heavenly Father giving us spiritual life. From all eternity, God as Father elected us, gave his Son to redeem us, and sent his Holy Spirit to regenerate us. We experience God the Father in a mighty way. To put it differently, we could never be born or saved without him. You say, "How do I know God is Father?" Look at yourself: you could not be who you are without him. We rejoice in faith to believe this.

Now, we turn to the person of the Son. Of him is said: "the Son is our Savior and Redeemer by his blood" (Article 9). Doesn't that make the second person of the holy Trinity close to our hearts? He went to the cross for us, and in his human nature suffered the curse of God upon our disobedience. The Father received his obedient work on the cross, declared us to be righteous in him, and raised him from the dead to demonstrate his approval. This same Son ascended into heaven and applies to us the benefits of his death and resurrection.

And of the third person, the Holy Spirit, the article states: "The Holy Ghost is our Sanctifier by his dwelling in our hearts" (Article 9). Certainly, he can't get any closer to us than that. We experience repentance from sin and the joy of forgiveness as he works salvation in our hearts and lives.

Yes, the doctrine of the Trinity is profound.

Yet, it is close to our hearts. Our faith is the evidence of his work.

Jason Kortering

March 2 — The Truth of the Trinity Defended by the Church

Are ye so foolish? having begun in the Spirit,
are ye now made perfect by the flesh? —Galatians 3:3

Two things impress us when we look at the history of the church and how the church dealt with the doctrine of the Trinity.

First, from the very beginning of creation, through the New Testament era and all the way to the present time, the universal church of Christ embraced the doctrine of the Trinity. That says something to us, as the Spirit of Christ dwelt in his church this way.

The second thing is that this doctrine was attacked from without and within, and yet the faithful church maintained her confession of the Trinity. Article 9 gives some details. "This doctrine of the Holy Trinity hath always been defended and maintained by the true Church, since the times of the apostles to this very day." Then, it lists some of the opponents which were "justly condemned by the orthodox fathers." Let's say a brief word about each.

The Jews rejected Jesus Christ as the Messiah and the divine Son; the Muslims insisted Allah was the one only god, and Jesus was a prophet subjected to Mohammed; Manes (Mani) believed that Jesus failed in the crucifixion to give light, but was semi-god, who salvaged his ministry through Manes and his followers; Praxeas said there were no three persons, but modes of revelation: that is to say, Christ on the cross was the Father suffering for sin; Sabellius also taught three modes of revelation, not persons; Samosatenus taught that the man Jesus was adopted by God and not truly God; Arius taught that Jesus was created by God and less than God. All these men taught their lies during the first three centuries of the early Christian church.

These few sentences do not adequately explain their heresies. I gathered the information above from the book *With Heart and Mouth*, by Daniel Hyde.[*] He has a more detailed chapter on the Trinitarian controversies which is helpful to read.[**]

There are a few things to conclude from these early controversies over the Trinity.

First, the devil attacked the fundamental doctrine of the Trinity. How smart of him. A church that denies the Trinity loses the gospel; it's that simple.

Second, God saw to it that his church understood clearly this cardinal truth and expressed it well in her early confessions. Thus, this truth stands to this very day.

Jason Kortering

---

[*] Hyde, *With Heart and Mouth*, 133-135.
[**] Hyde, *With Heart and Mouth*, 123-135.

March 3 — The Church Confesses the Truth of the Trinity

Are ye so foolish? having begun in the Spirit,
are ye now made perfect by the flesh? —Galatians 3:3

I want to make a comment on this verse. Paul admonished the Galatians for allowing the Judaizers to take from them the joy of salvation in Jesus when they insisted that new converts had to keep the law of Moses. They were foolish. In many ways, the early Christian church faced this same issue when they had to deal with controversy over the doctrine of the Trinity. All of salvation is joined to God triune.

Thanks be to God; the early Christian began in the Holy Spirit and continued in the Spirit by defending and confessing God as Father, Son, and Holy Spirit.

This was done in the confessions written by the early Christian church, which are listed in Article 9: "Therefore, in this point, we do willingly receive the three creeds, namely, that of the Apostles, of Nicea, and of Athanasius; likewise that which, conformable thereunto, is agreed upon by the ancient fathers."

We call these three creeds listed here the Ecumenical Creeds. The Apostles' Creed was the summary of the teaching of the apostles and was written in the early second century. The Nicene Creed was the summary of the church's teaching of the Trinity after they answered many attacks; it was adopted by the Council of Nicea in A.D. 325. The Athanasian Creed goes beyond the doctrine of the Trinity and includes a good defense of the Deity of Christ through his incarnation and union of both divine and human natures. Athanasius was a strong defender of these truths during the fourth century, yet this confession was a summary of his teaching and was included in the church's confession around the seventh century.

Not only did the devil attack the fundamental truth which would successfully destroy the gospel of salvation, but the Holy Spirit also used this attack to enable the church to formulate their understanding; as a result, church fathers gave biblical defense of these doctrines in a clear manner. As you may know, controversy can be painful, yet God uses it to advantage. The church grows in understanding and, by the Holy Spirit's work, makes perfect the doctrines begun in simple form.

The statements of faith contained in these ecumenical confessions have stood the test of history.

Rejoice! God is the God of history, and all things work for good.

Jason Kortering

March 4 — The Believer Embraces the Truth of the Trinity

But these are written, that ye might believe that Jesus is the Christ, the Son of God; and that believing ye might have life through his name.
—John 20:31

We close our consideration of the Trinity itself with a more personal response. The next two devotionals focus upon the divinity of Jesus and the divinity of the Holy Spirit. These are two crucial areas affected by our understanding of the Trinity. However, before we get into this aspect, I want to pause and reflect upon our own personal response to what we have considered.

I ask you directly, do you believe that God is triune, and how important is that to you?

Take as an example the Apostles' Creed, which is mentioned in this article as a wonderful statement of the church's confession. The Heidelberg Catechism describes it as our "catholic, undoubted Christian faith."* It adds that it is a summary of what is necessary for us as Christians to believe. The articles are divided into three parts: "The first is of *God the Father and our creation*; the second, of *God the Son and our redemption*; the third, of *God the Holy Ghost and our sanctification*."**

No wonder we recite the Apostles' Creed in our worship services!

The point I want to make is that all our Christian faith is intricately woven into the doctrine of the Trinity. Think about that for a moment. Father—creation. Son—redemption. Holy Spirit—sanctification. Deny any one of these persons, and you deny your salvation.

No teaching is more difficult to understand, and hence, to accept, than that of the Trinity.

No teaching requires of us more humble submission to God and his word than this teaching.

In response, the Christian says, "I believe." I accept this as truth. I embrace the Father, Son, and Holy Spirit as my God and Father.

These are written that ye might believe that Jesus is the Christ, the Son of God, and that, believing, ye might have life through his name.

God give us humility to bow before him.

Jason Kortering

---

*   Heidelberg Catechism 22, in Schaff, *Creeds of Christendom*, 3:314.
** Heidelberg Catechism 24, in Schaff, *Creeds of Christendom*, 3:315.

Article 10

JESUS CHRIST IS TRUE AND ETERNAL GOD

We believe that Jesus Christ, according to his divine nature, is the only begotten Son of God, begotten from eternity, not made nor created (for then he should be a creature), but coessential and coeternal with the Father, *the express image of his person, and the brightness of his glory*, equal unto him in all things. He is the Son of God, not only from the time that he assumed our nature, but from all eternity, as these testimonies, when compared together, teach us. Moses saith that *God created the world*; and John saith that *all things were made by that Word*, which he calleth God. And the apostle saith that *God make the worlds by his Son*; likewise, that *God created all things by Jesus Christ*. Therefore it must needs follow that he who is called God, the Word, the Son, and Jesus Christ did exist at that time when all things were created by him. Therefore the prophet Micah saith: *his goings forth have been from of old, from everlasting*. And the apostle: *He hath neither beginning of days nor end of life*. He therefore is that true, eternal, and almighty God, whom we invoke, worship, and serve.

March 5 — Jesus the Only Begotten Son of God

No man hath seen God at any time; the only begotten Son, which is in the bosom of the Father, he hath declared him. —John 1:18

We now focus our attention on Article 10 of the Confession. It begins this way: "We believe that Jesus Christ, according to his divine nature, is the only begotten Son of God, begotten from eternity, not made nor created (for then he should be a creature)."

The subject matter of this article challenges our faith to accept what the Bible teaches, even though we may not be able to comprehend it.

Jesus Christ is the only begotten Son of God according to his divine nature.

We must not envision the triune God giving birth to a baby. No, the Father begets a Son, and the reference here is to the first two persons of the holy Trinity. To beget a son is different from making or creating a son. It spells out a relationship that persists, in that the Father was never without the Son; rather, they enjoyed a personal fellowship between themselves.

Jesus described it this way: "No man hath seen God at any time; the only begotten Son, which is in the bosom of the Father, he hath declared him" (John 1:18). Jesus is the person of the Son who reclined upon the bosom of the Father, or, more accurately, continues to recline upon the bosom of the Father. This indicates to us that there is a beautiful relationship of love and friendship between the person of the Father and the person of the Son. As we saw before, this included the person of the Holy Spirit, by which God breathed this love within himself.

This makes Jesus unique; he is the only begotten Son of God. We are adopted, but he is naturally God's Son by this eternal begetting.

Because this is true, Jesus possesses the nature of God, for the person of the Father and the person of the Son are equally divine. We speak of this as being his divine nature, which he possessed as the second person of the holy Trinity. We will take time to see that this is important for our understanding of Jesus as our savior. He is not a man among men; he is the Son of God.

This is taught us in the Bible, and we receive this instruction by faith.

Jason Kortering

March 6 — Jesus, the Eternally Begotten Son of God

> *For this Melchizedek, King of Salem…who met Abraham…*
> *To whom also Abraham gave a tenth part of all…King of peace;*
> *without father, without mother, without descent,*
> *having neither beginning of days, nor end of life;*
> *but made like unto the son of God; abideth a priest continually.*
> —Hebrews 7:1–3

We add a few thoughts to this opening sentence of Article 10: "We believe that Jesus Christ, according to his divine nature, is the only begotten Son of God, *begotten from eternity*, not made nor created."

The idea of the first person of the Trinity, the Father, begetting a second person, the Son, emphasizes for us the intimate relationship of love between these two persons. Begetting must not be viewed as childbirth, for then the earthly father begets a son, and the son never existed before this act. The figure of "begetting" used here emphasizes instead that the Father is the author and originator of life within the Trinity, and the Son receives his life from the Father. Sometimes the verb *generates* is used to describe this passing on of life: the Father generates the Son, and the Son is generated by the Father. It stands to reason that if this begetting or generating should end, it would mean the end of the existence of the Son. Hence, we must follow the example of this article and embrace the doctrine that holds: "We believe that Jesus Christ, according to his divine nature, is the only begotten Son of God, begotten from eternity."

Hebrews 7 makes comparison between Melchizedek of the Old Testament and Jesus Christ. The point of comparison is that according to the Aaronic priesthood, establishing genealogy was crucial. Melchizedek had no genealogy (no father or mother), he came out of nowhere, and there is no record of his end. His priesthood is continual. The comparison is that Jesus also is such a priest after the order of Melchizedek, without beginning of days nor end of life, but abides a priest continually. How can this be? Jesus is the Son of God, eternally generated by the Father according to his divine nature.

It is true that Jesus was conceived by the Holy Spirit when he took on his human nature. Yet we know that he existed long before he was born. He existed personally within the Godhead, enjoying fellowship with the Father and the Spirit. In addition to this, he took on our flesh.

Jesus is both God and man, a perfect mediator.

Jason Kortering

March 7 — Jesus, Co-essential and Co-eternal with the Father

I and my Father are one. —John 10:30

It is important for us to ask, who is our savior? By this question, we do not imply that we do not know who he is among the children of men. Rather, we ask, what is his character?

We ask this especially as a sequel to the assertion that Jesus is the only begotten Son of God. He is begotten not for a brief moment at conception, but he enjoys eternal begetting as the Father infuses his love into the Son, and, together with the Holy Spirit, shares in the covenant life of the triune God.

This has a significant impact upon our understanding of who Jesus is. He partakes of the divine nature. It is one thing to say this in the setting of a class on Reformed doctrine. We must draw from the Scriptures that Jesus is very God, who possesses all the virtues of the Godhead. This makes him very special.

The practical significance of this comes to the fore when we consider what work Jesus had to accomplish for us when he came into this world to die as our mediator. More than that, he now continues to work on our behalf in heaven, in the presence of his heavenly Father. Because he possesses the divine nature and is in truth the co-essential and co-eternal God, he is abundantly qualified and capable of accomplishing the tasks which the Father gave him to do.

Jesus said in John 10:30, "I and my Father are one." Note with me, briefly, the context in which he spoke these words. He referred to himself as the good shepherd. He spoke those words which we still cherish: "My sheep hear my voice, and I know them, and they follow me" (v. 27). In response to this teaching, some of the Jews accused him of blasphemy and took up stones to kill him. Did this make Jesus a weakling, a victim of enemy assault? No, he said: "My Father, which gave them me, is greater than all; and no man is able to pluck them out of my Father's hand. I and my Father are one" (v. 28). His Father was sovereign over all men, and Jesus was one with his Father in possessing all power to accomplish his work.

He was this in his divine nature.

He had this power because he was begotten eternally of the Father. Our salvation is secure in him.

Jason Kortering

March 8 — Jesus, the Express Image of the Father

God, who at sundry times…Hath in these last days spoken unto us by his Son…
Who being the brightness of his glory, and the express image of his person,
and upholding all things by the word of his power, when he had by himself purged
our sins, sat down on the right hand of the Majesty on high. —Hebrews 1:1–3

Sons look like their fathers, some more than others. The genes take care of this. What the Belgic Confession is saying in this article is that something of this "look" applies to Jesus, the Son of God. It states that because Jesus is the only begotten Son of God, begotten not created, he is *"the express image of his person, and the brightness of his glory,* equal unto him in all things. Who is the Son of God, not only from the time that he assumed our nature, but from all eternity" (Article 10). The author of Hebrews expresses this in the above text.

If we pursue this figure of speech a bit more, we can see how this was true. The second person of the holy Trinity possessed the image of the first person—like Father, like Son. The Father imparts his glorious virtues unto the Son through the work of the Holy Spirit. The same truth applies to the incarnation of Jesus in the flesh. There he took on, in addition to his divine nature which he possessed personally, the human nature. At such a time, Joseph did not father Jesus; thus, it is abundantly established in the New Testament that Joseph was at first upset that Mary was pregnant because he knew he did not father that child, so there had to be someone else. He contemplated to put her away (divorce her) privately. However, the angel made clear to Joseph that the power of the highest came upon Mary and that which was conceived in her was of the Holy Spirit. God had fathered his own Son according to the flesh.

Hence, Jesus is called "the express image of his person [the Father]" (Heb. 1:3). This related to his divine nature, which he retained when he took on, in addition to it, the human nature.

As an aside, we can say that he took on his human nature from the virgin Mary. He was truly human. In this way, God qualified his Son to be our savior.

Jason Kortering

March 9   **Jesus, the Creator of the World**

> *God, who at sundry times and in divers manners spake in time past unto the fathers by the prophets, hath in these last days spoken unto us by his Son, whom he hath appointed heir of all things, by whom also he made the worlds.*
> —Hebrews 1:1, 2

The Confession continues to demonstrate from the Bible that Jesus is the Son of God, eternally generated by the Father. It reasons this way:

> Moses saith that *God created the world*; and John saith *that all things were made by that Word*, which he calleth God; and the Apostle saith that *God made the worlds by his Son*; likewise, that *God created all things by Jesus Christ*. Therefore it must needs follow that he—who is called God, the Word, the Son, and Jesus Christ—did exist at that time when all things were created by him. (Article 10)

Reference is made to the sublime words of John 1:3, "All things were made by him; and without him was not anything made that was made."

Jesus obviously existed prior to his birth in Bethlehem; he lived in the presence of the Father as the Son of God, called the *logos* or the Word. As such, he participated in the creation. God as Father called forth the creative word: "Let there be light" (Gen. 1:3). The Son, as the Word, echoed that call throughout the abyss of space. The Holy Spirit effectively brought into existence what the Father and Word called forth. Jesus was intimately connected with the person of the Son of God. Hence, the confession says they all refer to the same person: God the Son, the Word, and Jesus Christ.

Take a moment to reflect on this.

Our Savior not only existed before he was born, he participated in the origin of this world. As the Word, he brought forth this perfect world, free from sin. No wonder then that our Reformed forefathers say that when Adam fell into sin, he fell into the arms of Jesus. Jesus was there, and Adam was told that there was hope for a sinner who had listened to the devil and was flattered by his lie that "ye shall be as gods" (Gen. 3:5).

Jesus, creator, is also savior. The blood of the slaughtered animal covered sins, which the fig leaves could not. Put your trust in him alone.

Jason Kortering

March 10 — Jesus is True, Eternal, and Almighty God

But thou, Bethlehem Ephratah, though thou be little among the thousands of Judah, yet out of thee shall he come forth unto me that is to be ruler in Israel; whose goings forth have been from of old, from everlasting. —Micah 5:2

There are two more thoughts which bring to a close this detailed article of the Belgic Confession on the important truth that Jesus is true and eternal God. We have this summary statement at the end: "He therefore is that true, eternal, and almighty God, whom we invoke, worship, and serve" (Article 10). At this time, we will consider the summary of his deity: true, eternal, and almighty God. Next time, we will consider what our response must be: to "invoke, worship, and serve" him.

Let's say something in conclusion on each of these three descriptions.

Jesus is truly God. Though we cannot comprehend what this really means, we can at least get the sense of importance. How could Jesus ever make atonement for our sins on the cross except he is truly God? Our sins carry the guilt for everlasting punishment. No mere man, no matter how important he may be, can bear God's wrath against sin in a few hours of time. Jesus is truly God, and thereby qualified to accomplish such satisfaction of divine justice. Likewise, who can break the stubborn will of fallen man and move him in such a way that influences him to desire God and turn from the pleasure of sin? Only Jesus, who is truly God, can make such a spiritual change.

Jesus is eternal God. The prophet Micah makes the point in the quote above: "Whose goings forth have been of old, from everlasting" (Mic. 5:2). We considered how important it is for us to think of Jesus as the Son of God, comprehended in the second person of the holy Trinity. As such, Jesus is before creation and much involved in the work of God from everlasting. Within all the years of time, Jesus is actively involved. His goings forth include creation, salvation in the old covenant, his incarnation, his exaltation, and the on-going gathering of the church.

Jesus is almighty God. All his work involves power that is beyond human understanding and ability. Because Jesus is true, eternal, almighty God, he not only proposes to save, he does save.

And he is your Savior.

Jason Kortering

March 11 — **Jesus, the Object of Our Worship and Service**

And after eight days again his disciples were within, and Thomas with them: then came Jesus, the doors being shut, and stood in the midst, and said, Peace be unto you. Then saith he to Thomas, Reach hither thy finger, and behold my hands; and reach hither thy hand, and thrust it into my side: and be not faithless, but believing. And Thomas answered and said unto him, My Lord and my God.
—John 20:26–28

Our Reformed fathers bring to a close their consideration of the deity of Christ with a statement of awe and wonder: "He therefore is that true, eternal, and almighty God, whom we invoke, worship, and serve."

That was the response of Thomas who doubted when he was told that Jesus had risen from the dead. The other disciples had seen him, for he had appeared in their midst towards the end of the first resurrection Sunday. Thomas was not present with them. How could Jesus be alive when they all admitted he had been crucified, dead, and buried? Thomas was so adamant that he said: "Except I shall see in his hands the print of the nails, and put my finger into the print of the nails, and thrust my hand into his side, I will not believe" (John 20:25). And there, Jesus stood before him and took the initiative to insist that Thomas do as he said he must in order to believe. Thomas' response was: "My Lord and my God" (v. 28).

Thomas is not alone. Believing in the divinity of Christ is beyond our comprehension. Jesus understood this and gently accommodated Thomas without harsh reprimand. This is encouraging for us as well. We come to Jesus with our struggles and doubts, and here Jesus says to each of us: "Behold my hands and feet." Yes, it is true, Jesus is more than a man, for no man ever entered the grave and came out alive. Because he is true and eternal God, he is almighty to save.

Worship is a proper and beautiful response to the truth of the gospel of Jesus, the Son of God!

We invoke him—that is, we pray to him. We pray to God as our Father in the name of Jesus our Savior. Everything we can say to God as our Father is because of Jesus his Son and our Savior.

We worship him, daily and every Lord's Day.

We serve him as our Lord. We say to him: "Speak, Lord, for thy servant heareth" (1 Sam. 3:9).

Jason Kortering

Article 11

THE HOLY GHOST IS TRUE AND ETERNAL GOD

We believe and confess also that the Holy Ghost from eternity proceeds from the Father and Son; and therefore is neither made, created, nor begotten, but only proceedeth from both; who in order is the third person of the Holy Trinity; of one and the same essence, majesty, and glory with the Father and the Son; and therefore is the true and eternal God, as the Holy Scripture teaches us.

March 12 — **Faith in the Holy Spirit**

> *Go ye therefore, and teach all nations,*
> *baptizing them in the name of the Father,*
> *and of the Son, and of the Holy Ghost.*
> —Matthew 28:19

Our Reformed fathers open Article 11, which is entitled "The Holy Ghost is True and Eternal God," with the words: "We believe and confess also, that the Holy Ghost, from eternity, proceeds from the Father and Son."

This leads us to the consideration of the third person of the Holy Trinity. We quoted from the well-known baptism formula above. We baptize persons in the name of the Triune God: Father, Son, and Holy Ghost.

We might raise the question, what is the proper name for this third person? Is he "Holy Ghost" or "Holy Spirit"? Our King James Version of the Bible uses *Holy Ghost* ninety times and *Holy Spirit* an additional seven times. By all indications, there is no reason why one or the other must be used. Historically, *Holy Ghost* is an older English phrase, while more modern translations reflect the more current use by naming him Holy Spirit.

The significance of this is two-fold.

First, the use of *ghost* has been commonly associated with the spirits of the dead and even the demons of the underworld. Obviously, we must make a strong disassociation from these notions and not add *holy* to the name of the third person of the Trinity simply to distinguish him from demons or the spirits of the dead. This is important in the Singaporean culture in a special way.

Second, the name Holy Ghost or Spirit indicates to us that he is a person, and he is not embodied in any way in a physical body. In fact, it is good to reflect upon the character of the Holy Spirit as breath. That is the original meaning of the word in Scripture. As the Holy Spirit within the Godhead, he is the life or breath of God. Reverently speaking, when the Father loves the Son and the Son returns love to the Father, they express this love for each other in the breath of the Holy Spirit. We use human terms, but we say that the Holy Spirit animates God; he gives life to the persons of the Godhead.

Because he is personally God and he also has an important place in our salvation, our faith is in him, and we are baptized in his name as well.

Jason Kortering

March 13 — The Holy Spirit Proceeds from the Father and the Son

But when the Comforter is come,
whom I will send unto you from the Father,
even the Spirit of truth, which proceedeth from the Father,
he shall testify of me. —John 15:26

Today, we are focusing our attention on this sentence: "We believe and confess also that the Holy Ghost, from eternity, proceeds from the Father and Son" (Article 11).

There are two ways in which we speak of the Holy Spirit proceeding from the Father and the Son, often called "Double Procession" in the history of the Christian church.

First, within the holy Trinity itself, the person of the Holy Spirit proceeds from the person of the Father and the person of the Son. You recall in the case of the Son, it is said, the Father begets or generates the Son and the Son is so begotten. Now, in the case of the Holy Spirit, it is not said that the Father begets the Spirit, but that the Spirit proceeds from the Father and also the Son. The language of the confession (and Scripture) accommodates us to help form some sort of visible picture of the relationship between the persons of the Godhead. As the Father generates the Son (and the language must be viewed with all its limitations, for it uses temporal language as applied to the eternal Godhead), he does this in the person of the Holy Spirit. So also the Son, being begotten, returns affection to the Father who begot him in the person of the Spirit. Thus, the Spirit proceeds from both the Father and the Son in the Godhead.

Second, outside of the Holy Trinity, the Holy Spirit is given to Christ to powerfully realize the work he legally established on the cross and now must realize in the salvation of the people for whom he died. Hence, the Father gave to his Son, upon the completion of his redemptive work and his ascension into heaven, the Holy Spirit to finish the work. This Jesus referred to in the text quoted above, that is, "the Comforter...whom I will send unto you from the Father...which proceedeth from the Father, he shall testify of me" (John 15:26). The exalted Christ in the person of the Son sent the Holy Spirit as his Spirit to the church to finish the work of salvation. This too is Double Procession, from the Father and the Son.

Think on the important role the Holy Spirit has in our salvation.

Jason Kortering

March 14 — The Holy Spirit is the Third Person of the Trinity

The Spirit of God moved upon the face of the waters.
—Genesis 1:2

We now want to meditate a bit on the statement in the article which says: "who in order is the third person of the Holy Trinity" (Article 11).

One of the things that needs to be stressed over and over is that the Holy Spirit is not a force or spirit, but a person. We often fall into the error of referring to him as "it." The above quoted verse illustrates this, with the idea that a power moved over the earth. It is bad to refer to the Holy Spirit as "it," for "it" limits our ability to direct our attention to the relationship which he realizes in our salvation. If he is simply a power who works, we will soon think of our relationship to him as very impersonal and formal. This contributes to historical faith, in which we focus so much attention on our belief system that we ignore our salvation. The Holy Spirit as a person so works in us that we interact with him as we do with the Savior. We love Jesus and we love the Holy Spirit, for both enable us to have a love relationship with the Father (the triune God as our Father). Give this some thought. Do you really appreciate the Holy Spirit as a person?

The other thing which needs mentioning is that he is the third person of the holy Trinity. Again, when we speak of first, second, and third, we immediately think in temporal terms; after all, the words describe a succession of moments or events, and we cannot think differently. Keep in mind, however, that while the use of these terms when applied to the Godhead helps us with our thinking, the reality is that there never has been a moment when there was no Son or Holy Spirit. First, second, and third describe the relationship between each of these persons. The Father is first as the source of all things, the Son is second as the one who benefits from the Father and enjoys this special relationship with him. So also, the Holy Spirit is third not in rank but in relationship, for he is the one who breathes the life of the Father into the Son, and he is the person through whom the Father generates his Son.

This means all three persons are equally God and each one has his own personal role in the work of God. Rejoice in God the Father, God the Son, and God the Holy Spirit.

Jason Kortering

March 15 — The Holy Spirit is Equally Divine

Know ye not that ye are the temple of God,
and that the Spirit of God dwelleth in you? —1 Corinthians 3:16

Reflect a moment on this quotation from the Bible. When God works in us by his Holy Spirit, he works a saving work, and that work is described here as making us the temple of God, the place where God dwells. That is amazing, isn't it? What an incentive for us to be holy, for the God of our salvation is the holy God, and he performs his work of salvation by his Holy Spirit. It is significant that in the same breath in which God says that we are the temple of God, he indicates that we are so because the Spirit of God is dwelling in us. Both "temple of God" and "Spirit of God dwelleth in you" (1 Cor. 3:16) are used in the same sentence as phrases of equal value. As the Spirit of God dwells in us, God is dwelling in us. Both "Spirit of God" and "God" himself are used on the same level as well. The Spirit of God is God himself.

This Article 11 of the Belgic Confession states:

> We believe and confess also that the Holy Ghost from eternity proceeds from the Father and Son; and therefore is neither made, created, nor begotten, but only proceedeth from both; who in order is the third person of the Holy Trinity; of one and the same essence, majesty, and glory with the Father and the Son; and therefore is the true and eternal God, as the Holy Scripture teaches us.

The Holy Spirit is equally divine with the Father and the Son, or, as the article states, "the same essence." The confession mentions some of these qualities: majesty, glory, true, and eternal. *Majesty* refers to the amazing wonder of his work which stirs us to bow in reverence. *Glory* describes the beauty of God shining through his works. *True* tells us that he is faithful to his values. *Eternal* reminds us that he is without beginning or end. These attributes or virtues of God apply equally to the Holy Spirit.

This we acknowledge as we consider his works: creation and his providential care of it, the conception of Jesus, and most of all, his saving work in us. He gives sight to our blind eyes and calls life out of death.

The Holy Spirit is truly God. What a joy to believe this.

Jason Kortering

March 16 — Scripture Reveals to Us Who the Holy Spirit Is

Come ye near unto me, hear ye this;
I have not spoken in secret from the beginning;
from the time that it was, there am I: and now the Lord GOD,
and his Spirit, hath sent me. —Isaiah 48:16

In connection with the Holy Spirit, as was also true with the entire Trinity, the confession emphasizes that what we believe and teach about the three persons of the holy Trinity is derived from the teaching of the Holy Bible. Only God is able to tell us who he is, and he does that through the Bible itself, as it is his revelation. The importance of this is obvious: no human being would invent the idea of three persons in one being, because it defies human imagination and understanding.

This idea, that the word of God alone guides us in our understanding of him, is explained when God tells us about the third person of the Godhead, the Holy Spirit.

Consider the above quote from Isaiah. In it, God is speaking through the prophet Isaiah. He calls us to come near and listen to what he has to say. What he says is not new; he spoke from the beginning. He did this through the Holy Spirit, and this same Spirit sent Isaiah to be his mouthpiece.

In Genesis 1:2 we read: "And the spirit of God moved upon the face of the waters." In creation, God as Father spoke, and he did that through the Word, his Son. The Holy Spirit as God's breath brought it into existence.

Of the conception of Jesus, we read in Luke 1:34–35, "Then said Mary unto the angel, How shall this be, seeing I know not a man? And the angel answered and said unto her, The Holy Ghost shall come upon thee, and the power of the Highest shall overshadow thee, therefore also that holy thing which shall be born of thee shall be called the Son of God."

The Holy Spirit demonstrated his power at Pentecost; the doubting and unbelieving disciples were now able to preach the gospel of the living Lord. "And it shall come to pass in the last days, saith God, I will pour out of my Spirit upon all flesh: and your sons and your daughters shall prophesy" (Acts 2:17). What glory and power of God is demonstrated when the Holy Spirit works!

The Bible is reliable, the Holy Spirit is God. Your salvation is secure.

Jason Kortering

March 17 — We Believe and Confess that the Holy Spirit Is True and Eternal God

Sirs, what must I do to be saved? And they said,
Believe on the Lord Jesus Christ, and thou shalt be saved,
and thy house. —Acts 16:30–31

Our Reformed fathers remind us in this article that "we believe and confess *also* that the Holy Ghost from eternity proceeds from the Father and Son."

This is something beautiful to ponder as our consideration of Article 11 draws to a close.

Do you believe this? You accept for truth that the third person of the holy Trinity is true and eternal God? Do you understand that unless you believe this, your own salvation is impossible? I do not mean by this statement that you have to believe in the divinity of the Holy Spirit, which is true enough. Rather, I mean that unless the Holy Spirit is truly God, your salvation is impossible. Such is the sad teaching of those who deny the Reformed faith concerning the sovereignty of God and insist on the free will of man. Man without the Holy Spirit is nothing but an enemy of God, and that is true of you and of me as well. Rejoice that God the Holy Spirit is qualified and powerful to save us, and hence, our salvation is secure.

This we confess because we, like Paul, are not ashamed of the gospel of sovereign grace. Rather than draw back and speak softly, we eagerly shout it from the mountaintop. Because the Holy Spirit is true and eternal God, the work of salvation he began in us is God's work, and what God begins, he will finish. This is our comfort and hope for the future.

When the jailer, referred to in Acts 16, asked, "What must I do to be saved?" (v. 30), the apostle did not say to him: "You are asking the wrong question, because you cannot do anything to be saved." He admitted that the question was worked in the jailer by the Holy Spirit, and the always-important question demanded an answer: "Believe on the Lord Jesus Christ, and thou shalt be saved, and thy house" (v. 31). When the Holy Spirit arouses such a question, he provides a solid answer.

What about you? Do you believe and confess that the Holy Spirit is true and eternal God? You stand on solid, biblical ground when you do.

Jason Kortering

March 18 — A Final Reflection on the Holy Spirit, Another Comforter

And I will pray the Father and he shall give you another Comforter, that he may abide with you forever. —John 14:16

Would you agree with me that we do not give enough acknowledgment to the Holy Spirit of his role in our salvation?

The very name *Father* evokes in us thoughts of intimacy and love. From creation to Calvary, his love defies understanding. He calls us unto himself as our heavenly Father. The same is true of the name *Son*. This is Jesus, who was born in Bethlehem, climbed the hill of Golgotha, gave his very life for the sins of the world. Now, he is the exalted Lord of Lords who ministers to our needs. Since he was "touched with the feeling of our infirmities" (Heb. 4:15), he can minister to our needs very well.

But what of the Holy Spirit? How close do you feel towards him? Admittedly, we have to work harder to give him his due.

Reflect a few moments on the text quoted above. Jesus here assures us that he will pray to the Father to give us "another Comforter" (John 14:16). To be sure, Jesus came to earth to function as our first comforter. How precious are his words to us as we meditate upon the gospel record. We cling to his atonement and exalt in his resurrection and ascension into heaven. We derive comfort from every assurance of his redeeming love.

He knew that when he departed from the midst of his beloved church on earth, they would need continuing comfort. Thus, he prayed to the Father that he would send this Comforter, the Holy Spirit, to his beloved church on earth. By his abiding with us forever, we enjoy comfort until we enter everlasting life and glory in the day of his coming.

Comforter! Yes, when we struggle with our faith and sometimes cannot understand or discern truth from error, the Holy Spirit draws near to us, guides us into the truth, and gives us direction and conviction.

Comforter! Yes, when the demands of life go contrary to our desires and we struggle with disease and heartache, even death itself, he is our great Physician who is able to give healing and deliverance.

Comforter! Yes, when we face persecution and opposition for our faith, what will be the cost? Only God knows, but the Holy Spirit will take care of us.

I believe, help my unbelief, also regarding the Holy Spirit!

Jason Kortering

Article 12

OF THE CREATION

We believe that the Father, by the Word—that is, by his Son—created of nothing the heaven, the earth, and all creatures, as it seemed good unto him, giving unto every creature its being, shape, form, and several offices to serve its Creator; that he doth also still uphold and govern them by his eternal providence and infinite power for the service of mankind, to the end that man may serve his God. He also created the angels good, to be his messengers and to serve his elect: some of whom are fallen from that excellency, in which God created them, into everlasting perdition; and the others have, by the, grace of God, remained steadfast, and continued in their primitive state. The devils and evil spirits are so depraved that they are enemies of God and every good thing to the utmost of their power, as murderers watching to ruin the Church and every member thereof, and by their wicked stratagems to destroy all; and are therefore, by their own wickedness, adjudged to eternal damnation, daily expecting their horrible torments. Therefore we reject and abhor the error of the Sadducees, who deny the existence of spirits and angels; and also that of the Manichees, who assert that the devils have their origin of themselves, and that they are wicked of their own nature, without having been corrupted.

March 19 — Faith and the Creation

*Through faith we understand that the worlds
were framed by the word of God, so that things which are seen
were not made of things which do appear.* —Hebrews 11:3

Where did we come from? How did the world come into existence? How were the trees and the animals, the flowers, fish, and birds formed? What about the stars and the planets, and the galaxies; how were they formed? When did this happen? And why?

Nearly all religions and ancient cultures have vague stories, passed down from one generation to the next, of a creation work by their gods. These are myths and folk stories that few would believe today. Because people of every age ask such questions, scientists, philosophers, and theologians are still seeking answers to these questions today.

The Christian religion has a clear written record of how and why all things came into being. This creation account is found in the Bible. Christians believe this record with all their hearts. This article in the Confession states it exactly that way: "We believe that the Father…created…the heaven, the earth, and all creatures" (Article 12).

The Christian knows God (by faith) as his or her own heavenly Father in Jesus Christ. Because Christians have this faith in God, they know that God's record in his word is both true and accurate. Christians sing, "This is my Father's world."[*] And it is God's, for he made it.

Hebrews 11:3 states: "Through faith we understand that the worlds were framed by the word of God." Only faith understands this. Only faith can answer the questions that people of all ages have asked. Sad to say, no matter how brilliant a scientist or philosopher may be, if he does not have faith, he will not be able or willing to ascribe the creation to the power of God.

This faith is confirmed by what we see in the world around us. From the glory of the morning sun to the exquisite beauty of the flower to the power of the wind and sea, all things point to God their maker. Faith, therefore, is not a blind belief in old myths and stories that we cannot prove. Rather, faith is the firm conviction concerning a reality so clear to the Christian that is it beyond proof.

We join with the church of all ages by confessing our faith in "God the Father, Almighty, Maker of heaven and earth."[**]

Russell Dykstra

---

[*] By Maltbie D. Babcock (1901).
[**] Apostles' Creed, in *The Psalter*, 80.

March 20 — "We believe that the Father...hath created..."

*And because ye are sons, God hath sent forth the Spirit of his Son
into your hearts, crying, Abba, Father.* —Galatians 4:6

God is confessed in this article as Father. God, in his word (the Bible) to us, gives us the privilege to call him by that name. In the Old Testament, God's word to Pharaoh, king of Egypt, was "Israel is my son, even my firstborn" (Ex. 4:22). Jesus expanded on that, teaching his disciples to address God in prayer as "Our Father" (Matt. 6:9). In God's covenant of grace, he promises his people: "I will be a Father unto you, and ye shall be my sons and daughters, saith the Lord Almighty" (2 Cor. 6:18). And to make that possible, "God hath sent forth the Spirit of his Son into your hearts, crying, Abba, Father" (Gal. 4:6).

It is noteworthy that in connection with the work of creating, the Confession uses the name Father. That name indicates the source of life. As in the world of people, the father is the source of life in the family. So also in the work of creation, God gave himself the name *Father*, first of all, to teach us that he is the source of life and indeed, of all things, for he made all that exists.

Second, a good father in this life cares for his family. So likewise does God take care of his entire creation. He provides for every living thing that he has made. God does not create and then abandon his creation. Nor did God create all and then step back to allow the universe to run on its own, as a clock wound up.

On the contrary, God is deeply involved in his creation: he upholds and governs all things (Article 12), as the Confession puts it. There are bad fathers in this life who forsake their children. God, the one true Father, never neglects his creation.

Yet, although God is the creator of all men, women, and children, he is not the Father of all. For in the sin of Adam, all have lost the right to call God "Father." God is the Father of his people in and through his Son, Jesus Christ. All those who confess their faith in his Son, Jesus, belong to him eternally, and have the right to call God "Father."

Let us with confidence call upon the Creator of heaven and earth, as our Father.

Russell Dykstra

March 21 — Creation by the Word

By the word of the LORD were the heavens made;
and all the host of them by the breath of his mouth. —Psalm 33:6

The Confession sets forth the Bible's clear teaching that the Triune God, our Father, created all things by his Son, Jesus Christ. This Jesus is very God and very man. He came into the world in order to save his people from their sins by redeeming them on the cross.

Jesus is called "the Word" in John 1. God gave Jesus that name to teach us about his Son. Words teach and enlighten; they give knowledge. Jesus came into the world to teach, to give a perfect revelation of his Father.

The Bible also teaches that the Word of God is powerful. When God spoke in his judgment, "the earth melted" (Ps. 46:6). He sends forth his commands, and the earth is covered with snow and ice; he speaks his word again, and the ice melts (Ps. 147:15–18).

By that same powerful Word, God created all things. Genesis 1 records it all. "And God said, Let there be light: and there was light" (v. 3). He spoke, and his Word called into existence the firmament in the heavens, dry land and plants, the sun, moon, and stars, etc. Psalm 33:6 explains: "By the word of the LORD were the heavens made."

John 1:14 indicates that the Word is Jesus, who "was made flesh, and dwelt among us." And the inspired apostle wrote of that Word: "All things were made by him; and without him was not anything made that was made" (John 1:3).

Writing to the Colossians, the apostle Paul teaches that all things were made not only by Christ Jesus, but for him (Col. 1:16).

God made all things—oceans and streams, the mammoth grey whale, the butterfly, the tiger, and the lizard—all for Christ. For he enthroned his Son Jesus as king over all the creation. He rules over all for the glory of God. This same Jesus will rule forever and ever.

Before anything was created, God had a perfect plan in his own mind. In that plan, he determined to make the whole universe for his Son. Accordingly, "he spake, and it was done; he commanded, and it stood fast" (Ps. 33:9).

This bears out how serious it is to deny that God created all things. It is a denial of Christ, the Creator and the King of creation.

How blessed it is to confess that our Lord Jesus Christ is not only our Savior, but also the one who made all things for us so that we may serve God with all things for those who believe in Christ (1 Cor. 3:21-23).

Russell Dykstra

March 22 — Created out of Nothing

In the beginning God created the heaven and the earth.
—Genesis 1:1

Many and varied are the talents that people possess to create beauty. A carpenter selects his mahogany wood and fashions a beautiful table. The artist takes a brush in hand and fills the canvas, painting a lovely flower. A jeweler selects gold and precious stones and carefully crafts a diamond ring.

But none of them can ever do what God did. God created the world out of nothing. All that man can do is work with existing materials, be it gold, wood, paint, or canvas. Only God creates something out of nothing.

The church has confessed this since the beginning of time. Creation is *ex nihilo*—a Latin phrase meaning "out of nothing." This is the meaning of Genesis 1:1, "In the beginning God created the heaven and the earth." That is not a mere heading or description of the creation account. It is the creating act where God called into existence a new thing. From all eternity, "before" the beginning described in Genesis 1:1, only God was. God spoke, and there was a mass of material, a physical substance, distinct from God. It was not a substance that flowed or emanated out of the being of God. It was, rather, created by God.

That is why Hebrews 11:3 states that "things which are seen were not made of things which do appear." The carpenter, the painter, the jeweler, all need visible materials to make something visible. God does not. In another connection, Paul writes of God's almighty power not only to quicken or make alive the dead but also to call "those things which be not as though they were" (Rom. 4:17).

Only God is able to create out of nothing.

This truth contradicts a fundamental premise of the theory of evolutionism, namely, that matter always existed. Evolutionism teaches that the world as we know it formed from an existing mass of particles or gases; that somehow, life rose out of non-living material. This is a denial of the biblical truth that God created out of nothing.

What a tremendous power Jehovah God possesses! The Almighty God, the eternally living God, merely by speaking the word, brought into being the unformed mass covered with darkness and water. From this, he would fashion all creatures.

The church rejoices to confess that her "help is in the name of the Lord, who made heaven and earth" (Ps. 124:8).

Russell Dykstra

March 23 — Created in Divine Wisdom

The Lord by wisdom hath founded the earth;
by understanding hath he established the heavens.—Proverbs 3:19

"We believe that the Father…hath created…all creatures as it seemed good unto him" (Article 12). Considerable discussion has been held about whether a superior being, an intelligent designer, fashioned the universe and all creatures in it. Many scientists, recognizing the total impossibility of evolutionism explaining the universe, espouse belief in an intelligent designer, but distinguish that sharply from the sovereign, personal God of the Bible.

How foolish that is. The Bible not only reveals the Creator, but also sets forth his wisdom in creating. The Confession points to this with the words "as it seemed good unto him."

The Bible stresses the truth that the Creator formed all things in wisdom. "O Lord, how manifold are thy works! in wisdom hast thou made them all" (Ps. 104:24). The Psalmist sings the praises of God "that by wisdom made the heavens" (Ps. 136:5). Wise Solomon acknowledged this: "The Lord by wisdom hath founded the earth; by understanding hath he established the heavens" (Prov. 3:19). The inspired prophet Jeremiah twice reminded apostatizing Israel that their God "hath made the earth by his power, he hath established the world by his wisdom, and hath stretched out the heavens by his discretion" (Jer. 10:12; 51:15).

Wisdom is the exact opposite of folly. A foolish builder does not reckon with reality. Jesus describes the foolish man who builds his house on sand; when the heavy rains come, the house collapses. The wise builder understands this and constructs his house on a rock (see Matt. 7:24-27).

God is infinitely wise. His fashioning of the universe was not haphazard or without forethought. All was planned and executed with perfect wisdom.

The entire creation testifies of this perfect order. The sun, the planets, the seasons, and all living things of land and ocean were made to fit into the whole of the creation in perfect wisdom. What a thrill for the believer to look into God's creation and behold it! Be it the astounding complexity of the cell and the atoms, the depths of the ocean, the rocks in the desert, or the vastness of space—every discovery fills him with awe for the wisdom of the Creator.

But understand, wisdom has a goal. A wise man builds not only with foresight, but with purpose. So does God. And what is that goal? His own glory (Rev. 4:11).

Christ, the one for whom and by whom all were created, is the wisdom of God (1 Cor. 1:24). As King, he rules now and forever, for the glory of God.

Russell Dykstra

March 24 — "...giving unto every creature its being, shape, form, and several offices to serve its Creator"

Lift up your eyes on high, and behold who hath created these things, that bringeth out their host by number: he calleth them all by names by the greatness of his might, for that he is strong in power; not one faileth. —Isaiah 40:26

The believer stands in awe and reverence of the unspeakable wisdom and power of the Creator. God created out of nothing the mass of material, the physical substance. From that unformed, dark, and watery mass, God called forth all the creatures that he determined to fill his universe. Everything he made is a creature. God is Creator; all else—giraffe, mountain, shark, or star—is creature.

God gave existence to each creature by his almighty word. And God gave to each its shape and form. The orangutan with its man-like features, fingers, and toes. The fish with its fins and scales. The lizard with its flicking tongue and sweeping tail. The star with its burning light. Each creature has its existence, shape, and form from God.

And each creature exists for a purpose. Each one has an "office." The idea of office is that one is appointed or set in a position, with the authority and responsibility to perform certain tasks. A prime minister in a country has a certain recognized position with authority and responsibility to rule the country well. The minister in the church has an office with authority and responsibility to preach.

Similarly, every creature that God has made has an office. God made each creature with a purpose. It fills a certain function in the creation. The office of many creatures we can readily observe. The sun is to give light and life to the earth in the day. The moon gives its lesser light for the night. The herbs are created for food for man. Birds sing God's praises. The rock provides a solid foundation for the skyscrapers, and a picture of the unchanging steadfastness of God (Deut. 32:4). Trees are a source of food for man, homes for the birds, and shelter for the beasts. They are also a picture of a believer, planted by the river, bringing forth much fruit (Ps. 1).

By fulfilling its office, each creature serves his Creator. Rocks and rivers, without thinking. Fish, birds, and animals, without conscious activity. Man is the one creature that was formed by God to serve and glorify God consciously and deliberately. He was made to rule over the creation, develop the powers imbedded therein, and use it in the service of God.

May God give us eyes to behold the wonders of his creation, his wisdom and power, and to worship the one, only Creator and Lord.

Russell Dykstra

March 25 — The Creator's Care for His Creation

Who being the brightness of his glory, and the express image of his person, and upholding all things by the word of his power, when he had by himself purged our sins, sat down on the right hand of the Majesty on high. —Hebrews 1:3

"That he doth also still uphold and govern them by his eternal providence" (Article 12).

Jehovah is a wise creator. Eternally he planned the perfect creation for the glory of his name. Eternally he also planned to uphold and govern the whole creation. This is providence. There is an eternal decree or plan of providence. And there is a working out of that providence in time by God's "infinite power" (Article 12).

God provides for—cares for—his creation. This is what one would expect of a wise creator. Every builder knows that his finished project will need to be maintained, or else it will fall into ruin. God, the perfectly wise builder, maintains and cares for all the creatures that he has made (Article 13 will explain this truth more fully).

God created all things to be creatures, dependent on God. Nothing exists on its own power. Each creature is formed "by the word of God's power" and must be upheld by the same powerful word so that it continues to exist (Heb. 1:3). Were God to cease speaking his sovereign word, all would disappear into nothingness.

God's providence also governs. God created each creature with a purpose. Each thing fits into God's creation and fulfills a certain function. God's sovereign providence governs each creature so that it fulfills God's foreordained purpose. Not only do palm trees in general serve God's purpose, but also each individual palm tree does so, in God's providence.

Fallen man is willingly ignorant of this astounding reality, namely, that God upholds him day by day, minute by minute, and rules him sovereignly. For if "the king's heart is in the hand of the Lord, as the rivers of water: he turneth it whithersoever he will" (Prov. 21:1), surely every man is ruled by God. This is a great mystery, yet the Bible is clear on this. By his providence, God upholds and governs the whole universe, and every creature in it, including man.

A believer is most grateful for this knowledge. God upholds us. He controls all creatures great and small. God's providence so serves the salvation of his people that the believer knows from experience the truth of Romans 8:28, namely, "that all things work together for good to them that love God, to them who are the called according to his purpose."

Russell Dykstra

March 26   **"...to the end that man may serve his God"**

And God said, Let us make man in our image,
after our likeness: and let them have dominion over the fish of the sea,
and over the fowl of the air, and over the cattle, and over all the earth,
and over every creeping thing that creepeth upon the earth. —Genesis 1:26

God crowned his majestic work of creation by forming man. Man is unique among all the creatures of God's hand. In one way, man is like the animals—he is part of the earth, formed from the very dust. Yet by breathing into man the breath of life (Gen. 2:7), God instilled in man something more and different, namely, a spiritual aspect. Man is able to know more than he can see, hear, and touch—he is able to know God and spiritual things.

Everything about man's creation indicates that he is unique. First, before God created man in the sixth day, he paused and communed within himself about what he was about to do: "Let us make man in our image" (Gen. 1:26). Then, rather than call man into existence as he had done with every other creature, God formed man, as it were, with his own hands. Thus, both male and female were created in God's image, possessing the true knowledge of God, righteousness, and holiness.

One reason why God created Adam to be different from all other creatures is that Adam was created king of the creation. God specifically gave Adam dominion over all other creatures on the earth (Gen. 1:26, 28).

As king, under God, Adam was to "subdue" the earth (Gen. 1:28), that is, develop in God's service the powers that God had placed in the creation. The Bible indicates that this started almost immediately with Jabal's advances in agriculture (raising cattle), Jubal's development of musical instruments, and Tubal-cain's fashioning of metal tools (Gen. 4:20–22). Over the centuries, man has harnessed the power of water, fire, wind, and the atom, and has made many inventions.

The problem is that Adam fell from his lofty state as righteous friend-servant of God, and thus lost his right to rule the creation. Fallen man rules the creation for his own benefit and pleasure. Every new development is pressed into the service of sin, whether it be printing, cars, radios, computers, televisions, music, or art—man uses each to cultivate new ways to break God's laws.

This is not as it ought to be. God submitted every creature to man so that man might serve his Creator—use the whole of the creation to praise God. That is proper cultural development.

Only the believer, renewed in the image of God and sanctified by the Spirit, can use the developments of man to serve God. By God's grace, he presses into the service of God all the powers and inventions of the creation.

Believers seek to do that out of love and gratitude. Yet, we long for the life in the new heaven and earth when we will finally do that perfectly.

Russell Dykstra

March 27 — God Created Also Angels

But to which of the angels said he at any time,
Sit on my right hand, until I make thine enemies thy footstool?
Are they not all ministering spirits, sent forth to minister for them
who shall be heirs of salvation? —Hebrews 1:13–14

In that first week of time when God created the material world and all that is in it, he also made creatures that belong to a different world. He created angels. And God created a place for the angels to dwell: heaven. In distinction from the material such as earth, sky, water, roses, pineapples, and foxes, angels are spiritual. They are creatures, not gods, yet their realm is not the earth or sky, but the spiritual heaven.

What are angels? To begin with, the word *angel* means messenger. They are servants of God sent out with an official message to convey, or a work to accomplish.

Angels were created sinless. They love what is holy and pure and are zealous for God's glory. They can see that glory when we cannot. Isaiah beheld that in a vision of God on his throne, high and lifted up, and "one [angel] cried unto another, and said, Holy, holy, holy, is the Lord of hosts: the whole earth is full of his glory" (Isa. 6:3).

The angel's special function is to serve God's elect people (Heb. 1:14). How they serve his people, God does not fully explain. It is obvious that they serve the spiritual benefit of his people. They are sent to protect them not from physical danger and destruction, as is evident from the reality that God's people are injured and die just as the ungodly do. Rather, angels preserve God's people from spiritual dangers.

Angels ministered to Jesus at crucial times in his earthly ministry. They rejoice in heaven at the repentance of even one sinner. They will be involved in the final judgment, sent by Christ to gather the elect from the four corners of the earth, and then gather the ungodly unto destruction.

No one can see angels ordinarily. In Bible days, God sometimes gave them visible bodies so that they could accomplish God's appointed tasks, such as delivering Lot from Sodom or announcing Jesus' birth and, later, his resurrection.

Some have insisted that each believer has a guardian angel because the Bible on a couple of occasions speaks of "his angel." Understandably, parents like the thought that each of their children is protected from physical danger by one guardian angel. Yet, it is far more significant and comforting to hold to the Bible's teaching that all the angels, myriads of powerful spiritual agents, are engaged full-time in serving us, keeping us from spiritual destruction, and preserving us unto eternal life.

At death, they will escort us into the presence of Jesus. And we will join the throng of angels praising God perfectly.

Russell Dykstra

March 28 — **The Spiritual World**

Read: Acts 23:1–10

The Confession rejects errors from long ago that are still found in the world today. For that reason, it is worthwhile to examine them.

The first is the heresy of the Sadducees, a Jewish sect that existed in the days of Jesus. Jewish rulers of the people in that day were predominantly Sadducees, including the High Priests.

The error of the Sadducees was deadly serious. They denied the existence of any spiritual beings (angels or devils). They also denied the resurrection of the dead. For the Sadducees, this world and this life was all there was. They claimed to believe in the God of the Bible, but denied the afterlife—no heaven, hell, or resurrection.

Jesus taught us important information about heaven in response to a tempting question from the Sadducees. They invented a story of a woman who had legitimate marriages to several different men and posed the question: "In the resurrection, whose wife shall she be?" (Matt. 22:28). Jesus' stern reply was: "Ye do err, not knowing the Scriptures, nor the power of God. For in the resurrection they neither marry, nor are given in marriage, but are as the angels of God in heaven" (vv. 29–30). Then, Jesus effectively demolished the error of the Sadducees: "But as touching the resurrection of the dead, have ye not read that which was spoken unto you by God, saying, I am the God of Abraham, and the God of Isaac, and the God of Jacob? God is not the God of the dead, but of the living" (v. 31–32).

Many today claim to believe in God but deny that there is a heaven or hell apart from this world. They teach people to live for this world and this life. Some of these believe that there is nothing after death. Others believe they will make this world into heaven.

This is a denial of the one true God who created not only the heavens, the earth, and all creatures in it, but also angels and the spiritual heaven. And God has clearly revealed that there is a resurrection of the body. Jesus promised that "all that are in the graves shall hear his voice, and shall come forth; they that have done good, unto the resurrection of life; and they that have done evil, unto the resurrection of damnation" (John 5:28–29).

Jesus' instruction to Martha near the grave of her brother Lazarus is decisive: "Jesus said unto her, I am the resurrection, and the life: he that believeth in me, though he were dead, yet shall he live" (John 11:25).

Russell Dykstra

March 29 — The Origin of Devils

God spared not the angels that sinned,
but cast them down to hell, and delivered them into chains of darkness,
to be reserved unto judgment. —2 Peter 2:4

God created the material universe in which we live, the world that we can see, touch, study, and enjoy. God also created a world we cannot see: a spiritual realm. In that spiritual world, angels and devils live. Angels are holy creatures formed by the perfectly holy God. Devils are evil spirits. Where did devils come from?

An ancient heresy called Manichaeism, after a man named Mani, claimed that "devils have their origin of themselves, and that they are wicked of their own nature, without having been corrupted" (Article 12). Mani taught that eternally there was good and there was evil. God is good. Opposed to God, and independent of God, is another power which is evil. The devils come out of the evil substance.

According to this view, there is a constant battle between these two forces, both seeking to overcome the other. The outcome of the battle is uncertain.

These ideas exist yet in the twenty-first century. Many believe this battle continues between the good and the evil—two independent powers fighting for domination and victory.

This dualism is contrary to everything that Scripture teaches. The Bible proclaims the truth that God is sovereign. He is Creator. Everything else is creature, and dependent on his power. Man, angels, and, yes, devils too, are creatures.

But the question yet remains—what are devils and where did they come from? Devils are angels who fell into sin and became totally evil. Jesus indicated that the devil was at one time good but left that. Jesus said of the devil that he "was a murderer from the beginning, and abode not in the truth" (John 8:44). And 2 Peter 2:4 testifies that these devils were created angels: "God spared not the angels that sinned, but cast them down to hell."

God is in control. God determined Adam's fall into sin. He also determined that some of the angels would rebel against him. The rest of the angels God preserved in holiness. Paul calls the latter "elect angels" (1 Tim. 5:21). But God created all the angels good, holy, and sinless.

The devils are not independent of God. They are creatures whom God upholds, preserves, and governs—all for his purposes, in spite of themselves.

The believer never underestimates the power of the devil. Yet, he has every confidence that God rules supreme, also over the evil spirits.

Russell Dykstra

March 30 — What Do Devils Do?

Read: Ephesians 6:10–18

Devils are evil spirits. The Confession teaches that "they are so depraved that they are enemies of God and every good thing" (Article 12).

People all over the world are convinced that evil spirits abound. Anything bad that happens to them is attributed to evil spirits—accidents, diseases, loss of a business, death in the family, or anything they consider to be "bad luck." Such people are continually seeking to placate evil spirits or drive them away by charms, offerings, incense, or the like.

Devils are evil spirits, and they are real. They desire to bring evil on men, most definitely. But the essence of their evil nature is that they are opposed to God. Jehovah God is everything good, including truth, purity, wisdom, love, righteousness, and mercy. God is infinitely good. Devils oppose God because he is perfectly just, righteous, and good. Devils are so corrupt that they can only oppose all that is good and right.

Thus, the evil that devils seek in anyone's life is not disease, financial ruin, or death. It is rather the spiritual destruction of man that the devils pursue relentlessly. The devils are united in their opposition to God and desire to destroy God and his rule. Failing that, they desire to bring the entire human race into the pit of everlasting destruction with them.

Devils are rightly called evil spirits. They love iniquity because they hate the holy God. They seek "to ruin the church and every member thereof" (Article 12).

Devils will use anything in their war against God and his church. Being deceivers, they use the lie to draw men into the full bondage of sin. They make sin appear attractive. They use friends to entice to sin. Recall how the devil used Peter to tempt the Lord to forsake the obedient walk to the cross. Devils use peer pressure from society to make people conform to evil thinking and corrupt living. They will use government laws passed by evil men to encourage or compel citizens to sin.

The devil has an ally in each human being, for all are born totally depraved, willing slaves to sin and to the devil. The regenerated child of God still has that wicked nature, and the devils work in and through that.

Do not fear the evils of sickness, poverty, or even death. Fear rather the spiritual power of devils. "Give [no] place to the devil" (Eph. 4:27). "Resist [him], and he will flee from you" (James 4:7).

Russell Dykstra

March 31 — The Devil's Power Is Real, and It Is Great

*Put on the whole armour of God, that ye may
be able to stand against the wiles of the devil.* —Ephesians 6:11

Satan is the head of all the fallen angels. It is possible that God created Satan head of all the angels. Therefore, he was given tremendous gifts, power, and authority. He was chief over a myriad of angels, created to lead the band in service to the glorious God.

But Satan began to look too much at his own glory and power and lifted himself up. In his pride, Satan sinned and became a rebel against his creator and Lord. From that moment on, all his power and gifts have been pressed into the rebellion that he led among the angels that fell with him. They seek to destroy God and all that God has created.

Satan is, therefore, a formidable foe. He is called "the prince of the power of the air, the spirit that now worketh in the children of disobedience" (Eph. 2:2). He has legions of angels at his command. His status is evident from the fact that even "Michael the archangel, when contending with the devil...durst not bring against him a railing accusation, but said, The Lord rebuke thee" (Jude 9).

The Bible instructs the church to recognize the devil as a dreadful enemy. He is described "as a roaring lion...seeking whom he may devour" (1 Pet. 5:8). The church is warned not to open up any place in their lives for the devil (Eph. 4:26–27; 1 Cor. 7:5; 2 Cor. 2:11). Under him is one kingdom, fully devoted to the destruction of God, his kingdom, and his church.

Over the centuries, Satan has done great spiritual harm in and to the church. He introduces the lie into the church using false teachers. He sows tares (evil men) among the wheat (the elect). He rouses up the ungodly to persecute and kill believers. He strives to get ungodly men into the offices of the church so that evil men lead the church as preachers, elders, and deacons. In the days of Jesus' earthly ministry, there were many instances of demon possession, a dreadful picture of the spiritual power that a devil can have over a person.

All believers are called to be engaged in the spiritual battle. We are to put on the spiritual armor of God and stand for the cause of God (Eph. 6). We do this in the confidence that we are purchased with the blood of Christ. We are in his hand, and no one is able to pluck us out of his or his Father's hand (John 10:28, 29).

Russell Dykstra

April 1 — God's Plan for Devils: Eternal Destruction

And the devil that deceived them was cast into
the lake of fire and brimstone, where the beast and the false prophet are,
and shall be tormented day and night for ever and ever. —Revelation 20:10

Satan is the dreadful foe of the church of Jesus Christ. He is powerful, and his legions obey his command. He rules among the children of men. His greatest triumph (so he thought) was the crucifixion of the Lord Jesus.

Yet, Satan and his host have been eternally predestined for destruction in hell. And the all-wise God is using Satan for his purposes. Satan always wills and does evil. But he is an instrument in God's hand, accomplishing God's will. A prime example of that is God using a "lying spirit in the mouth of [the false] prophets" to convince wicked king Ahab to go out and fight the Syrians, leading to Ahab's God-determined death and overthrow (1 Kings 22:23).

Satan's end is certain. Genesis 3:15 already prophesies it, in the seed of the woman (Christ) crushing the head of the serpent (Satan). The Confession teaches: "by their own wickedness, adjudged to eternal damnation, daily expecting their horrible torments" (Article 12). Jesus speaks of hell as "everlasting fire, prepared for the devil and his angels" (Matt. 25:41). Notice: it is prepared for them.

Jesus has overthrown Satan's kingdom. Jesus, overcoming the devil's temptations, showed that Satan could not defeat Jesus. The cross was the triumph, as Paul writes: "And having spoiled principalities and powers, he made a shew of them openly, triumphing over them in it" (Col. 2:15). At his ascension into heaven, Jesus cast Satan and his host out (Rev. 12:9).

Destruction awaits them. Knowing that they have but a little time, they go after the church. This fits God's purpose, namely, that we fight in this spiritual battle.

We must fight. And yet, we fight not for the victory. The victory is accomplished in Christ's cross and resurrection. All believers are in Christ and have the victory. We fight in victory.

Satan's sure destruction is revealed in a vision of the end: "And the devil…was cast into the lake of fire and brimstone…and shall be tormented day and night for ever and ever" (Rev. 20:10). Likewise his followers (v. 15).

In the new creation that Jesus will form, there will be no place for Satan or his host. For "there shall in no wise enter into it anything that defileth, neither whatsoever worketh abomination, or maketh a lie" (Rev. 21:27).

What a glorious day when God brings his people into the everlasting kingdom of Jesus Christ! No adversary will torment us there, and we will live with God in perfect covenant life eternally.

Russell Dykstra

Article 13

OF DIVINE PROVIDENCE

We believe that the same God, after he had created all things, did not forsake them, or give them up to fortune or chance, but that he rules and governs them, according to his holy will, so that nothing happens in this world without his appointment; nevertheless, God neither is the author of, nor can be charged with, the sins which are committed. For his power and goodness are so great and incomprehensible, that he orders and executes his work in the most excellent and just manner even when the devil and wicked men act unjustly. And as to what he doth surpassing human understanding we will not curiously inquire into it further than our capacity will admit of; but with the greatest humility and reverence adore the righteous judgments of God which are hid from us, contenting ourselves that we are disciples of Christ, to learn only those things which he has revealed to us in his Word without transgressing these limits.

This doctrine affords us unspeakable consolation, since we are taught thereby that nothing can befall us by chance, but by the direction of our most gracious and heavenly Father, who watches over us with a paternal care, keeping all creatures so under his power that not a hair of our head (for they are all numbered), nor a sparrow, can fall to the ground, without the will of our Father, in whom we do entirely trust; being persuaded that he so restrains the devil and all our enemies that, without his will and permission, they can not hurt us.

And therefore we reject that damnable error of the Epicureans, who say that God regards nothing, but leaves all things to chance.

April 2 — **The Providence of God**

Read: Acts 17:24–28

In the next series of twenty-one meditations, we are going to consider what the Belgic Confession has to say about the great truth of the providence of God. This is a subject so wonderful we can with great benefit meditate on it for twenty-one days and even much longer. The "providence of God" is his willing, active and personal care for all his creatures. The God of providence is everywhere present in all the universe. He is at no time absent from it nor ignorant of any of the events that take place in the world. He himself has created the world and remains active in it. He is not himself part of the universe. He is highly and gloriously exalted above the entire universe. He is the sovereign almighty God, ruling over all the universe according to his own will and good pleasure. The Psalmist absolutely distinguishes the true and living God from idols by declaring: "But our God is in the heavens: he hath done whatsoever he hath pleased" (Ps. 115:3). By his almighty hand, God upholds the very existence of every creature. The creature cannot exist by itself. To speak of an independent and self-existent creature is to use contradictory language. Without the active and willing operations of God's providence, the creature would return to nothing.

The providence of God includes his daily care and provision for all his creatures by his Fatherly hand. One of the most beautiful and detailed Psalms speaking of the providence of God is Psalm 104. This Psalm speaks of all creatures waiting upon the Lord. He gives each creature the food it needs at the time of need and according to the nature of every creature.

In his amazing providence, God guides the whole of his vast creation that is millions and millions of miles broad and occupied by creatures, the largest of which are far larger than the small planet we live on. God guides the stars in their courses. The moon and the stars arise and set at a definite time every day at his command. This does not happen by chance or by some so-called natural law inherent to the universe.

The providence of God includes his guidance of the history of the nations of the world and all the events that take place in time. God has a purpose in this history, and by his sovereign almighty power he ensures that this purpose is realized without fail. We cannot understand the meaning and significance of history without knowing the truth of God's providence.

The providence of God includes his care and protection as the Lord and savior of his people in the world. Nothing in the whole of our life happens outside of the providence of God. "Even the very hairs of [our] head are all numbered," and not one of them falls to the ground without the will of our heavenly Father (Luke 12:7). "In him we live, and move, and have our being" (Acts 17:28). When we know the truth of the providence of God, we rely on him and trust in him completely. We find our comfort and peace in the truth of the providence of God. Even when God sends us very difficult trials and when enemies seem fierce and strong, we need not be afraid.

There are great mysteries about the truth of God's providence. There is great comfort in always being conscious of this truth in all of our lives.

Arie den Hartog

April 3 — Faith in the Providence of God

Read: Matthew 6:25–34

We know the truth of the providence of God only by faith. Every article of the Belgic Confession either begins with or implies the statement "We believe"! This is important to take note of and to remember as we consider the wonderful aspects of the providence of God, spoken of in this article of our confession.

The natural man who is an unbeliever cannot and does not know the providence of God, even though his whole life is determined by and controlled by the providence of God. The unbeliever often mocks the providence of God. God will judge this man by the daily operations of his providence, even though he refuses to acknowledge God. Psalm 73 speaks of how God sets the rich, prosperous, proud, and evil men of the world "in slippery places" and casts "them down into destruction" (v. 18). This is also part of the fearful, mighty, and constant operation of the sovereign providence of God.

We know the amazing truth of the providence of God only through faith in God and in his word. There are so many passages in the Bible that speak of the reality and operations of the providence of God. We shall consider these in the course of our twenty-one meditations on this wonderful subject. We should read these passages over and over and be comforted again and again by the amazing truth of the providence of God.

When we say, "We believe in the providence of God," we say this with great amazement and wonderment, and with fear and trembling. There are great and fearful truths regarding the providence of God that cause us to worship God in humility with godly fear.

The God of providence is Spirit and invisible in his being. The operations of God's providence are hidden to the eye of the natural man and known only by the children of God through the faith that God himself works in our hearts. There are mysteries in the providence of God that are far beyond our understanding. God's ways and God's thoughts in his works of providence are higher than our ways and our thoughts. Read Isaiah 55:6–10.

Sinful man cannot know the truth of God's providence through mere natural reason or scientific investigation. The providence of God is seen in the order and harmony in all the universe. However, there is in the world also much that seems confusing and hard to reconcile with the truth of God's providence. We believe the truth through humble faith in our hearts even when we cannot fully understand.

We are called to submit to the operations of God's providence in faith and obedience. This is especially important when there are operations of God's providence in our lives which involve trials and sufferings for us and mysteries beyond our understanding. Our faith must be stirred up by the constant reading of the word of God and meditation on its truth. Only then will the truth of God's providence be the source of great comfort and peace for us.

May the Lord give us daily the blessed comfort and assurance of knowing the providence of God in our lives.

Arie den Hartog

April 4 — The Mystery of the Providence of God

Read: Isaiah 55:8–13

I am still making some general comments on the wonderful subject of the providence of God before we enter into a discussion of some of the specific wording of the Belgic Confession in Article 13.

The truth of the providence of God explains for the believer why certain events take place in the world in which we live and in our personal life. The truth of God's providence is reasonable to the child of God. The things that take place in the providence of God cannot be explained by unbelieving human philosophy and the investigation of human science. In fact, such philosophy and science, because it is developed by the unbeliever, constantly strives to overthrow the truth of God's providence and somehow to deny it. Sinful man does not want to acknowledge the truth of the providence of God. He would rather entertain the imagination that he is free in all of his life in the world. He mocks the whole idea of the providence of God ruling over and directing all the events that take place in the world.

The child of God wants by faith to learn and consider the truth of the providence of God, and even in a measure to understand the ways of the Lord. Such a consideration of faith fills the child of God with wonder, amazement, and the worship of God.

But there are also truths of the operations of God's providence that are far beyond our very limited and small understanding. God is greater than our understanding. He is infinite in his own being and wisdom and goodness. He is absolutely sovereign in his providence, doing all things according to his own good pleasure.

We must humbly submit to the truth of God's providence in our lives, even when the ways of the Lord are mysterious and deep and beyond our understanding. The Psalmist declares concerning the works of God: "Thy way is in the sea, and thy path in the great waters, and thy footsteps are not known" (Ps. 77:19).

In considering the truth of the providence of God in the world and in our own personal lives, we always need to remember what Moses wrote in Deuteronomy 29:29, "The secret things belong unto the Lord our God: but those things which are revealed belong unto us and to our children for ever, that we may do all the words of this law."

Faith in the providence of God makes us greatly interested in the truths of God's providence that he has revealed to us in his word. We want to know these truths more and more. Knowing these truths is important for our life of obedience to God and service unto him.

But there are also truths of God's providence too high for us. There are mysteries in the operations of God's providence. These we receive and submit to in quiet faith and humility without always demanding understanding.

The truth of God's providence means that God rules. He does whatsoever he pleases. His wisdom is absolutely perfect. To believe the providence of God, we must have quiet trust in him even when we cannot understand. We may not seek with ungodly desire to pry into the things that God has not revealed and that are greater than all human understanding.

Arie den Hartog

April 5 — God Does Not Forsake the Creatures of His Hand

Read: Psalm 104:1–24

I hope you take the time to read all of Psalm 104. It is a marvelous Psalm about the providence of God!

Article 13 of the Belgic Confession makes many great statements about the truth of God's providence. In our series of meditations, we are going to consider some of these statements in the light of the word of God. A confession is of value only when it summarizes and explains the word of God. In the first three meditations, I made more general comments on the truth of the providence of God. In the rest of the series of articles, I will call your attention to the specific statements and truths outlined by the Belgic Confession.

The truth of the providence of God is intimately related to the truth of creation. One who does not believe in the truth of God as the creator of the universe cannot know and believe the truth of God as ruler and caretaker of the universe. Denials of the truth of creation as revealed in holy Scripture are common even in the church world today. Many have wrongly given way to what is called "theistic evolution," which tries to explain the truth of creation by trying to harmonize it with the unbelieving theories of modern science. This is impossible. We say: "we believe in God the creator." We also then confess: "we believe in God who is the God of providence."

The same God who created the universe and all creatures in it also upholds all things continually by the word of his power. God surrounds the being of every single one of his creatures. He guides the whole course of the existence of his creatures. He continually provides for the need of all his creatures according to the nature he gave each creature by his work of creation.

The creature cannot exist by itself. It is absolutely dependent on its Creator for all things. God must give to every creature its food and all things needful. See Psalm 104:27. If you have the time, you should read all of Psalm 104. How beautiful is this Psalm in its vivid description of the wonderful operation of God's providence in all of his creation.

The providence of God is the revelation of his goodness, faithfulness, and love for his creatures. If God failed to provide for the creatures of his hands, he would not truly be God, and his faithfulness could be called into question. The providence of God is about God's everlasting and unchangeable love and goodness.

God's providence in relation to the care of his children is wonderful. The providence of God is his constant and unfailing personal care and provision for us. We cannot care for ourselves by our own wisdom, power, and intelligence, for even these must constantly come from God. Believing this truth of God's faithfulness is absolutely essential for us as his children. We need to be constantly reminded of the care of God for his children. Such reminders will deliver us from anxiety in our lives.

Let's end this meditation today by meditating on the beautiful description of the care of God in his providence. Read and meditate on Matthew 6:25–32. May the words of this passage be your comfort in the day that is before you.

Arie den Hartog

April 6 — **Not by Chance, but by the Sovereign, Wise, and Good Providence of God**

Read: Matthew 6:25–31

There are really only two possibilities: either all things come by mere chance or fortune, or they come by the wonderful providence of God. The latter we know when we believe in God. When men reject the truth of God and his providence, they are given over to a world governed by cold and blind fate, determinism, chance, and fortune.

It is awful to be in the darkness of unbelief and to imagine that all things in our life and in the world are by chance. This is the hopelessness of atheism. It means that one is without hope or comfort, because one has no God. These will live in fear and have no certainty at all for anything that takes place in their lives. There is for them no purpose and meaning in life. They end their lives in pessimism and utter despair.

Imagining that all things happen by mere fate or chance has over the years taken the form of various philosophies. Ancient pagan philosophy and religion teach that the events of our life are determined by the movement of the stars. Those in such darkness check their horoscopes for the predictions of the day. Pagan religions trust in a multitude of deities, each vying for the attention, worship, and service of men. These deities often are at war with one another. Today one wins, tomorrow another. But an idol is nothing. Idols of wood and stone have eyes, "but they see not: they have ears, but they hear not… they have hands, but they handle not" (Ps. 115:5–7). The idol gods of the heathen cannot hear or help those who call upon them.

Many in our modern-day world have rejected every idea of God. They look to science to give them guidance. These believe that everything is ruled by natural law. They try hard to somehow influence natural law for their advantage. But the "forces of nature" are powerful. If everything is governed by the blind force of natural law, then the whole idea of chance is impossible. Then the world is determined by the laws of nature and by the rule of cause and effect. What awful darkness and despair finally engulfs the life of unbelieving and ungodly men. Even the most highly educated of our modern world live in this deep darkness of meaninglessness, despair, and confusion.

The believer boldly confesses from his heart through the faith God has graciously given, *I believe in God!* The God whom we believe in is sovereign, almighty, good, and wise. He accomplishes all things according to his good pleasure, for his glory and for the good and salvation of his people.

We believe that whatever takes place in the world and in our own personal life is firmly in the hands of the Lord. We know that God is good and wise. He loves us as a father loves his children. He knows and does only what is good for us, his children. He is able to work all things for the good of those who love him. Even though there are many things which we cannot understand, we know that God rules, and that we have nothing to fear. Even the deepest troubles in this life and the fierce enemies that we face are under the control of the great and wonderful God of providence. Believing this, we have peace, comfort, and the final and blessed hope of eternal life and glory.

Arie den Hartog

April 7 — God Rules Over the Great Things of the Universe

Read: Psalm 8

The Belgic Confession states: "We believe that the same God, after he had created all things, did not forsake them, or give them up to fortune and chance, but that he rules and governs them according to his holy will" (Article 13). The two most important words which we want to pay special attention to in our meditation for the next few days are "all things." In order to think about the providence of God "in all things," we need to remind ourselves what is all included in those things governed and ruled by God according to his will.

One way in which we consider the greatness of the providence of God is to look to the heavens and consider the stars. He created the greatest of the creatures of the universe, and he rules over them continually by the almighty power of his amazing providence. The Bible uses the number of stars to illustrate something that is beyond all human ability to number. The promise of God to Abraham was that his descendants would be greater in number than the stars (Gen. 15:5).

In considering this illustration, I decided to do an internet search on my computer. I was astounded by the answer to a question about the number of the stars. With the unaided human eye on a clear night, we can see several thousand stars. To get an idea about how many stars there are, you would need to travel to several places in the world from which to view the stars in the heavens above you. Of course, not all the stars are visible from one standing place on the earth. You would have to travel to various parts of the earth to be able to count all the stars visible to the naked eye. Perhaps you can count thousands of stars tonight by just seeing them with your own eyes.

With a good pair of binoculars, you could perhaps count as many as 200,000 stars. If you could look through a telescope of average power and took the time to count, you could see as many as 15,000,000 stars. Many of these stars are larger than our sun. The Milky Way, the galaxy in which we live, is over 120,000 light years across, according to astronomers. A light year is how far light travels in a year at the speed of 186,000 miles per second. Roughly, this would be about six trillion miles. Astronomers estimate that the Milky Way alone has about four hundred billion stars. There are giant galaxies that are estimated to have more than one hundred trillion stars. Again, according to the observable universe, astronomers estimate that there may be as many as 170 billion galaxies. All of these numbers boggle our minds.

Can you count the stars? To our greatest human imagination, they are more than we could ever number. God created them all! And God rules over them all. God is greater than all. He is absolutely sovereign in his rule over all of his creation. Every single one of the multitude of these stars is guided and controlled by God and moves according to his will and good pleasure. God is almighty to uphold all of these stars. If God would withdraw his power from these billions and billions of stars, they would all return to nothing. This is what they were before he created them.

The Psalmist in Psalm 8, in great amazement and astonishment, asks the question: "What is man, that thou art mindful of him? and the son of man, that thou visitest him?" (v. 4). The great God of the stars cares for every detail of our life. How wonderful it is to know this!

Arie den Hartog

April 8 — God Rules Over the Smallest of His Creatures

Read: Matthew 6:25–34

God created very tiny creatures. All creatures are made up of tinier creatures such as atoms, electrons, and protons. These are so small that they cannot be seen by the naked eye. Our bodies, too, are made up of thousands and thousands of cells. In a very short time, these cells die and are replaced by others. Some say that most of our body cells are replaced between every seven to ten years of our lives. God rules over all of this. He never changes. He is the same yesterday, today, and forever.

From the day of our birth, we are invaded by germs and organisms, which destroy our bodies and cause diseases to come into our bodies. We are born as babes and grow to maturity. In just sixty, seventy, or eighty years—and, in few cases, ninety years—our bodies have been so much under attack by these invading creatures that we die. After we die, worms destroy our bodies in the grave, and we return to the dust out of which we were created.

All these things are also under the providential control of the Lord. He has formed us from our conception in our mother's womb. Our members, according to Psalm 139:16, were all written in God's book. God made us as tiny babes, helpless and defenseless of ourselves. From our mothers' wombs, we were cast upon the Lord (Ps. 22:10).

The classic example of how detailed the providence of God is in our own lives is the truth that even "the very hairs of your head are all numbered" (Matt. 10:30). This passage is given to us to comfort us with regard to our enemies who persecute us and threaten our lives. Luke 21:16–18 records similar words of our Lord Jesus for our comfort in connection with the fearful things that will happen in the last days shortly before the return of our Lord. "And ye shall be hated of all men for my name's sake. But there shall not an hair of your head perish" (v. 17–18).

The control of God's providence is contrasted with the many things totally outside of our own control. In Matthew 6:25, Jesus tells us not to be anxious about "what [we] shall eat, or what [we] shall drink…or what [we] shall put on," because the Lord in his providence cares for us. He is the God who takes care of the common sparrow, so that none "fall on the ground without [the will of our heavenly] Father" (10:29). He is the God who clothes the lilies of the valleys with array grander than Solomon's (6:28–29). In both Matthew 6 and Matthew 10, Jesus tells us that in comparison to God's small creatures, we are in the sight of God of much greater worth and greater concern. His love and constant personal care of us is also much greater. This is the wonder of the providence of God.

And there are so many things that are outside of our control. We cannot make one of our hairs white or black. And we cannot by "taking thought…add one cubit to [our] stature" (Matt. 6:27). We cannot add even one moment or hour to our lives. Our whole lives are in the providence of God. Our lives will come to their conclusions on the day God has determined for us.

There have been those in the world that have mocked the very idea of such intimate and total control of the providence of God in our lives. But we believe what the Lord tells us and find great comfort in it. How amazing is the providence of our God.

Arie den Hartog

April 9 — **God Rules Over the Powers of Creation and the Seasons of the Year**

Read: Psalm 147

When we confess that God by his providence rules and governs all things, we need to think about what "all things" includes. We sometimes experience in the world in which we live the mighty forces of nature: the wind, storm, sea, lightning and thunder, and sudden, fearful earthquakes. All these are under God's control.

The most dramatic judgment that ever came upon this world was the flood. There may have been between two and three million people on the earth at the time of the flood. God destroyed them all. He only saved alive believing Noah and his family—only eight people altogether. After the flood, God declared that "while the earth remaineth, seedtime and harvest, and cold and heat, and summer and winter, and day and night shall not cease" (Gen. 8:22). Implied is that all these times are in the hands of the God of providence.

We are interested in what the weather will be. We say, "It will rain," or, "It will be sunny," or, "It will be cold." We commonly use language that ignores the truth of the providence of God. When we experience in our daily life the various kinds of weather and the changing of the seasons of the year, we should think about the providence of God. Even the rising and setting of the sun, the passing of day into night, these also are according to the abundant testimony of the word of God in the providence of God. Our bodies are dependent on the cycles of nature for rest and rejuvenation. The changing of the seasons is very important. Man must cultivate the land and plant the seed at just the right time to expect a harvest. He is entirely dependent on the providence of the Lord for the harvest. God must send the rain and the sunshine for the harvest. Without such operations of God's providence, man will die.

We often complain when inclement weather spoils our plans for the day. If you live in an area of the world similar to mine, you have experienced times when there was so much ice and snow that you could not even get out of your house to go to church. The Lord in his providence rules over the so-called regular seasons and climate changes through the year. Scripture makes plain that God in his providence also sends violent disturbances in nature. He sends earthquakes, violent storms, and the eruption of mountains. Droughts, famines, and pestilences also are controlled by the Lord. In some of these events, thousands of the inhabitants of the earth die.

The book of Revelation, as well as other parts of Scripture, makes clear that what man calls natural disasters are in fact the signs of the judgment of God on the earth and the coming of our Lord Jesus Christ. For example, the world has become familiar with what is called a tsunami. Earthquakes take place in the depth of the sea, creating huge waves. Large land masses can suddenly be inundated by water. Whole seaside villages, and even large sections of the great cities of the world, can be utterly destroyed, suddenly. The world in recent years experienced a tsunami that took away the lives of thousands of people in a fearful day.

Are such mighty events also in the providence of God? Many would vehemently deny this. But what does Scripture say? There are many questions that need to be answered. Think about it. Meditations should cause us to do this.

Arie den Hartog

April 10 — God Rules Over the Rise and Fall of the Nations

Read: Daniel 2:19–23

What is included in the "all things" that are governed and ruled by the providence of God? The answer to this question reveals how mighty and how significant the providence of God really is. God gives us the understanding and wisdom to know about the truth of God's providence in the world in which we live. We are taught to fear the Lord and his mighty power and judgments in the earth.

The book of Daniel tells of the rule of God's providence among the nations of the world. God gave a dream to the heathen king of Babylon. He had built a mighty world empire after his seemingly invincible army had conquered one nation after another, including Judah, the special chosen nation of God's people. After the proud heathen king Nebuchadnezzar had built his great kingdom, he walked in his stately palace and boasted: "Is not this great Babylon, that I have built for the house of the kingdom by the might of my power, and for the honour of my majesty?" (Dan. 4:30). Immediately after this boasting, in a moment, God made this proud king insane and drove him out from his palace to live like a wild beast of the field until he had acknowledged the sovereignty of the God of heaven.

In the book of Isaiah, we read of the greatness of God over the nations of the world.

13. Who hath directed the spirit of the Lord, or being his counselor hath taught him?
14. With whom took he counsel, and who instructed him, and taught him in the path of judgment, and taught him knowledge, and shewed to him the way of understanding?
15. Behold, the nations are as a drop of a bucket, and are counted as the small dust of the balance: behold, he taketh up the isles as a very little thing.
16. And Lebanon is not sufficient to burn, nor the beasts thereof sufficient for a burnt offering.
17. All the nations before him are as nothing; and they are counted to him less than nothing, and vanity. (Isa. 40:13–17)

In America and Singapore, many of us enjoy a great measure of wealth and prosperity. There are other nations of the world in which this is not the case. All of this is included in the providence of God. Have you thought about this? We must not be proud, boasting in the prosperity and glory of the nation in which we might be living. Even the very fact that we are living in such a nation was determined by the providence of God in our lives. Revelation 19:19 prophesies that at the end of the world, all nations will be joined together in the kingdom of antichrist. The kingdom of antichrist will in the providence of God be allowed to exercise dominion over the whole world for a very short time.

But the time will come suddenly when the kingdom of antichrist will be destroyed in one day. No powerful earthly nation or ruler will be able to prevent this from happening. The inhabitants of the world will mourn over the end and destruction of the kingdoms of the world. The truth of God's providence over the history of the nations is a fearful thing. We are called by the word of God to be wise. We are called to separate ourselves from the ungodly world, to submit ourselves to God and consecrate our lives to him. We are called to look for the glorious coming of the kingdom of Christ.

Arie den Hartog

April 11 — God Rules and Governs the Personal Life of Each One of Us

Read: Deuteronomy 8:7–20

When we think about all the things that are ruled and governed by the providence of God, we certainly must think of our own personal lives. We have already in past meditations considered the truth of that in Psalm 139. God in his wonderful providence formed us in our mother's womb. The Lord saw our substance from the very beginning of our existence, and all our members were written in his book (v. 16). How different each one of us is. We did not make ourselves. It is the Lord who has made us. All the differences of our characters and personalities were determined in the providence of God. All the gifts that we have, our intellects, and our talents were all determined at the very beginning of our lives by the providence of God. There are vast differences in our lives, such as the occupation we have, whether we are married or not, and whether we have children in our marriage. Yet, we all can look back at the very beginning of our lives and consider how all things in our lives were directed by the providence of God.

The measure of wealth each of us has is determined by God. Some have much more than others. Some have much less. God did not create us all equal. Some achieve great heights in their earthly occupations and establish themselves in a career in which they are able to amass great wealth and glory in the world. Others live a very minimal existence. These have a life-long struggle to earn a living. Think about how poor people are in so-called third world countries. If we have been born to a rich family in a prosperous nation of the world where there is freedom and lots of opportunities for us in our lives, we should always remember to acknowledge the Lord.

According to the passage in Deuteronomy 8, there is a great danger, strangely, when we get rich and prosperous in the world, with a position of power and honor, that we forget the Lord and boast in ourselves. This is due to our sinful nature. God reminds us in his word that it is he, not we ourselves, that gives us power to get wealth, and establishes us in our lives, and perhaps, gives us much more than the neighbor. Thus, we ought not boast in our own wisdom and great achievements, because our position in life is not at all because of who and what we are by ourselves. Rather, we ought to be thankful to the Lord and remember to serve him in humility and thankfulness. We are to use all the wealth that God has given us in his service for his glory and for the cause of his church and kingdom in the world. "Unto whomsoever much is given, of him shall be much required" (Luke 12:48). We are to give of the gifts that God has given to us to the poor, those who have less than we have, or perhaps those who have great need in their lives.

Those who are given great wealth have the calling of God to give liberally to support the church of Jesus Christ, of which they are members, and the causes of his kingdom in the world. The rule of the New Testament is not merely to give a tithe of one-tenth as our obligation unto the Lord. We must give cheerfully and thankfully to the Lord according as the Lord has prospered us. God does not always send us peace and prosperity and happiness in our lives. Nowhere in his word does he promise this. Are we ready also to accept this truth of the providence of God? We want to consider this soberly in our next meditations.

Arie den Hartog

April 12 — **God Rules Over Sin and Evil**

Read: Genesis 3:1–19

When the Belgic Confession says that God rules over all things, this includes also the sin and evil that is in the world. Many do not believe this. When one takes this position, one is often accused of maintaining that God is the author of sin. Can one maintain that God rules with absolute sovereignty over sin and evil without maintaining the blasphemous position that God is the author of sin?

When we enter into thinking about this aspect of the world of God's providence, we are confronted by great mysteries. The very language that we use in talking about this subject and the thoughts we have on it must be carefully formulated.

God is holy. He is absolutely, perfectly good. There is no evil in him whatsoever. Sin and wickedness cannot have its origin from the nature of God. In 1 John 1, we read that "God is light, and in him is no darkness" (v. 5). If God is the author of evil, then it must be the case that there is evil in God himself. To even suggest this is to blaspheme God. Blasphemy is the greatest imaginable sin. May God keep us from committing such great evil. God cannot be charged with the evil that is in the world.

There is no doubt that this world is full of evil and great wickedness. We know from Genesis 3, the literal, sober, and dreadful history from whence this evil came. Shortly after God had created the world good and perfect, the devil, a fallen angel and the great enemy of God, tempted man, who fell into sin. Fallen man brought all the evil into the world when he agreed with the lie of the devil that he could become God himself. Fallen man became the servant of the devil and perpetrator of all evil.

The fall brought terrible misery into the world. It brought the suffering and anguish of sickness and disease that ends in the judgment of death for man.

When man rebelled against God, his heart was filled with enmity against God. This act was also the beginning of man's enmity of the heart against his fellow man, his neighbor. The fall of man brought pride, jealousy, selfishness, and hatred into the heart of man against his fellow human being. As a result of the fall, there would be hatred, murder, and crime and bloodshed among man. There would be hatred, oppression, greed, and violence of all sorts by man against fellow human beings.

Shortly after the fall, we read in the book of Genesis,

5. And God saw that the wickedness of man was great in the earth, and that every imagination of the thoughts of his heart was only evil continually.
11. The earth also was corrupt before God, and the earth was filled with violence.
12. And God looked upon the earth, and, behold, it was corrupt; for all flesh had corrupted his way upon the earth. (Gen. 6:5, 11–12)

It is clear from this account that God judged that the sin characterizing the world after the fall had come from man's own wickedness and corruption. But where was God when this happened? Did God leave his throne when the fall took place? Answering this question in the right way is very important.

Arie den Hartog

April 13 — God Rules Over the Natural Evil that Takes Place in the World

Read: Isaiah 45:1–13

When we consider the rule of God over the evil of this world, we should distinguish between moral and natural evil. Moral evil is sin, when one misses the mark of God's moral law or breaks the commandments. Natural evil comprises such things as the suffering of man in the world, including the many hundreds of diseases that can befall him. It includes the great tragedies that can take place in his life, such as car accidents or being the victim of some violent crime at the hands of the wicked people of the earth.

These natural evils include natural disasters—earthquakes, famines, violent storms, plagues, and epidemics. In recent years, there was a huge tsunami in the Indian Ocean. Its mighty force killed over 250,000 people in a very short space of time. In the history of the world, there have been earthquakes and worldwide plagues that killed hundreds of thousands of people. Great misery, sorrow, and anguish came into the lives of thousands of seemingly helpless people, including women and children. The reports of such horrific natural disasters fill us with terror and dread. We are immediately filled with profound sympathy and anguish for those whose lives are affected by great calamities in such ways that they are never again the same.

Is God in control of such events that take place in our world? Or do they happen outside of his sovereign control? If God is in control of these, is he not some kind of a monster (which to say so would be the height of blasphemy)? If God is good, almighty in power, and absolutely sovereign in his rule in all of the vast universe, why does he not prevent these great tragedies from taking place in the world and spare so many thousands from all this sorrow, misery, suffering, and death?

These are many difficult questions which are not easy to answer. Some are questions that cannot be answered, nor should we seek to answer them. Some things must be left in the secret providence of God. We must remain silent and certainly not challenge God in his righteous judgments in the world. God's works of providence are full of mystery, and some of them are very dark. As much as man might be unwilling to admit it, the natural disasters that take place in the world are in part his holy and righteous judgment on the wicked men of the world. It is not God, but man who is evil, rebelling against God his creator, and not fearing his name, worshiping, or serving him as he is solemnly obligated to do. We tremble before the judgments of God in the earth.

In his just and holy wrath, God always remembers mercy. He shows us his mercy in the great salvation of his people in Jesus Christ. We all deserve to be destroyed everlastingly. From these judgments, God saves his people in his sovereign goodness and mercy. Our only comfort is that he rules over all, and we cry unto him for mercy for ourselves and also for our fellow man. And God is always merciful.

Arie den Hartog

April 14   **God Rules Over the Devil**

Read: Job 1

Are there two gods in the universe or is there only one true and living God who is absolutely sovereign over all his creatures, including even the devil? Heathen religion teaches that there is more than one god: supposedly, there are evil gods and good gods. The Christian religion teaches that there is absolutely only one God. This means that the devil, as powerful as he might be, is not God. He is not almighty. He is not able to do whatsoever he pleases in the world. The devil brought about the great tragedy of the fall. But even when he did this, he was ruled by God. The devil cannot even move outside of the providence of God.

There are three main characters in the book of Job: God, the devil, and Job. Of Job, it is said that he "was [a] perfect and [an] upright [man who] feared God, and eschewed evil" (v. 1). The devil falsely accused Job of serving God simply because God had given Job great prosperity in the world. The book of Job proves that this was a false and slanderous accusation against the godly and upright man. God allowed the devil to send dreadful trials in the life of Job. In one day, Job lost all of his riches and even all of his children. His wife urged him to "curse God, and die" (Job 2:9). He sat in what would be called today the garbage dump. Job's life, which had once been so full of joy and happiness, was now suddenly full of sorrow and misery.

Job suffered the most dreadful imaginable misery and suffering. After the devil could not succeed in destroying the faith of Job and turning him away from God, God allowed the devil even to grievously afflict his body. Job's body was covered with boils and sores. He was in torment and absolutely miserable. Besides our Lord Jesus Christ, there has never been a man who suffered like Job. The devil was involved in all of this! Yet, God was in complete control. The devil could do absolutely nothing to Job without the sovereign permission of God. As long as God did not permit it, the devil could not destroy Job. Job at times became very discouraged. He even cursed the very day of his birth, wishing he had never even been born, so miserable was he in all of this (Job 3:1–3).

To add to the great misery of Job, three men appeared on the scene who were supposedly long-time friends of Job. These so-called friends explained the misery of Job by maintaining that Job had committed some great sin in his life, and now God was punishing him. Job never denied that he was a sinner. Read his confession in chapter 42: "Wherefore I abhor myself, and repent in dust and ashes" (v. 6). Job was ashamed and confessed that he had sinned when he complained against the providence of God in his life and accused God of dealing with him in an evil way.

Several great lessons can be learned from the book of Job. The first is that even the devil is completely under the control of God's providence. He can do nothing even when he does his most evil works, and he can do nothing except by the permission of God. Though the trials of Job were very severe, ultimately Job knew that God was with him. Job confessed: "I know that my redeemer liveth, and that he shall stand at the latter [last] day upon the earth" (Job 19:25) to raise Job from the dead, deliver him from all evil, and cause his life to be blessed forever in the presence of his God.

Arie den Hartog

April 15   **Ye Thought Evil Against Me, But God Meant It for Good**

Read: Genesis 50:15–21

The Belgic Confession maintains that God's providence rules over all things. It even rules over the purposes of wicked men and causes these purposes to work for a great good. In the passage I ask you to read today, we have an amazing example of the above truth from the history of Joseph in the Old Testament. It is hard to tell this story in a very short form. I hope you can persevere in reading a longer meditation today.

Joseph was the second youngest son of Jacob. Jacob probably wrongly favored Joseph over all his other sons. He showed this special favor by making a coat of many colors for Joseph. God sent Joseph dreams that prophesied of a day that was coming when he would rule over his own father and over his brethren. These events made Joseph's brothers jealous of him. They hated him. So cruel was their hatred that they sold their own brother into slavery. The hearts of Joseph's brethren were so hard and cruel that even the bitter crying and anguish of Joseph did not make them pity him.

Joseph was sold into slavery in Egypt. An amazing chain of events took place, all under the sovereign control of God's providence. In this, God even used human trafficking, one of the greatest evils among men. Joseph was purchased by the captain of Pharaoh's army, whose name was Potiphar. Joseph proved himself to be a wise and faithful servant. He was made the chief servant in the house of Potiphar. His master trusted him and committed his whole estate to Joseph's care. But Potiphar had an evil and wicked wife who accused Joseph of trying to force her into adultery with him. She made this charge to cover up her own evil, lustful enticement of Joseph to go to bed with her. Because of the false charges of this evil woman, Joseph was thrown into prison where he suffered for a number of years. This whole chain of events could have made Joseph bitter, even against God. Joseph might have rotted in despair while in prison. But Joseph continued to trust in the sovereign God of providence. As a result of this, God gave Joseph wisdom even while in prison. Joseph was given the responsibility to rule over his fellow prisoners. While all of these were happening, God sent the dreams to the heathen king Pharaoh about the seven years of plenty and prosperity that were to come, which would be followed by seven years of severe famine. This is in itself an amazing testimony of the providence of God ruling over the seasons of the year—in times of prosperity and plenty, and also in times of famine and great distress.

In the midst of all this history, faithful Joseph was exalted from prison to become the chief ruler in Egypt. Joseph now had occasion to reveal himself to his brethren when they came to Egypt to buy food during the days of the famine. Another amazing series of events happened, also ruled by the providence of God. The culmination of these events was that Jacob and his entire family, who in spite of their sinfulness were the special covenant people of God at the time, moved to Egypt. This move was in order to keep the whole company of Jacob and his family alive in the providence of God.

The passage that you were asked to read was the confession of Joseph at a crucial time in all of this history. Father Jacob died of old age and was buried. After this, the brothers of Joseph greatly feared that Joseph would avenge himself of all the evil that his brothers had done to him in past years. Surely, he could not have forgotten their cruel and evil deeds of the past. But God gave Joseph an amazing and wonderful understanding of his providence. The providence of God ruled over evil not only for the great good of Joseph in his personal life. Joseph was exalted, as God rewarded him for his faithfulness. The providence of God ruled over all the seemingly evil things that took place for the salvation of God's people. What an amazing thing! Many are the applications of God's providence to our own lives and the history of the world in which we live. How wonderful is the providence of God, even ruling over the desperately evil purposes of wicked men for the good and salvation of his people. What a great comfort for us to know this truth of God!

Arie den Hartog

April 16 — God's Sovereign Counsel in Christ Ruling Over the Most Wicked Deeds of Men

Read: Acts 2:22–33

The passage that I ask you to read for this meditation contains the most amazing record of God's sovereign, providential rule over the sin and wicked deeds of men for the accomplishment of the great good of the salvation of his people. God sent his beloved Son into the world for the salvation of his people. We would have expected the world to receive the Son of God with joy and exultation, and to have given him the honor and glory of which he was worthy.

During all the years of his ministry, Jesus did nothing but good, healing the sick, making the blind to see, the deaf to hear, the lame to walk, and even raising up the dead to life again. The miracles that Jesus did clearly demonstrated that he was the Son of God, for no mere man could ever have done the mighty works that he performed. Yet, Jesus was hated and despised by men, even by those he came to save. This hatred was totally unreasonable. This hatred came to its culmination when the most wicked men of the world came together and condemned the perfect and holy Son of God to the accursed death of the cross. No greater evil has ever been done. Surely it was all inspired by the devil himself. The death at the cross involved dreadful agony and torment for our beloved Lord. In the midst of its great darkness and suffering, Jesus cried: "My God, my God, why hast thou forsaken me?" (Matt. 27:46). When they had crucified Jesus, and they saw him dead on the cross, the enemies of Christ imagined that they had triumphed over him.

But God raised up Jesus his Son from the dead and exalted him to the highest glory and honor at his own right hand in heaven. The exaltation of Christ was the reward for his perfect obedience, love, and amazing self-sacrifice on the cross. The death of Jesus Christ, the exaltation that followed, and the salvation that was accomplished surely did not happen by chance. Those evil men who crucified Jesus, contrary to their imagination, did not act independently and totally free of God's control. In fact, because of the providential rule of the sovereign God of heaven and earth, it all happened in order that Christ could become the mighty savior of his people and be made glorious in God's own presence. The inspired writer of the book of Acts declares that all these events took place according to the "determinate counsel and foreknowledge of God" (Acts 2:23). The meaning of these precise words is very significant. God did not passively allow wicked men and the devil to do their great evil. The truth is that God determined all of these things in his own sovereign and eternal counsel for the highest good.

The wicked men who performed the evil work of crucifying the Christ of God stand responsible and justly condemned for their evil work. We shiver even to think of the dreadful judgment all these wicked men will receive on the day of judgment and forever in hell. But God ruled over all of these things to accomplish the exaltation of his Son and the great good of salvation of his people. What a blessed and comforting truth with the greatest implications, showing that God is absolutely God!

Arie den Hartog

April 17 — **God Cannot Be Charged with Evil**

Read: Deuteronomy 32:1–6

In our last few meditations, we have been considering the truth that God's providence governs even the great evils that take place in the world. The supreme example of this, certainly, is that God ruled over the most wicked deed that men have ever done in the entire history of the world, namely, the crucifixion of the glorious and blessed Son of God. We considered in this connection what Acts 2:23 teaches. It is important to believe what Scripture says about God's rule over evil. If God does not rule over evil and over the works of the devil, then evil and the devil are independent powers. If evil is independent from God, then we cannot be certain that God will gain the victory over the devil in the end and that the devil will not be able to overthrow the work of the cross of Jesus Christ.

In the personal circumstances of our life, God is in complete control not only over the good things which he sends us but also in the difficult providences of sickness, trials, and troubles in our life. These things are not controlled by the devil or some blind, evil force independent from God, but by our loving heavenly Father. He rules over these things with such absolute sovereignty that he turns all evil which he sends for our good and salvation.

That God rules even over all the evil that is in the world does not make God the author or source of evil. To charge God with being the author of any evil in the world is the height of blasphemy. Yet, proud and wicked man does indeed sometimes charge God with being responsible for the evil that is in the world. Defiantly, he holds his fist in the face of God. He becomes angry with God because of the troubles of his life. Scripture makes clear that all the misery and suffering that is in the world is due to the fall of man and the curse of God upon this sin. The devil is the author of all evil in the world. The history of the fall as recorded in Genesis 3 makes this very plain.

When God rules even over the devil and even over the great sin and wickedness of man, he does so in such a way that he never in any way becomes tainted with sin himself. "God is light, and in him is no darkness at all" (1 John 1:5). He remains absolutely and perfectly holy, the embodiment of all perfection and glory.

The mysteries of God's absolute sovereignty even over evil are far greater than the limits of human understanding. When God rules over evil, he justly condemns—and in his holy wrath destroys—those who do evil, including the devil and all his host. God shows himself to be absolutely and fearfully just when he sends his judgment on the world of wicked men. This should cause all of us to tremble and fear before him.

God rules and triumphs over all evil. He has planned all things in his counsel, even the fall and the evil works of men. He is able to rule over them and destroy the wicked in such a way that they serve his own glorious purposes. Thus, his justice is revealed. The greatness of the salvation of his people and the wonderful work he has accomplished in the cross, resurrection, and exaltation of Christ—everything in the history of the world—will finally serve the glory of Christ and the salvation of his people. How great and absolutely sovereign is our God! We worship and adore him with fear and trembling.

Arie den Hartog

April 18 — God's Works in Providence Are Incomprehensible

Read: Isaiah 40

I have asked you today to read a long section of Scripture. This is good, and we should at times do just this with great benefit for strengthening our faith in God. Isaiah speaks powerfully of the greatness of God. He does so in order to comfort God's people in their troubles and in the severe trials of life that God sometimes sends in their lives.

Man is sinful and proud when he demands to understand all the works of God. In this demand, he is really imagining himself to be equal with God. But God is indeed infinitely greater than man. The works of God are greater than the limits of our human understanding. We are so small in the presence of God. He is so infinitely great! God's word calls us to faith when we consider his almighty providence in the world. Job states this truth when he declares: "Canst thou by searching find out God? Canst thou find out the Almighty unto perfection? It is as high as heaven; what canst thou do? Deeper than hell; what canst thou know? The measure thereof is longer than the earth, and broader than the sea" (Job 11:7–9). Job spoke these words by the inspiration of God while he was suffering the greatest imaginable trials. Even so, he believed that all of these were in the providence of God. He confessed that the ways of God in his life were very deep and beyond all understanding. He comforted himself through faith in the greatness of God.

Isaiah the prophet comforted Judah in the midst of the great trials of the Babylonian captivity, when the people of God were in despair and at times thought that God was not strong enough to save them.

In the rest of today's meditation, let's consider again some of the amazing passages in the prophecy of Isaiah. God spoke through the prophet Isaiah of his incomprehensible, amazing, and wonderful greatness in his providential dealings with his people:

> 12. Who hath measured the waters in the hollow of his hand, and meted out heaven with the span, and comprehended the dust of the earth in a measure, and weighed the mountains in scales, and the hills in a balance?
>
> 15. Behold, the nations are as a drop of a bucket, and are counted as the small dust of the balance: behold he taketh up the isles as a very little thing. (Isa. 40:12, 15)

A few verses later, we read: "It is he that sitteth upon the circle of the earth, and the inhabitants thereof are as grasshoppers; that stretcheth out the heavens as a curtain, and spreadeth them out as a tent to dwell in" (Isa. 40:22). "Lift up your eyes on high, and behold who hath created these things" (Isa. 40:26). In a later chapter, when the people of God were in deep despair because of the great trials they were experiencing in the providence of God, God said to his people: "For my thoughts are not your thoughts, neither are your ways my ways, saith the Lord. For as the heavens are higher than the earth, so are my ways higher than your ways, and my thoughts than your thoughts" (Isa. 55:8–9).

In order to believe in the truth of God's providence in our deepest trials—and in thinking about our own weaknesses and helplessness before forces and powers in the world—we need to remember and believe with deepest humility, fear, and trembling, the infinite greatness, almighty power, and absolute sovereignty of God in all of his ways.

Arie den Hartog

| April 19 | **The Proper Attitude Towards the Incomprehensible Works of God's Providence** |

Read: Job 42:1–6

Because the works of God are so much greater than the limits of our human understanding, we should not demand to fully understand them. We should not become discouraged and despair because we cannot fully understand them. We also should not in human pride seek to pry into the mysteries of God's providence which are greater than our understanding. God is greater than our understanding. We should expect that. We should humbly accept that by faith. We should not judge God when the works of his providence in our life, or in the world in which we live, are beyond our understanding.

We must simply believe what should be obvious, that God is greater than we are. We are ever so small and so limited in our understanding. God sent Job many difficult trials in his life. At times, Job complained and questioned God's dealings with him in his trials. At the end, when God brought Job to his senses, he made the confession in the passage which I have asked you to read for this meditation.

Moses by inspiration of God gave this admonition to Israel in Deuteronomy 29:29, "The secret things belong unto the Lord our God: but those things which are revealed belong unto us and to our children for ever, that we may do all the words of this law."

God has revealed many wonderful truths concerning his power, goodness, and mercy. He has revealed these things in his word, the infallible Scriptures, the Bible. We need to read and believe his word daily so that we might know and trust in him, do his will, and know his calling for us in our lives. We must also teach our children the wonderful truths of God for their great benefit and faith in him.

Before the mysteries of God's providence, we are to acknowledge with fear and trembling that God is infinitely greater than our understanding, and that we are before him but dust and ashes. Such faith gives us the proper reverence before God and proper humble knowledge of our own smallness and the severe limitations in our own lives. We are absolutely dependent on God's sovereignty. "It is he that hath made us, and not we ourselves" (Ps. 100:3). In his providence, God gives us life, breath, and all things. "In him, we live, and move, and have our being" (Acts 17:28).

Especially when we consider that God even rules over the wicked deeds of men and over all their evil devices against him, we must be careful of our own attitude. Never must we judge God for being evil nor demand of him that we must be able to fully understand the wonderful works of his providence.

The inspired apostle Paul writes about God's absolute sovereignty in the saving of his people and the severity of his justice in condemning the ungodly reprobate wicked. Afterwards, Paul in his utter amazement and astonishment makes this declaration concerning God.

33. O the depth of the riches both of the wisdom and knowledge of God! how unsearchable are his judgments, and his ways past finding out!
34. For who hath known the mind of the Lord? or who hath been his counselor?
35. Or who hath first given to him, and it shall be recompensed unto him again?
36. For of him, and through him, and to him, are all things: to whom be glory for ever. Amen. (Rom. 11:33–36)

Arie den Hartog

April 20 — The Care of Our Gracious and Heavenly Father

Read: Psalm 73:11–24

The truth of the providence of God is not an abstract doctrine. According to Article 13, "this doctrine affords us unspeakable consolation." This comfort is particularly for those who are the children of God in the world. These have the right to call the living God, the creator and ruler of the universe, their God and Father for Jesus' sake. The providence of God is his constant personal care for his dear children. He knows them by name and constantly watches over every circumstance of their lives. God is not the universal Father of all men (Eph. 2:2–3). The ungodly refuse to acknowledge God and serve him. They are said to be "children of wrath" (v. 3). What could be more dreadful than to pass the days of one's life in the holy wrath of God!

We are the children of God by grace. The grace of God is his unmerited favor towards us who are undeserving, in Christ Jesus. Without the grace of God, we too would be children of wrath, dead in trespasses and sin. But now, God loves us and cares for us! The providence of God is to be considered with adoration by those who are his children!

God in his providence sometimes sends prosperity to the wicked. He might even give greater riches and prosperity to the wicked than to his children. While he sends prosperity to the wicked, God might even send severe trials to his children in the world. This might cause us to be in great distress, as was the case with the psalmist of Psalm 73.

But what a mighty difference between God's dealings with the wicked and his dealings with his children! When God sends prosperity to the wicked, he sets "them in slippery places" and in the end casts "them down unto destruction" (Ps. 73:18). The blindness of sin causes the wicked to be ignorant of these things. At the same time, God directs all things in the lives of his dear children in his fatherly goodness and mercy. He causes all things in their lives to work for their good and salvation.

This God who cares for his children dwells in the highest heavens. He is a God of sovereign almighty power, and transcendent glory and majesty. He is the ruler over the vast universe which he created. He upholds and directs all the creatures in this universe so that none can even so much as move without his will and providence.

This God has set his love upon us. In this amazingly fatherly love, he has made us his children by his adoptive grace and his work of regeneration in our hearts. By his love, God has distinguished us from the billions of people on this earth to be his children. He has distinguished us to be his children in his Son Jesus Christ, for we were by nature children of wrath. We are the objects of God's love continually, as he beholds us as his dear children, redeemed by grace in his beloved Son Jesus Christ.

He loves us as no earthly father could ever love one of his children. This is true because he is God. Even the greatest earthly father is so limited in his power to protect and care for his children. There are so many things outside of the control of earthly fathers. These earthly fathers are often filled with anguish when they see their children in the midst of great suffering and trouble. But the God of providence is the sovereign almighty Lord of heaven and earth. What a comfort to know this blessed truth as children of the heavenly Father!

Arie den Hartog

April 21 — By His Will and Constant Loving Care

Read: Luke 12:1–12

In the passage I ask you to read today, Jesus comforts us with the truth of God's providence. He does so in connection with his prophesying that in this ungodly world, the Christian has many enemies. They persecute us, and when their hatred for us grows fierce, they may even kill us. This is an ever-increasing, fearful reality. The wicked world, under the instigation of the devil, wants to destroy the children of God spiritually. The devil is constantly attacking us. According to 1 Peter 5:8, the devil goes about "as a roaring lion…seeking whom he may devour."

We need not fear even the greatest of enemies nor any danger in the world. We have the Almighty Sovereign of heaven and earth taking care of us continually. He loves us in his capacity as our heavenly Father. He has distinguished us from the world, setting us apart by sovereign grace and adopting us as his children. He demonstrated the amazing greatness of his love to us by sacrificing his only begotten Son in order that he might redeem us forever to be his own.

It is inconceivable that God the Father could ever forsake any of his children. No enemy or power in all the universe can separate us from his love. Romans 8:38–39 declares "that neither death, nor life, nor angels, nor principalities, nor powers, nor things present, nor things to come, nor height, nor depth, nor any other creature, shall be able to separate us from the love of God, which is in Christ Jesus our Lord."

The providence of God involves the continual moment to moment operation of the will and power of God, directed by his amazing love, for our good and salvation. God is constantly active in his care for his people. He never slumbers nor sleeps. He will preserve us from all evil. He never lets us out of his sight.

God never desires anything else than the good and salvation of his people. He does not ever change his purpose and desire. He sometimes chastens us because of our sin. He is grieved with our sin, but even then, he does not change his love for us, nor turn against us to destroy us.

The providence of God has the final goal of our eternal salvation. That goal has been fixed in the eternal counsel of God. Our lives in all his perfect plan will lead us to the final realization of that goal. God's purpose of saving his people through Jesus Christ will not, nor can ever fail. The Psalmist confesses before God: "Thou shalt guide me with thy counsel, and afterward receive me to glory" (Ps. 73:24).

Even "the hairs of [our heads] are all numbered" (Matt. 10:30). Who ever thinks about the number of hairs on their head? Hair usually falls to the ground without our will and without our care. The providence of God is so all-knowing, so all-inclusive, that even the smallest details of our life are under the amazing and wonderful control of the providence of God.

There are so many mighty and significant things that happen in our daily life and in the world in which we live. There are so many forces greater than we are. There are so many things totally outside of our control. There are so many things in the future that God does not reveal to us now. All of these also are completely under the control of the wonderful providence of God. We are perfectly safe in the hands of our heavenly Father. What a comfort it is to know this blessed truth!

Arie den Hartog

April 22 — Trusting Completely in the Providence of God

Read: Psalm 27

With today's meditation we conclude the series of meditations on the wonderful truth of the providence of God in Article 13. It is not good enough that we have a certain intellectual knowledge and understanding of the truth of the providence of God. We must constantly hold this truth in our hearts by the conscious exercise of our faith. This truth must live in our heart and be our daily comfort and peace, no matter what happens in our lives.

We are so easily distracted because of the weakness of our faith. We are so easily frightened by the great evils and dangers of the world in which we live. We are at times overwhelmed with fear and even despair because of the enemy. We are discouraged and troubled because of the trials and difficulties that we experience in our lives. We sometimes think that everything and everyone is against us. We fear that God is against us or that he has forgotten us.

Remember that the Belgic Confession was composed at a time of great trials for the church of the Lord. Christians in Belgium, where this confession was composed, were experiencing severe persecution. The Spanish inquisition was being orchestrated by the church of Rome to destroy the cause of the Reformation. Sometimes the followers of the Reformation were expelled from their places of worship. They continued, however, to worship God, sometimes even in the open fields. During worship services, some congregations were surrounded by soldiers for protection. During this period, thousands of saints of God died as martyrs. Their faith, however, was in God, and they were not afraid. Many of them died for the faith that was more precious to them even than their own life. The Lord rewarded their faith with everlasting salvation. They believed that in life and in death, God would take care of them. In such circumstances, the wonderful statements about the providence of God recorded in Article 13 of the Belgic Confession were composed.

To have the truth of God's providence as our own real comfort, we need to exercise the faith God gives us. God himself must work faith in our hearts. We do not have it of ourselves. Our faith is often weak. One of the miracles that Jesus performed when he was yet on earth was to deliver the son of a man from a demon. The disciples of Jesus could not deliver the poor man's son from the devil. Therefore, when this man saw Jesus, he ran to him and fell down before him. He cried to the Lord to deliver his son. Jesus answered him: "If thou canst believe, all things are possible to him that believeth" (Mark 9:23). In turn, the man answered Jesus: "Lord, I believe; help thou mine unbelief" (v. 24; see Mark 9:14–29 for the whole account).

Faith requires deep humility on our part. We must not rely on our own wisdom or strength to overcome our troubles or to prevail over our enemies. We must rather trust completely in the wonderful God of providence. He is ever present with us. Let us not be afraid. When we realize our own weakness and trust completely in him, the knowledge of the truth of God's wonderful providence makes us strong.

Read the last two verses of Psalm 27 again: "I had fainted, unless I had believed to see the goodness of the LORD in the land of the living. Wait on the LORD: be of good courage, and he shall strengthen thine heart: wait, I say on the LORD."

Arie den Hartog

Article 14

OF THE CREATION AND FALL OF MAN, AND HIS INCAPACITY TO PERFORM WHAT IS TRULY GOOD

We believe that God created man out of the dust of the earth, and made and formed him after his own image and likeness, good, righteous, and holy, capable in all things to will agreeably to the will of God. But being in honor, he understood it not, neither knew his excellency, but willfully subjected himself to sin, and consequently to death and the curse, giving ear to the words of the devil. For the commandment of life which he had received he transgressed; and by sin separated himself from God, who was his true life; having corrupted his whole nature; whereby he made himself liable to corporal and spiritual death. And being thus become wicked, perverse, and corrupt in all his ways, he hath lost all his excellent gifts, which he had received from God, and retained only a few remains thereof, which, however, are sufficient to leave man without excuse; for all the light which is in us is changed into darkness, as the Scriptures teach us, saying: *The light shineth in darkness, and the darkness comprehendeth it not*, where St. John calleth men darkness.

Therefore we reject all that is taught repugnant to this concerning the free will of man, since man is but a slave to sin, and has nothing of himself, unless it is given from heaven. For who may presume to boast that he of himself can do any good, since Christ saith, *No man can come to me except the Father, which hath sent me, draw him*? Who will glory in his own will, who understands that to be *carnally minded is enmity against God*? Who can speak of his knowledge, since *the natural man receiveth not the things of the Spirit of God*? In short, who dare suggest any thought, since he knows *that we are not sufficient of ourselves to think anything as of ourselves, but that our sufficiency is of God*? And therefore what the apostle saith ought justly to be held sure and firm, that *God worketh in us both to will and to do of his good pleasure*. For there is no will nor understanding conformable to the divine will and understanding, but what Christ hath wrought in man, which he teaches us, when he saith, *Without me ye can do nothing*.

April 23 — **Creation of Man**

Read: Genesis 2:4–7

God created man!

Man often asks "Who am I?" Long has man been fascinated with the questions, "What is man?" and "Whence is man?" Man, the unbelieving anthropologists tell us, is an organism of the class *Mammalia*. Man is the most advanced of all animals. He is intelligent. He is self-conscious. He can think, reflect, infer, imagine, speculate, argue, and debate. He has discovered many of the mysteries and powers of the universe. He has harnessed them for his own use. Man, however, is not essentially different from the animals, and so must be classed among them. Man, we are told, is the result of millions of years of evolution. Evolution created man. Man traces his origin back to the apes, but only proximately. Ultimately, he originates from the more primitive microscopic organisms that first sprung to life in the primeval swamps of the early earth. Man is the product of luck. Man, in this view, is nothing but stardust looking at stars.

But no! *God* created man! Over against this absurd unbelief of Darwinism, we believe: "God created man" (Gen. 1:27). God, who calls "the things which be not as though they were" (Rom. 4:17), called forth man. God, who eternally decreed to create man, gave existence to man in time.

But God created man not in the way he created the other creatures. God made all other things, "heaven and earth, the sea, and all that in them is," by his word, by omnipotent fiat (Ex. 20:11). He said, "Let there be," and there was. "He spake, and it was done; he commanded and it stood fast" (Ps. 33:9). He uttered the word, and that word brought forth out of nothing all things that are. But God used a different mode of operation to create man. He first paused and said within himself: "Let us make man" (Gen. 1:26). God conferred with himself, for he is a plurality of persons, Father, Son, and Spirit in one being. God conferred with himself, not to make a plan before embarking on this significant endeavor, for he already had a plan. But he did so to reveal that we are his crowning achievement and the centerpiece of his creative work.

God then formed man. God did not create man out of nothing by means of speech but shaped him out of something by his own hand. He, as it were, scooped up a handful of the earth he had just made and carefully fashioned a body with head and torso, arms and legs, eyes and ears, nose and mouth. He made man's body out of earth. But he was not finished. He breathed into that body, through the nostrils, to fill it with the breath of life. The lungs began to breathe. The heart began to pump blood. The brain began to send impulses. But still he was not finished. He did something more. He made man a living soul. No, not just a living body, but a living soul. He gave man a spiritual side. He made man different from the animals, a creature related intimately to himself, thinking and willing, choosing and rejecting, knowing and desiring, understanding right and wrong.

God created man! Do you ask, "What is man?" Man is a creature of God with a physical and spiritual nature, a rational and moral soul. Man is the centerpiece and culmination of God's creative work. Man is the creature through whom and to whom God would glorify himself in the highest way.

"What is man, that thou art mindful of him? and the son of man, that thou visitest him? For thou hast made him a little lower than the angels, and hast crowned him with glory and honour…O Lord our Lord, how excellent is thy name in all the earth!" (Ps. 8:4–5, 9).

Daniel Holstege

April 24 — **Creation of Woman**

Read: Genesis 2:18–25

God created man, but also woman.

"Male and female created he them" (Gen. 1:27). Such is the brief statement of the creation of woman in Genesis 1. But Genesis 2 tells the story.

On that sixth day of creation, God said: "It is not good that the man should be alone" (Gen. 2:18). This reality God made known to man. He revealed it to him in an unmistakable way. He made the beasts of the field and the birds of the air come before him, two by two. Every animal had a partner, a companion. But Adam had none. In the words of the Preacher, he was "one alone, and there [was] not a second" (Eccl. 4:8). This, according to the Lord, was not good, not ideal, not complete, because man was a creature made for fellowship, but he was all alone. As the Preacher would later say: "Two are better than one" (Eccl. 4:9). Companionship is better than solitude. Friendship is better than isolation. Therefore, God said: "I will make him an help meet for him" (Gen. 2:18). That is, I will create another of Adam's kind, a helper meet for him, no mere subordinate, but a helper to meet Adam's deep need for fellowship and to complement and complete him: a companion and a friend. God put Adam into a deep sleep, reached into his chest, and removed a single rib. He made out of that rib, by a mind-defying wonder, a woman. Woman she was called because out of man she was taken.

God created man, but also woman.

God had a purpose, a significant purpose, in creating the woman. Look: God "brought her unto" the man (Gen. 2:22). God then said: "Therefore shall a man leave his father and his mother, and shall cleave unto his wife: and they shall be one flesh" (Gen. 2:24). Marriage was instituted as the fundamental human relationship. Marriage is the intimate union of one man and one woman whom God has brought together and joined in an unbreakable, life-long bond of friendship. "What therefore God hath joined together, let not man put asunder" (Matt. 19:6). Let all young people who seek marriage wait patiently for the Lord to bring them their mate and marry one with whom they are one in the Lord. Let all married people understand that they are "no more twain, but one flesh" (v. 6). Let the evil thought of divorce never enter our minds. Let us husbands love our wives as our own cherished bodies and live joyfully with them all our days. Let wives love their husbands, reverence, and submit to them as their God-given heads.

For only then is marriage an accurate reflection of "the mystery" (Eph. 5:32). God had a deeper purpose in creating woman than merely to give Adam a friend. Adam had a Friend already. God's purpose was to create a relationship among men to reflect the relationship between himself and his people, his beloved in Christ Jesus. "The mystery" is the marriage between Christ and the church, the intimate union of the Lamb and his bride, whom God brought together in election, and through the cross, in an unbreakable and everlasting bond of friendship. This is the covenant of grace. Christ our bridegroom now takes us by the hand into this covenant of marriage through his Spirit. Christ, your bridegroom and mine, will come again to rescue us from this present evil world, to consummate his marriage with us, raise it to perfection, and inaugurate the marriage supper that will last forever!

Then we will shout with unbounded joy: "Let us be glad and rejoice, and give honour to him: for the marriage of the Lamb is come, and his wife hath made herself ready" (Rev. 19:7).

Daniel Holstege

April 25 — Made in the Image of God

Read: Genesis 1:24–27

Imagine yourself standing on the shore of a clear, pristine lake on a bright, sunny day, the water perfectly calm. Now, look into the lake. What do you see? You see yourself looking back at you. You see a reflection of yourself there on the surface of the water. You see an image of yourself. You are looking, as it were, into creation's mirror. But there is more. For the water is calm. And therefore, you see an image which is also a likeness, don't you? No ripples or waves distort your reflection. An accurate reflection of you, a likeness, stares back at you. The color of your hair and eyes, the shape of your head and body, the length of your arms and legs are all discernible. Should you toss a small pebble into the lake, however, the resemblance would vanish in an instant. Your reflection would become distorted. The likeness would disappear. Then the water would return to its settled state, and your likeness would reappear. Image and likeness reunite.

God made and formed man after his own image and likeness. What a marvel! We were created as a reflection of God that resembled God! What a wonder!

No other creature was made in God's image: not light or the firmament or earth or sea or plants. Not the tall majestic redwood trees or the bright beautiful orchids. Not the sun or moon or stars. Not the fish or fowl, not the beast or reptile. Oh, to be sure, all creatures "declare the glory of God" and show forth "his handywork" from day unto day (Ps. 19:1). Surely "the invisible things of him from the creation of the world are clearly seen, being understood by the things that are made" (Rom. 1:20). No doubt creation is a revelation of God, bearing the stamp of its creator. But apart from man, no creature was made to be an image and likeness of God. Only man was made as the mirror of God or, in the terms of my illustration, the image in that lake. Man is unique.

No myth of primitive man is this! Modern man scoffs at this truth. Says he: it is a mere myth from primitive times, the product of the fertile imagination of ancient humans and primitive man's answer to the question, "What is man?" Man noticed the stark contrast between himself and the animals and reasoned that he was special and different, and that too by divine order. He imagined to himself: "I may not be God, but surely I am like God, an image and likeness of God." But now, says modern man, we know better: man is no image of God, but a descendent of the ape.

But we vehemently reject this.

We believe Scripture: God created man, made and formed him after his own image and likeness. Do you believe that? You, my fellow Christian, have been re-created in the image of God by the Spirit of Christ. You are a reflection of *God!* You look like God! You are a special creature among all God's creatures. You are a beautiful image of God, created in righteousness, holiness, and knowledge of God. You are a marvel of God's grace. Believe it!

Daniel Holstege

April 26   **Image of God in Particular**

Read: Ephesians 4:17–24, Colossians 3:8–10

Man was originally made in the image and likeness of God. But how in particular did man reflect and resemble God?

We may be tempted to accept the opinion that man was an image of God by virtue of his spiritual-rational-moral nature. After all, God is a spirit, God has intellect, and God is a moral being. Thus, man's spiritual-rational-moral nature must be the image. But perhaps we feel this is insufficient and that more needs to be included. Then perhaps we would be drawn to make a distinction between the image in the broad sense and the narrow sense, the former referring to man's rational-moral nature, the latter to man's original goodness. Such is the doctrine of many concerning the image of God. According to this view, man lost the image only in the narrow sense through the fall and still reflects the nature of God in the broad sense. I say, we may be drawn to such an opinion as a sensible explanation of this truth.

But we must resist such an explanation. Such is the product of human philosophizing. Such is not founded on Scripture or our confessions. The Genesis account does not tell us what the image was. But the Reformers argued that the new man created in us is the same as that image of God. How did man originally reflect and resemble God? In the same ways regenerated man once again reflects and resembles God according to Scripture: in righteousness, holiness, and knowledge (Eph. 4:24, Col. 3:10). Such is the explanation of all three of our forms of unity: "God created man good, and after his own image—that is, in righteousness and true holiness."* "Man was originally formed after the image of God. His understanding was adorned with a true and saving knowledge of his Creator, and of spiritual things; his heart and will were upright."** God "made and formed him after his own image and likeness, good, righteous, and holy, capable in all things to will agreeably to the will of God" (Article 14). Or, we may say, man reflected and resembled the communicable attributes of God: love, grace, mercy, justice, righteousness, holiness, knowledge, wisdom, truth.

What then of man's rationality and morality? It is not the image of God, but the canvas on which the image is portrayed. Image and canvas are two different things. When I go to an art museum and look at a beautiful painting, I do not suppose that the frame and canvas are part of the painting. They are only the neutral substratum on which the painting appears. If I were to take white paint and brush it all over the painting, the image would disappear, but the substratum would remain. Something ugly could be painted on that same substratum. Such is man's rationality and morality: the substratum of the image, that which makes man capable of bearing the image. But the image itself is the beautiful artwork of God's marvelous virtues which man originally reflected in paradise.

Adam and Eve were good: not at all inclined to evil but loving and desiring to do good. They were righteous: not guilty of a single trespass but in a state of perfect innocence and obedience to God's law. They were holy: utterly opposed to sin and devoted to God as the highest and only good. They knew God: not just facts about him but personal communion with him.

Such was the image of God. Such was lost in the fall. Such was restored to us, to you and me, the elect of God, by Christ through his cross and Spirit. "Seek" therefore the "things which are above" (Col. 3:1), today and every day, as one bearing the image of God.

Daniel Holstege

---

* Heidelberg Catechism 6, in Schaff, *Creeds of Christendom*, 3:309.
** Canons of Dort 3-4.1, in Schaff, *Creeds of Christendom*, 3:587.

April 27 — The Cultural Mandate

Read: Genesis 1:26–31

God made man in his own image, capable in all things to will agreeably to the will of God, to obey God and do what God commanded.

God expressed his positive will for man in what is often called the cultural mandate: "Be fruitful, and multiply, and replenish the earth, and subdue it: and have dominion over the fish of the sea, and over the fowl of the air, and over every living thing that moveth upon the earth" (Gen. 1:28). Three commands entered the listening ears of Adam and Eve on that sixth day of history, which came thereby to the whole human race: First, God said, "Be fruitful, and multiply, and replenish the earth." God did not create all men in the beginning. He created two. He built into them the power, when joined together in the act of marriage, to reproduce. God intended for man to bring forth man, and for all men to be organically connected. God commanded Adam and Eve to reproduce, to multiply through children, and to fill the earth with people. God's primary purpose was not merely to bring the human race into being, but to bring forth his elect in the human race. Therefore, this mandate, as it now comes to us as believers in Christ, is a high and noble calling. Let us, to whom God has given the ability and right, be fruitful and fulfill this calling. God will gather his people through our seed!

Second, God said: "Subdue the earth." God created a mature universe full of diversity and possibility, atomic and molecular particles, galaxies and star systems. God built into it laws and principles regarding matter, space, time, motion, light, life, and so forth. God intended that these laws would be discovered, harnessed, and put to use by man. God did not create man with innate knowledge of all these things. Adam and Eve did not understand everything about the world at the moment of their creation. But God made man capable of understanding. God then commanded man to subdue this vast world with its deep mysteries and possibilities. Man was to subdue it, subject it to discovery, to understanding, and to his own use and benefit, and to do so to the glory of God. But though man still eagerly seeks to fulfill this mandate, and is quite successful from an outward point of view, he now does so in defiance of God, for his own glory and in the service of Satan, and his work will culminate in the kingdom of antichrist. But we Christians must seek to fulfill this mandate in our vocations—in science, industry, technology, agriculture, and so forth—for the glory of God.

Third, God said: "Have dominion over the fish of the sea, and over the fowl of the air, and over every living thing that moveth upon the earth." God created man as the pinnacle of the created order. God made man, under himself, the king of all creatures. God created man as his officebearer, his prophet-priest-king, in the midst of the world. God endowed man with intelligence and goodness and made him capable of ruling well over the other creatures. God then mandated man to exercise dominion, to uphold order in the animal world and to care for the animals, as a steward takes care of the property of his master. This was to be done with wisdom and benevolence, not cruel tyranny. But since the fall, man rapes and pillages, pollutes and destroys, tortures and brings to extinction the creatures God put under his care. Man rules the animals, whether as poacher or environmental activist, in proud defiance of God and for his own sinful purposes. We, as God's people, must be good stewards of God's creatures, exercising wise dominion for the glory of God, who is our Father for Jesus' sake.

Daniel Holstege

April 28 — The Commandment of Life

Read: Genesis 2:8–17

Adam received a commandment of life. But he received it as a commandment of death: "And the LORD God commanded the man, saying, Of every tree of the garden thou mayest freely eat: but of the tree of the knowledge of good and evil, thou shalt not eat of it: for in the day that thou eatest thereof thou shalt surely die" (Gen. 2:16–17). Disobey and die. Obey and live. That was the commandment of life.

From this commandment of life, many derive the elaborate doctrine of the covenant of works between God and man in paradise. But most who speak of the covenant of works are sorely mistaken. We do not see God and man as two contracting parties making a pact with each other. We read only of a command issuing from the sovereign Lord to his human creature. We do not hear God promise to give Adam life, much less eternal life, on the basis of his merits. We only hear God warn Adam that he will surely die, and lose the life he had, should he disobey. Nor does our Confession, by this phrase we are now considering, so much as hint at the idea of the covenant of works.

What then? Pay close attention to the text. God breathed into man the breath of life. God made man a living soul. Man had life. Life was a gift to man from God "who was his true life" (Article 14). What is life? Life in its lowest form is mere physical energy expressed in physical motion. But life in its highest creaturely form is spiritual energy expressed in spiritual activity. Man had life, spiritual life, communion with God. Man's life was a covenant life. But this covenant was no pact. It was a bond of intimate communion, a relation of close fellowship, a friendship of love. God was Adam's God, and Adam was God's man. God was Adam's sovereign friend, and Adam was God's friend-servant. God and Adam walked and talked together in deep, intimate fellowship. God gave Adam this life. Adam owed him a debt of gratitude. Adam had to obey the commandment of life, not to merit life, but in thankfulness for the life he had been given.

Obedience must always flow out of gratitude, not out of the desire to merit. Obedience must always be done because I have received, never in order to get. Obedience never deserves anything from God but is always a debt to God. Disobedience flows from ingratitude. Disobedience deserves something, namely, death, the revoking of life.

Adam could not merit eternal life by obeying the commandment of life.

Only one man in all of history could do that. Only our Lord Jesus Christ obeyed to merit. He alone obeyed to merit, because he alone is God in our flesh. He alone, as God, did not have to obey, but chose to obey. He alone, as God, was able to merit with God for willingly humbling himself and obeying unto the death of the cross. He alone obeyed God perfectly on behalf of God's elect. He alone sustained the wrath of God and earned eternal life for all those in him. He alone could and did obtain everlasting, immortal, incorruptible, irrevocable life. Look not backward with longing eyes to the Garden of Eden and that life, but look forward with eagerness to the blessed life of the new creation earned for us by Christ. And rejoice now in the foretaste of that life which we enjoy in his Spirit.

Daniel Holstege

April 29 — The Fall

Read: Genesis 3:1–7

Man has fallen. Falling is that harmful experience in which one plunges downward from a higher to lower position. Man has fallen in the spiritual-ethical sense of the word. What a high position man formerly occupied! What a marvelous life he lived! What a lofty and wonderful privilege to be created at all, and then in the image of God! What heights of honor and excellency belonged to him! But he understood it not, nor knew it. Oh, I think he understood it in his mind, but not in his heart. He did not view it as precious. He stumbled. He willfully tripped and plummeted into spiritual ruin.

The fall was man's first sin. His sin was multi-faceted disobedience. It was apostasy from the truth. Eve distorted what God said when she told the serpent: "God hath said, Ye shall not eat of it, neither shall ye touch it, lest ye die" (Gen. 3:3). God never said, "Ye shall not touch it," only, "Thou shall not eat of it" (2:17). It was carnal lust, for she "saw that the tree was good for food, and that it was pleasant to the eyes," and she longed for the pleasure of eating the forbidden thing (3:6). It was wicked pride, for she viewed the tree as "a tree to be desired to make one wise" (v. 6) and she desired to become "as gods, knowing good and evil" (v. 5). Quite simply, the sin was disobedience to the law of the Most High. God said: "Of this tree thou shalt not eat." Man said: "Of that tree I will eat." Man took the outlawed thing "and did eat" (v. 6). He transgressed the commandment of life. And note well, this is our sin, our apostasy, our lust, our pride, our disobedience. This is not just the sin of Eve, or of Adam, but of *man*. This is the sin every man would commit, did commit in Adam, and does commit in his actual life.

Man willfully subjected himself to sin. He, and we, chose to sin. Man was faced with a choice: to sin or not to sin. He chose to sin. He did not act in ignorance, nor did he have an accident, nor did he simply fall victim to the devil's overpowering charms. But he, in the full knowledge of what he was doing, and with heart, mind and will, chose to sin. How is that possible? Many explanations to this mystery have been attempted. Augustine observed that man was not created *non posse peccare* (not able to sin), but *posse peccare* (able to sin). Man was originally able to choose to sin, even though he was righteous. But how was it that man did sin? Was he not perfectly righteous? He certainly was. But note well that he was not absolutely righteous. He was not righteousness itself. He did not possess the attribute of righteousness in himself but had received it from God. God alone is absolutely righteous. God cannot sin. Man could sin. Man's righteousness was losable. But why did man choose to sin? Man sinned because God willed it in his counsel and realized it by his providence, for God works "all things after the counsel of his own will" (Eph. 1:11). He did not force man to sin, nor was he responsible for it, but he certainly caused it, not out of a love for sin, but to glorify himself by saving us from sin through Christ.

Adam and Eve, and all of us who are elect in Christ, fell into the arms of Christ. Praise God that we have not fallen into the everlasting abyss, but into his saving arms, from which we can never fall!

Daniel Holstege

April 30 — **The Words of the Devil**

Read: Genesis 3:1–5, John 8:44

Man gave ear to "the words of the devil" (Article 14).

The devil is the ancient angelic enemy of God and God's kingdom. He did not always exist but was created with the other angels, perhaps on day one of creation. He was called Lucifer (Isa. 14:12). He was the "anointed cherub" (Ezek. 28:14). He was one of the most powerful, beautiful, and wise of all angels. But pride arose in him, and he said: "I will be like the Most High" (Isa. 14:14). Thus, he fell and became the dragon, Satan (adversary), and the devil (slanderer). He drew one-third of the angelic realm to his side over against God (Rev. 12:4). He desires but one thing: to destroy God and to enthrone himself as god.

And man gave ear to his words! The words of the devil are words of falsehood and deceit. "He was a murderer from the beginning, and abode not in the truth, because there is no truth in him. When he speaketh a lie, he speaketh of his own: for he is a liar, and the father of it" (John 8:44). He brought forth the lie, the deliberate twisting and distorting of truth, as a way to beguile man and turn him against God. He did not waste any time. Immediately, he entered paradise. From the world of animals, he selected the most subtle, the serpent, and inhabited it. Creeping through the garden, he looked for the woman, and finding her, he spoke. He began with a deceitful question subtly designed to cast doubt into her mind: "Yea, hath God said, Ye shall not eat of every tree of the garden?" (Gen. 3:1). Deceitful it was, because he knew that God never forbade them to eat of every tree, but only of one tree. She gave ear to his words. She did not flee but listened. She did not rebuke but discussed. Therefore, he gleefully ensnared her with a bold lie of terrible implications: "Ye shall not surely die: for God doth know that in the day ye eat thereof, then your eyes shall be opened, and ye shall be as gods, knowing good and evil" (Gen. 3:4–5). Ye shall be as God! Ye shall obtain divine power, wisdom, and blessedness!

Man gave ear to these words of the devil. And man fell.

Beware of the words of the devil! He speaks still today. He still speaks the same old lie: Ye shall not die from a little sin! On the contrary, sin is the secret to success and happiness! God is a cruel tyrant who does not want you to find happiness. He hides the secret by forbidding sin. But I, says the devil, am on your side! I know what really satisfies, what fulfills, what gives happiness: Do what you want! If you want the fruit, eat it. If money is what you like, seek it. If cursing makes you feel better, do it. If you dislike your neighbor, kill him. If you want to have sex before marriage, go ahead. If you enjoy drinking booze or doing drugs, indulge. You are God! Do not let anyone tell you what to believe or how to behave. Believe and do what you want. Such words the devil whispers into our ears. Beware! Do not give him your ear. But "put on the whole armour of God, that ye may be able to stand against the wiles of the devil" (Eph. 6:11). Pray for strength to resist. Give ear, beloved saints, to the words of the Lord Jesus Christ who died for you and crushed the head of the serpent.

Daniel Holstege

May 1 — By Sin, Separated from God

Read: Genesis 3:7–10, Psalm 51

By sin, man separated himself from God. By sin, we too separate ourselves from God.

Sin is a dark and dreadful reality. This dark and dreadful reality goes by many names in Scripture. "Sin is the transgression of the law" (1 John 3:4) and the "filthiness of the flesh and spirit" (2 Cor. 7:1). It is evil and darkness. It is disobedience and rebellion. It is iniquity and wickedness. But sin is also the willful choice to separate oneself from God. By sin, man separated himself from God in the garden of Eden. By sin, we too separate ourselves from God. Dark and dreadful reality! Horrible choice!

But what is meant by this? After all, we cannot separate ourselves from *God*, can we? From some points of view, that is certainly true. We cannot separate ourselves from God spatially. Of course not. God is everywhere present. We can never escape from him. We cannot run or hide from him. We cannot flee from the universe or move beyond the bounds of his all-searching eye. "If I ascend up into heaven, thou art there: If I make my bed in hell, behold, thou art there" (Psa. 139:8). Adam and Eve tried to escape from God and to hide from his presence "amongst the trees of the garden" (Gen. 3:8). But what folly! Man can never separate himself from the presence of God. Nor, we might add, can those who were predestinated unto eternal life separate themselves "from the love of God, which is in Christ Jesus" (Rom. 8:39).

What then does our Confession mean that by sin man separated himself from God? This: By sin man separated himself from God in the moral and spiritual sense of the word. Man separated himself from the deep, intimate fellowship he enjoyed with God as his friend. Man sought to erect a barrier, a thick wall, between himself and God. He burned the bridge, as we say, and tried to undo the covenant of friendship between himself and God. He betrayed his friend-sovereign and violated the covenant. He alienated himself from God, became at odds with him. He joined himself to the devil. He forsook God, who was his true life, and chose the way of death; for to separate from God is not to choose one of two equally legitimate modes of life, but to choose the way of death. To opt for sin is to make oneself the object of the wrath of God, the recipient of certain and eternal death in hell. Dark and dreadful reality! Horrible choice!

But, beloved saints, every time we sin, we make that same choice to separate ourselves from God. We forsake God, who is our true life, and choose the way of death. We turn against him and reject him. We grievously violate the covenant of friendship he has established with us. We opt for the devil. Horrible choice! So, let us give thanks to God for Christ who broke down that "wall of partition" which we erected, who "abolished in his flesh the enmity," who reconciled us to "God in one body by the cross" (Eph. 2:13–16). Let us give thanks to God for not casting us "away from [his] presence" (Ps. 51:11). Let us give thanks to God for forgiving our sins and for his Holy Spirit who enables us to choose not to sin, but to enter into sweet covenant fellowship with our God through Christ Jesus our Lord. Wonderful reality! Marvelous blessing!

Daniel Holstege

May 2 — Death and the Curse

Read: Genesis 3:14–24

The consequence of sin is death. Death is the result of the curse. The curse is the word of divine wrath, the pronouncement by God of his extreme displeasure, the proclamation of condemnation upon the sinner. The curse is the verdict of the Almighty upon the sinner that he is guilty and damnworthy. The curse is an invincible decree that the sinner shall be punished for his sin. That punishment which follows is death: "For the wages of sin is death" (Rom. 6:23).

Death descended upon man in the day that he ate of the tree. Death swooped down on him in that instant and devoured him. But did man really die at that moment? After all, Adam lived for 930 years before he died (Gen. 5:5). But the question is, did he really live? Yes, in a certain sense he did live, for the Bible says he "lived." But he "lived" in the midst of death. He "lived" under the power of death. His "life" became nothing but a continual death. He entered the sphere and process of death which terminates inevitably in the rending asunder of body and soul, in the return of the body to the dust of the ground whence it was taken. He began to suffer the signs and effects of death: pain, sickness, sorrow, and struggle. He came under the dark cloud of vanity and hopelessness and despair. He suffered in the knowledge of this reality: "that which befalleth the sons of men befalleth beasts; even one thing befalleth them: as the one dieth, so dieth the other…for all is vanity" (Eccl. 3:19). Death devoured man, entrapped him, surrounded him, and laid claim on him. And not on him only, but on all the sons of men in his loins, including you and me. Death threatens to destroy us, too. We too feel its effects. We smell its awful odor. We recoil at its painful sting. And especially when we stare into the graves of our deceased loved ones.

But there is still more.

Death descended upon man not only in the corporal (physical) sense, but also in the spiritual sense. And that is the deepest sense. Man's life was not primarily or essentially his physical power and energy of movement and activity. But it was his spiritual power to know and commune with God in love. Death destroyed that power. Death in the spiritual sense rendered man incapable of doing any good and inclined to all evil. Man became "dead in trespasses and sins" (Eph. 2:1; see also Col. 2:13). He entered the sphere of darkness which terminates inevitably in hell, "the second death" (Rev. 20:14). He became through sin the slave of sin, chained up in the bondage of sin, making himself thereby liable to more and more death, greater and deeper punishment, in body and soul, in time and eternity. And not him only, but all the sons of men, including us, as we are by nature totally depraved. We experience our natural depravity in our daily struggle with sin, and the commandment which was ordained unto life, we find to be unto death, and we daily cry out: "O wretched man that I am! who shall deliver me from the body of this death?" (Rom. 7:24).

Then, we look to Jesus Christ our Lord, who died and rose again. Him God promised already to Adam and Eve soon after they fell into sin and death (Gen. 3:15). Him God sent in our flesh. He died for us, in our place, as the perfect sacrifice for our sins. He suffered the penalty of death, in the fullest sense of the word. He was cursed by God for us. He entered death and conquered it. He arose. Therefore, we cry out in faith: "I thank God through Jesus Christ our Lord" (Rom. 7:25).

Daniel Holstege

May 3 — Become Corrupt in All His Ways

Read: Psalm 53, Romans 3:9–19

Human nature has become, and is, morally corrupt in the fullest sense of the word. Man has become, and is, wicked and perverse in all his ways.

But is not this being a bit too harsh? After all, does not experience teach us that man is basically good? Oh, no doubt there are some "bad eggs" out there, men who are morally degenerate through and through, who inexplicably seem to delight in committing atrocious crimes, inflicting pain and suffering on others, reveling in debaucheries of the worst sort, who seem to have no conscience and no remorse in doing any kind of evil. But they are only a small minority, are they not? Surely, most of mankind is guided by an inner moral compass to do what is right? Surely if given a chance, if properly taught, or perhaps reeducated, most men will be morally upright, will they not? Just look around you. What do you see? You see some evil men, but many good men: faithful spouses, hard workers, brave soldiers, devoted mothers, generous givers, and polite neighbors. Is it not a bit too harsh to say that man is wicked, perverse, and corrupt in all his ways? So reasons the Pelagian, ancient and modern alike, who denies the depravity of man's nature.

But we may not be taught first by experience. We must be taught first by the word of God, and experience always confirms the word of God if we look below the glittery surface of human nature into the pitch blackness of the soul.

The Scriptures teach that man has become, and is, morally totally corrupt in all his ways:

1. Corrupt are they, and have done abominable iniquity: there is none that doeth good.
2. God looked down from heaven upon the children of men, to see if there were any that did understand, that did seek God.
3. Every one of them is gone back: they are altogether become filthy; there is none that doeth good, no, not one. (Ps. 53:1–3; see also Rom. 3:10–12)

Every man, woman, and child on the planet today is by nature morally corrupt. That means you! That means me! And not just part, but our whole nature is corrupt: our body and soul, our mind and will, and, apart from grace, our deepest heart, too. Our nature is wicked, perverse, and corrupt. It is totally unable to think, will, or do what is good in God's eyes. It is wholly inclined to what is evil and despicable in God's eyes. Your nature is. Mine is. It may produce actions which appear good in our eyes: acts of heroism, generosity, and achievement. But it cannot, and does not, produce actions that are actually good in God's eyes. Such is the case, because every outward act has an inward cause. That inward motive is inextricably linked to that act in God's eyes. That motive and that act are one. If that motive, in the deepest sense, is evil, the act is evil too in God's eyes. Man cannot, does not, and will not keep any of God's commandments in his heart. You, by nature, do not. I do not, Man can only, does only, and will only grossly transgress all of God's commandments. And man is corrupt in all his ways. Man is morally depraved in all that he sets himself to do or be, in private and public life, in home, work, or school, and in all his human relationships.

Man is totally depraved. This article teaches the T of the TULIP of Calvinism. This biblical truth is one of the pillars, dark and ugly though it is, of the Reformed faith. The other pillar is the truth that God is sovereign in salvation. God has saved us from our moral corruption by his irresistible grace (the I of TULIP). That grace flows to us from the cross of Jesus Christ. Bow down, then, in humble thanks to God for saving you by his grace through Christ.

Daniel Holstege

May 4 — **Excellent Gifts All Lost**

Read: Romans 1:16–25

Man "hath lost all his excellent gifts" (Article 14).

What a sad fact for man! Let me try to illustrate. On our wedding day, my wife gave me two excellent gifts, a telescope and a tungsten wedding ring, and I gave her a pearl necklace and a diamond ring. How sad it would be if we should lose those excellent gifts! Especially sad it would be if we lost our wedding rings, the symbols of our marriage-bond. But how much more sad it would be if one of us lost those gifts not by accident, but on purpose! Such is the case with man. What excellent gifts God gave him. He had the gifts of a powerful intellect, a flawless memory, and a boundless creativity. Still more, he possessed the gifts of the knowledge of God, moral goodness, and perfect blessedness. But he lost these gifts. He lost all of them! He did not lose them by accident, but he intentionally threw them away. How sad, how horribly sad for man!

But wait. Did he really lose all these excellent gifts? According to our Confession, he lost *all* of them. But does that not imply an absurdity, namely, that man lost intellect and memory, rationality and morality? An absurdity this would be because man clearly still retains these powers. Man still thinks. He still reasons. He still creates. He still knows the difference between right and wrong. Man still employs the powers of human nature, and impressively so. Witness the history of human thought, of science and philosophy, of religion and politics. Witness the advance of civilization, the growth of industry and technology. Witness the modern inventions and achievements of man: the computer and internet, the airplane and spacecraft, and countless machines to make life better. Oh yes, man still retains the powers of the mind. But if you can grasp it, man only retains "a few remains thereof" (Article 14). He has lost the gift of intellect he once had in Eden. He has lost the ability to wield his full brainpower. He only retains a few remnants, a few tiny specks, a few glimmerings of his natural gifts. He only wields a tiny percentage of his total brainpower. He retains just enough of his natural gifts to remain a man.

But those remaining sparks are not the gifts of some common grace of God, as some have interpreted this article. Those few remnants do not enable man to do anything good in God's eyes. They are not sufficient to empower man to perform good deeds. Oh no, man has lost all his excellent moral-spiritual gifts. He retains none of those gifts. He has no remaining moral goodness. But he even presses the few remnants of his natural gifts into the service of sin. Those few remnants are sufficient only to leave man "without excuse" (Rom. 1:20; see also 2:1). They leave man with some knowledge of God and of right and wrong, so that he knows better when he sins. Therefore, when man comes before the judgment seat of God, he will not be able to make any excuses for his sins. He will have to say: "My sentence is just." And God will be glorified.

But to us who are in Christ Jesus, God has restored those excellent gifts by pouring out his Spirit into our hearts. What a joyous fact! And he will perfect those gifts in us in the new paradise of eternity. What a marvelous and thrilling hope!

Daniel Holstege

May 5 — The Light in Us Changed into Darkness

Read: John 1:1–14

"All the light which is in us is changed into darkness" (Article 14).

Physical light, which now shines on us from the sun, was originally created by God as an entity by itself. "God said, Let there be light: and there was light" (Gen. 1:3). God "commanded the light to shine out of darkness" (2 Cor. 4:6). God, moreover, "saw the light, that it was good" (Gen. 1:4). It was perfectly adapted to give life to the physical world and knowledge, fellowship, and joy to the world of men. But it was also created to symbolize a perfection of his own being. "God is light, and in him is no darkness at all" (1 John 1:5). God is light in the deepest sense of the word. This is the same as to say that God is good. God is goodness itself. God is the very implication of all virtues. God is the standard of moral goodness among men. Moreover, God created man in his own image, reflecting the light: good, righteous, and holy. The light shined from God into the heart of man and was reflected outward in his morally excellent thoughts, words, and deeds. Light, and only light, beamed forth from man. That light gave life. That light resulted in knowledge and fellowship with the source of that light. That light yielded perpetual joy.

But that all changed. Darkness descended on man.

Physical darkness is the absence of light. Darkness did not always exist, but it too was formed by God in the beginning. "In the beginning God created the heaven and the earth. And the earth was without form, and void; and darkness was upon the face of the deep" (Gen. 1:1–2). Darkness is the antithesis of light. It yields death. It obstructs knowledge. It impedes fellowship. It produces fear and sorrow. Physical darkness is therefore an apt symbol of sin and evil. Spiritual darkness is moral corruption. It is disobedience and rebellion, pride and hatred, lust and greed. Darkness first entered the created sphere in the rebellion of Satan. Henceforth, he is the Prince of Darkness. Darkness first entered the world when man gave ear to his words and chose sin. Right at that moment, all the light that was in us was changed into darkness. The light went out. The light was instantly extinguished. We plunged into darkness. Only pitch blackness remained in us, only sin and evil. We became in our very nature utterly lost in thick darkness.

Thus, when "the light of the world" came (John 8:12) and shined in the midst of this thick darkness, "the darkness comprehended it not" (John 1:5). Of course they did not comprehend him! Of course the world knew him not! "Men loved darkness rather than light…Every one that doeth evil hateth the light, neither cometh to the light, lest his deeds should be reproved" (John 3:19–20). Thus, when the Light of the world came, the world of darkness received him not. Nor would we receive him if left to ourselves.

But that too has changed for us who were chosen in him before the foundation of the world. "For God, who commanded the light to shine out of darkness, hath shined in our hearts, to give the light of the knowledge of the glory of God in the face of Jesus Christ" (2 Cor. 4:6). We of course did not restore that light in ourselves. But he did so. God has shined his light in us his chosen ones, through Christ. But even now, the darkness remains in our flesh. We have, if you will, a dark side. Therefore, let us pray that more and more, we might "walk as children of light" (Eph. 5:8) and "let our light…shine before men" (Matt. 5:16).

Daniel Holstege

May 6 — **Man Not Free, But a Slave to Sin**

Read: John 8:31–47, Romans 6:15–18

The Pelagian rejects the truth of total depravity and teaches what is repugnant to that truth: the free will of man. The Pelagian means by "free will" not merely that natural man has a will, makes choices, and is not forced in his choices; namely that he has a free will in the general or formal sense of the word. Of course that is true. Man makes choices in day-to-day affairs: to work or play, run or walk, eat or sleep. He does not have freedom in the absolute sense, for only God has absolute, sovereign freedom, but man has freedom in the relative sense, within the bounds of God's will. But the Pelagian means far more when he speaks of "free will." He affirms that natural man has the freedom to choose between good or evil. He teaches that fallen man has moral-ethical freedom. He denies that you and I, or anyone else, is by nature "wicked, perverse, and corrupt." He believes man can still choose to do good or evil. The Semi-Pelagian and Arminian are really no better. They too reject total depravity and teach free will. Though they speak of the necessity of grace, yet they teach that man can resist or accept that grace, and thus has a free will to do good or evil.

This we reject.

This our Confession rejects. This the holy Scriptures reject.

Natural man, including you and me in our flesh, is but a slave to sin. "Whosoever committeth sin," says our Lord, "is the servant of sin" (John 8:34). "Know ye not," says the apostle Paul, "that to whom ye yield yourselves servants to obey, his servants ye are to whom ye obey; whether of sin unto death, or of obedience unto righteousness?" (Rom. 6:16). Natural man is the servant of sin. He still has a will and can choose between many alternatives, but he cannot choose to obey God. He can choose many different ways to sin, but he can only choose to sin. Sin is his lord. Sin has dominion over him. Yet, though he is a slave to sin, he is a willing slave! He does not resist his master. But he freely chooses and delights in sin.

And such are we by nature.

Therefore, beloved, we have nothing of ourselves, but whatever we have has been given to us from heaven. Who of us, then, may presume to boast that we of ourselves can do any good? None of us came to Christ by our own free choice, for Christ says, "No man can come to me, except the Father which hath sent me draw him" (John 6:44). Who of us will glory in our own will? None of us, if we understand what Paul says: "The carnal mind is enmity against God" (Rom. 8:7)—and this is true of us by nature. Who of us can speak of our own acquisition of saving knowledge when Scripture states: "The natural man receiveth not the things of the Spirit of God: for they are foolishness unto him: neither can he know them, because they are spiritually discerned" (1 Cor. 2:14)? In short, who among us dare to suggest any thought other than this, that all our salvation is of God, since Scripture puts these words into our mouths: "Not that we are sufficient of ourselves to think any thing as of ourselves; but our sufficiency is of God" (2 Cor. 3:5)? Let us never boast in ourselves, for we are totally corrupt, but "he that glorieth, let him glory in the Lord" (1 Cor. 1:31). For the apostle says: "It is God which worketh in you both to will and to do of his good pleasure" (Phil. 2:13). And our Lord said the same thing when he told his apostles: "Without me ye can do nothing" (John 15:5). Let us therefore look away from ourselves unto Christ and his cross. And let us shout with joy: "God forbid that I should glory, save in the cross of our Lord Jesus Christ!" (Gal. 6:14).

Daniel Holstege

Article 15

OF ORIGINAL SIN

We believe that, through the disobedience of Adam, original sin is extended to all mankind; which is a corruption of the whole nature and an hereditary disease, wherewith infants themselves are infected even in their mother's womb, and which produceth in man all sorts of sin, being in him as a root thereof, and therefore is so vile and abominable in the sight of God that it is sufficient to condemn all mankind. Nor is it by any means abolished or done away by baptism, since sin always issues forth from this woeful source, as water from a fountain; notwithstanding, it is not imputed to the children of God unto condemnation, but by his grace and mercy is forgiven them. Not that they should rest securely in sin, but that a sense of this corruption should make believers often to sigh, desiring to be delivered from this body of death. Wherefore we reject the error of the Pelagians, who assert that sin proceeds only from imitation.

May 7   **Our Misery: Sinners by Nature**

That which is born of the flesh is flesh.
—John 3:6

In Article 15, we continue to look at the humbling truth of our sinfulness. The Bible teaches that we have sinned, which means that by committing acts of disobedience against God, we have transgressed his law and are guilty before him. But that, to use a figure, is only the tip of the iceberg. Our sinful deeds are the bitter fruit of an even more bitter root. We are sinners by nature.

Some men today try to excuse their sins by appealing to their nature. "It is natural for me to have lustful thoughts," they say; "I am just naturally bad-tempered; I am a habitual liar, blasphemer, thief, etc. Therefore I cannot be blamed." In today's increasingly liberal legal system, a judge can be convinced to be lenient because a criminal "could not help" doing what he did. There are even calls to recognize certain sinful dispositions as natural and therefore good and acceptable.

But that is not what the Bible teaches. It is true that we are sinners by nature—fallen nature—but that in no way excuses our sin. It makes it worse! Habitual, incorrigible thieves belong in prison! Habitual, incorrigible sinners belong in hell! And that is humbling. As sinners, we are always trying to excuse ourselves, but God never does. God forgives sinners, not by excusing their sin, but by making satisfaction to his own justice for sin. Only when we understand how sinfully corrupt we are will we seek God's mercy in Jesus Christ.

According to Article 15, "original sin is extended to all mankind." Sin began with an unlawful bite of a fruit. That one sin has produced thousands of years of misery, death, and destruction; and it has completely ravaged the entire human race. The presence of pain, disease, and suffering; the cruelty of mankind in violence, murder, and war; the corruption of every good ordinance of God; and even the overturning of the whole creation can be traced back to that one terrible act of rebellion against God by Adam. When God said, "In the day that thou eatest thereof thou shalt surely die" (Gen. 2:17), he meant exactly that!

The explanation for our sinful nature is our fall in Adam with the original corruption of our nature. Quite simply, we are born sinners because our parents pass on to us a sinful nature, which their parents passed on to them. That corrupt line goes all the way back to Adam, our first father.

But even that does not answer the question: Why does the sin of Adam, which he committed in the garden of Eden, affect us, so that every child is born into the world with original sin? Why do we have death working in us from the moment we are conceived in our mother's womb? How is that fair? How can God punish us for something Adam did, and in which we had no part? These are important and perplexing questions. And I will answer them next time.

Martyn McGeown

May 8 — Adam Our Federal Head

[Adam] is the figure of him that was to come. —Romans 5:14

Original sin is the corruption of our nature with which we are born. Yesterday, I asked the question of how Adam's sin could have such a devastating effect on us. The answer is federal headship.

A federal head is a legal representative who acts on our behalf and whose actions have a direct impact on us. If your father squanders your inheritance, you are poor because of him. If you give someone power of attorney over your legal affairs, that person has the right to act as your legal representative. He may sign checks, make investments, and enter into legal contracts in your name. If he makes poor investment choices, you suffer; if he is an astute investor, you benefit. That is why it is foolish to give power of attorney to an untrustworthy man. Or, take the example of world leaders. When the president of a country declares war, he plunges the whole country into war, and every man, woman, and child under him suffers the consequences of that decision. Similarly, everyone reaps the benefits of a good decision by the president.

God has appointed two, and only two, federal heads. The first is Adam. He represented all mankind in the garden of Eden. As a head, he failed. He fell into sin and brought everyone down into death with himself. But, says Paul in Romans 5:14, Adam is "the figure of him that was to come." That second head (also called "the last Adam" in 1 Corinthians 15:45) is Jesus Christ. He represents all the elect. His obedience has a direct effect upon us.

If we do not understand federal headship, we will never understand original sin.

Adam was not a private person when he acted in the garden. He was our representative. Adam did not volunteer for the position of federal head. God created him as federal head. Nor did God ask our permission before he appointed Adam to represent us. He was appointed without our consent. In the same way, Christ became our representative on the cross without our consent. If we do not complain about the latter, why should we complain about the former? Besides, we have no right to complain about God's dealings with us, which are always just: "O man, who art thou that repliest against God? Shall the thing formed say to him that formed it, Why hast thou made me thus?" (Rom. 9:20).

But consider the representative God gave us. Adam was made in the image of God—endowed with true knowledge of God, righteousness, and holiness (Eph. 4:24; Col. 3:10). Adam was created in a covenant of friendship with God. God loved Adam and showered his love upon him. Adam delighted to serve God and enjoyed sweet fellowship with his Creator. God gave Adam every reason to obey and fair warning on what would happen if he did not obey. But Adam disobeyed. And because Adam represented us, his disobedience had immediate—and devastating—consequences for us. We became sinners in him!

Martyn McGeown

May 9 — **Guilty of Adam's Sin**

For as by one man's disobedience many were made sinners,
so by the obedience of one shall many by made righteous. —Romans 5:19

Because Adam was our federal head or legal representative, we are guilty of his sin of taking the forbidden fruit. This is not because we were physically there in the garden—we were not even born—but because Adam sinned for us or on our behalf. Article 15 has this in mind when it says: "through the disobedience of Adam, original sin is extended to all mankind." The disobedience of Adam is that one act of disobedience in the garden, whereby Adam, acting on behalf of himself and of all mankind, willfully transgressed God's holy commandment. That act is imputed to us, we are guilty of that one act, and we are liable to punishment for that one act.

That explains, also, why we are not guilty of all of Adam's other sins. Adam lived for 930 years, and, like us, he sinned every day of his life from the point of eating the fruit of the knowledge of good and evil. But God does not impute those sins to us. That is because Adam ceased to be our representative when he fell. Adam's fall meant his deposition from his glorious position as head of the earthly creation, his dismissal as God's officebearer and image-bearer, and the end of his covenant relationship with God. Only by the grace of God in Christ was Adam not entirely cast off, and his covenant relationship with God, although greatly marred, was restored (Gen. 3:15).

As soon as Adam sinned, he became guilty. And God, as he had threatened, punished Adam with death. We think of death so often in very narrow terms. Death is the end of earthly life. But Adam lived for 930 years after he sinned. Death means more. Adam began to die as soon as he became guilty of sin. Sin and death immediately were at work in his body, and some 930 years later he finally succumbed to death and returned to the dust. But worse than physical death is spiritual death. With that death, God punished Adam, and us. That death was the loss of the image of God and the corruption of Adam's own nature. In other words, Adam became corrupt as a punishment for the guilt of his first sin! He was no longer worthy to bear the image of his Creator. And because we are guilty in Adam, we are punished with corruption, too. Therefore, God is just in bringing us into the world already totally depraved.

That is Paul's meaning in Romans 5:19, "For as by one man's disobedience many were made sinners." That word *made* means *legally constituted*, placed into the category of, sinners. But that is only the bad news. The opposite is true, because Paul goes on to write: "So by the obedience of one shall many be made righteous." Christ's obedience becomes ours in the same way in which Adam's disobedience becomes ours—by imputation! No wonder Paul can conclude: "Where sin abounded, grace did much more abound" (Rom. 5:20)!

Martyn McGeown

May 10 — Original Guilt and Original Corruption

For the wages of sin is death.
—Romans 6:23

Reformed theology distinguishes between original guilt and original corruption. Strictly speaking, original corruption is what we, and Article 15, mean by original sin. However, there is no original corruption (original sin) without original guilt.

Guilt, remember, is liability to punishment. When a court of law finds a person guilty, the next step is sentencing. How will the guilty person be punished? With a fine? With a prison sentence? Imprisoned for how long? With the death penalty, even? Guilt and punishment go together. There can be no punishment without guilt; there can be no guilt without punishment. At least, that is the case when justice prevails. God is just. Therefore, he only ever punishes the guilty, never the innocent.

Perhaps you say: but did God not punish Christ, who was innocent, and forgive us, who are guilty? It is not as simple as that. In fact, what happened was this: God imputed our guilt to Christ so that he was legally (although not personally) guilty of our sins, and then (and only then) he punished his Son in our place. On the basis of what Christ did, God then imputes to us the perfect righteousness and innocence of Christ and forgives us. All guilt is punished, one way or another. Either Christ bears the punishment on the cross, or the sinner bears the punishment in hell forever.

Adam was no exception.

Adam would never have become corrupt unless he was first guilty. When Adam became guilty, God in righteous judgment took away from him the gifts with which he was created. The knowledge of love which Adam had was turned into horrible blindness of heart, the uprightness of Adam's character was twisted into an awful perversion, and the holiness of Adam's being was changed into corruption, impurity, and vileness. As a result, Adam became totally depraved, unable to do anything good and inclined to all wickedness. In the words of Genesis 6:5, "God saw that the wickedness of [Adam] was great in the earth, and that every imagination of the thoughts of [Adam's] heart was only evil continually."

What a dreadful fall from such a great height!

The point we make with original guilt is this: God was perfectly just in inflicting such punishment on Adam. Adam's original guilt in eating the forbidden fruit earned for him the punishment of original corruption. Adam forfeited all God's good gifts and richly deserved the misery that came upon him. That is one of God's most dreadful punishments: to punish sin with more sin, to give sinners over to sin. That is how God dealt with Adam.

Adam's guilt earned for him corruption. The same is true for us. Adam's guilt is our guilt. Therefore, we too deserve original corruption. That is why every human being who comes into this world is already guilty and already corrupt before he or she takes his or her first breath. That is why salvation is utterly impossible for man. We are, quite literally, dead upon arrival, spiritually dead upon arrival!

Martyn McGeown

May 11 — The Proud Error of the Pelagians

There is a generation that are pure in their own eyes,
and yet is not washed from their filthiness. There is a generation,
O how lofty are their eyes! and their eyelids are lifted up. —Proverbs 30:12–13

At the end of Article 15, our creed declares: "we reject the error of the Pelagians, who assert that sin proceeds only from imitation." Before we proceed in our discussion of original sin, it is good for us to defend the truth against this heresy. Pelagianism, named after a fourth-century British monk named Pelagius, is an ancient but deeply-rooted heresy which has plagued the church almost from the very beginning. In the Middle Ages, Pelagianism morphed into a less radical semi-Pelagianism, and our Canons of Dordt charge the Arminians with "bring[ing] again out of hell the Pelagian error."*

Pelagianism is an outright rejection of the truth of original sin. Pelagius taught that Adam's sin has no effect whatsoever upon the nature of man; that man did not in any sense lose the image of God; that neither Adam's own nature nor the nature of any of his descendants was corrupted by the fall; and that every person born into the world enters it as morally neutral. In fact, taught Pelagius, every person not only must, but can—if he strives hard enough and uses the light of nature, the law of God, and the good example of Christ—lead a sinless life and merit heaven for himself.

What explains the universal prevalence of sin, then? Pelagius taught that men sin because Adam gave his descendants a bad example. He argued that children sin only because they see others sin. Pelagianism is the underlying theory of many unbelievers today: they argue that if only we could make man's environment better, he would be a better person. They argue, therefore, that education, urban regeneration, and other social programs are the answer to man's moral problems. Man, they say, is basically good! Not so, says the word of God! Man is not basically good. Man is totally depraved, utterly corrupted, vile, and polluted. Sin is not a matter of the environment; it is a matter of the heart. Jesus said: "make the tree good, and his fruit good" (Matt. 12:33). It is foolish, wishful thinking to expect good fruit from a corrupt tree. Only God, by the powerful work of regenerating grace, can and does make evil trees good.

Semi-Pelagianism modified this view. Pelagianism was so obviously unbiblical that very few could hold to it, especially after Augustine had fought this heresy so vigorously. Semi-Pelagianism concedes that man's nature has been affected by Adam's sin—man is very far gone from original righteousness. However, semi-Pelagianism contends that man is only sick, not dead in sin, and that man still retains the power of free will with the ability to do good. Where Pelagianism taught that grace is useful but not necessary, semi-Pelagianism teaches that grace is necessary but not irresistible. To be saved, say the semi-Pelagians, man must cooperate with the grace of God, which is given to everyone as a help towards salvation. Final salvation, however, depends on man. Pelagianism teaches that salvation is entirely the work of man; semi-Pelagianism teaches that salvation is the work of God working with man; the Bible teaches that salvation is entirely the work of God. How important it is for us to understand, and rightly to confess, our sinful nature!

Martyn McGeown

---

* Canons of Dort 2, error and rejection 3, in *The Psalter*, 66.

May 12 — Original Sin Extended to All Mankind

And so death passed upon all men, for that all have sinned.
—Romans 5:12

All human beings born into this world enter it already in the state of original guilt and with original pollution (or original sin). This is because, as we have seen, Adam represented us all in the garden of Eden when he ate the forbidden fruit. To this universal rule there is one, and only one, exception. Although this will be treated in Article 18 on the incarnation of Jesus Christ, it is necessary that we mention it here also.

Christ was not guilty of Adam's original transgression. That guilt was not imputed to him, and he was not punished with original pollution. There are various important reasons for the sinlessness of Christ. First, as to his person, Christ is the eternal Son of God. It is unthinkable that the eternal Son of God could be stained with sin. Second, in the virgin conception and birth, Jesus Christ was shielded by the Holy Spirit and preserved from sin. Therefore, explains the angel Gabriel, "That holy thing which shall be born of thee shall be called the Son of God" (Luke 1:35). These are good reasons why Jesus must be an exception to the rule of original sin.

But there is another more important reason which is fundamental to the doctrine of original sin. Christ was not under the headship of Adam. When Adam sinned as our representative, he did not act as Christ's representative. Adam represented only human persons, and Christ is not a human person. He is a divine person. Therefore, God could not impute the guilt of Adam's sin to Christ and then punish Christ with original pollution. In fact, Christ was Adam's representative or federal head.

But all other persons—being human persons—were represented by Adam, and therefore all other persons are implicated in Adam's guilt and are consequently born totally depraved with original pollution (or original sin). No human person can escape this. Some of the details of this are difficult to understand. How does sin pass from mother or father to child? In what way exactly is this a "hereditary disease" (Article 15)? Suffice to say that all those who are born of a woman—except Jesus Christ—come forth from the womb already unclean. How humbling!

In 1854, Pope Pius IX issued a decree declaring Mary, the mother of Jesus, to be another exception. This Roman Catholic dogma is called the immaculate conception of Mary. However, such a dogma is impossible. The Bible does not teach it, the Bible allows for only one exception, not two, and, since Mary was represented under the federal headship of Adam, she must also have both original guilt and original corruption (original sin). Mary confessed that Jesus was her savior, not (as Rome contends) because God, by a singular grace, kept her from falling into sin in the first place, but because God forgave her sins in the blood of Jesus Christ. Thus, we do not look to Mary as a sinless fountain of grace, but we look to the sinless Son of God, "full of grace and truth" (John 1:14), who of all mankind alone is exempt from the pollution of original sin.

The good news is that Mary's original and actual sins—and ours—are forgiven through the atoning work of the only sinless savior, Jesus Christ.

Martyn McGeown

May 13 — A Corruption of the Whole Nature

The whole head is sick, and the whole heart faint.
From the sole of the foot even unto the head there is no soundness in it;
but wounds, and bruises, and putrifying sores: they have not been closed,
neither bound up, neither mollified with ointment. —Isaiah 1:5–6

Having seen the basis for our original sin (Adam's federal headship) and its universality (Christ only excepted), we consider its extent. Article 15 teaches that original sin is a "corruption of the whole nature" (Article 15). One of the most graphic figures of corruption in the Bible is that of a leper. A leper is a mass of walking, putrid flesh. Leprosy is a disease that eats the flesh, making the leper vile. In fact, God sets forth leprosy as a picture of the vileness of sin—it makes a man unclean, unfit for fellowship with God or his church; it causes him to stink, as from his wounds oozes the putrefaction of his own flesh. No wonder a leper had to stand afar off and cry out in dreadful anguish, "Unclean! Unclean!" Isaiah 1 describes Israel as a leper: "from the sole of the foot even unto the head there is no soundness in it; but wounds, and bruises, and putrifying sores" (v. 6). Spiritually, that describes us. Every faculty of our being is corrupted by sin—totally corrupted by sin. Our heart is deceitful and desperately wicked; our mind is darkened, blinded, and hardened by sin; our will is stubbornly opposed to God and to all that is good; our affections are directed toward evil; and we flee from the light because we hate the light and love darkness. Moreover, we defile everything we touch and spread corruption everywhere we go.

And this is all true before we even do anything! Sin is not simply in the deed. Before the sinner begins to conceive a sinful thought; before the sinner's lips begin to frame a sinful word; before the sinner's hand or foot begins to move in the direction of performing an evil deed, sin is already in the nature. To put it very bluntly, we sin in our sleep; we even sin if we are in a coma! We are not sinners because we sin. We sin because we are sinners.

Sometimes we are tempted to think highly of ourselves, usually because we compare ourselves against the wrong standard. When we compare ourselves with others, we think that we are pretty good. But compare yourself against God's law, compare yourself against Adam before the fall, compare yourself against Jesus Christ!

Original sin, if rightly understood, is the end of all free will theology. How can a man have free will when his entire nature has been corrupted? How can a man choose good, when he will not come to the light because his deeds are evil (John 3:19–20)? The answer of the one who clings to the notion of free will is that there remains some good in man even after the fall, some inclination in man toward God. Then he is like a leper who says, "Oh, but I am still a little bit clean." Such a leper dresses himself in a white robe and for a moment appears to be respectable, but before long, corruption begins to ooze out of him, and the beautiful pure white robe is ruined. That is the folly of the sinner who denies his own corruption and dresses himself in his own works—only to discover that he corrupts even his best works.

A corruption of the whole nature makes salvation by human works or even by free will utterly impossible. The answer to our depravity is not our works and not our supposed free will, but grace: sovereign, particular, saving grace found only in Jesus Christ.

Martyn McGeown

May 14 — A Hereditary Disease Infecting Even Infants

*Behold, I was shapen in iniquity; and in sin
did my mother conceive me.* —Psalm 51:5

Probably one of the most controversial aspects of the doctrine of original sin is that it affects infants, newborns, even unborn children in the womb. There is no such thing, therefore, as an "innocent child." A child may be innocent relatively speaking—he is not guilty of any crime recognizable by the state—but he is not innocent with respect to God. Reformed parents confess this when they present their children for baptism. The Form for the Administration of Baptism puts these words into the mouth of Reformed parents as they carry their infant children in their arms: "Our children are conceived and born in sin, and therefore are subject to all miseries, yea, to condemnation itself."* We might not like to think of our children this way, but this is exactly what the Bible explicitly teaches: "in sin did my mother conceive me" (Ps. 51:5); "The wicked are estranged from the womb: they go astray as soon as they be born, speaking lies" (Ps. 58:3).

There are many mysteries about children. How does God knit a child together in its mother's womb? How does God create a new person with a body and soul? How does God breathe a soul into the body of a new person? These are mysteries we cannot fathom. We confess: "I am fearfully and wonderfully made" (Ps. 139:14). We know that a child is a human person from the very moment of conception—and that therefore abortion is a horrible crime, the taking of a real, defenseless human life. We also know that God imputes the guilt of Adam's sin to each human person from the moment of his conception, on the basis of which God causes the child to be born totally depraved with original sin.

Therefore, we reject the notion of "an age of accountability." Every child is accountable for the sin of Adam and for his own original corruption not at the age of seven, eight, nine, or ten years, but from the moment of conception.

There is one very compelling proof of this: babies die. Children, even unborn children, are subject to death. And if babies die, they must be guilty, because a just God could never cause the guiltless to die. Writes Paul: "death reigned from Adam to Moses, even over them that had not sinned after the similitude of Adam's transgression" (Rom. 5:14).

Reformed believers have hope, however, not in the "innocence" of their children, but in God's covenant promise to save us and our elect children by his grace and mercy: "I will establish my covenant between me and thee and thy seed after thee in their generations for an everlasting covenant, to be a God unto thee, and to thy seed after thee" (Gen. 17:7). That is why we have comfort as our Canons of Dordt 1, Article 17 teaches us: "godly parents have no reason to doubt of the election and salvation of their children, whom it pleaseth God to call out of this life in their infancy."**

Our children are not exempt from original sin. They receive nothing but sin from us. From God alone they receive grace.

Martyn McGeown

---

* Form for the Administration of Baptism, in *The Psalter*, 87.
** Canons of Dort 1.17, in Schaff, *Creeds of Christendom*, 3:585.

May 15 — The Spread of Sin

Fill ye up then the measure of your fathers.
—Matthew 23:32

From tiny acorns, mighty oak trees grow. A seed, which starts small, gradually develops over a long period of time into something much greater. The seed has in principle the entire oak tree contained within it—to speak in terms of modern science, the DNA for the trunk, bark, leaves, and every other part of the tree is already inside the acorn when it is planted into the ground. Something very similar is the case with original sin: the one transgression of Adam contained within it, in principle, all sins and transgressions committed in the history of the world. Human history is the record of the sad development of that first principle of sin.

Sin develops throughout history and even in the lives of individuals. God's purpose with sin is that man fills up the cup of his iniquity: man must develop his sin to its full potential, so that sin can be manifested as exceedingly wicked, and God can be seen as just in punishing sin. There are three cups which are being filled up. The first is the cup of iniquity. In Abraham's day, "the iniquity of the Amorites [was] not yet full" (Gen. 15:16). The second is the cup of the sufferings of God's people, which is filled as the wicked fill their cup of iniquity (Col. 1:24; Rev. 6:11). The third is the cup of God's wrath, which will finally overflow the wicked in terrifying intensity (Rev. 14:10).

It is the folly of unbelieving evolutionary philosophy to imagine that man is improving. He may be becoming more technologically advanced, but morally he is degenerating. He was always totally depraved—ever since Adam sinned and plunged all mankind into ruin—but that depravity unfolds and expresses itself in new ways in every generation. Quite simply, humanity is developing in sin; it ripens the fruits of iniquity. Men can commit sin today in ways in which sinners of former generations never thought possible. As man develops in his technology, science, and culture, and as he explores and subdues the creation under him, he does so in the service of sin. God commanded man to do this—to "be fruitful, and multiply" and to subdue the earth (Gen. 1:28), the so-called cultural mandate—but originally man was called to do so to the glory of God. Instead, man takes the good gifts of creation and presses them into the service of sin to build for himself a kingdom in defiance to God. That defiance was first seen at the Tower of Bebel and will culminate in the coming kingdom of Antichrist.

Sin is a destructive force which has infected mankind. And yet the devil promised fulfillment, satisfaction, even happiness, in sin. Eve was deceived; Adam rebelled; and we have been developing in sin ever since. But what about "common grace"? Many teach today that God curbs sin by means of a non-saving, common grace which works in the hearts of men so that they do not sin as much as they could or would and even gives them the ability to do some good in the development of a godly culture. This view is wrong: there is only one grace of God, and that is the saving, particular, efficacious, irresistible grace, rooted in election and displayed on the cross. God's restraint of sin is merely outward—it never improves man's nature; it is never grace to the reprobate; it simply acts as a muzzle upon a rabid dog or a straitjacket upon a serial killer. Men do not commit every possible sin because of fear of punishment or lack of opportunity, not because of any operation of so-called common grace. Without the grace of regeneration, all we do—and all we can do, and all we want to do—is sin!

Martyn McGeown

May 16 — Original Sin Sufficient to Condemn All Mankind

We...were by nature the children of wrath, even as others.
—Ephesians 2:3

How many sins must we commit before we are worthy of hell? The answer, surprisingly, is none! We come into the world already worthy of hell. We are, as Ephesians 2:3 expresses, "by nature the children of wrath." That is a very difficult confession, and we would not dare confess that unless we knew the forgiveness of sins. One of the great sins of the unbeliever is his refusal to confess that he is a sinner—a sinner according to the Scripture's definition of a sinner.

But how can that be true? How can we all from birth and even from conception already be worthy of hell? The answer is that we come into the world burdened with the original guilt of Adam and infected with the "hereditary disease" of original pollution or original sin. Article 15 warns us that God does not take our original sin lightly. On the contrary, it is "so vile and abominable in the sight of God that it is sufficient to condemn all mankind" (Article 15). God created man upright in our first father and representative, he warned Adam about sin and sin's terrible consequences, and he was angry when Adam sinned. Sin, even original sin, is vile and abominable in God's sight. Words can scarcely express God's abhorrence of sin. God speaks of it in terms of loathsomeness, of depravity, of filth; he uses some incredibly offensive words to describe it (*dung* is one of the milder words!). And for Adam—who had been created as God's friend—to sin against God was base treachery. Had God opened up the earth to swallow Adam and Eve into hell, he would have been perfectly just.

All of us come into this world guilty of Adam's sin. Therefore, all of us come into this world under the wrath of God with a vile and abominable nature. Our very nature is a swirling whirlpool of iniquity. The Canons of Dordt speak of "the propagation of a vicious nature."* Therefore, we ought not expect anything good to proceed from our nature. Nor should we be surprised—we should be saddened but not surprised—to see our little children sinning as soon as they are born. And as our children grow, they simply develop in sin: in selfishness, in envy, in hatred, in malice, and in pride. Especially humbling for parents is when our little children develop in our own particular ways of sinning. The Form for the Administration of Baptism expresses it in these words: "And although our young children do not understand these things, we may not therefore exclude them from baptism, for as they are without their knowledge, partakers of the condemnation in Adam, so are they again received unto grace in Christ."**

Original sin alone, without any actual sins of our own, is enough to condemn us all!

Martyn McGeown

---

* Canons of Dort 3–4.2, in Schaff, *Creeds of Christendom*, 3:588.
** Form for the Administration of Baptism, in *The Psalter*, 86.

May 17

By No Means Abolished or Done Away by Baptism

Purge me with hyssop, and I shall be clean: wash me, and I shall be whiter than snow. —Psalm 51:7

The Catechism of the Roman Catholic Church says the following about original sin and baptism:

> [Original sin] is a deprivation of original holiness and justice, but human nature has not been totally corrupted: it is wounded in the natural powers proper to it, subject to ignorance, suffering and the dominion of death, and inclined to sin—an inclination to evil that is called concupiscence. Baptism, by imparting the life of Christ's grace, erases original sin and turns a man back towards God, but the consequences for nature, weakened and inclined to evil, persist in man and summon him to spiritual battle.*

Several days ago, we looked at the Pelagian error. Clearly, the Roman Catholic Church is semi-Pelagian: it teaches not that human nature is totally corrupted by sin, but that it is "wounded" and "deprived" of some of its powers. In the same paragraph, the Catechism says: "Original sin does not have the character of a personal fault in any of Adam's descendants." Thus, Rome denies both original guilt and original pollution, and, although Rome speaks of "original sin," she denies the Scripture's teaching on the subject.

Not surprisingly, Rome, who misdiagnoses the condition of fallen man, errs grievously in understanding the cure. Semi-Pelagian Roman Catholicism teaches salvation by the cooperation of man's free will with God's grace. This grace is especially dispensed through the sacraments of the church—in particular, baptism.

According to Rome, baptism "erases original sin." For an adult, baptism also removes all actual sins. A baptized person, then, according to Rome, is basically innocent and pure before God. Total depravity is a concept utterly foreign to the Roman Catholic mind. If you have this basic view of yourself, you will never see the urgency of the grace of God in Jesus Christ. In fact, the average Roman Catholic believes that (by virtue of his baptism and membership of the church which supposedly has all the means of grace) he is not good enough to go to heaven, nor bad enough to go to hell. Why? Because baptism has dealt with his sin, but he still has weaknesses and tendencies toward sin. That's all! That is the tragic blindness caused by semi-Pelagianism.

Article 15 of the Belgic Confession vehemently rejects this error: "Nor is [original sin] by any means abolished or done away by baptism." Astutely, the Confession proves this from the fact that the baptized continue to sin. If baptism really removed original sin, then surely the sinful, depraved, corrupt nature of man would be gone, and man would no longer sin. Both Scripture and our own experience tell us that the opposite is true. A baptized person has the same sinful nature as one who is not baptized. He too is inclined to all kinds of evil. He too is by nature proud, selfish, and malicious. Watch a group of children, some baptized and others not baptized, and you will see no essential difference. They are all sinners by nature and very quickly show that nature in their practice. None can deny that baptized children—even the children of Christian parents who are rightly baptized—still sin after baptism.

Baptism has no effect whatsoever on our nature. Sin is too deeply rooted in us to be removed by a few drops of water. That's why we need the blood of Jesus Christ.

Martyn McGeown

---

* *Catechism of the Catholic Church* paragraph 405, Second Edition (Città del Vaticano: Libreria Editrice Vaticana, 1997).

May 18 — The Ever-Flowing Fountain of Corruption

But the wicked are like the troubled sea,
when it cannot rest, whose waters cast up mire and dirt. —Isaiah 57:20

We have within us a bubbling fountain of corruption, a spring of pollution that continually casts up filth. This means that sin is not only—or even primarily—in the deed. This is true even of Christians, for those are in mind when Article 15 states that "sin always issues forth from this woeful source, as water from a fountain." Since we are corrupt at our very source, all our works are defiled. If the source has polluted water, the streams from that fountain must also be corrupted. Even if we passed pure water through such a stream, the pure water would be defiled by the pollution of the stream. In the book of Job, Eliphaz asks: "What is man, that he should be clean? and he that is born of a woman, that he should be righteous?…How much more abominable and filthy is man, which drinketh iniquity like water?" (Job 15:14, 16).

It is true, of course, that Christians are regenerated by the Spirit of Jesus Christ, but that does not mean that our sinful nature is gone, or even that it has been improved. Our sinful nature (also called the "flesh" or the "old man") coexists with the new life of Jesus Christ (also called the "spirit" or the "new man") in the one person of the believer. But there can be no peaceful coexistence between these two principles. Instead, there is war. The old man of the sinful flesh struggles against the new man of Jesus Christ. This truth concerning our sinful nature explains why we are so easily attracted to wickedness, why it is a struggle for us to do good, to pray, to worship God, to read Scripture, while we find sinful pleasure well-nigh irresistible. Paul explains it this way: "I delight in the law of God after the inward man: but I see another law in my members, warring against the law of my mind" (Rom. 7:22–23), and, "The flesh lusteth against the Spirit, and the Spirit against the flesh: and these are contrary the one to the other: so that ye cannot do the things that ye would" (Gal. 5:17). "The things that ye would" are the things that you want to do. We want to keep God's commandments, but our flesh resists, and our flesh even pollutes our best works.

Therefore, since we have an active sinful nature, we must never underestimate our capacity for sin. Sinners, fallen in Adam and totally depraved by nature, are capable of every sin, even the vilest and most abominable of transgressions. And Christians, because that sinful nature remains, are still capable of the vilest of sins. Sin is deceitful. We must be constantly on our guard, watching and praying as Christ commands us.

The good news for Christians is that the old man is crucified—not eradicated but crucified—with the result that sin is no longer a ruling principle in our lives. It is an active principle, it is the source in us of all our sins, but by the grace of God, sin shall not have dominion over us.

Martyn McGeown

May 19 — **Sighing Over Our Corruption**

O wretched man that I am! who shall deliver me from
the body of this death? —Romans 7:24

Both believers and unbelievers are sinners. Both believers and unbelievers are sinful by nature. Both believers and unbelievers have original guilt and original pollution. About believers Paul writes: "by nature children of wrath, even as others" (Eph. 2:3). The difference, by the grace of God, is in their attitude to their sin. Unbelievers deny, seek to minimize, or excuse their sins, or give themselves over to enjoy their sins. An unbeliever loves sin as a pig loves mud! We must never think that unbelievers are forced to sin against their will. They love sin, they are attracted to sin, sin is their delight, and they hate all righteousness. Paul writes about the unbelieving Gentiles, that they "have given themselves over unto lasciviousness, to work all uncleanness with greediness" (Eph. 4:19).

But sinners do not like the evil consequences of sin. If there was a way in which sinners could sin with impunity—without a guilty conscience, without the sense of the wrath of God, without diseases and other judgments of God, without shame or civil penalties by the state, without death, and without hell—they would gladly accept it. Those considerations restrain many unbelievers in their sin without making them one whit better in the depravity of their nature.

But it is different with the believer. By the grace of God, the believer is sorry for his sin and desires to be rid of it. Sincerely, the believer desires to serve God according to the new man, but he finds himself hindered by his sinful nature. His attitude is to be humbled over his sin, over his remaining depravity, and to cry out to God for grace to subdue his iniquities under him. Paul describes his own experience vividly in Romans 7, and every Christian echoes Paul's cry because every Christian experiences the same thing. We all know the wretchedness of our own inner corruption. All of us struggle with that nature. We all have our own particular sinful inclinations—for some, it is a bad temper; for others, it is lust; for others, it is greed. Paul did not do what he wanted to do but did what he did not want to do (v. 15). Paul was willing to do good, but he did not find the strength (v. 18). The good that Paul wanted to do, he did not do; the evil he did not want to do—and even hated—he did do! (v. 19). Wherever he turned to do good, "evil [was] present with" him (v. 21).

Paul's attitude was the same as ours, as outlined in Article 15: he did not "rest securely in sin." Instead, a sense of corruption made him "often to sigh, desiring to be delivered from this body of death."

Is that your experience? Do you sometimes despair that you never seem to have victory over sin? Do not think that you are abnormal. The fact that you are truly sorry for your sins—which is nothing more than poverty of spirit, spiritual mourning, hungering and thirsting after righteousness, and a broken and contrite spirit—shows that you are a child of God. Then believe Paul's triumphant conclusion: "I thank God through Jesus Christ our Lord" (v. 25)!

Martyn McGeown

May 20 — Our Original Sin Graciously Pardoned

Where sin abounded, grace did much more abound.
—Romans 5:20

Perhaps two weeks of meditations on the corruption of our nature is a bit depressing for some. The subject of original sin is hardly uplifting or heart-warming, is it? Go to most Christian bookstores and look at the devotional works, and sin will hardly be mentioned. Certainly, no one would think of spending two weeks concentrating on the subject! But such an attitude is shortsighted and wrong. Remember our Heidelberg Catechism: it says that a knowledge of how great our sins and miseries are—and that certainly includes our original sin—is necessary if we are to "live and die happily."* The subject of sin, and of original guilt and pollution in particular, is not a pleasant topic, but it is the necessary background to the gospel.

Article 15 does not tell us about our sin so that we can wallow in misery and self-pity. We insist as Reformed Christians on a thorough knowledge of sin, so that we understand our need for God's grace and are deeply thankful for it. As Jesus said: "They that are whole need not a physician; but they that are sick. I came not to call the righteous, but sinners to repentance" (Luke 5:31–32). The doctrine of original sin, when rightly understood, drives us to despair of ourselves. We see that we are a mass of corruption, dead in sin from birth, guilty and depraved by nature, unable to do anything good and wholly inclined to all evil. We see that God is just in condemning us to eternal damnation in hell, not only for the evil deeds which we have performed but even for the very loathsomeness of our nature. And then we are ready to hear the good news of Christ.

"Notwithstanding," says Article 15, "it is not imputed to the children of God unto condemnation, but by his grace and mercy is forgiven them." God would be just to lay our original and actual sins to our charge—but he does not. God does not hold our sins against us so as to punish us for them. God, our merciful Father, does not treat us as guilty offenders and loathsome creatures in light of our sin. But neither does God sweep our sins under the carpet, as it were, and pretend that we have never sinned and have no sin. God does not hold our sins—and even our sinful nature, the source in us of all our transgressions—against us; he held them against Jesus Christ.

The Son of God came into this world laden with the guilt of our sins, burdened under the heavy weight of our iniquities. He knew the oppressive sense of God's wrath bearing down upon him as he walked the long and difficult way that his Father had mapped out for him—a way which led to the cross on Calvary's hill. Christ's entire life, including his death, is summed up in one word by the apostle Paul in Romans 5:19, "obedience." Adam sinned; he disobeyed—and we are condemned. Christ never sinned; he obeyed for us—and we are justified and forgiven. But, remember, you cannot have Christ without Adam. That was God's good and wise purpose. When Adam fell, he did not fall into hell as he deserved. He fell into the arms of Christ, whom God had mercifully prepared and provided to be the savior (Gen. 3:15). And we fall into Christ's arms, too, we who believe on him!

Martyn McGeown

---

* Heidelberg Catechism 2, in Schaff, *Creeds of Christendom*, 3:308.

Article 16

OF ETERNAL ELECTION

We believe that all the posterity of Adam, being thus fallen into perdition and ruin by the sin of our first parents, God then did manifest himself such as he is; that is to say, merciful and just: merciful, since he delivers and preserves from this perdition all whom he, in his eternal and unchangeable council, of mere goodness hath elected in Christ Jesus our Lord, without any respect to their works: just, in leaving others in the fall and perdition wherein they have involved themselves.

May 21 — Time and Eternity

Read: Psalm 90

In Article 16, our Confession leaps backward from time into eternity. So far, we have confessed our faith in the one, true God revealed in holy Scripture, who of nothing created heaven, earth, and all things, governs them by his providence, and made man in his own image. We have confessed that man willfully subjected himself to sin and death; became wicked, perverse, and corrupt in all his ways; and this corruption has extended to all mankind. These things have taken place in time. But now we leap backward into eternity to the truth of God's "eternal and unchangeable counsel."

Time and eternity: Scripture does not define them but does speak of them. It speaks of eternity as "before the foundation of the world" (Eph. 1:4; 1 Pet. 1:20). We often think of eternity as time before time, as the period of time stretching from the beginning of our world infinitely backward, as the era that had no beginning but always was. Thus, we think of eternity not as qualitatively but only quantitatively different from time. That is, we think of it as an infinite amount of time. Nor is it surprising that we think of it that way because we are bound by time. We exist, and can only exist, in time. We think, and can only think, in terms of time. We cannot imagine anything outside of time. Therefore, we assume that eternity is the infinite time stretching backward and forward before and after earth's history.

Yet this is a mistake.

Scripture does speak of eternity as "before the foundation of the world," which seems to imply a period of time, but Scripture only speaks this way because we cannot think in any other way. But eternity is not infinite time. It is fundamentally different from time. Time is a creature. Time was created by God "in the beginning" (Gen. 1:1). Before the beginning there was no time. Before the beginning there was only God. Therefore, eternity is not infinite time before time, but it is an attribute of *God.* Scripture testifies that "one day is with the Lord as a thousand years, and a thousand years as one day" (2 Pet. 3:8) because God is not bound by days and years, but he creates days and years. God names himself I AM THAT I AM (Ex. 3:14), the "Alpha and Omega, the beginning and ending...the first and last" (Rev. 1:8, 11).

We confess that as God is eternal, so his counsel is eternal. God carries out his eternal counsel in time. All history flows from him and to him. All people enter history by him and for him. We too who have lived only a few years, who will live only threescore years and ten, or perhaps fourscore, who will soon be cut off and fly away, exist by him and for the glory of him who "hath made every thing beautiful in his time" (Eccl. 3:11).

Daniel Holstege

May 22 — God's Counsel

Read: Isaiah 46

According to Article 16, we believe that the one true God who is revealed in Scripture has an "eternal and unchangeable counsel."

Many deny this. Process theism believes in a god who is in the world, but not above the world; a god who cannot control the world but can only attempt to lure it along in a never-ending process of becoming. Open theism believes in a god who does not know or control the future but is open to endless possibilities. Others believe that blind fate has determined the destiny of every man. Arminians believe God has an eternal counsel, but it is changeable and dependent on the will of man.

However, all these are mistaken. We believe the Bible, which reveals the one true God and his "eternal and unchangeable counsel." "The counsel of the Lord standeth for ever, the thoughts of his heart to all generations" (Ps. 33:11). "Remember the former things of old: for I am God, and there is none else; I am God, and there is none like me, declaring the end from the beginning, and from ancient times the things that are not yet done, saying, My counsel shall stand, and I will do all my pleasure" (Isa. 46:9–10). God "worketh all things after the counsel of his own will" (Eph 1:11).

God has a will. He is not a blind power. He is a living, personal, volitional being. He has a purpose regarding all things. God's counsel is his will, purpose, and good pleasure determining all things that exist in time. It is the perfect idea in his infinite mind, and the eternal will to realize it outside himself. It includes absolutely all things, persons, and events that have existed, do exist, and will exist. It aims at the highest and greatest glory of God. It purposes to accomplish this by manifesting God "such as he is; that is to say, merciful and just" (Article 16), and to do so in the highest way, the antithetical way of sin and grace. Therefore, the death and resurrection of Christ, which most clearly manifest the justice and mercy of God, stand at the very heart of God's counsel.

God's counsel includes you. God willed your existence. God determined to create you for his glory. God has a purpose for your life. God intends to reveal and glorify himself through you and to you. God has determined the exact way to do that through you. And his counsel shall stand!

Daniel Holstege

May 23 — The Eternity and Immutability of God's Counsel

Read: Hebrews 6:13–20

God's counsel, according to our Confession, is eternal and unchangeable.

God's counsel is eternal, not temporal like ours. We too make plans and set goals, but we do so in time. There was a time when our plans did not exist and when our goals were not yet formed. When we were children, we did not yet have a comprehensive life-plan. But when we grew older, such a plan gradually emerged in our minds. Today we might not have a plan for tomorrow. But when tomorrow comes, we will form our plan for the day. Not so with God. His counsel is above time. It exists as an eternal reality outside of time. It is eternal because God himself is eternal. There was never a time when his plan did not exist. There was never a time when his goal was not in place.

God's counsel is also unchangeable. It cannot be altered or amended. Our plans can be changed, and they often are. Children plan to be policemen or firefighters or doctors, but when they grow up their plans may change, and they may pursue some other career. We might plan to take a vacation, but then a loved one dies, and our plan changes. We might plan to go to work tomorrow, but then we get sick, and our plan changes. Not so with God. His counsel is unchangeable. He does not and will not change it, because it is his perfect idea. Nor can anything or anyone stand in his way or thwart his plan, for he is almighty. God does not have any "Plan B" or "C." He only has a "Plan A." It is unchangeable because God himself is unchangeable: "For I am the Lord, I change not; therefore ye sons of Jacob are not consumed" (Mal. 3:6).

To some, this makes God cold and aloof. It makes him unsympathetic to our cries. It implies that our prayers cannot change him. He is rigid. He is set in stone. He is immovable. But to us, this view of God is a source of great comfort and encouragement. It means God is faithful. It means he will never change his love toward us. He will never change his mind about us. He will never turn his back on us. He does indeed hear our prayers, and he always answers them.

God's counsel is eternal and unchangeable! Be thankful!

Daniel Holstege

May 24 — Predestination

Read: Romans 8:28–39

How vast is the sea of humanity that fills the earth! Consider this for a moment. As I write this, I see scores of people through my window driving by and going about their daily routines. If I fly across the country in an airplane, I see thousands of homes containing thousands of people below me. If I look at statistics, I learn that the world is home to billions of men, women, and children. If I consider all who have lived in the past and all who will yet be born, I am astonished at the vastness of humanity. Now consider this too: each one has a destiny, either heaven or hell, which was determined before the foundation of the world and is eternally and unchangeably fixed in the counsel of almighty God.

This is the decree of predestination which we confess in Article 16 on the basis of holy Scripture. Almighty God has, before the foundation of the world, determined the eternal destiny of every rational-moral creature, of men and angels. He determined the existence of each one, the place of each one in his perfect plan, and the final destiny of each one, whether eternal life or death. He determined the time, place, nation, and culture in which each one would be born and live. He determined all the relationships each one would sustain toward others and all the influences each one would exert upon and receive from others. He determined whether or not one would be born and live in the sphere of the covenant or in the world; whether one would be faithful in the covenant or forsake his covenantal training; whether one would remain in darkness and unbelief or be called "into his marvellous light" (1 Pet. 2:9); whether one would believe in Christ and be saved or reject him and be damned.

That is the eternal and unchangeable decree of predestination.

This decree, according to Scripture and our Confession, is twofold. On the one hand, some men "were before of old ordained to this condemnation, ungodly men, turning the grace of our God into lasciviousness, and denying the only Lord God, and our Lord Jesus Christ" (Jude 4). That is the aspect of the decree known as reprobation. But on the other hand, some whom God "did foreknow, he also did predestinate to be conformed to the image of his Son, that he might be the firstborn among many brethren" (Rom. 8:29). That is the aspect of predestination known as election.

For us who believe in Jesus Christ, this decree is a tremendous comfort! We too have a destiny. Our destiny is that we should be conformed to the image of God's Son! Our destiny is that we should be called, justified, and glorified. Our destiny is that all things in this life must work together for our good. Our destiny is not condemnation but everlasting life. Nothing can separate us from that destiny. Nothing can separate us from the love of Christ. We who seem to be but a handful of people in the vast sea of humanity are the objects of the predestinating love of God!

Daniel Holstege

May 25 — The Importance of the Doctrine of Predestination

Read: Titus 1

The doctrine of predestination is a central doctrine of holy Scripture. It is no minor doctrine. It is not one we may simply ignore.

And this makes it difficult to explain why our Confession is so incredibly brief in its treatment of predestination in Article 16. It is even more difficult to explain when we recall that the author of the Confession, Guido de Brès, was a disciple of John Calvin who strongly maintained and defended this truth. But although the Confession is certainly brief on this matter, we must remember that the Lord in his providence also gave to the Reformed Churches the Canons of Dordt, in which the doctrine of predestination is much more fully explained. Therefore, we must not be misled by the brevity of the Confession. We must not think that this doctrine is a minor one. On the contrary, the doctrine of predestination is revealed throughout sacred Scripture.

It was revealed in the Old Testament in God's choice of Abraham out of those living in Ur of the Chaldees (Neh. 9:7); his choice of Isaac over Ishmael as the one with whom he would continue his covenant (Gen. 21:12, Rom. 9:7); his choice of Jacob whom he loved over Esau whom he hated (Rom. 9:10–13); his choice of Israel over Egypt, Assyria, Babylonia, and all the other nations of the earth (Deut. 7:6). Throughout the Old Testament, God revealed that he did not choose or love all men and nations, but that he chose and loved Israel alone and that he rejected and hated the heathen nations. In the New Testament, God revealed the truth of predestination more deeply and fully. Our Lord Jesus Christ preached this doctrine repeatedly. He told certain Jews that they did not believe on him because they were not of his sheep, the ones whom the Father had given him, who would never perish but have eternal life (John 10:25–28). He told his disciples that "it was not given to" some men "to know the mysteries of the kingdom, and that he taught in parables so that "seeing [they would] see not" and "hearing [they would] hear not" (Matt. 13:11–13). He also said that "many are called, but few are chosen" (Matt. 22:14). Moreover, Jesus' apostles also taught this doctrine repeatedly in their epistles. The apostle Paul taught it especially in that clearest and most avoided chapter of Scripture, Romans 9. He also assumes it in his other epistles, as in Titus 1:1, where he speaks of the "faith of God's elect."

The importance of this doctrine must be emphasized today because many, if not most, Reformed people de-emphasize it practically into non-existence. It is not preached from their pulpits. It is not discussed at their Bible studies. It is not taught in their seminaries. It is not part of their theological or devotional thinking. We must beware, and take care, that this does not happen in our circles. We must preach this doctrine and love to hear it preached. We must study this doctrine and devote ourselves to understanding it. We must embrace this doctrine for the great comfort it gives to us and for the great glory of God. May we hold fast to sound doctrine. May we be able to exhort and convince the gainsayers. May we not have itching ears longing for something new. May we love and stand fast in the truth!

Daniel Holstege

May 26 — The Primacy of Predestination in God's Counsel

Read: Colossians 1:12–20

Predestination is the primary purpose of God with all things. God's one all-encompassing purpose, of course, is the glory of his name, or in the words of Article 16 of our Confession, to "manifest himself such as he is…merciful and just." But there is one central way in which God determined to manifest himself unto his glory.

Some, such as Abraham Kuyper and Herman Bavinck, claim that God has two or more distinct and equally significant purposes for the realization of his glory. They deny that predestination is God's central purpose to realize the glory of his name. They claim that God purposes to realize his glory through election and reprobation and through creation and providence, through particular grace and through common grace, through Christ and through human culture. They condemn as one-sided the view that makes predestination the central purpose of God. But in so doing, they make the counsel of God two-sided. They introduce dualism into the mind of God by teaching that God has two utterly distinct and equally significant purposes with this world. They deny that God's counsel focuses on one purpose in Christ. They imagine two purposes in the counsel of God, which run like two railroad tracks side by side, never joining together as far as the eye can see. They exclude Christ from one of the two great purposes of God (as they say) with all things: namely, the development of culture through common grace. You see, this gives them a theological basis for bridging the gap between the church and the world, so that they may cross over that bridge, enter the world, and enjoy the ungodly, Christless, man-centered culture of the world.

But this is not scriptural. Rather, according to Scripture, predestination is the central and primary purpose of God in his eternal counsel. God has

9. made known unto us the mystery of his will, according to his good pleasure which he hath purposed in himself:
10. That in the dispensation of the fulness of times he might gather together in one all things in Christ, both which are in heaven, and which are on earth; even in him:
11. In whom also we have obtained an inheritance, being predestinated according to the purpose of him who worketh all things after the counsel of his own will:
12. That we should be to the praise of his glory. (Eph. 1:9–12)

And by Christ

16. were all things created, that are in heaven, and that are in earth, visible and invisible, whether they be thrones, or dominions, or principalities, or powers: all things were created by him, and for him:
17. And he is before all things, and by him all things consist.
18. And he is the head of the body, the church: who is the beginning, the firstborn from the dead; that in all things he might have the preeminence. (Col. 1:16–18)

God gathers together in one all things in Christ, in whom we have been predestinated. All things were created by Christ and for Christ. In all things Christ has the preeminence. God clearly has one great purpose with all things, and it revolves around Christ and his salvation of his people in Christ, and thus the decree of predestination. All things serve that one great purpose: the stars in the sky and the sand of the seashore, the beasts of the field and the fowl in the air, and also the development of human culture. All things serve God's one great purpose to glorify himself in Christ through the salvation of his elect and the damnation of the reprobate.

"For it pleased the Father that in him should all fulness dwell" (Col. 1:19).

Daniel Holstege

May 27 — Election

Read: Ephesians 1:1–8

God chose us! How often, beloved, do you meditate on that wondrous reality? How often do you ponder that beautiful truth? Does that truth shape your whole life, your behavior, your choices?

How often is it not the case that others do not choose us? Perhaps as a child or young person you were not chosen to play on the sports team or to go to a birthday party but were left out. Perhaps a young man or young woman to whom you were attracted chose to date someone else and not you. Perhaps a company to which you applied for a job selected another applicant and passed you by. Perhaps you and another man were nominated to the office of elder, but the congregation elected the other and not you. Often we are not chosen. And that can hurt at times.

But God chose us!

How wondrous! How joyful! For he chose us to everlasting life!

He chose us "before the foundation of the world" to be the recipients of life eternal (Eph 1:4)! He chose us as the ones whom he would bless with all spiritual blessings in heavenly places in Christ. He predestinated us unto the adoption of children. He chose to lead us through this life, bestow upon us the gift of faith, shower us with his grace, and take us into heavenly places. He chose us as the bride of Christ, "loved [us], and gave himself for [us]" (Eph. 5:25). He determined to bring us to Christ our bridegroom to dwell with him in perfect fellowship at the marriage supper of eternity. He chose us as the body of Christ (Eph. 1:23). He did not choose a disordered and chaotic horde of individuals, but a body with a Head and members who each have a place and role. He gave us spiritual gifts and appointed us to our own unique offices in that body. God chose us!

Let that, fellow believer, encourage you in the midst of the pain of being rejected by men. You may not be chosen by men. You might be left out or passed by. You may even be fiercely rejected, hated, and condemned. But as a child of God, you have been chosen. God chose you! God has not left you out in the cold, in the darkness. God has taken you into his church. God has not passed you by in favor of others but has determined to choose you. God has elected you in Christ. Your destiny is bound up with Christ's. You are crucified with Christ. You are raised up with Christ. You are united to Christ even now by his Spirit. You shall never be separated from Christ.

Because God chose us.

Daniel Holstege

May 28 — The Order of God's Decrees

Read: Isaiah 55

Did God choose us in his eternal counsel as fallen and sinful people or totally apart from sin and the fall? Oh, do not misunderstand the question. I do not ask whether God chose us in time, after he created man, after man fell into sin. Oh no, God surely chose us before time in his eternal counsel. But did God choose us in his counsel as people or as sinful people? Did God first determine to create mankind, then determine that mankind would fall, and only then determine to choose us in Christ out of that fallen mass of mankind? Or did God first determine to choose us in Christ, then determine that we and all mankind would fall into sin, and only then determine to create mankind and the world itself as the arena in which to carry this all out? This is the debate between infralapsarianism and supralapsarianism. Our Confession of Faith evidently takes the former view, as do our Canons of Dordt. Notice: the Confession does not treat election in the first articles in the section on theology, but much later, after treating creation and the fall. By this placement it shows its preference that election follows the fall in the counsel of God.

Both views have commendable features, and neither has ever been condemned as heretical. According to the infra view, God chose us as fallen, sinful people. This magnifies the electing grace of God as favor to undeserving sinners. God then did not choose us merely as men and women, but as wicked, rebellious, and corrupt men and women with no right to live, worthy of death and hell. That is indeed an "election of grace" (Rom. 11:5). But according to the supra view, God chose us in Christ in distinction from other men, totally apart from sin and the fall, and determined the latter only as a means of glorifying himself in the highest possible way by delivering us from it. This magnifies the sovereign freedom of God to choose one man as a "vessel of mercy" and to determine that another would be a "vessel of wrath" (Rom. 9:22–23). He chose us and not others. He could have chosen others and not us. He is absolutely free to do as he pleases. What gratitude must we then have that he chose us!

Which view is correct? Although I admit that I favor the supra view, and was even taught it in the home, I also see truth in the infra view, which I cannot discard. I do not usually like to sit on the fence, but in this regard, I find myself lingering there, hesitant to leap fully to one side or the other. I sometimes wonder whether this debate should be viewed as an either-or proposition at all. Is it not possible that both views contain truth and both a bit of error? This we may know with certainty: God's thoughts are not our thoughts, and his ways are not our ways, but his ways are higher than our ways, and his thoughts than our thoughts (Isa. 55:8–9). God's counsel is one idea and has one purpose concerning all things. He determines the order and relations of all the parts. He sees it all in one eternal present. He does not first determine one thing, and then another. But he conceives and determines everything at once with all the causes and effects, ends and means, and perfectly glorifies himself in Christ through all things. What an incredible privilege we have to be included in his perfect plan, and to be the objects of his eternal and sovereign election!

Daniel Holstege

May 29 — Unconditional Election

Read: Deuteronomy 7:6–8, John 15:16, Romans 9:11, Ephesians 1:3–5

Of his mere goodness God chose us in Christ Jesus our Lord—without any respect to our works!

Do you ever wonder why God chose you of all people in the world? If you were an Arminian, you would not wonder. You would feel quite confident that you know why you were chosen. You would simply point out that you are a believer, that you have accepted Christ into your heart, that you have chosen Christ by your own free will, and therefore you are elect. If you were an Arminian theologian, you would probably say that your election is a conditional thing, that it all hinges on your faith and obedience, and that only God knows if you will still be elect at the end of your life. You are elect now because now you choose Christ. But in the future…who knows? Maybe you will forsake Christ. Then you will no longer be elect. It all depends on you! Your choice is first. God's choice is second. You choose your own fate. Therefore, you would never wonder why God chose you. You would believe that he chose you because you have made yourself to differ, because you have shown yourself morally superior to other men, because you have chosen Christ.

But you, beloved saints, are not Arminians. You are Reformed.

Therefore, you might wonder why God chose you. After all, you know that God did not choose you because you chose Christ. But you confess in Article 16 that God chose you "without any respect to [your] works." God did not gaze from his eternal viewpoint into the future and take notice of the fact that you believe in Christ and then choose you because of it. God does not choose anyone on the basis of foreseen faith and obedience. God did not choose us on the basis of our works! God chose us without any respect to our works. God's election is unconditional. And thank God that it is! For if it was not, we could have no assurance of our salvation. We could never be sure that we would persevere in faith to the end of our lives. Thank God that he did not consider our works when he chose us!

Thus, we wonder: why did God choose us? Our Confession tells us very simply that he chose us "of mere goodness" (Article 16). We could say, "of mere grace," or "of mere love." God chose us because he loved us. He longed to be gracious to us. He longed to do good to us. He longed to deliver us from sin and perdition and to give us eternal life.

But why us? That question always seems to return unanswered! Why did God love us? Why did God long to do good to us? Our Confession does not go any further in answering that question. But our Canons of Dordt do (Canons 1, Art. 10). God chose us "according to the good pleasure of his will" (Eph. 1:5). God chose us merely because he was pleased to do so. Beyond that we cannot go. Scripture bars us from intruding any farther into the mind and will of God. But we do not need to go any farther! This is far enough. It is enough for us to know that he chose us and loved us because he was pleased to do so. Thus, we continue to stand amazed at the love and goodness of our God to us, and to say until our dying day: "To God be the glory!"

Daniel Holstege

May 30 — Election of a Certain and Great Number

Read: Genesis 13:14–18; 15:1–6

The number of God's elect is certain and limited, but it is more than we can count, a multitude which no man can number.

Have you numbered the grains of sand on the seashore? Take just a handful of sand next time you are by the sea and try to count all the grains. There is no doubt that the number of grains is definite and limited. But what that exact number is, you will never know. It is too great to count. God promised that Abraham's seed would be not just as many as a handful of sand, but as many as the sand of the seashore!

Have you seen the stars in the sky on a clear evening, far away from the bright city lights which drown them out? Try to count the stars. They too are a definite and limited number. But there are millions, or perhaps billions, or even more, so we could never count them all. Even if you could count every star in the night sky, you still would not have counted all the stars, for faraway galaxies which appear as only a speck of light contain billions more! And God promised to make Abraham's seed as many as those stars! And who are Abraham's seed? The Jews? No, not just the Jews, but all who belong to Christ, all who are chosen in him, all who believe in him (Gal. 3:29). The number of God's elect is great!

It is true that the number of the elect is often small. "Many are called, but few are chosen," says our Lord (Matt. 22:14). Many walk the broad path which leads to destruction, but few follow the narrow way that leads to life (Matt. 7:13-14). Most often in the world, including today, the wicked seem to be an overwhelming horde, while there is only "a remnant according to the election of grace" (Rom. 11:5).

Nevertheless, Scripture also emphasizes that the total number of the elect is very great. God saves the whole world in the elect. God saves all men in the elect. That is, God chose a great throng from all nations, tribes, and tongues, throughout all history. We will never see this vast multitude as long as we walk by faith in this world. We will always see the elect as a little flock, hated, persecuted, and oppressed. But we believe God's promise. And soon our faith will become sight. Soon we will pass from this world into heaven and see that great multitude which no man can number worshiping God and the Lamb (Rev. 7:9–10). Soon afterward we will witness the full ingathering of the whole body of the elect, as many as the sand and stars, in the new heavens and earth. Soon, and very soon, we will see that God's elect are indeed a very great number. What a day that will be!

Daniel Holstege

May 31 — Reprobation

Read: Romans 9:1–24

God did not choose all men but determined to leave some in the fall and perdition wherein they involved themselves. We believe the doctrine of reprobation, too, on the basis of Scripture.

We admit that from our human viewpoint this is a hard doctrine to accept. Even Calvin called the decree of reprobation horrible or dreadful.* It is not hard to accept because Scripture is unclear about it. Scripture is crystal clear about it! But it is hard to accept because of the horrible implications for a vast number of human beings. We shudder at the awful reality that multitudes will perish eternally in hell. We shrink from the thought that our God determined this from eternity. We struggle to understand why he did so. We find it difficult to answer the deep questions that arise: If God is love, then why does God also hate (Rom. 9:13)? If God wanted to reveal his justice, why was it not sufficient to do so through the cross of Christ? Why would God create some men intending to destroy them? We admit that this is a hard doctrine.

Perhaps this explains why our Confession presents the doctrine in a manner that seems less harsh. For it does not say, as the Bible does, that God hardens the wicked in their sin and unbelief unto their destruction (Ex. 4:21, Rom. 9:18). Nor does it make the biblical confession that the wicked were appointed unto disobedience (1 Pet. 2:8) or that heretics were "before of old ordained to this condemnation" (Jude 4). But it says only that God leaves some men in the fall and perdition in which they have involved themselves. It attempts to present reprobation in a softer light: God leaves some sinners in their sins and lets them go their own way, which ends in hell.** God determined to do so in his eternal counsel. This is an attempt to soften a hard doctrine. It seeks to emphasize that people go to hell because of their own willful sins. People willfully involve themselves in sin, and deserve to perish in hell, and God merely leaves them on that path to hell. God is passive. He does not do anything. He just leaves them alone to their own destruction.

Now, the motive for presenting reprobation this way is admirable: the desire to guard against the lie that God arbitrarily throws men into hell, or that God forces people to sin against their will and then damns them for it. God does nothing of the sort. God puts sinners into hell, people who love sin and hate God. We must always take care to maintain that all who go to hell go there on account of their own sins.

Nevertheless, although God does leave some men in their sin and perdition, he does more. God is active in all his works and decrees. God is no mere onlooker at the lives of the reprobate. But God is active in realizing his decree of reprobation. He hardens them. He gives them over to sin (Rom. 1:24–32). Yet he is not the author of their sin. God determined some men to be "vessels of wrath" (Rom. 9:22), and he carries out that decree in time. He is God. He does his own good pleasure. We shudder at it. We struggle with it. But we do not deny it. "Nay but, O man, who art thou that repliest against God?" (v. 20).

Daniel Holstege

---

* Calvin, *Institutes of the Christian Religion*, 3.23.7.
** See Canons of Dordt 1.15, in Schaff, *Creeds of Christendom*, 3:584.

June 1 — Why Reprobation?

Read: Genesis 25:19–34, Romans 9:10–13

Why did God decree some men to be vessels of wrath? Why did he determine not to save all men from sin and hell? Why did he decide to create some to be enemies of him and his people? Why Esau? Why Pharaoh? Why reprobation?

The simple scriptural answer, of course, is that the "Lord hath made all things for himself: yea, even the wicked for the day of evil" (Prov. 16:4). He made the wicked for his own glory. He raised up Pharaoh for the glorification of his power (Ex. 9:16; Rom. 9:17). He wills to show his wrath and to make his power known, and therefore he endures the "vessels of wrath" (Rom. 9:22). And as our Confession points out, he leaves some in their sins to manifest himself such as he is, that is, just. He manifests his justice very clearly through the reprobate. He shows that he is a God who hates sin and punishes it with everlasting damnation. He makes known to all that he is holy and that he maintains himself as such over against the sinner. He would have been perfectly just to leave us in our sins, too, but he also willed to manifest his mercy, which he has done in Christ.

But that does not exhaust the answer to this question. After all, did not God manifest his justice in Christ at the cross by punishing our sins in him? Of course! That is exactly what we confess in Article 20 of this same confession! But why did God determine to manifest his justice also through reprobation? Why reprobation? Does Scripture say anything more about this? Yes, for God told Rebecca concerning her twins that "the elder shall serve the younger" (Gen. 25:23; Rom. 9:12). The reprobate Esau would serve the elect Jacob. Reprobation serves election.

Let this be understood properly. God determined to glorify himself in the highest way, the antithetical way of election and reprobation, sin and grace, life and death, salvation and condemnation, heaven and hell. God decreed the existence of the reprobate, sin, death, judgment, and hell to serve the realization of election and salvation through Christ to the highest glory of his name. For the grace of election stands out in the greatest glory only against the background of reprobation. Only when I realize that not all men were chosen do I appreciate the grace of God to me and my profound debt of gratitude to him. Only then do I truly stand in awe before him who possesses absolute freedom and who does all things for his own glory. Only then do I truly marvel at the depths of the mystery of his unsearchable will (Rom. 11:33).

Thus, God willed reprobation to serve election, and the reprobate to serve the elect, Esau to serve Jacob, Pharaoh to serve Israel. He decreed that there would be two peoples in the earth, one seed of the woman and one of the serpent (Gen. 3:15), which would exist in spiritual contrast and opposition to each other. He willed that the one people would follow Satan and would have enmity toward his people. He willed this conflict of all ages as the means of showing his sovereign grace in his people by their endurance to the end and as the means of showing his power over the wicked in his judgment upon them.

This is a comfort to us as God's people when we find ourselves viciously attacked and persecuted by the reprobate men of the world. We may be assured that they are unwittingly serving our higher glory and salvation! Why reprobation? For the highest glory of God and the greatest salvation of his people.

Daniel Holstege

| June 2 | **Predestination and the Covenant** |

Read: Genesis 17:1–8, Galatians 3:15–18

Although Article 16 does not discuss the relation between election and the covenant, this is such an important subject that we ought to devote at least one meditation to it.

In Reformed and Presbyterian churches today, there is fierce debate over this fundamental question: with whom does God establish his covenant? Is it with those chosen in Christ before time or with all those baptized into the Christian church in time? Is it with the elect alone or with all who profess faith in Christ and all their baptized children?

Let us see what Scripture teaches: God established his covenant with Abraham and his "seed after [him] in their generations" (Gen. 17:7). Who is Abraham's seed? Is it all of Abraham's physical offspring or all who were circumcised? Many say yes. They say God establishes his covenant with all of the physical, baptized offspring of believers, but only those who fulfill the conditions of faith and faithfulness till the end of their lives are saved. But we say no. Scripture says: "Now to Abraham and his seed were the promises made. He saith not, And to seeds, as of many; but as of one, And to thy seed, which is Christ" (Gal. 3:16). Abraham's Seed is Christ! God established his covenant first of all with Christ. But not only with Christ: Abraham's seed includes all who belong to Christ: "And if ye be Christ's, then are ye Abraham's seed, and heirs according to the promise" (v. 29). God established his covenant with Christ and all those in Christ, that is, the elect (Eph. 1:4). God did not establish his covenant with every individual in Israel of old at Mt. Sinai (Deut. 5:2–3). For Scripture tells us: "They are not all Israel, which are of Israel: neither, because they are the seed of Abraham, are they all children…They which are the children of the flesh, these are not the children of God: but the children of the promise are counted for the seed" (Rom. 9:6–8). God establishes his covenant with Christ and with all the elect in Christ.

Generally, God establishes his covenant with the elect in the lines of believers and their seed. Sometimes the children of believers show that they are reprobate, like Esau, by abandoning Christ. They never were members of the covenant, though they grew up in the sphere of the covenant. They are the tares in the wheat field, the chaff of the grain, those who are not Israel, though "of Israel" (Rom. 9:6). They will be separated from the wheat at the end of time and cast into hell (Matt. 13:41–42). But generally, God establishes his covenant with his elect in the lines of the continued generations of believers.

Therefore, we view the faithful congregation of Jesus Christ, of believers and their seed, as the covenant people of God. We know that election and reprobation cut right through the visible church on earth, and that the antithesis exists even within her walls. Yet we also know that God promises to make his covenant with believers and their seed. Therefore, we do not suspiciously eye our fellow members and try to find the reprobate chaff. Rather, we view each other as brothers and sisters in Christ. And we look forward to the day when all God's people will be brought into his everlasting covenant, when his tabernacle will be with us, and when we will dwell with him and each other forevermore!

Daniel Holstege

June 3 — Delivered and Preserved!

Read: John 10:22–31

God delivers and preserves us!

In my first meditation on Article 16, I pointed out that in this article, our Confession leaps backward from time into eternity and considers God's eternal and unchangeable counsel. In this same article, however, we confess that God carries out his decree of predestination in time. He does so, according to Article 16, not by leaving some in the fall and perdition wherein they have involved themselves, but by delivering and preserving us his elect from that fall and perdition.

God delivers us! We fell into sin in Adam. We fell thereby into perdition and ruin, because "the wages of sin is death" and hell (Rom. 6:23). We were born into this world as sinners, dead in trespasses, and we add more and more sins every day. But God has delivered us! He sent his Son to die on the cross and make atonement for our sins. Christ died for us. Christ endured God's wrath against our sins. Christ has delivered us (Gal. 1:4). Therefore, God delivers us now in our present experience. He sends his Spirit into our hearts to unite us with Christ and bestow on us all the blessings of salvation! The Spirit regenerates us, translating us in principle "out of darkness into [God's] marvellous light" (1 Pet. 2:9), implanting in our hearts the seed of the new life of Christ. The Spirit quickens faith in us, whereby we experience justification and deliverance from our sins. But that is not all.

God also preserves us! We would surely go lost again if he did not preserve us. We are like foolish sheep because we constantly go astray. We love sin by nature. We love the pleasures of this world according to our flesh. We sometimes wish we could have the lifestyle of the world. We sometimes long to enjoy the pleasures of sin. But God preserves us! He never entirely forsakes us to our carnal lusts. He never lets the seed of regeneration in our hearts perish. He never wholly withdraws his grace and Holy Spirit from us. He preserves us even when we fall into enormous, heinous sins, as David and Peter did, and as we might have done. Even when we are seduced by the temptations of Satan, beguiled by unbelief or doubt, and enticed by the powerful allurements of sin, God preserves us. He will not let us go. He will not give us over to Satan. He holds us in the palm of his hand, and Jesus assures us that "no man is able to pluck [us] out of [his] Father's hand" (John 10:29). He guards us "as the apple of his eye" (Deut. 32:10). He finishes the good work which he has begun in us (Phil. 1:6). He keeps us from ultimate apostasy. He preserves us by his irresistible grace so that we persevere, so that we continue in faith, so that we cleave to Christ throughout our lives until we are finally taken out of this world into glory!

What a comfort, beloved, in the midst of a world of fierce spiritual warfare. We do not need to fear. "We are more than conquerors through him that loved us" (Rom. 8:37). We can never be separated from his love (v. 39). Unto all eternity!

Daniel Holstege

Article 17

OF THE RECOVERY OF FALLEN MAN

We believe that our most gracious God, in his admirable wisdom and goodness, seeing that man had thus thrown himself into temporal and spiritual death, and made himself wholly miserable, was pleased to seek and comfort him when he trembling fled from his presence, promising him that he would give his Son, who should *be made of a woman, to bruise the head of the serpent*, and would make him happy.

June 4 — Our Admirably Wise and Good God

O give thanks unto the LORD; for he is good:
for his mercy endureth for ever. —Psalm 136:1

In Article 17, we begin to look at what our gracious God has done for our salvation. Scripture teaches that we do not save ourselves. Salvation is the purpose and work of God alone. We have already seen in the previous article that God planned salvation before the foundation of the world. In this article, we see what God has done in time for our salvation.

It is important to notice that the Belgic Confession addresses the whole subject of salvation from the perspective of its revelation in time. This was the case in Article 16 also. There we read: "We believe that, all the posterity of Adam being thus fallen…God then did manifest himself." God, of course, planned salvation before the creation and fall of man. Indeed, God's decree to save some and reprobate others is eternal. When Adam fell, our Creator did not begin scrambling for a solution to an unforeseen problem, as if salvation in Christ were a "Plan B" after "Plan A" went awry. It never was God's purpose that Adam and Eve should remain forever in the garden of Eden in a state of innocence. God had something much better, much richer, and much more glorious in mind. God's plan was, and is, to reveal his "admirable wisdom and goodness" (Article 17), as well as his just severity, in saving some from the fallen race of men, and condemning others to everlasting punishment. In short, God's plan always was Christ (1 Pet. 1:20).

But to make way for Christ, Adam had to fall. Adam fell in such a way that God was sovereign over his fall, but Adam was guilty for his sin. Article 17 emphasizes the latter: man's responsibility and guilt. In this God displayed his incomparable wisdom. God ordained all things so that he would be glorified to the highest possible degree.

The Bible teaches us very clearly, then, that salvation is the seeking God coming to save the sinning man. What a display of God's "admirable wisdom and goodness"! Salvation must be by the seeking and saving God because man cannot save himself. In fact, so far is man from saving himself, that he does not even desire salvation.

And behold, how quickly God came to seek his fallen friend, Adam. Adam had rebelled against God and had made himself miserable. Of himself there was no hope or desire of reconciliation with God, no possibility of restoring that friendship which Adam had violated by his disobedience, and no hope of annulling the relationship he now had with the devil, God's archenemy. But no sooner do we read of Adam's shameful fall than we hear God's call to Adam: "Where art thou?" (Gen. 3:9).

What could Adam hope to receive from God now? Had God not threatened Adam with death? Had not Adam's eyes been opened to the horror of what sin really is? Would Adam and Eve not now be swallowed into everlasting hell?

Surely, all Adam could expect from God was the swift sentence of death. But our admirably wise and good God had something very different in mind.

Martyn McGeown

June 5 — The Misery of Temporal and Eternal Death

The wages of sin is death.
—Romans 6:23

Article 17 magnifies the grace of God by describing the awful effects of the fall, through which Adam—and in him all men—plunged himself into misery. The more we understand our misery, the more thankful we are to hear about deliverance. An incomplete or wrong diagnosis of our condition leads to an incomplete or wrong understanding of the work of salvation from sin.

God had threatened Adam with dire consequences in the event of his disobedience. One word sums up God's threat: death! This was no empty threat: God did indeed judge Adam—and all of us in him—with death.

The Confession speaks of two kinds of death: "temporal and spiritual death" (Article 17). Temporal death is the death of the body. This might at first appear puzzling. Had God not said: "In the day that thou eatest thereof thou shalt surely die" (Gen. 2:17)? But Adam did not drop dead at the foot of the tree in the garden on that very day. In fact, Adam lived for 930 years. Had God reprieved Adam and not inflicted the judgment of death? The truth is that Adam began to die physically as soon as he transgressed God's commandment. In the very day of his transgression, Adam did indeed die. Death began to gnaw away at his very existence; death began to be active in his members; and his body began to decay. This is true with our bodies also. The judgment of God is the cause in the world of all sicknesses, infirmities, and pains in the body of man long before his body and soul are violently torn apart at the moment of death. Literally, God had said in Genesis 2:17, "Dying, thou shalt die." And Adam did die, as do all men that descended from Adam.

The second sense in which Adam died was to suffer eternal death. Eternal death, in the original French of the Belgic Confession, is "spiritual death." Eternal death is everlasting death under the wrath of God in hell, something Revelation 20:14 calls the "second death." But before a lost sinner perishes in hell, he or she is spiritually dead. Adam would have died eternally in hell if God had not saved him by his grace. About all sinners born into the world we can say that they are already born spiritually dead because of the guilt of Adam's sin (Rom. 5:12; Eph. 2:1–3; Col. 1:21–22). Spiritual death, then, is the death of the spirit or soul. Spiritual death is alienation from God, the source of all life. Spiritual death is the corruption of the whole nature of man, making him unfit to be the friend of God, no longer in the state of original righteousness in which he was created.

One in such a state of death is miserable, wholly miserable. Adam was miserable, and all mankind in him is miserable, too. Do not let the outward façade of happy-go-lucky sinners fool you. Sinners without God are miserable. They know that they are guilty before God, and yet they hate the God who made them. They know that without God they can never be happy, but they do not want to know God. They seek in vain to find satisfaction, meaning, and fulfillment in the creation while they suppress the knowledge of God the Creator, and seek to drown out their accusing conscience; and they know when their miserable life is over—in which they have desperately sought to eat, drink, and be merry—that they will fall into the hands of an angry God.

Martyn McGeown

June 6 — Our Fatal Plunge into Misery

*Know therefore and see that it is an evil thing and bitter,
that thou hast forsaken the Lord thy God,
and that my fear is not in thee.* —Jeremiah 2:19

Article 17 is transitional. It comes between the article on election—what God decreed to do in eternity—and the article on the incarnation of Jesus Christ—what God has actually done in Jesus Christ to save his people. In Article 17, we read of God's promise to do what he actually does in the sending of his Son.

This promise is all the more admirable when we remember Adam's guilt, which, as we learned in a previous article, is also our guilt. Article 17 underlines the deliberate and willful nature of Adam's transgression. Sometimes the word *fall* gives us the wrong impression. A fall is something tragic, a dreadful accident. A man might fall down the stairs, out of a tree, or even off a tall building. Some falls can be very serious; others, less so. But a fall is usually not deliberate. We tend to pity a man who falls as we see him with a broken leg or other injury. But Adam did not merely fall. He jumped! Article 17 explains it this way: "man had thus thrown himself into temporal and spiritual death." The idea is of a fatal plunge. When a man deliberately destroys himself, he is no longer to be pitied. He is to be condemned. Adam was not a victim of the deception of the serpent. Adam walked wide-eyed into death. God had warned him in unmistakable words: "In the day that thou eatest thereof thou shalt surely die" (Gen. 2:17). Adam chose death, therefore. Not even the devil could have forced Adam to sin against his own will.

The result of Adam's deliberate plunge into evil was his—and our—misery. The serpent had lied. He had promised Eve a much better result: "Ye shall not surely die: For God doth know that in the day ye eat thereof, then your eyes shall be opened, and ye shall be as gods, knowing good and evil" (Gen. 3:4–5). In a way, the serpent was right: Adam's eyes were opened, but not as he might have hoped. He experienced evil for himself, and the experience was bitter. Much later, Jeremiah would exclaim: "Know therefore and see that it is an evil thing and bitter, that thou hast forsaken the Lord thy God, and that my fear is not in thee" (Jer. 2:19). Adam was miserable. He had cut himself off from God, the only source of life and joy. And yet Adam did not want to return to God. He loved sin, although it made him miserable; he hated God; and he was allied to the devil, although Satan was a wicked tyrant who held him in cruel bondage.

That is the folly of sin. The sinner knows that sin will destroy him, but he will not give it up. He knows that the wages of sin is death, but he would rather receive those wages than repent. But God did not abandon Adam to his doom. Adam deserved to die, both temporally and eternally. Adam deserved to remain miserable forever. But, although God was justly offended by man's sin, and although God had every just cause to destroy mankind, he came with the promise of salvation to trembling, fleeing Adam—and to us who are in Jesus Christ!

Martyn McGeown

June 7 — Adam Fleeing, God Seeking

Adam and his wife hid themselves from the presence of the Lord God amongst the trees of the garden. And the Lord God called unto Adam, and said unto him, Where art thou? —Genesis 3:8–9

Adam had known the sweetness of the friendship of God. Made in God's image, Adam had been righteous and holy, "that he might rightly know God his Creator, heartily love him and live with him in eternal happiness to glorify and praise him."* But all that changed the moment he ate the forbidden fruit. The knowledge of God was changed into horrible blindness of heart; the righteousness and holiness of nature were stripped from him, and he became corrupt and vile. In such a condition, Adam could no longer fellowship with God, for the holy God will not fellowship with sinners.

Adam knew his own nakedness and hurried to cover himself with fig leaves and to hide among the trees (Gen. 3:7–8). Article 17 reminds us that Adam "trembling fled from [God's] presence." Before Adam's rebellion, Adam had gladly communed with God in the cool of the evening. But not now! Now he was afraid. Now he trembled! That's his own confession: "I heard thy voice in the garden, and I was afraid, because I was naked; and I hid myself" (Gen. 3:10). The voice in which he had delighted before the fall now was a fearful voice summoning him to give account of himself. How could a naked sinner stand before a holy God? And yet how foolish of Adam to hide from God. Shall any sinner hide from the omniscient, everywhere-present God who searches the hearts and who lays bare the motives of all men? Adam was the first sinner to attempt to hide from God, and he will not be the last. Sinners on the Last Day will cry out in terror: "Fall on us, and hide us from the face of him that sitteth on the throne, and from the wrath of the Lamb: For the great day of his wrath is come; and who shall be able to stand?" (Rev. 6:16–17).

Adam hid in vain, but God sought Adam out. God did not wait for Adam to seek him—that would never have happened; Adam would have fled forever if he could have done so—but God, as had been his custom before the fall, came to walk "in the garden in the cool of the day" (Gen. 3:8). Adam, his erstwhile friend, was not there. God knew why Adam was not there. He had seen what Adam had done. But Adam had to be taught a lesson, brought to repentance, and restored to fellowship. Therefore, God called, "Where art thou?" (v. 9). Then, on hearing Adam's response, he asked Adam: "Who told thee that thou wast naked? Hast thou eaten of the tree, whereof I commanded thee that thou shouldest not eat?" (v. 11).

Thus God seeks out all his children. He does not wait for us, for "there is none that seeketh after God" (Rom. 3:11). He calls after us and shows himself to be the admirably good God in promising to us salvation.

Martyn McGeown

---

* Heidelberg Catechism 6, in Schaff, *Creeds of Christendom*, 3:309.

June 8 — God Pleased to Seek His People

In hope of eternal life, which God, that cannot lie,
promised before the world began. —Titus 1:2

Salvation is rooted in the good pleasure of God. Article 17 says: "We believe that our most gracious God...was pleased to seek and comfort [man]." God's good pleasure in Scripture is not a whim but his eternal good purpose, what he is pleased to decree in eternity and therefore pleased to do in time. Long before Adam was created, and certainly long before Adam sinned, God was pleased to promise salvation.

Titus 1:2 speaks about God promising eternal life before the world began. This begs the question: "To whom did God make such a promise?" To the angels? No! They had not yet been created! To man? No! Man did not yet exist. The answer is that God made that promise to Christ. Christ, remember, is the eternal Son of God, the second person of the blessed Trinity. In eternity, then, the Father promised eternal life to the Son in the Holy Spirit. This eternal life he promised to give to the elect whom he chose eternally in Christ (Eph. 1:4). The Father promised to give unto the Son a people, who would be his body and bride, a people chosen in him before the world began. The Son promised to become a man to save his people, who, in the decree of God, would fall into sin and misery. The Son promised to bear the sins of his people, to take the place of condemnation and punishment into which his people would plunge themselves. The Spirit promised to apply the work of the Son to the people of God so that they would possess the salvation decreed for and merited for them. And the Father promised to exalt the Son in the human nature to the highest possible glory in heaven, and in so doing to glorify his people.

We teach this in distinction from some Reformed and Presbyterian theologians who speak of an agreement within the Godhead, as if the Father and the Son entered into an agreement: "I will do this, if you do this; and you will do this, if I do this." The relationship between the persons of the Trinity is not an agreement, but a close, blessed covenant fellowship in love.

Of course, Adam and Eve knew nothing of this glorious promise. As they hid trembling among Eden's trees, the last thing on their minds was a promise from a merciful God. God had threatened death and they already knew death was at work in them. They knew that there was no way back into God's favor and blessing. The only thing they could do was flee further and further away from God. Therefore, Adam must have been terrified when he heard the voice of God that fateful evening: "Where art thou?" (Gen. 3:9).

However, God had not come to destroy, but to save. God would not let them go. They had been God's friends in the covenant, and God never breaks his covenant. Now was time to reveal his promise. Titus 1:3 goes on to teach concerning this promise made in eternity: "But hath in due times manifested his word through preaching." And the first preacher of the first promise was God himself, by which he was pleased to seek and comfort us in our misery.

What admirable goodness!

Martyn McGeown

June 9 — The Mother of All Promises

Unto which promise our twelve tribes,
instantly serving God day and night, hope to come. —Acts 26:7

Genesis 3:15 is the *protevangel*, the first gospel or the "mother promise." It is the first promise which God made to his people, and out of it all the other promises in Scripture flow. Every promise of salvation really is a development and further unfolding of this one mother promise.

A promise is a sure or certain word. Even children know the difference between an ordinary word and a promise. Often when a parent indicates to a child that he intends to give the child something, the child asks: "Do you promise?" A promise is a solemn declaration that a person will do something. Therefore, a promise may never be taken lightly. Men might lie when they promise, men might have no intention of keeping their promises, or men might promise in good faith but later be unable to fulfill the promise. The mother promise of Genesis 3:15, however, is God's promise. God cannot lie (Titus 1:2), and nothing in heaven, earth, or hell can prevent the fulfillment of God's promise.

God came to Adam and Eve just after the fall and promised to them salvation. That was his sure and certain word. They had ruined themselves. God would save them from their self-inflicted misery and make them happy. Happiness for miserable sinners is to be delivered from sin and reconciled to God. It is to be again in a covenant relationship with God where we know God as our God and experience the blessedness of being his people. Happiness is to have life in the presence of God without sin forever. That happiness God promised Adam and Eve, and he makes that same promise to all his children.

What would Adam and Eve have to do to procure this happiness, to make this promise happen? Nothing! God did not come to Adam with a salvation plan, which Adam and Eve would have to ratify, for which Adam and Eve would have to work, which Adam and Eve would be able to merit. He came with a promise: "I will." He did not come with a command: "Thou shalt." The mother promise, then, teaches us that salvation in the Old Testament as well as in the New Testament will be by the free grace of God, based on the work of Christ, whom God promised to send in the *protevangel*, the first gospel or the mother promise.

Genesis 3:15 is pivotal to understanding the Old Testament. God promised the seed of the woman. This seed, who is Christ, was the hope of every believing child of God in the Old Testament. In the early years after the fall, this was the only gospel to which the saints could cling. What did Abel, Enoch, and the generations before Noah know about the gospel except what they learned in this one promise? But this promise was enough to sustain their faith. Over the centuries, God gradually revealed more about this promise. He would be the seed of the woman; he would be the seed of Abraham; he would be the seed of Isaac, Jacob, Judah, and David. He would be a real man—the seed of the woman—and he would be more powerful than any creature—he would bruise the head of the serpent, the devil himself. He is Christ. Look for him in the Old Testament and see him fulfilled in the New Testament. And marvel at the wonder of God's promise!

Martyn McGeown

June 10 — The Promise of Two Seeds in Enmity

*And I will put enmity between thee and the woman,
and between thy seed and her seed; it shall bruise thy head,
and thou shalt bruise his heel.* —Genesis 3:15

It is a striking thing that the first promise, while spoken in the presence of Adam and Eve, was spoken to the serpent, or the devil, as part of God's curse upon him. This is because God's promise to save his people was at the same time a pronouncement of doom upon the devil and his seed.

The promise of the *protevangel* is enmity. Enmity means hostility or hatred. It is the opposite of friendship and is related to the word *enemy*. God promises a twofold enmity. First, there will be enmity between the serpent and the woman (and also between the serpent and the man). This does not mean that people will hate snakes and flee from them, although many people are repulsed by snakes. The serpent is the devil or Satan. God will put enmity between the devil and the woman (and the man). This means that God will destroy the friendship which the devil has made between himself and the woman (and the man). Adam's and Eve's sinful alliance with the devil will be overturned, and God's friendship with Adam and Eve will be restored. Second, there will be enmity between "thy seed and her seed," that is, between the seed of the devil (ultimately the devil himself and all those who belong to him, the reprobate wicked) and the seed of the woman (ultimately Christ and all those who belong to him in eternal election). The promise of salvation, then, is not made to all men without exception, but by virtue of the promise, two lines of people develop in fallen mankind—the line of God's elect friends in covenant with him in Christ, and the line of God's reprobate enemies, allied with the devil in opposition to God.

This enmity would manifest itself very clearly in Old Testament history. Eve had a son (whom she called Cain) because she mistakenly believed that he would be the promised seed. In fact, Cain was the first manifestation of the seed of the serpent, the first of the devil's brood. John explains this enmity: "Not as Cain, who was of that wicked one, and slew his brother. And wherefore slew he him? Because his own works were evil, and his brother's righteous" (1 John 3:12). Later, Adam and Eve had more children, and two lines, of Cain on the one hand and Seth on the other, developed in the earth. The devil was behind every attempt of the seed of the serpent to destroy the seed of the woman. The ultimate purpose of the devil was to use his seed to prevent the coming of the great Seed of the woman, who is Christ.

That was the ultimate enmity. Christ was the enemy of Satan and came to destroy Satan. He did this in a way Satan did not expect. He crushed Satan's head on the cross while Satan was bruising his heel. Christ had to suffer in order to destroy the devil and to reconcile us to God.

That was God's promise. He would send his Son. The devil would be crushed, but only in the way of terrible suffering for the Son of God. And for that, the incarnation was necessary.

Martyn McGeown

Article 18

OF THE INCARNATION OF JESUS CHRIST

We confess, therefore, that God did fulfill the promise which he made to the fathers by the mouth of his holy prophets when he sent into the world, at the time appointed by him, his own only-begotten and eternal Son, *who took upon him the form of a servant, and became like unto men*, really assuming the true human nature, with all its infirmities, sin excepted, being conceived in the womb of the blessed Virgin Mary, by the power of the Holy Ghost, without the means of man; and did not only assume human nature as to the body, but also a true human soul, that he might be a real man. For since the soul was lost as well as the body, it was necessary that he should take both upon him, to save both. Therefore we confess (in opposition to the heresy of the Anabaptists, who deny that Christ assumed human flesh of his mother) that Christ is become *a partaker of the flesh and blood of the children*; that he is a *fruit of the loins of David* after the flesh; *made of the seed of David according to the flesh*; *a fruit of the womb* of the Virgin Mary; *made of a woman*; a *branch* of David; a shoot of *the root of Jesse*; *sprung from the tribe of Judah*; *descended from the Jews according to the flesh: of the seed of Abraham, since he took upon him the seed of Abraham, and became like unto his brethren in all things, sin excepted*; so that in truth he is our Immanuel, that is to say, *God with us*.

June 11 — **Christ Coming According to Promise**

*Yea, and all the prophets from Samuel
and those that follow after, as many as have spoken,
have likewise foretold of these days.* —Acts 3:24

All Christians believe in the incarnation. All Christians believe that the Son of God entered this world as a tiny baby. This is the greatest and most astounding of all miracles. But Article 18 gives an important perspective on this truth. The incarnation did not happen "out of the blue," but was something promised by God.

In Article 17, we took note of the fact that immediately after the fall of man, God promised a savior "to bruise the head of the serpent [Satan]" and to "make him [man] happy." This was only the beginning of many precious promises made by God to his people. The promise—a sure and certain word which depended only on God for its fulfillment—must be understood. Many Christians today (like the Jews before them) totally misunderstand the promise which God made and therefore misunderstand the reason for Christ's coming into the world. The mother promise of Genesis 3:15 promised salvation in the way of two things: destruction for the devil and suffering for the savior. Therefore, the rest of the promises in the Old Testament, which unfolded or developed the one promise, contained one or both of these aspects of the promise.

On the one hand, the promised savior would be victorious. He would destroy the enemies of God and establish a kingdom of righteousness. Genesis 49:10 promises this: "The sceptre shall not depart from Judah, nor a lawgiver from between his feet, until Shiloh come; and unto him shall the gathering of the people be." Isaiah 9:6 promises this: "For unto us a child is born, unto us a son is given: and the government shall be upon his shoulder." Thus, the Old Testament saints were taught to expect a king who would crush Satan and all God's enemies. On the other hand, the promised savior would suffer. He would be despised, rejected, bruised, and he would even die. All the sacrifices—from the daily offerings to the passover feasts—foreshadowed this, and there were many prophecies about the sufferings of Christ. Isaiah 53:5 promises this: "He was wounded for our transgressions, he was bruised for our iniquities: the chastisement of our peace was upon him; and with his stripes we are healed." Zechariah 13:7 prophesies concerning the Messiah: "Awake, O sword, against my shepherd, and against the man that is my fellow, saith the Lord of hosts: smite the shepherd, and the sheep shall be scattered."

When Christ was born, Israel groaned under Rome's oppressive yoke. Many Israelites who looked for the Messiah—and remember, no prophecy of the Lord had been given for four hundred years after Malachi—longed for the wrong kind of deliverance. Since a suffering Messiah made no sense to them, they ignored the passages about a suffering savior and clung to a wrong interpretation of passages about a conquering king. This was true not only of the unbelieving multitudes, but even of the disciples themselves. Not until after the death and resurrection of Christ did they understand how the twofold promise of a conquering and suffering savior made sense, and how Christ was victorious in his sufferings.

Thus, Christ rebuked them: "O fools, and slow of heart to believe all that the prophets have spoken: ought not Christ to have suffered these things, and to enter into his glory?" (Luke 24:25–26). All the promises of God in the Old Testament are fulfilled in Jesus Christ in the New Testament. Thus, we see that our God is faithful, and we have good hope to trust in him!

Martyn McGeown

June 12 — Christ Coming at the Appointed Time

But when the fulness of the time was come, God sent forth his Son, made of a woman, made under the law. —Galatians 4:4

God, unlike us, is never in a hurry. Sometimes, in our foolishness and impatience, we think that God is unnecessarily slow in the fulfillment of his promises. About the incarnation—the great miracle by which God, sending his own Son into the world, was made flesh and dwelt among us—Article 18 says that it occurred "at the time appointed by him [God]."

The time of the incarnation—as is the time of every event in history—is eternally determined by God. Paul explained this to the Athenians: God "hath determined the times before appointed" (Acts 17:26). God determined the time of your birth, and he has determined the point of your death. If that is true of us, how much more did God not appoint the time of the birth, death, resurrection, and second coming of his Son, upon whom our salvation depends?

Eve did not understand this. When she exclaimed in joy, "I have gotten a man from the Lord" (Gen. 4:1), she believed that Cain was the seed of the woman. This was understandable in the circumstances, and it was a testimony to the fact that hope lived in her heart. But Eve and all God's people had to learn by bitter experience that God's promise is not fulfilled according to our timetable. God exercised the patience of his people for many centuries before Christ came. God promised Abraham a son, but he made Abraham wait for a long time before Abraham saw the promised Isaac, and Isaac himself was not the promised Christ. Much later, God promised David that the Messiah would be of the fruit of his loins, but Solomon was not the promised Christ either.

Why did God—from our perspective—delay his promise?

First, he would teach his people to long for the coming of the promised Christ. The closer we come to the end of the Old Testament, the greater is the longing of God's elect. The heyday of David and Solomon lasted less than a century; the kingdom was divided, and the ten tribes of the northern kingdom perished; the southern kingdom of Judah was decimated in Babylon, and only a miserable remnant returned. Never again did a Davidic king sit on Jerusalem's throne. Between the return under Zerubbabel and the coming of Christ, the royal line was preserved, but it never became prominent again. Even the rebuilt temple paled in significance before Solomon's temple, and the ark of the covenant was never restored. God would take the eyes of the people away from the types and shadows of the Old Testament and have them long more earnestly for Christ (see Heb. 8:13).

Second, God would teach his people that they could not produce the promised savior. God brought the line of David almost to extinction to prove that only he had the power to fulfill the promise. David's line ended with a virgin, living when a cruel Edomite ruled over Israel by the authority of Caesar. Surely, she could not bring forth the promised savior!

When the condition of God's people was at its darkest, when hope was all but extinguished, God sent forth his Son. God delights to do this so that his glory, power, wisdom, and grace shine all the brighter. Are you able to trust him even now as you wait for the second coming?

Martyn McGeown

June 13 — Christ Coming in the Wonder of the Incarnation

And the Word was made flesh, and dwelt among us.
—John 1:14

Having seen that the incarnation was promised and that the entire Old Testament was preparation for it—although many of the Jews did not understand what God had actually promised and expected a Christ according to their own carnal desires—we examine the incarnation itself.

The word *incarnation* comes from the Latin word for *flesh* and means that God took upon him human flesh. John 1:14 tells us: "And the Word was made flesh." The Word is the eternal Son of God, one who was and is "in the bosom of the Father" with God, and "who was God" (vv. 1–2, 18). We must understand that the incarnation is not the birth of a mere man, nor is it even the birth of an extraordinary, supernatural man. The incarnation is nothing less than the birth of one into our world as a real human being who is God.

God, without ever ceasing to be God, became man. The incarnation presupposes the doctrines which the Belgic Confession has already taught us. It presupposes the doctrine of the Trinity, for the Son, and not the Father or the Holy Spirit, became flesh. One of the three persons of the Godhead—who are coequal, coeternal, and coessential with one another, and yet distinct from one another—became a man. It presupposes the deity of the Lord Jesus Christ, that the one who became incarnate was not a mighty angel or even the greatest of all creatures, but the eternal, only begotten Son of God. It presupposes, too, the depravity of man, because so great is our sin and so deep is our misery, that only the extreme measure of the Son becoming flesh in order to suffer for our sins is sufficient to deliver us from sin, death, and the curse.

The incarnation was the Son coming into the world and the Father's sending him into the world through the power of the Holy Spirit. The triune God purposed the incarnation in his eternal counsel. The Father would send the Son, the Son would go and suffer, and the Spirit would perform the work necessary for the Son to become incarnate.

We must understand this for our salvation and comfort. The little baby born in Bethlehem was the Son of God. The little boy who played with the other boys in the streets of Nazareth and who submitted to his mother and Joseph was the Son of God. The young man, the carpenter's son, was the Son of God. The man who was baptized, tempted, and who preached for some three-and-a-half years was the Son of God. The man who struggled in prayer in Gethsemane, was arrested, tried, beaten, spat upon, mocked, and finally crucified, was the Son of God. The man who died on the cross after crying out, "Father, into thy hands I commend my spirit" (Luke 23:46), was the Son of God. The man who rose from the dead, ascended into heaven, sits at God's right hand, and will come again to judge the living and the dead, is the Son of God. He was (and is) the Son of God in our human nature, but he was (and is) also the Son of God in heavenly glory.

Article 18 sums it up in these words: "[God] sent into the world, at the time appointed by him, his own, only begotten and eternal Son."

This means that the Son, who is eternally in the bosom of the Father, without losing or laying aside his divinity, took to himself a human nature, thus becoming what he was not before, a man. And he did this for our salvation!

Martyn McGeown

June 14 — The Son of God Really Assuming the Human Nature

Every spirit that confesseth that Jesus Christ is come in the flesh is of God: and every spirit that confesseth not that Jesus Christ is come in the flesh is not of God. —1 John 4:2–3

How could God become man? Around this question swirled controversy in the early church. First, it seemed to be impossible. There is an infinite gulf between the essence of God and the nature of man. The Son of God as God is eternal, unchangeable, and infinite. The nature of man is limited by time and space, dependent and weak. How could God become man? Second, it seemed to be unfitting. This was especially true because of false notions about spirit and matter among the pagans. Many held the notion—and brought that false idea into the church—that matter (such as flesh and blood) is evil. How could God become flesh and blood? To the first objection, Scripture responds in Luke 1:37, "With God nothing shall be impossible." We cannot understand it, but we believe it. To the second objection Scripture responds in 1 Timothy 4:4, "Every creature of God is good." Flesh and physical matter are not evil.

The incarnation of the Son of God was attacked and denied, and it still is today. One popular heresy was to say that Christ did not have a real human nature. He just seemed to be a man. He was a phantom, a spirit, an apparition, but not a real man. John refutes that heresy in his first epistle: "That which was from the beginning, which we have heard, which we have seen with our eyes, which we have looked upon, and our hands have handled, of the Word of life" (1 John 1:1). Notice how Scripture insists that Jesus Christ had a real human nature.

How important this is for our salvation! When Jesus wept, he wept real human tears. When Jesus sweated, he sweated real human sweat. When Jesus bled, he bled real human blood. When Jesus was scourged, his real human flesh was torn. When Jesus suffered, real human pain receptors from real human nerves sent messages to a real human brain. Yet the one who wept, sweated, bled, was wounded, suffered, and felt pain was the Son of God! Jesus had to be a man in every sense in which we are humans because he came to satisfy the justice of God for the sins of his people which we have committed in the human nature.

Another error concerning the incarnation was to deny the completeness of Christ's humanity. Various heresies existed in the early church. One man denied that Jesus had a human soul; another denied that he had a human will. Article 18 answers all these objections in these words: "[the Son of God] did not only assume human nature as to the body, but also a true human soul, that he might be a real man. For since the soul was lost as well as the body, it was necessary that he should take both upon him, to save both."

This, too, was important for our salvation. Jesus had a real, human soul. This means that Jesus thought the thoughts of a real human mind. When Jesus experienced emotions, such as sorrow (Matt. 26:38) and joy (Luke 10:21), he experienced real human emotions. When Jesus wrestled in prayer "with strong crying and tears" in the garden of Gethsemane (Heb. 5:7), he was consciously submitting his real human will to the divine will (Matt. 26:39, 42). In none of this was Jesus playacting. We should also notice, for this will help us understand the gospel accounts of our Savior, that Jesus did not have an omniscient soul, for that would not be a human soul. Therefore, the man Jesus, although he is God, did not know everything in his human mind: he learned (Heb. 5:8), he "increased in wisdom" (Luke 2:52), and he was ignorant (Mark 13:32).

No wonder Paul exclaims: "And without controversy great is the mystery of godliness" (1 Tim. 3:16)!

Martyn McGeown

June 15 — The Son of God Taking Upon Him the Form of a Servant

But made himself of no reputation, and took upon him the form of a servant, and was made in the likeness of men. —Philippians 2:7

What kind of human nature did the Son of God take to himself in the incarnation? We have seen it was a real human nature. Jesus Christ was as really human as you or I. We have seen that it was a complete human nature. Since we are flesh and blood, Jesus took upon himself our flesh and blood. Since we are body and soul, Jesus took upon himself body and soul, so that he could both sympathize with us as our high priest (Heb. 2:17–18, 4:15–16), and so that he could save us body and soul.

There are two other adjectives commonly used to describe Christ's human nature. First, it was a weakened human nature; and second, it was a sinless human nature. A weakened human nature is one which is subject to the effects of man's fall. We must not think by the word *weakened* that the human nature which Christ assumed was fallen or sinful, but it was weakened by the fall. This means that Christ could feel pain, that he could suffer, and that he could die. Adam, although human, had not felt pain, suffered, or been subjected to death before the fall, and Jesus, although still human, cannot feel pain, suffer, or die in heaven. Therefore, we confess with Article 18 that Christ assumed "the true human nature, with all its infirmities." Although Christ's human nature was weakened by the effects of the fall, it was not sinful. To Christ was not imputed the original guilt of Adam. Christ's human nature was not ruined by original corruption, pollution, or total depravity. Thus, Article 18 adds "sin excepted." Romans 8:3 expresses it succinctly in this phrase: "in the likeness of sinful flesh." It was real human flesh, but it was in the likeness of sinful flesh.

This weakened human nature was part of Christ's humiliation. In the doctrine of Christ, we distinguish two states of Christ. For a time, from his conception to his death and burial, the Son of God was in a state of humiliation. This means that he was, in a legal position before God, guilty of the sins of his people. God reckoned or imputed the sins of all the elect to Christ. That was the only legal basis for Christ's suffering. Only as one guilty of our sin could Christ, the Son of God, suffer. From his resurrection and forever into eternity, the Son of God is in a state of exaltation. This means that he has removed from himself—and from us whom he represents—all guilt, so that he is beyond all possibility of suffering or shame.

The humiliation of the Son of God in our human nature is astounding. We might imagine that when the Son of God became a man, he chose for himself the human nature and the earthly splendor of a king or of an emperor. Jesus chose—because we must remember that as the eternal Son of God he orchestrated all the events surrounding his birth—to be born of an obscure virgin in a backward village called Nazareth. Furthermore, he chose to be born into abject poverty, and even to be born in a stable and laid in a manger, a feeding trough for animals. Moreover, he chose to be a servant—the lowliest slave—and to suffer the most shameful and painful death, the death of crucifixion.

And he did that for us and for our salvation. Truly a wonder worth celebrating!

Martyn McGeown

June 16

Christ Descended from the Jews According to the Flesh

For verily he took not on him the nature of angels;
but he took on him the seed of Abraham. —Hebrews 2:16

If you had seen Jesus as he walked on the earth and taught in the villages and synagogues of Israel, you would have seen a Jew. The man Jesus Christ worshipped the God Jehovah or Yahweh. The man Jesus Christ grew up in the home of a Jewish mother and his adopted Jewish father. The man Jesus Christ had Jewish siblings (Matt. 13:55–56). Jesus also attended the obligatory feasts of the Jews in Jerusalem and attended the public worship of the Jews in his local synagogue (Luke 4:16).

The Son of God—as a real, complete, weakened, and sinless human being—worshipped God and called God his God and his Father (Matt. 26:39; John 20:17). The Son of God does not worship, pray to, or prostrate himself before the Father in the Godhead—the three persons of God are coequal—but the Son of God in our flesh, our mediator, does.

But there is more to Christ's Jewishness than his worship. Jesus Christ was biologically a Jew. If you had seen him, he would not have looked as many misleading artworks depict him. He had a typical Semitic appearance, and Isaiah 53:2 indicates that he was not particularly attractive in his physical appearance: "when we shall see him, there is no beauty that we should desire him."

In God's remarkable providence, the biological line of God's people was preserved. The man Jesus can trace his genealogy all the way back to Abraham (Matt. 1:1) and even to Adam (Luke 3:38). This, too, is the fruit of God's promise. Why had God preserved the biological line of his people through Abraham, Isaac, Jacob, Judah, David, and all the way to Mary, if not to fulfill his promise that the Christ would be organically related to his people? Thus, Article 18 lists a number of phrases taken from the Scriptures to prove that Jesus Christ was not a nondescript man, but a man who came from the covenant line. According to the flesh, the man Jesus Christ is "a fruit of the loins of David." The human nature of Jesus can be traced back to David, so that biologically Jesus Christ is related to David and can be called David's son. Since Jesse was David's biological father, Jesus Christ, the son of David, is called "a shoot of the root of Jesse." Since Abraham is a distant biological ancestor of David, or David is a distant biological descendant of Abraham, Jesus Christ is called "of the seed of Abraham, since he took on him the seed of Abraham."

Even more distantly, Jesus Christ is biologically related to us, because we (like him) can trace our biological line all the way back to Adam, our first organic father. For this reason—but especially because we are adopted by grace as the children of the Father, for, remember, it is of no benefit to be biologically related to Christ if we remain unbelieving—we can call Jesus Christ, the Son of God in our flesh, our elder brother.

Astounding are the words of Hebrews 2:11, "he is not ashamed to call them brethren." Do you believe—whether as an ethnic Jew or Gentile—in this Savior? He, by virtue of his incarnation and his death on the cross for your sins, is not ashamed to call you his brother or sister.

Martyn McGeown

June 17   **Of the Flesh and Blood of the Virgin Mary**

The Holy Ghost shall come upon thee,
and the power of the Highest shall overshadow thee: therefore also that
holy thing which shall be born of thee shall be called the Son of God. —Luke 1:35

We have partially answered the question already concerning the origin of the human nature of Jesus Christ. The human nature, we have seen, was real, complete, weakened, and sinless, and biologically of the line of God's covenant people through Adam, Abraham, and David. This emphasis was necessary because of the heresy of the Anabaptists who "deny that Christ assumed human flesh of his mother" (Article 18). One of the purposes of Article 18 which we have seen was to repudiate the Anabaptist position. At that time, the Roman Catholic authorities used the Anabaptist error as a pretext to persecute the Reformed. The Anabaptists were a radical sect who not only denied infant baptism, but also claimed direct revelation from the Spirit and had revolutionary tendencies. One Anabaptist notion concerned the human nature of Christ.

The Anabaptists believed that it was impossible for the human nature of Jesus Christ to be holy if it was the human nature derived from Mary's flesh. Therefore, some of them taught that the Holy Spirit brought heavenly flesh and deposited it in the womb of Mary. The Anabaptists said that Christ was conceived by the Holy Spirit, born in the virgin Mary, but they did not want to confess that Christ was born of the virgin Mary. Do you see the difference between *in* and *of* here? Mary was therefore simply a basket in which the Spirit deposited Christ, or Mary was a pipe through which Christ flowed. But Christ had no biological relation to Mary, and certainly did not derive his flesh from Mary. This is a serious error. It really is a denial of the true humanity of Jesus, for "heavenly flesh"—whatever that is—is not real human flesh and blood.

We confess that Mary was the true biological mother of Jesus according to the flesh. We must not, however, err on the other side by elevating Mary. Mary was not sinless, as the Roman Catholic Church teaches. She did not even need to be sinless to give birth to the sinless Christ. How is it possible that the Son of God, in uniting himself to the human nature of Mary, a sinner, remained sinless? The angel answered thus to Mary: "The Holy Ghost shall come upon thee, and the power of the Highest shall overshadow thee: therefore also that holy thing which shall be born of thee shall be called the Son of God" (Luke 1:35). The Holy Spirit shielded the human nature, which he formed in the womb of the virgin Mary, from any pollution of Mary's flesh.

What a great mystery is this! How did God knit you together in your mother's womb? How does God form the soul and unite it to the body? The greatest minds among men have not been able to understand that fully. How much greater is the conception of the Son of God! The Holy Spirit formed a human embryo from the flesh and blood of Mary "without the means of man" (Article 18), and he united the human nature (body and soul) which he formed to the person of the Son of God, overshadowing the miracle and producing a real, complete, weakened, and sinless human nature.

Thus, the holy Son of God was conceived and born in our human nature. "For unto us a child is born, unto us a son is given" (Isa. 9:6), to be our Savior, our Immanuel, that is to say, God with us!

Martyn McGeown

Article 19

OF THE UNION AND DISTINCTION OF THE TWO NATURES IN THE PERSON OF CHRIST

We believe that by this conception the person of the Son is inseparably united and connected with the human nature; so that there are not two Sons of God, nor two persons, but two natures united in one single person; yet each nature retains its own distinct properties. As then the divine nature hath always remained uncreated, without beginning of days or end of life, filling heaven and earth, so also hath the human nature not lost its properties, but remained a creature, having beginning of days, being a finite nature, and retaining all the properties of a real body. And though he hath by his resurrection given immortality to the same, nevertheless he hath not changed the reality of his human nature; forasmuch as our salvation and resurrection also depend on the reality of his body. But these two natures are so closely united in one person, that they were not separated even by his death. Therefore that which he, when dying, commended into the hands of his Father, was a real human spirit, departing from his body. But in the mean time the divine nature always remained united with the human, even when he lay in the grave; and the Godhead did not cease to be in him, any more than it did when he was an infant, though it did not so clearly manifest itself for a while.

Wherefore we confess that he is very God and very Man: very God by his power to conquer death, and very man that he might die for us according to the infirmity of his flesh.

June 18 — Understanding Christological Terms

Verily, verily, I say unto you, Before Abraham was, I am.
—John 8:58

Jesus Christ is both God and man. That is the simple, but profound, confession of Christianity. He, who is and remains the eternal Son of God, became and remains a real, complete man forever. The subject of Article 19 is the relationship between Christ as God and Christ as man.

To understand this great truth, we must be clear about religious terminology. First, the person of Jesus Christ is the eternal Son of God. We encountered the term *person* in Article 8–11 when we studied the doctrine of the Trinity. There we noted that God, although one in his divine essence (there is but one God), is three persons, the Father, the Son, and the Holy Spirit. God is three persons. We are one person. Christ is one person. But your pet cat is not a person; a tree is not a person; a rock is not a person. A person is a conscious and self-conscious individual, distinct from other individuals, who says *I*. The Greek word *person* (*hypostasis*) means *that which stands under*. Your person, therefore, is that which "stands under" all your activity. In the Godhead, there are three persons, each one distinct and individual from—but not independent of—one another. The Father says, "I," but he is neither the Son nor the Holy Spirit. The Son says, "I," but he is neither the Father nor the Holy Spirit. As a human person, you say, "I," and you can know yourself, and you can know and interact with other persons, but you are distinct from other persons.

Now, who is the person of Jesus Christ? Is Jesus Christ a human person, or does he have a human person? Is the one who says, "I," in Jesus Christ a man? Or is the one who says, "I," in Jesus Christ God? Is Jesus Christ, therefore, a divine person? Or is Jesus Christ two persons, each saying "I," a kind of dual personality or schizophrenia? The Reformed position is that "the person of the Son is…united…with the human nature, so that there are…two natures united in one single person."

The second technical, theological term we must understand is *nature*. Jesus Christ, who as to his person is the eternal, only begotten Son of God, has two natures. The nature of something is what it is: it is the sum total of the qualities or attributes of a thing. So, the human nature of Christ is his being man, his body, flesh, blood, soul, will, and everything else that makes someone human. Christ is as human as you or I—he is, as our creeds put it, "very man." Everything that man is (except sin, of course, which is not essential to the being of man), Jesus Christ is. The divine nature of Christ is his being God, his infinite divine essence or being. Christ is as divine as the Father or the Holy Spirit—he is, as our creeds put it, "very God." Everything that God is, Jesus Christ is. Thus, Jesus Christ possesses the essence, the names, and the attributes, and receives the worship of God.

This was the confession of the Christian church from the beginning. The difficulty the church had was to understand the relationship between the divine and the human in Jesus Christ. The church came to an understanding of this truth only through great struggle.

And we must understand this for our salvation and comfort because only one who is both God and man, in two distinct natures, in one divine person, can be our savior.

Martyn McGeown

June 19 — The Errors of Nestorianism and Eutychianism

He saith unto them, But whom say ye that I am?
—Matthew 16:15

There are two main errors, which the early church rejected, with respect to the relationship between the two natures of Christ. We must remember that the Bible does not provide for us the theological terms *person* and *nature*. Therefore, as the Holy Spirit led the church into all truth, the church coined her own terms so that she could give a coherent confession of her faith. But before the church officially defined the doctrine of Christ, men arose with wrong ideas, ideas that had to be rejected.

The first error was Nestorianism. Nestorius (c. 386–451 AD) concluded that since Christ has two natures, Christ must be (or have) two persons. Thus, Nestorianism teaches two Christs, one a divine Christ, and the other a human Christ, and a dual personality. Nestorius tried to explain the union between the two natures in Christ as that of a marriage—just as a man and a woman become "one flesh" in marriage (Gen. 2:24), so the human and divine are one in Christ. Another illustration helpful in explaining Nestorianism is two peas in a pod, or two eggs sitting side by side in a basket. The problem, of course, is this: in Nestorianism, there is no connection between the human and divine in Christ. They are separate, even independent of one another. Nestorianism is condemned in Article 19: "The person of the Son is inseparably united and connected with the human nature, so that there are not two Sons of God, nor two persons, but two natures united in one single person."

Nestorianism is a dangerous heresy because it separates what God has united in the incarnation of the Son of God. If Jesus Christ is (or has) two persons, what he does in one nature has no relationship with what he does in the other nature. And this has serious implications for the cross. If the sufferings of Jesus Christ are the sufferings of a mere man—in whom somehow a separate person called the Son of God lived—how can they have any value for our salvation? If the human nature and divine nature are not personally united, how could the man Jesus Christ bear up under the infinite weight of the wrath of God? The Heidelberg Catechism has this in mind: "Why must he be at the same time true God? That by the power of his Godhead he might bear, in his manhood, the burden of God's wrath, and so obtain for and restore to us righteousness and life."*

The other error was Eutychianism. Eutyches (c. 380–456 AD) concluded that since Christ is one person, Christ must have one nature. Notice how the truth lies between the middle of two extreme errors. Nestorius taught two natures, two persons. Eutyches taught one person, one nature. The truth is one person, two natures. The nature of Christ, concluded Eutyches, is neither human nor divine, but a humanized divinity or a divinized humanity. If Nestorius imagined two eggs lying side by side in a basket with no real connection to one another, Eutyches imagined two substances blended to form a third substance. Thus, the Christ of Eutychianism is neither human nor divine. Article 19 answers Eutychianism in these words: "each nature retains its own distinct properties." Eutychianism also endangers our salvation because a Christ who is neither God nor man cannot suffer in the human nature—he does not have a real human nature distinct from the divine nature—on the cross.

How important is our confession of Christ: one Christ, in two distinct natures, in one person forever! And how thankful we are for the Spirit's work in leading the church into the truth!

Martyn McGeown

---

* Heidelberg Catechism 17, in Schaff, *Creeds of Christendom*, 3:312.

June 20 — The Distinct Properties of the Divine Nature

For in him dwelleth all the fulness of the Godhead bodily.
—Colossians 2:9

Jesus Christ, by virtue of the incarnation, has two natures. The Son of God is, was, and always has been God. The Son of God became, was, and remains forever man. These two natures are united in the one Christ in the person of the Son of God, and therefore they cannot be separated from one another. However, they can and must be distinguished from one another.

The divine nature of Christ is everything which a divine nature must be. Article 19 lists some of its qualities. First, it is eternal because it "hath always remained uncreated, without beginning of days or end of life." Therefore, Christ, according to his divine nature, has no beginning. He always is. He is unchangeable: he is not born, he does not grow, and he can never die. Jesus declared to the Jews who scoffed at his claim to have seen Abraham: "Before Abraham was, I am" (John 8:58). Not only does Jesus Christ, as the Son of God have preexistence, he eternally is, as eternal as the Father and the Holy Spirit. Second, it is omnipresent, "filling heaven and earth." Christ, according to his divine nature, is not limited by time or space, and he is simultaneously on earth and heaven, and indeed his divine essence (which is the same divine essence of the Father and the Son in the holy Trinity) is present everywhere. Therefore, Christ, according to his divine nature, does not move from one location to another. He did not descend, and he did not ascend. Jesus puts it very strikingly in John 3:13, "And no man hath ascended up to heaven, but he that came down from heaven, even the Son of man which is in heaven." As Jesus Christ spoke to Nicodemus in Jerusalem he could claim as the Son of man that he was dwelling in the very presence of God! Later, Jesus says to the Jews: "Ye shall seek me, and shall not find me: and where I am, thither ye cannot come" (John 7:34). Jesus does not say, "Where I shall be," but, "Where I am." And he is speaking about heaven. Jesus is, as to his divine nature, both in heaven and on earth. Third, we can mention other divine attributes not mentioned by Article 19. Jesus Christ, as to his divine nature, was and is omniscient, knowing all things with perfect knowledge. He was also omnipotent, possessing the power not only to do mighty miracles—raise the dead, heal the sick, calm the sea, cast out demons—but also to sustain the heavy burden of God's wrath on the cross, to conquer death, to crush Satan's head, and to raise himself from the dead on the third day.

This divine nature never changed. Never did the Son lose any of the attributes of his divine nature. Article 19 gives two striking instances of this: in his birth and childhood, and in his death and burial. "The Godhead did not cease to be in him [when he lay in the grave], any more than it did when he was an infant, though it did not so clearly manifest itself for a while" (Article 19).

But at the same time, the one who was eternal, unchangeable, omnipresent, omniscient, and almighty, the one who never laid aside or lost any of his divine attributes, was a true and complete man. About this Jesus Christ the apostle Paul writes, "God was manifest in the flesh" (1 Tim. 3:16) and "in him dwelleth all the fullness of the Godhead bodily" (Col 2:9).

Thus, the man Jesus Christ is God.

And his human nature we will consider next time.

Martyn McGeown

June 21 — The Distinct Properties of the Human Nature

I thirst. —John 19:28

Yesterday, we saw that Jesus Christ has two natures, and we looked at the properties of his divine nature. As the Son of God, Jesus Christ is eternal, unchangeable, omnipresent, omniscient, and almighty in his divine nature. The man who lived on earth for some thirty-three years is God in human flesh.

But we are not finished. The divine nature must be distinguished from his human nature.

Just as the divine nature must possess divine attributes to be divine, so the human nature of Christ must possess human qualities to be human. Quite simply, when Jesus Christ lived on earth, his human nature possessed essentially the same human qualities which your human nature does. Article 19 explains: "So also hath the human nature not lost its properties, but remained a creature, having beginning of days, being a finite nature, and retaining all the properties of a real body."

We must not think that, because the human nature was (and is) united to the divine nature, some of the divine attributes were passed on to it. For example, with respect to Christ's human nature, he changed. He began as a tiny baby, and he grew physically until he reached a certain height and weight. This was not true of his unchangeable divine nature. With respect to his human nature, he was limited by both time and space. Christ could not exist in his human nature in two places at once. He had to travel from Jerusalem to Nazareth, and this took him time, just as when you walk from one place to another, it is a real change of time and place. Christ's human nature had a beginning—unlike his divine nature—so that the body and soul of the man Jesus Christ did not exist before the incarnation. In fact, Article 19 calls the humanity of Christ "a creature." As the eternal Son of God, Christ is the creator. As the man Christ Jesus with respect to his humanity, Christ is a creature!

This explains what we read in the Gospel accounts. Jesus Christ was born as a human being, but as the Son of God he is eternally begotten (Luke 2:11; John 1:18). Jesus Christ hungered, thirsted, sweated, grew tired, slept, and experienced pain as a human being, but as the Son of God, he is impassible, unable to suffer, the God who is never weary and is utterly independent of the creation (Matt. 21:18; John 19:28; Luke 22:44; John 4:6; Mark 4:38; 1 Pet. 2:23; Isa. 40:28; Ps. 50:12–13). Jesus Christ was ignorant of things because as a man he did not have an omniscient soul, but as the Son of God he is omniscient (Mark 13:32; John 1:48, 4:29, 21:17). Jesus Christ prostrated himself before the Father, worshipping him as his God and submitting himself to the divine will, because as a man he was the servant of God, but as the eternal Son of God, the second person of the holy Trinity, he is subordinate to none and is himself worshipped (Matt. 26:39–44; Matt. 8:2; John 9:38). Finally, Jesus Christ died, which can only be true of him with respect to his human nature. The divine nature neither sheds blood—there is no such thing as divine blood—nor dies, but the man Christ Jesus died. "Therefore," explains Article 19, "that which he, when dying, commended into the hands of his Father, was a real human spirit, departing from his body."

Behold our Savior! God in the flesh, possessing all the powers, attributes, and glory of God. A real man, with flesh and blood as real as ours. A real man with a real human soul, mind, and will. Who can fully comprehend the mystery? Ours is to worship and adore him.

Martyn McGeown

June 22 — The Hypostatic Union

Had they known it, they would not have crucified the Lord of glory. —1 Corinthians 2:8

We have seen that the doctrine of Christ is complicated. First, the terminology we use—*person* and *nature*—is not found in Scripture but was developed by the church from scriptural principles. Second, we must avoid falling into the error of Nestorianism—two natures, two persons—on the one hand, and Eutychianism—one person, one nature—on the other hand. The orthodox view is one person, two natures. Third, a careful distinction must be maintained between the human and divine in Jesus Christ. He is both omniscient and ignorant; both infinite and limited; both omnipotent and weak; both without a beginning and with a beginning. The only way in which this makes sense is to confess that Christ is omniscient as God with respect to his divine nature, and that he is ignorant as man with respect to his human nature.

These two natures are united, joined, or connected. We must consider this next. The union of the two natures is unique. It is not the "one flesh" union of a man and a woman in marriage because that is the union of two persons. It is not the union of two chemical substances, which, when they react together, form a third substance, such as the union of hydrogen and oxygen to form water. The theological explanation for this union is the hypostatic union. The word *hypostatic* comes from the Greek word *hypostasis* which means *person*. Hypostatic union, therefore, means personal union.

Remember what (or who) the person of Christ is: Christ's person is the conscious and self-conscious subject of all of Christ's activity. That sounds complicated, but remember that the subject is the one performing the action. Therefore, the subject is the one who says, "I." When Jesus Christ said, "I," or when he did or experienced anything, the person of Christ—the eternal Son of God, the second divine person of the Trinity—was the one doing the action or experiencing the thing. At the same time, the one person of the Son of God acted in and through the two distinct natures, human and divine. We must remember this because, strictly speaking, the nature of Christ does not perform the activity. Only the person does. This is true with us too, although our person is not divine. For example, when you feel hungry you do not say, "My stomach feels hungry," but, "I feel hungry." When you sleep, you do not say, "My body slept," but, "I slept." When you cry, you do not say, "My eyes are crying," but, "I am crying." Think similarly of Christ: the person of the Son of God was hungry, tired, slept, wept, and died! Be very careful not to misunderstand. We did not write, "God was hungry, tired, wept, and died." But notice also that we did not write, "The human nature of Christ was hungry, tired, wept, and died." Christ did these things, and he did them as the Son of God! On the other hand, when we say that Christ created, we do not mean that the divine nature of Christ created; we mean that the person of the Son of God created (which is only true of his divine nature, not his human nature).

So close therefore is the union of the divine and human in the one Christ that what can be said of either nature—he wept, he thirsted, or he created the universe—can be said of the one person. Thus, it was proper of Paul to write, "They...crucified the Lord of glory" (1 Cor. 2:8) or to speak of "the church of God, which he hath purchased with his own blood" (Acts 20:28).

When we speak, therefore, of Christ, we say: "The Son of God acted according to his [human or divine] nature." Always the one Son of God acts according to, in and through, his natures. Never are these natures confused, and never are they separated.

Martyn McGeown

June 23 — The Glorified Human Nature Really Human

Who shall change our vile body, that it may be fashioned like unto his glorious body, according to the working whereby he is able even to subdue all things unto himself. —Philippians 3:21

Article 19 has its eye on the Lutherans. At the time of the Reformation there were three main groups in Christendom. The Roman Catholics were the persecuting majority. Guido de Brès, who wrote the Confession, died a martyr's death at the hand of Romish authorities. The Anabaptists, as we have seen, were a radical group, some of whom espoused various heresies, such as Christ's heavenly flesh, direct revelations of the Spirit, a denial of infant baptism, and rebellion against the state. They are condemned in several articles of the Belgic Confession. The third group, with whom the Reformers had very much in common, were the Lutherans. The tragic error of Luther and the Lutheran churches concerned Christ's presence in the Lord's supper, an error which spawned a Christological error.

The question which exercised the minds of the Lutherans was this: How can Christ be bodily present in the Lord's supper? The Reformed denied such a bodily presence, for good reason as we shall see in Article 35. The Lutherans concluded that the human nature of Christ became ubiquitous or immense at his ascension. *Ubiquitous* means *present in many places at once* and is akin to the word *omnipresent*. But how is it possible for a real human nature to be ubiquitous? The answer of Lutheranism was that by virtue of the hypostatic union the divine nature communicated (or shared) some of its properties with the human nature. Lutheranism illustrated it thus: just as iron when placed into a fire becomes red hot and glows with the properties of fire, although the fire does not receive any of the properties of the iron, so the human nature when united with the divine nature glows with the divine attributes and thus becomes ubiquitous. Most Lutherans say that this communication of properties happened at the ascension. Lutheranism also caricatured the Reformed view: the Reformed, said the Lutherans, view the two natures as two boards glued together where neither board confers anything upon the other board (see the Formula of Concord, Art. 8, para. 5). You can probably see that the Lutheran view is a form of Eutychianism—a blending of the two natures—and that the Lutherans accuse the Reformed of a form of Nestorianism—a separation of the two natures.

The divine nature does not share its attributes with the human nature. A ubiquitous or omnipresent human nature is impossible because a human nature, by definition, must be finite and limited by space. There was (and is), however, a close personal union between the two natures, such that the one person of the Son could sustain his human nature on the cross by the power of his divine nature. Similarly, the weight of glory and the fullness of the Spirit, with which the Son of God is glorified in his human nature, are only possible because the Son of God is both human and divine.

Nevertheless, the human nature of Christ remains human even after it is glorified and after it becomes immortal in the resurrection. "The human nature [hath] not lost its properties…He hath not changed the reality of his human nature, forasmuch as our salvation and resurrection also depend on the reality of his body" (Article 19) If our human nature—not a divinized, immense, or ubiquitous nature—is not in heaven, we have no hope of going there. But because Christ took our human nature, not to lay it aside at his resurrection but to glorify it, we have confidence that he will take us body and soul to heaven to be with him.

Martyn McGeown

June 24 — The Two Natures Never Separated

Fear not; I am the first and the last: I am he that liveth, and was dead; and, behold, I am alive for evermore. —Revelation 1:17–18

The hypostatic union, the personal union of the two natures in Jesus Christ, shall never end. That union began at Christ's conception by the Holy Spirit in the womb of the virgin Mary. At that time, the Son of God became a man. The Son of God remained a man throughout his thirty-three years on earth, in his death on the cross and in his resurrection and ascension. He remains a man today and shall be a man forever. The orthodox teach this about the Son of God, that remaining what he was, he became what he was not. The Son of God became and remains forever man without ever ceasing to be God.

Article 19 contains some of the most striking language concerning this inseparable union found in any creed.

> These two natures are so closely united in one person, that they were not separated even by his death...The divine nature always remained united with the human, even when he lay in the grave; and the Godhead did not cease to be in him, any more than it did when he was an infant, though it did not so clearly manifest itself for a while. (Article 19)

In death, the human nature of Christ was divided, which means that his real human soul or spirit separated from his real human body. The same thing happens to us when we die. For three days his spirit or soul—which, being a real human soul, and therefore not an omnipresent soul—was in heaven (Luke 23:43, 46), and his real human body, lifeless and dead, remained under the power of death in the grave. But what about his divine nature? What about the person of the Son of God? The divine nature of Christ is omnipresent, so he is everywhere present with respect to his divine nature. But Article 19 is not speaking about mere omnipresence, it is speaking about the union of the human and divine natures. The divine nature of Christ remained united to the whole human nature of Christ—to his real human body and soul—and therefore it was united to both his soul in heaven and to his body in the grave. Not even death could sever the hypostatic union between the divinity and humanity in the one Christ!

Where the human nature of Christ is—even when that human nature is divided in death—there the divine nature is inseparably united to it. But the opposite is not true. We cannot say, where the divine nature is, there the human nature is. Why not? Because that would make the human nature omnipresent. Is the human nature of Christ now in heaven and also on earth? Does the human nature of Christ fill heaven and earth? Of course not, but the divine nature does! Can the human nature appear in many different locations on earth and in heaven at the same time? No, because then it would not be a human nature!

The Heidelberg Catechism explains:

> But are not, in this way, the two natures in Christ separated from one another, if the Manhood be not wherever the Godhead is? By no means; for since the Godhead is incomprehensible and every where present, it must follow that it is indeed beyond

the bounds of the Manhood which it has assumed, but is yet none the less in the same also, and remains personally united to it.*

Perhaps you wonder about the necessity of such deep, complicated theology. Why must we believe this about Christ? Article 19 explains: "Wherefore we confess that he is very God, and very man: very God by his power to conquer death; and very man that he might die for us according to the infirmity of his flesh."

Only this Christ can save sinners such as we are!

Martyn McGeown

---

* Heidelberg Catechism 48, in Schaff, *Creeds of Christendom*, 3:322.

Article 20

GOD HATH MANIFESTED HIS JUSTICE AND MERCY IN CHRIST

We believe that God, who is perfectly merciful and just, sent his Son to assume that nature in which the disobedience was committed, to make satisfaction in the same, and to bear the punishment of sin by his most bitter passion and death. God therefore manifested his justice against his Son when he laid our iniquities upon him, and poured forth his mercy and goodness on us, who were guilty and worthy of damnation, out of mere and perfect love, giving his Son unto death for us and raising him for our justification, that through him we might obtain immortality and life eternal.

June 25 — God Perfectly Merciful and Just

Mercy and truth are met together;
righteousness and peace have kissed each other. —Psalm 85:10

Christians believe—rightly—that God is love. But for many Christians, God is only love. The other attributes of God, which are equally important, are often neglected or only begrudgingly confessed. Many in the church do not like to think about God's justice, righteousness, holiness, or wrath. Some even imagine that the God of justice was the Old Testament God, and the God of mercy is the New Testament God. Others believe that God is an angry, vindictive deity, but that Jesus came to persuade God to be merciful to us.

The Belgic Confession already taught us in Article 1 that God is simple. God's simplicity means that he is one in being and one in his attributes. The simple God cannot be a confusion of characteristics so that his love, mercy, and grace are in conflict with his justice, righteousness, and holiness. God does not overcome his justice by his mercy. God's mercy does not swallow up his justice. God's mercy is just, righteous, holy mercy. God is both justice and mercy at the same time. We have difficulty understanding that, perhaps, because we are a confusion of complicated emotions. We often find ourselves conflicted. Our hearts are in turmoil at times. But God is the ever blessed one. He is not like us. He is perfectly at harmony within himself.

God's mercy is not well-understood. Many have defined it as the delay in punishment, not giving a man the punishment he deserves. But not all delay in punishment is mercy. When God delays the punishment of the wicked it is so that they might fill the cup of iniquity and receive the heavier punishment in the end. That is not mercy! Mercy is a positive attitude of pity or compassion upon one who is miserable. God's mercy in the Bible is often called his tender mercy or his lovingkindness. When God has mercy on a sinner, he not only desires to relieve misery—and remember that our misery is our sin—but he actually, powerfully delivers from misery and makes blessed. Scripture tells us that God is "rich in mercy" (Eph. 2:4). We sing of God's mercy: "The Lord is merciful and gracious, slow to anger, and plenteous in mercy" (Ps. 103:8).

God is perfectly—eternally, unchangeably, infinitely—merciful!

And God is just. God's justice is his unswerving commitment to himself as the ultimate standard of perfection. When we say that a person or an action is just, we have in mind a standard. A judge is called just when he legislates in such a way that he upholds the law. A law might be said to be just when it is in harmony with existing legislation. There is no standard or measurement outside of God himself to which God must conform. God is the standard. God's justice is his harmony with himself. Because God is just, he must punish sin. He must be against everything that does not harmonize with himself: "For the righteous Lord loveth righteousness" (Ps. 11:7); "He is the Rock, his work is perfect: for all his ways are judgment: a God of truth and without iniquity, just and right is he" (Deut. 32:4).

That is our God—the only true God. He is perfectly merciful, overflowing in goodness and compassion for miserable sinners; and he is perfectly just, committed to righteousness and truth, incapable of the slightest deviation from perfection. This God will save sinners—for he is merciful—and he will do so in such a way that sin is punished—for he is just.

Merciful and just in Jesus Christ. Do you know this God by faith in his Son?

Martyn McGeown

June 26 — God's Son Making Satisfaction

Even as the Son of man came not to be ministered unto,
but to minister, and to give his life a ransom for many. —Matthew 20:28

God is perfectly merciful and just. God has compassion on miserable sinners and does not punish us. And God punishes sin so that salvation never contradicts his justice. This happens through satisfaction. *Satisfaction* means *to do or pay enough*. When God is satisfied—and he must be if sinners are to be saved—all the righteous demands of his law are met. God's demands are twofold.

First, God demands that the creature—man—render full, perfect, lifelong obedience. This means that we must love the Lord our God with our whole heart, soul, mind, and strength, and our neighbor as ourselves (Mark 12:30–31). That was the demand which Adam was able to fulfill by virtue of his creation in the image of God—until he fell. That demand was never revoked, and it can never be revoked. If God were to revoke that demand, he would be saying that it no longer matters to him that he be loved by his creatures. He would then be saying that he is something less than the ever-blessed God, worthy of all glory, honor, and praise. In short, God would be denying himself. The creature—whether in a state of innocence or fallen—is eternally obligated to adore God with everything that is in him. Anything less is sin.

Second, now that man has fallen into sin, God demands full payment for all sins committed against him. This means that God can never ignore the fact that we have committed sin. He can never let us get away with sin, as if sin—which is a crime against the infinite God—were nothing serious.

If God's demands are to be met, there are several possibilities. First, it might be possible that we pay what we owe to God, that we satisfy God for our own sins. But we have nothing with which to pay such a debt, and that debt increases every moment we fail to render obedience and with every transgression of God's law, not to mention that we are corrupt in our very nature! Second, it might be possible to find among men, angels, or the animals a being which could pay for our sins. God's word tells us "it is not possible that the blood of bulls and of goats should take away sins" (Heb. 10:4). Animals are not a substitute for sinful men. Angels cannot bear the punishment we deserve either because it would be unjust for God to punish an angel for the sins committed by man. Another man cannot pay our debt and bear God's punishment for our sins for two reasons. First, no man is powerful enough to endure the infinite weight of the wrath of God so that he could deliver himself—or others—from it. Second, all men are sinners, so that they could not even begin to satisfy for their own sins, never mind attempt to satisfy for our sins.

There is, therefore, only one other possibility. God satisfies his own justice in the human nature. That is exactly what God has done in Jesus Christ. God "sent his Son to assume that nature, in which the disobedience was committed, to make satisfaction in the same" (Article 20).

That is why the Son of God became a man in the incarnation. He came in our human nature to bear the punishment which we deserve to suffer forever in hell. We could never bear that punishment. God would not leave our sin unpunished.

Salvation in a substitute! What admirable goodness and mercy!

Martyn McGeown

June 27 — The Father Sending the Son

For God so loved the world, that he gave his only begotten Son,
that whosoever believeth in him should not perish,
but have everlasting life. —John 3:16

Sometimes it is said that the Son came to save us from the Father's wrath, as if God was angry with us, and Jesus by his sacrifice persuaded God to love us. It is true that the Father was angry with us, justly wrathful because we have sinned against him. But we must remember that the triune God—the Father, the Son, and the Holy Spirit—is a God of mercy and justice. We cannot pit the one person (the Father) against the Son, any more than we can pit one attribute (mercy) against another attribute (wrath).

Jesus did not have to do something to persuade the Father to love us. Jesus did not by his satisfaction persuade God not to destroy us. The Father loved us eternally, and that is the reason for his sending the Son! Here is the relationship—the Father sent the Son in love, and the Son willingly came in love. That is the teaching of Article 20: "We believe that God…sent his Son." God was the one "giving his Son unto death for us." The word of God speaks of the gift of God in sending his Son, and in the love of Christ in coming. God's love is the cause of the coming of the Son. The coming of the Son is not the cause of God's love. "For God so loved the world, that he gave his only begotten Son" (John 3:16); "Herein is love, not that we loved God, but that he loved us and sent his Son to be the propitiation for our sins" (1 John 4:10).

We must understand that the sending of Christ into the world was the promise, purpose, and plan of God from the very beginning. The Belgic Confession has taught us that already: God promised to give his Son in eternity (Titus 1:2–3); God revealed that promise to send his Son just after our first parents sinned (Gen. 3:15); God repeated that promise throughout history in various ways (through the shadows of the Old Testament law and by clear prophecies), and in the fullness of time Jesus Christ came according to that promise. God promised his Son because this is the only way in which sinners can be saved. Only in this way can God's admirable mercy be put on display, and God's strict justice be satisfied.

We must also understand that the Son of God who was sent in the incarnation came most willingly. Although the Son knew, of course, how much it would cost him to come—humiliation, shame, suffering, and death—he came willingly because of his love for the Father. This, too, is clearly revealed in Scripture: "Sacrifice and offering thou didst not desire…Then said I, Lo, I come: in the volume of the book it is written of me, I delight to do thy will, O my God: yea, thy law is within my heart" (Ps. 40:6–8; see also Heb. 10:5–10). Jesus said to his disciples: "My meat is to do the will of him that sent me, and to finish his work" (John 4:34).

And the wonder is this: Jesus was willing to perform the will of the Father, knowing all along that the will of the Father is that he satisfy God's justice with respect to the sins of all his people! Paul sums it up: "For scarcely for a righteous man will one die: yet peradventure for a good man some would even dare to die. But God commendeth his love toward us, in that, while we were yet sinners, Christ died for us" (Rom. 5:7–8).

Martyn McGeown

June 28 — The Son Assuming the Nature in which the Disobedience Was Committed

Forasmuch then as the children are partakers of flesh and blood, he also himself likewise took part of the same; that through death he might destroy him that had the power of death, that is, the devil. —Hebrews 2:14

We have seen thus far that our God is both perfectly merciful and perfectly just. We have seen that in his admirable mercy, he sent his own only begotten Son into the world. We have insisted that this was a free sending by the Father and a willing coming of the Son. Now we ask the question—why? What was exactly the purpose of the Son becoming a real human being, of the Son adopting or assuming our human nature of flesh, blood, and soul? And why could the Son not have assumed the nature of the angels? Why did he have to assume our nature and none other? Article 18–19 already began to answer these questions: "since the soul was lost as well as the body, it was necessary that he should take both upon him, to save both" (Art. 18); "that he might die for us according to the infirmity of his flesh" (Article 19). Therefore, we know from previous Articles of the Belgic Confession that the incarnation was necessary for our salvation, that he might die. Article 20 elaborates: the Son assumed a human nature—as opposed to, let's say, an angelic nature—because it was in the human nature that man's disobedience was committed.

All of our sins are committed in the human nature. That should be obvious since we are only human nature. Unlike Christ, we are not both human and divine, only human. Our sins are committed in our bodies and souls. Paul reminds the Roman Christians that they had employed the members of their bodies for sin: "ye have yielded your members servants to uncleanness and to iniquity unto iniquity" (Rom. 6:19). Paul warns the Corinthians not to disobey God with their bodies: "he that committeth fornication sinneth against his own body" (1 Cor. 6:18); "glorify God in your body, and in your spirit, which are God's" (v. 20). The calling of Christians is to mortify (put to death) the sinful deeds of the flesh: "Mortify therefore your members which are upon the earth..." (Col. 3:5). Even when our bodies are resting, our human souls (our mind, heart, and will) are defiled by sin.

Jesus Christ assumed a human body of flesh and blood with all the human members which we have—hands, feet, etc.—with which we sin. In that human body and with that human body, Jesus Christ avoided sin and followed after righteousness. Never did his hands perform a sinful deed. Never did his feet walk the path of unrighteousness. Moreover, Jesus Christ assumed a human soul of heart, mind, and will. With that human soul Jesus Christ loved God with all of his being. Never did his human heart lust after sin. Never did he set his human will on evil. Never did one impure thought defile his human mind. What perfection there is in the Son of God!

But there is more to the Son's assuming our human nature than his rendering in that human nature the perfect obedience we have failed—indeed, refused—to give God. Jesus Christ assumed that human nature of body and soul so that he might make satisfaction by suffering what we deserved to suffer.

Satisfaction through suffering. That is the salvation which Christ has wrought for us!

Martyn McGeown

June 29 — The Son Making Satisfaction in the Human Nature

He shall see of the travail of his soul,
and shall be satisfied —Isaiah 53:11

Last time, we began to see that the Son of God assumed the human nature because that was the nature in which the disobedience of man was committed. We also saw that the Son came to make satisfaction in that nature. We looked yesterday at the positive aspect of that satisfaction, that in the human nature (of body and soul) the Son rendered to the Father the perfect obedience which we could not—and would not—render of ourselves.

But there is also the matter of our transgressions and sins against God's law. We have employed, as we saw from Romans 6, the members of our body (our hands, feet, etc.) to sin against God. Therefore, all the members of our body must suffer the punishment of God. We have sinned willfully, deliberately, and even greedily with our souls (our mind, will, heart, emotions, etc.). Therefore, we must experience in our souls the anguish of God's wrath. That is the fearful punishment of hell—in the lake of fire, the damned are punished, body and soul, for all the evil done in the body and soul in this life. That punishment is awful, but it is also just. No one who suffers such eternal punishment does not deserve it. We deserve it also, and we shall suffer it, unless a way be found to satisfy God's justice.

Suffering and punishment in body and soul came upon Christ in his human nature as he dwelled upon the earth and especially as he died upon the cross. That is why our Savior had to have a human nature. The Son of God could not suffer in the divine nature. The Son of God as he dwells in heaven in the bosom of the Father knows no suffering. He cannot know suffering. The Son of God in heaven is adored by myriads of angels. He cannot know shame or sorrow of any kind. It was only in humbling himself, in taking upon himself the form of a servant, in being in the likeness of sinful flesh, that the Son of God could suffer. Christ suffered in his body of flesh and blood. Christ suffered those things which are common to man—hunger, thirst, fatigue, physical pain—but he knew them with greater intensity than other men. This was especially true at the end of his life. In Christ's final hours he suffered dreadful torments in his body. His flesh was torn to pieces with the Roman scourge; nails were pounded into his hands and feet; and he was hanged on a cross for six hours suffering excruciating pain. Add to that the awful sufferings of soul—sorrow, grief, anguish. Who can fathom the depth of the sufferings of our Lord Jesus Christ? "My soul is exceeding sorrowful, even unto death," he said (Matt. 26:38). Hebrews 5:7 says that Christ "offered up prayers and supplications with strong crying and tears" and then he submitted his own human will (which shrank from suffering) to the divine will.

But we have not yet described the worst sufferings of Christ. The agonies of body and soul of a victim of crucifixion were truly dreadful. But Christ, in addition to those sufferings and through those sufferings, bore the wrath of God in order to make full satisfaction for all our sins.

What incomparable suffering! What incomparable obedience! What incomparable mercy!

Martyn McGeown

June 30 — The Father Laying Our Iniquities Upon Him

But he was wounded for our transgressions,
he was bruised for our iniquities —Isaiah 53:5

There is one subject about which we must be clear before we proceed—the justice in God's punishing of his Son for our sins. How could the sinless, innocent Son of God be made to suffer? How is it right that the Son of God experience pain and anguish in body and soul? How is it possible that the Son of God should know the wrath of the Father? Could it be true that the Father was angry with his own Son?

The answer is given in Article 20: "God therefore manifested his justice against his Son when he laid our iniquities upon him." It was because God laid our iniquities upon Christ that he could be just in punishing Christ. To lay our iniquities upon Christ means to impute the guilt of our iniquities to Christ. Legally, the guilt of all our sins became Christ's. Imputation is an extremely important word in theology. We believe in a threefold imputation. First, we believe, as we already saw in Article 15, that God imputed the guilt of Adam's sin to the entire human race. Adam's sin rendered us all guilty because Adam represented us. Second, we believe, as we will learn in Article 20–21, that God imputed the guilt of all our sins to Jesus Christ. Our sins rendered Christ guilty—not personally guilty, but legally guilty—before God, and God treated Christ accordingly as a guilty man, guilty of all the sins of all those whom he represents. "For he hath made him to be sin for us, who knew no sin; that we might be made the righteousness of God in him" (2 Cor. 5:21). Third, we believe, as we learn in Article 22–23, that God imputes the righteousness of Jesus Christ to us by faith. Christ's righteousness renders us, whom he represents and who believe in him, righteous before God. "For as by one man's disobedience many were made sinners, so by the obedience of one shall many be made righteous" (Rom. 5:19).

This explains how it was possible for Christ to suffer. He had the capacity to suffer because he had a human nature. He had the right to suffer—or God had the right to inflict suffering upon him—because our sins were imputed to him. Otherwise, to speak reverently, God had no legal right even to have Christ stub his toe, and it would be a moral outrage for Christ to experience the slightest pang of anguish. Anguish, pain, and suffering are the experience only of sinners. As a person, Christ is the sinless Son of God, the righteous one. If he is not, he cannot be our mediator and savior. But legally—with respect to the law, with respect to his position before God's law—Christ became guilty when the sins of all his people, whom he represented, were made his by imputation.

And since Christ was loaded down with the guilt of our sins, he became the object of God's just wrath. He lived under the shadow of that wrath his whole life, and that wrath came upon him—justly—when he died on the cross.

But we must never forget that Christ willingly adopted that position of guilt before the law for us. Christ made himself of no reputation; Christ humbled himself for our salvation.

Martyn McGeown

July 1 — God Pouring Forth His Mercy and Goodness on Us

For ye know the grace of our Lord Jesus Christ, that,
though he was rich, yet for your sakes he became poor,
that ye through his poverty might be rich. —2 Corinthians 8:9

In our place, Christ stood as guilty with the guilt of our sins. The sufferings which he bore were "the punishment of sin by his most bitter passion and death." When Christ died on the cross, God "manifested his justice against his Son." The blessed result of this was that God "poured forth his mercy and goodness on us, who were guilty and worthy of damnation, out of mere and perfect love."

It was always God's purpose to pour out his mercy and goodness upon his people. In fact, God created our first parents in his mercy and goodness. We remember how Adam and Eve knew and loved God, and how they experienced his mercy and goodness. That mercy and goodness were not yet extended to sinners, of course, but God's attitude towards our first parents before they sinned was mercy and goodness. He gave them to taste and know him as God. But the fullness of the riches of God's mercy and goodness was prepared in eternity only in Jesus Christ. What Adam and Eve knew in the garden of Eden is not what we now have in Jesus Christ—we have a better, higher, richer experience and possession of mercy and goodness! We have, in short, "immortality and life eternal." It took the profound and mysterious way of sin and grace to bring us into the full experience of eternal life.

By our sins we have forfeited mercy and goodness. Because of our sins, we have no right to life at all. "But God, who is rich in mercy, for his great love wherewith he loved us" (Eph. 2:4). By our sins we have earned the bitter wages of death, the curse, and destruction: "For the wages of sin is death; but the gift of God is eternal life through Jesus Christ our Lord" (Rom. 6:23). "For to be carnally minded is death…if ye live after the flesh, ye shall die" (Rom. 8:6, 13). We cannot even begin to satisfy God for our sins. We cannot pay for even the least of our transgressions. Even one of our iniquities is enough to plunge us into damnation forever. But Christ bore our punishment and earned for us eternal life.

He did that by obeying where we could not—and would not—obey. He did that by dying the death we could never die. He did that by removing from himself—and therefore from us, whom he represented—the guilt of those sins imputed to him and loaded upon him. When he cried, "It is finished" (John 19:30), the debt was paid.

We know that the debt is paid and that eternal life has been procured for us because Christ rose again on the third day. Christ was "declared to be the Son of God with power, according to the spirit of holiness, by the resurrection from the dead" (Rom. 1:4). Christ was "raised again for [on account of] our justification" (Rom. 4:25). Look to the cross. See the Son of God suffering there for sinners and believe in him. Look to the empty tomb. See that the Son is the victor over death, sin, hell, and the devil. Death could not hold him. Sin could not bind him. The grave could not keep him. He has paid it all. And God will demand nothing more from the one for whom Christ died, who trusts in him for full and free salvation.

Martyn McGeown

Article 21

OF THE SATISFACTION OF CHRIST, OUR ONLY HIGH PRIEST, FOR US

We believe that Jesus Christ is ordained with an oath to be an everlasting High Priest, after the order of Melchizedek; and that he hath presented himself in our behalf before the Father to appease his wrath by his full satisfaction, by offering himself on the tree of the cross and pouring out his precious blood to purge away our sins, as the prophets had foretold. For it is written: *he was wounded for our transgressions, he was bruised for our iniquities: the chastisement of our peace was upon him, and with his stripes we are healed. He was brought as a lamb to the slaughter, and numbered with the transgressors*, and condemned by Pontius Pilate as a malefactor, though he had first declared him innocent. Therefore, *he restored that which he took not away*, and *suffered, the just for the unjust*, as well in his body as in his soul, feeling the terrible punishment which our sins had merited; insomuch that *his sweat became like unto drops of blood falling on the ground*. He called out, *My God, My God, why hast Thou forsaken me?* and hath suffered all this for the remission of our sins. Wherefore we justly say with the apostle Paul, *that we know nothing but Jesus Christ, and him crucified; we count all things but loss and dung for the excellency of the knowledge of Christ Jesus our Lord*, in whose wounds we find all manner of consolation. Neither is it necessary to seek or invent any other means of being reconciled to God than this only sacrifice, once offered, by which believers are made perfect forever. This is also the reason why he was called by the angel of God, Jesus, that is to say, Savior, because he would save his people from their sins.

July 2   Christ the Only Everlasting High Priest

Consider the Apostle and High Priest of our profession,
Christ Jesus. —Hebrews 3:1

The holy God has ordained that he should be approached through a priest. The first man named a priest in Scripture is Melchizedek (Gen. 14:18). Often the heads of households functioned as priests (Job 1:5). Later God instituted an order of priests, the sons of Aaron of the tribe of Levi. Throughout Israel's history, God's people relied on priests to officiate in the tabernacle and the temple. The task of a priest was to act as a representative of the people to bring the people into fellowship with God (Heb. 5:1).

The work of a priest was threefold. First, on the altar of burnt offering the priest offered sacrifices to cover the sins of the people. Of course, the sins of the people were only covered ceremonially. However, the requirement of blood atonement reminded the people of the holiness of God and of the need for satisfaction for sin. Second, the priest took some of the burning coals from the altar of burnt offering, mixed them with a carefully prepared mixture of spices, and then offered the mixture on the altar of incense. A cloud of sweet-smelling smoke called incense would ascend to heaven. While he offered incense, the priest interceded for the people. Thus, incense was symbolic of intercessory prayer. Third, on the basis of the sacrifice offered and after the intercessory prayer, the priest would bless the people in the name of God.

God gave priests in the Old Testament to prepare his people for the coming of Christ who would, as the everlasting high priest, perform a threefold work. Christ offered one final sacrifice on the cross; Christ intercedes for us in heaven at God's right hand, and Christ blesses us with all spiritual blessings in heavenly places. In Article 21, the focus is on Christ's priestly work of atonement. The title is "The Satisfaction of Christ, Our Only High Priest, For Us." Article 26 will deal with Christ's intercession, which we shall study in future meditations.

One very important point, often missed today, is that Christ died for, intercedes for, and blesses the very same people. There is an essential unity in Christ's priestly work. Christ makes this clear in his well-known "high priestly prayer" where he says: "I pray for them: I pray not for the world, but for them which thou hast given me; for they are thine" (John 17:9). If Christ does not pray for every single human being, he did not die for every single human being, and therefore he neither procures nor bestows blessings upon every single human being. To teach that Christ only prays for some but that he died for all is to imagine an impossible division in Christ's priestly work.

In the New Testament, there is no longer an order of priests, but only one high priest, Jesus Christ himself. The priesthood of Jesus Christ is a major theme of the epistle to the Hebrews. In that epistle, the inspired writer proves the superiority, uniqueness, and permanence of Christ's priesthood by comparing Christ to the Old Testament priests. Therefore, the priests of the Roman Catholic Church and the priests of the Mormon cult must be rejected as imposters.

Do you know this one, only, everlasting high priest? Trust no other priest but him!

Martyn McGeown

July 3 — Christ's Melchizedekian Priesthood

The LORD hath sworn, and will not repent, Thou art a priest for ever after the order of Melchizedek. —Psalm 110:4

In Scripture there are only two orders of the priesthood: the priesthood after the order of Aaron of the tribe of Levi, and the priesthood after the order of Melchizedek. Christ was not, and never could be, a priest after the former order, because he was not born of Levi's tribe but of Judah's (Heb. 7:13–14). Indeed, since in the Old Testament the priests were from Levi and the kings were from Judah, it was not possible to be simultaneously king and priest. Yet God promised a savior who would be priest (Ps. 110:4), and king (Gen. 49:10), as well as prophet (Deut. 18:18).

The writer to the Hebrews takes a relatively obscure prophecy in the Psalms and from it expounds the priesthood of Christ according to the order of Melchizedek. In so doing, he proves the superiority of Christ over the Old Testament priesthood. The reader should study carefully Hebrews 7.

There are many reasons for the superiority of the Melchizedekian priesthood of Christ over the Levitical or Aaronic priesthood. First, Melchizedek precedes Levi and Aaron in time. He appears in Genesis 14:18–20 after Abraham's slaughter of the kings and successful recovery of the captives, including his nephew Lot. Second, Abraham recognizes Melchizedek's superiority by giving him a tenth of the spoils of war, and in a way—this is the argument of the inspired writer to Hebrews—Levi (who was in Abraham's loins) gave tithes to Melchizedek (Heb. 7:4–9). Third, since Melchizedek is—at least on the pages of Scripture, for he disappears as suddenly as he appeared—"without father, without mother, without descent, having neither beginning of days, nor end of life; but made like unto the Son of God, abideth a priest continually" (Heb. 7:3), he is a fitting picture of the real Melchizedek, of whom the historical Melchizedek was a picture. Thus, the Levitical or Aaronic priesthood was temporary and imperfect; the Melchizedekian priesthood is eternal and perfect (Heb. 7:8, 24). Fourth, the Melchizedekian priesthood of Christ is significant because he is ordained with an oath to be an everlasting high priest. In Scripture, God's promise or oath is always superior to the law. The fact that God swears an oath in Psalm 110 after he has ordained the Levitical or Aaronic priesthood shows that the law and its priesthood would pass away (Heb. 7:15–18, 28).

How blessed we are to have a high priest after the order of Melchizedek. Unlike the Old Testament priests, Christ does not die but is made a priest "after the power of an endless life" (Heb. 7:16). Since Christ never dies, he is never replaced, and his priesthood does not pass on to successors (Heb. 7:23–24). This is in accordance with God's solemn oath: "The LORD hath sworn, and will not repent, Thou art a priest for ever after the order of Melchizedek" (Ps. 110:4). God will not repent or change his mind. Christ will be a priest forever with a priesthood that shall have no end. Besides this, Christ, again unlike the Old Testament priests, is "holy, harmless, undefiled, separate from sinners, and made higher than the heavens" (Heb. 7:26). Therefore, Christ can offer one sacrifice for sins forever, unlike former priests who had to offer ineffectual sacrifices repeatedly (Heb. 7:27; see also 9:25–26; 10:11–14).

One perfect high priest; one perfect sacrifice; one perfected people!

Martyn McGeown

July 4 — Christ Presenting Himself Before the Father

No man taketh it from me,
but I lay it down of myself—John 10:18

Sometimes we think of Jesus as a victim upon whom God inflicted terrible sufferings. Some have scoffed at Christianity, calling it "slaughterhouse religion." More recently, certain wicked men—even within Evangelical Christianity—have accused God of "cosmic child abuse." But all such objections to the gospel of the cross are based on a deliberate refusal to see that what Christ suffered was voluntary.

When we see the awful sufferings of Christ in Scripture, let us never lose sight of that great truth. Christ was arrested in the garden of Gethsemane only because he willingly consented to his arrest and gave himself into the hands of his captors (John 18:4–9). Christ was beaten, spat upon, and mocked, but remember his words in Isaiah 50:6, "I gave my back to the smiters, and my cheeks to them that plucked off the hair: I hid not my face from shame and spitting." Christ was arraigned before the Jews and then Pontius Pilate, but only because he himself permitted it. Christ was crucified and suffered the indignities and agonies of the cross, but only because he personally embraced those sufferings as part of the will of God. All of this he sums up in John 10:17–18, "Therefore doth my Father love me, because I lay down my life, that I might take it again. No man taketh it from me, but I lay it down of myself. I have power to lay it down, and I have power to take it again. This commandment have I received of my Father." Indeed, Christ did not actually die until the moment determined by himself. He could not have died one second earlier or later than the one appointed by the Father and to which he willingly submitted.

Article 21 explains this in these words: "He hath presented himself in our behalf before the Father to appease his wrath by his full satisfaction." The Son of God, as it were, appeared before the Father and declared: "Here I am, send me." And we must be abundantly clear that the Son of God knew exactly the import of his words: "Send me, Father, and I will be born of a virgin, in humble and miserable circumstances. Send me, Father, and I will grow up in relative obscurity and poverty. Send me, Father, and I will preach thy gospel, do good, and keep thy law, under which I will be born. Send me, Father, and I will be rejected by many, despised and abhorred by men, betrayed, denied, and finally put to death. Send me, Father, and I will submit to the indignities of arrest, false imprisonment, a wicked, unjust, public flogging, rejection by the people in favor of a murderer, and finally the agony of crucifixion. Send me, Father, and I will bear in my own body the full weight of thy wrath against the sins of which my elect are guilty." The book of Hebrews sums it up, quoting Psalm 40:7, "Then said I, Lo, I come (in the volume of the book it is written of me,) to do thy will, O God" (Heb. 10:7).

Something legal happened when Christ presented himself before the Father. The guilt of all our sins was transferred to the account of God's Son. He undertook full responsibility for what we had done and did what we had left undone and had refused to do.

What amazing love is this! Praise Christ, our self-giving, self-sacrificing Savior!

Martyn McGeown

July 5 — Feeling the Terrible Punishment which Our Sins Had Merited

It pleased the LORD to bruise him.
—Isaiah 53:10

To understand the death of Christ, we must see that Christ did not suffer merely at the hands of ungodly men. There is no doubt that Christ's physical sufferings were excruciating, a word which comes from the Latin word *crux* for *cross*. Crucifixion was an extremely painful, humiliating, and slow way to die. The Romans developed it as a form of execution to terrorize those whom they conquered. No Roman citizen could be crucified. Indeed, the words *crucify* or *cross* were not uttered in polite conversation. When the readers of the gospel accounts read the words "they crucified him" (Mark 15:25), they knew exactly what that meant.

But we would miss the gospel of the cross if we did not see beyond the physical anguish of our Savior caused by the "contradiction of sinners" (Heb. 12:3). There have been various theories about what Christ's death on the cross means, but many of them fall short. Some have seen Christ's death as an inspiring example to moral courage, the death of a martyr for a good cause. The lesson they draw from Christ's death is that we must be willing to suffer bravely for our principles. There is truth to that, of course (1 Pet. 2:21; 4:1, etc.). But there is more to it than that. Others have seen Christ's death as the way to receive inspiration to love God and our neighbor. The sufferings of Christ are supposed to melt our heart in love for him. This is the moral influence theory. This, like many errors, has a grain of truth to it (2 Cor. 5:14). Still others teach that by the cross, Christ has conquered the devil and the power of sin, the so-called *Christus victor* theory. While it is true that Christ has conquered the devil as promised (Gen. 3:15; Col. 2:15), there is more to the atonement than that. A fourth view is the governmental view. This is the view that Christ died on the cross as an example of the justice of God. The idea is that God punished Christ instead of punishing us to "make an example of him." This is what God will do to you if you do not repent! Because Christ has suffered instead of you, God can be just in forgiving you.

But do not be fooled by these false views of the atonement. None of them is the truth, although they all have an element of truth in them. The truth is penal substitutionary atonement. *Penal* means *pertaining to punishment*. A country might have a penal code, which detail the punishments mandated by law for certain crimes. A prisoner might be sent to a penal colony or be incarcerated in a penal institution. Those are places of punishment. Article 21 teaches us that Christ "[felt] the terrible punishment which our sins had merited." The second word in *penal substitutionary* refers to the fact that Christ was the substitute, that he stood in the place of sinners and endured the punishment which those sinners should have endured.

The wonder of the sufferings of the cross is this: they were inflicted on Christ by the Father who punished his Son to the full extent of the law in our place. The punishment he felt was not a general punishment, but the punishment which our sins merited.

Thus, the prophet can write: "He was wounded for our transgressions, he was bruised for our iniquities…the LORD hath laid on him the iniquity of us all" (Isa. 53:5, 6). When we contemplate the sufferings of Christ, we must not think abstractly. We must remember our own sins—our lies, our pride, our anger, our envy. Those were the sins which brought him to Calvary.

Martyn McGeown

July 6

Satisfaction, Atonement, Redemption, Reconciliation, and Propitiation

He shall see of the travail of his soul, and shall be satisfied.
—Isaiah 53:11

To understand what Christ accomplished by his sufferings and death, we must examine the rich language of the Bible. All too often this is not done, which leads to confusion and error about the cross of our Savior. The more we rightly understand what Christ has done for us, the more we are filled with gratitude.

Consider this illustration. A man and his wife are enjoying a pleasant stroll along the pier. Suddenly, the man says to his wife: "Darling, I want to show you how much I love you." And he jumps into the sea and drowns. Would the wife view that as an act of love? Of course not: she would view that as a senseless waste of life. But if that same man jumped in front of a gunman to save his wife, that would be a heroic act even if the man was killed in his act of courage. If the death of Christ was not necessary, and if it did not accomplish anything, then how can we glory in it? The Bible tells us that the death of Christ was both necessary and powerfully effective. It does that in the various words it uses to denote the sufferings of Christ.

First, the death of Christ was real satisfaction. To satisfy means to make a full payment of a debt so that the creditor receives the amount he is owed. We owe a debt to the justice of God which we cannot even begin to pay. Jesus satisfied God by paying on our behalf. "He shall see of the travail of his soul, and shall be satisfied" (Isa. 53:11). Article 21 speaks of "appeasing his [the Father's] wrath by his full satisfaction."

Second, the death of Christ was atonement. To atone means to cover over by means of a sacrifice. Many times that word is used with respect to the sacrifices of the Old Testament, for example, "he shall put his hand upon the head of the burnt offering; and it shall be accepted for him to make atonement for him" (Lev. 1:4). What the sacrificial lambs did typically, Christ did actually by shedding his blood on the cross.

Third, the death of Christ was redemption. To redeem means to release from slavery by the payment of a price, a ransom. The only ransom costly enough to redeem lost sinners is the life of the Son of God. "Ye were not redeemed with corruptible things…but with the precious blood of Christ" (1 Pet. 1:18, 19).

Fourth, the death of Christ was reconciliation. To reconcile is to restore parties at variance with one another to fellowship by the removal of the cause of their estrangement. Quite simply, reconciliation is the restoration of a broken friendship. Christ reconciled us to God by removing our sin. "When we were enemies, we were reconciled to God by the death of his Son" (Rom. 5:10).

Fifth, the death of Christ was propitiation or an appeasing of the wrath of God by means of a sacrifice to cover over the sin. The anger of God was turned away from us by the sacrifice of Christ. God "sent his Son to be the propitiation for our sins" (1 John 4:10).

Therefore, we can say that the death of Christ is a satisfaction which really satisfied the justice of God; an atonement which really atoned and covered over our sins; a redemption which really delivered us from death, sin, hell, and the devil; a reconciliation which really brings us into fellowship with God; and a propitiation which really turns away God's wrath from us.

That is the rich meaning of our Savior's death.

Martyn McGeown

July 7 — A Particular, Effectual Atonement

For God so loved the world,
that he gave his only begotten Son, that whosoever believeth in him
should not perish, but have everlasting life. —John 3:16

Did Christ die for everybody, did Christ die for those who are never saved, or did Christ die only for God's elect people? The answer to that question is determined by more than numbers—*all* versus *some* or *many*—but depends on what the death of Christ actually is.

In the providence of God, this has become a debate between limited and unlimited atonement. But that terminology is unfortunate. It leads one to imagine that the Reformed, who believe in limited atonement, are limiting the atonement while the Arminians, who believe in unlimited or universal atonement are not limiting the atonement. The opposite is true.

Christ's death is real satisfaction, atonement, redemption, reconciliation, and propitiation. If that is true, the question about the extent of the atonement should be easy to answer. The Arminians claim that Christ redeemed all men without exception, that God was in the world reconciling it to himself and that Christ is the propitiation for the sins of the whole world. But do not let Arminianism fool you. If Christ redeemed all men without exception, but not all men are not delivered from sin and the devil, then his redemption was worthless because it did not redeem! If God was "reconciling the world to himself"—which according to 2 Corinthians 5:19 means "not imputing their trespasses unto them"—but not all are brought into his fellowship and many perish as his enemies, then his reconciliation did not reconcile! And if Christ propitiated God with respect to the sins of the whole world, but some still bear God's wrath in eternal hell, then Christ's propitiation did not propitiate! It is the Arminian who limits the atonement of Christ by robbing it of its efficacy and therefore of its meaning.

The answer of Arminianism is that Christ did these things for everyone, but we must accept it to make it real for us. Thus, we have the Christian cliché of "accepting Jesus as your own and personal savior." However, the Bible does not speak in those terms. "We were reconciled to God by the death of his Son" (Rom. 5:10); "Christ hath redeemed us" (Gal. 3:13). Christ "loved us, and washed us from our sins in his own blood" (Rev. 1:5). The Bible is clear: Christ either redeemed his people effectually by his death, saving all those for whom he died, or Christ redeemed no one. There is no merely potential or possible atonement in Scripture.

The great objection of Arminianism is that the Bible says that Christ died for "*all*" or for the "world." Arminians assume that these terms mean everybody, the entire human race without exception. But this is not true. In Scripture, the word *world* rarely means all without exception (John 7:4, 12:19, 15:18–19, 16:20). It is a word used to denote all nations. Similarly, the term *all men* means all in a specific group and rarely means everyone without exception (Mark 1:37, 11:32; John 11:48; Acts 2:45, 4:21, 19:19, 21:28). This is not unusual language even in English. Consider these examples: "The world was shocked by the earthquake." "Does everyone have a copy of the book?" "There is a lunch for everybody on the table." "I do not want anyone to be late." "Everybody was at church." Context determines meaning.

The beautiful truth of Scripture is this: Christ died for all his people, he redeemed his sheep, he purchased his bride, and he redeemed us from every nation. He did so effectually for all those for whom he died, and he saves to the uttermost all those who believe in him.

Martyn McGeown

July 8 — Christ's Agony in Gethsemane

My soul is exceeding sorrowful, even unto death.
—Matthew 26:38

For every Christian, the sufferings of Christ are fascinating. We love to hear how our Lord Jesus Christ gave himself for our sins. We love to ponder all the details and to marvel at his wondrous love. Although Christ suffered his whole life, we might say that his sufferings begin to peak as he reached the point of Gethsemane.

Gethsemane means *oil press*. It was an enclosed garden on the Mount of Olives. Jesus and his disciples knew the place. How fitting, as the Son of God was about to be pressed with the dreadful, crushing burden of God's wrath, that he would come to Gethsemane—the oil press! Christ came to that location for two main reasons. First, it was a place of refuge, a place of seclusion, and he needed time to be alone with his Father in prayer. Second, Christ knew that the place was familiar to Judas Iscariot, his betrayer (John 18:2). Christ made no attempt to hide from Judas or to evade arrest. He was waiting for Judas when the betrayer arrived with his mob of soldiers. "Behold, the hour is at hand, and the Son of man is betrayed into the hands of sinners. Rise, let us be going: behold, he is at hand that doth betray me" (Matt. 26:45–46).

When Christ entered Gethsemane for the last time, a change came over him. Christ, the beloved Son, who was always so calm and reposed, began to tremble with fear. A great and holy dread came upon him, which we must try to understand. The gospel writers describe Christ in very moving words: he "began to be sorrowful and very heavy" (Matt. 26:37); he "began to be sore amazed, and to be very heavy" (Mark 14:33); he was "in an agony" (Luke 22:44). Christ himself describes how he is feeling to his disciples: "My soul is exceeding sorrowful, even unto death" (Matt. 26:38). Luke tells us that "his sweat was as it were great drops of blood falling down to the ground" (Luke 22:44). In Hebrews we read: "Who in the days of his flesh, when he had offered up prayers and supplications with strong crying and tears unto him that was able to save him from death, and was heard in that he feared" (Heb. 5:7).

Was Christ, who before this had so often spoken in solemn terms about his upcoming death in Jerusalem, now suddenly afraid to die? Had his courage left him? Was he less courageous—I speak as a fool—than others who had suffered the horrible death of crucifixion? Not at all! Christ was afraid of something worse—infinitely worse—than physical death. Christ feared the cup. That was the focus of his prayer in the garden of Gethsemane. "O my Father, if it be possible, let this cup pass from me: nevertheless not as I will, but as thou wilt…O my Father, if this cup may not pass away from me, except I drink it, thy will be done" (Matt. 26:39, 42). In Gethsemane, Christ was wrestling with the horror of drinking the cup. He knew what was in the cup, and he shrank back in dread from the contents of the cup. In Scripture, a cup is an appointed portion of something, either of blessing or of wrath. "In the hand of the Lord there is a cup, and the wine is red; it is full of mixture; and he poureth out of the same: but the dregs thereof, all the wicked of the earth shall wring them out, and drink them" (Ps. 75:8).

Now that cup was handed to Christ. In Gethsemane, Christ took it and began his last steps to the cross where he would drink every last drop of it.

Martyn McGeown

July 9 — Christ Condemned Though Declared Innocent

Take ye him, and crucify him: for I find no fault in him.
—John 19:6

After his arrest in the garden of Gethsemane, Christ suffered the indignity of a trial. His trial took place in several stages. First, he was questioned by Annas, the father-in-law of Caiaphas, the high priest (John 18:13). Then he was arraigned before the entire Sanhedrin in Caiaphas' house in the middle of the night. Multiple laws of Jewish jurisprudence were transgressed that night because Christ's enemies were desperate to convict Christ and kill him. After trying threats and intimidation and using the testimony of false witnesses, Caiaphas demanded that Christ answer a question under oath: "I adjure thee by the living God, that thou tell us whether thou be the Christ, the Son of God" (Matt. 26:63). Christ responded truthfully that he was. The Sanhedrin, having rejected Christ as the Son of God for some time, now officially pronounced Jesus guilty of blasphemy: "Then the high priest rent his clothes, saying, He hath spoken blasphemy; what further need have we of witnesses? behold, now ye have heard his blasphemy. What think ye? They answered and said, He is guilty of death" (Matt. 26:65–66). Then Jesus' enemies unleashed their fury upon him: "they [did] spit in his face, and buffeted him" (v. 67). All this Jesus bore patiently, not speaking a word!

Condemned by the religious leaders, Jesus was taken to Pilate to be tried before the civil powers. At this time only the Romans had the authority to put a person to death. The Sanhedrin needed some excuse to have Pilate, the Roman governor, execute Jesus. Pilate was not convinced. Having examined Jesus, Pilate declared repeatedly that he was innocent: "I find in him no fault at all" (John 18:38); "I bring him forth to you, that ye may know that I find no fault in him" (John 19:4); "Take ye him, and crucify him: for I find no fault in him" (John 19:6). Pilate even tries to absolve himself of the guilt of unlawfully sentencing Jesus to death by washing his hands symbolically before the people. "I am innocent of the blood of this just person: see ye to it" (Matt. 27:24). Others testified to the innocence of Jesus: Pilate's wife (Matt. 27:19); Judas Iscariot (Matt. 27:4); one of the thieves who was crucified alongside Jesus (Luke 23:41); and the centurion whose soldiers crucified Jesus (Luke 23:47).

Article 21 takes note of this: "[he was] condemned by Pontius Pilate as a malefactor, though he had first declared him innocent." But why was such a trial necessary? First, God would have the innocence of his Son thoroughly examined and publicly testified. No one was able to find the least fault in Jesus. This was necessary because he was our substitute who must be "a lamb without blemish and without spot" (1 Pet. 1:19). Second, God would confront the powers of that day, both the religious and civil powers, as well as the common people, with the question: "What will ye do with Jesus which is called Christ?" No one can escape that question, although Pilate desperately tried to do so. Third, and most significant, God himself condemned Jesus, using sinful men as his instruments. When Jesus heard those words, "He is guilty of death" and "Take ye him, and crucify him," Jesus heard in his own consciousness the terrible sentence of death coming from God himself.

As Jesus stood before God, he was bearing the sins of all his people whom he represented. Therefore, the only fitting verdict was guilty. Guilty of all the sins of thy people! Guilty of our sins!

Martyn McGeown

July 10 — Christ Wounded and Bruised

But he was wounded for our transgressions,
he was bruised for our iniquities. —Isaiah 53:5

From Pilate's judgment hall, Christ made his way to the place of execution on the hill of Calvary. Before crucifixion, the condemned man was scourged. Sometimes, a Roman scourging was so severe that the victim died. A cruel whip lacerated Jesus' back, and the soldiers added to Christ's suffering and indignity by mocking his kingship with a crown of thorns, bowing in contempt before him, beating him, and spitting in his face! Then upon his bleeding back they laid a heavy piece of wood. Our Savior had to carry the instrument on which he himself would be crucified. When he could carry the burden no longer, they forced a man, Simon of Cyrene, to carry it for him. When they reached the hill, the soldiers began their grisly work, pounding nails into his hands and feet and hoisting him up on the cross. And there he hung for six dreadful hours, in excruciating agony, from nine in the morning to three in the afternoon while his enemies looked on until darkness descended upon the scene.

Isaiah the prophet, writing centuries before the events took place, describes the sufferings of our Savior in vivid language. First, there are words which speak of severe injury. Stricken! Smitten! Oppressed! Afflicted! Bruised! Wounded! The servant of Jehovah received one dreadful blow after another, each one more crushing than the former. The imagery in Isaiah 52–53 is of one beaten so severely that men can barely recognize him, of one whose sufferings are so awful that men will turn away their faces in horror at the sight (Isa. 52:14, 53:3). Second, there are words which speak of an intolerably heavy burden, a burden designed to crush a man under its weight. The suffering of Jesus was suffering which almost overwhelmed and engulfed the Servant of Jehovah, the Messiah. "Surely he hath borne our griefs, and carried our sorrows…The Lord hath laid on him the iniquity of us all" (Isa. 53:4, 6). Never in the history of the world did any carry a load as heavy as this man. Third, there are words which describe the effect of this suffering upon the Savior. We saw already how the anticipation of this suffering affected Jesus in Gethsemane. Now, on the cross, he feels acutely every blow, every wound, every laceration of his flesh, the agonizing thirst, the oppressive heat and the torment which pierces his very heart and soul with sorrow. He is afflicted, a word which means *bowed down, humbled, made low* (v. 7). Verse 11 speaks of "the travail of his soul." To suffer there was grievous toil, hard labor which exhausted him physically and emotionally as his soul was poured out unto death.

But the physical torment was only the beginning of Christ's suffering. If mere men had stretched forth their hands against him, he would not have felt such anguish. The horror of Calvary for the Son of God was this: God bruised him; God crushed him; God punished him for our sins. "Yet, it pleased the Lord to bruise him…" (Isa. 53:10). When Christ looked beyond the Jews and the Romans, he saw the hand of his Father. That hand was not gentle; that hand did not spare him; that hand dealt him crushing blow after crushing blow.

And yet, the Savior did not complain but submitted himself to the righteous judgment of the Father. He knew that God was just and holy, and he loved the one who bruised him.

Isaiah says that it was the "chastisement of our peace" (v. 5). We deserved that punishment, and that punishment brought us peace, peace with God, and eternal life.

Martyn McGeown

July 11   **Forsaken for the Remission of Our Sins**

My God, my God, why hast thou forsaken me?
—Matthew 27:46

From the depths of Christ's agonies came the cry of abandonment: "My God, my God, why hast thou forsaken me?" (Matt. 27:46). These words spoken by Christ from the cross are among the most profound, mysterious, and sacred in Scripture. The Son forsaken by the Father! What could this mean? How could this be possible? What is its significance?

We must remember the events of the cross. For three hours, Jesus had hung on the cross as a spectacle before men, and men had been active in mocking him. It was not enough for his enemies that they had brought him to the cross. They gathered like bloodthirsty wolves to growl at him. "He saved others; himself he cannot save. If he be the King of Israel, let him now come down from the cross, and we will believe him" (Matt. 27:42). Even the two thieves—one of whom would later repent and be forgiven by Jesus (Luke 23:43)—mocked him (Matt. 27:44). But the blasphemous chatter at the cross ended when God plunged the earth into darkness for three hours (Matt. 27:45). This was a miraculous darkness which lasted from high noon until three o'clock, when the sun was normally at its hottest. During those three hours of darkness, God was judging sin and the sinbearer, Jesus Christ. Judgment came to Calvary that day in the form of thick, impenetrable, oppressive darkness. That darkness was upon Jesus Christ because he was the object of the righteous and holy judgment of God against all the sins of God's people. Only after Jesus had purged our sins and exhausted the wrath of God against our sins did the light return.

It was as Jesus plumbed the depths of that darkness—the outer darkness of hell itself—and just before he emerged from it, that he cried with a loud voice the words of abandonment. At this point, Christ was being crushed by the heavy hand of God; the billows of God's wrath, like a raging ocean of fire, were flooding and overwhelming him; Jesus was tasting, drinking, and emptying the bitter cup which God had given him. At that point, inexpressive horror gripped Christ's soul. God had forsaken him. In that horror, Christ called out in agony, seeking for fellowship with his God: "My God, my God…" But there was no fellowship possible. God did not answer his Son with his favor. Our Mediator, who had always known and enjoyed communion with his Father, who was the object of the Father's delight, who dwelled eternally in the Father's bosom, was now without the presence of God's love.

This does not mean that there was suddenly a schism in the being of the Trinity. This does not mean either that the Father now hated his Son. The Father loved the Son even when he did not spare him. The Son loved the Father even as the Father inflicted suffering upon him. It means that the Son of God experienced in his human nature of body and soul that God was not his benevolent Father but the avenging and righteous judge. It means that in his capacity as judge, God showed no mercy to his Son but punished him to the fullest extent, pouring out the full fury of his wrath.

The presence of God in wrath, but the absence of God's favor, was intolerable for the holy Son of God. But that was necessary for our salvation. Christ experienced hell that day so that we would never experience hell, we who believe in him.

Martyn McGeown

July 12 — Appeasing the Father's Wrath

He loved us, and sent his Son to be
the propitiation for our sins. —1 John 4:10

Have you ever tried to propitiate someone? The word means to appease or to placate by offering a gift. The effect of propitiation is that the anger of an offended person is turned away. Jacob found himself in that position when he returned from Haran. He knew that his brother Esau was angry with him but he hoped to propitiate him: "I will appease him with the present that goeth before me" (Gen. 32:20).

Christ is our propitiation (1 John 2:2; 4:10). This means that Christ has turned away the wrath of God which justly rested upon us. We were "children of wrath, even as others" (Eph. 2:3). God was angry with us, and we were deserving of that anger. Christ removed that wrath from us by taking that wrath—and the guilt which was the ground for that wrath—upon himself. Thus, especially on the cross, Christ became the object of God's just and righteous wrath. As he was loaded down with our guilt, he felt that wrath burning against him. That sense of God's wrath reached its lowest and most bitter point when Christ from the depth of his anguished soul cried out: "My God, my God, why hast thou forsaken me?" (Matt. 27:46). When Jesus died, the wrath was removed. Now there is no wrath for any sinner for whom Christ died.

On the cross, then, God was angry with Jesus Christ. This does not mean that God hated his Son, or that God was personally angry with him. The Son always pleased his Father, even when he was actively laying down his life on the cross. God was judicially angry with Jesus Christ, that is, God was angry with his Son in his capacity as the judge. Jesus was justly the object of God's wrath because Jesus was legally—but not personally—guilty of all the sins of the elect whom he represented. Paul writes in 2 Corinthians 5:21, "For he hath made him to be sin for us, who knew no sin; that we might be made the righteousness of God in him." The Son of God was made to be sin! This does not mean that Jesus Christ became sinful. It means that he became legally guilty and therefore liable to be punished with God's wrath.

We must understand God's wrath as righteous wrath. God is not a vengeful God who enjoys inflicting pain upon his creatures. Rather God inflicts suffering on sinners according to strict justice. When God inflicted suffering on Jesus, which he felt as terrible punishment in body and soul, he was inflicting only what the law required. Perhaps a person might object: why cannot God simply forgive without requiring that someone be punished in our place? The answer is that God's justice demands it. Perhaps an illustration might help. If you break your neighbor's window, he might choose to forgive you and not ask you to pay for the broken window. But does that mean that no payment will be made? Actually, your neighbor, by forgiving you, will pay to repair the window from his own money or his insurance company will pay. But there must be a payment made by someone! When God's law is transgressed, it is an affront to God's holiness. If God chooses not to punish us for our sins, someone will still have to pay. And, in grace, God paid for our sins himself in the person of his own Son.

The result of Christ's death as propitiation is that the wrath of God is turned away from us. Because "Christ hath presented himself in our behalf before the Father, to appease his wrath by his full satisfaction," we have no need to fear when we stand before him.

Christ has died, and God is satisfied forever!

Martyn McGeown

July 13 — Offering Himself on the Tree of the Cross

Who his own self bare our sins in his own body on the tree. —1 Peter 2:24

Does it matter how Jesus Christ died? Could he have atoned for our sins by being stoned to death by a Jewish mob? Could his death have come about by drowning? Could he have died of natural causes at a ripe old age? The manner of Christ's death does matter: he had to be crucified.

The cross was the means by which Christ offered himself as a living sacrifice to God for the sins of his people. In the Old Testament, all the animal sacrifices were unwilling. They were slaughtered, their blood was sprinkled, and their bodies were burned on the altar. The altar which Jesus chose for the place of his sacrifice was the cross. Article 21 describes it in these words: "He hath presented himself…to appease [God's] wrath…by offering himself on the tree of the cross and pouring out his precious blood to purge away our sins."

There are many reasons why death by crucifixion was necessary for the Son of God. But the main reason is the most humbling. He must be crucified because we have sinned. Sometimes we tend to think that our sins are very minor. Often, we try to excuse our sins. Sometimes, and more often than we care to admit, we love our sins and do not want to turn from them. We are so perverse by nature that we enjoy sin, although we know that it will bring shame, misery, and ultimately death. When we are tempted to love our sins, we must look at the cross. Our sins are so vile in the sight of the holy God, that only the death of the Son of God could atone for them.

But there are other reasons why crucifixion was the kind of death Jesus died. First, the cross acted as an altar on which the Lamb of God could offer himself. Consider some of the similarities between this sacrifice and the Old Testament sacrifices. The cross was a bloody, violent, traumatic death. In this way, Jesus shed his blood. On the cross Jesus was "burned" or consumed by the wrath of God in a way reminiscent of the burning of the flesh of animals on the altar.

Moreover, death by crucifixion was slow, deliberately so. Had Jesus been stabbed quickly with a dagger or received a quick blow to the head, he would not have been able actively to take to himself the death which we deserved to bear. And let us never forget that Christ gave himself over into the power of death. We do not find him cowering among the trees when men came to arrest him. He goes forth to them (John 18:4). We do not find him loudly protesting his innocence and seeking to escape from the men who tried him. "As a sheep before her shearers is dumb, so he openeth not his mouth" (Isa. 53:7). When he was offered a sedative to dull his senses, he refused to drink it (Matt. 27:34). He was determined to be fully alert when he offered himself on the cross.

In a very real sense, therefore, we must view the cross as an altar. On that altar, the sacrifice to end all sacrifices was offered. A lamb was slain there, the Lamb of God. Blood was sprinkled there, the blood of our Savior. Redemption was secured there, the redemption of our souls and bodies from eternal damnation.

Let us flee from all other altars to the cross of Christ, where the only perfect sacrifice was made.

Martyn McGeown

July 14 — Redeeming Us from God's Curse

For it is written, Cursed is every one that hangeth on a tree. —Galatians 3:13

Paul says about the gospel of Christ crucified that it was "a stumblingblock" to the Jews (1 Cor. 1:22–23). It was offensive to them that the Christians should believe and preach a crucified Messiah. The reason for this offense was that the law of Moses taught that a crucified person was cursed by God.

> 22. And if a man have committed a sin worthy of death, and he be to be put to death, and thou hang him on a tree:
> 23. His body shall not remain all night upon the tree, but thou shalt in any wise bury him that day; (for he that is hanged is accursed of God;) that thy land be not defiled, which the LORD thy God giveth thee for an inheritance. (Deut. 21:22–23)

In the Old Testament, the Jews stoned a man to death and then the corpse was hanged on a tree to expose it to open shame. Thus, the corpse decomposed in the hot sun and was eaten by vultures. The idea was that such a person had no place in the land of the living and was utterly rejected by God. He was under God's curse! Crucifixion was worse than that because a person was hanged on a tree, a piece of wood, while he was still alive. Thus, a man who was crucified bore God's curse while he still lived.

For the Jews, those two concepts—God's curse and the Messiah of God—did not fit together. The idea that God could curse his own Son was blasphemy. Therefore, that Jesus Christ was crucified and thus cursed proved to the Jews that he could not be the Messiah. But Paul explains how these two concepts fit together. The Son of God was made a curse for others. We, who deserve by our sins to be under God's curse, receive God's blessing because Christ bore the curse which we deserved. "Christ hath redeemed us from the curse of the law, being made a curse for us" (Gal. 3:13). God's curse is the word of his destructive wrath. To curse means to speak evil of or evil upon or against someone. God does not "say bad words," as we forbid our children from doing. God's curse is the righteous, holy word of his wrath which pronounces misery upon his enemies, devoting them to destruction and banishing them from him so that they are eternally miserable. That curse must come upon all lawbreakers for, as Paul explains: "as many as are of the works of the law are under the curse: for it is written, Cursed is everyone that continueth not in all things which are written in the book of the law to do them" (Gal. 3:10).

That curse came in all its horror upon Jesus Christ. As one under God's curse, he must be deprived of the favor of God. That happened on the cross. As one under God's curse, he must be enveloped in darkness and taste the full misery of banishment from God. That, too, happened on the cross. Although God loved his Son, when Christ became the sinbearer, he became the object of God's just and holy wrath. The word of God's wrath was directed against him and thus made Christ unspeakably miserable.

Behold Christ on the cross! He is there as a public spectacle of accursedness so that we might know that we have been redeemed from that curse which he bore on our behalf. The Jews stumbled at it and the Gentiles scoffed at it (1 Cor. 1:23), but we glory in it. God therefore will not and cannot curse one who is in Christ because to be in Christ is to be blessed. "Christ hath redeemed us from the curse of the law…That the blessing of Abraham might come on the Gentiles through Jesus Christ; that we might receive the promise of the Spirit through faith" (Gal. 3:13–14).

Christ was cursed so that we who believe in him are blessed. Do you know the blessing of God? Believe in the crucified Savior!

Martyn McGeown

July 15 — Finding Consolation in His Wounds

But God forbid that I should glory,
save in the cross of our Lord Jesus Christ, by whom the world
is crucified unto me, and I unto the world. —Galatians 6:14

Christianity appears to be foolish to the world. We glory in the cross! Why would people glory—boast or rejoice—in the cross which was an instrument of cruel torture and agonizingly painful death? But we do not glory in the cross as a piece of wood. We rejoice in the cross because of what it has accomplished for us and what it means to us.

The death of Christ on the cross was the greatest evil ever perpetrated by man. Peter confronts the inhabitants of Jerusalem with that sin: "Ye have taken [him], and by wicked hands have crucified and slain" (Acts 2:23). That same accusation comes to us—our sins have crucified the Lord of glory. Our transgressions nailed the Son of God to the accursed tree. Our iniquities brought down upon the perfect Lamb of God the bruising, crushing, killing wrath of God. He felt the terrible punishment which our sins have merited. We were the unjust for whom he, the Just One, died. He poured out his precious blood to purge our sins.

Jesus did not die so that we might feel sorry for him. As he made his way to the cross, he rebuked those who bewailed him: "Daughters of Jerusalem, weep not for me, but weep for yourselves" (Luke 23:28). Jesus does not need our pity. Jesus demands our repentance.

The reason we rejoice in the cross of Christ is because his death is the only and effectual atonement for our sins. Had Christ simply died as an example, we could not glory in his cross because we would still be in our sins. Had Christ died merely to show us how righteous or loving God is—but without making satisfaction for our sins—we would have no reason to glory in his cross because it would not be the reason for our salvation. If Christ had died to make it possible for us to save ourselves, we would not glory in the cross, but in ourselves.

Article 21 glories in the cross of Christ, "in whose wounds we find all manner of consolation." We find consolation or comfort in the wounds of our Savior because he was wounded, bruised, and crushed for us—in our place! If he had not died, we would perish. When we consider what Christ suffered, we rejoice because his death means that we do not suffer for our sins. Instead, death is a passageway for us into eternal life. When we remember that he was made a curse for us, we know that this means that we will never suffer God's curse. When we understand that he bore the wrath of God for us, we know that this means that we will never bear the wrath of God ourselves. What a difference that little word *for* makes!

Since Christ has paid it all, we need not—and indeed we cannot—pay anything ourselves. What a burden this truth lifts from our conscience. There is no need for us to pay penance, to punish ourselves for our own sins. There is no horrible prospect of purgatory after death where we would have to suffer for our own sins. "Neither is it necessary to seek or invent any other means of being reconciled to God, than this only sacrifice, once offered, by which believers are made perfect forever," is the joyful conclusion of Article 21.

Let us derive comfort from Christ's wounds. We who are covered by his blood can never perish. All the blessings of salvation are ours—freely, because Christ has paid for them!

Martyn McGeown

Article 22

OF OUR JUSTIFICATION THROUGH FAITH IN JESUS CHRIST

We believe that, to attain the true knowledge of this great mystery, the Holy Ghost kindleth in our hearts an upright faith, which embraces Jesus Christ with all his merits, appropriates him, and seeks nothing more besides him. For it must needs follow, either that all things, which are requisite to our salvation are not in Jesus Christ, or, if all things are in him, that then those who possess Jesus Christ through faith have complete salvation in him. Therefore, for any to assert that Christ is not sufficient, but that something more is required besides him, would be too gross a blasphemy: for hence it would follow that Christ was but half a Savior. Therefore, we justly say with Paul *that we are justified by faith alone, or by faith without works*. However, to speak more clearly, we do not mean that faith itself justifies us, for it is only an instrument with which we embrace Christ our righteousness. But Jesus Christ, imputing to us all his merits and so many holy works which he has done for us and in our stead, is our righteousness. And faith is an instrument that keeps us in communion with him in all his benefits, which, when become ours, are more than sufficient to acquit us of our sins.

July 16 — **The True Knowledge of This Great Mystery**

And without controversy great is the mystery of godliness.
—1 Timothy 3:16

Paul writes to Timothy that the Christian faith is a mystery (1 Tim. 3:16). Some have thought that this means that Christianity is an incomprehensible riddle or an enigma. Since that is so, they have concluded, there is no point in trying to understand the Christian faith. It is beyond human comprehension. Others have said that Christianity can only be understood by the initiated—those who are "let in" to the secret by means of special ceremonies and rites.

If that were true, we and our children could not be Christians. We are very thankful that that is not what the Bible means by mystery.

A mystery in the Bible is something which had not been revealed before but now has been revealed; or, a mystery is something hidden in God's counsel—God's eternal plan for all things—which had been known before only in part, but now has been fully disclosed to God's people in the light of the fullness of New Testament revelation. Paul develops this idea in Ephesians 3. There he tells the Ephesians that in the past the Gentiles' inclusion in the church of God was a mystery in the Old Testament: "Which in other ages was not made known unto the sons of men, as it is now revealed unto his holy apostles and prophets…that the Gentiles should be fellowheirs" (vv. 5-6). It is not that the salvation of the Gentiles was completely unknown in the Old Testament, but it was not known as clearly or fully as it is known now. Thus, it was a mystery.

A mystery, then, is a truth of God's counsel which we cannot know except by revelation and which now has been made known, but which had not previously been made known to the extent to which it is now known by New Testament Christians.

The great mystery of the gospel has been explained in the previous articles of the Belgic Confession—the incarnation of Jesus Christ, the union and distinction of the two natures in the one person of Christ, and the manifestation of God's justice and mercy in the satisfaction of Christ on the cross. These truths were not completely unknown in the Old Testament. They were depicted in types and shadows, and God gave some remarkably explicit prophecies concerning these truths. But in the New Testament, the veil has been removed and we see clearly what was known only dimly in the Old Testament. We are partakers of a great mystery!

Article 22 deals with a new question. Given what Christ has done in his incarnation, his life of obedience and his atoning death, how do the benefits of his death and resurrection become ours personally? If Christ has done everything on the cross which is necessary for our salvation, how are we actually saved?

To this question there have been several answers. Some teach that Christ has done all that he can, and now you must do your part. The common presentation of this view is of a Christ who now offers salvation to whomever will accept it. But this is a denial of the power of Christ. The Biblical, Reformed, and confessional answer is that the same Christ who purchased salvation applies that salvation to his people by working faith in them.

And saving faith is the subject of Article 22: what is faith; where does faith come from; what does faith look to; and how does faith bring us into possession of salvation? These questions I will address in future meditations.

Martyn McGeown

July 17 — Faith's Knowledge of Christ

Ye shall neither be barren nor unfruitful in the knowledge of our Lord Jesus Christ. —2 Peter 1:8

Unlike our Heidelberg Catechism, the Belgic Confession does not give a definition of faith, but we can certainly find the main elements of faith in Article 22. We must be clear, however, at the beginning that there is a distinction between objective faith (what we believe) and subjective faith (our activity of believing). The focus of the Confession is on the latter: by the activity of faith, we become partakers of Christ. What kind of faith is that?

First, we read of faith as knowledge (by faith we "attain the true knowledge"); second, we read of faith's object ("an upright faith, which embraces Jesus Christ with all his merits, appropriates him"); third, we read of the confidence of faith which finds all things in Christ ("and seeks nothing more besides him").

There is much confusion about faith today. For some, faith is simply a vague feeling, but it has no content. For others, faith is a leap in the dark, a step out into the unknown and unknowable. For still others, faith is belief without evidence or belief in the face of all contrary evidence. An atheist, such as Richard Dawkins, derides faith in Jesus Christ as credible as belief in the "flying spaghetti monster" or the "tooth fairy"!

The first element of saving faith is knowledge. A believer knows not only about God, but a believer knows God in Jesus Christ. In fact, so precious is this knowledge that Christ calls it eternal life: "And this is life eternal, that they might know thee the only true God, and Jesus Christ, whom thou hast sent" (John 17:3).

We must stress this point in our anti-doctrinal age. We who believe know who God is and what God has done in Jesus Christ, and the more we know, the stronger our faith becomes. To claim faith without knowledge is to worship an unknown God as did the heathen in Athens (Acts 17:23) or to worship what we do not know as did the Samaritans (John 4:22). Faith is not ignorance.

The source of this knowledge is the word of God. We cannot know anything of God without the Bible. Faith believes everything revealed in the word of God—the history, the miracles, the doctrines, the promises—and faith is informed and increased by the word of God, especially by hearing the preaching. That is why preaching must have content—the minster may not bring silly stories and moral lessons to entertain the people of God. That is why, too, we must hear preaching. A Christian who absents himself from preaching and does not read the Scriptures at home must expect to have weak faith. A Christian who diligently attends the means of grace ought to expect an increased and strengthened faith.

But none of this means that faith is merely intellectual. The knowledge of faith is the knowledge of love, the knowledge of a personal relationship, the knowledge of the covenant. The covenant is friendship. Friends know about one another. They know one another's likes, dislikes, and interests. And friends know one another. They have communion, they share one another's lives, they spend time together, and they communicate.

What a privilege that the infinitely glorious God would condescend to know us and to permit us to know him through faith in Jesus Christ!

Martyn McGeown

July 18 — An Upright, Not Counterfeit, Faith

The devils also believe, and tremble.
—James 2:19

The story is told of an interview between a minister of a church and a prospective candidate for membership. "What do you believe?" the minister asked. "I believe what the church believes," was the answer. Somewhat confused, the minister asked again, "What does the church believe?" "Oh, the church believes what I believe," was the reply. Somewhat frustrated, the minister asked again, "But what do you and the church believe?" To this final question the man replied, "The church and I believe the same thing!"

That is not the upright faith described in our creed. The word *upright* simply means *true*. There is true or saving faith, and there are other species of false or non-saving faith. It is very important that we know the difference between these things because without faith it is impossible to please God, and one can certainly not please God by a counterfeit faith.

The first species of false faith is implicit faith. One with implicit faith blindly follows what the church says. In fact, it is not even necessary for a man with implicit faith to know what the church teaches. Implicit faith is found in many who entrust their soul to the church. They assume that the church has the truth, and because they are in some sense connected to the church, they will be saved. You might discuss doctrine with such a person, and he will tell you that he does not need to bother with doctrine because the minister or priest studies these things, and he simply trusts him. This species of faith makes ignorance a virtue and denies that faith is knowledge. It is because we reject implicit faith that we insist on thorough catechism for our members.

The second species of false faith is temporary faith. Temporary faith is the response of some to the gospel. They are initially very excited—a mere emotional response—but when difficulties come, they are offended and fall away. They were never truly converted. Christ says that they have no root (Matt. 13:21). Having no root, they do not live out of Christ. Emotional faith is not faith.

The third species of false faith is historical faith. The demons have such faith. They know that there is one God, and they tremble (James 2:19). A man with historical faith knows the facts of the Bible and he even believes them—he believes that there was a man called Jesus; he believes that there is a place called heaven—but he does not appropriate these things to himself (Acts 8:18–24). He does not trust in the Christ revealed in Scripture. He cannot say, as Paul did, "I know whom I have believed, and am persuaded that he is able to keep that which I have committed unto him against that day" (2 Tim. 1:12).

The fourth, and final, species of counterfeit faith is miraculous faith. Multitudes had this faith in the days of Jesus (John 2:23–25). They believed that he could perform miracles; they were recipients of miracles; and some even performed miracles in his name; but they did not believe in Jesus Christ (Matt. 7:22–23). When the miracles ended and the truth of Christ was presented, they turned away.

True faith, unlike all these counterfeits, is a certain knowledge and hearty confidence in Jesus Christ, a faith which expects all things necessary for salvation from Christ alone. It is that upright faith of which Article 22 speaks.

Martyn McGeown

July 19 — Faith Keeping Us in Communion with Christ

Abide in me, and I in you. —John 15:4

"Faith is an instrument that keeps us in communion with [Christ] in all his benefits" (Article 22). By these words the Belgic Confession teaches the same truth as the Heidelberg Catechism: that the Holy Spirit unites us to Jesus Christ and that we receive his benefits by believing in him. This implies that by nature we are not united to Jesus Christ. Something must happen to us so that we become united to him. The illustration of Scripture, especially in John 15 and Romans 11, is of a branch which is engrafted into the living vine. The illustration comes from horticulture or gardening. A gardener is able to take a branch from one plant, make an incision in the trunk of another plant, and join them so that a bond is formed between the two plants. The branch then begins to live out of the life of the new plant, and it bears fruit from the life of the new plant, even if the plant is a different species! This living connection between the two plants is called a graft. The process of making a graft is called engrafting.

Perhaps you have encountered other illustrations—faith is like a water pipe conveying water from a reservoir, or faith is like a socket connecting an appliance to an electricity supply. These illustrations, although useful, are inferior to the one the Bible uses because they are not living connections. A graft, unlike a water pipe or electric socket, is not a mechanical or static connection. In grafting, the gardener does not simply glue a branch onto a trunk. That would not create a living bond. For the bond to be effective, the branch must live out of the trunk of the other plant; it must receive the goodness from the sap of the Vine.

However, the graft which the human gardener is able to create by skilled horticulture is still a limited illustration. Can the gardener pick up an old, dead, withered twig and attempt to make a graft with a living tree? No, because the twig is dead! It must be living before it is attached to the trunk of a new tree.

The miracle of salvation is greater. God is not limited as is the human gardener. In salvation, the Holy Spirit takes a sinner—who is like an old, dead, withered stick lying on the ground, severed from the only source of life—and he unites that sinner to Jesus Christ (John 15:1–2). The sinner certainly does not have any power of himself to unite himself to Jesus Christ. Nor, in fact, does the sinner even desire it. He is dead! The Holy Spirit gives to the sinner the life of Jesus Christ in uniting him or her to Jesus Christ.

We call that vital connection, bond, or union, the mystical union. The Holy Spirit works in us the mysterious gift of the faculty of faith, so that we receive Jesus, whom we would otherwise reject. That aspect of our salvation is much neglected today by many who see faith simply as something we do. Before we do something—before we become active in faith—God does something. And our activity depends entirely on his activity. The mystical union is a fruitful union not a passive, lifeless bond. Out of it, we believe.

To express this theologically, before the activity of faith—looking to and believing in Christ—there must be the faculty of faith, or the bond of faith. Another illustration is that of sight. Before a man sees, he must have the faculty of sight. You can no more expect an unbeliever to believe without the faculty of faith than a blind man to see without the faculty of sight. And once we are united to Jesus Christ by the Holy Spirit we begin to believe: we begin to live out of the Savior to whom we are united. As Romans 11:17 puts it, we partake "of the root and fatness." What a wonder!

Martyn McGeown

July 20 — Faith Expecting All Things from Christ

Now faith is the substance of things hoped for,
the evidence of things not seen. —Hebrews 11:1

Hebrews 11 is the great chapter on faith—it describes the activity of faith of a "great... cloud of witnesses" from the Old Testament Scriptures (Heb. 12:1). The opening verse gives the closest we have in Scripture to a definition of faith. It is two things: substance and evidence.

Substance is not the word we might have expected to read. We think of substance as the stuff out of which things are made. Clearly, that is not the meaning of *substance* here. When the Bible speaks of faith as substance, it means something substantial, solid, weighty. The idea is steadiness of mind, a firm and solid resolution and assurance concerning things which are not seen. The things "not seen" are not unicorns or leprechauns or hobgoblins (imaginary, mythical, nonsensical things), but things "hoped for," that is, things promised by God and therefore confidently expected—the spiritual realities of salvation and eternal life (Heb. 11:1).

Thus, it is fitting that Article 22 speaks of the expectation of faith. In faith we look to someone from whom we expect good things.

The believer expects all good things from Christ alone. By faith, he can see them, those invisible things come clearly before his mind. Thus, the Confession declares with unshakable confidence, "those who possess Jesus Christ through faith have complete salvation in him" and "when [Christ and all his benefits] become ours, are more than sufficient to acquit us of our sins" (Article 22). Therefore, by faith the believer knows—knows with an absolute, unshakable, undeniable certainty—not only that there is a heaven, eternal life, future glory, kingdom of God, and everything else promised in the gospel, but that these things are ours, even ours!

Do you know that? Believer in Jesus Christ, you do, and you must!

Second, faith is evidence. We all know that science likes to boast of solid evidence. We hear that unbelieving scientists mock Christians because we believe without evidence or contrary to the evidence. Not so! Faith is evidence. The word *evidence* in Hebrews 11:1 means *conviction* or *proof*. Through faith the believer is convinced that what God has promised is true. The believer does not require any other evidence than the word of God itself. This is something we must remember. When an unbeliever asks for evidence, we cannot give it to him in the form in which he demands it. Was Noah able to give evidence to the world of his day? Was Abraham able to give evidence? Neither should we expect to give (or be given) evidence today. The words of Abraham to the rich man are true: "If they hear not Moses and the prophets, neither will they be persuaded, though one rose from the dead" (Luke 16:31).

A believer is convinced by faith itself. An unbeliever can never be convinced, because he has no faith. To try to convince an unbeliever without faith to believe is akin to trying to convince a blind man without the faculty of sight to see. Faith is a miracle—certain knowledge, assured confidence, absolute conviction—worked in the heart of man, worked in our hearts and in the hearts of our children.

Martyn McGeown

July 21 — Faith as Assurance

For I know whom I have believed, and am persuaded that he is able to keep that which I have committed unto him against that day. —2 Timothy 1:12

One who has faith knows that he has eternal life. One who has faith knows that he belongs to Jesus Christ now and forever. One who has faith knows that nothing will "separate [him] from the love of God, which is in Christ Jesus our Lord" (Rom. 8:39). In other words, faith is personal assurance of salvation and personal assurance of eternal election. Without this assurance, a man cannot live—and he certainly cannot die—for Christ. In fact, without this knowledge, we dare not die at all.

Assurance of salvation is something which God desires for all his children. In giving us faith, he gives us assurance because faith is assurance. About this, there should be no doubt. What father would be happy if only a few of his children really believed that he loved them and that he was their father? How would a loving father react if he knew that many of his children were afraid to come to him because they believed that there was a distinct possibility that they did not really belong to him? If earthly fathers find such a thought intolerable, how could our heavenly Father be pleased that his children live and die without any assurance of his love? And how cruel would God be to leave his children in suspense about such an important thing? Without such assurance, no prayer, good works, or worship are possible.

The devil knows that if he can cause God's children to doubt their salvation, he can ruin their experience of the Christian life, cut the throat of their comfort, and lead them to despair. Doubts are part of the "fiery darts of the wicked" which can only be quenched with "the shield of faith" (Eph. 6:16).

The Bible presupposes that the people of God know that they are saved and that they know that they are among the number of God's elect. Everywhere, the apostles address God's people this way. Often the apostles urge believers to make their calling and election sure. Doubts are not normal, healthy, or useful in the Christian life. Doubt is sin, the enemy of faith. Jesus rebuked his disciples more than once for doubt. To Peter he says, "O thou of little faith, wherefore didst thou doubt?" (Matt. 14:31). To Thomas, whom we call "Doubting Thomas," Jesus says: "Be not faithless, but believing" (John 20:27). James rebukes the man who prays with doubts: "But let him ask in faith, nothing wavering" (James 1:6).

The ministers of the gospel must never foster or encourage doubts. There are preachers who do this. They encourage a morbid self-examination, a spiritual navel-gazing. "Are you really converted?" they ask. In such churches, the number of doubters is so great that very few church members come to the Lord's supper! That is a travesty, the fruit of preaching which discourages faith and encourages doubt. Apostolic preaching does not encourage doubt. It rebukes doubt. It urges to faith. It seeks to strengthen and build up faith.

How, then, can I know that I am an elect child of God? I do not look for assurance in experiences or in feelings. I know that I am elect by faith. Only the elect have faith. Faith itself is the assurance of salvation. And when I have doubts—and remember that all Christians struggle with doubts in one form or another and at various times in their lives, especially when they fall into sin or are vexed by some affliction—I view that doubt as sin, confess it as such, and cry to God: "Lord, I believe; help thou mine unbelief" (Mark 9:24).

Martyn McGeown

July 22

Faith Kindled by the Holy Spirit

For unto you it is given in the behalf of Christ,
not only to believe on him. —Philippians 1:29

We have seen in the previous meditations that faith is, first, knowledge and, second, confidence (expectation). There are many professing Christians who believe that a sinner can work up this knowledge and confidence by the exercise of his own freewill.

According to this view—Arminianism—every sinner has in himself the capacity to believe, and all that is necessary to bring him to faith is persuasion. This explains Arminian evangelism—the emotional appeals, the high-powered evangelist, the music, the atmosphere. Everything in such evangelism is designed to appeal to the sinner's emotions and especially his will. If some less radical Arminians find a place for the Holy Spirit, they still insist that the sinner has the possibility to resist or cooperate with the wooing of the Spirit. The work of the Spirit is not, and cannot be, according to Arminianism, irresistible or effectual.

This is not at all the truth of the biblical concept of faith as explained in Article 22. That is set forth in a beautiful expression: "to attain the true knowledge of this great mystery, the Holy Ghost kindleth in our hearts an upright faith."

That the Holy Spirit kindles faith in us means, first, that without the kindling power of the Holy Spirit we are dark and cold. To *kindle* means *to ignite, to start a fire*, which brings both light and heat. Our hearts are cold; in them there is no affection for Jesus Christ. Quite the contrary. We "love darkness rather than light," and we will not come to the light because our deeds are evil (John 3:19–20). Our hearts are dark; in them there is no knowledge of the true God or of Jesus Christ, but horrible darkness and blindness. Can such a heart—cold, dark, lifeless—produce the slightest spark of faith? Of course not!

For this reason, the Bible speaks consistently of faith as a gift, a gift which God breathes into us and works in us, or kindles in us. Ephesians 2:8 teaches that faith is "not of yourselves: it is the gift of God," and Philippians 1:29 teaches that "it is given"—graciously and freely granted—to us to believe.

But the Arminian has a subterfuge. He says: "Yes, faith is a gift, but you must accept it." Notice how the Arminian changes faith from a gift into an offer. But notice, too, the absurdity of that position. How do we supposedly accept this gift of faith? By believing! So, we can have the gift of faith if we believe. That would be to say to a blind man, "I will give you the gift of sight, if you see!"

What a difference the work of the Holy Spirit makes! In a dead, lifeless, cold, dark heart the Spirit kindles a true and living faith. Now there is the light of the knowledge of God in Jesus Christ. Now there is an assured confidence in the Savior. Now there is hope and joy in believing. Let us never be tempted to rob the Spirit of his glory by attributing that great miracle of kindling saving faith to ourselves!

Martyn McGeown

July 23 — Faith Seeking Nothing More Besides Christ

The life which I now live in the flesh
I live by the faith of the Son of God. —Galatians 2:20

Faith is not common to all men. Often we hear that all men have faith—that faith is simply trust in something. Thus, people say that when you sit on a chair you exercise faith in the chair that it will not collapse under you. But that is not faith. That is a weighing up of probabilities. You assume that the chair was built to sustain your weight, no one has broken the chair before you, you have no reason to think that the chair will break now.

When we say that we believe in Jesus Christ we mean much more than that. Faith confidently and with full assurance seeks all good things from Jesus Christ. That is because we know Jesus Christ. Therefore, when our faith in Jesus Christ brings us hardship—and it will—we do not cast away our confidence. Faith is childlike trust. Why does a child trust his father? Because he knows his father—he knows his father's character, and he knows his father's love. This knowledge gives the child confidence in the presence of his father. The same child behaves differently around strangers because he does not know strangers. As Jesus said about his sheep who know him as shepherd: "And a stranger will they not follow, but will flee from him: for they know not the voice of strangers" (John 10:5).

The New Testament teaches that faith is confidence by means of two prepositions—small words which indicate position or movement. First, the New Testament speaks about believing *into* Jesus Christ; second, the New Testament teaches that we live *out of* Christ and that we are justified by (literally, out of) faith. These expressions teach us that the source of life for the believer is Jesus Christ, and that by believing he partakes of the benefits of Jesus Christ.

Moreover, the believer has faith exclusively in Jesus Christ. He does not believe in other saviors, and he does not divide his allegiance between saviors. If all things necessary for salvation were not found in Christ, Christ would be but "half a Savior." Of course, the Belgic Confession, a Reformation creed, has Roman Catholicism in mind—Rome taught that the saints, especially Mary, contributed to salvation. But we must not forget the error of self-salvation—the error that we can contribute something to our salvation in the form of good works.

The answer to all self-salvation is the sufficiency of Christ. Remember the vine and the branches. The branches receive the sap from the vine through the graft. The branches do not suck the sap from the vine and from some other plant at the same time. For the branches there is no other source of life. If the branch ever became separated from the vine—which, of course, could never happen—it would die. The same is true for us. We live out of Jesus Christ, not out of ourselves, nor out of Jesus Christ and someone else. "Without me," says Christ, "ye can do nothing" (John 15:5).

Let us seek all things in Jesus Christ alone, by faith alone.

Martyn McGeown

Article 23

OUR JUSTIFICATION CONSISTS IN THE FORGIVENESS OF SIN AND THE IMPUTATION OF CHRIST'S RIGHTEOUSNESS

We believe that our salvation consists in the remission of our sins for Jesus Christ's sake, and that therein our righteousness before God is implied; as David and Paul teach us, declaring this to be the happiness of man, that God imputes righteousness to him without works. And the same Apostle saith, *that we are justified freely by his grace, through the redemption which is in Jesus Christ*. And therefore we always hold fast this foundation, ascribing all the glory to God, humbling ourselves before him, and acknowledging ourselves to be such as we really are, without presuming to trust in any thing in ourselves, or in any merit of ours, relying and resting upon the obedience of Christ crucified alone, which becomes ours when we believe in him. This is sufficient to cover all our iniquities, and to give us confidence in approaching to God; freeing the conscience of fear, terror, and dread, without following the example of our first father, Adam, who, trembling, attempted to cover himself with fig-leaves. And, verily, if we should appear before God, relying on ourselves or on any other creature, though ever so little, we should, alas! be consumed. And therefore every one must pray with David: *O Lord, enter not into judgment with thy servant: for in thy sight shall no man living be justified.*

July 24 — Salvation: The Remission of Sins

Blessed is he whose transgression is forgiven,
whose sin is covered. —Psalm 32:1

Articles 22–23 of the Belgic Confession belong together because Article 23 is a continuation of Article 22. Both deal with justification by faith alone. The peculiar emphasis of Article 23 is the utter graciousness of justification. From it, all of our works must be excluded.

First and foremost, says Article 23, "we believe that our salvation consists in the remission of our sins for Jesus Christ's sake, and that therein our righteousness before God is implied." Remission is another word for forgiveness. Salvation is forgiveness of sins because it is the chief blessing and the blessing without which we have nothing. That is David's emphasis in Psalm 32. As a king he had experienced many good things in life—he lived in a beautiful palace, he had many faithful servants, he had riches, and in his kingdom there was peace. But none of those things meant anything to David when he did not know the forgiveness of sins. David fell into gross public sin for a time and refused to repent. During a prolonged period of impenitence, David experienced the opposite of the blessedness of forgiveness. God's heavy hand of chastisement was upon him, and he knew no peace, no joy, and no satisfaction in God (Ps. 32:3–4). But in the way of confession and repentance, David had come again to experience the joy of the forgiveness of sin. That was the occasion of his writing Psalm 32.

The conclusion of Psalm 32 is really the first verse: "Blessed is he whose transgression is forgiven, whose sin is covered." In the Psalm, which Paul quotes to prove gracious justification in Romans 4:6–8, David describes sin using three words: *transgression*, *sin*, and *iniquity*. A *transgression* is the crossing of a boundary, in this case the boundary of God's law. In transgressing the law, David deliberately, willfully, and wickedly rebelled against God. The law said, "Thou shalt not." David said, "I will disregard the law, and I will do what I want." This was a rebellious shaking of the fist in the face of God! And this sin arose from hatred of God in David's heart. A *sin* is a *missing of the mark*. Observe an archer. He has a target, but instead of aiming at the target, he turns his bow and shoots in the opposite direction. That's sin. When we sin, we refuse to aim at the mark that is the glory of the God. We shoot at a different mark, the mark of our own pleasure, our own glory. *Iniquity*, the third word David uses—behold how manifold sin is that the Bible uses so many words to describe it!—means *something twisted, perverse, or bent*. Our calling is to conform to the standard of God, but we pervert our way and refuse to walk uprightly according to God's commandments.

Transgression, sin, iniquity! High-handed rebellion against the Almighty!

The wonder—the great blessedness of which Psalm 32 speaks—is that God forgives. The word *forgive* in Psalm 32:1 is *to lift up* or *to carry away*. Sin, like a heavy burden, was crushing David, and God carried that burden away, bringing relief to David's soul. What blessedness! The last word in Psalm 32:1 is *covered*. The word means *to blot out* or *to conceal*. When God forgives our sins, he covers them up so that he does not see them with a view to punishing us for them. David had tried to cover his own sins, but this had led only to misery.

God lifts our sins; he carries them away; he covers them; he blots them out. That's forgiveness. And we who know that forgiveness are blessed above measure.

Martyn McGeown

July 25 — **Forgiven for Jesus Christ's Sake**

The blood of Jesus Christ his Son
cleanseth us from all sin. —1 John 1:7

Yesterday we rejoiced in the forgiveness of sins, and we especially noticed what sin is and what it means for God to forgive us our sins. God lifts, or carries away, and God blots out, or covers over, our sins, transgressions, and iniquities and does not punish us for them. But the question which begs to be asked is this: how can that be possible?

The answer Article 23 gives is "for Jesus Christ's sake." That expression, which we hear so often, especially at the end of many prayers, contains a wealth of meaning. God forgives us for the sake of Christ, or because of Christ, or on the basis of what Christ has done for us.

Both Abraham and David, who lived in the Old Testament before the coming of Christ, understood that. Every child of God has understood that to a greater or lesser degree. Every believer in Israel, who stood before a sacrifice of a bleeding lamb and trusted in God for the forgiveness of sins, understood that. We must understand that, too, and we do by faith.

No child of God trusts in himself for the forgiveness of sins. Pardon is found in another, namely, Jesus Christ. Take the example of David. He stands before God, defiled by the sin of adultery, his hands dripping with Uriah's blood. What is his plea, or, on what does he base his hope for pardon? God does not say to David, "You have sinned, but I am willing to overlook your sin and hopefully you will do better in the future." God does not say to David: "Your sins are very serious, and my law says that the sinner must die, but I will take into account your good works. At the end of your life I will look at how you have done, and if your good works outweigh your bad works, I will forgive you then." David did not have any good works. He did not plead any good works. The only works David mentions are transgressions, sins, iniquity, and guile.

Moreover, Psalm 32 declares that David was a passive recipient of, not an active participant in, salvation. "Blessed is he whose transgression is forgiven" (v. 1). Not "blessed is the man who forgives his own transgressions," or "blessed is the man who carries away his own burden of transgressions," or even "blessed is the man who helps God carry away his own transgressions." "Blessed is he…whose sin is covered" (v. 1). Not "blessed is he who covers up his own sins" (David had tried that—it was called guile or deceit—and that had made him miserable).

How, then, can God bless the sinner and make him happy by forgiving his sins? The answer is that another—Jesus Christ—carried away our sins, blotted them out, and thus covered them over in the sight of God. Upon Jesus Christ, the great son of David, and the eternal Son of God in our flesh, God piled the load of David's guilt—and ours! Imagine that burden! That heavy load of guilt which would have crushed a mere man, Christ carried to the cross, and there he suffered under the heavy wrath of God. God removed the load of guilt from us and placed it on the shoulders of Christ. On the cross, too, Christ blotted out our sins. No amount of scrubbing and no amount of soap could have removed one stain of our sin. Christ covered our filthy stains, not by "brushing them under a rug," but by fully satisfying God's wrath for them, and then rising again from the dead, having conquered the power of death, sin, hell, and the devil.

Thus, God is satisfied, Christ is glorified, and we are blessed!

Martyn McGeown

July 26 — Justification: God as Judge

They shall justify the righteous, and condemn the wicked.
—Deuteronomy 25:1

Justification by faith alone is the heart of the gospel. By it the Reformers answered from the Bible the urgent question: "How can I, a sinner, be right with God?" The answer is that God justifies us freely by his grace alone through faith alone in Christ alone.

To understand the doctrine expounded here, we must understand several key concepts. The very first thing we must comprehend is that in justification, God acts as the judge.

A judge is one who examines a defendant with respect to the law, and then, having examined him, determines whether he is innocent or guilty; and, if the defendant is guilty, the judge determines and officially pronounces the sentence of punishment. If the defendant is innocent, the judge officially pronounces him innocent and free from punishment. When the Bible reveals that God is judge, we must understand that God evaluates all his rational, moral creatures with respect to his law. Have men and angels kept his law or not? God evaluates all of us with respect to that great question. In fact, God is always judging, and man must know (and does know) that he is always being judged. The conscience of a man—remember that man's conscience is that little judge in his heart, a judge placed there by God himself—either accuses or excuses a man with respect to the moral worth (or demerit) of his actions (Rom. 2:15). The eyes of the Judge are everywhere (Prov. 15:3), and no man can escape him!

It is important that we stress this at the very beginning. Justification deals only with a man's relationship to the law of God. Every other subject, although important in its own place, is irrelevant to the subject of justification. When we consider the great doctrine of the justification of sinners, therefore, we must think of God only as judge.

Perhaps an illustration will help. Imagine for a moment that you stand before a human judge. The judge in the courtroom will examine you with respect to the question of your guilt or innocence. He will weigh up the evidence and make a judgment, and the one question he will ask himself will be this: "Has this person committed a crime, or has he kept the law?" The judge will not be interested in your character—that you are generally a nice person. The judge will disregard the fact that you have up to this point been law-abiding—that you have had a clean driving record, let's say. The question will be, "Have you committed the crime?" If you have—and if the judge is a just judge—the verdict will be, and it will have to be, "Guilty!" If you have not, the verdict will be, "Not guilty!" This is the case even if the judge before whom you stand is a friend, a close relation, or even your own father.

That was God's requirement for judges. They had to condemn the wicked, that is, declare that the wicked were guilty and punish them accordingly. They had to justify the righteous, that is, declare that the righteous were innocent and deal with them accordingly. God forbade them to justify the wicked by turning a blind eye to their crimes or by accepting bribes; or to condemn the righteous by accepting false testimony against them.

The astonishing truth is that God justifies those who are sinners. The question we must answer is: how is that possible? That question only the glorious doctrine of justification by faith alone answers.

Martyn McGeown

July 27 — **Justification: God's Legal Declaration**

He that justifieth the wicked,
and he that condemneth the just, even they both are
abomination to the Lord. —Proverbs 17:15

Yesterday, we considered the important truth that in justification, God is the judge, and we began to examine what exactly God does in his capacity as judge. Judges examine evidence, determine guilt or innocence, and then declare a verdict.

We could define justification briefly thus: Justification is God's legal declaration of righteousness.

First, justification is legal. It pertains to the law, to things judicial or forensic. All of those terms are used in theological works on justification. Notice first the words *legal* and *judicial*. They mean *pertaining to law*. That word *forensic* may be less familiar, but it too pertains to law. Forensic medicine, for example, is medical examination with a view to presenting a case in court. Blood samples, traces of hair, DNA, and fingerprints are part of the forensic examination of a crime scene. Thus, the language of a court of law is prevalent in texts which deal with justification. The issue in justification is only guilt or innocence, only acquittal or condemnation. A person may be accused of a crime—a transgression of God's law in this case—but is acquitted and justified before God's judgment seat. How that happens we will examine later. For now, we want to stress that that is what happens.

Second, justification is a declaration, or an official pronouncement, verdict, statement, or judgment. When God justifies, he speaks about a person's relationship to the law. If the person is not in harmony with the standards of God's perfect law, God pronounces him guilty, and thus God condemns him. If the person is in harmony with the standards of God's perfect law, God pronounces him innocent, and thus justifies him. The fact that in the Bible, *justify* and *condemn* are opposites proves that justification is a declaration. When God condemns the sinner, he does not make the sinner wicked or ungodly. Similarly, when God justifies us, he does not make us morally good.

That explains, too, Proverbs 17:15. God abominates the wicked judge who "justifieth the wicked" and "condemneth the righteous." The judge must not declare the wicked to be righteous, or the righteous to be wicked. His legal declaration must be in truth. And, as we shall see, God's righteous declarations are in truth. To summarize: justification is the declaration from God's judgment seat that a person is righteous, not guilty, and therefore not worthy of punishment. It is not something which God does inside a sinner to make him morally good but is a declaration concerning his position with respect to the law. Someone has wisely remarked that when God justifies, he acts in his capacity as the judge, not as a surgeon!

Third, justification is God's legal declaration. When the almighty God justifies, that verdict is final. It cannot be overturned, appealed against, changed, increased, decreased, or lost. A man is either justified or he is condemned. There is no middle ground. Thus, Paul dares anyone to overturn the justifying verdict of God: "Who shall lay anything to the charge of God's elect? It is God that justifieth. Who is he that condemneth?" (Rom. 8:33–34).

Justification: God's legal declaration concerning us that we are righteous. What a wonder!

Martyn McGeown

July 28 — **Justification: A Declaration of Righteousness**

Even the righteousness of God which is by faith
of Jesus Christ unto all and upon all them that believe. —Romans 3:22

Yesterday we did not finish explaining our short definition of justification: God's legal declaration of righteousness. We need also to define and explain righteousness because righteousness is absolutely vital in justification.

Righteousness is conformity to a standard or a norm. The word *righteous* in Scripture means *straight, level,* or *even*. Something righteous conforms to and is in harmony with a given standard. The opposite of righteous is crooked, twisted, bent, or perverse. Thus, the word *iniquity* (one of the words for sin in the Bible) means *crookedness* or *perversity*. Scripture says that God is righteous or just. That raises a question: if God is righteous, and righteousness is harmony with a standard, with what standard is God in harmony? The answer is himself: God is unswervingly committed to himself as the highest and only standard. There is no higher standard outside of God to which he would have to conform. Therefore, whatever or whoever is in conformity to God's standard of righteousness is righteous and is declared righteous; and whatever or whoever deviates from God's standard is unrighteous and is declared unrighteous. It really does not matter if you conform to the standards of society, or even to your own standards. Do you conform to God's standard?

Clearly we do not, for we are sinners. Therefore, it would appear that our justification is impossible.

God is righteous. Therefore, he must punish sin and sinners for their unrighteousness. That is one way in which the Bible speaks of righteousness. Martin Luther knew that aspect of God's righteousness, and it troubled him greatly. He understood that, since God is righteous, God will and must punish all those who do not conform to the standard that God has revealed in his perfect law. Imagine Luther's confusion, therefore, when he read in Romans 1:16–17, "For I am not ashamed of the gospel of Christ... for therein is the righteousness of God revealed from faith to faith." Luther could not make sense of this. On the one hand, the gospel is good news for poor sinners. On the other hand, the gospel reveals the righteousness of God, which, as Luther understood it, is God's perfect character according to which he punishes sinners. How could God's righteousness possibly be good news for a sinner such as Luther?

Luther could have no peace until he understood that the righteousness of God means more than that, and that it is something which God gives to sinners so that they can stand before him without fear of condemnation. Article 22 has this in mind when it states that "Christ...is our righteousness."

Romans 3 gives the answers to Luther's problem. There Paul speaks of the righteousness of God again. This righteousness is "manifested, being witnessed by the law and the prophets" (v. 21). And, crucially, this righteousness is "unto all and upon all them that believe" (v. 22). The righteousness of God, then, is not merely one of God's perfect attributes, but something he bestows upon us. It is the righteousness from God, the only righteousness which satisfies the demands of God's holy law.

Do you have that righteousness? Believer in Christ, you do!

Martyn McGeown

July 29 — Christ Our Righteousness

And this is his name whereby he shall be called,
*the L*ORD *our righteousness.* —Jeremiah 23:6

In previous meditations, we have seen that justification is God's declaration that we are in perfect harmony with the standard of God's perfect law, free from all guilt, and worthy of eternal life. In other words, justification is God's legal declaration of righteousness.

The issue that we must address is this: on what basis can God justify us? We noticed earlier that the calling of a judge is to justify the righteous and to condemn the wicked (Deut. 25:1; Prov. 17:15). We also know that God always justifies "according to truth" (Rom. 2:2). Could an opponent of the Reformed faith argue that we are teaching that God does what no human judge may do, that he is justifying the ungodly (Rom. 3:26; 4:5)? How can God do that and remain just? Does God simply pretend that we are righteous when in reality we are not? Does God turn a blind eye to our sins and bless us anyway? We answer with the blessed truth that the basis of our justification is the righteousness of another, namely, Jesus Christ.

We are not righteous in ourselves. We certainly are not in perfect harmony with or in perfect conformity to the law of God. And yet, when he justifies us, God declares that we are righteous! He does so because Christ, whose righteousness becomes ours in justification, is our righteousness. That is how the Belgic Confession explains it, "Jesus Christ, imputing to us all his merits and so many holy works, which he has done for us and in our stead, is our righteousness" (Article 22), and our justification rests on "the obedience of Christ crucified" (Article 23).

For Christ to be our righteousness, he must meet all the demands of the law for us and in our place. We can never meet these demands, and, since God will never set aside his demands without denying himself, Christ humbled himself to meet those demands for us.

First, Christ paid for all our transgressions against the law of God. He did that by suffering the wrath of God especially on the cross and by dying under God's curse. Second, Christ obeyed all the commandments of God's law and never deviated from the path of God's righteousness. This—Christ's lifelong obedience and his atoning death which satisfied God's justice—is our righteousness before God. On the basis of this, God accepts us as righteous, without any guilt and worthy of all the blessings of salvation. God declares concerning us: "This one, whom I see in my beloved Son Jesus Christ, is righteous. I see no sin in him. I see only the merits of my Son and the many holy works which he has performed. And because of what I see, I am perfectly satisfied that this one is in harmony with me and with my law, and I pronounce blessings upon him."

That was Paul's confession in Philippians 3. Paul had tried to be justified by "mine own righteousness, which is of the law" (v. 9). That righteousness, hypothetically speaking, would come to one who by hard work had managed to live in harmony with God's law. Paul called that "mine own righteousness (v. 9). Paul rejected that righteousness as an impossibility—he even calls it loss or dung! (v. 7–8)—and clings to the righteousness of Jesus Christ, the righteousness which Christ himself had wrought for Paul and for all believers by his life and death.

That righteousness—the righteousness which comes from Christ and not from us—is the only basis for justification.

Martyn McGeown

July 30 — The Error of Romish Justification

I tell you, this man went down to his house justified rather than the other. —Luke 18:14

In previous meditations, we have carefully defined the elements of the Reformed doctrine of justification. We have done this deliberately because justification by faith alone is the heart of the gospel, the article of a standing or a falling church, and the hinge on which salvation turns. We have also done this so that we can contrast it with the doctrine of the Roman Catholic Church. Truth is always clearer against the background of error.

It should not surprise us that the Roman doctrine of justification is the antithesis of what we have been learning from the Belgic Confession.

First, in Roman Catholicism justification is not so much a legal declaration as a moral renewal, or a legal declaration based on a moral renewal. Roman Catholicism downplays the legal aspect of justification. Instead of a *declaration* of righteousness, Rome speaks of a *making righteous*. Rome teaches that justification is a moral, cleansing work in the soul which brings about a change in the one justified. This may sound reasonable and even biblical, but remember, a judge does not improve the moral character of a person in his courtroom: he simply makes a declaration concerning him. Remember, also, that we do not deny that God changes our moral character when he saves us. However, that change has nothing whatsoever to do with justification. Thus, according to Rome, in justification God pours (or infuses) virtue into the sinner's heart, which makes him inwardly holy and good. The devilish nature of Rome's doctrine is that she calls the virtue infused into the soul "grace." And this "grace" is dispensed through the church in her sacraments and increased in the soul by the performance of pious exercises.

Second, on the basis of the change wrought in the sinner by the infusion of virtue (grace) into his soul, God declares the sinner to be justified and worthy to receive more grace. Thus, grace is increased in the soul, and the sinner is further justified. However, if the sinner commits a serious sin (mortal sin), he loses grace, loses justification, and must be re-justified by the infusion of more grace, again through the sacraments. Hear what Rome herself says in the *Catechism of the Catholic Church*: "No one can merit the initial grace of forgiveness and justification, at the beginning of conversion. Moved by the Holy Spirit and by charity, *we can then merit* for ourselves and for others the graces needed for our sanctification, for the increase of grace and charity, and for the attainment of eternal life."*

We draw several conclusions. First, Rome teaches that justification is a process. The Bible teaches that it is the finished act of God. Second, Rome teaches that justification is a moral work in the sinner. The Bible teaches that it is a declaration concerning the sinner's status before the law of God. Third, Rome teaches that the basis of justification is the sinner's own righteousness—a righteousness wrought by the Spirit by means of faith, the use of the sacraments, and good works. The Bible teaches that the basis of justification is only the righteousness of Christ—all the merits and holy works that Christ has performed in his living and dying for us.

Rome's doctrine of justification destroys comfort. How can we know if we are righteous enough to gain salvation? Any sinner who trusts in his own righteousness—whether the works of the law or even those works supposedly wrought by charity and the Spirit in his heart—is lost because his works can never reach the standard required by God's law.

This is a standard that only Christ has met. Away with any other righteousness!

—*Martyn McGeown*

---

* *Catechism of the Catholic Church*, paragraph 2010.

July 31 — Righteous by Faith Alone

Therefore we conclude that a man is justified by faith without the deeds of the law. —Romans 3:28

In justification, God declares elect sinners to be righteous—to be in perfect harmony with and conformity to the standard of God's law and thus with God himself—on the basis of the righteousness of another, namely Jesus Christ. That righteousness consists of the "merits and so many holy works" (Article 22) of Christ: his obedience.

The issue we address now is: how does that righteousness become ours? And the answer of the Bible is: by faith.

Remember that the Holy Spirit unites us to Jesus Christ so that we believe in him. Faith is that spiritual activity which consists of certain knowledge and a hearty confidence in him (see Heidelberg Catechism, question and answer 21). The Belgic Confession teaches that faith "embraces Jesus Christ with all his merits, appropriates him, and seeks nothing more besides him" (22). Notice the verbs: faith seeks (and therefore finds) Christ, embraces him, and appropriates him; and in so doing faith lays hold of Christ's righteousness. Moreover, Article 22 states, faith is "an instrument with which we embrace Christ our righteousness," and "faith is an instrument that keeps us in communion with him in all his benefits, which, when become ours, are more than sufficient to acquit us of our sins."

Faith is only an instrument: it is the appropriating organ by which we lay hold of Jesus Christ. Without faith, what Christ has done for us in life and death cannot become ours. Remember the graft: the branch itself is nothing without the graft, but even the graft itself is nothing without the vine into which we are engrafted.

When the Bible speaks of justification by faith—or through faith or out of faith—it contrasts the truth with the false teaching of justification by works or justification by the law (or out of the law). We do not become possessors of a righteousness pleasing to God by works. We cannot work hard enough to produce such a righteousness of our own; we cannot even work so that we can purchase Christ's righteousness. This is true for two reasons. First, we can never meet the demands of the law for perfect obedience. Second, we can never satisfy the demands of the law for a payment of our sins. Therefore, justification by works must forever remain an impossibility for sinners.

Paul speaks of the "righteousness of God without the law" (Rom. 3:21) and insists that we are justified "without the deeds of the law" (v. 28). That word *without* means that the law is completely excluded from justification. No law of any kind, not the law of Moses, not the moral law, not the law of love, not the civil or ceremonial law, not the law of nature, no law at all, justifies a sinner. When it comes to justification, all law is excluded. The righteousness by which we are justified has nothing to do with our keeping the law. Law is completely out of the picture.

Justification by faith and not of works is necessary to exclude boasting. We come to be justified, not bragging about our obedience, but clinging to the obedience of Jesus Christ; and through believing we are justified. Only through believing.

Martyn McGeown

August 1 — Faith: Not the Basis of Justification

But to him that worketh not, but believeth on him that justifieth the ungodly, his faith is counted for righteousness. —Romans 4:5

Justification is the legal declaration of God that a person is in harmony with his law. The basis for this legal declaration is the righteousness of another, namely, Jesus Christ. We receive this righteousness by faith alone without works.

You may have noticed that Articles 22–23 overlap somewhat. That is because they both teach justification by faith alone. In a systematic treatment, some issues must still be addressed. What do we mean by "justification by faith alone"? What exactly is the role of faith? That must be clarified.

In every age there have been those who have twisted or perverted the doctrine of justification. The Arminians are guilty of this perversion when they teach that faith itself is our justification before God, that is, faith itself is our righteousness. Article 22 rejects this error: "However, to speak more clearly, we do not mean that faith itself justifies us, for it is only an instrument with which we embrace Christ our righteousness." Notice the careful distinction: faith is not the basis or ground of justification, but the instrument or means of justification. This careful distinction comes from a careful study of God's word: the Bible teaches repeatedly that we are justified by faith (or through faith), but it never teaches that we are justified on account of (or on the basis of) faith.

This is true for a number of reasons. First, our faith cannot be the ground of our justification because our faith is imperfect. The faith of the strongest Christian is very weak. Mixed in with our faith is much unbelief and sin. Every Christian can identify with the man who cried out to Jesus with tears: "Lord, I believe; help thou mine unbelief" (Mark 9:24). Our faith is, therefore, not a righteous basis for our justification. Second, our faith cannot be the ground of our justification because our faith does not fulfill the demands of God's law. Even if our faith were perfect—not weak, imperfect, unstable, changing, and faltering—it would not answer the charges of God's law against us (we have sinned and deserve death) or the demands of God's law concerning us (we owe God lifelong, perfect obedience in love with our whole heart, soul, mind, and strength). Only Christ has done that, and therefore only his obedience can be our righteousness or the basis of our justification. The Arminians' error is to deny God's justice. They imagine that God will accept something less than perfect obedience—our faith. But then God would deny himself and would not be just. Such is impossible.

The Arminian objects by quoting Romans 4:5, "his faith is counted for righteousness." In verse 3, Paul quotes Genesis 15:6, "Abraham believed God, and it was counted unto him for righteousness." It would appear that the basis for Abraham's justification was Abraham's faith, that faith itself was Abraham's righteousness. But that is emphatically not what Paul is teaching here. First, as with us, Abraham's faith was weak and faltering. Read Genesis to observe how God had to test and purify Abraham's faith through trials. Second, *faith* in verse 5 refers to the object of Abraham's faith, which is Christ. Abraham, even in the days of types and shadows, saw Christ and believed in him. God reckoned to Abraham not his faith—as if that were something meritorious—but that which Abraham embraced by faith: Jesus Christ and his righteousness.

The same is true for us. Our righteousness is Christ's righteousness received by faith alone.

Martyn McGeown

August 2 — The Blessed Non-Imputation of Iniquity

Blessed is the man unto whom the Lord imputeth not iniquity.
—Psalm 32:2

Justification, which is the subject of Article 23, is not merely the forgiveness of sins. Let us remind ourselves that justification is God's legal declaration of righteousness. In justification, God the judge makes an official legal declaration that the sinner who stands before him is righteous, that is, that the sinner conforms perfectly to and is in complete harmony with the absolute standard of God's holy law. That means, negatively, that the sinner is not guilty of any sin—no sin can be laid to his charge. Positively, the sinner possesses legally a status of perfect, positive righteousness because he possesses all of the "merits and so many holy works" (Art. 22) of Jesus Christ by faith.

If we might so speak, forgiveness of sins is only half a justification. Think of a man who stands before a judge accused of a crime. He is found not guilty and is free to go. But he is not positively righteous! If God merely forgave our sins, we would not go to hell, but we would not be worthy of heaven either. To go to heaven, we must not merely have no sins to our account. We must be positively righteous. That is why Article 23 adds: "in the remission of our sins…our righteousness before God is implied."

This brings us to the last great biblical and theological word which we must know to understand the doctrine of justification. We looked at *legal, judicial* and *forensic* (pertaining to law); *declaration* or *pronouncement*; *righteousness*. Now we consider *imputation*, that is, "Christ, imputing to us all his merits" (Article 22) and "God imputes righteousness to him without works" (Article 23).

To impute means to reckon, to consider, to account something to someone. When something is imputed, it is counted as legally belonging to someone, so that either a person bears the responsibility for another's guilt or receives the credit for another's virtue. Paul wrote to Philemon: "If he [Onesimus] hath wronged thee, or oweth thee ought, put that on mine account; I Paul have written it with mine own hand, I will repay it" (vv. 18–19). Imputation concerns accounts or records, therefore; and in justification, imputation concerns legal accounts or records. Imputation answers these questions: How can the perfect record which Christ wrought in his righteous life become mine; and how can my sinful record of horrible crimes against the law of God become Christ's, so that I am not punished on account of my own sins but am rewarded for the virtues, merits, and holy works of Christ?

In justification God performs a twofold imputation. First, he imputes, reckons, or accounts all of our sins to the record of Jesus Christ. Imagine that for a moment! To the sinless, holy, righteous Son of God are imputed all our sins. As it were, Christ says of us, "If my people, whom I love, have wronged thee or owed thee anything, Father, put it on my account. I, thy only begotten and ever beloved Son, have written it in my own blood. I have repaid it." That is why David speaks of the blessedness of the man "unto whom the Lord imputeth not iniquity" (Ps. 32:2). The Lord has already imputed our iniquity to Christ. Christ, entering the world with our iniquity on his account, was punished for that iniquity—not his iniquity, but ours! That was the solemn responsibility Christ assumed for us in his life and death.

The second imputation—Christ's righteousness to us—I will address in the next meditation.

Martyn McGeown

August 3 — Righteousness Freely Imputed

The blessedness of the man, unto whom God imputeth righteousness without works. —Romans 4:6

Yesterday, we began to treat the subject of imputation. We saw that one part of imputation is that God imputed or reckoned the guilt of our sins to the account of Jesus Christ, who thus took full legal responsibility for our sins and whom God punished accordingly. Only the doctrine of imputation explains how God was just in punishing his own, only begotten, ever beloved Son in our flesh for our sins, which he personally never committed. Legally, in imputation, Christ assumed the position of one guilty for our sins. And he remained in that state of condemnation—a state of guilt before the law of God—until he fully satisfied God's justice.

But there is more to imputation: the positive aspect. Remember that Jesus Christ lived a perfect life of obedience to the law of God. He did more than die on the cross: in the words of the Belgic Confession, Jesus Christ performed "many holy works…for us and in our stead" (Article 22). That is the "obedience of Christ crucified alone, which becomes ours when we believe in him" (Article 23). We know that the righteousness of Christ becomes ours when we believe in him because we have seen that the Holy Spirit unites us to Christ and makes us partakers of all his benefits. But how exactly does the righteousness of Christ become ours by faith? God imputes that righteousness to us. God reckons to us the righteousness of his Son, which is called the righteousness of God. God credits that righteousness to our account.

Think of a legal transaction. We enter the courtroom of God with a criminal record, a rap sheet as it is called colloquially by some. On that record are all of our crimes against the law of God—a very long list of felonies. We are guilty of breaking all of God's commandments, of keeping none of them, and therefore we are worthy of the ultimate penalty, eternal death. In addition, we are guilty—as we learned in Article 15 on Original Sin—of the original guilt in Adam. God does not reckon any of those crimes to our account. He expunges the record. Those crimes are imputed to another, who himself has a perfect record—no crimes of any kind, only perfect righteousness. But now we have no record at all—nothing in the negative column, but also nothing in the positive column. In double-imputation, God takes the perfect record of Christ—all his holy works, merits, and obedience, which we have not performed, and which he performed for us during his life and death—and reckons it to our account. Now, so to speak, we have nothing in the negative column and have perfect righteousness in the positive column.

That imputation of Christ's righteousness is the basis for our justification. As far as God's law is concerned, we are righteous and therefore worthy of all the blessings of eternal life. We are even worthy—because of double-imputation—to be adopted as God's beloved children. Here, then, is the wonder of justification. A condemned sinner facing the death penalty is, after the legal transaction called justification, declared to be an adopted son and an heir of eternal life. The only response to that truth is to cry out with David: "Blessed is the man!" (Ps. 32:1).

Are you that blessed man or woman? Believer in Jesus Christ, you are!

Martyn McGeown

August 4 — Alien Righteousness

> *And be found in him, not having mine own righteousness, which is of the law, but that which is through the faith of Christ, the righteousness which is of God by faith.* —Philippians 3:9

Alien righteousness! This is not the title of a science fiction novel or of a Hollywood blockbuster movie, but is an expression made famous by Martin Luther to describe the righteousness which is the basis of our justification.

When we encounter the word *alien*, we might immediately think of little green men from outer space. The word *alien* is also used in immigration law to denote a foreigner. The idea of *alien* here, however, is that the righteousness which forms the basis of our justification before Almighty God our judge has its source outside of us, and indeed outside of this world. It is, in the highest sense, "the righteousness of God." In Romans, Paul writes about the righteousness of God, "even the righteousness of God which is by faith of Jesus Christ unto all and upon all them that believe" (3:22). Notice those words: "unto all and upon all." Righteousness is not only something which God has and is—he is the God of perfect justice—but something which God gives to and confers upon others.

The righteousness on the basis of which we are justified is called the righteousness of God, first, because the person whose righteousness it is, and who works that righteousness for us, is God. In fact, only the eternal, only begotten Son of God, the second person of the Holy Trinity, could and did work such righteousness. That righteousness is, as Article 23 explains it, "the obedience of Christ crucified alone." It is called the righteousness of God, second, because the Holy Spirit, who also is God, worked that righteousness in the life and death of Jesus Christ, the Son of God made flesh. It is called the righteousness of God, third, because it is a perfect, utterly flawless, and pristine righteousness, sufficient to cover all the sins of all the elect from the beginning to the end of the world. This—the righteousness of God, the alien righteousness of Jesus Christ—is the only righteousness which will be able to satisfy God. God satisfies himself with his own righteousness.

We can see now why Luther chose "alien righteousness" to describe the righteousness of our justification. This righteousness in no way has its origin in us. We did not produce one scrap of this righteousness. "All our righteousnesses"—not just all our sins, but all our righteousnesses!—"are as filthy rags" (Isa. 64:6). Although Paul as a Pharisee could claim that as "touching the righteousness which is in the law, [he was] blameless," he counted all his legal achievements as "loss" and as "dung" (Phil. 3:5–8). Why? Because in comparison to the pristine, perfect, heavenly, alien righteousness of Christ, his so-called righteousness was dung. What a vivid picture that is: a man who stands before Almighty God trusting in the righteousness of the law stands before God dressed from head to toe in filthy, dung-covered rags, and thus is a foul stench in the nostrils of the holy God!

The Reformers rejected all righteousness but the alien righteousness of another, Jesus Christ. God does not justify us on the basis of our personal moral character. We are sinners! God does not justify us on the basis of our imperfect obedience to the law. He demands perfection because he is righteous. God does not even justify us on the basis of the work of the Holy Spirit in us. That work is never perfect or complete in this life. God does not first infuse goodness into us and then on that basis justify us. That goodness is never perfect this side of heaven. Only the righteousness of another—the alien righteousness of Christ—is the sure ground for justification.

Martyn McGeown

August 5 — The Righteousness which Is of the Law

For Moses describeth the righteousness which is of the law,
That the man which doeth those things shall live by them. —Romans 10:5

We are justified only on the basis of the alien righteousness of another, Jesus Christ, which, as Article 23 explains it, "becomes ours when we believe in him," and adds, "is sufficient to cover all our iniquities, and to give us confidence in approaching to God." A major question and controversy swirling around the time of the apostle Paul (as the church was emerging from Judaism) and at the time of the Reformation (as the church was emerging from the gloom of medieval Roman Catholicism) was: What about the law?

We have seen that the law must be excluded from justification—that is, we have seen that our obedience to the law must be excluded from justification. This gospel of justification and righteousness without the law was offensive to the Jews, who highly revered the law; and one of the charges against the Christians was that they were enemies of God's law. This was the false charge against Stephen: "This man ceaseth not to speak blasphemous words against this holy place, and the law" (Acts 6:13). But Paul, although he spoke against the error of finding righteousness and justification in obedience to the law, never spoke against the law itself: "The law is holy, and the commandment holy, and just, and good" (Rom. 7:12). The problem is simply this: the law of God is good, but we are sinners. The law, Paul writes elsewhere, "was added because of transgressions," and "if there had been a law given which could have given life, verily righteousness should have been by the law" (Gal. 3:19, 21).

The law of God, then, is good. It perfectly reveals God's perfect standard and sets forth how a man should behave if he would live in fellowship with God. But, first, the law can only show us what God demands. It cannot give us the strength to perform what God demands. Paul writes that the law "was weak through the flesh" (Rom. 8:3). The law itself was not weak, but man's flesh—his sinful nature—is unable to keep the law; even the believer is unable to keep the law perfectly. Second, since the law demands perfection, God will curse and condemn the man who does not keep the law to perfection. Paul challenges the man who says he wants to be righteous by keeping the law to realize the terms under which he will be judged. God does not grade on a curve. He demands a perfect score! "For as many as are of the works of the law are under the curse: for it is written, Cursed is everyone that continueth not in all things which are written in the book of the law to do them" (Gal. 3:10). James makes a similar statement: "For whosoever shall keep the whole law, and yet offend in one point, he is guilty of all" (James 2:10). You may have heard the expression, "Three strikes and you're out!" With God's law, it is, "One sin and you are damned!" In fact, as we saw in Article 15, we enter the world under God's condemnation already because of Adam's sin.

To seek righteousness in keeping the law, then, is arrogant folly. It is to trample underfoot the righteousness of Christ, it is to insult the Spirit of grace, and it is to bring down upon oneself the full burden of the wrath of God and the curse of his law. What blessedness that we have the righteousness of Christ—the one who was cursed for us.

Let us come empty-handed into the judgment of God, trusting only in that righteousness.

Martyn McGeown

August 6 — The Judaizing Error

For I testify again to every man that is circumcised,
that he is a debtor to do the whole law. —Galatians 5:3

We have seen that the righteousness of the law cannot justify us because, although the law reveals to us God's perfect standard, we cannot perform it. To this argument, theologians in the Roman Catholic Church have replied, "But the law to which Paul refers is only the Old Testament ceremonial law. Good works in obedience to the moral law are not excluded from justification." In the Old Testament, there was a threefold law—that will be the subject of Article 25. First, there was the moral law of the ten commandments. That law is summed up in the command to love God and the neighbor. Second, there is the civil law which governed Israel as a nation. This included rules concerning agriculture, commerce, and civil penalties, such as capital punishment by stoning for various offenses. Third, there is the ceremonial law which governed Israel's worship. This included dietary laws, laws concerning cleanness and uncleanness, and all the ordinances pertaining to the priests, the tabernacle, and the temple.

In the early New Testament church, Gentiles were being saved. This was a source of controversy among the Judaizers, certain Jews who professed Christianity but who were really false brethren and heretics. These Judaizers said: "Except ye be circumcised after the manner of Moses, ye cannot be saved" (Acts 15:1). These men, also called the Pharisees, insisted that "it was needful to circumcise [the Gentile converts], and to command them to keep the law of Moses" (Acts 15:5). The church met in Jerusalem, and the Holy Spirit guided them to reject the teachings of the Judaizers and Pharisees. The doctrine of justification by grace alone through faith alone was preserved!

However, the Judaizers did not give up easily. They infiltrated the churches in Galatia and began spreading their heresy there. Paul's response was the epistle to the Galatians. In it he exclaimed that those who had turned away from the gospel of grace to be circumcised had followed another, that is, a false gospel (Gal. 1:6); and he pronounced the curse of God on teachers of any other gospel (Gal. 1:8–9).

Why did Paul make such an issue about circumcision? Because circumcision represented the works of the law. You might say that the tiniest, most insignificant work of the law—the simple act of circumcision—was the first step on the slippery slope of apostasy from Christ. "Behold, I Paul say unto you, that if ye be circumcised, Christ shall profit you nothing" (Gal. 5:2). By being circumcised, says Paul, you are not merely submitting to one Jewish ceremony: you are signing up to a plan of salvation which will obligate you to keep the whole law. "For I testify again to every man that is circumcised, that he is a debtor to do the whole law. Christ is become of no effect unto you, whosoever of you are justified by the law; ye are fallen from grace" (Gal. 5:3–4). And, as we have already seen, with the law it is an "all-or-nothing proposition." If you put your trust in circumcision, you must keep all the laws of God perfectly.

Instead of putting our trust in circumcision—or in our modern context, instead of putting your trust in baptism, church ordinances, good works, the keeping of the ten commandments, or any other work of man—we find all our salvation in Jesus Christ.

Christ will not be half a savior, providing only some of the righteousness as the basis of our justification: "If righteousness come by the law, then Christ is dead in vain" (Gal. 2:21).

Martyn McGeown

August 7 — The Error of the New Perspective

Except your righteousness shall exceed the righteousness of the scribes and Pharisees, ye shall in no case enter into the kingdom of heaven. —Matthew 5:20

There is a movement in the church world today which denies justification by faith alone. This movement is called the new perspective on Paul (NPP). The Belgic Confession does not address the NPP as such—how could it when the error in its present form did not exist?—but we should. The most popular contemporary proponent of the NPP is N. T. Wright.

Wright redefines the concepts we have carefully studied—justification and righteousness—and rejects imputation. Wright removes justification and righteousness from soteriology (the doctrine of salvation) and places them in ecclesiology (the doctrine of the church). For Wright, justification is not about how a person is saved from sin and blessed with eternal life, but how a person is declared here and now to be a member of the church. In the Old Testament, the badge or mark of membership among God's people was circumcision. Gentiles who became Jews in the Old Testament had to be circumcised. In the New Testament, with the coming of Christ, the new badge or mark must be one that does not exclude Gentiles—as circumcision did—that is, the new badge or mark is faith. Therefore, in the New Testament both Jews and Gentiles are justified—declared to be members of the people of God, the church—by faith. Thus, when Paul argued with the Judaizers about circumcision, he was not arguing about salvation; he was arguing about who is a member of the church.

Righteousness for Wright is God's faithfulness to his people in putting the world right by the cross and resurrection of Christ. Wright does not believe that God imputed our sins to Christ and punished him in our place. For Wright, the cross is simply a display of how righteous God is, and the resurrection is a vindication of that righteousness. Moreover, righteousness, according to Wright, cannot be imputed to a guilty sinner to be the basis of his justification. Thus, Wright denies the gospel and tears down the foundation of our justification before God, leaving us exposed to God's wrath and curse.

Wright's "gospel" is that God declares believers part of his people on the basis of faith. However, their remaining as his people depends on their faithfulness to him (i.e., on their good works). Wright's conclusion is this: "Future justification, acquittal at the Last Assize, always takes place on the *basis* of the totality of the life lived."* The "Assize" is the judgment.

We repudiate Wright by "relying and resting upon the obedience of Christ crucified alone" (Article 23). Any follower of Wright's advice who enters the judgment relying on the "totality of [his] life lived"—or even on one work—will be damned. Why? Because the good works of the sinner can never even begin to compare with the perfect standard which God demands in his holy law. What good, then, is a "gospel" which tells us that we might be in God's favor today, but which announces to us that our remaining in fellowship with God depends on us? If a man understands his sin, he must be utterly beside himself with terror to enter the judgment relying on himself, and we urge him to flee instead to the perfect righteousness of Christ our Lord. We reject Wright's "righteousness," and we abominate Wright's "justification" as Paul does—dung!

Let us beware of slippery—but popular—heretics such as N. T. Wright!

Martyn McGeown

---

* N. T. Wright, "The Law in Romans 2," in *Paul and the Mosaic Law*, ed. James D. G. Dunn (Grand Rapids, MI: Eerdmans, 2001), 129.

August 8 — The Error of the Federal Vision

Not as though the word of God hath taken none effect.
For they are not all Israel, which are of Israel. —Romans 9:6

Hot on the heels of the new perspective on Paul, which we considered yesterday, comes the federal vision (FV). These two errors are modern (that is, current) and dangerous, and are a repudiation of the Reformation gospel of justification by faith alone as summarized in our creeds, such as the Belgic Confession.

But some might ask, is it really appropriate to include polemics in meditations? Polemics is the art of theological warfare, the defense of the truth and the repudiation of error. First, the truth always shines more brightly against the background of error. Second, one who loves the truth will fight or contend for it (Jude 3). Third, one who loves the church will not hesitate to raise the alarm when danger threatens. The devil is always seeking to rob the church of truth and thus of comfort. And if the church has no comfort, there can be no heartwarming meditations—which I hope these articles are. Devotional material is not fluff because the Holy Spirit does not comfort us by means of fluff but by means of the truth applied to our hearts (John 14:16–17).

The FV is an error concerning the covenant. We should remember that the covenant is the gracious relationship of friendship that God establishes with us and our children in Jesus Christ, in which he declares himself to be our God and takes us to be his people. First, the FV teaches a conditional covenant, that is, a covenant with many more than the elect, which depends upon man for its maintenance and fulfillment. In practice, this means that all the children of believers are elect, regenerated, and justified in Christ. But by *elect* and *in Christ*, the FV does not mean unconditionally chosen in Christ in eternity and guaranteed salvation. Election in the FV is temporal (pertaining to time), temporary (not necessarily permanent), and therefore can be lost; and since justification—the subject of Article 23—is a blessing which flows from election, it too can be lost.

Therefore, it is perfectly possible, according to the FV, for a person to be justified for a time, but then to forfeit justification by his sinful behavior. It is possible for the spiritual union, by which the Holy Spirit supposedly joins all baptized children to Jesus Christ, to be severed by sin. It is possible, says the FV, for a person who is saved in the present to be damned on the last day, and thus to perish forever. In fact, it is possible, says the FV, for every believer—for you, the believing reader, and for me, the believing writer—to perish forever. How, then, are we justified, and how do we remain justified, according to the FV? By covenantal faithfulness! By faithfully keeping the conditions of the covenant—faith and the good works which flow from faith. What, then, is the basis for justification? Not the perfect, imputed righteousness of Jesus Christ—the men of the FV in general oppose the concept of imputed righteousness—but one's own Spirit-worked, faith-inspired works. All that theological fancy footwork—the works are the Spirit's works in us, and they flow from faith and operate by love—does not hide the fact that justification in the FV is by works! If justification is in any sense by works, it is not the utterly gracious justification of the Scriptures. Thus, the FV, too, is a repudiation of the gospel and an attempt by Satan to move us away from the only sure foundation—the alien righteousness of Christ, imputed to us.

The only answer to the FV is that the covenant is unconditional. The blessings earned by Christ on the cross are for the elect only (whether elect adults or children), and they can never be lost. That's the firm foundation of our salvation—not the treacherous quicksand of the FV!

Martyn McGeown

August 9 — *Simul Iustus et Peccator*

> *But to him that worketh not, but believeth on him that justifieth the ungodly, his faith is counted for righteousness.* —Romans 4:5

Simul iustus et peccator is Latin, and, like the term "alien righteousness," was coined by Martin Luther. The phrase means, "at the same time justified and a sinner." Justification is God's legal declaration that a believing sinner is righteous—for the sake of the imputed, alien righteousness of the Son of God, which Christ wrought in his lifelong obedience and atoning, sacrificial death on the cross—that is, that the sinner is in perfect conformity to and in complete harmony with the law of God. Upon this believing sinner the holy God pronounces the verdict: "Righteous! Not guilty! Worthy of eternal life!"

But the justified person is still a sinner. Paul expresses this very strikingly in Romans 4:5—the one whom God justifies is ungodly! We might have expected Paul to write that "God justifieth the godly," or, at the very least, "God justifies the man whom he has made godly," but instead Paul writes, God "justifieth the ungodly," that is, God justifies the one who is, and who remains, ungodly, impious, and wicked. The word *ungodly* is consistently used of the wicked in the book of Proverbs, for example. The reader will immediately see the problem: according to Romans 4:5, God does what God himself forbids human judges to do—"they shall…condemn the wicked" (Deut. 25:1); "he that justifieth the wicked…[is] abomination to the Lord" (Prov. 17:15)! But the problem quickly evaporates when we remember that when God justifies the sinner and declares him to be righteous, he does so on a righteous basis: the perfect righteousness of Jesus Christ. That is why Paul writes: "that he might be just, and the justifier of him which believeth in Jesus" (Rom. 3:26). He is the justifier, and he is just in so justifying!

Therefore, we say that the sinner is both righteous and at the same time a sinner, *simul iustus et peccator*. As far as his legal status is concerned, he is righteous. As far as his actual condition—the real circumstances of his life—he is a sinner. In this life we are justified—that is, our status before the law—but we only begin to enjoy the blessings of freedom from the bondage and corruption of sin in this life. We only begin to be holy, and that holiness does not contribute one whit to our justification, which because it is based upon an alien righteousness, is complete and unchanging.

Thus, we confess that justification is only a declaration of righteousness. It is only the official verdict from the Judge concerning the legal status of the sinner, his relationship to the law of God. Justification does not change the sinner's character. This does not, however, mean that the justified sinner will forever remain ungodly, or that he will continue to walk in ungodliness; but it does mean that justification has nothing to do with God's making the ungodly sinner godly. The justified sinner does indeed become godly, but that is a distinct work of God, the work of sanctification, the subject of Article 24.

Our legal status as justified believers never changes, and God continually testifies of that to us in the gospel. But, despite our legal status, we are still sinners. We still struggle with and commit sin. Sin does not affect our justification—we are not more justified when we do good works or less justified when we sin—but it does affect our enjoyment and experience of salvation. That is why we, even as justified sinners, continue to pray for the forgiveness of sin.

Simul iustus et peccator. The confession of every believing sinner!

Martyn McGeown

August 10 — Legal Fiction!

For they being ignorant of God's righteousness,
and going about to establish their own righteousness, have not submitted
themselves unto the righteousness of God. —Romans 10:3

We noticed in an earlier meditation the Roman Catholic view of justification. Instead of imputed righteousness, Rome teaches infused or imparted righteousness, the idea that the Spirit works grace in the heart of the sinner who uses the sacraments of the church. Then, on the basis of virtue in the heart—an acquired, internal righteousness—the church member is justified. The more grace in the heart, the more justified a person becomes, but even the most justified person in this life—with very few exceptions—must be purified in purgatory after death. The result is that no member of the Roman Catholic Church can ever know if he has accrued enough grace in his heart to merit justification now and on the last day. The result for the sinner, who understands sin and the holiness of God, is and must be terror.

Rome scoffs at the Reformed, biblical, and confessional view of justification by imputed righteousness as "legal fiction." Rome is especially offended by the "as if" language of Reformed theologians. We believe that God views us in justification "as if [we] had never committed nor had any sin, and had...accomplished all the obedience which Christ has fulfilled for [us]."* To "as if," Rome cries out, "Legal fiction!" Modern heretics have also criticized the doctrine of imputation, characterizing it as "the shuffling about of heavenly ledgers" (or accounting books); and have said that it is impossible for righteousness to be transferred to a guilty sinner from the sinless Christ. These objections come from the NPP and FV movements, as we have seen.

The Reformed believer is not afraid of the charge of "Legal fiction." First, if our justification is legal fiction, how can we possibly explain the cross of Christ? If it is impossible for God to impute Christ's righteousness to us, it is also impossible for God to impute our sins to Christ and for Christ to bear the punishment for them. Then we must satisfy God's justice for our own sins, and that is impossible. Was God playing legal fiction at the cross? God forbid! Second, the legal fiction argument supposes that God is playing pretend in his judgment hall. God would be pretending that the sinner is righteous when the sinner is, in fact, not righteous. But God is not pretending because the righteousness which is the basis of our justification is not a make-believe righteousness but Christ's righteousness. Christ's righteousness is real. Christ's lifelong obedience is real. Christ's atonement on the cross is real. And God's act of imputing that righteousness to us is real. Third, it is not that the demands of the law are not met—they must certainly be—but that the demands of the law are not met by us. It is not that God agrees not to enforce the demands of his law—he insists on them most strongly—but that God does not demand them from us. And the reason God does not demand perfect obedience from us is that Christ has already fulfilled the demands for us. That is not legal fiction, but grace!

Let us turn the "legal fiction" charge back on our detractors. All who deny that justification is by faith alone based on the imputed, alien righteousness of Christ alone must face this question. On what basis are you justified before God? On what basis can God declare you—here and now, and in the final judgment—to be righteous? If God—as Rome, NPP, and FV contend—justifies sinners on the basis of an imperfect obedience to his law, God is unjust. Imperfect righteousness as the basis of justification is the real legal fiction!

Martyn McGeown

---

* Heidelberg Catechism 60, in Schaff, *Creeds of Christendom*, 3:326.

August 11 — A Conscience Free from Terror

Therefore being justified by faith,
we have peace with God through our Lord Jesus Christ. —Romans 5:1

Article 23 ends by rejoicing in the subjective effect of justification upon the conscience of the believing sinner. In one word, justification gives peace.

Peace is to found only in God because God is "the God of peace" (Rom. 15:33). This means that, first, God is peace, harmony, and perfect blessedness within himself. Imagine a tranquil lake on which there is not the slightest ripple. That is a wonderful image of God in whom there is no agitation, anxiety, confusion, or tension. As the God of peace, he is at peace with himself, and he is at peace with all that which is righteous, all that which conforms to and is in harmony with God himself.

However, the same God of peace is the God who is at holy war against the wicked. Within God there is no agitation, but between God and sinners there is enmity. Sinners hate God and show their hatred daily by their sins, and God is justly offended by man's rebellion and will punish sinners both in time and in eternity in his terrible wrath.

Man is not at peace because man is not righteous. And since man is not righteous, God is at war with man and pursues sinful man with his wrath and curse. "The wicked are like the troubled sea, when it cannot rest, whose waters cast up mire and dirt. There is no peace, saith my God, to the wicked" (Isa. 57:20–21). All of man's attempts, therefore, at creating peace are doomed to failure—Christ himself who takes peace away from the earth (Rev. 6:4) smashes their false peace to pieces—because man is unrighteous and at war with God himself. But in justification, God establishes peace between himself and his people. He does this by removing the cause for the enmity, which is our sin. Christ "is our peace" (Eph. 2:14). Christ is the righteous basis for peace between us and the holy God.

The conclusion is obvious. We who are justified by faith are not only not at war with God, but we know ourselves not to be at war with God, and we know that God looks upon us in peace. We know that there is true harmony between us and our God. We enjoy blessed fellowship with the triune God in Jesus Christ by the Holy Spirit. In other words, we have both objective peace in the cross and subjective peace in our own consciousness.

Contrast that with one who is attempting to justify himself before God by his own works, and who is not relying on the perfect obedience, righteousness, and merits of Jesus Christ alone. He is following the example of Adam, who "trembling, attempted to cover himself with fig-leaves" (Article 23). Every child of God knows: "If we should appear before God, relying on ourselves, or on any other creature, though ever so little, we should, alas! be consumed" (Article 23). And we can add the testimony of Article 24: "we should always be in doubt, tossed to and fro without any certainty, and our poor consciences continually vexed, if they relied not on the merits of the suffering and death of our Savior."

What about your conscience, reader? Is it "continually vexed," or do you have peace with God? If you are relying upon yourself for justification, you cannot know peace, and God himself will not declare you righteous and give you peace. That peace, "which passeth all understanding" (Phil. 4:7) and which enables a sinner to live and die happily, is the treasured possession of all believers whose only plea is the perfect, imputed, alien righteousness of Jesus Christ alone. Is it yours?

Martyn McGeown

August 12 — Ascribing All Glory to God

*If Abraham were justified by works, he hath
whereof to glory; but not before God.* —Romans 4:2

Justification is a humbling doctrine. That is why our flesh hates it and unbelievers—especially religious unbelievers—reject it. One who truly believes and understands this doctrine must be humble. Article 23 urges us to humility by reminding us that in our salvation all the glory is God's. Of course it is! God determined salvation in his eternal decree; God set his love upon us, and sent his only begotten Son to work out a perfect righteousness for us as the basis of our justification; God punished his own Son on the cross in our place, thus removing from us the curse of the law and satisfying his own justice; and God even worked faith in our hearts by the Holy Spirit in order to impute to us by free grace the righteousness of Jesus Christ. "And therefore," declares Article 23, "we always hold fast this foundation, ascribing all the glory to God, humbling ourselves before him."

What an abomination to be proud in the presence of God! Are we, perhaps, proud in the presence of man? Do we continue to compare ourselves with others and imagine in the vain imagination of our mind that we are better than others? Never look at the unbeliever with disdain and say to yourself, "I thank God that I am not as other men are. I am glad that I believe in Jesus." Remember that you have believed in Jesus because God graciously opened your eyes, kindled in your heart a true faith, and united you to Jesus Christ. Remember that you are just as sinful as any unbeliever you meet. The only difference is that your sins are covered by the blood and righteousness of Christ, and his are not. Will a man on death row, who has been graciously pardoned, boast because he did something to earn his pardon? Therefore, we must never boast as if we contributed something to our justification and salvation. And we may never assume a haughty attitude towards unbelievers.

There is a place for glorying and boasting: it is not before God, but it is in God. We boast in the grace, mercy, and love of God. We boast in the spotless righteousness of God imputed to us. We boast in the unchangeable decree and verdict of justification from God's judgment seat. But we never boast of what we have done. Our justification is not based upon our works. Will a man boast in filthy rags and dung? Our works do not even contribute one stitch to the spotless, seamless robe of Christ's righteousness.

Here is a good test in evaluating any doctrine, including the doctrine of justification. Does it lead to boasting, or does it give all glory to God? Article 23 states that we do not presume "to trust in anything in ourselves, or in any merit of ours," but that we rely and rest "upon the obedience of Christ crucified alone." Does your doctrine lead you to that conclusion? If it does not, you must quickly reevaluate it, repent, and believe the truth.

"Where is boasting then?" asks the apostle. "It is excluded. By what law? of works? Nay: but by the law of faith," and later, he adds, "If Abraham were justified by works, he hath whereof to glory; but not before God" (Rom. 3:27; 4:2).

Let us then humble ourselves in the presence of our God, praising and thanking him that in Jesus Christ he has given us perfect righteousness, and let us never rob God of any part of his glory by daring to ascribe even the smallest part of that righteousness to our own works.

"He that glorieth, let him glory in the Lord" (1 Cor. 1:31).

Martyn McGeown

Article 24

OF MAN'S SANCTIFICATION AND GOOD WORKS

We believe that this true faith, being wrought in man by the hearing of the Word of God and the operation of the Holy Ghost, doth regenerate and make him a new man, causing him to live a new life, and freeing him from the bondage of sin. Therefore it is so far from being true, that this justifying faith makes men remiss in a pious and holy life, that on the contrary without it they would never do any thing out of love to God, but only out of self-love or fear of damnation. Therefore it is impossible that this holy faith can be unfruitful in man: for we do not speak of a vain faith, but of such a faith as is called in Scripture *a faith that worketh by love*, which excites man to the practice of those works which God has commanded in his Word. Which works, as they proceed from the good root of faith, are good and acceptable in the sight of God, forasmuch as they are all sanctified by his grace: howbeit they are of no account towards our justification. For it is by faith in Christ that we are justified, even before we do good works, otherwise they could not be good works any more than the fruit of a tree can be good before the tree itself is good.

Therefore we do good works, but not to merit by them (for what can we merit?)—nay, we are beholden to God for the good works we do, and not he to us, *since it is he that worketh in us both to will and to do of his good pleasure*. Let us therefore attend to what is written: *When ye shall have done all those things which are commanded you, say we are unprofitable servants: we have done that which was our duty to do.*

In the meantime we do not deny that God rewards good works, but it is through his grace that he crowns his gifts. Moreover, though we do good works, we do not found our salvation upon them; for we can do no work but what is polluted by our flesh, and also punishable; and although we could perform such works, still the remembrance of one sin is sufficient to make God reject them. Thus, then, we should always be in doubt, tossed to and fro without any certainty, and our poor consciences would be continually vexed if they relied not on the merits of the suffering and death of our Saviour.

August 13 — Regeneration by Faith?

*By the washing of regeneration,
and renewing of the Holy Spirit.* —Titus 3:5

Perhaps your Reformed antennae quivered when you read Article 24: "We believe that this true faith, being wrought in man by the hearing of the word of God and the operation of the Holy Spirit, doth regenerate." Faith doth regenerate? Surely the Belgic Confession is mistaken. We must understand, however, that we can speak of regeneration in two senses: the narrow and the broad sense. Regeneration in the narrow sense is usually what modern Reformed theologians mean by regeneration. We might call it regeneration proper. The Belgic Confession does not speak much about it. It is that first work of God in which he implants, imparts, or breathes life into a spiritually dead sinner. Scripture calls it the new birth (John 3:3). Faith certainly does not regenerate a sinner in that sense. It is impossible for a sinner who is dead in trespasses and sins to regenerate himself by the activity of faith. Similarly, it is impossible for an unborn child to give birth to itself, a man to give himself a new heart, or a dead man to raise himself from the dead—all illustrations of regeneration in Scripture (Ezek. 36:27–28; 37:5; John 3:6–8; etc.). Regeneration is a sovereign work of God in which man's activity of faith has no part.

Article 24 is not treating that aspect of regeneration. Regeneration in the broad sense is the entire life of renewal which flows out of regeneration itself. 1 John 3:9 speaks of God's seed in the believer—that is, the life of Jesus Christ, regeneration in the narrow sense. If regeneration in the narrow sense is the seed, regeneration in the broad sense is the tree with its leaves, blossoms, and fruit. In that sense, Article 24 declares rightly that "this true faith…doth regenerate and make him a new man, causing him to live a new life, and freeing him from the bondage of sin."

That new life which flows out of the principle of faith in the believer—which faith, remember, is kindled in his heart by the Holy Spirit, thus uniting him to Jesus Christ—is the theme of Article 24. This article necessarily follows because the Reformed faith needs to answer the charge hurled against it by the Roman Catholics and others that justification by faith alone without works leads to a careless and profane life. Their argument is very simple: if, as we have demonstrated, a man is justified without works, a justified believer needs not and will not produce good works, and instead will live an ungodly life.

The answer of the Reformed faith is this: yes, it is true that God has justified us—legally declared us to be perfectly righteous before him on the basis of the imputed, alien righteousness of Christ alone—but God has not finished our salvation at that point. God also sanctifies us or makes us holy. Sanctification (the subject of Article 24) must be distinguished from justification (the subject of Article 23) but they cannot be separated. God justifies no one whom he does not also sanctify.

So, where do good works fit into our justification? They are excluded: "they are of no account towards our justification…We do not found our salvation upon them" (Article 24). But does that mean that there is no place for good works in the Christian life at all? Absolutely not!

Good works have a place—a very important place—as we shall see in future meditations.

Martyn McGeown

August 14 — Whom God Justifies He Also Sanctifies

But of him are ye in Christ Jesus, who of God is made unto us wisdom, and righteousness, and sanctification, and redemption. —1 Corinthians 1:30

The subject of Article 24 is "Man's Sanctification and Good Works." Sanctification, like justification, is part of salvation, and endless confusion will be avoided if we carefully distinguish between these two aspects of our salvation. Sin, like a many-headed monster, has different parts, and when God saves us, he gives us complete deliverance from sin.

Justification is a legal declaration that we are righteous based on the alien, imputed righteousness of Christ alone and received by faith alone. Justification, therefore, delivers us from sin's guilt. Sanctification is God's work of making elect, believing, justified sinners holy. Sanctification, therefore, delivers us from sin's defilement. Both justification and sanctification are necessary because we need deliverance from both the guilt and defilement of sin.

Salvation is, in its entirety from beginning to end, the work of God. Therefore, God alone justifies, and God alone sanctifies. Just as we cannot justify ourselves, so we cannot make ourselves holy. Sanctification is the peculiar work of the Spirit, which is why he is called the Holy Spirit. Justification is God's act as judge in declaring us righteous. Sanctification is a work which God performs in our souls, in which he works holiness in us. Justification changes our legal state or status. Sanctification changes our actual moral condition. God never simply justifies us and then leaves us in our sins. Whom God justifies, he also sanctifies. Justification is the once-for-all, final legal verdict of Almighty God as judge: justification cannot be overturned, changed, annulled, increased, or decreased. Sanctification is a progressive work of God in us, by which we are transformed into the image of Jesus Christ, progressively devoted and dedicated to God in love, and increasingly separated from sin. Sanctification is never completed in this life. Perfect sanctification (glorification) awaits the last day.

There are other differences between justification and sanctification as well. In justification we are passive. God declares concerning us that we are righteous. We did nothing at all. In sanctification we are active. God does not sanctify us without means: he uses prayer; he uses the means of grace (the preaching and the sacraments) received by faith in order to make us more and more holy. We must not imagine that we will simply be zapped with holiness as we sleep! Sanctification requires of us that we fight against sin in ourselves and produce good works. In sanctification, says Article 24, God "make[s] him [the believer] a new man, causing him to live a new life, and freeing him from the bondage of sin." However, we must also understand that sanctification is never dependent on us. Sanctification is not even a cooperative effort between God and us. In sanctification, we are active, and God will not sanctify us without our activity, but God produces activity in us.

If you understand that as a sinner you are not only guilty, but also defiled, polluted, and enslaved by sin, you will rejoice in sanctification as much as in justification. You will pray: "Lord, sanctify me. Make me holy. Cause me more and more to die unto sin and to live unto righteousness. Cleanse me and create in me a new heart."

What man who stands accused before the law is content merely to hear the justifying verdict from the judge without also experiencing freedom? Sanctification is the blessedness we experience as we leave God's court, free to serve him in thankfulness for what he has done for us. Let us live thus to God's glory.

Martyn McGeown

August 15 — Remissness Impossible in the Justified

*What shall we say then? Shall we continue in sin,
that grace may abound? God forbid. How shall we,
that are dead to sin, live any longer therein?* —Romans 6:1–2

The doctrine of justification by faith alone has many enemies. The greatest of all enemies is our own prideful flesh. Sinners are offended when they hear that their works are not good enough to please God, so that, as Article 24 explains it, "they are of no account towards our justification," "we can do no work but what is polluted by our flesh, and also punishable," and "the remembrance of one sin is sufficient to make God reject them." Remember, those phrases in the Confession describe our works, as believing children of God!

It takes a miracle of God's grace to transform a proud, self-seeking sinner into one who humbly cries out to God, "God be merciful to me a sinner" (Luke 18:13), and who then, out of thankfulness, goes forth and lives in all good works. It takes the almighty Holy Spirit himself to break our pride, which is so rooted in our hearts, before we can confess our unworthiness and receive the truth that our justification is grounded in the righteousness of another.

The objection voiced in all ages to this doctrine is this: "But that doctrine will make men careless and profane! But that doctrine gives no incentive to good works! If salvation is guaranteed simply through believing in Jesus, and if Jesus has done it all already for us, why should we do good works?" Paul heard the same objection in his day: "What shall we say then? Shall we continue in sin, that grace may abound?" (Rom. 6:1). Paul's answer is an indignant, "God forbid" (v. 2). Article 24 answers the same objection: "it is so far from being true, that this justifying faith makes men remiss in a pious and holy life, that on the contrary, without it they would never do anything out of love to God."

Justified sinners are not remiss in a pious and holy life. That can never be because justification is never in isolation from the other benefits of salvation. Justification must be distinguished from the other benefits of salvation, but it cannot be separated from it. Romans 8:30 teaches us: "whom [God] did predestinate, them he also called, and whom he called, them he also justified: and whom he justified, them he also glorified." Glorification is not merely going to heaven but is "to be conformed to the image of [God's] Son" (v. 29). Glorification is the end goal of sanctification, a lifelong process of God making us holy. In Romans 6, Paul shows how absurd it is to teach that justified sinners could be remiss in piety and holiness. By virtue of our union with Christ—that union created by the Holy Spirit by which all the benefits of Christ including justification become ours—we are "dead to sin" (v. 2); we are "baptized into [Jesus'] death" (v. 3); "we are buried with him" (v. 4); "we are planted together in the likeness of his death" (v. 5); "our old man is crucified with him" (v. 6). What are the effects of such a fundamental change? Surely, it is not that we are remiss in holiness, or that we actively walk in the ways of sin as before! Listen to the word of God: "even so we also should walk in newness of life" (v. 4); "that henceforth we should not serve sin" (v. 6); "sin shall not have dominion over you" (v. 14); "ye became the servants of righteousness" (v. 18).

This is exactly what Article 24 teaches. You will find that faith "doth make [us] a new man, causing [us] to live a new life, and freeing [us] from the bondage of sin."

Let unbelievers scoff, and hypocrites misuse this doctrine to their own spiritual ruin. We, who know the mercy of God in justification, will be rich in good works to his glory.

Martyn McGeown

August 16 — Good Works Impossible without Justifying Faith

Whatsoever is not of faith is sin. —Romans 14:23

There are two commonly held false views on the place of good works in the Christian life. The first is legalism, that good works contribute to a sinner's justification before God. The other view is antinomianism, that good works are not necessary in the Christian life and that the law of God is not a guide for the Christian. The Belgic Confession avoids both errors and sets forth the real place of good works in our lives.

The first thing we notice is that Article 24 emphatically denies that "justifying faith makes men remiss in a pious and holy life." In fact, insists Article 24, "it is impossible that this holy faith can be unfruitful in man." Therefore, it is impossible for a justified sinner not to bring forth good works as the fruit of faith.

The second assertion is that, on the contrary, it is impossible without faith to please God, and therefore it is impossible for one not justified by faith to produce any truly good works. When we think about good works as the fruit of salvation, we need to consider the source of these good works. A sinner cannot produce good works of himself. Of ourselves we are nothing but sin and depravity. The only way in which a sinner can produce good fruit is through union with the source of all goodness, Jesus Christ himself. Jesus teaches that in John 15 with the figure that he is the true vine and we are the branches. A branch can only produce fruit when it lives out of the vine and absorbs the succulent sap from the vine. Without that vital connection to the Vine—which the Holy Spirit creates, and out of which flows the activity of faith by which we are justified, and out of which we live and are made partakers of all Christ's benefits—we are dead, withered sticks lying on the ground. Therefore, for anyone to suggest that we could be justified on the basis of our works is to reverse the order. First we are justified by faith alone, then, as a consequence, we begin to produce the good fruits of faith. That is the argument in Article 24: "Without it [justifying faith] [we] would never do anything out of love to God, but only out of self-love or fear of damnation."

Many people in the world think that a good work is any work which is useful to society. To feed the hungry is a good work, to find a cure for disease is a good work, to help an old lady to cross the street is a good work. Men often boast in their good works. Witness the celebrities of our day with their benefit concerts, raising money for charity! Surely these are good works. There are others who think that good works are religious activities. Prayers, fasting, pilgrimages, giving to the church are good works, they say. Others try to be active in good works by doing no harm to their neighbor. We do not, of course, mean to discourage charitable behavior in society. Better to help an old lady than to steal her purse! But there is more to genuine "good works" that please God than that!

Jesus warned the Pharisees: "Ye are they which justify yourselves before men; but God knoweth your hearts: for that which is highly esteemed among men is abomination in the sight of God" (Luke 16:15). The Pharisees—for all their seeming piety—were abominable in God's sight. They had not produced one good work, not one! Why? They did not believe in Jesus Christ, and because they were not united to him by faith, they could not produce any fruit, nor did they even desire to produce any good fruit. As Jesus said, "Without me ye can do nothing" (John 15:5)—not "a little imperfect something," but nothing!

Good works from a dead branch! Impossible!

Martyn McGeown

August 17 — Evil Motives in the Unjustified: Self-Love

And that he died for all, that they which live should not henceforth live unto themselves, but unto him which died for them, and rose again. —2 Corinthians 5:15

What insight the Belgic Confession has into the human condition! It identifies two main motives for so-called good works in those not justified by faith alone—self-love and fear. When you examine the works of unbelievers—especially religious unbelievers—those are the two motivating factors. Either a sinner desires to earn for himself some great good—self-love—or he desires to avoid some great evil—fear of damnation. But those two motives are not the motives behind truly good works. A truly good work is done out of love for God which flows out of gratitude for salvation.

As sinners, we are naturally selfish. Before doing something we ask: "What is in it for me? How will that affect me?" That is true even in our best works. A husband might love his wife only because she makes him feel good. Friends might be friends only because of what they can do for one another. But when such love and friendship either become inconvenient or begin to cost something, often the relationship feels the pressure. That is a test—do you love someone only because of what that person gives to you? When that person stops giving what you want, is the result anger and resentment? And what about God? When God gives you everything you want, do you serve him? But when he begins to take away certain things, are you bitter against him? Alas, the idol of self has too prominent a place in our lives!

The works of unbelievers are not merely tainted by selfishness. Their primary motive is selfishness! Many live in an outwardly moral fashion because they love the praise of men and because they value their reputation. That is the motive behind much charity work—people want to be seen to be charitable. No wonder Article 24 says that without faith we act "only out of self-love."

Self-love can only be rooted out of our hearts by Christ's cross. This is the teaching of 2 Corinthians 5:14–15. According to verse 15, sinners "live unto themselves;" Christ died so that "they which live should not henceforth live unto themselves, but unto him which died for them, and rose again" (v. 15). About us for whom Christ died, Paul writes that we now live unto Christ. That is the fruit of the death of Christ in our lives. This is not something that might possibly happen, but this is the certain fruit of the death of Christ with respect to all those for whom Christ died. So true is this, that if a person does not live unto Christ, there is only one explanation—Christ did not die for him, and he is an unbeliever.

This must be so because of the intimate union between Christ and the elect. The explanation is given in 2 Corinthians 5:14, "If one died for all, then were all dead." A more accurate translation is "therefore all died." When Christ died, he did so as the head of his people. Therefore, we died with him and in him. Although we were not personally present at the cross, we were there legally. This means, first, that Christ died for our sins, bearing our punishment. Second, our sinful flesh was crucified with Christ, so that it no longer has dominion over us to rule us. Therefore, by the cross, we are delivered from the terrible idol of self.

But for that—the death of Christ received by faith—we produce no works which are not born of selfishness. The love of Christ—not selfishness—constrains us to do good works to his glory, who selflessly lived and died for us to deliver us from our sins!

Martyn McGeown

August 18 — Evil Motives in the Unjustified: Fear of Damnation

And it came to pass, when Ahab heard those words,
that he rent his clothes, and put sackcloth upon his flesh, and fasted,
and lay in sackcloth, and went softly. —1 Kings 21:27

There are many in the church today who are impressed by the lives of some unbelievers. They conclude—wrongly—that unbelievers are able to do genuinely good works. Yesterday we examined the first of the evil motives of unbelievers—self-love. The second evil motive of unbelievers is fear, especially fear of damnation.

Not all unbelievers sin in the same way. Not all unbelievers are murderers, for example. But all unbelievers are murderers at heart—and so are we (Matt. 5:21–22). One reason why many who are murderers at heart do not commit the act of murder is fear of being caught and punished. The same is true with respect to many other crimes. It is not that people would not like to commit certain crimes, but that they dare not risk being caught; the shame, the court appearance, the prison sentence—these are active deterrents. But that is not the Christian motivation for doing good works or for avoiding sin.

Others do not commit sins—at least not outwardly—because they are afraid of God's judgment, which is so much greater than man's judgment. Fear of hell keeps many people religious and acts as a bridle for many sinners. "If any one saith, that he will for certain, of an absolute and infallible certainty, have that great gift of perseverance unto the end—unless he have learned this by special revelation: let him be anathema."* The message of Rome was to keep the people guessing, not to give assurance—to keep them on their toes.

King Ahab in 1 Kings 21 was afraid of the judgment of God. Elijah the prophet had declared that God would "bring evil" upon Ahab and "cut off" Ahab's house (v. 21). In response, Ahab did not repent, but he did put on sackcloth. When Ahab—the worst of Israel's kings—wore sackcloth and appeared to repent, he did not perform a good work pleasing to God. Ahab had already rejected God by marrying the heathen Jezebel and worshipping Baal. He thought a show of humility and sackcloth would turn away God's anger. But Ahab was not sorry for his sin, merely for the evil consequences of his sin. Ahab would have gladly sinned further if he could have escaped punishment. There was no love for God in Ahab's heart—he acted out of self-love and fear of damnation.

Self-love and fear of damnation are the only motivations of the wicked with respect to God. That is why unbelievers cannot understand the motivation of the Christian, which is love. The unbeliever who does not know the love of God never acts out of love for God, but the believer who knows God's love lives out of thankfulness. That is why the believer does not need to be threatened with hell and damnation. The heart of the Christian melts because of love!

These are two very different motives. One is the motivation of a slave. A slave obeys the master because he fears his master's wrath, but he does not love his master. He only obeys out of necessity. The other is the motivation of a son who obeys his father out of love. A son does not serve his father because he fears being beaten and even disowned as a son if he does not perform well enough as a son. A son serves his father because he loves his father and because he is thankful for all the good things that his father has given to him.

Thus it is with us. We keep God's commandments and we perform good works because we are filled with thanksgiving. That is the only true motivation. Is it yours?

Martyn McGeown

---

* The Canons and Decree of the Council of Trent, in Schaff, *Creeds of Christendom*, 2:113–114.

August 19 — True Faith Is Excited by Love

Wherefore I say unto thee, Her sins, which are many, are forgiven; for she loved much: but to whom little is forgiven, the same loveth little. —Luke 7:47

It is impossible for any unbeliever—who is not engrafted into Jesus Christ by the Holy Spirit with the result that he believes—to bring forth anything but dead works: works that are either rooted in selfishness or slavish fear. But the believer has a different motivation—love.

Article 24 speaks of this activity of faith as the fruit of justification. It is not that the works, which are the fruit of faith, justify us or contribute to our justification. How could they? We are already justified before we can begin to do any good works motivated by love. Without free and gracious justification received by faith alone, we would never "do anything out of love to God, but only out of self-love or fear of damnation." The Judge utters the verdict—"Not guilty! Righteous! Worthy of eternal life!"—and that verdict has an effect upon the one justified.

Try to imagine the scene for a moment. A homeless beggar is led into the courtroom. He knows that he is guilty of crimes that are worthy of death. He has no reason to expect anything else but condemnation. The indictment is made, and the evidence of guilt is unmistakable. Trembling, the beggar waits for the judge to read out the sentence of doom. But the judge does not condemn him. Instead, he says to him: "I know you are guilty, but another has been punished in your place. You are free to go. The law has been satisfied." What relief must flood that man's soul! As the man turns to leave the courtroom, the judge speaks again: "I have more to say. These papers in my hand are adoption papers. I have signed them. You will live with me, sit at my table, and become part of my family. You will inherit everything I possess." What surprise, what wonder, what joy will flood the soul of that beggar! Before his justification, he had nothing. Now he has the title to a great inheritance. That is but a faint picture of what happens in justification—and we have seen how that happens in earlier meditations.

Such an experience will have an effect upon the beggar. He will be filled with thanksgiving. He will desire to show his gratitude by the way in which he lives in the home of the judge—the home of his father! That is the point of Article 24. What is true of our imaginary beggar is infinitely truer of the child of God. This is because when God justifies us, "the love of God is shed abroad in our hearts by the Holy Ghost which is given unto us" (Rom. 5:5). What the judge cannot do to the imaginary beggar—make him love him—God does to those whom he saves from sin. He sends the Holy Spirit into our hearts, and he fills our hearts with love—his own love, which returns from our hearts as ardent love to him.

Article 24 explains the relationship between faith and love. We are not justified by love—because we loved God or our neighbor. We cannot love God and our neighbor by nature, and even the love we have as regenerated believers is weak, imperfect, and tainted with self-love and fear. But the faith by which we are justified—by which the perfect righteousness of Christ becomes ours, being imputed to us—"worketh by love" (Gal. 5:6). That love "excites man to the practice of those works which God has commanded in his word."

Is that not true for you, believer in Christ? Is it not your chief delight—now that you are justified by free grace—to live out of gratitude to him who loved you so?

From the one who has been forgiven, the only response is love!

Martyn McGeown

August 20 — Paul and James

Ye see then how that by works a man is justified,
and not by faith only. —James 2:24

Do James and Paul contradict one another on the subject of justification? Paul writes: "We conclude that a man is justified by faith without the deeds of the law" (Rom. 3:28). God justifies the believing sinner on the basis of "the righteousness of God without the law" (Rom. 3:21). In Galatians, he is equally emphatic: "a man is not justified by the works of the law…for by the works of the law shall no flesh be justified" (Gal. 2:16). Moreover, Paul proves the doctrine of justification by appealing to the example of Abraham: "if Abraham were justified by works, he hath whereof to glory; but not before God" (Rom. 4:2). About Abraham, Paul writes: "but to him that worketh not but believeth, his faith is counted for righteousness" (Rom. 4:5) and points out that Abraham was justified by faith before he was circumcised (Rom. 4:10)!

James, however, writes something which on the face of it seems contradictory to Paul. James writes that Abraham was "justified by works" (James 2:21) and then adds this conclusion, which would appear to be devastating to the Reformed position: "Ye see then how that by works a man is justified, and not by faith only" (v. 24). Even today you will meet Roman Catholics who will say: "The phrase 'justified by faith alone' is not found in the Bible. The only place where Scripture mentions it is to condemn it, as in James 2:24, 'Not by faith only.' Case closed. The Reformation was wrong."

But, before we address the question, we must stress the truth that James and Paul do not contradict one another. How could they, when they both wrote "as they were moved by the Holy Ghost" (2 Pet. 1:21)? Moreover, both were present at the Jerusalem Council as recorded in Acts 15, and there was no hint of disagreement between Paul, Peter, and James. Remember, the subject of that council was justification (Acts 15:10–14, 19)!

Both Paul and James use the same Greek word for *justify*. They appeal to the same Old Testament example of Abraham. Both Paul and James quote Genesis 15:6, "And he believed in the Lord; and he counted it to him for righteousness."

We must understand that Paul and James are addressing two very different situations. Paul is addressing the question of a sinner's justification before God. Carefully, systematically, and in great detail, Paul explains the utter depravity of man, that "there is none righteous" (Rom. 3:10), and that therefore God himself has provided the only righteousness that is acceptable before him (Rom. 3:21). Therefore, Paul deals with great theological concepts such as righteousness and imputation which we have already studied in some detail. He sets forth the glorious work of Jesus Christ as the only ground on which the believer's justification rests; and, although he does not use the phrase "by faith alone," he emphatically and repeatedly excludes works from justification.

Therefore, to understand justification, we must start with Paul, not with James. This does not mean that James is less authoritative, less important, or less inspired than Paul. However, if you want to study a subject, you must first study that place where the subject is treated at length. James' main point is not justification, but the role of faith in the believer's life.

Tomorrow, we will examine what James is teaching in context, and we will conclude that James and Paul are in complete harmony. Both teach justification by faith alone, and both teach that there is an important place for works—but not in justification before God.

Martyn McGeown

August 21 — If A Man Say He Hath Faith

What doth it profit, my brethren, though a man say he hath faith, and have not works? can faith save him? —James 2:14

Yesterday, we began to deal with the relationship between Paul and James, and I insisted that there is no contradiction. But I still must explain what James means by "justified by works" (James 2:21, 24–25).

In chapter two of his epistle, James is addressing the man who says that he has faith but who has no works to demonstrate his faith. "What doth it profit…though a man say he hath faith, and have not works?" (v. 14); "…you say…and give them not" (v. 16); "A man may say, Thou hast faith, and I have works: shew me thy faith without thy works, and I will shew thee my faith by my works" (v. 18). Faith, you see, is invisible. But the fruits of faith are not invisible. True faith—as opposed to "dead" faith (v. 17)—always displays itself to others by means of works. The examples in the chapter are striking: one with true faith does not ignore the needs of a destitute brother or sister in the church (v. 15–16). He goes beyond the mere intellectual knowledge of devils (v. 19)—who know many facts about God but hate and fear him. And one with true faith is willing to deny himself, as did Abraham and Rahab (vv. 21, 25). All of this simply means that you know a believer not by the loudness of his profession, but by the fruit of his faith. Our faith in Jesus Christ will lead us to love God and the neighbor; it will bring us to true sorrow for sin and hearty thankfulness to our Savior manifested in obedience. One without true faith—a hypocrite or a "vain man" (v. 20)—will lead an ungodly life.

James uses the example of Abraham. Abraham was justified by faith some seven chapters and thirteen years before the test of his faith on Mt. Moriah (Gen. 15:6; 22:16). Both Paul and James teach this (James 2:23; Rom. 4:3). What was God doing on Mt. Moriah then? He was not justifying Abraham again. He was proving to Abraham, to us, and to all in the world that Abraham had true faith, that Abraham's faith was not a pious-sounding sham. So strong was Abraham's faith—a faith which God worked in him and perfected through this trial and by which he had already justified him—that he was willing, when commanded, to sacrifice his son (Rom. 4:19–22; Heb. 11:17–19). Thus, writes James concerning the trial, "Faith wrought with his works, and by works was faith made perfect…And the scripture was fulfilled which saith, Abraham believed God, and it was imputed unto him for righteousness" (James 2:22–23). Genesis 22 proves the genuineness of the testimony of Genesis 15!

The same is true with Rahab, the harlot of Jericho. She believed in the true God (Josh. 2:8–13), but how did she demonstrate to the spies of Israel the genuineness of her faith? By siding with Israel, helping Israel's spies, saving them from death, and betraying her own city in a time of war and at great risk to herself (James 2:25).

So, in what sense were Abraham and Rahab—and in what sense are we—justified by their works? Is it in the sense that their works are part of or even all their righteousness before God? Or is it in the sense that God accepts their imperfect obedience as a suitable alternative to the perfect righteousness of Christ? Absolutely not (see James 2:10)! We are justified by works in that our good works (which flow from faith) vindicate or prove the genuineness of our faith before men. Those who have no good works and who live in an ungodly manner show by that very fact that their faith is counterfeit, or as James puts it, that their "faith…is dead" (James 2:17, 20, 26).

But, says Article 24, "we do not speak of a vain faith." Thank God that true faith in Jesus Christ can be neither dead nor vain!

Martyn McGeown

August 22 — Holy Faith Never Fruitless

He that abideth in me, and I in him, the same bringeth forth much fruit. —John 15:5

It is impossible for any unbeliever, without the gift of true faith, to bring forth anything but dead works—works motivated by self-love or fear. It is equally impossible for a believer who is engrafted into Jesus Christ by a true faith not to bring forth the fruit of good works.

In Matthew 12, Jesus illustrates this: "Either make the tree good, and his fruit good; or else make the tree corrupt, and his fruit corrupt: for the tree is known by his fruit" (v. 33). By nature, says Jesus, we are all evil trees. In fact, some trees are trees not planted by the Father. They will be uprooted and destroyed (Matt. 15:13). How does an evil tree change into a good tree? Its very nature must be changed, and that happens by God's grace. The inevitable result, fruit, and evidence of that change in the believer are the bringing forth of good works. A similar illustration is used in John 15, which we have already seen. The inevitable result of being engrafted into Jesus Christ by the bond of faith is good fruit. It simply cannot be any other way.

The good works in the life of the believer come from Christ! Without Christ—that is, severed or separated from Christ—we can do nothing, but as we abide in Christ, and continue to live out of him, we will produce fruit, indeed "much fruit" (John 15:5).

Article 24 gives several reasons why justifying faith cannot be "unfruitful in man." First, justifying or holy faith is not "a vain faith." Vain faith is the subject of James 2—it is mere belief in God, which is no better than the faith of devils (v. 19); it is faith which refuses help to a fellow church member in need (vv. 15–16); it is the faith of one who says he has faith but really has no faith at all (v. 14). By that faith no man is justified. It is a vain faith because it is an empty, useless faith, a faith which does not unite a sinner to Jesus Christ but to some other object in which there is no salvation. It is the rootless faith of the stony-ground hearer in Matthew 13:21. Second, the holy, justifying faith is not an idle, dead faith (James 2:17), but "such a faith which is called in Scripture, *a faith that worketh by love*, which excites man to the practice of those works which God has commanded in his word" (Article 24). We are not justified by faith, but faith—which looks to and lives out of Jesus Christ—is excited, spurred on, or energized by love. One who understands what Christ has done and who truly believes and embraces Christ as his own hope will love God and keep his commandments. One who has no appreciation for what Christ has done really has no faith, and he will have no motivation for avoiding sin or for obedience to God but for self-love and fear. Third, and most importantly, good works flow from faith because true faith is a root which is embedded deeply into Christ. A tree rooted in the ground will produce fruit. A Christian rooted in Jesus Christ will produce the fruit of good works. "As ye have therefore received Christ Jesus the Lord, so walk ye in him: rooted and built up in him, and stablished in the faith, as ye have been taught, abounding therein with thanksgiving" (Col. 2:6–7).

Therefore, good works are not only necessary in the Christian life: they are inevitable. There is not, and never shall be, a Christian anywhere in the history of the world who has not produced good fruit. Some produce more and better fruit than others, but none is entirely fruitless. Remember also what the Heidelberg Catechism teaches: "It is impossible that those, who are implanted into Christ by a true faith, should not bring forth fruits of thankfulness."*
Are you thankful for gracious salvation? You shall produce fruit!

Martyn McGeown

---

* Heidelberg Catechism 64, in Schaff, *Creeds of Christendom*, 3:328.

August 23 — Genuinely Good But Not Perfect Fruit

Even so every good tree bringeth forth good fruit;
but a corrupt tree bringeth forth evil fruit. —Matthew 7:17

There are only two kinds of people in the world—one kind as represented by good trees which bring forth good fruit, and the other kind as represented by evil trees which bring forth evil fruit. By nature, we are all evil trees, but God transforms us into good trees when he saves us. We have also seen that every believer must bring forth good fruit because he is united to Jesus Christ, and no unbeliever can bring forth good fruit because he lacks that union. There are also others—hypocrites—whose professions of faith are false. The counterfeit nature of their dead faith is seen in its fruitlessness. One whom God justifies freely by his grace, God also sanctifies by producing in him good fruit unto God's own glory. Jesus said: "Herein is my Father glorified, that ye bear much fruit" (John 15:8).

The best description of this fruit is found in Galatians 5:22–23, "But the fruit of the Spirit is love, joy, peace, longsuffering, gentleness, goodness, faith, meekness, temperance: against such there is no law." This fruit may not seem spectacular, and it will not bring the praise of men, but this fruit—of the Spirit, because the Spirit produces it in us—is, in the sight of God, of great value and worth and is well-pleasing to him. The works of faith "are good and acceptable in the sight of God," says Article 24. We stress this point because there are some who, in misplaced zeal to protect the doctrine of total depravity and man's inability to do good, deny that the believer ever produces genuinely good works. "All our righteousnesses are as filthy rags!" is the cry of such people. "Our righteousnesses are as filthy rags" (Isa. 64:6), but our good works as fruit of our justification are not to be placed in the same category as our "righteousnesses." Remember that righteousness pertains to justification. Righteousness is perfect conformity to God's law. The believer in his best works never conforms perfectly to God's law, but that does not mean that he never does a genuinely good work.

Article 24 puts works in the right perspective. Our good works are something God as our Father delights in, yet they could not withstand his scrutiny as judge. "They are of no account to our justification. For it is by faith in Christ that we are justified, even before we do good works." In fact, says Article 24, "we can do no work but what is polluted by our flesh, and also punishable; and although we could perform such works, still the remembrance of one sin is sufficient to make God reject them." We produce by the Spirit genuinely good fruit, but not fruit able to withstand the strict judgment of God. This is not because there is something wrong with the fruit the Spirit produces. There is something wrong with us. We pollute our good works by the sinfulness of the flesh. That is why the Spirit must sanctify our good works.

By way of illustration, imagine a little girl who sincerely loves her mother. She desires to please her mother by making her a bouquet of flowers. She lovingly arranges some weeds, wilted blossoms, and a variety of leaves, and places them into a plastic cup. The mother is genuinely pleased with the child's efforts to please her and does not chide her daughter for the many imperfections in the bouquet. But bring that bouquet under the scrutiny of the judge of a formal flower show, and the result will be very different!

Similarly, our good works are genuinely good, but they could never withstand the judgment of God. Our Father accepts them in his goodness as tokens of our gratitude, only after his justice has been satisfied, and we are justified by the finished work of Christ.

Martyn McGeown

August 24 — No Merit in Our Good Works

So likewise ye, when ye shall have done all those things which are commanded you, say, We are unprofitable servants: we have done that which was our duty to do. —Luke 17:10

"We do good works, but not to merit by them (for what can we merit?)—nay, we are beholden to God for the good works we do." With that sentence, Article 24 condemns and denies all possibility of mere creatures to merit with God. Merit is something earned or deserved. It was part of the whole scheme of medieval salvation—and still part of Roman Catholicism today—that sinners could merit with God.

Merit is only possible for one who can give God more than he already owes God. Therefore, merit is impossible for a mere creature. Adam could not merit with God—every moment of his existence he owed to God. Imagine that Adam comes to God at the end of the first day of his service in the garden of Eden, saying, "God, thou owest me!" How absurd and wicked that would be! Rather, Adam's attitude was this: "God, thou art my creator. I owe everything to thee. Everything I have is thine already. I have nothing to give. I live only to serve thee in love. It is my joy and my privilege to serve thee!"

If Adam before he fell could not merit with God, how much more impossible it is for fallen sinners to merit with God. Jesus illustrates this with a parable in Luke 17. A slave has worked all day in the fields of his master. He comes home, hungry and weary, but his time of service is not finished. All his time belongs to his master. Will the master say to his slave, "Go and sit down to meat" (v. 7)? Of course not! Before the slave can have his dinner, he must prepare a meal for his master—he must wait upon his master, filling his plate and cup as is required, and then clear the table and wash the dishes. Only then, after he has completed all the work, may the slave sit down and attend to his own supper. The entire time that the slave has been working, he has simply been doing his duty. He deserves no credit, no reward, not even a thankful acknowledgment from his master: "Doth he thank that servant because he did the things that were commanded him? I trow [think] not" (v. 9). The application to us is clear: we must never be tempted to think that our good works somehow make God our debtor, so that we have a claim on God, a right to his favor. Even if we have done everything which is commanded us—and we have not—we would be "unprofitable servants" (v. 10). Unprofitable servants are useless, good-for-nothing servants! Our good works add nothing to God; they give nothing to God which he needs; they never make God indebted to us! Instead of seeking to merit with God, we need to be in prayer: "Father, bear with our infirmities. Forgive the impurities of our best works. Do not impute to us our endless imperfections but receive us in mercy and receive our good works as a genuine expression of our love for thee. Look upon us in thy favor for Jesus' sake."

Instead of our good works meriting with God, Article 24 reminds us that we are "beholden to God for the good works we do." Why? Because he works them in us by his grace, and he purifies them by the blood and Spirit of Jesus Christ.

In our best work, there is enough sin to damn us, but yet God receives us in mercy for the sake of Christ. What a wonder of grace our salvation is!

Martyn McGeown

August 25 — **Beholden to God for Our Good Works**

For it is God which worketh in you both to will and to do of his good pleasure. —Philippians 2:13

What is the place of good works in our salvation? That has been the theme of Article 24. They are "of no account towards our justification." We have seen several reasons for this. First, we cannot do any good works before we are justified. The only works performed before justification are dead, damnable works—the evil fruit of an evil tree! They are evil because they do not flow out of faith and are not to the glory of God out of gratitude, but they are only out of the evil motives of self-love and the fear of damnation. Second, even the best works that we—as believers—perform are imperfect, "polluted by our flesh, and also punishable." They can never withstand the scrutiny of the righteous Judge: "The remembrance of one sin is sufficient to make God reject them." Indeed, such are our best works that they must be "all sanctified by his grace." Third, we can never merit any part of justification because we can never merit at all. We can never give to God something he does not already have. All we have, we already owe to him.

Perhaps, then, we might be able to say—as many who are otherwise orthodox in their doctrine of justification do say—that we contribute something to our sanctification. Perhaps by our good works we sanctify ourselves, we make ourselves holy. Not so, says the Belgic Confession! On the contrary! "We are beholden to God for the good works we do, and not he to us." *Beholden* means *indebted*. We are indebted to God for our good works. We owe God a debt of gratitude we cannot even begin to pay, and on top of that, we owe God a debt of gratitude even for the good works which we do.

Consider Christ the vine. Do the branches in Christ boast that they have produced fruit by their own efforts? The only reason we can produce any fruit at all is that we are in Christ the vine. The only reason we are in the vine is the gracious work of God in engrafting us into the vine. The sap and fatness from Christ the vine flow to us through the mystical union created by the Holy Spirit—that union is not our work, either! No wonder, then, Article 24 teaches that we are "beholden to God" for our good works!

Paul makes a very profound point in Philippians 2, a passage quoted in Article 24. Paul exhorts the Philippians to "work out" their salvation (v. 12). But how and why? "For it is God which worketh in you both to will and to do of his good pleasure" (v. 13). God works the willing in our hearts, causing us to have the desire to do good works. That sigh of repentance, that sorrow over sin, that hunger and thirst after righteousness, that desire to meet your Savior in prayer—all of that is from God! How absurd, then, to teach that man, by his own freewill, can bring himself into a state of salvation. Not even the believer—who is already justified—is able to will a good thought without the working of God's grace! God also works the doing in our lives. He gives us the opportunity, the ability, and the gifts necessary to perform the good works. And when we do the good works that God has worked in us—and we do indeed perform them and produce fruit—we do not congratulate ourselves, but we return thanks to God: "Lord, thou hast willed and performed these good works in me by thy Holy Spirit. Receive them as tokens of my love and gratitude and forgive the many imperfections and pollutions of my flesh."

Thus, all the glory—both for justification and sanctification—is given to God alone.

Martyn McGeown

August 26 — God's Gracious Reward of Our Good Works

And, behold, I come quickly; and my reward is with me,
to give every man according as his work shall be. —Revelation 22:12

God promises to reward his people for their good works. In the last judgment, we see Jesus Christ rewarding Christians for the good work of feeding the hungry, giving drink to the thirsty, taking in the stranger, clothing the naked, and visiting the sick and prisoners (Matt. 25:34–36). Some have concluded that our good works do indeed merit with God, and that they are part of our justification. Article 24 has a very different explanation of reward: "In the meantime we do not deny that God rewards our good works, but it is through his grace that he crowns his gifts."

Grace upon grace upon grace! That is Scripture's message of salvation. How it offends the self-righteous, but what a thrill it is to the believer! Graciously, God gives us his Son to die on the cross and to work a perfect righteousness for us. Graciously, God works faith in us, uniting us to Jesus Christ. Graciously, God imputes, through that instrument of faith he worked in us, the perfect righteousness of Christ. Graciously, God works in us by the Holy Spirit, "both to will and to do of his good pleasure" (Phil. 2:13), so that we produce—by his grace—the fruit of good works which he has "before ordained that we should walk in them" (Eph. 2:10). Graciously, God rewards the works he has produced in us with more grace!

Notice how Article 24 describes our good works—"his gifts." Now notice what the gracious God does—"through his grace he crowns his gifts." The Heidelberg Catechism so succinctly expresses it: "This reward is not of merit, but of grace."*

Recall the little girl who made a bouquet of flowers for her mother. She went out into the mother's garden, picked the mother's flowers, mixed the flowers with weeds, and gave the finished product to her mother. As a reward, the mother graciously gives the child a treat. Did the child merit that treat? Is the bouquet—a mixture of weeds, wilted blossoms, and badly-arranged flowers—worth anything? Is the mother obligated to reward the child? No. That bouquet in no way makes up for the huge amount of money and time the mother has invested in bringing up her little girl from infancy. Consider the servants in Luke 17:10—their master might in his generosity give a reward, but the master does not owe the servants a reward. If the master gives a reward, it will only be a further display of his generosity.

Thus it is with us and our relationship to our heavenly Father. The paltry works we perform are nothing in comparison with the great salvation he has bestowed upon us. We would be embarrassed to mention our good works in the day of judgment. Look at the reaction of the justified saints on that Day: "Lord, when?" (Matt. 25:37–39). When we shall look back on our life, we shall exclaim: "But, Lord, I do not deserve a reward. The reward is too much. I am overwhelmed by it." And the Lord shall answer: "I know you do not deserve it, but I am pleased to give it. You may have forgotten the services you rendered to me, but I have not forgotten. Come, ye blessed of my Father, into the kingdom prepared for you. You did not merit it. I merited it for you. I washed you in my blood, and I justified you by my righteousness. And I worked grace in you so that you bore good fruit, and now I crown my grace with more grace and with glory."

An eternal weight of glory, an everlasting crown of righteousness and life—these are the rewards of grace which God bestows upon his people. What wondrous grace!

Martyn McGeown

---

* Heidelberg Catechism 63, in Schaff, *Creeds of Christendom*, 3:327.

August 27 — Our Consciences Neither Tossed Nor Vexed

Let us draw near with a true heart in full assurance of faith, having our hearts sprinkled from an evil conscience. —Hebrews 10:22

In its treatment of faith, justification, sanctification, and good works, Article 24 ends with an appeal to the conscience. What effect does the teaching of gracious justification without works—and what effect does the opposite doctrine of justification partly or wholly by works—have upon the conscience? What effect does this doctrine have upon your conscience?

Lack of assurance in the one not trusting in Christ is devastating: "Thus, then, we would always be in doubt, tossed to and fro without any certainty, and our poor consciences continually vexed, if they relied not on the merits of the suffering and death of our Savior."

Always in doubt! Tossed to and fro! Our consciences continually vexed! What an awful description of a sinner who does not know the peace through believing in Christ! The image is of one lying on a bed, tossing and turning, unable to get to sleep because of the many doubts which assail his conscience. The image is of a "troubled sea, whose waters cast up mire and dirt" (Isa. 57:20). The image is of one who is tormented—vexed—with the awful possibility that he will be cast into hell by an angry God. Such a person has no joy in living and cannot serve God but dares not die.

Irreligious people try to drown the conscience in alcohol, drug use, and wanton pleasure. They even try to convince themselves that there is no God, or if there is a God, he does not care how they live. Religious people try to silence their accusing conscience by fervent religious exercises—performed, as we have seen, out of the fear of damnation. But none of these things give peace. God will not give peace through these things.

Doubts and fears are to be expected as the bitter fruit of unbelief. No person can know that he has performed enough works of sufficient quality to merit a justifying verdict today and on the last day. When his own conscience accuses him that he has broken God's law, he has no plea. Perhaps he might say that he has tried his best. But our best is not good enough, and besides, we have not tried our best. We could have tried harder, we could have sacrificed more, we could have been more diligent. Perhaps one might say that he will try harder tomorrow, but God's law will not be satisfied with a promise of a better tomorrow. No judge will accept that: "Your honor, I know that I have broken the law, but I will try harder tomorrow." The judge will answer: "But you have broken the law, and must be punished." Perhaps that one might even say that his good works will cancel out his bad works. But that is impossible, too. Even if we could do good works—and we have seen that outside of Christ, we cannot—our "good works" would not cancel out our sins. No judge will accept that: "Your honor, I know that I have broken the law, but I would like to mention the many years of faithful service I have given to the community." The judge will answer: "This is irrelevant! You must answer for the crimes you have committed!"

But all doubt and vexation of conscience disappear when we approach God clothed in the righteousness of Christ. Have we done enough? No, but Christ has! Have we answered for our sins? No, but Christ has! The knowledge that Christ has done everything to secure our justification frees our conscience from fear and frees us to serve God in gratitude. The unbeliever will scoff at this free justification, and the hypocrite will abuse it, but the believer rejoices in it. Christ is the end of a vexed conscience: "Let us draw near with a true heart in full assurance of faith, having our hearts sprinkled from an evil conscience" (Heb. 10:22).

Sprinkled from an evil conscience, by the blood of Christ!

Martyn McGeown

Article 25

OF THE ABOLISHING OF THE CEREMONIAL LAW

We believe that the ceremonies and figures of the law ceased at the coming of Christ, and that all the shadows are accomplished; so that the use of them must be abolished amongst Christians; yet the truth and substance of them remain with us in Jesus Christ, in whom they have their completion. In the meantime we still use the testimonies taken out of the law and the prophets, to confirm us in the doctrine of the gospel, and to regulate our life in all honesty to the glory of God, according to his will.

August 28 — The Threefold Law Given to Israel

He sheweth his word unto Jacob,
his statutes and his judgments unto Israel. —Psalms 147:19

Articles 22–24 have dealt with faith, justification, sanctification, and good works. The question naturally arises—what about the law? In Reformed theology, the law of God has an important place and role to play in the life of the church and of the Christian. Although, as we have seen, the law in no way contributes to our justification or righteousness before God, it remains binding upon all sinners and remains the rule by which Christians are called to live. "As many as have sinned without law shall also perish without law: and as many as have sinned in the law shall be judged by the law" (Rom. 2:12). Paul quotes many of the ten commandments as binding upon New Testament believers (Rom. 13:9–10; Eph. 4:25, 28; 6:1–3).

But we need to understand what the law is. First, the law refers to the Torah, the first five books of Moses (Genesis through Deuteronomy). Second, the law refers to all the commandments, statutes, and ordinances contained in the Old Testament. Third, the law refers to the threefold division of the law: the moral law, the civil law, and the ceremonial law. All of these laws were received while Israel camped at Mount Sinai. It is especially the ceremonial law which is the focus of Article 25.

Israel's sojourn at Mount Sinai was memorable. Who could forget the smoke, the fire, the thunderings, the lightnings, the terrible quaking of the entire mountain, and the awe-inspiring voice of the Almighty which sounded like a long trumpet blast (Ex. 19:18–19; 20:18)? Even Moses confessed: "I exceedingly fear and quake" (Heb. 12:21). At the same time, Israel sinned grievously at Sinai by making and worshipping a golden calf. But the highlight of Sinai was the giving of the law. To no other nation did God give such a righteous law. This law was designed to regulate every aspect of Israel's life, to teach her how God was to be worshipped, and to show what a life of thankfulness should look like.

Two parts of the law have passed away. The first is the civil law. These are the laws which pertained to Israel as a nation. For example, God legislated through Moses how the Israelites should do farming—do not sow fields with mingled seed; do not crossbreed cattle (Deut. 22:9–10; Lev. 19:19). God legislated concerning property rights and laws of indemnity—if your animal causes damage to another man's property or destroys his life, you must make restoration (Ex. 21:28–36). God gave laws concerning punishments for various crimes—including the death penalty (Lev. 20:8–22).

The second is the ceremonial law. These are the laws which pertained to Israel's worship. There were instructions on constructing the tabernacle (Ex. 25–31); there were detailed instructions on the different kinds of sacrifices, apparel for the priests, laws concerning cleanness and uncleanness, and laws concerning the special feast days. Most of these laws are detailed in the book of Leviticus—a book which impresses upon us the holiness of God.

New Testament believers do not need to—indeed, they may not—observe these Old Testament ceremonial laws. They were all fulfilled in the coming of Christ, of whom these laws were but a shadow.

We live in full gospel light. We have no need to keep those laws.

Martyn McGeown

August 29 — The Perpetual, Binding, Moral Law

And he gave unto Moses, when he had made an end of communing with him upon mount Sinai, two tables of testimony, tables of stone, written with the finger of God. —Exodus 31:18

Since the Biblical nation of Israel no longer exists, the detailed civil laws which governed the Old Testament saints have passed away. God no longer regulates our farming methods or determines death by stoning for certain gross offenses. The New Testament church is catholic, or universal, gathered from all nations. The church and state are no longer intertwined. Therefore, the Christian must live in the world and obey the laws of the nation in which he lives. Moreover, since the religion of Israel has been fulfilled in the coming of Christ, the ceremonial law—with the sacrifices, the priesthood, the festivals and stated solemnities, the food laws, and many other ordinances—has passed away also. The Christian may eat pork or shellfish, indeed, all things are clean unto us (1 Tim. 4:4; Tit. 1:15; Col. 2:16, 20–22). This is the freedom of the Christian, which the Old Testament saints did not enjoy.

But this does not mean that God's moral law has passed away.

The moral law belongs to a different category. It is altogether unique. First, the moral law—as it is summarized in the ten commandments, which in turn are summarized in Christ's command to love God and the neighbor—is the revelation of the unchanging will of God for his creatures. We may eat pork—abomination in the Old Testament. We may wear a garment of mixed fabrics—forbidden in the Old Testament. We may approach God without a Levitical priesthood—unthinkable in the Old Testament. Nevertheless, the commandment to love God and the neighbor has not been abrogated. Murder, adultery, theft, lying, idolatry, blasphemy, and covetousness are still sins. The sabbath day—now the Lord's day, the first day of the week—is still the day God requires for public worship, although the sabbath days (i.e. rest days, which were different from the weekly Sabbath which is now our Lord's day), the new moons, and the seven Levitical feasts (see Lev. 23) are no longer to be observed.

Second, the moral law is set apart as unique in the Pentateuch itself. God spoke the words of the ten commandments personally to the people (Ex. 20:1). The rest of the law, God gave through the mediator Moses. God wrote these ten commandments on two tables of stone with his own finger (Ex. 31:18). The number ten signifies their completeness and perfection, the finger of God signifies their binding authority, and the tablets of stone signify their perpetuity.

Third, of the laws, only the ten commandments—the two tables—were placed inside the ark of the covenant. Everything in Scripture points to the unique importance of the ten commandments—the decalogue, or "ten words," the moral law.

How do we show love for God and the neighbor? Not by abstaining from pork; not by offering sacrifices; not by keeping the Feast of Tabernacles. We show love by keeping the commandments of God's moral law (John 14:15). Which commandments? The ten commandments, as Paul summarizes them in Romans 13: "He that loveth another hath fulfilled the law. For this, Thou shalt not commit adultery, Thou shalt not kill, Thou shalt not steal…and if there be any other commandment, it is briefly comprehended in this saying, namely, Thou shalt love thy neighbour as thyself" (vv. 8–9).

How will you show your love for Christ who has given such a great salvation? Keep the ten commandments!

Martyn McGeown

August 30 — Not Under the Law

For ye are not under the law, but under grace. —Romans 6:14

Invariably, when someone raises the question of the law as a rule of gratitude in the Christian life, the objection is heard: "But we are not under the law, but under grace" (Rom. 6:14). Therefore, it is vital that we understand the role of the law in the New Testament.

First, the law reveals our sin. "By the law is the knowledge of sin" (Rom. 3:20). It is true that we all have a conscience, and we all have some idea of right and wrong because God has written the work of the law—not the law itself—in the hearts of even the heathen (Rom. 2:15). Nevertheless, the law increases our knowledge of sin. Paul experienced this himself when the law began to work upon him. "I had not known sin, but by the law: for I had not known lust, except the law had said, Thou shalt not covet" (Rom. 7:7).

Second, the law increases our sin. This does not mean that the law is sinful or that the law promotes sin. But the sinful flesh of man hates God's law and cannot be subject to it (Rom. 8:7). Therefore, when God reveals his law to us, we are incited to sin even more. "Sin, taking occasion by the commandment, wrought in me all manner of concupiscence…When the commandment came, sin revived, and I died…For sin, taking occasion by the commandment, deceived me, and by it slew me" (Rom. 7:8–9, 11). This is because the law is "weak through the flesh" (Rom. 8:3).

Third, the law reveals to us our need for a savior, and in that way "the law was our schoolmaster to bring us unto Christ, that we might be justified by faith" (Gal. 3:24). The law reveals to us what God's requirements are, but the law does not give us any strength to obey the commandments of God. The only thing that the law can do is condemn and curse the transgressor of the law. Therefore, we need a savior who delivers us from the condemnation and curse of the law. That savior is Jesus Christ (Gal. 3:13).

Fourth, the law is the guide of our thankfulness. We do not know without the revelation of God's law how we ought to show our gratitude to God for the salvation he has given us. Sometimes we think that we know, but we discover that our so-called good work of thankfulness has no warrant from the word of God because God has not commanded it. Unbelievers might have a "zeal of God," but if it is "not according to knowledge," what value is it (Rom. 10:2)? Indeed, some men have even committed great sins because they believed that in so doing, they were serving God (John 16:2). Paul was an example of this when he was a persecutor of God's people.

So, in what sense are we "not under the law, but under grace"? This phrase comes from Romans 6:14. Often it is quoted only in part without considering the context. Paul mentions our not being under the law as a reason for our not serving sin! We are not under the law for condemnation. The law cannot curse or damn Christians because Christ was cursed in our place. We are also not under the law in the sense that sin does not have dominion over us. We have been delivered from the power of sin, and therefore are free to serve God—by keeping his commandments with a new heart and a purified conscience.

The liberty of the Christian is not lawlessness, but freedom from condemnation (Rom. 8:1). Lawlessness is a spiritual bondage. "Ye were the servants of sin, but…ye became the servants of righteousness" (Rom. 6:17–18).

What a privilege is ours—to serve the Lord Jesus Christ with "the perfect law of liberty" (James 1:25), "the royal law" of the King of kings (2:8)!

Martyn McGeown

August 31 — The Figures or Shadows of the Law

For the law having a shadow of good things to come,
and not the very image of the things, can never with those sacrifices
which they offered year by year continually make the comers
thereunto perfect. —Hebrews 10:1

The Old Testament saints lived in the days of types and shadows.

A type is an Old Testament person, thing, or event which points to a higher, spiritual reality in the New Testament. David was a type of Christ. In a certain sense, he resembled and pointed to Christ—he was a mighty warrior, he was a man after God's own heart, he had a zeal for God's worship—but he was not Christ. When the Old Testament saint studied him and his life, they could see something of Christ in him, but the real Christ was always future. The land of Canaan was a type of heaven. It had some similarities to heaven—it was freely given to Israel as her inheritance, it was the land which God set apart as holy, it was the place where God dwelled with his people—but it was not heaven. The Old Testament saints understood that the real land promised to them was heavenly (Heb. 11:10, 16). The exodus from Egypt and the passing through the Red Sea were types of redemption—it was deliverance from bondage by a mediator, it separated Israel from the Egyptians, it consecrated them to God and to Moses (1 Cor. 10:2)—but this was not redemption in the blood of Jesus.

We must be careful, however, not to overanalyze the Old Testament and find types where God has not placed types. A type will be indicated by Scripture: there will be clear points of comparison between the type and the reality (the antitype), and there will be a point where the type fails to be the reality. There are too many speculative Christians whose overactive imaginations lead them to make the Bible into a collection of fanciful pictures. This dishonors the word of God and makes the Bible mean whatever we want it to mean.

A shadow is a shape produced by an object when light shines upon it. That shadow, however, is not real. We have all seen shadows. Perhaps as children we have even chased shadows. The object (or body) is real, but the shadow itself is not real. In the Old Testament, Christ was casting many shadows, but those shadows were never the reality. Christ, who stood behind the shadows, was the reality. God's people saw the shadows, but they longed to get behind the shadows to the reality. Hebrews 10:1 says: "The law having a shadow of good things to come, and not the very image of the things, can never with those sacrifices which they offered year by year continually make the comers thereunto perfect."

Article 25 addresses this subject in these words: "We believe that the ceremonies and figures of the law ceased at the coming of Christ." What, then, were the tabernacle, the temple, the ark of the covenant, the incense, the priesthood, the day of atonement, and the passover feast? Shadows, types, pictures, images, but not the reality.

And if you look very carefully at those shadows, you will see Christ; rejoice that Christ's coming has dispelled the shadows and that you walk in his light!

Martyn McGeown

September 1 — All the Shadows Are Accomplished

Which are a shadow of things to come; but the body is of Christ.
—Colossians 2:17

In Galatians 3–4, Paul develops the truth that God has one people—Israel or the church—and that this one people has reached her maturity in the New Testament age. In Galatians 3:23, Paul describes the strict confinement of Old Testament Israel: "before faith came, we were kept under the law, shut up unto the faith which should afterwards be revealed." That "shutting up" meant Israel's entire life was controlled by the boundaries of the law of God.

Parents understand this. When your children are small, you determine everything for them. You set the boundaries—and this is good for children. Parents determine their children's food; what they wear; where and when they sleep; where, when, and with whom they go. Parents hedge in their children for their own good—childproof locks, fences, and gates are all necessary when children are small. Israel in the Old Testament was a child. She needed to be told what to eat and what to wear, and she needed regulations for every aspect of her existence. "The heir, as long as he is a child, differeth nothing from a servant, though he be lord of all; but is under tutors and governors until the time appointed of the father" (Gal. 4:1–2). But the New Testament church does not need such rules—she has matured, she has inherited the inheritance, she enjoys the full freedom of gospel privileges.

Moreover, a little child cannot be taught in the same way as a mature adult. A child needs illustrations and pictures. God gave Israel a beautiful picture book called the Old Testament—Canaan was a picture of heaven; food laws and laws concerning cleanness and uncleanness were pictures of the defilement of sin; the temple was a picture of fellowship with God. This truth ought to give us pause when we are tempted to read Old Testament prophecy too literally. Israel always needed to be taught in terms of pictures with which she was familiar. To attempt to teach her about the full realities of gospel truth would have confused her—as if you would attempt to teach a three-year-old with an encyclopedia.

What changed? The answer is that Christ came. Galatians 4:2 speaks of "the time appointed of the father." That time was the coming of Christ, his death, resurrection, and outpouring of his Holy Spirit (Gal. 4:4–7). The coming of Christ marked the church's coming of age.

The transition from Old Testament to New Testament was painful. Most Jews remained unbelieving and rejected Christ altogether. They clung to their beautiful picture book but refused to believe that Christ had fulfilled every picture therein. Even believing Jews were reluctant to come out of the shadows—they had never known anything else. Through patient instruction, the apostles encouraged them to embrace the promises of Christ.

Article 25 is clear: "all the shadows are accomplished; so that the use of them must be abolished amongst Christians." Are you still chasing shadows? The substance is Christ!

Martyn McGeown

September 2 — The Truth and Substance Remain

Think not that I am come to destroy the law, or the prophets:
I am not come to destroy, but to fulfill. —Matthew 5:17

The truth that the Old Testament law—especially with respect to the ceremonial or civil law—was a shadow, which has now been fulfilled, must not cause us to despise the Old Testament. What we have is better, richer, and more glorious than anything the Old Testament saints ever knew, but what they had was good, necessary, and still profitable for us. Article 25 reminds us: "yet the truth and substance of them remain with us in Jesus Christ, in whom they have their completion."

There are many in the church who despise the Old Testament. "Oh, that's just the Old Testament!" they cry, "We live in the New Testament." Perhaps ministers are reluctant to preach the Old Testament for this reason. Modern Christians are woefully ignorant of the Old Testament Scriptures. But remember that for Christ and the apostles the Old Testament was the only Bible they knew. When Paul urged the inspired, God-breathed Scriptures upon Timothy (2 Tim. 3:16), he meant the Old Testament. When Christ quoted, "it is written" and "Have ye not read" to his enemies, he wielded the Old Testament (Matt. 4:4, 19:4). Indeed, without the Old Testament, our understanding of the gospel would be greatly impoverished. Much of the New Testament presupposes the Old Testament. Christians must be familiar with creation, the fall, the flood, the exodus, the passage through the Red Sea, the wilderness wanderings, the psalms, the prophets, and so much more to understand the New Testament gospel of Jesus Christ. Think of only one chapter: Hebrews 11!

The truth and substance of the ceremonies remain. Take circumcision. We do not—we must not—circumcise our children for religious purposes. But the truth of original sin, sanctification, the covenant, and the forgiveness of sins in the blood of Christ remains. Take the sacrifices of the Old Testament Levitical priesthood. We must not offer animal sacrifices today, but Jesus is the Lamb of God. Without the shedding of blood, there is no remission, and Christ is not our great high priest. Take the law against eating the meat of pigs or other unclean animals. We are not so restricted today, but the truth and substance of God's holiness and our spiritual separation from the world remain. The truth and substance remain in every Old Testament ordinance, although the shadow has been dispelled by the appearance of Christ. And when we search the Scriptures diligently, we will find Jesus Christ there to the comfort of our souls. Jesus expects us to find him there. "And beginning at Moses and all the prophets, he expounded unto them in all the scriptures the things concerning himself" (Luke 24:27) and, "These are the words which I spake unto you, while I was yet with you, that all things must be fulfilled, which were written in the law of Moses, and in the prophets, and in the psalms, concerning me" (v. 44).

Consider the picture book illustration. As the church in its maturity, we no longer need to be taught exclusively by means of pictures, but pictures are even useful for adult believers. It is true that we have the reality, but the pictures of the Old Testament can still teach us much about our Savior. And we can understand those pictures better than the Old Testament saints ever could.

There is a saying—"do not throw out the baby with the bathwater." Do not throw away the Old Testament with the coming of the New Testament. Both are God's precious word to us.

Martyn McGeown

September 3 — **Using the Testimonies of the Law to Confirm Us in the Doctrine of the Gospel**

> *What advantage then hath the Jew? or what profit is there of circumcision? Much every way: chiefly, because that unto them were committed the oracles of God.* —Rom. 3:1–2

One final use of the law is to "confirm us in the doctrine of the gospel, and to regulate our life in all honesty to the glory of God, according to his will" (Article 25).

When we look at many of the laws contained in the books of Exodus, Leviticus, and Deuteronomy, we might wonder, what possible relevance do they have for us? Perhaps it would help to look at a few examples of how specific laws do have relevance to us today.

In Leviticus 16, the great day of atonement is described. We know from the New Testament that "it is not possible that the blood of bulls and of goats should take away sins" (Heb. 10:4). This does not mean that the day of atonement can be cut out of our Bibles. Without an understanding of the day of atonement, the different sacrifices, the scapegoat in the wilderness, and the sprinkling of the blood on the mercy seat, our appreciation of the real atonement of Christ is greatly impoverished. The same is true of the awesome account of the passover in Exodus 12. How would we appreciate the last supper (and therefore the Lord's supper) and the cross itself without understanding the historical and religious significance of the passover? "Christ our passover is sacrificed for us" (1 Cor. 5:7).

Take also the laws concerning leprosy in Leviticus 13. This rich instruction gives us a very profound understanding of the filthiness and defiling nature of sin. Cleanness and uncleanness were very important concepts to the Old Testament saint. We are no longer to think of cleanness and uncleanness in terms of eating, drinking, wearing different clothes, or various diseases, but the concept of sin is still one which must profoundly affect us. Do you need a vivid picture of sin which you and your children can understand? Go to Isaiah 1:6, "From the sole of the foot even unto the head there is no soundness in it; but wounds, and bruises, and putrifying sores: they have not been closed, neither bound up, neither mollified with ointment." Then turn to Psalm 51:7, "Purge me with hyssop, and I shall be clean: wash me, and I shall be whiter than snow." The hyssop is a reference to Leviticus 14:4 and verses 51–52!

Do you know how serious sin is? Examine the many offenses in the Old Testament punishable by death—even the picking up of sticks on the sabbath day (Num. 15:32–36). And having seen how serious your sin is, flee to Christ who has borne the sins of his people.

There are many other laws in the Old Testament, which—although they do not apply to our lives today—apply in a general sense. A Presbyterian creed called the Westminster Confession explains the applicability this way: "To them [the Jews] also, as a body politic, he gave sundry judicial laws, which expired together with the state of that people; not obliging any other now, further than the general equity thereof may require."* General equity is general justice or honesty, something Article 25 mentions. The general principles of merciful provision for the poor, protection of one's neighbor from injury, restoration of goods when lost or damaged, and such-like can be derived from the Old Testament. Read the books of Exodus, Leviticus, and Deuteronomy in that light!

When the law of God is properly understood, every Christian can surely sing: "O, how love I thy law! it is my meditation all the day" (Ps. 119:97).

Martyn McGeown

---

* The Westminster Confession of Faith 19.4, in Schaff, *Creeds of Christendom*, 3:641.

Article 26

OF CHRIST'S INTERCESSION

We believe that we have no access unto God save alone through the only Mediator and Advocate, Jesus Christ the righteous, who therefore became man, having united in one person the divine and human natures, that we men might have access to the divine Majesty, which access would otherwise be barred against us. But this Mediator, whom the Father hath appointed between him and us, ought in nowise to affright us by his majesty, or cause us to seek another according to our fancy. For there is no creature, either in heaven or on earth, who loveth us more than Jesus Christ; *who, though he was in the form of God, yet made himself of no reputation, and took upon him the form of a man and of a servant for us, and was made like unto his brethren in all things.* If, then, we should seek for another mediator, who would be well affected towards us, whom could we find who loved us more than he who laid down his life for us, even when we were his enemies? And if we seek for one who hath power and majesty, who is there that hath so much of both as *he who sits at the right hand of his Father,* and who hath *all power in heaven and on earth*? And who will sooner be heard than the own well-beloved Son of God?

Therefore it was only through diffidence that this practice of dishonoring instead of honoring the saints was introduced, doing that which they never have done nor required, but have, on the contrary, steadfastly rejected, according to their bounden duty, as appears by their writings. Neither must we plead here our unworthiness; for the meaning is not that we should offer our prayers to God on account of our own worthiness, but only on account of the excellence and worthiness of our Lord Jesus Christ, whose righteousness is become ours by faith.

Therefore the Apostle, to remove this foolish fear or, rather, distrust from us, justly saith that *Jesus Christ was made like unto his brethren in all things, that he might be a merciful and faithful high-priest, to make reconciliation for the sins of the people. For in that he himself hath suffered, being tempted, he is able to succor them that are tempted.* And further to encourage us, he adds: *Seeing, then, that we have a great high-priest that is passed into the heavens, Jesus the Son of God, let us hold fast our profession. For we have not a high-priest which can not be touched with the feeling of our infirmities; but was in all points tempted like as we are, yet without sin. Let us therefore come boldly unto the throne of grace, that we may obtain mercy, and find grace to help in time of need.* The same Apostle saith: *Having boldness to enter into the holiest by the blood of Jesus, let us draw near with a true heart in full assurance of faith,* etc. Likewise, *Christ hath an unchangeable priesthood, wherefore he is able, also to save them to the uttermost that come unto God by him, seeing he ever liveth to make intercession for them.* What more can be required? since Christ himself saith: *I am the way, and the truth, and the life; no man cometh unto the Father but by me.* To what purpose should we then seek another advocate, since it hath pleased God to give us his own Son as our Advocate? Let us not forsake him to take another, or rather to seek after another, without ever being able to find him; for God well knew, when he gave him to us, that we were sinners.

Therefore, according to the command of Christ, we call upon the heavenly Father through Jesus Christ, our only Mediator, as we are taught in the Lord's Prayer; being assured that whatever we ask of the Father in his name will be granted us.

September 4 — No Access to God

Who only hath immortality, dwelling in the light which
no man can approach unto. —1 Timothy 6:16

We have all seen "No access" signs blocking doorways and entrances. To get beyond that point, you need a special pass. Perhaps you need an ID badge, or you must key in a specific code. Ever since the fall of man in the garden of Eden, there has been no access to God for sinful man. A flaming sword barred the way back into Eden. At Mount Sinai, when God's glory descended in a cloud, the people had to stay behind the fence. No man could come near on pain of death. In the tabernacle and temple, a thick curtain blocked the entrance to the Holy of Holies. The message was clear: stay away, keep back, no access! And we read of terrifying examples in the Bible of men who tried to push past the "No access" sign and meet with God without the proper mediator: Nadab and Abihu (Lev. 10:2); Korah, Dathan, and Abiram (Num. 16:32); the men of Bethshemesh (1 Sam. 6:19).

Before Article 26 introduces us to the mediator, our Lord Jesus Christ, it reminds us that we need him: "we have no access unto God but alone through the only Mediator" and "access [to the divine Majesty] would otherwise be barred against us."

We have no access to God because God is holy. God dwells "in the light which no man can approach unto" (1 Tim. 6:16). "God is light, and in him is no darkness at all" (1 John 1:5). No man has ever seen God, and no man can ever see God (John 1:18). Even the angels must shield their faces in the awesome, glorious, majestic presence of God. In our age of irreverence, we have lost sight of that. We think we can buddy up to God. We imagine God on our level. But when God appears in the fullness of his glory, no man will be able to stand. If the angels cannot look upon the majesty of God, how can we, who are sinful dust? Any sinner standing in the presence of God Almighty will be consumed by God's holy wrath which burns like a fire against sin and sinners. Our "God is a consuming fire" (Deut. 4:24; Heb. 12:29). Can we "dwell with everlasting burnings" (Isa. 33:14)? An unholy, guilty, depraved sinner cannot meet with God or have access to his majesty. That is why we need a mediator, one who will bring us into the very presence of God.

Such a mediator was promised and anticipated in the Old Testament and has been revealed in the gospel. The Old Testament believer had a typical and incomplete access to God. God dwelled among his people, but access to him was restricted to one man (the high priest) who represented God's people. Complete access could be enjoyed only when sin was dealt with. And so, God's people longed for the coming of the promised Messiah who would bring them to God.

Martyn McGeown

September 5 — The Only Mediator

For there is one God, and one mediator between God and men, the man Christ Jesus. —1 Timothy 2:5

Have you ever offended someone? Have you ever been offended? Has there been a time in your life when such offense caused a friendship or a harmonious relationship to break down? Have you, children, ever been playing happily with your friend when one friend said something or did something hurtful to another friend so that the fun and games ended? Have husband and wife argued so much that they were no longer on speaking terms? In such situations, reconciliation is needed. *Reconciliation* means *the restoration of fellowship*. To have reconciliation, we need a mediator.

The word *mediator* means *one who stands between or in the middle*. The most common earthly example is a marriage counsellor. Such a person brings estranged spouses together. But the mediator of Article 26 is the mediator who stands between us and God. He brings sinners who have been estranged from God by their sins and who are under the wrath of God back into fellowship with God. This is only possible when the barrier which prevents fellowship is removed. That barrier is our sin: "Your iniquities have separated between you and your God" (Isa. 59:2).

It is important to remember that this mediator, who is Jesus Christ, is the one given by God. Article 26 says that several times: "whom the Father has appointed," "it hath pleased God to give us his own Son," and "God well knew, when he gave him to us, that we were sinners." We are not at liberty to seek another mediator. There is no other mediator acceptable to God who qualifies! Thus, Paul writes: "There is one God, and one mediator between God and men, the man Christ Jesus" (1 Tim. 2:5). If there were more than one God, there might conceivably be more than one mediator, but there is one God, and the only way of access to him is through the one mediator he approves of and has provided. We should notice, too, that whereas with human cases of mediation (such as marriage counselling) there are almost always two parties at fault, here only man is at fault. God is in every sense the innocent offended party. We have offended God by our sins. God therefore dictates the terms according to which we will be reconciled to him. We do not reconcile ourselves to God. God reconciles us to himself. "God was in Christ, reconciling the world unto himself" (2 Cor. 5:19).

This mediator, Jesus Christ, comes from God, acts in God's interests, displays God's glory, vindicates God's justice, and represents us before the Father. The mediator comes to us in the grace, love, and mercy of God. He is our Lord Jesus Christ. Let us come to God by him, only by him.

Martyn McGeown

September 6 — The Only Advocate

And if any man sin, we have an advocate with the Father,
Jesus Christ, the righteous. —1 John 2:1

You and I have a court date before the Judge. To stand on the judgment day, we need an advocate. The word *advocate* ought to be familiar to us from human law. Usually, when a man stands accused of a crime before a judge, he needs someone to defend and represent him before the law. That person is an advocate, a defense attorney, a lawyer. The advocate is the person who comes alongside the accused man to help him; and that is what the word *advocate* in Scripture means: *one called alongside*. The advocate visits the accused man in his cell, discusses with him his legal possibilities, advises him on court procedures, prepares a defense, and seeks, to the best of his ability, to obtain for his client the best possible outcome.

Who is our advocate? When we stand before God, what will our plea be? Many do not like to think about that day of judgment. They die unprepared and without an advocate. Or they imagine that they can defend themselves. They vainly hope that they can find a legal loophole by which they will escape God's judgment. Others trust in unauthorized advocates. Some flee to the Virgin Mary, or to one of the saints; others hope that their loved ones who have died will put in a good word for them. Others imagine that God will have pity on them because they were sincere or made some effort to be good, or because they are not as bad, they think, as other "serious sinners."

All such defenses are vain. The Judge before whom we stand on the last day is no fool, he is not blind, he is not corrupt, he will not be moved by excuses; there are no legal loopholes.

But the Judge, our heavenly Father, is merciful to his people. Thus, says Article 26, he has given our poor defenseless souls "his own Son as our advocate." The apostle John says: "And if any man sin, we have an advocate with the Father, Jesus Christ the righteous" (1 John 2:1). Jesus' defense of us is simple and beautiful: "Father, these are my people. They plead guilty. They have broken all thy commandments and kept none of them. Their very nature is corrupt. And, although they have a small beginning of the new obedience, even that cannot stand the scrutiny of thy holiness. My people deserve everlasting damnation in hell." Thus, Christ makes no excuses for us, and he upholds God's justice.

But that is not the end of Christ's defense. If it were, it would be a hopeless defense and would secure only our condemnation.

"Father, in order to uphold the justice of the law, I have accomplished all the obedience that they would not and could not accomplish, and I have borne the punishment that they cannot bear. Since I have met all the legal obligations for my people, I move to dismiss the case against them."

And the Judge shall say: "Case dismissed! I declare this people innocent and worthy of eternal life." What a privilege to have Jesus Christ as our advocate!

Martyn McGeown

September 7 — **The Mediator Qualified by Two Natures**

And without controversy great is the mystery of godliness:
God was manifest in the flesh. —1 Timothy 3:16

Article 26 teaches us about our "only Mediator and Advocate, Jesus Christ the righteous." His work is to bring us back into fellowship with God. He does that by taking upon himself our legal obligations (what we owe God) and by suffering and dying in our place. But who is he, and how does he do that?

This section of Article 26 gets to the heart of why Jesus Christ is and can be the only mediator. Jesus is altogether unique. No other has "united in one person the divine and human natures." That is the great "mystery of godliness: God was manifest in the flesh" (1 Tim. 3:16); "In the beginning was the Word, and the Word was with God, and the Word was God. The same was in the beginning with God…And the Word was made flesh, and dwelt among us" (John 1:1–2, 14). That is the wonder of our salvation. Whom did God give to be our mediator and advocate? Was it an angel—one of the archangels, perhaps—or the best specimen of humanity that he could find, the wisest, the noblest, the worthiest of all men? No, he gave us his own Son. This Son of God, "which is in the bosom of the Father" (John 1:18)—"he was rich," rich with all the riches of the Godhead (2 Cor. 8:9); he was blessed; he was "in the form of God" (Phil. 2:6).

First, our mediator must be God.

Salvation is a divine work: it requires almighty power, perfect wisdom, and infinite goodness. Only if the mediator is God will his work be of value before God. Only if the mediator is God will he be able to perform the difficult work of perfect obedience and suffering which is necessary to reconcile us to God.

Second, our mediator must be man.

The Son of God could not be the mediator by remaining in the bosom of the Father. He became a man by taking to himself a human nature (body and soul). He became a man to represent poor sinners before God, to stand between poor sinners and God, to bring poor sinners into fellowship with God. We, the poor, guilty sinners, have sinned. We must be punished. Jesus was punished in our place in a true human nature which could suffer. God's justice demanded it.

But third, our mediator must unite in one person the divine and human natures.

That is a deep mystery. But we understand it this way. We do not have two mediators, a human mediator and a divine mediator. We have only one mediator, who is both God and man. We do not have a mediator who is a mixture of God and man, a kind of super-man. Then, we have neither God nor man, but a third species. We have as our mediator the Son of God who combines the human and divine natures so that, on the one hand, he performs mighty miracles, and, on the other hand, he becomes hungry and tired, he sleeps and he weeps, he experiences real pain, and he dies.

One mediator, in one person, and two distinct natures, forever!

Martyn McGeown

September 8 — Access to Divine Majesty

*By whom also we have access by faith into
this grace wherein we stand.* —Romans 5:2

Our first examination of this beautiful article concentrated on the negative: We have no access to God. But, says Peter: "Christ also hath once suffered for sins, the just for the unjust, that he might bring us to God" (1 Pet. 3:18). With our only mediator and advocate, our Lord Jesus Christ the Son of God, uniting the two natures in one person, we have access to the very presence of God. Thus, the Son of God became man "that we men might have access to the divine Majesty" (Article 26).

Access to the divine majesty means, firstly, that we can stand in God's presence without fear. We do not need to be terrified to approach God as if he would destroy us if we come too close. We have access. We have the right and ability to approach God. In fact, and here is the wonder of it all, we have a greater, freer, and richer access to God than have even the angels. We have the same access to God as Christ himself does. Perhaps you would like to meet someone very important. What you need is someone who will introduce you, who will recommend you. But we have the very Son of God who introduces us to the Father. By his work as mediator (his perfect life and atoning death, as well as his resurrection, ascension, rule at God's right hand, and continual intercession), he gains us access to God.

Access to the divine majesty means, secondly, that we have fellowship with God. Think of a mighty king. His servants have access to him: they may approach him to serve him. The common citizens do not have that access. But our access is more than that of servants. That is the access which angels have. Our access is the access of children to a father. That is a sweeter, closer, more intimate access. The children sit on the father's lap, whisper in his ear, sit at his table, and share his life. That, to speak reverently, is the kind of access we have through our mediator. We enjoy the Father's love, he draws us into his fellowship and communion, he calls us to pray to him, he speaks to us in the word, he lives in our hearts by his Spirit, he showers us with blessings, and he has promised that we shall dwell with him. "Surely goodness and mercy shall follow me all the days of my life: and I will dwell in the house of the LORD forever" (Ps. 23:6).

This access is ours because Christ has purchased it for us. We, who are poor, guilty sinners, Christ has justified, and the Father has adopted. The adoption papers are signed in the blood of Christ, our elder brother, who brought us into the Father's house. And we enjoy that access by faith in Jesus Christ, our only mediator and advocate!

Martyn McGeown

September 9 — Not Affrighted by His Majesty

And when I saw him, I fell at his feet as dead.
And he laid his right hand upon me, saying unto me, Fear not;
I am the first and the last: I am he that liveth, and was dead; and behold,
I am alive for evermore. —Revelation 1:17–18

The Belgic Confession is a Reformation creed. It was written just as the church was emerging from the darkness of the Middle Ages. It might be difficult for us as Evangelical and Reformed Christians to imagine, but one of the reasons sinners were reluctant to believe in Jesus Christ, the only mediator and advocate, was that they were afraid of him. The picture of Jesus common in the Middle Ages was one of a stern judge. When the church of the Middle Ages taught "He shall come to judge the quick [the living] and the dead," the average member quaked in terror. Judge Jesus would come in all the fury and vengeance of God and cast poor sinners into hell. Therefore, many concluded, we cannot, we dare not, come to him.

Affrighted by his majesty! That was the common experience of many.

This fear was encouraged by the church because the church wanted the people to seek help and salvation through the church itself. The church promoted penances, works of charity, religious devotions, and pilgrimages. Salvation would come through faithful use of the sacraments and other ceremonies of the church. This fear was understandable, too, because few had a Bible of their own. Did not Scripture teach that Judge Jesus would send some "away into everlasting punishment" (Matt. 25:46)? Are there not terrifying scenes in the book of Revelation? "And [men] said to the mountains and rocks, Fall on us, and hide us from…the wrath of the Lamb: for the great day of his wrath is come; and who shall be able to stand?" (Rev. 6:16–17). Is not Judge Jesus God? Will he not condemn poor, defenseless sinners?

But, says Article 26, although it is true that Jesus possesses all the majesty of God, this ought not to "affright us by his majesty." His majesty is not against us, but for us. His majesty makes him the only suitable mediator for us. His majesty gives his work of mediation infinite worth. His majesty makes his work effectual, so that he really does save us. Instead of being affrighted by the majesty of Christ, we rejoice in it.

Perhaps you are affrighted of Jesus' majesty. Perhaps you say that you are not worthy to come to God through such a majestic Jesus. But how then shall you come? Will you wait until you have made yourself worthy? When would that be? Jesus is the only mediator, the only one God has appointed, the only one qualified. To refuse to come to Jesus because you are affrighted by his majesty is really a twisted form of pride. And besides, God gives poor sinners every reason, every encouragement, to come. "Come unto me, all ye that labor and are heavy laden, and I will give you rest" (Matt. 11:28). Poor, contrite sinners need not be affrighted by his majesty.

Martyn McGeown

September 10 — Not Seeking Another According to Our Fancy

Let no man beguile you of your reward in a voluntary humility and worshipping of angels, intruding into those things which he hath not seen, vainly puffed up by his fleshly mind, and not holding the Head. —Colossians 2:18–19

Because many are affrighted by the majesty of the one mediator and advocate Jesus Christ, they seek another. But, warns Article 26, to seek another is to act "according to our fancy." Our fancy is our imagination. Men have always been attracted to fanciful religion, to a religion of their own imagination. Some men fancy a god who is not holy, whose standards are not so high as to require that we come through this mediator. Other men fancy a god who will accept our best efforts. Other men fancy a god whose mercy will somehow outweigh his justice. But we must never worship a god of our own imagination. We must always follow what God has revealed to us in his word.

The fact is that human fancies could never have conceived of this mediator. None of the pagans, worshipping the gods of their own imagination, ever imagined Jesus Christ. None of the wisest of philosophers ever conceived of God sending his own Son in our flesh to be our mediator. When Christ came, few were able to understand it. We see the first man who tried to worship God by seeking another mediator according to his fancy. He was Cain. He refused to come to God in the way of the revealed and promised mediator by refusing to bring a lamb; he brought the works of his own hands, the fruit of the ground. And God rejected Cain's offering, and Cain perished. But Abel, rejecting his own fancies, clinging to the Lamb of God who should come, offered a lamb, and Abel was saved.

Everything in the Old Testament pointed to this mediator. Every detail of Old Testament worship was necessary to teach the people about the mediator who would come. No wonder, then, that God was so strict and so terrible in his just judgment against those who, according to their fancy, tampered with the details of God's worship. Every fanciful change in worship obscured Christ.

Do you worship God according to your own fancy or according to the revealed will of God? Have you embraced Jesus Christ by faith or do you cling to your own works, or to some other mediator, as a passport into heaven? Be not deceived. All other mediators are according to our fancy. And our fancies will not take us to heaven. Colossians 2 speaks of this fanciful worship as "will worship" (v. 23). It led some in Paul's day to worship angels—they fancied that they could communicate with God via angels—and a "voluntary humility" in which they claimed to be unworthy to come to Christ and sought a different, fanciful route to God (v. 18).

Article 26 calls Jesus Christ the mediator "whom the Father hath appointed." The Father knows the mediator we need, and the Father has provided the uniquely qualified mediator. Since the Father appointed him, it would be to insult his wisdom to seek another mediator not appointed by the Father but according to our fancy. "He is able also to save them to the uttermost that come unto God by him, seeing he ever liveth to make intercession for them" (Heb. 7:25). Come to God through him, only through him!

Martyn McGeown

September 11 — No Creature Loves Us More Than Jesus Christ

May be able to comprehend with all saints what is the breadth,
and length, and depth, and height; and to know the love of Christ,
which passeth knowledge, that ye might be filled with
all the fullness of God. —Ephesians 3:18–19

This beautiful Article 26 answers the objection of some who are afraid to come to God through Jesus Christ, the only mediator and advocate. They are affrighted by his majesty. Such fright drives them into the arms of other, supposedly less frightening and more merciful mediators. This was especially (and still is) the case with many Roman Catholics. But, says Article 26, there is no reason for the believer to be frightened of Jesus Christ. Instead, we must have firm confidence. The reason is Christ's love. "There is no creature, either in heaven or on earth, who loveth us more than Jesus Christ."

Compare the love of mere creatures to the love of Jesus Christ. Look up into heaven for a moment! Do the angels love us? We might suppose that they do. They certainly love God, and they live to serve God. They are "ministering spirits, sent forth to minister for them who shall be the heirs of salvation" (Heb. 1:14). The angels are keenly interested in our salvation (1 Pet. 1:12). We might be tempted, then, to seek them as our mediators since they seem less frightening than Jesus. But, do not! John the apostle, the disciple whom Jesus loved, was tempted and fell down to worship before the feet of an angel, but the angel said: "See thou do it not" (Rev. 22:9). What about the departed saints, all the believers who have gone before us in to heaven (Abel, Noah, Abraham, John, Peter, Mary)? Do they even know our names? Do any of those, who are mere creatures, love us more than Jesus Christ? Would you dare say that any creature in heaven loves us more than Jesus Christ? Would not such a thought be so absurd, even a blasphemy, that no child of God could utter it?

If heaven contains no creature who loves us more than Christ, will we find such a creature upon the earth, where our best love is tainted by sin, selfishness, and envy? Believer, do your pastor, elders and deacons, spouse, children, or parents, does anyone on earth love you more than Jesus Christ?

O, the love of Christ! Who can measure it? Christ is "well-affected" toward us, says Article 26. But, surely, "well-affected" is too weak an expression. What is it to be loved by Jesus Christ? It means that Jesus Christ ardently and passionately breathes after us in holy zeal. It means that Christ takes pleasure in, treasures, and prizes us as his chief desire. It means that Christ cleaves to, clings to us, and reaches out to us to embrace us with the love of God. It means that Christ will not rest until we are saved from all our sins, washed and free, and enjoying everlasting blessedness with him where he is. Will we be affrighted by his majesty? Surely not!

Martyn McGeown

September 12 — Christ's Humiliating Love

The life which I now live in the flesh I live by the faith of the Son of God, who loved me, and gave himself for me. —Galatians 2:20

Article 26 urges us to seek the one mediator, Jesus Christ, by appealing to the love which he has for us, a love which surpasses understanding, cannot be measured, and to which the love of all creatures in heaven and earth cannot be compared. Instead of being affrighted by his majesty, let us embrace him in confident faith.

How do we know that Christ loves us? Surely not in word only? He demonstrated it. Christ showed that love in an act of self-giving. He "made himself of no reputation" (Phil. 2:7). He assumed the position of a lowly slave before his Father. He "humbled himself" to "the death of the cross" (v. 8). Compare what Christ had and what Christ became for us, we who belong to him! He was in the very form of God. Jesus "is the image of the invisible God" (Col. 1:15); Jesus is the "brightness of [the Father's] glory, and the express image of his person" (Heb. 1:3); in Christ dwells "all the fullness of the Godhead" (Col. 2:9). Paul writes that Christ Jesus did not think it "robbery to be equal with God," yet "made himself of no reputation, and took upon him the form of a servant, and was made in the likeness of men" (Phil. 2:6–7). That means he did not think that his position of glory and honor in heaven, equal with God, was something to be held on to, to be grasped on to, so that he would never let go of this glorious privilege.

Unfathomable! Mysterious! Jesus was rich; he became poor: cringingly, beggarly poor. Jesus willingly took our human nature in all of its weakness. Jesus adopted the position of the lowest slave. Jesus humbled, lowered, humiliated himself as none else has ever done. And why? Because he loved us!

He did all that for our salvation. God had said: "You must love me perfectly or you perish. You must keep all my commandments, or you incur my wrath." And Jesus said: "Father, I will pay what they owe. And I will bear the consequences of what they have done." And the Father said: "In that case, you must live a perfect life before me, and suffer your whole life, and then at the end of your life, you must die under my curse. And all the time you must love me with your whole heart, soul, mind, and strength, even when I am pouring out my just wrath on you against the sins of my people." Jesus did that, especially on the cross.

Christ did that, willingly, joyfully, obediently out of love for us.

And he did that, mind you, while we were his enemies, while we hated him, while we wanted nothing of his love, nothing of his salvation. And he still loves us, even though we continue to sin against him in the weakness of our flesh. Will one die for a righteous man? Perhaps a heroic person could be found to do that. Will one die for a good man? The possibility might just exist (Rom. 5:7). But Christ surpassed all such possibilities: "God commendeth his love toward us, in that, while we were yet sinners, Christ died for us" (v. 8).

Martyn McGeown

September 13 — The Mediator with Power and Majesty

And set him at his own right hand in the heavenly places, far above all principality, and power, and might, and dominion, and every name that is named, not only in this world, but also in that which is to come: and hath put all things under his feet, and gave him to be the head over all things to the church. —Ephesians 1:20–22

In the previous meditations we have looked at the love which our mediator has for us, which should give us every reason to trust in him and to not be affrighted by his majesty. Now, we return to the majesty of our mediator because both love and majesty are needed in the mediator who will represent us before the Father.

Article 26 asks: "If we seek for one who hath power and majesty, who is there that hath so much of both as [Jesus Christ]?" Jesus has power to save, power to bless, power to obtain for us all of the blessings of salvation from his Father.

The love of Christ is not sickly sentimentalism but almighty, majestic love. He has power and majesty because he is the Son of God. As the Son of God, he is equal in power and glory with the Father and the Holy Spirit. That's his power and majesty within the Godhead. As the mediator, the man Jesus Christ, he has power and majesty because God has "highly exalted him" (Phil. 2:9). How highly has God exalted him? "Far above all principality, and power, and might, and dominion, and every name that is named, not only in this world, but also in that which is to come" (Eph. 1:21).

Jesus, the Son of God in our human nature, then, is infinitely exalted above all men, kings, mighty rulers, unions of nations, and above all angels, archangels, and, certainly, above all devils. He is exalted above all the saints. He is the head of the whole church. He sits at the right hand of the Father, which is not a physical place, but a position of honor. He has all power and authority (the ability and the right to rule) in heaven and in earth. He, and he alone, directs the history of this world, so that all things great and small serve the one great purpose of glorifying the triune God through the salvation of the church. If all things are in his hands, because the Father has committed them such, and if the one in whose hands are all things is our savior, our Lord, our mediator, our advocate, what have we to fear? Nothing!

Do you see how Jesus combines in one person the power and majesty of God and the tenderhearted love of a heavenly bridegroom? Do you see that God has provided us with the mediator who meets our every need? What foolishness to seek another! Let us not be affrighted by his majesty but rejoice in it and draw confidence from it, and let us come to him, the one who loved us so!

Martyn McGeown

September 14 — The Mediator Who Has the Father's Ear

Father, I thank thee that thou hast heard me.
And I knew that thou hearest me always. —John 11:41–42

We have seen how Article 26 piles up reasons why we should flee from all other would-be mediators and find refuge alone in Jesus Christ. He is qualified as the Son of God made flesh; he is authorized and appointed by God himself, so that all other mediators are fanciful; he is powerful and majestic, and his majesty must not frighten us away from him because he loves us more than all creatures in heaven and earth do. And now Article 26 adds a further reason: Jesus, as the Son of God, has the Father's ear: "Who will sooner be heard than the well-beloved Son of God?"

God loves his Son. The relationship between the mediator and the triune God is not a cold, detached, official relationship like the relationship between a judge and a defense attorney, but the warm, intimate, loving relationship of a father with his son. Everything the Son does pleases the Father. And the heart of the Father is toward the Son. Since the Son brings those people whom he represents in his heart before the Father, we can be sure that the Father hears whatever the Son asks on behalf of his people. Remember the Old Testament high priest: he wore an ephod on which were engraved the names of the twelve tribes of Israel. In the tabernacle, there were loaves called shewbread which represented the same twelve tribes (Lev. 24:5–9). The whole system of priests, tabernacle, and offerings reminded the people that God loved Israel and dwelled among them. Jesus Christ is the fulfillment of all that. Now there are no longer loaves of shewbread or engraved stones. Now Christ himself enters into the presence of God with our names written on his heart. And the Father, who loves us in Jesus Christ, loves the Son, and hears him always. That was Jesus' own confession: "I knew that thou hearest me always" (John 11:42).

But we must not misunderstand. Christ does not make the Father love us. The Father already loves us, and he loves the Son, and he loves what the Son has done for our salvation.

And the Father has good reason, a compelling reason, to hear what the Son asks for us. Christ has died for us, and on that basis alone he intercedes for us and obtains for us, again on that basis alone, all the blessings of salvation.

Do not tremble, therefore, believer in Jesus Christ. It is true "that God heareth not sinners" (John 9:31), but he hears his only begotten, dearly beloved Son; and because he hears him, who died for us and now represents us at the Father's right hand, he hears us, who come to God through him.

Martyn McGeown

September 15 — The Intercession of Saints Forbidden

Doubtless thou art our father, though Abraham be ignorant of us, and Israel acknowledge us not. —Isaiah 63:16

If we are wrongly affrighted by the majesty of the one mediator and advocate Jesus Christ, we will be tempted to seek a mediator according to our fancy. This, according to Article 26, is the reason why many had (and still have) recourse to saints.

A saint is a holy one. In the Bible all of God's children are called saints: every member of the church on earth (as well as in heaven) is a saint (1 Cor. 1:2; Eph. 1:1). But the Roman Catholic and Eastern Orthodox churches have a very different understanding of saints. Only a select few of very faithful church members are saints, and usually only after death. To be a saint, a person must be an especially holy person whose holiness has been recognized by the church. There is a definite process by which a person is recognized as a saint: miracles must be attributed to that person, the person will be declared blessed, and finally a person is beatified. These saints, ancient and modern, are objects of veneration. Statues and pictures of these saints are used in worship. And most importantly, ordinary church members pray to these saints. Since these saints are supposedly closer to God than we are, they can supposedly obtain favor for us on the earth. The most popular and exalted saint of all is the Virgin Mary, who is called the Holy Mother of God, the Queen of Heaven, and the mediatrix (the female version of *mediator*) of all graces.

This practice of praying to, venerating, and seeking help from saints is condemned in our Belgic Confession. It is nothing but idolatry. It dishonors true saints who steadfastly rejected such veneration (e.g. Peter in Acts 10:26 refused the worship of Cornelius). Believers in the Bible never had recourse to departed saints, and certainly never required others to pray to them. Where, for example, do we ever read of a man like David praying to Abraham, or a man like Paul praying to Daniel? When Stephen was dying, he committed his spirit to Jesus, not one of the departed saints (Acts 7:59). In fact, in the Bible, all contact with the dead is strictly forbidden, as ungodly king Saul found out to his cost (1 Sam. 28:15–16). If Asaph had recourse to a whole host of departed saints, why does he ask rhetorically, "Whom have I in heaven but thee [Jehovah]?" (Ps. 73:25).

Besides, it is impossible for a saint to be a mediator.

Consider that countless millions of Roman Catholics are offering up prayers to the Virgin Mary and to other saints. Think of the common prayer, the Rosary ("Hail Mary") being offered all over the world, in many different languages. How could Mary, a mere creature, and therefore not omniscient, hear and answer all those petitions? Moreover, none of the saints has a ground or basis to be petitioned to. Remember that Jesus Christ intercedes for us on the basis of his perfect work on the cross. On what basis could Mary, Monica, or Mother Teresa intercede for us? We can never separate the intercessory work of Christ from his atonement on the cross. "If any man sin, we have an advocate with the Father, Jesus Christ the righteous: and he is the propitiation for our sins" (1 John 2:1–2); "It is Christ that died…who also maketh intercession for us" (Rom. 8:34).

Only one who does not understand the glory of the only mediator and advocate Jesus Christ could possibly be tempted to pray to saints.

Martyn McGeown

September 16 — Our Unworthiness No Excuse

Come unto me, all ye that labor and are heavy laden, and I will give you rest. —Matthew 11:28

Some justify seeking other mediators by a kind of feigned humility. We are unworthy to come to Christ, they say. That is why we come through the Virgin Mary, Monica, or some other saint. Article 26 anticipates this objection also: "Neither must we plead here our unworthiness." Let us review the reasons Article 26 has already given: only Jesus Christ is qualified by his two natures united in one person to be the mediator; only Jesus Christ is appointed by the Father to be the mediator; we have no reason, as poor sinners, to be affrighted by his majesty because he does not destroy us by his majesty but saves us; no creature in heaven or in earth loves us more than Jesus Christ; Jesus Christ has demonstrated that love by his self-humiliation at Calvary; and this mediator alone has the Father's ear.

Despite all those reasons, there remain some who refuse to come to God by Jesus Christ.

The excuse, "I am unworthy," may sound pious but is really the expression of foolish pride. Article 26 exposes the pride when it counters the objection: "for the meaning is not that we should offer our prayers to God on the ground of our own worthiness." One who refuses to come to Jesus Christ really harbors the notion that he can make himself worthy in some other way. Perhaps he is unworthy now, but with a little bit more effort he can make himself worthy of being heard by God. But Jesus says that those who try to come another way are thieves and robbers (John 10:1)! Jesus consistently calls people to come directly to him. He will bring us to the Father. Never does he even hint that we should come to him through others.

This is the fundamental sin of those who have recourse to saints. They believe that by praying to the saints they can obtain enough spiritual virtue to stand approved one day before God. By thinking that way, they have never relinquished the notion that they can somehow become worthy of God's salvation. That is pride: deadly, devilish, God-insulting, damning pride!

Away with any idea that we are worthy, or, to put it more subtly, that we can somehow (perhaps with the help of others) make ourselves worthy! We will never be worthy! Those who are saved will always be debtors, saved by grace. Our worthiness is in Jesus Christ. Our worthiness is always and only in Jesus Christ! That is the beautiful argument of Article 26: "only on account of the excellence and worthiness of our Lord Jesus Christ, whose righteousness is become ours by faith."

Do not seek to make yourself worthy. Come as you are. Embrace Christ, the worthy one, the excellent one, by faith!

Martyn McGeown

September 17 — Our Foolish Fear or Mistrust Removed

Yea doubtless, and I count all things but loss for the excellency of the knowledge of Christ Jesus my Lord. —Philippians 3:8

The subject of the perfect intercession of Jesus Christ is so important to our salvation and to our daily comfort that Article 26 leaves no stone unturned in answering all the foolish objections of our sinful hearts. We have seen that Article 26 has medieval Roman Catholicism in mind (the Catholic Church, by the way, has not improved doctrinally since that time) with its idolatrous doctrine and practice of the veneration of saints.

There are two ways to convince a child to relinquish an object which he holds dear. One method is to scold the child and tell the child to stop doing what he is doing. We explain what is wrong with the object to which the child is clinging. Often, however, the more we scold a child, the more stubbornly the child clings to the object of his trust. Another approach is to describe to the child how much better another object is so that the child sees the beauty of that object and willingly gives up what he has so that he can have this new thing. Often the child becomes so enamored with the new thing that he forgets about the old thing.

This is what we must imagine as we try to convince a Roman Catholic friend to give up venerating Mary or the saints and to find recourse in the only mediator and advocate, Jesus Christ. But Article 26 does not only have Roman Catholics in view here. We, too, are prone to foolish fear and sinful pride. We, too, are prone to doubt God's love and Christ's salvation.

We should explain that Mary and the saints do not have the powers that our friend believes that they have; we can point out the terrible sinfulness of trusting in saints and the wickedness of self-trust. Such calls to repentance certainly have an important place in preaching. But the other approach is to explain the excellency of Jesus Christ as mediator, advocate, and intercessor that we are so captivated by him that we never think of anyone else.

In a way, Article 26 adopts both approaches. On the one hand, it warns us against false mediators, but mainly it sets before us in glowing, heartwarming words the glories of Jesus Christ. Of course, only the Holy Spirit can truly convince us of these things, but the preaching of the gospel, which the Spirit uses, sets forth Jesus Christ in a captivating way. That is how Paul described his preaching. When he preached, he could say that "Christ hath been evidently set forth, crucified among you" (Gal. 3:1). Paul himself testifies to the effect of Christ on him: "I count all things but loss for the excellency of the knowledge of Christ Jesus my Lord…and do count them but dung, that I may win Christ, and be found in him, not having mine own righteousness" (Phil. 3:8-9).

What foolish fear, or rather mistrust, prevents you from coming to Christ? Is it your sin, some bitter experience or grudge? Is it pride, pleasure, religion? Does anyone, can anyone, give richer salvation than does Jesus Christ? Has anyone done more for poor sinners than has Christ?

Martyn McGeown

September 18 — Our Merciful High Priest

Who can have compassion on the ignorant,
and on them that are out of the way; for that he himself also
is compassed with infirmity. —Hebrews 5:2

Jesus Christ is our only mediator and advocate, and Article 26 has given us many reasons why we must come to God through him and why we must not come to God through any other. In addition, as we shall notice in the next few meditations, Jesus Christ is our high priest.

The name Christ is our mediator's official name, and it refers to the work he is authorized by the triune God to perform: he has one office (official position), that of prophet, priest, and king. We are interested especially in his priestly office.

In the Old Testament, God instituted a class of priests. It was by these priests that the sinful, impure people of Israel were brought into fellowship with the spotlessly holy God. To put it very simply, a priest is holy and brings God's people to God. The holiness of the Old Testament priests was typical and ceremonial. It consisted in holy garments, sacred ceremonies, special washings, and various kinds of purifications (Heb. 9:10). But the sprinkling of pure water, of blood, of the ashes of a heifer, and other ordinances could never purify the conscience. There was always a remembrance of sin. Even the highest and most solemn ceremony which the high priest performed once a year on the great day of atonement had to be repeated year after year. The people of God looked for something better.

The priests' work had three main parts. First, they offered sacrifices on the altar of burnt offering. Second, they mixed burning coals from that altar with carefully prepared incense on the altar of incense. This was a picture of intercession, an offering up of prayers for the people. This was what Zacharias the priest was doing when the angel Gabriel announced the birth of John the Baptist (Luke 1:9). Third, they obtained and bestowed the blessing of God upon the people (Num. 6:23–27). These three things Jesus Christ has done: he died on the cross to purchase our salvation, on the basis of that sacrifice he intercedes for us, and he obtains and bestows all the blessings of God upon us.

Hebrews 4–5 concentrate on the mercifulness of our high priest. One who is merciful is one filled with pity or compassion, one who sees our misery and is touched by the feeling of our infirmities, one who desires to remove our misery from us, and one who has not only the desire, but also the power, to make us blessed.

In order to be our merciful high priest, Jesus Christ was made like us in all things. We do not have an aloof, distant, uncaring high priest, but one "taken from among men," one "who can have compassion on the ignorant," one who "also is compassed with infirmity" (Heb. 5:1–2). Christ became a man and entered the misery of our human condition to lift us out of misery and to make us blessed.

Jesus Christ, the merciful high priest for poor, miserable sinners! Let us not be afraid to come to him!

Martyn McGeown

September 19 — A High Priest Who Was Made Like Us

Wherefore in all things it behooved him to be made like unto his brethren, that he might be a merciful and faithful high priest in things pertaining to God, to make reconciliation for the sins of the people. —Hebrews 2:17

Have you ever been in a severe affliction and found that a well-meaning fellow believer could not help you? Did you impatiently push him or her aside with the words, "You could not possibly know how I feel"? We can never say that about our high priest, Jesus Christ. Quoting Hebrews 2:17–18, Article 26 reminds us that Christ became just like us (sin excepted) in order to be able to sympathize with us.

Before the incarnation, the Son of God did not experience suffering. On earth, he experienced it in abundance. No man ever suffered as Christ did. Christ's calling was to suffer and remain fully obedient to his Heavenly Father. He was called to love God with all his heart, soul, mind, and strength, and his neighbor as himself, even while he suffered. And he did so! He did this perfectly.

We cannot fathom what it was like for the perfectly spotless and sinless Son of God to come into this sin-cursed world. How must he have felt to have opened his eyes in Bethlehem as a helpless baby, born into poverty? What humiliation for the Son of God! How his sinless soul must have been vexed to be surrounded by sinners! He experienced the full range of human suffering: poverty, physical pain, emotional pain, hunger, physical exhaustion, shame, fear, and sorrow. He was "despised and rejected" (Isa. 53:3), scorned and mocked. He was rejected by his friends who thought he was mad (Mark 3:21; John 7:5). He was forsaken by his closest disciples on the day of his arrest. He suffered agonizing physical pain at the hands of the Roman soldiers and was crucified, which was the most cruel and painful death of that day. Worst of all, he was forsaken by God on the cross so that he no longer experienced that blessed covenant fellowship and love which he had always known (Matt. 27:46).

All of this he did for his people so that he would be a sympathetic high priest to them. All of this prepared him for his role as benevolent intercessor. Do you feel weary? He knows what that is like. Are you poor? He knows what that is like, too. Do you suffer from a crippling and painful disease? He hung on a cross in unspeakable agony and knows what suffering is like. Are you misunderstood, scorned, and mocked? No man was so held in derision as Jesus Christ! In no situation can we ever say, "Jesus Christ, my merciful and faithful high priest, does not understand what I am going through." Let us therefore come to him in all our times of need.

Martyn McGeown

September 20 — A High Priest Who Knows Our Temptations

For we have not an high priest which cannot be touched with the feeling of our infirmities; but was in all points tempted like as we are, yet without sin. —Hebrews 4:15

Part of our suffering as Christians is temptation.

In the Bible, there are two meanings to the word *temptation*. Sometimes, the word refers to a trial, which means a test. When God tries us, he tests us with the purpose of revealing the genuineness of our faith. An illustration might make this clearer. A certain rich man has a nugget of gold. He knows that it is gold, but he also knows that there is some impurity in that gold that needs to be purged out to make the gold even purer. He places the gold in a hot fire, which melts the gold and burns up the dross. Thus, the gold comes out approved, tried, having passed the test and become stronger for it. That is God's purpose in trying our faith. God knows that we have faith. Of course he does! He gave us that faith! But he also knows the infirmities of our flesh, so he tries us, often with much suffering (sickness, disappointment, sorrow, etc.). Through the trial, our faith is purified and strengthened (1 Pet. 1:7).

But the devil has an altogether different purpose when he tempts. He will use the trial which God sends as an occasion to tempt us to doubt God's love and faithfulness. Satan's hope is that we will curse God to his face, as he hoped with Job (Job 1:11; 2:5). The devil's purpose in temptation, then, is our failure, that our faith be exposed as counterfeit, that we come out weakened and disapproved. Thus, the devil entices us to sin, encourages us to doubt, and lures us away from the way of obedience and faith.

What should we do when we are tempted? What should we do when sin becomes so attractive to us that it becomes practically irresistible? We should go to Christ. Perhaps we object, but what does he know about temptation? Would he understand?

Article 26, echoing the book of Hebrews, says that he does! "For in that he himself hath suffered being tempted, he is able to succour them that are tempted" (Heb. 2:18); "For we have not an high priest which cannot be touched with the feeling of our infirmities; but was in all points tempted like as we are, yet without sin" (Heb. 4:15).

Temptation for Christ was real suffering. Sin was something peculiarly vexing to Jesus, something abhorrent to his sinless soul. And the devil reserved his most subtle temptations for the Son of God. When the devil tempted Jesus to turn stones into bread, Jesus was genuinely and agonizingly hungry. He was not attracted to disobedience (he abhorred that), but he was attracted to bread. When the devil tempted him in Gethsemane to refuse to take the cup of suffering, Christ struggled to submit his will to the Father's. He cried out "with strong crying and tears" (Heb. 5:7). These were real, difficult, dreadful temptations.

And Jesus came victoriously through all the temptations. And then as the sinless, victorious Son of God, he went to the cross to pay for our sins. When we are tempted, we must flee to him to obtain mercy and grace for help; and when we fall into sin, we must flee to him for forgiveness. And to none other!

Martyn McGeown

September 21 — Entering the Holiest

*But into the second went the high priest alone
once every year, not without blood.* —Hebrews 9:7

The epistle to the Hebrews teaches the superiority of Christ over all the ordinances of Old Testament Judaism. This does not mean that the worship of Old Testament Israel was bad. How could it be when God himself gave it in detail to Moses? But it means that New Testament Christianity is the fulfillment of the Old Testament and therefore superior, or better. Christ is "better than the angels" (Heb. 1:4); Christ is "worthy of more glory than Moses" (3:3); Christ is better than Abraham (7:6–7); Christ is the mediator "of a better testament" (7:22); Christ has a more excellent ministry and serves "a better covenant, which was established upon better promises" (8:6); Christ has offered "better sacrifices" (9:23); the blood of Christ speaks "better things than that of Abel" (12:24).

The Old Testament saints had something good, something excellent, something blessed; but the coming of Christ in the New Testament age brought something better. This means that in the New Testament, we have a better and clearer knowledge of Christ; we have closer fellowship with God; we have a richer experience of grace; we have a greater understanding of the plan of salvation; we have freer access to God without the need of priests, sacrifices, and cleansing rituals. In short, we have the same salvation but administered in a higher, richer, fuller way. They had the shadow; we have the reality or the substance.

One startling difference (at least for a Jewish reader of the book of Hebrews) is a "boldness to enter into the holiest." That was impossible, inconceivable in the Old Testament. The holiest (or the most holy place) was a small room in the center of the tabernacle or temple in which the ark of the covenant was found. Above the ark between the two golden cherubim on top of the mercy seat was the cloud of God's holy presence. No one, upon pain of death, could enter into that place. There was only one exception and only one occasion, when one person, carefully prepared, could enter that place.

No non-Israelite could enter there. No woman could enter there. No person with any kind of physical defect could enter there. Of the twelve tribes of Israel, only a man of the tribe of Levi could enter there. Thus, eleven tribes were barred, including even the kings and prophets. Of the Levites, only the priests could come anywhere near there, for they alone were permitted to enter the holy (but not the most holy) place. Of the priests, only the high priest could enter there. The high priest (he alone) could enter the holiest only once a year. And he had to bring blood to sprinkle on the mercy seat in the most holy place.

Now, with the coming of Christ, all believers can enter the truly most holy place, which is not found in an earthly tabernacle or temple, but in heaven itself. Christ has torn down the barrier by his death on the cross (Matt. 27:51).

And now we come boldly: not timidly, not reluctantly, not fearfully, but boldly, confidently, joyfully, because we know that we are received through Christ. What a privilege is ours! Let us never forget what it cost our Lord Jesus, and let us never neglect it.

Martyn McGeown

September 22 — Entering with Boldness

*Having therefore, brethren, boldness to enter
into the holiest by the blood of Jesus.* —Hebrews 10:19

Yesterday, we noted that we, unlike the vast majority of the Old Testament saints, may come into the very presence of God through our one mediator, advocate, and high priest, Jesus Christ. We may do so with boldness. It is one thing to be able to come into the presence of God, and even more significant that we can do that boldly.

Boldness is not presumption or recklessness. There is an expression, "Fools rush in where angels fear to tread." We do not rush into the presence of God without thinking about what we will say, without being properly awestruck by the majesty and the holiness of our Father in heaven. When we enter God's presence, we are coming to the holiest! It would be presumption to enter God's presence if we were not called to do so. But we must enter through the right way, the only way, through Jesus Christ. The Old Testament high priest knew, when he entered on the appointed day, with the appointed preparations, that he and the people he represented would be received. We have "boldness to enter into the holiest by the blood of Jesus, by a new and living way, which he hath consecrated for us, through the veil, that is to say, his flesh" (Heb. 10:19–20).

The way by which we draw near to God is a way sprinkled with the blood of our savior. The thick veil which blocked the way into the holiest has been torn down with the tearing of the flesh of Christ, the suffering and death of the Son of God. On the cross, Christ made satisfaction to the Father for all our sins. Now, we must not doubt that God will receive us.

Presumption would be to imagine that we could come to God another way, as if the blood of Christ were not necessary or insufficient to pay for our sins. Presumption would be to expect God to accept us on our own merits, on the basis of our worthiness, our works, our prayers, or our religious observances. But we are not presumptuous; we are bold, we are assured, we are confident.

To be bold means, negatively, not to be timid. We do not stand afar off and bemoan our unworthiness. We are unworthy, but Christ is our worthiness. To be bold means that we are not fearful or reluctant, that we do not think that God will refuse us, that we are not afraid that God will destroy us if we come too close, that we do not feel the need to cover our faces in horror at the idea of approaching God. Boldness is, positively, a freedom of access, a confidence that we will be received, a fearless approach, not to stand before a terrifying judge, but to come into close fellowship with a loving Father.

Do you know such boldness? Do you come in that manner to God? Believer, you can, and you must, through Jesus Christ! Only through Jesus Christ!

Martyn McGeown

September 23 — Christ's Unchangeable Priesthood

But this man, because he continueth ever,
hath an unchangeable priesthood. —Hebrews 7:24

Article 26 has given compelling reasons for us to trust in our only mediator, advocate, and high priest, Jesus Christ. He is the high priest who brings us into the very presence of God.

Another way in which Christ's priesthood is superior to that of all other priests is its unchangeableness.

In Scripture there were many priests and high priests. Perhaps you can name some: in the Old Testament, Aaron, Eli, Abiathar; and in the New Testament, during the time of Christ and the apostles, Annas, Caiaphas, Ananias. Some of these men were godly high priests; some were ungodly. But none of them had an unchangeable, permanent, everlasting priesthood. They died; their priestly office ended and was passed to successors. In addition, even the godliest of high priests were sinners. And the sacrifices which they offered could never take away sin. For that reason, the same sacrifices had to be offered repeatedly, and they could never cleanse the conscience (Heb. 9:9; 10:11).

What an excellent high priest we have in Jesus Christ! Where the priests of Israel failed, Christ excels. Christ is the eternal, ever-living, holy Son of God. Christ died, but not even his death interrupted his priesthood, for in dying he was exercising his priesthood. The Old Testament priests had to cleanse themselves and cleanse the altar; then, they offered sacrifices for their own sins; and finally, they offered sacrifices for the people's sins. Christ had no sins of his own. His sacrifice is perfect because he offered himself, a sacrifice of infinite worth and value in the sight of God. The sacrifices of the Old Testament could never cleanse a sinner and give him assurance in his conscience that he was forgiven. God was simply passing over his sins until the true sinbearer would come (Rom. 3:25). Christ's sacrifice actually saves all those for whom it was offered.

Given all these beautiful truths, how could we look for another high priest? How could Christ's priesthood pass to a successor? Christ will never die! Christ's sacrifice will never be repeated by a future priest! Christ's sacrifice will never lose its value or its power to save! And Christ continues his priestly work in heaven, not by sacrificing (that aspect of his work is finished) but by his continual intercession and his applying, by the Holy Spirit, all the blessings purchased by his sacrifice. Right now, Jesus is in heaven presenting before the Father our names, we who believe in him, and his prayer is the same as it was when he uttered it in John 17:24, "Father, I will that they also, whom thou hast given me, be with me where I am; that they might behold my glory, which thou hast given me: for thou lovedst me before the foundation of the world." All for the sake of Calvary, only for the sake of Calvary.

Martyn McGeown

September 24 — What More Can Be Required?

Lord, to whom shall we go? thou hast the words of eternal life.
—John 6:68

Only one who clings stubbornly to his sinful pride and who refuses to submit to the clear word of God can fail to see the glory, excellency, and unique suitability of the one, only, true mediator, advocate, intercessor, and high priest, Jesus Christ. But, alas, we are blind, foolish, stubborn, proud, and unbelieving by nature!

And so Article 26 ends its treatment of Christ's intercession with rhetorical questions and urgent admonitions: "What more can be required?" "To what purpose should we then seek another advocate?" "Let us not forsake him to take another, or rather to seek after another, without ever being able to find him."

We have seen all conceivable objections answered. We have seen that Christ is the only possible mediator. Only he, combining the human and divine in one divine person, is qualified; of him alone can it be said, "it hath pleased God to give us his own Son." We have seen that he possesses power and majesty unlike any other, and yet, with that majesty, he is filled with love and tenderhearted mercy for miserable sinners. Therefore, we have been admonished not to be affrighted by his majesty, nor to doubt his love, which is so great that he humbled himself even to the cross. We have seen the solid basis for his intercession, mediation, and advocacy: his perfect work of atonement on the cross, by which he has blotted out all our sins, answered the demands of the law and the accusations of Satan, and restored us to blessed fellowship with the triune God, into whose presence we have free and open access.

"What more can be required?" Who could possibly compare with Jesus Christ? Whose person is more perfect; whose work is more complete; whose love is deeper; whose access to the Father is closer; who else meets all our needs as sinners? Shall we go to Mary, when the Son calls us to go to him? Shall we flee to one of the saints, who themselves were sinners and needed Christ to cleanse them? Shall we seek the advocacy of angels when the Father has appointed only Christ?

Surely, to refuse Christ is the greatest depravity and the deepest folly! Shall we cling to our own self-righteousness and conceal it under a false humility? Do not say, "But we are sinners. Surely we could never come to him." Did God design a mediator for sinners without taking into account our sinfulness, our unworthiness, our utter hopelessness? Do not charge the only wise God with folly, as if he did not know what kind of mediator we needed. As Article 26 so eloquently explains it: "God well knew, when he gave him to us, that we were sinners."

Let no niggling doubts remain! Let us not think that the Father left something undone—that the Father overlooked something—when he made Jesus Christ our mediator.

The Father knows our every need. And in infinite grace and mercy, our Father has met our every need in Christ. Only in Christ. Thanks be to God for the gift of his Son!

Martyn McGeown

Article 27

OF THE CATHOLIC CHRISTIAN CHURCH

We believe and profess one catholic or universal Church, which is a holy congregation and assembly of true Christian believers, expecting all their salvation in Jesus Christ, being washed by his blood, sanctified and sealed by the Holy Ghost.

This Church hath been from the beginning of the world, and will be to the end thereof; which is evident from this, that Christ is an eternal king, which, without subjects, he can not be. And this holy Church is preserved or supported by God against the rage of the whole world; though she sometimes (for a while) appear very small, and, in the eyes of men, to be reduced to nothing: as during the perilous reign of Ahab, when nevertheless *the Lord reserved unto him seven thousand men, who had not bowed their knees to Baal.*

Furthermore, this holy Church is not confined, bound, or limited to a certain place or to certain persons, but is spread and dispersed over the whole world; and yet is joined and united with heart and will, by the power of faith, in one and the same spirit.

September 25   **Christ the Head of the Church**

Read: Matthew 28:18; Ephesians 1:20–23, Philippians 2:9–11, Colossians 1:18

As believers, we are blessed to belong to the church. But what is that church to which we belong? Article 27 provides the answer. The church of which Article 27 speaks is the church as the universal body of Christ. We are taught here concerning the church of the elect, chosen from all nations of the earth, and gathered during all the ages of history. We are privileged to belong to that church and thus to be among the elect.

A consideration of the truth of the church must begin with this fundamental question: "Who is the church's head?" This has tremendous significance for us as regards our comfort of being members of that church. Many men claim to themselves the position of head of the church. The pope does in the church of Rome. Bishops do in Episcopal churches. World rulers do in the Erastian form of church government. And many ministers of the word sinfully do, especially in Independentism.

But no man has this right or may make this claim. The only head of the church is the Lord Jesus Christ. He is the church's "eternal King" (Article 27). Christ has the right to be the head of the church on account of who he is. He is the Son of God. No man is his equal. No mere man is qualified to be head of the church. No mere man has any claim to this honorable position. Thus, if any man makes this claim, or else acts as though he is the church's head, he is guilty of the greatest pride and of greatly dishonoring the Son of God.

Christ also has the right to be the church's head because of all he has done for her. He is her redeemer. He gave himself for her. He submitted himself to the wrath of God and the eternal torments of hell in order to save the church unto himself. Who else has done so much for the church? Who else is even able to do such things for her? No one! Christ alone has the right to be head.

As our head, Christ has absolute authority in the church. He rules the church and us, the members. He decides things in his church and thus for us. His word is the law in his church and thus our law. He tells us the members what to believe and how to live.

This confession gives comfort. Christ's headship means we are his body. We are joined to him. We can never be separated from him, for he is sovereign, almighty, and wise. And he, our head, loves us. Because of him, we are now and will forever remain living members of his church. May we give thanks to God today and every day for Christ our head!

> Jehovah reigns in majesty;
> Let all the nations quake.
> He dwells between the cherubim;
> Let earth's foundations shake.
> Supreme in Zion is the Lord,
> Exalted gloriously;
> Ye nations, praise His name with awe,
> The Holy One is He.*

Daniel Kleyn

---

* No. 265:1, in *The Psalter*.

September 26 — The Church's Oneness

Read: John 17:20–21, Romans 12:3–10, 1 Corinthians 12:12–27, Ephesians 4:1–7

Because Christ is the church's head, the church has certain characteristics. These things characterize the body of the elect because these things characterize Christ our head. The first of these is that the church is one.

In Article 27 we confess this oneness when we say: "We believe and profess one… church!" Article 27 also affirms this by speaking not of "churches," but of "church," and by stating that the church is "joined and united with heart and will, by the power of faith, in one and the same spirit." What does it mean that the church is one? The basic idea is that there is only one church of Christ.

We may wonder: "Is this really true? Then why are there so many different congregations and denominations—literally thousands upon thousands?" There are many earthly reasons why the church's oneness is not fully manifested. One reason is that God's people are in many different nations around the world and have many different languages. Another reason (to our shame) is sin—departure from the faith, the pride of man, the failure of God's people to be united in the faith, etc. But none of this takes away from the reality that there is only one church of Christ. Although Christ's elect are scattered throughout the world, and although they are in many different congregations and denominations, there is only one church. Christ does not have two, or five, or fifty, or five thousand bodies, but only one.

And therefore, we who are members of Christ's one body are united to each other and have many things in common. We all expect our "salvation in Jesus Christ," being "true Christian believers" who have all been "washed by his blood" and "sanctified and sealed by the Holy Spirit." Regardless of all earthly differences, all believers have a common life in Christ, a common enemy, common struggles, common goals, common spiritual blessings, etc.

Sometimes when we look at the church with earthly eyes, we do not see unity, but instead schism, division, and separation. We even find ourselves guilty of causing these things—by pitting ourselves against fellow believers, or congregation against congregation, or Christian school against Christian school. But this does not negate the reality of the church's oneness. It is a matter of faith. We believe it is a reality, even if we cannot always see it.

Because we contribute to the lack of unity, there is an urgent need to strive with all our might to maintain and manifest the oneness of the church—within the congregation to which each of us belong, within our respective denominations, between sister churches, and through always seeking out others who are one with us in the truth of God's word.

Be thankful for what Christ has done in establishing unity in his body. And always strive, by his grace, to manifest it.

> How pleasant and how good it is
> When brethren in the Lord
> In one another's joy delight
> And dwell in sweet accord.*

Daniel Kleyn

---

* No. 369:1, in *The Psalter*.

September 27 — The Holiness of Christ's Church

Read: Numbers 23:21, 2 Corinthians 6:14–18, Ephesians 2:21, 1 Peter 2:9

Because Christ the king and head of the church is holy, the church is also holy. Christ's body is "a holy congregation" (Article 27). She is a church that hates and is separated from sin. She is devoted to Christ her head. And she is made up of members who are holy—in and because of Christ their head.

The holiness of the church does not mean that a particular congregation is perfect. You will never find a perfect congregation of Christ's church in this world. Sin will always be present in every church, even in the most faithful on earth.

This is also true regarding the church's members. None of them is personally perfect. The elect cannot be sinless in this life. We will all continue to manifest unholiness until the day we die. Even the holiest of men have, in this life, only a very small beginning of the new obedience.

Nevertheless, the church, and we her elect members, are holy in the eyes of God. God sees the church as sanctified by the Spirit of Christ. God views the members of the church as saints—"holy ones." For God sees the church and her members not as we are in ourselves, but as we are in Christ our head—"a glorious church, not having spot, or wrinkle, or any such thing…holy and without blemish" (Eph. 5:27).

What a wonder of grace. God says concerning the church that "he hath not beheld iniquity in Jacob, neither hath he seen perverseness in Israel" (Num. 23:21). God views you, an unholy sinner, as a saint.

This implies a calling for all members of Christ's church. God says: "Be ye holy; for I am holy" (1 Pet. 1:16). Since Christ our head is holy, we his body must be holy, too. We must separate ourselves from all that is unholy. We must hate sin and love what is good. In one word, the church and her members must be antithetical. Constantly we must say, "No," to sin and, "Yes," to God.

Do this today and every day. Say, "No," to sin on the television and internet. Say, "No," to sinful thoughts and desires. Say, "No," to other gods. Say, "No," to hatred, lying, adultery, and covetousness. And say, "Yes," to God and the things of God. Say, "Yes," to obedience to God and to all in authority over you (at home, work, and in the church). Say, "Yes," to prayer and reading the Bible. Say, "Yes," to loving your neighbor. Say, "Yes," to loving the Lord your God with all your heart, soul, mind, and strength.

> Who, O Lord, with Thee abiding,
> In Thy house shall be Thy guest?
> Who, his feet to Zion turning,
> In Thy holy hill shall rest?
> He that ever walks uprightly,
> Does the right without a fear,
> When he speaks, he speaks not lightly,
> But with truth and love sincere.*

Daniel Kleyn

---

* No. 24:1, in *The Psalter*.

September 28 — **The Catholicity of Christ's Church**

Read: Psalm 22:27; Psalm 87; Galatians 3:16, 28; Revelation 7:9

If you have ever had the privilege of meeting (or living among) the people of God from a different land, you will have experienced firsthand the wonder of the catholicity of the church. In spite of earthly differences, you sense within minutes the bond that unites in Christ and the wonder of belonging to the same church—a church from every nation under heaven. For Christ's "church is not confined, bound, or limited to a certain place or to certain persons, but is spread and dispersed over the whole world" (Article 27).

Christ is a catholic king and savior. He died on the cross to save his people from every nation, tribe, and tongue. Thus, the church which is his body is also catholic.

This means the church is universal. It is not limited or restricted by anything earthly—not race, language, skin color, social status, intellect, age, etc. The church is made up of whites and blacks, Europeans and Asians, and believers who speak French and English and Chinese and any other language. The church has in it both young and old, male and female, rich and poor, employer and employee, great and small.

The catholicity of the church also means that the church is made up of God's people from every age of history. We confess in Article 27 that "this Church hath been from the beginning of the world, and will be to the end thereof." All God's people, from every age, belong to the same church. You and I belong to the same church as Adam, Abraham, Moses, and David.

The reason the church is catholic is because God's election crosses all barriers. God does not choose his people on the basis of physical or earthly characteristics. His gracious choice and the saving work of Christ on the cross break down all walls between races. The church is made up of people from every nation, language, and status under heaven. It transcends all national boundaries and distinctions.

The fact of the church's catholicity condemns racism and prejudice in the church. We must resist the temptation to reject or look down upon others because of their nationality, skin color, language, or customs. Instead, we must view all these differences as adding to the church's beauty. Each race has something to contribute to the church of Christ. If we were all the same, the church would be bland and colorless. But each race of God's people can be thought of as a different color of the rainbow. When all these colors are placed next to each other, the glory and beauty of the church as the body of Christ shines brightly to the praise of Christ our head.

> The ends of all the earth shall hear
> And turn unto the Lord in fear;
> All kindreds of the earth shall own
> And worship Him as God alone.[*]

Daniel Kleyn

---

[*] No. 49:1, in *The Psalter*.

September 29 — **The Apostolicity of Christ's Church**

Read: Matthew 16:16–18, John 8:32, Ephesians 2:19–22

What is the church's foundation? On what is the church built? What is it that gives the members of the church a solid rock on which to stand and keeps them from being led astray and away from their sure and only comfort? The answer lies in understanding the truth of the church's apostolicity.

We confess that the church is apostolic. This is implied in Article 27 when it states that the church is made up of "true Christian believers" and that they are united "by the power of faith, in one and the same Spirit."

What is apostolicity? It refers to the fact that the church is built upon the foundation of the apostles and prophets.

Apostolicity does not mean that the church is built on the apostles themselves (as Rome claims). But it means that the church confesses the doctrines and truths that were taught by the apostles and prophets. And what are those truths? They are the truths written down in the Scriptures. The solid rock on which the church is built is the inspired scriptures of the Old and New Testaments.

However, since the central truth of the Scriptures is Christ, an apostolic church is built upon Christ himself. "The church's one foundation is Jesus Christ, her Lord."* He is the chief cornerstone of the church. Everything in a truly apostolic church centers around Christ. He is the content of the preaching. In every sermon and in every Bible study, the gospel of salvation in him is set forth. The church and her members are "determined not to know anything…save Jesus Christ, and him crucified" (1 Cor. 2:2).

An apostolic church is therefore one that is thoroughly biblical. The truths of the Bible are preached. The members know the truth, love the truth, believe the truth, confess the truth, and live the truth. Such a church is also confessional. The Reformed creeds are an integral part of the church's confession and life. The Heidelberg Catechism is preached. And the other creeds do not die from disuse but are regularly referred to and studied.

If by God's grace the church to which you belong is truly apostolic, give God thanks. For then you are receiving the preaching that powerfully saves. Then you are being fed by the truth that sets you free from the bondage and punishment of sin. Then you are being nourished and fed unto life eternal. Then you are being comforted by Christ himself. And then you are spiritually safe, for the church to which you belong has a foundation against which not even the gates of hell will prevail. Thanks be to God for membership in such a church.

> The precepts of the Lord are right;
> With joy they fill the heart;
> The Lord's commandments all are pure,
> And clearest light impart.**

Daniel Kleyn

---

* By S. J. Stone (1866).
** No. 42:2, in *The Psalter*.

September 30 —— **The Church Gathered by Christ**

Read: John 10:16, Acts 13:48, Romans 9:24, Romans 10:14–15

Why are you a saved child of God? Why are you in the church? How did you become a member? This did not happen because of a work of man. We do not add ourselves to the church. Preachers do not save the church, no matter how powerful or persuasive their preaching.

> Not human strength or mighty hosts,
> Not charging steeds or war-like boasts
> Can save from overthrow.*

The salvation of the church is exclusively the work of Christ. He and his work are the only reason any one of us is a member of his body. He did it all.

This saving work of Christ is part of his care for his body. The elect are scattered throughout the world. Unless Christ gathers them, they are not and will not be saved. Unless Christ saves them, the elect will never know that they are elect and will never know that they belong to Christ and his church.

And so, King Jesus Christ sends out the preaching of his word and his mighty Spirit. Those he has washed by his blood, he sanctifies and seals by his Holy Spirit. He brings us to conscious faith in himself. He gives us all the benefits of salvation he purchased by his death. He causes us to know his love. He assures us of forgiveness and life eternal. He works in us the confident assurance that we are members of his church.

This is not to deny that Christ uses men. He uses ministers and missionaries who faithfully declare his gospel. He uses believers and the witness they give by their life and confession. He uses parents as they carry out their calling to teach their children the works and ways of Jehovah. He uses Christian schools and Christian school teachers. But the truth is that Christ does not need any of these. He does not need you, or me, or anyone. He does not need our work, abilities, zeal, wisdom, insights, money, and tireless efforts. His work is not dependent on us. The only reason the church or any member of her is saved is because of Christ.

That's how it needs to be. For Christ alone knows who the elect are. Christ alone knows where the elect are in this world. And Christ alone is able to save them. If it were not his work, heaven would forever remain empty. But because it is his work, not one of his elect will be overlooked, forgotten, or lost. And because it is his work, you can be confident that you and your elect children will be saved.

> O sing ye Hallelujah!
> 'Tis good our God to praise;
> 'Tis pleasant and becoming
> To Him our songs to raise;
> He builds the walls of Zion,
> He seeks her wandering sons,
> He binds their wounds and comforts
> The brokenhearted ones.**

Daniel Kleyn

---

* No. 87:2, in *The Psalter*.
** No. 402:1, in *The Psalter*.

October 1 — The Church Preserved by Christ

Read: Matthew 16:18, Luke 12:32, John 10:28–29, Philippians 1:6

The church of Christ is constantly under attack. The devil and world do not leave her alone. The elect are always objects of their hatred and persecution. They make our way in this world very narrow. They tempt us on every side. And none of us can deny that the temptations appeal to us. Frequently, therefore, it appears that the church and the cause of Christ in this world will be destroyed and disappear.

But that will never happen. For, according to Article 27,

> this holy Church is preserved or supported by God against the rage of the whole world; though she sometimes (for a while) appear very small, and, in the eyes of men, to be reduced to nothing: as during the perilous reign of Ahab, when nevertheless *the Lord reserved unto him seven thousand men, who had not bowed their knees to Baal.*

That was the confident confession of the sixteenth-century church while she was in the very middle of severe persecution. It may be our confident confession, too.

Christ loves his church. She is most precious to him. He cares for his beloved body and bride. Therefore his church will always exist in the world—it "hath been from the beginning of the world, and will be to the end thereof" (Article 27).

The church needs Christ's protection because of her many enemies. Consider the devil. Sometimes he rages against the church and severely persecutes her members. Other times he attacks by appearing as an angel of light. He introduces tares among the wheat. He causes the ungodly to mingle closely with the elect so as to weaken them and lead them astray. He introduces false doctrine. He tempts believers with the world and all its lusts. Without Christ, the church would not exist. Without him, none of the elect would survive. But with him and because of him, the church is safe. Our enemies cannot so much as touch us except that Christ wills it. Not one elect will ever be snatched out of the church of Christ. Not one elect will go lost. Every child of God will be preserved unto the end.

Christ also preserves the members of the church in their salvation. We sometimes doubt. On account of sin or great sufferings, we wonder: "Am I really one of the elect?" But Christ does not leave us to fend for ourselves. By means of his word and Spirit, he strengthens our faith and removes the doubts. When we sin, he lifts us up again by his almighty grace. He forgives; he restores; he comforts.

May we praise God for Christ's protection and preservation. Because of him, the gates of hell will not prevail against us. Because of him, you will never perish, but will forever remain a member of his church.

> Thou wilt stretch forth Thy mighty arm
> To save me when my foes alarm;
> The work Thou hast for me begun
> Shall by Thy grace be fully done;
> Forever mercy dwells with Thee;
> O Lord, my Maker, think on me.[*]

Daniel Kleyn

---

[*] No. 381:4, in *The Psalter*.

Article 28

EVERY ONE IS BOUND TO JOIN HIMSELF TO THE TRUE CHURCH

We believe, since this holy congregation is an assemblage of those who are saved, and out of it there is no salvation, that no person of whatsoever state or condition he may be, ought to withdraw himself, to live in a separate state from it; but that all men are in duty bound to join and unite themselves with it; maintaining the unity of the Church; submitting themselves to the doctrine and discipline thereof; bowing their necks under the yoke of Jesus Christ; and as mutual members of the same body, serving to the edification of the brethren, according to the talents God has given them. And that this may be better observed, it is the duty of all believers, according to the Word of God, to separate themselves from those who do not belong to the Church, and to join themselves to this congregation, wheresoever God hath established it, even though the magistrates and edicts of princes be against it; yea, though they should suffer death or bodily punishment.

Therefore all those who separate themselves from the same, or do not join themselves to it, act contrary to the ordinance of God.

October 2 — Salvation Only in the Church Institute

Read: Ephesians 4:11–12, Psalms 133 & 134

Article 28 makes a bold statement concerning the church, namely, that "out of it there is no salvation." What does this mean? Is Article 28 referring to the church from the viewpoint of the universal body of Christ? No, that is not the case. This is clear from the fact that Article 28 states that the believer has a duty to join himself to a true church. And we do not join ourselves to the universal body of Christ—God did that in his eternal decree of election.

Article 28 is speaking of the church institute. It has in mind the church as an organized congregation in a specific location. And Article 28 teaches that there is no salvation outside the church institute. In order to be saved, one must join a true church of Christ. Why is this the case? Why is it so important for the child of God to be a member of such a church? The reason is because Christ has given the means of grace to the church institute. You will not find the means of grace (the preaching and the sacraments) anywhere else. They are found only in a true and faithful church of Christ. And it is only in such a church that the Spirit of Christ works through the means of grace (especially the preaching) to save our souls.

Someone may say: "But is that really true? Is it really necessary to be a member of a church in order to be saved? Do you mean to say that God cannot and does not save people who are not members of a local church?"

Our answer to these questions is this: It is not a matter of what God is able to do, but simply a matter of what God has willed to do. God teaches us in his word that he has decided to save his people by means of their being members in the church institute.

Therefore, there is no substitute for membership in a local church. Corporate worship with the people of God cannot be replaced by home worship or by small group Bible studies. We need to join a true church of Christ, for we need to hear the faithful preaching of the gospel, which is the power of God that saves (Rom. 1:16; 10:13–15). We need to be in a true church, for "this holy congregation is an assemblage of those who are saved" (Article 28).

All of this is beautifully expressed in Psalms 133 and 134. These psalms speak of Zion (the church) and of God's people standing "in the house of the Lord" (134:1). These psalms also mention the oil of anointing, which represents the Holy Spirit at work in the faithful, instituted church of Christ (133:2). Finally, these two psalms point out that Jehovah blesses his people "out of Zion" (134:3). It is in Zion that Jehovah "commanded [his] blessing" upon his people, even "life for evermore" (133:3). Salvation is not found outside the church, but within the walls of Zion.

> Such love in peace and joy distils,
> As o'er the slopes of Hermon's hills
> Refreshing dew descends;
> The Lord commands His blessing there,
> And they that walk in love shall share
> In life that never ends.*

Daniel Kleyn

---

* No. 370:2, in *The Psalter*.

October 3 — **Called to Be Members of the Church**

Read: Psalm 87, Hebrews 10:25

Because there is no salvation outside the church institute, the child of God has a calling to join himself to a true church of Christ. "No person of whatsoever state or condition he may be, ought to withdraw himself to live in a separate state from it; but that all men are in duty bound to join and unite themselves with it" (Article 28). It is the duty of every believer to be a member.

Church membership is not optional for us. It is not something we decide to do (or not to do) depending on how much we think we need it (or don't need it), how much we like a particular congregation, how personable the pastor is, or how friendly the members are. Regardless of all these things, it is our duty to join. Not only do we have the duty to join, but we also have the duty not to separate ourselves from a true church. This has clear biblical warrant in Hebrews 10:25, where we are commanded not to forsake "the assembling of ourselves together."

One may be tempted to leave a church for various earthly reasons. Young people may be tempted to do so for the sake of college, work, voluntary service in the military, marriage, or a more suitable place to live. But a child of God may not willfully leave a true church—either temporarily or permanently. His duty is to remain an active member in that church.

Reformed churches and Reformed believers must have a high view of church membership. Earthly choices, earthly goals, and earthly needs must never take precedence. What must always come first is obedience to the command of Christ to be a member in a church in which is found (more clearly than in any other church) the three marks of a faithful church of Christ: the pure preaching of the gospel, the pure administration of the sacraments, and the proper exercise of Christian discipline (see Article 29). The child of God must never willfully separate himself from that church.

The reason we must take our church membership so seriously is that it is necessary for our salvation. It is in a true church of Christ that the Spirit works to save us through the preaching of the gospel. Church membership ought to be as important to us as the forgiveness of sins, the comfort of our hearts, the joy of our salvation, and the hope of eternal life. And this is important not only for ourselves personally, but also for our families. We need to be members for the sake of the salvation of our children and grandchildren.

If someone either refuses to join a true church or else abandons it, in reality he is saying, "The salvation of my soul, and of the souls of my loved ones, is insignificant and unimportant to me. Earthly things are far more necessary for me to have and pursue." May God preserve us from ever having such a careless attitude toward our salvation and thus toward membership in a true church of Christ.

> When the Lord shall count the nations,
> Sons and daughters He shall see,
> Born to endless life in Zion,
> And their joyful song shall be,
> "Blessed Zion,
> All our fountains are in Thee."*

Daniel Kleyn

---

* No. 238:3, in *The Psalter*.

October 4 — A Member in Spite of Persecution

Read: Daniel 3:1–18, Acts 4:13–29, Acts 5:27–29

Membership in a true church of Christ is not always easy. Sometimes a very high price must be paid by the faithful member of a true church. But in spite of that, the child of God is called to join that church and always to remain a member. Why? Because he must obey God, rather than men.

Some of our fellow believers around the world face severe consequences for gathering together as a church in order to worship God. The government forbids it. Earthly rulers threaten them with extreme punishments. If they disobey, they can expect severe persecution, including imprisonment and even death.

Other children of God face milder forms of persecution. Parents threaten to disown children who abandon their pagan beliefs and join a faithful church of Christ. Family members mock a parent or child or sibling who lets nothing detain him from being in church twice every Lord's day. Former friends ridicule and do all they can to make life miserable for the believer who manifests his undying love for and devotion to Christ and his church.

Such suffering for the sake of Christ ought not surprise us. We can expect it, for unto us "it is given in the behalf of Christ, not only to believe on him, but also to suffer for his sake" (Phil. 1:29). The world hated Christ and put him to death. The world will do the same to those who belong to Christ and who confess his name (John 15:18).

But "even though the magistrates and edicts of princes were against it, yea, though [we] should suffer death or any other corporal punishment" (Article 28), we must never abandon Christ's church. Always we must obey God rather than men.

That means we must never separate ourselves from the church out of fear of what our earthly rulers might do to us. We must never stop attending a true church because the result will be constant mockery from those who are dear to us. We must ever remain faithful in our attendance, even if the earthly welfare not only of ourselves, but also of our own family, is at stake. Even if we might lose all our earthly possessions, earthly friendships, earthly peace, and even earthly life itself, still we must remain faithful members of a true church of Christ.

Why is this necessary? For the sake of our salvation. We need to be in church every Lord's day so our souls are fed with the bread of heaven. We must allow nothing to keep us from that.

But we do all this with confident trust and hope in God and Christ. We know that nothing (not mockery, hatred, imprisonment, or even death) will separate us from Christ and his love. We know that we are more than conquerors through Christ, and we will always have the victory. Yes, even death will be victory.

May this be our confession and song:

> The Lord with me, I will not fear
> Though human might oppose;
> The Lord my helper, I shall be
> Triumphant o'er my foes.
> No trust in men, or kings of men,
> Can confidence afford,
> But they are strong, and sure their trust,
> Whose hope is in the Lord.*

Daniel Kleyn

---

* No. 317:2, in *The Psalter.*

October 5 — A Member Who Submits to Christ

Read: Psalm 110, Matthew 11:15–30

Article 28 mentions an important characteristic and duty of the faithful members of a true church: "bowing their necks under the yoke of Jesus Christ." This points to the fact that as members of the body of Christ, we not only confess that Jesus is our savior, but also this: "Jesus is our Lord!" He is the supreme head of his church, and thus Lord over all the members of that church. As Article 28 points out, the duty to bow our necks to the yoke of Christ means especially two things: we submit to the doctrine of the church, and we submit to the discipline of the church. We do this not simply because it is the doctrine and discipline of the church itself, but because it is the doctrine and discipline of Christ.

First, submission to the doctrine of the church means submitting to all the truths of the word of God. That includes not only the Bible itself, but also the whole body of truth as it is set forth in our Reformed confessions. We must submit to all the truth, for it is the truth that makes us free (John 8:32). But submission to the doctrine of the church means submission especially to the preaching. That is crucial, for the true preaching of the word of God saves. When that word is faithfully preached, Christ himself preaches. His voice is heard in his church and by his people. And that voice is powerful to regenerate, to justify, to turn from sin, to sanctify, and to preserve us in our salvation. He who fails to submit to the doctrine of Christ in a true church not only commits the sin of refusing to submit to Christ, but also does it to the peril of his own soul.

Second, submission to the yoke of Christ means that we submit to the discipline of the church. Christ has appointed certain men in his church (the elders) to "watch for [our] souls" (Heb. 13:17). When elders faithfully carry out their work, Christ himself does that work. If a believer errs in doctrine or life, it is not merely a few men who come to visit him and speak to him, but Christ visits, Christ admonishes, and Christ calls him to repentance. We must submit to him.

If we are outside the church, we will be without the care of the preaching and elders. We need that care, for we all stray. If we are not members of a true church, who will correct us?

When we make a public confession of faith, we make promises regarding our submission. We say, "I promise to adhere to the doctrine that is taught here in this Christian church," and, "I promise to submit to church government and to church discipline."[*] This is a serious promise. It is a solemn vow made before God himself. May he strengthen us to be faithful in keeping it.

But let us remember, too, that it is a delight to submit to Christ, for his rule over his people is a rule of grace. He makes his people "willing in the day of [his] power" (Ps. 110:3). His "yoke is easy," and his "burden is light" (Matt. 11:30).

> Christ shall have dominion
> Over land and sea,
> Earth's remotest regions
> Shall His empire be.[**]

Daniel Kleyn

---

[*] See Public Confession of Faith, in *The Psalter*, 90.
[**] No 200:1, in *The Psalter*.

October 6 — A Member Who Edifies Others

Read: Romans 12:3–18, 1 Corinthians 12:12–27, Ephesians 4:16, Philippians 2:2–8

As members of a true church of Christ, we have the opportunity and privilege to use our God-given gifts for the welfare of the other members of Christ's body. We are able "as mutual members of the same body" to serve "to the edification of the brethren, according to the talents God has given" us (Article 28).

Every member of the church is unique. God makes it so, for God distributes among the members the different abilities and talents that the church needs. Romans 12 indicates what some of those different gifts might be. Some have the gift of prophecy, some of ministry, some of teaching, some of exhorting, some of giving, some of ruling, some of showing mercy. And we can easily add to this list such things as the gift of prayer, the gift of music, the gift of patience, etc.

You may sometimes think you do not have any gifts. You might say: "Others have special talents, but not I. Others can contribute to the church and to the welfare of their fellow believers, but I have nothing to give or do. I'm rather unnecessary in the church." But none of us may ever say that. The Scriptures plainly teach that Christ has given gifts to every single member of his church. If we think we do not have any, then perhaps we need to look harder to discover what Christ has given. Or perhaps we need to take more time to look at the needs that others have and think of concrete ways in which we can help them.

Having discovered our gifts, we may not be selfish with them. Those gifts are not given to us for our own advantage and advancement and praise. We must use our gifts for the benefit of others. Do the following with your gifts. Help those who are in need. Provide for those who are poor. Approach those who are lonely. Befriend those who have no friends. Comfort those who are sorrowful. Constantly look for ways to show love to your fellow saints.

To use our gifts for the sake of others especially refers to our calling to seek their spiritual welfare. Why? Because we are mutual members of the same body and must seek the edification of our fellow believers in everything we say and do. Let us speak with other church members about the Scripture and the preaching. Let us encourage our fellow believers to read the Bible and pray. Let us assist those who are struggling against temptation and sin. Let us speak of the love and faithfulness of God to those who are troubled or depressed.

One more thing we ought to do is to pray for our fellow believers. Every one of us is able to do this. Pray that God would bless, comfort, forgive, guide, protect, and save them. Be sure to pray for them every day. For when you do, then you will think about them. And if you think about them, then you will also remember to look for ways in which to use your unique gifts and talents for their physical and spiritual good.

May we take with us these beautiful words of Psalm 16:

> I love Thy saints, who fear Thy Name
> And walk as in Thy sight;
> They are the excellent of earth,
> In them is my delight.[*]

Daniel Kleyn

---

[*] No. 27:2, in *The Psalter*.

October 7 — A Member Who Lives Antithetically

Read: 1 Corinthians 5:9–11; 2 Corinthians 6:14–18; 2 Thessalonians 3:6, 14–15

Membership in a true church means being a covenant friend of God. God has established his covenant with us. God has included us by his grace in a covenant of friendship and fellowship. In that covenant, God and his people are friends. That is why membership in a true church involves also this calling: "It is the duty of all believers, according to the word of God, to separate themselves from all those who do not belong to the church" (Article 28). This is the antithesis. This is the antithetical life we must live. We must separate ourselves from the world of the ungodly and from the false church.

The true church of Christ lives in a world in which wickedness abounds. Every day we are bombarded and allured by the sins of the ungodly—through advertising, music, television, the internet, and through our constant contact with the ungodly at school, at work, in stores, etc. Our calling is to say, "No," to it all. Though we are sorely tempted by the lusts of the flesh, our response must be: "Let the world keep all that it offers—its language, music, riches, fornication, and pleasure. I don't want any of it. God calls me to live in spiritual separation from the ungodly."

This is necessary for the safety of believers and their children. Moses mentioned this just prior to Israel's entrance into Canaan. His words to the church were: "Israel then shall dwell in safety alone" (Deut. 33:28).

Moses was not speaking of physical safety for Israel, but spiritual. By dwelling alone, the church and the people of God are kept from being destroyed spiritually. We are kept safe from being dragged into greater evils. We are kept safe from being swallowed up by a world that is bent on destroying the church. We are kept safe in the enjoyment of our salvation in Jesus Christ.

A faithful antithetical life is necessary not only for our own welfare, but also for the church of tomorrow. If we fail in this duty, the real danger could be for the future generations of the church. That happened to Lot. He chose to dwell in Sodom. He joined the world. And although he himself was saved, his family was lost. That is the sad result when God's people do not remain spiritually separate from the world—they go lost in their generations.

It is not easy to be in the world but not of it. Our flesh longs for the treasures and pleasures of the world. We can also expect ridicule. But for the sake of the church's future, and for the sake of the honor of Christ's name, may we be faithful.

And there is encouragement in this. For the antithetical calling is not a negative but a positive thing. It is something the child of God loves and wants and is thankful for. For while it is true that we will be alone from the ungodly, being alone from them means being alone with God. What more could we want? God is at our side. God is with us. God is our friend.

> In sweet communion, Lord, with Thee
> I constantly abide;
> My hand Thou holdest in Thy own
> To keep me near Thy side.*

Daniel Kleyn

---

* No. 203:1, in *The Psalter*.

October 8 — **Blessings of Church Membership**

Read: Psalm 122, Ephesians 4:15–16

There are many (countless) blessings that follow from membership in a true church of Jesus Christ. Just think of all the blessings that have been mentioned (either explicitly or implicitly) in the previous meditations. Reflect on those blessings. Be thankful for them.

But consider also this blessing—that by means of church membership, we are able to worship God. The worship of our God is of central importance in our lives. It is also an important calling and duty. We often find it difficult to devote time to this during the week or to be consistent in doing so. However, in church on the Lord's day, we are able to do it without being distracted by our earthly cares. What a blessing to be part of an instituted church and to be able to give God the praise and thanks that is due to his name.

Another significant blessing of church membership is the fellowship of other believers. It is a great blessing to have fellow believers and to be part of the communion of saints. It is a blessing to be able to use our gifts for the welfare of others. It is also a blessing that our fellow saints use their gifts for our good. And it is a blessing to have fellow saints because then you do not need to be alone in this world.

Just think of how difficult your Christian life would be without other believers. Just imagine if no one else loved God, read the Bible, prayed, or lived as a Christian. Just imagine if when you came to church on Sunday, the building was always empty, for there was no one else interested in worshiping God. You were the only one there, and you had to worship God alone.

This would mean that the only people you could have any fellowship with would be the ungodly. That would be difficult and disastrous. It would be almost impossible to be a believer and to live a Christian life.

What a blessing, therefore, to have others with whom we are one in Christ. We do not have to be alone in this world. God has given us all the saints we know and have regular fellowship with, and many others besides. It is a gift we should be thankful for and that we should treasure.

But, as great a blessing as this is, the most important blessing that comes from church membership is salvation. By means of faithful membership and diligent attendance, we hear the true preaching of the gospel. And that saves us, strengthens us in our faith, comforts our souls, and preserves us unto the end.

All this being true, why would any true believer not want to be a member of a true church of Christ? Why would any child of God want to separate himself from that church? Why would any saint want to live separate from Christ and his people? Only in a true church will the believer find Christ and thus true happiness, comfort, safety, joy, and peace.

> Redeemed by Thee, I stand secure
> In peace and happiness;
> And in the Church, among Thy saints,
> Jehovah I will bless.*

Daniel Kleyn

---

* No. 69:7, in *The Psalter*.

Article 29

OF THE MARKS OF THE TRUE CHURCH, AND WHEREIN SHE DIFFERS FROM THE FALSE CHURCH

We believe that we ought diligently and circumspectly to discern from the Word of God which is the true Church, since all sects which are in the world assume to themselves the name of the Church.

But we speak here not of the company of hypocrites, who are mixed in the Church with the good, yet are not of the Church, though externally in it; but we say that the body and communion of the true Church must be distinguished from all sects who call themselves the Church.

The marks by which the true Church is known are these: If the pure doctrine of the gospel is preached therein; if she maintains the pure administration of the sacraments as instituted by Christ; if church discipline is exercised in punishing of sin; in short, if all things are managed according to the pure Word of God, all things contrary thereto rejected, and Jesus Christ acknowledged as the only Head of the Church. Hereby the true Church may certainly be known, from which no man has a right to separate himself. With respect to those who are members of the Church, they may be known by the marks of Christians, namely, by faith; and when they have received Jesus Christ the only Saviour, they avoid sin, follow after righteousness, love the true God and their neighbor, neither turn aside to the right or left, and crucify the flesh with the works thereof. But this is not to be understood as if there did not remain in them great infirmities; but they fight against them through the Spirit all the days of their life, continually taking their refuge in the blood, death, passion, and obedience of our Lord Jesus Christ, *in whom they have remission of sins through faith in him*.

As for the false Church, she ascribes more power and authority to herself and her ordinances than to the Word of God, and will not submit herself to the yoke of Christ. Neither does she administer the Sacraments, as appointed by Christ in his Word, but adds to and takes from them as she thinks proper; she relieth more upon men than upon Christ; and persecutes those who live holily according to the Word of God, and rebuke her for her errors, covetousness, and idolatry. These two Churches are easily known and distinguished from each other.

October 9   **Discerning the True Church**

Prove all things; hold fast that which is good.
—1 Thessalonians 5:21

Article 28 pressed upon every believer the solemn calling to find and join a true church. That naturally leads to questions: what is a true church, where can such a true church be found, and how can such a true church be recognized? Article 29 answers those questions with the doctrine of the three marks of the true church.

If you open your Bible, you will not find one verse or even one chapter in the word of God where the three marks are delineated. Instead, to answer the questions above, we will have to examine the whole word of God, compare Scripture with Scripture, and examine certain biblical principles. But before we do that, we should look at the subject more generally.

When you visit a new city and do some research, you will find that most places have a dazzling array of different churches on offer. This was true in the days of the Belgic Confession as well. "All sects which are in the world assume to themselves the name of the church" (Article 29). "The true church must be distinguished from all sects who call themselves the church" (Article 29). So true is this today that many Christians like to engage in "church shopping." This is often the case if they are dissatisfied with some aspect of their church life—they just leave their church with very little consideration of the marks of the true or false church and find a new church which suits their fancy. But, church membership is, as Article 28 taught us, a long-term commitment. We may not leave a church lightly—and we certainly may never leave a true church to join a false church.

For many, this whole discussion of true or false church is incomprehensible and even offensive. How dare you suggest that there could be false churches! What right do you have to question the veracity of the ministries of others! If a man or a woman says that his or her ministry is true, you must simply accept that. If a building has the sign "First Church of Anywhere," we must simply recognize that that is a church. For such people, the question is not over truth or falsehood, but the question is one of convenience or preference.

This is, however, a foolish and naïve attitude. Perhaps an illustration would help. If you visited a restaurant where the waitstaff was rude, the food was poorly prepared, and the conditions were unsanitary, would you return? Would you return every week for the next twenty years? Sadly, many Christians tolerate a poor church much more readily than they would a poor restaurant. They can discern a good restaurant, but they have no discernment whatsoever with respect to churches. Jesus and the apostles warn us about false doctrine. They warn us that when false doctrine is tolerated, it spreads like leaven. They warn us that Christ will remove a church's candlestick so that it no longer shines as a pillar of truth in the world. "I know the blasphemy of them which say they are Jews, and are not, but are the synagogue of Satan" (Rev. 2:9). "So then because thou art lukewarm, and neither cold nor hot, I will spue thee out of my mouth" (Rev. 3:16).

It is therefore of the utmost importance that we can discern and know the true church from the false—for our spiritual welfare and our children's, and for the glory of God.

Martyn McGeown

October 10 — Distracted by the Wrong Marks

Thou hast tried them which say they are apostles, and are not, and hast found them liars. —Revelation 2:2

Yesterday, we began to look at the concept of examining churches as to their truth or falsehood. While many object to this practice as unloving, harsh, and judgmental, the Bible makes clear that such an examination is necessary.

When we begin to examine the churches around us, we are tempted to look for the wrong marks. If you ask professing Christians today why they are in a particular church or denomination, you will receive various answers. The problem with the vast majority of these answers is that they are subjective, not objective, criteria. In other words, people who examine various options do so based on their feelings and emotions more than on what is true or false. Since we are emotional creatures by nature, it is difficult for us to avoid this. Therefore, the word of God gives us objective standards of truth and falsehood for which we must look.

Most people attend a church out of custom. I have heard people say: "I was born in this church. I will die in this church." Such loyalty to one's congregation is good—if the church is true! But if the church is false—and we will examine that possibility later—such an attitude is sinful stubbornness. Others attend a church for social reasons. If they examine their hearts, the reason they attend the worship services is not to worship God or to hear the preaching, but so that they can see their friends and family. An interest in fellowship with the saints is good—if the people there are saints and the church is true. But the church is not a social club. When social activities become more important than the worship of the Almighty, we have sinned. Others attend a church out of loyalty to their family. Their family and friends attend there, and they enjoy a whole social network there. Loyalty to family is good—if the church is true. But family must not become idols, and one must be less concerned with displeasing family than displeasing Christ (Luke 14:26). Still others attend church because it is convenient. The church is close by. No long drive is necessary to attend the services. But if that church is false, no amount of convenience can justify membership there. Christianity—true Christianity—is not always convenient! (Matt. 16:24–25).

Besides this, many attend churches because of the programs they offer. If the church is lively—and even if the preaching is false—they will attend it. But the mark of a true church is not lively worship, but true, biblical, reverent worship. If the church offers activities for the children and the young people—but no pure preaching—they will attend it. Youth work is important—that is why Reformed churches have catechism—but it is not a mark of the true church either. Some prefer a mission-minded church, or one which permits them to use and develop their gifts. Missions and gifts are important, but in themselves are not marks of the true church either. Others say that love must surely be the mark of the church. If the people are friendly, loving, generous, and kind, such church-shoppers will be tempted to join. Love, however, like beauty, is in the eye of the beholder. Love is undoubtedly important, but who can discern how loving a church is? Many true churches have been slandered as unloving because of the impression of one visitor.

While many claim the name of church, we need objective standards. Thankfully, the word of God gives us such standards.

Martyn McGeown

October 11 — The False Mixed with the True

For they are not all Israel, which are of Israel.
—Romans 9:6

When people first hear the terms "true church" and "false church," they might misunderstand, and in such misunderstanding the natural reaction might be anger or indignation. Therefore, some clarification is necessary.

First, when we speak of the true church, we do not mean that there is only one true church in the world. There is one church with respect to the universal body and bride of Christ, but there are many churches with respect to the institute. In Paul's day, for example, there was a true church in Corinth, another in Ephesus, and another in Antioch—and probably multiple true churches in those cities. Today, there are true churches throughout the world. We would never be so arrogant as to assert that we are the only true church, or worse, that we are the only ones who are going to heaven!

Second, when we speak of the true church, we do not mean that all the members of that church are Christians and therefore saved. The Bible makes clear that even in the purest churches under heaven there are hypocrites. The church in Jerusalem had an Ananias and Sapphira (Acts 5:1–11), and we can be sure that in true churches today there are hypocrites. Article 29 speaks of these hypocrites "who are mixed in the church with the good, yet are not of the church, though externally in it." This is also true with respect to the children. Not all the children born and baptized in the church are elect children. "They which are the children of the flesh, these are not the children of God: but the children of the promise are counted for the seed" (Rom. 9:8). Nevertheless, because the church is the covenant community of God, it is not the calling of the church to flush out hypocrites—or to look upon everyone in the church with suspicion as a potential hypocrite—but to remain faithful to the word of God. Christ will expose hypocrites in his own way and in his own time. The carnal seed has a way of expressing itself.

When we speak of the false church, we do not mean that all the members of that church are unbelievers. The church itself is false, but God may have some of his children there. Some may be believers who are untaught and ignorant, others are careless and foolish, and others are elect and not yet converted. This in no way, however, justifies their remaining in a false church or outside a true church. We must admonish such Christians to depart from the false church and join a congregation which bears the marks of the true church. We must pray for them that God gives them the strength to obey this command.

The true/false distinction must never be an occasion for spiritual pride. If, by the grace of God, the church of which we are members remains faithful, we must thank God for preserving his church in our midst. We must also heed the earnest warnings of Christ in Revelation 2–3. Christ will take away the candlestick when a church is unfaithful. Where is the church in Ephesus today? She left her first love!

No church is immune from the threat of apostasy. Not even ours!

Martyn McGeown

October 12 — The Preaching of the Pure Doctrine of the Gospel

*Which is the church of the living God,
the pillar and ground of the truth.* —1 Timothy 3:15

The first and primary mark of the true church is the preaching of the pure doctrine of the gospel. Without this mark, a group may call itself a church, but it is not a church. Since this is the mark of the true church, this must be the priority for God's people when they seek a church.

How infrequently this is done! Often a Christian decides to move. Perhaps he moves for better employment possibilities or to be closer to family, but, before he moves, he does not even consider the question of which church he will go to. He assumes that when he gets to his new location, he will fit into one of the local churches. Then, when he starts looking seriously for a church—something he should have done before he considered moving away—he does not ask the right questions. He judges churches on their friendliness, liveliness, and service rather than on the doctrine preached.

The true church is called "the pillar and ground of the truth" (1 Tim. 3:15). This means that the calling of the church in the world is to hold up and support the truth in the world. The true church must display the truth of God's word so that her own members know it and the world around her sees it. We live in a day when "truth is fallen in the street" (Isa. 59:14), when God's "people are destroyed for lack of knowledge" (Hos. 4:6). The churches today have little interest in truth. Instead, the churches want to make the world a better place. Now, there is nothing wrong with the world becoming a better place—although it is naïve to expect the church to be able to achieve much in that area—and there is nothing wrong with Christians seeking to help the poor, but the church institute does not have that role in the world. The church has a much more important function—and one only she can do. She must preach the truth.

Notice, too, how Article 29 explains this first mark: "if the pure doctrine of the gospel is preached therein." The issue is not that there is preaching—there *must* be preaching. Churches without preaching or churches that replace preaching with entertainment are not churches according to the Bible. The issue is not that there is lively preaching, interesting preaching, or a preacher with a pleasing delivery—by all means, let the preaching be lively, interesting, and well-delivered. The issue is the content of the preaching. The issue is not that the preaching is perfect, but it must be pure, that is, it must not be mixed with errors.

Therefore, when we look for a church, we must ask this question: what does this church teach? Is there teaching—that is, preaching from the pulpit and instruction of the children in catechism? Is the teaching pure—is it biblical? Does the minister explain the Scriptures so that we and our children "grow in grace, and in the knowledge of our Lord and Saviour Jesus Christ" (2 Pet. 3:18)? Nothing else matters in a church.

Are you in such a church? Be thankful and support that church as a living member. Are you not in such a church? Seek that church without delay!

Martyn McGeown

October 13 — The Second and Third Marks

*Teaching them to observe all things whatsoever
I have commanded you.* —Matthew 28:20

The preaching of the pure gospel is the first mark of the true church. Without the preaching of the truth, there can be lively worship, interesting and friendly people, great programs for young people and the elderly, and zeal for missions and helping the poor, but there is no church! The Mormons can boast all of the above, but the Mormons are a cult. False religions and even atheistic humanists can provide much of the above, but we would not classify them as churches.

We will treat the second and third marks together because we will develop these points more at length in later articles of the Belgic Confession. Article 32 explains Christian discipline, and Articles 33–35 explain the two sacraments. These second and third marks depend on and flow out of the first. We simply cannot have the right administration of the sacraments without the pure gospel preached, and church discipline is impossible without preaching.

The two sacraments are baptism and the Lord's supper. A group of Christians without sacraments is not a church. The church must baptize and administer the Lord's supper. This is part of Christ's great commission, his instructions to his church. "All power is given unto me in heaven and in earth. Go ye therefore, and teach all nations, baptizing them in the name of the Father, and of the Son, and of the Holy Ghost: teaching them to observe all things whatsoever I have commanded you: and, lo, I am with you alway, even unto the end of the world. Amen" (Matt. 28:18–20). Notice Christ's instructions are not to engage in social work, not to entertain the youth, not to be politically active, but to preach and teach the commandments of Christ and to baptize. Part of the "all things" which Christ commanded were the sacraments (Matt. 26:26–29, 28:19) and Christian discipline (Matt. 18:15–20).

The relationship between preaching (the first mark of a true church) and the sacraments and Christian discipline (the second and third marks of a true church) is important. As we shall see in Article 33, the sacraments are signs and seals of the promises declared in the gospel. If the promises of the gospel are not preached, or if the promises of the gospel are corrupted in the preaching, how can the sacraments signify and seal those promises? Without the pure preaching of the gospel, the sacraments are meaningless! Moreover, the message proclaimed in the preaching and confirmed in the sacraments must be the same. Otherwise, there is confusion. Christian discipline enforces the doctrine and life demanded by the word of God. Without the preaching, discipline has no biblical basis. People will be placed under discipline not because their doctrine is false or their lifestyle is wicked, but because they do not please the church authorities. Moreover, without discipline, the pure preaching of the gospel will not be maintained in a church for long. There needs to be accountability, both for the pastor and the members.

Article 29 summarizes these three marks in these words: "if all things are managed according to the pure Word of God, all things contrary thereto rejected, and Jesus Christ acknowledged as the only Head of the Church."

There is the church because there is Christ—and where Christ and his church are, there must we and our children be.

Martyn McGeown

October 14 — Degrees of Truth and Error

Be watchful, and strengthen the things which remain.
—Revelation 3:2

Article 29 might give the impression that there is the true church (which is more or less perfect) and there is the false church (which is irredeemably evil) and nothing in-between. The marks of the true church are "pure doctrine," "pure administration of the sacraments," and "church discipline," which means that "all things are managed according to the pure word of God." Notice that word *pure*. It is also true that "these two churches are easily known and distinguished from each other," that is, we can know which is the true church and which is the false church.

Nevertheless, a church does not become false overnight. The sad history of Christianity tells us that a church can be a true church—even the Roman Catholic Church was true at one point—but it can depart from the truth over time. Almost all apostate churches in existence today would have been considered true churches some one hundred or two hundred years ago.

To add to our confusion, there are many more churches today than there were in 1561, when our Belgic Confession was written. In 1561, there were in Europe four kinds of churches: Roman Catholic, Reformed, Lutheran, and Anabaptist. Today, there are dozens of Presbyterian denominations, Baptist denominations, Pentecostal and Charismatic denominations, Roman Catholic, Lutheran, Anglican, and independent churches. The marks we are called to discern are the same three, but the number of possibilities is much larger. In addition, there are even within the same denomination pure and less-pure churches.

All of this makes discerning the true and false church more difficult—but not impossible. Some today try to use the "pure" and "less pure" church distinction as an excuse, saying that no church is perfect. It is true that there is no such thing as a perfect church, but that does not justify someone remaining in an obviously false church. Remember the illustration of a restaurant. There is no perfect restaurant. Does that make all restaurants equally good or suitable places to eat? Does the non-existence of a perfect restaurant mean that we should eat where there is poor hygiene, where the waitstaff are rude, and where the food is laced with poison? Of course not! You would rightly warn your friends and family against such a place. If we have discernment about our physical food, why do so few have discernment about their spiritual food?

Our calling, then, is to discern. Are the marks present in this or that church? Are the marks somewhat obscured? In what direction is that church going spiritually—is it declining or is it growing in truth? If the church is beginning to decline, how serious is the declension, and is a reformation of that church possible? Even Luther and Calvin thought long and hard before they left the Roman Catholic Church. In the end, of course, they were put out of the church.

Let us seek for wisdom—and if by the grace of God, as I believe is the case, we have true churches, let us watch and pray, lest we depart from the way of truth.

Martyn McGeown

October 15 — As for the False Church...

For the Jews had agreed already, that if any man did confess that he was Christ, he should be put out of the synagogue. —John 9:22

The false church is always a danger for Christians. The Christian has four main enemies—the flesh, the devil, the world, and the false church. The Bible is filled with warnings about "false brethren" (Gal. 2:4), false gospels (Gal. 1:8–9), false spirits and prophets (1 John 4:1–2), "false teachers" (2 Pet. 2:1), and "false apostles" (2 Cor. 11:13). Despite these warnings, many find it offensive to speak about a false church. In our tolerant age, we are supposed to accept all as true, and it seems very arrogant to call someone's church a false church.

Nevertheless, the false church does exist. Luther once said that where God plants a church, the devil builds a chapel beside it—and we could add that the devil's chapel (the false church) is often bigger, livelier, and more popular than the true church of Christ. Article 29 concludes, after identifying the marks of the true church, by warning against the false church. This is necessary because the false church never identifies itself as false. There is no "False Church of Anywhere" in your town, I assure you! The devil "is transformed into an angel of light" (2 Cor. 11:14), and his churches convince many that they are true churches.

The marks of the false church are the opposite of the marks of the true church. First, the false church despises the word of God. Where she will give the word of God lip service, her real interest is in promoting her own power. "She ascribes more power and authority to herself and her ordinances than to the word of God, and will not submit herself to the yoke of Christ" (Article 29). Thus, the false church is more concerned with pragmatism than the word of God—what works? What will make the congregation larger? What will make the church culturally acceptable? What will make the church rich and powerful? This is true of the mainstream apostate denominations as well as the megachurches. Therefore, obviously, you will not find true preaching in the false church.

Second, the false church corrupts the sacraments. She does not see the sacraments as a sacred trust, but she "adds to and takes from them as she thinks proper." The medieval Roman church did this when she corrupted the two sacraments, baptism and the Lord's supper, and added five sacraments. But Rome is not the only false church that corrupts the sacraments.

Third, the false church corrupts discipline. She "persecutes those who live holily according to the word of God, and rebuke her for her errors, covetousness, and idolatry" (Article 29). Where Christian discipline is neglected, tyranny soon follows. Such a church promotes an environment in which sin and error flourish, and when someone speaks out against sin, he will be persecuted. The Pharisees did this in Christ's day—they persecuted Christ himself. Rome did this at the time of the Belgic Confession. And churches still do this today: when a member protests against the sins of the church, he is branded a troublemaker and is expelled from the membership of the church.

When a church has departed so far from the truth that it manifests the marks of the false church, it is time to flee. God's judgment will fall on such a church. The calling is clear: "Wherefore come out from among them, and be ye separate, saith the Lord, and touch not the unclean thing; and I will receive you" (2 Cor. 6:17).

Let us pray for, seek, join, and remain in the true church!

Martyn McGeown

Article 30

CONCERNING THE GOVERNMENT OF, AND OFFICES IN, THE CHURCH

We believe that this true Church must be governed by the spiritual policy which our Lord has taught us in his Word—namely, that there must be Ministers or Pastors to preach the Word of God, and to administer the Sacraments; also elders and deacons, who, together with the pastors, form the council of the Church; that by these means the true religion may be preserved, and the true doctrine every where propagated, likewise transgressors punished and restrained by spiritual means; also that the poor and distressed may be relieved and comforted, according to their necessities. By these means everything will be carried on in the Church with good order and decency, when faithful men are chosen, according to the rule prescribed by St. Paul to Timothy.

October 16 — The Church Must Be Governed

Christ is the head of the church: and he is the saviour of the body.
—Ephesians 5:23

Articles 30–32 deal with a specific aspect of the church, the subject of church polity: "We believe that this true church must be governed." Church government is church polity. For many, church polity is a dry and boring subject, as dry and boring, they imagine, as politics are in the world. The writer of the Belgic Confession did not share such a view. He saw the necessity of good church government for the welfare of God's people.

When church authority is neglected and denied or abused and usurped, the church suffers. For many years before the Reformation, the church had suffered tyranny. The pope declared himself to be the head of the church on earth. Under him were a number of different men in different positions, each with their own rank. The Roman Catholic Church has the same governmental structure today. At the bottom are common church members without rights. They cannot appoint their own officebearers. They have no right to appeal the decisions of the church. In fact, strictly speaking, they are not the church. Only the clergy are the church. Indeed, only the pope is the church, and only they who are in communion with him can be called church. This is still Rome's position. We call it hierarchy, an ever-ascending succession of offices from parish priest through bishop, archbishop, and cardinal, to the pope himself. The Reformation rejected such a tyrannical government over the church.

On the other hand, without any government, the church suffers chaos and confusion. How is God to be worshipped? Who makes the decisions in the local congregations? Who are the members and the leaders of the church? What is their relationship? How are truth and purity to be preserved in the congregations? The Anabaptists were radicals at the time of the Reformation, who, rejecting the tyranny of the pope and his clergy, sought to rid themselves of all or almost all church government. The church became a free-for-all. There are churches today where there is no membership list, no oversight of members, no supervision of the worship services, preaching, or sacraments, and no discipline. Anything goes in the name of Christian freedom.

The Reformed churches reject both extremes. We teach freedom from the tyranny and abuse of hierarchy, but we also refuse to live in anarchy, a word which means *having no ruler*. Anarchy, both in church and state, is harmful.

We refuse anarchy because Christ is the head of his church. As the head, he is not only the source of the church's life, but he also rules the church. Without the headship of Christ, the church would be chaotic, and God would be dishonored. A body which refuses to listen to the head is a monstrosity. A body which seeks to rule itself without a head is impossible. How thankful we must be that Christ has not left us headless. He is our loving and sovereign head. Let us submit ourselves gladly to him in all things, including submission to the church government which he has appointed.

Martyn McGeown

October 17 — The Safety of Christ's Yoke

*Take my yoke upon you, and learn of me; for
I am meek and lowly in heart: and ye shall find rest unto your souls.
For my yoke is easy, and my burden is light.* —Matthew 11:29–30

Government is everywhere. In the family, the husband and father is the head of the home. Wives are called to submit to their husbands. Husbands are called to rule their wives in love. Children are called to obey their parents. Citizens are subject to civil magistrates and government officials. Government is essential for the well-being of any society.

The church must be governed also. Many Christians agree that the church universal is under the headship of Christ. All Christians are called to obey and serve him. But many Christians do not agree that they must submit to the government of a local congregation. This is because they fail to recognize that Christ rules his people by his grace and Holy Spirit through his word in the church institute. Article 28 has already mentioned this: being a member of the church includes "submitting [ourselves] to the doctrine and discipline [of the church], bowing [our] necks under the yoke of Jesus Christ."

The government that Christ has ordained for his church is neither tyrannical nor negligent. Christ loves his church, and therefore he has given to her a specific form of government for her edification. Paul writes: "For though I should boast somewhat more of our authority, which the Lord hath given us for edification, and not for your destruction, I should not be ashamed" (2 Cor. 10:8). Elsewhere, Scripture states: "Obey them that have the rule over you, and submit yourselves: for they watch for your souls, as they that must give account, that they may do it with joy, and not with grief: for that is unprofitable for you" (Heb. 13:17). And again, Paul beseeches: "Know them which labour among you, and are over you in the Lord, and admonish you; and to esteem them very highly in love for their work's sake. And be at peace among yourselves" (1 Thess. 5:12–13). No wonder the Bible calls church leaders shepherds. They must love and care for the sheep as Christ himself, who died for them, loves them, and cares for them. Peter writes: "Feed the flock of God which is among you, taking the oversight thereof, not by constraint, but willingly; not for filthy lucre, but of a ready mind; neither as being lords over God's heritage, but being ensamples to the flock" (1 Pet. 5:2–3). Paul warns the elders in Ephesus about this: "Take heed therefore unto yourselves, and to all the flock, over the which the Holy Ghost hath made you overseers, to feed the church of God, which he hath purchased with his own blood" (Acts 20:28).

The Christian needs to be in a church with good government because of the many false teachers who prey on Christians. Ordinarily, Christians not under the oversight of good elders will be easy prey for a convincing heretic. No wonder Jesus was so concerned for the people of Israel in his day: the spiritual leadership had degenerated so much that wolves instead of shepherds ruled over the flock. The flock was "as sheep having no shepherd" (Matt. 9:36).

Are you a member of a good Reformed church with a faithful pastor, wise elders, and compassionate deacons? Be thankful for that blessing! If you are not, seek shelter under the wings of Christ's church for the good of your own soul and that of your family!

Martyn McGeown

October 18   **That Spiritual Polity**

For the weapons of our warfare are not carnal,
but mighty through God. —2 Corinthians 10:4

Jesus Christ is king and head of his church. Every Christian is called to submit to his yoke, and this includes submission to him in the local congregation. Article 27 already taught us about the kingship of Christ: "This church hath been from the beginning of the world, and will be to the end thereof; which is evident from this, that Christ is an eternal King, which without subjects he cannot be." The subjects or citizens of King Jesus are the members of the church. Christ also rules over the wicked, but he rules over them in a different sense. We speak of Christ's rule of power over the whole universe, and his rule of grace over his people, the church. That distinction is very important in our consideration of church government.

Christ rules over the wicked with "a rod of iron; [he dashes] them in pieces like a potter's vessel" (Ps. 2:9), and he exerts his almighty power for the deliverance and safety of his church (Eph. 1:22; Rev. 19:15). It is not, therefore, the role of the church to Christianize the world, to bring all aspects of human society under Christian principles, or to bring heaven to earth. The kingdom of Christ, manifested in the church, is not carnal, that is, fleshly, or governed by fleshly, worldly principles such as brute force, political intrigue, or numerical strength (John 18:36–37). Jesus warned his disciples: "The kings of the Gentiles exercise lordship over them; and they that exercise authority upon them are called benefactors. But ye shall not be so: but he that is greatest among you, let him be as the younger; and he that is chief, as he that doth serve" (Luke 22:25–26). When men through selfish ambition seek to govern the church for their own personal advancement, they do damage to the church and dishonor the church's Lord.

For this reason, Article 30 reminds us that "this true church must be governed by the spiritual polity which our Lord hath taught us in his word." Notice that word *spiritual*. The three words we should remember when we speak of church polity are *grace, word,* and *spiritual*.

First, the power by which Christ rules in his church is the power of grace. Grace is that beautiful attitude of favor that God displays to unworthy and undeserving sinners. But grace is also a power. By the power of grace, God subdues our sins and renews us according to the image of Jesus Christ. Grace is a greater power than any power the world possesses: grace makes of a sinner a saint; of a blasphemer a singer of God's praises; of a mean-spirited, spiteful, selfish, hateful person a lover of God and his neighbor. Second, the standard by which Christ rules his church is the word of God, the Bible. This means that the church is not governed by the opinions of the powerful or more influential members of the church, by the whims of the young people, by the dictates of society; but that the whole church submits together to the word of God in all things. Quite simply, there is one voice to be heeded and obeyed in the church: Christ's as he speaks in holy Scripture! Third, this power can be summarized in one word: *spiritual*. The church does not rely on carnal means to bring people into the church or to keep them in the church. The Spirit, by his grace and word, is active in the church for the glory of God.

Is that how the church of which you are a member is governed? Then you may know yourself to be under the care of the Good Shepherd.

Martyn McGeown

October 19 — Ruled by Officebearers

That thou shouldest set in order the things that are wanting, and ordain elders in every city. —Titus 1:5

Paul left Titus on the island of Crete to deal with unfinished ecclesiastical business: he had to ordain elders in every city. For the apostle Paul, a church is not organized, and therefore something is wanting (or lacking) if officebearers, especially elders, have not been ordained to rule the local congregations. This is very enlightening for our modern age. It is not enough for a group of Christians to meet together in someone's house to have informal Bible studies or even to listen to sermons on the internet. Christian fellowship is good, but that in itself is not a church. A church institute does not exist without elders. A group of Christians might have a missionary working among them, but without their own elders, they cannot call themselves a church. They are a fellowship, and they should seek to be organized as a church. Until they do, there is something wanting there.

Article 30 makes the same point about the "spiritual polity" by which the true church must be governed: "namely, that there must be ministers…also elders and deacons, who, together with the pastors, form the council of the Church." These men—ministers, elders, and deacons—are officebearers. They are necessary for a church to exist in any given place.

An officebearer is one who occupies an office. By *office* we mean a position of authority. Specifically, an officebearer in the church is a man who is called by Christ through the church to occupy a position of authority in the church. As an officebearer, that man represents Jesus Christ, who, as the prophet, priest, and king, is the officebearer from whom all other officebearers derive their authority. In the Old Testament, God called and equipped men to serve him in the offices of prophet, priest, and king. In the New Testament, every Christian occupies the office of believer and is a prophet, priest, and king by the Spirit and grace of Christ. Besides the office of believer, there are the special offices of minister, elder, and deacon. These offices correspond roughly to the offices of prophet (minister), priest (deacon), and king (elder).

There are some who insist that the office of believer in the New Testament does away with the need for special offices in the New Testament church. Their cry is "every man ministry." But we must recognize that Jesus himself has ordained how he will govern his church. "Every man ministry" is not the rule of Scripture, but the cry of a rebellious spirit. It requires meekness and humility to submit to the church government which Christ has instituted.

An officebearer is not a mere functionary. He has real, spiritual authority. 1 Thessalonians 5:12 says that officebearers are "over you in the Lord." That authority comes from Jesus Christ himself. Christ preaches to us through the ministers; Christ governs us through the elders; Christ administers mercy to us through the deacons. We must, therefore, recognize Christ's authority in the godly officebearers whom he has sent. This means "that I…submit myself with due obedience to all their good instruction and correction, and also bear patiently with their infirmities, since it is God's will to govern us by their hand."* This also means that officebearers must give account to Christ for the way in which they have exercised their office. An awesome, but a blessed, responsibility indeed (Heb. 13:17; 1 Pet. 5:4)!

Do you love your officebearers, pray for them, and submit to them for Christ's sake?

Martyn McGeown

---

* Heidelberg Catechism, in Schaff, *Creeds of Christendom*, 3:345.

October 20 — Temporary, Extraordinary Officebearers

And he gave some, apostles; and some, prophets;
and some, evangelists; and some, pastors and teachers. —Ephesians 4:11

The subject of church office is very important. The question is often asked, "Which offices must the church have?" Some, such as the Roman Catholic Church, have many offices foreign to Scripture, such as the pope, cardinal, archbishop, archdeacons, and many others. Others, such as some modern megachurches, have multiplied positions in the churches—they have senior pastors, associate pastors, executive pastors, youth pastors, worship leaders, youth coordinators, and much more—but neglect the biblical offices. Others, such as the Charismatics, claim that the office of prophet, evangelist, and apostle remain in the church. The Reformed position is that Christ has appointed three permanent offices: minister, elder, and deacon. These three offices are sufficient for the good governance of the church.

Ephesians 4:11 lists several offices, some of which were temporary, extraordinary offices. The most significant of these is apostle. Even at the time of the writing of the New Testament, the office of apostle was limited to the eleven disciples, Matthias, and Paul (Acts 1:22; 9:15; 26:15–18). "Are all apostles?" asks Paul rhetorically in 1 Corinthians 12:29. The Bible is clear that the office of apostle passed away with the completion of the Bible by John when he received the Revelation. We see this, first, because the apostles were a foundational office: that is, the apostles were called to build the foundation of the New Testament church (Eph. 2:20). Once that foundation was built—upon the writings of the apostles and prophets—the need for foundation-builders passed away. Second, we know that no man occupies the office of apostle today because of the unique qualifications of an apostle. An apostle had to be an eyewitness of the risen Lord Jesus Christ (Acts 1:22; 1 Cor. 9:1–2). An apostle had to be able to prove his apostolic credentials by miracles (2 Cor. 12:12; Rom. 15:19; Heb. 2:3–4). No man today—despite the claims of modern Charismatics—can prove such credentials. Third, an apostle, by virtue of his office, had unique authority. This included infallible teaching authority, authority of government over all the churches, and authority of discipline (1 Cor. 7:17; 14:37; 2 Cor. 10:8; 11:28). No man today can claim such authority over all the churches. Thus, we must reject all modern claimants to the apostolic office (Rev. 2:2).

Besides apostles, there were evangelists and prophets in the New Testament church. An evangelist is not merely a church planter as we might understand that word today. An evangelist—such as Timothy, Titus, or Philip—was an apostolic assistant. The work of an evangelist today is included in the role of a minister (2 Tim. 4:5). A prophet was a person who, before the completion of Scripture, received and communicated direct messages from God. Agabus was such a prophet (Acts 11:28; 21:10). With the completion of Scripture, direct communication with God in the form of special revelation has ceased. This was another foundational office which is no longer necessary in the modern church (Eph. 2:20; Heb. 1:1–3).

The extraordinary offices have fulfilled their purpose. Now we have the fullness of the Spirit and the completed Scriptures (2 Tim. 3:16).

But the permanent, special offices of minister, elder, and deacon remain.

Martyn McGeown

October 21 — Male Officebearers Only

But I suffer not a woman to teach,
nor to usurp authority over the man, but to be in silence. —1 Timothy 2:12

Male headship is a doctrine of the word of God which brings the church into conflict with the world. Faced with modern feminism, many churches are tempted to open the offices of minister, elder, and deacon to women. The Reformed churches, in faithfulness to Christ, must resist. The passages which address the subject of officebearers in the New Testament church all teach that men, and not women, must be in those offices. The first deacons were men: "Look ye out among you seven men" (Acts 6:3). In the pastoral epistles to Timothy and Titus, Paul restricts the offices to men. The Belgic Confession speaks about "faithful men [being] chosen according to the rule prescribed by St. Paul in his epistle to Timothy" (Article 30). In 1 Timothy 3:1–13, Paul gives the qualifications for elders and deacons, one of which is that he be "the husband [if he is married] of one wife" (vv. 2, 12). Clearly, only men are included in this description. The same instructions are given in Titus 1:5–9. However, 1 Timothy 2 is even clearer. There Paul states expressly: "Let the woman learn in silence with all subjection. But I suffer not a woman to teach, nor to usurp authority over the man, but to be in silence" (vv. 11–12).

We must notice, of course, that Jesus was not anti-women. Christ had many female followers who were devoted to him and served him (Luke 8:2–3). Women were even privileged to be the first to see him alive after his resurrection (Matt. 28:5–10). Women were present in the upper room on the day of Pentecost (Acts 1:14). Women have been and still are members in the church and of great service to the church (Acts 5:14; 8:12; 9:36; 17:12; 21:9; Rom. 16:1–2; Gal. 3:28; Phil. 4:3). But for all that, Jesus appointed only men to be officebearers in his church. Women must not feel slighted by this, because godly women will humbly submit to Christ's will as it is revealed in Scripture; and, besides this, the offices of the church are not positions of prestige, but places of lowly service. Male officebearers, called to be pastors, elders, and deacons, must remember this. They are not called for their self-aggrandizement, but to serve the saints.

Feminists, however, object that the rule prescribed by Paul is only Paul's opinion, and that Paul was influenced by his rabbinical teaching as a Jew. This is an attack on the inspiration of the Bible. Paul is an apostle of Jesus Christ who speaks with the authority of the one who sent him. Before he introduces specific teaching on the position of men and women in the church, he underlines the authority he has as an apostle: "Whereunto I am ordained a preacher, and an apostle, (I speak the truth in Christ, and lie not;) a teacher of the Gentiles in faith and verity" (1 Tim. 2:7). Also, in 1 Corinthians 14—after he teaches that women are to be silent in the churches—Paul writes: "if any man think himself to be a prophet, or spiritual, let him acknowledge that the things that I write unto you are the commandments of the Lord" (v. 37).

A humble Christian woman will listen to the word of God, even when her flesh is offended by it. Christ ordained male officebearers for the church's good, including the good of the women of the church.

Martyn McGeown

October 22 — Pastors to Preach the Word

And how shall they hear without a preacher?
—Romans 10:14

The first of the three offices which Christ has given to his church is the minister or pastor. Many believe—and, sadly, some ministers do nothing to dispel this myth—that the minister is the boss of the congregation. Nothing could be further from the truth. Although the minister has real authority in the church, he is a servant of the congregation. The word *minister* means *to serve*. Woe to that minister who uses the ministry as the Pharisees did: they "love the uppermost rooms at feasts, and the chief seats in the synagogues, and greetings in the markets, and to be called of men, Rabbi, Rabbi" (Matt. 23:6–7)! Instead, a minister knows that he gives himself to the labors of the ministry so that he might serve the Lord Jesus by edifying the church. The other title of the minister is *pastor*. This word means *shepherd*. The minister or pastor must remember the words of the Lord Jesus to Peter: "Feed my lambs...Feed my sheep" (John 21:15–16). Woe unto the shepherd who feeds himself and neglects the sheep (Ezek. 34:2)!

The minister or pastor is a servant of Jesus Christ and a shepherd of the sheep with real, spiritual authority. He rules with the elders in the consistory of the church. The main work of a pastor, however, is to preach. The apostles summarized the minister's calling: "we will give ourselves continually to prayer and to the ministry of the word" (Acts 6:4). The minister is not a social worker but a preacher. Therefore, the bulk of his time and effort must be devoted to the preparing of sermons, as well as the other teaching he gives throughout the week. This includes catechism classes for the youth, Bible studies, public lectures, and writing projects. For this reason, a congregation must not be surprised or offended if their pastor spends a lot of time in his study. That is where he prepares the sermons and other materials with which he is called to feed the flock. Without that time in the study, he has very little to say when he is in the pulpit.

The main purposes of pastors, as outlined in Article 30, are first: "that by these means the true religion may be preserved" and, second, that "the true doctrine [be] everywhere propagated." Preaching, which, as Article 29 already explained, is the first mark of a true church, is necessary for the wellbeing—even the being—of the church. And preaching is not the task of just anybody. A man must be called through the church by Jesus Christ himself to preach. Paul asks the question: "And how shall they preach, except they be sent?" (Rom. 10:15). Only then is the word which the church hears the authoritative, official word of Jesus Christ. Anyone can speak about Christ, but only through a preacher does Christ himself speak.

Without the preaching, the church cannot continue. She lacks the main means by which she worships God. She lacks the chief means of grace. She lacks faithful instruction from the word of God. This is one of the main reasons why the modern churches are so weak. It makes one want to weep to see the confusion and ignorance of many Christians. Why? Because ministers are doing everything except preaching (Isa. 56:10)!

How thankful we must be for faithful preachers! How we must pray for our preachers! How we must pray that the Lord would raise up—even of our own sons—more faithful preachers so that the gospel can be preached to us, to our children and to the ends of the earth!

Martyn McGeown

October 23 — Preaching: The Voice of Jesus Christ

*My sheep hear my voice, and I know them,
and they follow me.* —John 10:27

There is much confusion about preaching. For some, preaching is that intolerably boring and seemingly endless part of the service where the minister drones from the pulpit. For others, preaching is the minister sharing a thought from the Bible. For others, preaching is a short, entertaining message or story on how to live a better life. If we do not know what preaching is, how will we ever learn our need for it and appreciate what a gift Christ has given to us?

First, the Greek verb *to preach* in the New Testament is *to herald*. A herald is an official commissioned messenger of the king. This means, first, that a preacher brings no message of his own. The calling of a preacher—and woe to the preacher who does not do this—is to communicate what the king announces to the people. He may not add something to the message to make it palatable to the hearers; he may not take something away from the message to make it more relevant. It is the word of the king! And the king of whom we speak is the Lord Jesus Christ. Since this is the case, the minister must preach the word of God. This does not mean that the minister merely mentions a Bible passage occasionally in his sermon or even uses a text as a peg on which to hang his message. This means that the sermon must be an explanation, an exposition of the Bible itself.

Second, as a herald, the preacher must be sent by King Jesus himself. No man has the right to send himself, to make himself a minister or a preacher. A man might be able to stand before the people and give a good explanation of the Bible, but that in itself is not preaching if that man was not sent by Jesus Christ. Only a herald has the right to speak authoritatively for the king. Only a preacher has the right to preach authoritatively for Jesus Christ. "And how shall they preach, except they be sent?" (Rom. 10:15).

Third, since a preacher is an authoritative herald of Jesus Christ, Christ himself is pleased to speak through him. Thus, when you hear faithful preaching, you do not merely hear the voice of a man. As wonderful as it might seem, you hear the voice of Christ himself. That is why the Reformed have said, "The preaching of the word of God is the word of God," or, "The preaching of the gospel is the voice of Christ." Believers hear the voice of Christ—as he himself promised (John 10:27)—not as voices in their heads but in the preaching. Paul makes this very clear in two passages. "How shall they believe in him whom they have not heard? And how shall they hear without a preacher?" (Rom. 10:14, my translation). The better translation is not "of whom they have not heard" but "whom they have not heard." In preaching, we do not merely hear of or about Christ; we hear Christ himself. "But ye have not so learned Christ; if so be that ye have heard him, and have been taught by him, as the truth is in Jesus" (Eph. 4:20–21). The Ephesians, who had never seen Jesus in the flesh, heard him (not merely about him) in the preaching of the gospel.

That gives preaching its authority. When preaching is faithful to the word of God, Christ himself speaks to the church. Christ commands; Christ rebukes; Christ instructs; Christ edifies; Christ comforts. Shall we neglect to hear—or even despise—the voice of Christ? We do when we neglect, despise, and refuse to hear the preaching of the gospel in a true church.

Martyn McGeown

October 24 — The Office of Elder or Bishop

*To all the saints in Christ Jesus which are at Philippi,
with the bishops and deacons.* —Philippians 1:1

The New Testament speaks of three offices in the church: minister, elder, and deacon. There are two words for elder in the New Testament. The first is *presbuteros*. From this word the term *Presbyterian* is derived. The second is *episcopos*. From this word the term *Episcopalian* is derived. Our Bibles usually translate *presbuteros* as *elder* and *episcopos* as *bishop*. But we must not imagine that the modern use of terms such as *Presbyterianism* or *Episcopalianism* accurately reflects the meaning of *presbuteros* and *episcopos* in the New Testament.

The term *elder* is already found in the Old Testament. There, the older, and therefore supposedly wiser, men of Israel exercised a leadership role among the people (Ex. 18:21–22). There were also judges among the people (2 Chron. 19:6–7). In the days of Christ, Israel had elders who joined with the chief priests to condemn Jesus (Matt. 27:1). This office passed over into the church of Jesus Christ. The term *elder* (*presbuteros*) means, at its most basic, an older man. Older men were generally chosen as elders because an elder required the gravity, soberness, and wisdom that come from experience and are often absent in younger men. The office of elder is further described by the second word, *episcopos*, often translated as *bishop* in the New Testament. The word means *one who looks over or oversees*.

Episcopalianism errs when it treats elder and bishop (overseer) as distinct offices. Episcopalianism (with Roman Catholicism) errs even more grievously when it treats the office of bishop as higher in rank than the office of elder. Although the Bible uses two words, they are used interchangeably of the one office. In Titus 1:5, Paul commands Titus to "ordain elders [*presbuteros*] in every city," and then immediately adds, "for a bishop [*episcopos*] must be..." (v. 7). In Acts 20, Paul calls the elders (*presbuteros*) of the church of Ephesus (v. 17), but he reminds them: "Take heed therefore unto yourselves, and to all the flock, over the which the Holy Ghost hath made you overseers [*episcopos*]" (v. 28). Peter makes the same point in 1 Peter 5 where he writes, "the elders [*presbuteros*] which are among you I exhort" (v. 1). Then he adds: "Feed the flock of God which is among you, taking the oversight [*episcopos*] thereof" (v. 2).

We can see what the work of an elder is from the name *episcopos*. An elder is (usually) an older, wiser, more experienced man who oversees the church. This means that elders have real spiritual authority over the whole church and over every member. They are the official representatives of Jesus Christ, through whom he is pleased to rule. Article 30 names some of the responsibilities of elders. They must see to it that the word of God is faithfully preached; that "true religion [is] preserved and the true doctrine everywhere propagated;" that "transgressors [in the congregation are] punished and restrained by spiritual means;" that "the poor and distressed may be relieved and comforted;" and that "everything will be carried on in the church with good order and decency."

This means that the elders in the church oversee the entire work of the church—the preaching, worship, sacraments, catechism classes, diaconate work, discipline, and even the property of the congregation. They do so for the welfare of the church.

Respect those men, pray for them, and submit to them for Christ's sake.

Martyn McGeown

October 25 — The Plurality of Elders

And when they had ordained them elders in every church...
—Acts 14:23

Elders are so important for the church that without elders, there is no church. A group of Christians without elders—even if they have a missionary working among them to preach the gospel—is not a church in the proper, official sense. Such a group of Christians may enjoy fellowship, but they cannot call themselves a church. They should seek to become organized as a local, instituted congregation of Jesus Christ with "bishops [elders] and deacons" (Phil. 1:1). Until they are organized, something is wanting (missing or lacking) there (Tit. 1:5).

Another important principle of Reformed church polity is the plurality of elders. A group of Christians must have, besides the minister, a minimum of two elders and one deacon to be an instituted church. Ideally, the church should have more. Assemblies of these officebearers have specific names. In the days of Christ, Israel's religious affairs were governed by the Jewish council or Sanhedrin. Today, Presbyterians speak of a session—a sitting of elders—and Reformed churches speak of a consistory. The consistory consists of the elders, usually with the minister who is also an elder (1 Tim. 5:17). The minister, elders, and deacons are together called the council. Thus, Article 30 teaches: "[there must be] elders and deacons, who, together with the pastors, form the council of the church."

Why a plurality of elders? First, this is the practice of the apostolic church as recorded in the New Testament. On Paul's first missionary journey, many believed in Christ in various cities of Antioch, Iconium, Lystra, and Derbe. On the way back through these cities, we read that "they had ordained them elders in every church" (Acts 14:23). Paul and Barnabas do not ordain one elder in every church. Nor does Paul ordain a bishop to rule over several churches in one area. Elders (plural) are ordained in every church (singular). Thus, we have example. We also have precept. Paul commands Titus to ordain a plurality of elders on the island of Crete. "For this cause left I thee in Crete, that thou shouldest set in order the things that are wanting, and ordain elders in every city, as I had appointed thee" (Tit. 1:5). Paul writes: "elders [plural] in every city [singular]." In fact, in every place in the New Testament where elders are mentioned in a local church setting, there is a plurality of elders—more than one elder per congregation (Acts 20:17; 1 Tim. 5:17; James 5:14; 1 Pet. 5:1). Paul only speaks of elder (singular) when he is outlining the various qualifications for an individual elder (1 Tim. 3:1–7) or where he is dealing with the discipline of an individual elder (1 Tim. 5:19).

There is great wisdom in the practice of the plurality of elders. One man—even well-intentioned—can be corrupted by power. Other men are a check on folly and sinful ambition. The Reformed have always feared placing too much power into the hands of one man. The irony is that when a church refuses to have biblical officebearers, often one man with great gifts and abilities will naturally rise to the top and become a tyrant. Better by far to adopt the government which Christ has ordained: "Where no counsel is, the people fall: but in the multitude of counsellors there is safety" (Prov. 11:14).

Martyn McGeown

October 26 — **Transgressors Punished and Restrained by Spiritual Means**

Whatsoever ye shall bind on earth shall be bound in heaven: and whatsoever ye shall loose on earth shall be loosed in heaven. —Matthew 18:18

We have seen that the elders and ministers together make up the consistory which rules the local congregation. Paul speaks of two kinds of elders in 1 Timothy 5:17, "Let the elders that rule well be counted worthy of double honour, especially they who labour in the word and doctrine." All the elders rule, and all the elders must have some capacity for teaching—in the absence of ministers, they may be called to teach catechism classes; they are required to teach the people by word and example, privately and from house to house (1 Tim. 3:2; Tit. 1:9). Among the elders, some are called to preach and teach full time. These men are the pastors or ministers, and for that work they are supported by the congregations (1 Tim. 5:18).

One important work that the consistory performs is discipline. This is the subject of Article 32, but we should mention it here because Article 30 makes a very important point about that work which falls under the remit of the eldership. "Transgressors [may be] punished and restrained by spiritual means."

For some modern Christians, such language is disturbing. Do the elders of the church really have the authority to punish and restrain transgressors? Punishment and restraint sound very medieval. Perhaps we have visions of the rack, thumbscrews, and other horrific torture devices! But the Belgic Confession is very careful in the wording: "by spiritual means." This is important to remember because Christ has given authority in various spheres. In the home, Christ has ordained that the husband be the head. In the state, Christ has ordained civil government and given to it the power of the sword (Rom. 13:3–4). Therefore, the civil government can use various physical means to restrain and punish criminals: fines, imprisonment, and even the death penalty. But Christ has not given the power of the sword to the church. In the Old Testament, in the nation of Israel, there was a blurring of roles. In Israel, the elders could inflict physical punishment, even death by stoning (Deut. 21:18–21). In the New Testament, the church has only spiritual means for punishing and restraining members who walk in sin. But those means must not be despised.

The church has spiritual means which are mighty in the hand of Christ. Through the spiritual means—which Christ calls "the keys of the kingdom" (Matt. 16:18–19; 18:18)—Christ opens the kingdom to some and shuts it against others. To be admitted into the kingdom of heaven is a far greater blessing than to receive a passport, visa, or citizenship in any earthly nation. To be excluded from the kingdom of heaven is far worse than banishment, imprisonment, or even death. This does not mean—as we shall see in Article 32—that the church has the right to throw out of the kingdom whomever the elders deem unworthy. When the spiritual means are used correctly, Christ himself admits some into and excludes some from the kingdom: "Whatsoever ye shall bind on earth shall be bound in heaven: and whatsoever ye shall loose on earth shall be loosed in heaven" (Matt. 18:18).

The preaching of the gospel and Christian discipline used as the keys of the kingdom of heaven are real, awesome, spiritual powers!

No kingdom on earth has power as great as that!

Martyn McGeown

October 27 — **Everything With Good Order And Decency**

Let all things be done decently and in order.
—1 Corinthians 14:40

In Corinth, chaos, confusion, and disorder were seriously threatening the welfare of the church. A survey of Paul's first letter to the Corinthians reveals disunity and schism (1:10–11), immaturity and carnality (3:1–3), gross sins tolerated in the congregation and not addressed by the elders (5:1–2), civil lawsuits among the members (6:1–2), confusion over the subject of marriage and divorce (7:1–39), confusion over meats offered to idols and idolatry itself (8:1–13; 10:19–33), gluttony and drunkenness at the Lord's table (11:20–22), confusion and misuse of spiritual gifts without the exercise of love, chaos in the worship services (12:1–14:40) and false views on the doctrine of the resurrection (ch. 15).

This survey might be surprising to some because many have an almost romantic idealism about the early church as it is described in Acts and the epistles. "If only we could go back to the way it was before so many man-made doctrines and practices were adopted," is the cry of many modern Christians. But take off those rose-tinted spectacles! Churches like Corinth and the churches in Galatia were seriously threatened by false doctrine and evil practices. Much of what Paul wrote to these churches—and we have not even considered the letters to the seven churches in Revelation 2–3—is rebuke! For example, Paul writes concerning the Corinthians' celebration of the Lord's supper: "When ye come together therefore into one place, this is not to eat the Lord's supper. For in eating every one taketh before other his supper: and one is hungry, and another is drunken…What shall I say to you? shall I praise you in this? I praise you not" (1 Cor. 11:20–22). Having described what the Corinthians did, Paul explained what the Corinthians ought to do. Later in the epistle, Paul described their worship. But this is not to give us an example of how we should worship God. Quite the opposite—he wrote this to show the Corinthians that they should not worship God that way because it is disorderly!

26. How is it then, brethren? when ye come together, every one of you hath a psalm, hath a doctrine, hath a tongue, hath a revelation, hath an interpretation. Let all things be done unto edifying…

33. For God is not the author of confusion, but of peace, as in all churches of the saints…

40. Let all things be done decently and in order. (1 Cor. 14:26, 33, 40)

Decency and order do not restrict the Spirit. The Spirit as God is not the author of confusion, but he is the Spirit of order and decency. Therefore a spiritual church is an orderly church. A disordered, chaotic church where everyone does what seems good to them, is not a spiritual church. The Spirit is grieved there.

Decency and *order* are watchwords in the Reformed churches. Christ has given officebearers to the churches so that the business of the church is conducted decently and in order. This decency and order apply to the lives of the members, the instruction given in catechism and from the pulpit, the worship services, including the administration of the sacraments, and the meetings of the officebearers in consistory and council. Does that sound stuffy and restrictive? On the contrary, it is good for the church. Be thankful for decency and order in the church and seek to promote it by your good behavior and submission to God-appointed officebearers for Christ's sake and God's glory.

Martyn McGeown

October 28 — The Office of Deacon

It is not reason that we should leave the word of God, and serve tables. Wherefore, brethren, look ye out among you seven men of honest report, full of the Holy Ghost and wisdom, whom we may appoint over this business. —Acts 6:2–3

Christ, who loves his church, has not only given himself for her salvation, but he has given her gifts at his ascension. These gifts are many, but one important gift is officebearers, in particular "pastors and teachers" (Eph. 4:8, 11). These officebearers are necessary for the good government and welfare of the church. We have examined ministers and elders. The third permanent special office in the church of Jesus Christ is the deacon. Collectively, deacons are called the diaconate. The word *deacon* comes from the Greek word *diakonos*. The non-technical meaning of *diakonos* is *servant*. It is important to understand that because not all references in the New Testament are to the office of deacon proper. Sometimes *diakonos* means only *servant*, and in those cases, even women are called deaconesses. Therefore, not all servants are deacons, but all deacons are servants.

The deacons, like the ministers and elders, hold an office, a position of authority. This is clear from 1 Timothy 3 where the qualifications of elders are set forth. Immediately after giving the qualifications for one office, the elder, Paul writes, "Likewise must the deacons be…" (v. 8). The deacons are also included with elders in Paul's greeting to the Philippians (Phil. 1:1). We must not think that the deacons are men who merely deal with some financial matters in the congregation by collecting and counting the offerings. Their work is official, important, ecclesiastical, spiritual work.

Many churches do not have deacons. Others call men deacons, but these men do not do the work of deacons. There is probably more confusion over this office than the other two offices. Does a deacon just look after the money? Is he just a charitable worker? What does the deacon do? How are the congregations supposed to relate to the deacons? The work of the deacons is outlined in Article 30 briefly thus: "there must be… deacons…that the poor and distressed may be relieved and comforted, according to their necessities." Reformed churches have often summed up that work in one phrase, the ministry of mercy.

First, deacons are called to collect the alms. The word *alms* means *mercy*. Many churches have a benevolent fund for monies particularly designated for the relief of the poor. Almsgiving is a Christian duty, calling, and privilege. Collecting the alms is a serious responsibility. Deacons must be honest men without covetousness. Second, deacons are called to distribute the alms. Deacons must be wise in this distribution so that the truly needy are not neglected, and the greedy, lazy, and irresponsible are not encouraged in sinful behavior. The deacons, therefore, do not simply give away "free money" without careful and prayerful thought, and this work, too, is supervised by the elders of the congregation.

Our calling toward the deacons is, first, to give generously. This makes diaconate work easier. Second, we must alert the deacons to needs in the congregation. The deacons are given by Christ to help the poor and distressed. But, they need to be told about poverty and distress! Third, there must be a willingness to seek help from the deacons. Let not shame keep us from Christ's ministers of mercy!

Martyn McGeown

October 29 — The Poor Relieved and Comforted

Let him labour, working with his hands the thing which is good, that he may have to give to him that needeth. —Ephesians 4:28

Poverty is a reality in this fallen world. The unbelieving world imagines that with enough social programs they will be able to eradicate poverty. Jesus Christ said that there would always be poverty (John 12:8). God has always commanded that his people show concern for the poor. However, what many Christians have not noticed is that the primary concern for the poor must be for the poor among the people of God. In Israel, God commanded that the poor brethren (fellow Israelites within the covenant community) be cared for by the generosity of fellow Israelites. There were various provisions in the law. For example, the poor could glean the fields of the rich (Lev. 19:10), the poor could be redeemed (25:25; Deut 15:7–11), and the sacrificial offerings were less demanding for the impoverished (Lev. 5:7). When the prophets preached against the exploitation of the poor by the rich, they had primarily the poor within Israel in mind (Amos 5:11–12; 8:4–6). In the New Testament, the apostle Paul did not seek to help all the poor of the Roman empire. He did help his neighbor when opportunity arose. Paul's primary concern, however (apart from the preaching of the gospel, of course), was the poor in the church. To that end, Paul organized collections for the impoverished saints in Jerusalem (Acts 24:17; Rom. 15:26; 2 Cor. 8–9; Gal. 2:10). Both James and John made the same application to the poor in the congregations (James 1:27; 2:14–16; 1 John 3:17–18). This does not mean that the church refuses to help the poor who are not members of the congregation, but it does mean that the primary focus of the work of the deacons is the poor of Christ.

The poor in the church of Jesus Christ must not be despised or neglected. They must not be viewed as a burden or a nuisance. It must be seen as a great privilege for us to help the poor, for in so doing we serve Jesus Christ himself (Matt. 25:34–40). But at the same time, we must not be naïve. It is not the Christian's calling to give money to everyone who claims to be poor. This is where the deacons need much wisdom. Paul gives some principles to Timothy in his first epistle. First, the primary responsibility for the poor within the congregation is with their own family. Paul has sharp words for Christians who neglect their impoverished relatives. The church should not be charged with their financial support (5:4, 8, 16). Second, Paul insists that people work, and those who refuse to work may not eat (2 Thess. 3:10). Idleness and dependency by the poor are to be discouraged (Eph. 4:28; 2 Thess. 3:10–12). Indeed, it is good for the deacons to encourage budgeting, thrift, and stewardship, for often poverty is caused by mismanagement of funds. Third, those who are poor indeed must be helped, not only financially and generously, but with comfortable words of Scripture.

The deacons are not mere social workers. They are not like the clerks in the social welfare office of the secular state. They are the official representatives of the merciful Christ who comes to relieve the poor in the churches. Their work is as spiritual as that of the ministers and elders.

Let them be received as such.

Martyn McGeown

Article 31

OF THE MINISTERS, ELDERS, AND DEACONS

We believe that the Ministers of God's Word, and the Elders and Deacons, ought to be chosen to their respective offices by a lawful election of the Church, with calling upon the name of the Lord, and in that order which the Word of God teacheth. Therefore every one must take heed not to intrude himself by indecent means, but is bound to wait till it shall please God to call him; that he may have testimony of his calling, and be certain and assured that it is of the Lord.

As for the Ministers of God's Word, they have equally the same power and authority wheresoever they are, as they are all Ministers of Christ, the only universal Bishop, and the only Head of the Church.

Moreover, that this holy ordinance of God may not be violated or slighted, we say that every one ought to esteem the Ministers of God's Word and the Elders of the Church very highly for their work's sake, and be at peace with them without murmuring, strife, or contention, as much as possible.

October 30 — Lawful Election by the Church

Wherefore, brethren, look ye out among you seven men of honest report. —Acts 6:3

It is a fundamental principle of Reformed church polity that the local church chooses her own officebearers—her own minister, elders, and deacons. Reformed churches differ sharply from hierarchical forms of church government. For example, in the Roman Catholic Church, the priests are appointed by the bishop. He determines—without any input from the local congregation—who shall be the priest. Therefore, the priest is imposed upon the congregation by a higher ecclesiastical authority. This is the case for all the offices in the Roman Catholic Church. The cardinals are appointed by the pope; the archbishop, bishops, and other offices—which are unbiblical offices—are in no way determined by the people. This kind of imposition from the outside is practiced by other types of churches as well, for example, by Episcopalianism and Methodism.

Article 31 condemns such an approach. No higher ecclesiastical authority—or even the civil authority of the state—has the right to determine the officebearers of the local congregation. This includes the pope, bishop, classis, or synod. "The ministers of God's Word, and the elders and deacons, ought to be chosen to their respective offices by a lawful election by the church" (Article 31). This is good and proper. Only the members of the local congregation, who know their own particular needs, can determine for themselves who their pastor should be. Only the members of the local congregation can elect their own elders and deacons. The elders and deacons must be fellow members of the congregation who know the flock and are able to minister to their spiritual needs. Peter speaks about this when he addresses the elders thus: "The elders which are among you…feed the flock of God which is among you" (1 Pet. 5:1–2). How could a man who is imposed against the will of the congregation know the flock? Additionally no man may impose himself upon the congregation. This was a problem in the days of the Reformation. Men felt themselves called to preach and started thrusting themselves forward. But a man must be called through the church and by the church to be properly called by God. This, too, is part of the good order and discipline demanded by Christ in his church. Paul explains this principle in Romans 10: "How shall they preach, except they be sent?" (v. 15).

The process for appointing officebearers is not set forth in all its details in Scripture. However, the principles are easy to determine and to follow. First, the Scriptures describe for us the kind of men we should seek, men who have certain spiritual qualifications (1 Tim. 3:1–13; Tit. 1:5–9). Let not the election of officebearers be a popularity contest! Let it not be determined by who has the most money! Second, the Scriptures demand that these men be examined ("proved") by the congregation (1 Tim. 3:10). Only after such examination and election can men say that they have been appointed by the church—and therefore by Christ himself—to their respective offices.

Martyn McGeown

October 31 — **That Order which the Word of God Teacheth**

And let these also first be proved.
—1 Timothy 3:10

In Acts 13, the church in Antioch was fasting and praying, seeking the will of the Lord. The Holy Spirit said: "Separate me Barnabas and Saul for the work whereunto I have called them" (v. 2). In response to the Holy Spirit's commandment, the church in Antioch "fasted and prayed, and laid their hands on them [and] sent them away" (v. 3). When Paul and Barnabas—and later Paul and Silas—returned from their missionary journeys, they reported to the church in Antioch concerning the work they had done (Acts 14:26–28; 15:40; 18:22–23).

From all this, we can draw several conclusions. First, the Holy Spirit calls a man to his office in the church, but he does not do this without the church. Acts 13:2 says that the Holy Spirit called Paul and Barnabas. Acts 13:3 says that the church in Antioch sent them out. And Acts 13:4 interprets this as their being "sent forth by the Holy Ghost." The same is true of the elders in Ephesus. Paul reminds them that the Holy Spirit had made them overseers (Acts 20:28), yet Acts 14:23 makes clear that the Spirit used the call through the church to place such elders—and by implication, also ministers and deacons—into their offices.

Second, elders should only be chosen after prayer—and even after fasting (Acts 13:1–3; 14:23). Article 31 has such passages in mind when it urges the church to elect officebearers "with calling upon the name of the Lord." Only by humbling ourselves before God and seeking his direction will we be enabled to elect godly officebearers. The Bible teaches us that God gives unsuitable officebearers to his church in his wrath when we are unfaithful to him. One needs only to think of King Saul: "I gave thee a king in mine anger, and took him away in my wrath" (Hos. 13:11).

Third, the election of officebearers is as spiritual an activity as any other ecclesiastical business. That is why God gives the spiritual characteristics of ministers, elders, and deacons. You will look in vain for the qualifications that modern churches seek: today, a man must be a good communicator, a people-pleaser, a good organizer and coordinator, a team player, and a charismatic leader. God bypasses all those qualities—some of which might be useful in an officebearer—and insists that officebearers be godly. Blamelessness, gravity, sobriety, honesty, fidelity in the family, and soundness in faith are the indispensable qualifications for a minister, elder, or deacon. Other gifts and talents may be useful—and could even be developed by a man—but godliness is vital. These are not the qualifications of a president or a manager, but they are the qualifications of an officebearer in Christ's church.

Fourth, the men who are elected to be officebearers must be proved (tested and examined) for their fitness (1 Tim. 3:10). Paul warns that no novice—one new to the faith and therefore lacking in experience and spiritual maturity—should be chosen (v. 6). This election of men to the offices should not be with undue haste (5:22).

When the election of officebearers happens according to this careful biblical pattern, we can be sure of God's blessing. When ungodly men are selected, the results will be disastrous.

Martyn McGeown

November 1 — The Need for a Lawful Call

And how shall they preach, except they be sent?
—Romans 10:15

The church needs ministers so that the word of God is preached. Ministers are the gift of the ascended Christ who gives these officebearers to his church for her spiritual good (Eph. 4:12). The question is, how does Christ give pastors to his church? The answer is, as Article 31 explains it, that a man "is bound to wait till it shall please God to call him."

The lawful call of a man to the ministry is felt as a subjective call. This is a desire to serve Christ in the office of minister. This desire, if it is a genuine call of Christ upon the life of that man, will not be a desire for glory, power, or wealth. Nor will this call come about through undue external force or pressure. What Peter writes concerning elders applies equally to ministers because ministers are elders, teaching elders (1 Tim. 5:17). "Feed the flock of God which is among you, taking the oversight thereof, not by constraint, but willingly; not for filthy lucre, but of a ready mind. Neither as being lords over God's heritage, but being ensamples to the flock" (1 Pet. 5:2–3). Notice, first, the office should not be forced upon a man against his will by the pressure of others ("not by constraint"). Second, the office should not be sought for monetary gain ("not for filthy lucre"). Third, that the office must not be desired for selfish ambition ("neither as being lords over God's heritage"). Rather, a young man will have a desire to serve Christ by feeding his flock. Such a young man will notice—and usually his fellow saints will notice it also—the presence of certain gifts for the ministry, and he will seek to develop those gifts for use in the pastorate.

But that is not enough. For many, this subjective call might seem like enough. Here is a young man. He feels called to serve Christ. But that cannot be enough. The church must have a role in determining the fitness of a man to occupy the office. No man can know himself to be called until he receives the external call from a local congregation "that he may have testimony of his calling, and be certain and assured that it is of the Lord," says Article 31. This principle is found in Scripture. About the deacons—and therefore also about the ministers and elders—Paul writes: "And let these also first be proved" (1 Tim. 3:10). In addition, Paul warns: "Lay hands suddenly on no man" (1 Tim. 5:22). That word *proved* means *examined* or *tested* with a view to determine fitness. Scripture does not specify how this examination should take place. In Reformed churches, a man is proved by rigorous seminary training followed by an examination before the church. The principle for this is found in 2 Timothy 2:2, "And the things that thou hast heard of me among many witnesses, the same commit thou to faithful men, who shall be able to teach others also." When the church is not able to have its own seminary, on-the-job training is provided for promising candidates. This was how Timothy and Titus were prepared for the ministry.

The important point is that the ordination of men by the laying on of hands (2 Tim. 1:6) must not happen with undue haste (1 Tim. 5:22). In this way, God will give to the church, for her edification, men who desire the office in sincerity.

Martyn McGeown

November 2   **No Intrusion by Indecent Means**

…but Diotrephes, who loveth to have the preeminence.
—3 John 1:9

Selfish ambition and pride are sins that have plagued the church from her earliest days. There have been, in the history of the church both in the Old and New Testaments, those who have sought to exalt themselves as leaders without a call from God. Moses, the meekest of all men (Num. 12:3), one who was called directly by God, saw his leadership challenged on several occasions. First, his brother and sister opposed him in Numbers 12. God struck Miriam with leprosy, and Moses had to pray for her. Later, a more serious rebellion brewed in the wilderness with Korah, Dathan, and Abiram (Num. 16:3). Judgment was swift and terrible upon the rebels. They were swallowed up by the earth (Num. 16:32–35; Ps. 106:16–18; Jude 11)! When God rebukes false prophets, he says that he did not send them: they spoke without his authority (Jer. 14:14–15). In the New Testament, Paul warns women not to usurp the offices (1 Tim. 2:12). Article 31 warns against a usurpation of office out of pride or some other base motive: "Therefore every one must take heed not to intrude himself by indecent means."

In his third epistle, the apostle John named a proud man called Diotrephes. We do not know how Diotrephes became an officebearer in the church. Perhaps he desired money, power, or prestige. Perhaps he desired to have the praise of men and to be popular. John said of him that he "loveth to have the preeminence" (3 John 1:9). This is a terrible indictment of the man. "In all things," Christ must "have the preeminence" (Col. 1:18). How different Diotrephes' attitude was from John the Baptist, who said of Jesus, "He must increase, but I must decrease" (John 3:30). Because Diotrephes loved the preeminence, he opposed any whom he perceived to be a threat to his power in the church. John wrote of Diotrephes: "Neither doth he himself receive the brethren, and forbiddeth them that would, and casteth them out of the church" (3 John 1:10).

There are men like Diotrephes in the church in every age. His name stands as a warning to us. Some of these men desire the office of the church but they are never elected. They then do everything in their power to undermine the work of the lawful officebearers. They become the chief critics in the congregation. Their envy embitters them. A Diotrephes in the pulpit, consistory, or diaconate is worse. The churches must be vigilant not to allow a Diotrephes to gain a position of authority where he can do damage to the congregation. One way in which this can be done is by heeding Paul's warning in 1 Timothy 3:6, "Not a novice, lest being lifted up with pride he fall into the condemnation of the devil." A novice is a recent convert. To thrust such a man into office—even with the best of intentions—could be ruinous for that man.

The greatest enemies of the church creep in using indecent means to gain a position of influence (Acts 20:29–30; Gal. 2:4; Eph. 4:14; Jude 4). Such men have no love for Jesus Christ or his sheep. Therefore, in the important task of calling officebearers, we must take heed that we do not intrude ourselves or permit others to intrude themselves by such indecent means.

Let us wait upon the Lord to give us officebearers for our good.

Martyn McGeown

November 3 — The Equality of Officebearers

Neither as being lords over God's heritage.
—1 Peter 5:3

We have seen several important principles of Reformed church government. First, there must be officebearers, men whom Christ calls through the church and to whom Christ gives real, spiritual authority. Second, there must be a plurality of officebearers, lest too much power be concentrated in one man. In the multitude of counselors, there is safety. Third, there must be no hierarchy: that is, in the church of Christ, there are no offices higher than others. Fundamentally, then, a bishop is not a higher-ranking office than an elder. The offices in Christ's church of pastor, elder, and deacon are distinct, but one office is not above the other.

The same is true of the individual officebearers. "As for the ministers of God's Word, they have equally the same power and authority wheresoever they are, as they are all ministers of Christ" is the explanation of Article 31. This means that the church must not have senior pastors, associate pastors, assistant pastors, or other kinds of pastors. All pastors have the same office. Each of them has the authority to preach, baptize, and administer the Lord's supper. One pastor may be more experienced, better gifted, and more popular than another, but they are equal in office. The church must be careful not to put one pastor above another. Paul warns of this attitude in 1 Corinthians 1:12–13, "Now this I say, that every one of you saith, I am of Paul; and I of Apollos; and I of Cephas; and I of Christ. Is Christ divided?" and again in 1 Corinthians 3:3–4, "For ye are yet carnal: for whereas there is among you envying, and strife, and divisions, are ye not carnal, and walk as men? For while one saith, I am of Paul; and another, I am of Apollos; are ye not carnal?"

The minister has his authority from Christ, and all ministers have that same authority. But Christ only permits a man to preach as he sends by the church. A man is accountable to the consistory of elders of that church. Thus, a man preaches with the permission and under the supervision of the elders. When a man preaches in another congregation, he must have the permission of the elders of that congregation. He may not thrust himself upon a congregation without the elders.

The same equality of office is true of elders and deacons. No elder may lord over a fellow elder. Every elder in the consistory—or at a broader assembly at which he is called to be a delegate—has equal right to speak and to vote. No deacon may assume an authoritarian attitude over the other deacons.

Let hierarchy in all its forms be rejected by Reformed churches. Let us be servants of one another and of the Lord.

Martyn McGeown

November 4 — Christ, the Only Universal Bishop and Head

For ye were as sheep going astray; but are now returned unto the Shepherd and Bishop of your souls. —1 Peter 2:25

Article 31 reminds us that all officebearers are servants of Christ and that he is "the only universal Bishop, and the only Head of the church." This creedal statement is an answer to the pretensions of the Roman Catholic pope.

The Roman Catholic Church makes very exaggerated claims for her popes. "The Roman Pontiff, by reason of his office as vicar of Christ, namely, and as pastor of the entire church, has full, supreme, and universal power over the whole Church, a power which he can always exercise unhindered."* These claims are based on several arguments. First, the Catholic Church argues that Peter was the prince of the apostles, the first bishop of Rome, and that the subsequent bishops of Rome are his rightful successors and exercise the supremacy that Christ gave to Peter. This argument has no basis in Scripture. Peter never claimed such supremacy for himself, and the other apostles never suggested it. Furthermore, there is no evidence that Peter was ever the bishop of Rome.

Second, there is, the Roman Catholic Church argues, an unbroken succession of bishops from Peter to the present pope. This argument, even if it were true—and history denies it—is irrelevant. A succession of persons does not guarantee a succession of gifts and authority. In fact, history shows that many of the popes were monsters of iniquity.

Third, Rome claims lofty titles for her popes, titles which belong to God, such as Holy Father and His Holiness (see John 17:11). Other titles which the pope claims are Supreme Pontiff, which means the bridge between God and men; Vicar of Christ, which means one who stands in the place of Christ; the Head of the Church on earth; and Universal Bishop.

Especially in the Middle Ages, the power of the popes in Rome was very great. The pope claimed the sovereign right to appoint bishops and even to depose kings who opposed him. At the pope's command, our spiritual forefathers were put to death. The popes of Rome are indeed "drunken with the blood of the saints, and with the blood of the martyrs of Jesus" (Rev. 17:6). As recently as 1870, the pope has been declared infallible when he speaks on faith and morals. There is little wonder that the Reformers viewed the pope, who usurped the power of both church and state, as the antichrist. Certainly, the pope is an antichrist, and every Reformed believer must reject his blasphemous claims.

Christ did not place one man over his church. He did not appoint one man to be universal bishop. That title he reserves for himself. He is the only head, the bishop, the mediator, and the savior of his church. For her welfare, he has appointed a plurality of officebearers of equal rank. For these reasons, we reject the pope. We will not allow ourselves or our churches to be brought again under such bondage.

Martyn McGeown

---

* *Catechism of the Catholic Church*, paragraph 882.

November 5 — The Esteem We Should Have for God's Officebearers

And we beseech you, brethren, to know them which labour among you,
and are over you in the Lord, and admonish you;
and to esteem them very highly in love for their work's sake.
And be at peace among yourselves. —1 Thessalonians 5:12–13

How do you view your pastor, your elders, and your deacons? Article 31, quoting 1 Thessalonians 5, urges us to "esteem the ministers of God's Word and the elders of the church very highly for their work's sake."

If the officebearers have been chosen as the word of God determines, they will be godly. Therefore, before they are officebearers, they are your brethren in the Lord. No unbeliever may be a member—and certainly no unbeliever may be an officebearer—in the church of Jesus Christ. Moreover, the officebearers have been elected by the congregation in a majority vote and approved by the congregation. Therefore, they have been lawfully called. This is true even if the men you desired in office did not receive sufficient votes. You had, at the time of election, the opportunity to raise any lawful objections with the consistory. If there were no lawful objections, you must consider that these men in office are a gift of the ascended Christ to you (Eph. 4:11). Therefore, you are called to obey them and submit to them in the Lord (Heb. 13:17). This is profitable for you because these men occupy the office for your edification.

In 1 Thessalonians 5:12–13, Paul urges the believers in Thessalonica to receive their officebearers. We can apply this instruction to our own churches. First, we must know them (v. 12). This should not be difficult for us because—especially in the case of elders and deacons—these men are, even before their election to office, members of the congregation. They live and work among us. Perhaps it is more difficult with respect to the pastor. Often, he comes from the seminary or is called from another church. But we must make the effort to know him. The pastor and his family will be keen to know the congregation—all the congregation.

Second, we must recognize their work. Paul calls it *labor*. The word means *toil*. Pastors, elders, and deacons work hard to carry out the calling of their respective offices. Pray for them in their work and show them that their work is appreciated by you and your children.

Third, we must "esteem them very highly" (v. 13). This esteem is the esteem of honor or reverence. We do this not because they have nice personalities—by all means, let the officebearers be affable, approachable, friendly men—but for their work's sake. We recognize the importance of the work. Where would we be without the preaching, without catechism instruction for our children, without pastoral care, without oversight, without the compassionate work of the deacons? We would stand exposed to every false teaching and be "tossed to and fro," easy prey for deceivers who seek to destroy the church (Eph. 4:14).

Fourth, we must love them. It is amazing how quickly a bond of love forms between the officebearers and the people. When the people see that the officebearers care, genuinely care, for their souls, they will love the officebearers greatly in return.

Finally, the greatest gift we can give the officebearers is to walk in the truth. John writes: "I have no greater joy than to hear that my children walk in truth" (3 John 1:4). Do not only believe the truth—that is the foundation—but also walk in the truth. Let the truth mold your life, your relationships, your marriage, your children, and your work.

This will make it true joy for your officebearers to labor among you.

Martyn McGeown

Article 32

OF THE ORDER AND DISCIPLINE OF THE CHURCH

In the mean time we believe though it is useful and beneficial that those who are rulers of the Church institute and establish certain ordinances among themselves, for maintaining the body of the Church; yet they ought studiously to take care that they do not depart from those things which Christ, our only master, hath instituted. And, therefore, we reject all human inventions, and all laws which man would introduce into the worship of God, thereby to bind and compel the conscience in any manner whatever.

Therefore we admit only of that which tends to nourish and preserve concord and unity, and to keep all men in obedience to God. For this purpose excommunication or church discipline is requisite, with the several circumstances belonging to it, according to the Word of God.

November 6 — The Usefulness of Ordinances

But if any man seem to be contentious, we have no such custom, neither the churches of God. —1 Corinthians 11:16

The Bible does not set forth in detail how the church should be organized in every age and culture. This does not mean that the Bible gives the church freedom to do whatever she desires, believe whatever she wants, and worship however she pleases. The church is not governed by public opinion or pragmatism (the idea that what works well should be done), but by the word of God. However, the Bible is neither a systematic theology, nor a directory for public worship, nor a church order. Instead, the Bible is the word of God, the revelation of who God is, what he has done for us in Jesus Christ, and how we must live in thankful response to his love.

We can contrast how the church was governed in the Old Testament with the government of the church today. Isaiah writes: "For precept must be upon precept, precept upon precept; line upon line, line upon line; here a little, and there a little" (Isa. 28:10). The Old Testament church was like a little child which had to be led by the hand and taught by means of pictures. She was spiritually immature because she did not yet have the outpoured Spirit of Christ (Gal. 4:1–7). Therefore, God imposed upon Old Testament Israel detailed ordinances, laws, and rules which hemmed her in on every side, determining every aspect of her life. In the Old Testament, God determined the times and manner of worship, what the people wore and ate, what was clean and unclean for them, and many other details. Parents know that a little child needs rules for everything. When a child grows, the rules are relaxed and there is more freedom. When a child becomes a man, he can determine for himself the details of his life according to the rules of God's word. In the New Testament, God's church has come of age, and with the freedom of the Spirit lives without certain defined parameters (Gal. 3:23–25). This has implications for the life of the church.

Article 32 declares that "it is useful and beneficial that those who are rulers of the church institute and establish certain ordinances among themselves for maintaining the body of the church." Some Christians do not like ordinances. And they refuse to accept the ordinances determined by the officebearers unless they can agree with every single one of them. The more extreme among this kind of Christian refuse to join any church and instead criticize many of the practices of the church as pagan because they cannot find a text of Scripture which explicitly supports any given practice.

Perhaps some examples will help. Where ought the church to meet? Churches have met in private homes, in the temple in Jerusalem, in rented rooms or halls, in the open air, and today, many erect their own buildings. Surely this should be a matter of Christian prudence. At what time on the Lord's day should churches have their worship services, and what should be the exact order of worship? Apart from general principles, the Bible does not determine these things.

Let us not confuse proof texts with principles. We must all agree on the principles of church government and on the elements of worship, but many of the details fall under the category of Christian liberty. Nevertheless, without ordinances, the church cannot function efficiently. And surely, it is wiser that the officebearers decide some of the details rather than there being a disorderly free-for-all every Sunday.

"Let [everything] be done decently and in order" is our motto (1 Cor. 14:40)!

Martyn McGeown

November 7 — The Rulers Instituting Ordinances

He that ruleth, [let him do it] with diligence.
—Romans 12:8

Yesterday, we noticed that ordinances are useful and beneficial for the smooth running of the church. Today, we take note of the fact that "those who are rulers of the church" should institute and establish these ordinances.

No organization can run smoothly unless there is a clear distinction between the rulers and the other members of the church. A congregation that elects officebearers must let them rule (1 Thess. 5:12–13; 1 Tim. 5:17; Heb. 13:17; 1 Pet. 5:1–3). This means that the members gladly submit to the decisions made by the officebearers without murmuring or complaining. One example is the time of the worship service. The elders of the congregation determine at what times the church meets for public worship on Sunday. Everyone will have his preference in the congregation. The members might even make suggestions. But, if after carefully considering the needs of the congregation, the elders decide on the times of 9:30 a.m. and 6 p.m., it would be folly for some of the congregation to arrive at noon. Nor should a member grumble and complain that he wanted the worship service at a different time and then refuse to come to church because the time is not ideal for him. The church consists of many members. It is impossible to please everyone all of the time. For the sake of the church's peace, let the members submit to the decisions of the elders. These ordinances, says Article 32, are "for maintaining the body of the church" and should be that which "tends to nourish and preserve concord and unity."

Another example is the order of worship. Those details are not set down in Scripture. In some churches, the reading of Scripture occurs immediately before the sermon. In others, the sermon is separated from the reading by the singing of a psalm. The important thing is, the order of worship having been decided by the elders, that all the members worship in the same manner. Paul criticizes the disorderly coming together of the Corinthians in this regard (1 Cor. 14:26, 33, 40).

A third example is the church budget. The Biblical principles are that the pastor be supported financially so that he can devote himself to the work, and that the church care for the poor in her midst (1 Cor. 9:14). The many activities of the church—such as evangelism, catechism of the youth, and even the upkeep of the church's property if it has any—require money. The rulers of the church should determine how much money the church needs, applying the biblical principles of prudence and stewardship, and the members of the church should contribute according to ability (1 Cor. 16:1–2; 2 Cor. 9:7).

Some Christians disagree with this approach. They believe that everything in the church should be decided by the people in common. This view of church government is called congregationalism. The congregation, and not the elders, rules. Such an approach fails to do justice to the offices which Christ has appointed. Officebearers have real authority in the congregation.

Let the elders rule diligently. They do it for our own good and for the maintenance of the body of the church. Let us esteem them and live in peace in the church of Christ.

Martyn McGeown

November 8 — Not Binding or Compelling the Conscience

But when ye sin so against the brethren, and wound their weak conscience, ye sin against Christ. —1 Corinthians 8:12

Article 32 contains a warning for all officebearers who seek to make rules for the maintaining of the body of the church. Do not bind or compel the conscience! Take care studiously not to depart from those things which Christ has instituted! Do not introduce human inventions! This is the danger when men begin to make rules for the church. A man-made rule can become more important and more binding than the word of God. The Reformation churches understood this very well and were very concerned to maintain the freedom of conscience.

The conscience is the testimony of God in the consciousness of every man, either accusing or excusing him in his actions. By the conscience, even the heathen without the word of God know that they have done something wrong. Because of conscience, every culture has an established morality or moral code. Every culture of man knows that to murder is evil, to steal is wicked, and to commit adultery is a sin against the Creator God (Rom. 2:15). Therefore, every culture of man has laws to punish evildoers to one degree or another. A guilty conscience is very difficult to endure because it accuses the sinner before God. Men seek all kinds of relief—except repentance towards God and faith in Jesus Christ—to escape the accusations of their guilty conscience. Some men have even so defiled their conscience that it has lost much of its sensitivity to evil. They are deeply hardened in sin and wickedness (1 Tim. 4:2; Tit. 1:15). Other men—usually weak believers—have an uneducated, uninformed, or overly-sensitive conscience. They imagine that some activity which God has not condemned is sin. Therefore, they cannot perform that activity with a good conscience. For example, some imagine that to drink wine or to eat meat is sin. Others, having a better grasp of Christian liberty, eat and drink (in moderation) without qualms (Rom. 14; 1 Cor. 8).

Throughout the Middle Ages, the Roman Catholic Church bound, compelled, and tyrannized the consciences of men with rules. For example, the church mandated times for fasting at Lent, and the church insisted that no meat could be eaten on Fridays. There were many more ways in which the church ruled over the people—often hanging the threat of damnation over them if they stepped out of line. In fact, the pope himself could place an interdict upon an entire people if the king defied him! This would stop ecclesiastical activity—for example, no masses could be said, no confessions heard—and this was fearful for medieval people, as it meant no means of grace and therefore no salvation. The Pharisees bound consciences in the day of Christ. They added to and expanded the laws of Moses to include ridiculously detailed prohibitions and obligations. This was particularly true concerning the sabbath day. For the Pharisees, to heal or to do good on the sabbath day was evil (Matt. 12:1–14; John 5:1–17; 9:1–16). Christ excoriates the Pharisees for this: "Ye lade men with burdens grievous to be borne, and ye yourselves touch not the burdens with one of your fingers" (Luke 11:46).

The church must take care, therefore, never to impose rules upon the members which might wound their consciences: "They ought studiously to take care that they do not depart from those things which Christ, our only Master, hath instituted" (Article 32). These considerations must be paramount in the consistory when rules are contemplated. Is this rule necessary? Will this rule offend the conscience? How will this rule minister to the needs of the church?

Let all things be done for the edifying of the body. Then, the church will have peace.

Martyn McGeown

November 9 — The Believer's Right to Appeal and Protest

Is it so, that there is not a wise man among you? no, not one that shall be able to judge between his brethren? —1 Corinthians 6:5

Reformed church government is not a tyranny but the benevolent rule of Jesus Christ in his church. Because the Lord has chosen to rule the church through officebearers, who, even with the best of intentions, remain fallible and sinful men, there are possibilities that the elders might impose rules upon the congregation which are not biblical, and which wrongly bind and compel the conscience. The Belgic Confession recognizes that there is that danger even with the wisest and most godly of elders. For this reason, there is the warning of Article 32: "they ought studiously to take care…" Some might wonder what redress a church member has when he believes that the elders have overstepped the bounds of their authority and made an unbiblical decision. No officebearer in Christ's church has the authority to contradict the will of Christ as revealed in Scripture. What can the church member do?

There are several principles at work here. First, the presence of the special offices of pastors, elders, and deacons in no way annuls or contradicts the office of believer. Every Christian shares in the anointing of Christ by the Holy Spirit and is therefore a prophet, priest, and king (Acts 2:17–18; 1 John 2:27). No officebearer can hinder the believer's relationship with Christ. Second, the conscience of the believer may not be violated by any church ordinance. The believer may not be forced against his conscience to comply with an ecclesiastical ordinance. The believer's conscience must be regulated by Scripture alone. Third, there is the possibility for every church member to appeal a decision of the consistory beyond the elders of the local congregation. In Reformed churches, there are broader assemblies of the church. Delegates from the area congregations form a classis; and delegates from various classes form a synod. Presbyterians call these assemblies presbytery and general assembly. The biblical principles behind broader church assemblies are found especially in Acts 15.

Imagine the following scenarios. A church member has heard something from the pulpit with which he disagrees, believing it contradicts the Scriptures. A church member disagrees with a decision made by the consistory in an ordinance for the maintenance of the body of the church. A church member feels aggrieved about the consistory's decision concerning church discipline. As a member of Christ's church, the believer has the right to approach the consistory and lodge an official complaint (often called an appeal or a protest). The consistory will then discuss his complaint and make a decision. Perhaps the consistory will agree with the church member and change their original decision. Perhaps the consistory will not be convinced by the appeal of the church member. Perhaps the consistory will even convince the church member that he is mistaken, and he will withdraw his appeal. If all parties can be satisfied from the word of God, agreement is reached and peace maintained. On the other hand, perhaps the consistory disagrees with the church member. That member has the right to bring his complaint to the meeting of classis and all the way to synod.

Let no one say, therefore, that Reformed church government tramples on the rights of church members.

Martyn McGeown

November 10 — The Nourishing of Concord and Unity

Do all things without murmurings and disputings.
—Philippians 2:14

Yesterday, we began to look at what redress a member of a Reformed church has when he feels aggrieved by the consistory's decisions. We noticed that the member has the right to protest or appeal the decisions of the officebearers. I insisted that the member has the right to the freedom of his conscience. In this meditation, our focus shifts from the rights of the church member to his responsibilities.

In a fallible church with fallible, sinful officebearers, there can be, even with the best intentions, times when there is friction between the officebearers and the members. We remember here the teaching of the Heidelberg Catechism in Lord's Day 39, question and answer 104, that I "submit myself with due obedience to all their good instruction and correction, and also bear patiently with their infirmities, since it is God's will to govern us by their hand."* This statement has application not only to parents, but also to officebearers in the church. This has several implications.

First, the church member must not be a complainer, always seeking for some reason to oppose the elders. He must bear patiently with the elders' weaknesses. "Do all things without murmurings and disputings" (Phil. 2:14); "Let us not be desirous of vain glory, provoking one another, envying one another" (Gal. 5:26). There are many things in the church that, although they might not be done according to our personal preference or convenience, are not sins. The calling in such situations is to learn to be content.

Second, when the member has a legitimate complaint, he must complain in an ecclesiastical manner: that is, in a church-orderly way. There are people who behave in disorderly ways: they openly accuse the elders of base motives, they seek to stir up a faction in the congregation against the elders, or they air their grievances before the ungodly world, ruining the good name of the church. This is the grievous sin of schism. If a complaint is serious enough to bring to the consistory's attention, let it be done in a way which seeks the glory of God and the peace of the church.

Third, let the complaint be brought humbly, with the recognition that the elders might be right and the church member might be mistaken. Proverbs 18:17 says: "He that is first in his own cause seemeth just; but his neighbor cometh and searcheth him." It is the responsibility of the church member not to prove to himself from the word of God that a given doctrine or practice is false, but to prove to the church, whether to the consistory, classis, or synod, that the church has erred in a doctrine or practice.

All of these assume, of course, that we are speaking of a true church. In an apostate or false church, it will not take long to discover that neither the people nor the officebearers care what the word of God says. When a concerned member has lodged a formal, ecclesiastical protest (assuming that the church still retains some semblance of biblical church government), and when the church has rejected the word of God, the member can leave the church in good conscience and seek a church which faithfully adheres to the truth.

The final judge in all ecclesiastical disputes is the word of God. Every member and every officebearer must humble himself before the will of God as it is revealed in Scripture. When that is done, there will be unity and concord in the truth.

Martyn McGeown

---

* Heidelberg Catechism 104, in Schaff, *Creeds of Christendom*, 3:345.

November 11 — Rejecting Human Inventions

Howbeit in vain do they worship me, teaching for doctrines the commandments of men. —Mark 7:7

"And therefore, we reject all human inventions, and all laws which man would introduce into the worship of God" (Article 32). In previous meditations we have noticed that Article 32 teaches that the leaders in the church should make various laws and ordinances for the church. These ordinances concern the "maintaining [of] the body of the church" and must be only "that which tends to nourish and preserve concord and unity, and to keep all men in obedience to God." We considered some examples, taking note of the caution not to bind the consciences of men by unnecessary and oppressive rules. We also noticed the rights and responsibilities of church members who think themselves aggrieved. Let us apply wisdom and love in all these things.

It is one thing for the elders to determine the time, venue, and order of the worship services. It is another thing for the elders to introduce innovations into the worship of God itself. It is one thing for the elders to determine the budget of the church. It is quite another for the elders to extort money from the members or to seek to rule their lives.

Article 32 gives expression to the Reformation principle called the regulative principle of worship. Who determines how God shall be worshipped in his church? The answer is that God himself determines it. We may only worship God according to what he has commanded. This means that we do not add to his worship.

Some teach that if God forbids something, you should not include it in worship, but that if something is not expressly forbidden, it is permissible in worship. The regulative principle goes further. If something is not expressly commanded, it may not be included in the worship of God. The elements of worship are clear from Scripture: the reading and preaching of the word of God, prayer, praise, confession of faith, sacraments, benediction, and the giving of alms. How these elements are applied, and the order in which they are to be used, are open to some interpretation. But to these elements, we are not at liberty to add our own ideas. The regulative principle shuts the door against all human innovations which plague the churches today.

Applying this principle, the Reformation purged the church of choirs, incense, altars, clerical vestments, holy water, consecrated oil, and many other innovations which had crept into the worship of God. These things are not forbidden in Scripture, but because there is no warrant for them in the word of God, they were rightly removed from the church's worship. Apply this principle to some modern worship practices. Youth bands, choir concerts, drama, puppet shows, props, and many forms of entertainment could—and should—be swept away if we rejected all human inventions in the worship of God.

It is a mark of the false church to corrupt the worship of God with unnecessary additions. The question is not, "What is wrong with it?" The question is rather, "Where has God commanded this?"

Not even the officebearers of the church may add to the worship of God.

Martyn McGeown

November 12 — Church Discipline

Put away from among yourselves that wicked person.
—1 Corinthians 5:13

Article 32 is entitled, "Of the Order and Discipline of the Church." We turn now to consider the subject of church discipline.

Church discipline has fallen into disuse. Many Christians are opposed to it. They suppose that it is out of place in our modern, inclusive, tolerant world. Nevertheless, the Bible clearly demands that the church use discipline. A church that refuses to use church discipline not only disobeys Christ, but she sows the seeds of her own destruction.

The purposes of church discipline are three. First, Christ commands church discipline so that God is glorified. God is glorified by the holiness of the church. When all things are done according to God's word, when sinners are saved and begin to obey God out of thankfulness, when redeemed sinners adorn the doctrine of the gospel with good works, God is glorified. But God's name is dishonored when sin is tolerated in the church. The world will see an unholy church and mock God. Today, much of the church is scandalously unholy in doctrine and life. Men preach error as they please and without constraint. Churches receive men and women who live in open, flagrant sin as members of the church, and without qualms allow them to partake of the Lord's supper. The Heidelberg Catechism warns against this in Lord's Day 30, question and answer 82: God's "wrath [is] provoked against the whole congregation" when his covenant is profaned. God's wrath was evident in Corinth: "For this cause many are weak and sickly among you, and many sleep. For if we would judge ourselves, we should not be judged. But when we are judged, we are chastened of the Lord" (1 Cor. 11:30–32).

Second, Christ commands church discipline for the sake of the church's purity. "Evil communications corrupt good manners" (1 Cor. 15:33). To allow a person to live in sin openly encourages the spread of sin throughout the congregation. Paul uses the figure of leaven. Leaven, when mixed into dough, spreads through "the whole lump" (1 Cor. 5:6; Gal. 5:9). Sin, when allowed to spread unchecked, corrupts the whole church. One who loves the church will not permit this to happen. Christ, who loves the church, commands that the wicked member be put out of the congregation by church discipline (Matt. 18:17).

Third, Christ commands church discipline for the sake of the sinning member. Many think that the elders take some kind of pleasure in putting a person out of the congregation. Nothing could be farther from the truth! It is with a heavy heart and many tears that the church, through her officebearers, puts away a member. But the church uses the means of discipline for the restoration of the sinning member. For this reason the church has traditionally called excommunication, which is the final step in discipline, the extreme remedy.

The Lord is pleased to use church discipline for the good of the church. It is good for the church that unbelievers and hypocrites be expelled. It is good for the church that members who walk in the way of sin be admonished, rebuked, and even excommunicated. It is good for the church that she has a reputation as a church that takes sin seriously and insists on holiness among her members. And it is good for the church when God is pleased to use discipline to turn a member from the folly of sin to reconciliation with the church and with God himself.

Martyn McGeown

November 13 — Church Discipline Is Requisite

And ye are puffed up, and have not rather mourned.
—1 Corinthians 5:2

The Corinthians harbored in their midst a man who was guilty of open, flagrant sin against the seventh commandment of God. He was living in fornication with his stepmother. "It is reported commonly that there is fornication among you, and such fornication as is not so much as named among the Gentiles, that one should have his father's wife" (1 Cor. 5:1). This sin was so scandalous that even the Gentiles blushed at the idea of it. Yet, the church in Corinth did nothing about it. Paul was shocked and wrote to the church that this man must be put out of the church by Christian discipline.

In Ephesus, a young pastor Timothy was laboring in the gospel ministry. There were two heretics in the congregation, openly denying the faith and teaching doctrines to subvert the truth. They had made shipwreck of the faith and were a risk to the other members in the church. Paul named these two men and "delivered them unto Satan, that they may learn not to blaspheme" (1 Tim. 1:20; 1 Cor. 5:5). "Delivered unto Satan" means church discipline.

These two passages teach us that those who refuse to walk in the doctrine and life of Christianity must be placed under church discipline, and if they do not repent, they must be excommunicated. However, very few churches today practice church discipline.

Paul highlighted the reason in 1 Corinthians 5:2, "Ye are puffed up, and have not rather mourned." To be puffed up is to be proud. The Corinthians were proud when they should have been ashamed. Perhaps they were proud that by their tolerance of sin they displayed the grace of God. Perhaps they were proud because they considered themselves to be an open, tolerant, affirming, inclusive church. Perhaps they were proud because they were more "loving" than another "judgmental" church. Instead, they ought to have mourned. They ought to have mourned that their sin was so well-known that it was the subject of the heathens' gossip—it was "reported commonly" (v. 1)—and that the sin which they tolerated was so vile that even the promiscuous pagans of Corinth were shocked by it: "fornication as is not so much as named among the Gentiles" (v. 1). They ought to have mourned that the name of the church, and therefore the name of the Lord Jesus Christ, was blasphemed among the wicked. Behold the "holy church" of Corinth! They ought to have mourned that the sin would soon spread through the congregation and destroy it as gangrene spreads through the body and eventually kills it (2 Tim. 2:17).

There are reasons for mourning in the church today. The statistics are shocking. For example, among evangelicals, divorce statistics are higher than among the general population. Divorce and unbiblical remarriage after divorce are tolerated and promoted. Rare is the church today that even knows what church discipline is. And when a church does dare to begin the process of discipline, more often than not the member under discipline leaves to join another church where he is permitted to join, no questions asked.

Let us not think ourselves wiser than God. Paul excommunicated that wicked man in Corinth for the glory of God, the good of the church, and for the man's salvation. Does the church of which you are a member practice discipline? Be thankful for that mark of faithfulness and pray for your elders in that difficult work.

Martyn McGeown

November 14 — Private Sins and Admonitions

Moreover if thy brother shall trespass against thee,
go and tell him his fault between thee and him alone. —Matthew 18:15

"Excommunication or church discipline is requisite, with the several circumstances belonging to it, according to the word of God." That is all that Article 32 says about church discipline. Previous articles have mentioned the subject also: one mark of the true church is "church discipline is exercised in punishing of sin" (Article 29). Government is necessary in the church, among other things, that "transgressors [be] punished and restrained by spiritual means" (Article 30). However, our Confession does not elaborate. Instead, it directs us to the Biblical principles. A wise church will adopt a church order so that the various circumstances of discipline and the procedure are determined from the word of God.

Church discipline concerns sin in the congregation, but not all sins necessarily become the occasion for church discipline. If every sin were brought to the attention of the elders to be dealt with by them in official church discipline, there would be no end to the elders' work! Life in the church is the life of fellowship in the truth. But because we are all sinners, there are times when sin begins to affect the relationships between the members. Although all sins are serious, we do not address all examples of sin in the same manner. Sometimes it is best to cover a sin, to refuse to bear a grudge concerning it. Perhaps a fellow church member does not greet you as you might desire, or speaks in a bitter, impatient tone. There are a thousand ways in which we can offend one another if we are ready to take offense! "And above all things have fervent charity among yourselves: for charity shall cover the multitude of sins" (1 Pet. 4:8). "Forbearing one another, and forgiving one another, if any man have a quarrel against any: even as Christ forgave you, so also do ye" (Col. 3:13). "In lowliness of mind let each esteem other better than themselves" (Phil. 2:3). If we applied these principles to our life in the church among the members, how blessed life in the church would be! Certainly, there is no need to run to the elders to demand discipline for every minor irritation fellow saints cause one another in the church.

Some sins, however, because of their nature, are more serious. Christ commands us to forgive our brethren when they repent. Peter asked the question once: "Lord, how oft shall my brother sin against me, and I forgive him? till seven times?" (Matt. 18:21). With the suggestion of seven times, Peter thought that he was generous. Christ answered: "I say not unto thee, Until seven times: but, Until seventy times seven" (v. 22). In the same chapter, Christ gives guidelines on how to deal with a sinning brother when the sin is so serious that we cannot simply cover it up with love. These guidelines refer only to private sins, sins in which no other party is involved and sins about which no one else knows.

First, we must approach the sinning brother and admonish him in private. This means that we do not make his sin public or the subject of gossip. If he repents, the issue is closed: "thou hast gained thy brother" (v. 15). But what happens if the brother does not repent?

We will consider that in future meditations.

Martyn McGeown

November 15 — Public Sins

Them that sin rebuke before all, that others also may fear.
—1 Timothy 5:20

We continue to look at church discipline "with the several circumstances belonging to it, according to the word of God." We noticed yesterday that not all sins are censurable sins. This is not because all sins are not damnable or serious. They are. But, not all sins require the elders formally to exercise church discipline. We also began to examine the way of Matthew 18.

Before we continue, we answer one misapplication of Matthew 18. The Lord's directions here apply only to private sins. A private sin is, as Christ describes it, a fault "between thee and him [the sinning brother] alone" (v. 15). No one else knows about or is affected by this sin. A public sin is different. Often men appeal to the way of Matthew 18 to avoid public rebukes for public sins. For example, a man publishes a heretical book, preaches false doctrine on the radio, broadcasts heretical views on the internet, or writes something heretical in the newspaper. Sometimes, a Christian will respond to public heresy with a public rebuke or will publish his answer in various media. This is perfectly good and proper because when that man went public with his views, his behavior does not come under the provisions of Matthew 18. Paul dealt with the public sin of Peter this way, although Peter was no heretic. "But when I saw that they walked not uprightly according to the truth of the gospel, I said unto Peter before them all..." (Gal. 2:14). Paul did not write Peter a private letter of admonition, nor did he take Peter aside into a corner. A public sin required a public rebuke. Elsewhere, Paul named and shamed men in the congregation whose heresies endangered the church. "Of whom is Hymenæus and Alexander; whom I have delivered unto Satan, that they may learn not to blaspheme" (1 Tim. 1:20). Doubtless, the friends and family of these two men were not pleased with Paul's approach. Nevertheless, this way was necessary for the peace and purity of the church. In another epistle, Paul named Hymenaeus, Philetus, Demas, and Alexander as sinners whose evil deeds must be exposed as a warning to others (2 Tim. 2:17; 4:10, 14–15). John did the same by exposing the evil deeds of Diotrephes (3 John 1:9).

The application of these words is clear in letters to Timothy and Titus: "Them that sin rebuke before all, that others also may fear" (1 Tim. 5:20) and, "This witness is true. Wherefore rebuke them sharply, that they may be sound in the faith" (Tit. 1:13).

Sins in the church can become public in various ways, and when such sins do become public, the way of Matthew 18 is no longer appropriate. Some sins, by their very nature, cannot be hidden for long. An obvious example is premarital or extramarital sex when the woman becomes pregnant. Another example is a sin where a church member has transgressed the law of the land and has been caught by the civil authorities. His sin will be front page headlines the next day in the local newspaper! Another example is where the sin of a member has become the occasion of (sinful) gossip either in the church or in the world.

When a sin is so public that even the world knows about it or when, as Paul writes, "it is reported commonly" (1 Cor. 5:1) that such sin exists in the congregation, the elders must act with firm, loving, Christian discipline for the glory of God, the purity of the church, and the salvation of the sinning member.

This is a difficult, often thankless, but necessary work.

Martyn McGeown

November 16 — But If He Will Not Hear Thee

But if he will not hear thee, then take with thee one or two more.
—Matthew 18:16

The first step in the way of Matthew 18 is private admonition. When a brother sins against you, and when there is no one else involved or affected by the sin, then go to him and tell him his sin. Do that only after prayer, after carefully searching your own heart; and with much humility, tell him what his sin is (he may not even have realized it), urge him to repent, and pray with him, if this is appropriate. Make every effort to be reconciled to the brother. If he repents, "thou hast gained thy brother" (v. 15). Then you must assure him that you forgive him; both you and he must be reconciled at the foot of the cross together. And when you forgive him, this means that you will never bring up his sin again, never hold it against him, and never treat him in the light of that sin. Also, that private sin must be kept private forever. Remember the proverb: "He that covereth a transgression seeketh love; but he that repeateth a matter separateth very friends" (Prov. 17:9).

Reconciliation is wonderful. Sadly, it is not always achieved at the first attempt. It may be necessary for you to approach the brother more than once. Your admonitions to him may need to be repeated. Christ does not specify this in verse 15. However, when it becomes apparent that the brother is stubbornly refusing to repent of his sin, it is time for the next step the Lord sets forth. Bring one or two witnesses. Clearly, these witnesses cannot be witnesses of the brother's sin. If they had been witnesses of the sin, the sin would not have been a strictly private one. These witnesses must be trusted fellow believers whom you can tell about the sin (and tell only them; do not be tempted to make the brother's sin the subject of gossip) so that they can come with you when you admonish him and be witnesses to the brother's impenitence.

Your arrival with your witnesses ought to give the brother pause. He ought to see, first, that you love him. Never may you approach your brother in a haughty, self-righteous manner, as if you are better than he. Never may you display the Pharisaical attitude. "Why beholdest thou the mote [speck] that is in thy brother's eye, but considerest not the beam that is in thine own eye?" (Matt. 7:3). "The Pharisee stood and prayed thus with himself, God, I thank thee, that I am not as other men are" (Luke 18:11). Instead, you must display real concern for his spiritual welfare: "Brethren, if a man be overtaken in a fault, ye which are spiritual, restore such an one in the spirit of meekness, considering thyself, lest thou also be tempted. Bear ye one another's burdens, and so fulfill the law of Christ" (Gal. 6:1–2). The brother ought to be able to see that rather than allow him to be ruined by his sin, you care enough for him to risk losing his friendship and favor in the very difficult calling of rebuking him. "Open rebuke is better than secret love" (Prov. 27:5). "Thou shalt not hate thy brother in thine heart: thou shalt in any wise rebuke thy neighbor, and not suffer sin upon him" (Lev. 19:17). He also ought to see when you arrive with your witnesses that you take his sin seriously. His folly has brought him to the second step of Matthew 18!

If the brother repents in front of your witnesses, you have gained him. If not, you have reliable testimony to bring to the elders of the brother's impenitence. With a heavy heart, and with confidence in the Lord's will, you tell it to the church—that is, to the representatives of the church, the elders.

Martyn McGeown

November 17 — Tell it to the Church

And if he shall neglect to hear them, tell it unto the church.
—Matthew 18:17

We have been examining the way of discipline, beginning with Matthew 18. We have noticed that this way is appropriate only for private sins. The church must deal with public sins in a different manner. The first and second steps having been taken (and the brother remaining impenitent in his sin despite repeated admonitions), the next step is to "tell it unto the church" (v. 17). This does not mean that we make a public announcement of the brother's sin to the whole church. One important principle in church discipline is to keep the sin as private as possible for as long as possible. There is, of course, an important exception: if the brother has committed a crime as well as a sin, there is an obligation to report that to the appropriate authorities. Ideally, the brother should be advised to confess his crime and accept the legal consequences of his actions. The reason we seek to keep sins private (in the cases where they are not crimes) is to spare the brother's reputation and to save him from shame. The church in Matthew 18:17 is the consistory of the local congregation. This is clear because Christ goes on to speak about binding and loosing, which is the work of the elders (vv. 18–19).

Therefore, at this stage in the discipline process, a maximum of four people know about the sin: the brother, the two witnesses, and you, the one who has admonished the brother. You and your witnesses must go to the meeting of the consistory. You must explain to the consistory several things. First, you must explain to the elders the nature of the sin. This will include what was done and when. Second, you must explain to the elders what you have done. This will include how you have admonished the brother and when. Third, you must identify your witnesses, who must then verify that they have witnessed the admonition and impenitence of the brother. Then, you must leave the matter with the elders for their further investigation. They may desire to question you or your witnesses further. Having fulfilled your Christian calling, you and your witnesses still must not make the sin public. It will only become public at a later stage in the disciplinary process, if the brother does not repent.

The brother will now receive a visit from the elders who will desire to speak to him about his sin. The elders will do this only after carefully examining the evidence that you and your witnesses have brought. Elders must be very careful to follow Proverbs 18:17, "He that is first in his own cause seemeth just; but his neighbor cometh and searcheth him." Having satisfied themselves that the brother has indeed sinned and that he remains impenitent, the elders will admonish the brother. They will come with the Scriptures and teach the brother the error of his ways. The brother must not spurn the admonitions of the consistory. These men are the officebearers of Christ's church and therefore Christ's representatives whose calling is to rule in the congregations. These men "watch for [the] souls" of the members (Heb. 13:17).

If, even at this stage, the brother repents, the consistory will bring it no further. The brother has been won! Great must be our rejoicing in that case. And, since the sin was never public, the consistory will not make the sin and the repentance public.

But if after being often brotherly admonished, that man "shall neglect to hear" the church (v. 17), discipline must be brought to the next step.

Martyn McGeown

November 18 — The Steps of Church Discipline

*A man that is an heretick after the first
and second admonition reject.* —Titus 3:10

A sin which began as a private sin against you alone has now reached, through the proper way laid out in Matthew 18, the attention of the elders. The Bible does not lay out for us in detail how the elders should proceed. In fact, if anything, the Bible appears to move very quickly to excommunication: "But if he neglect to hear the church, let him be unto thee as an heathen man and a publican" (Matt. 18:17). Paul writes: "A man that is an heretick after the first and second admonition reject" (Tit. 3:10). Whatever happened to the "forgive thy brother seventy times seven" policy of Matthew 18:22? It might seem more like a "two strikes and you're out" policy! Notice, however, first, that forgiveness is only appropriate when the brother repents. When the brother repents, forgiveness must be full and free. With repentance, we must desire forgiveness, work towards it, pray for it, and refuse to harbor bitterness in our hearts; but we cannot extend forgiveness to an impenitent person. Notice, second, that the admonitions of Titus 3:10 are official, and indeed, public, admonitions. Paul does not mean that after telling a brother twice, we cut the brother off. He is not saying that the elders visit the brother only twice. These two public admonitions come only after weeks, even months, of repeated, patient instruction and admonition in private. The one who is rejected in Titus 3:10 is a stubborn, impenitent sinner who is "subverted...being condemned of himself" (v. 11).

In Reformed churches, the first step of official discipline by the elders, which takes place after a number of private admonitions, is silent censure. The sinning brother is not permitted to come to the Lord's table. This prohibition is silent, secret, and discreet. Only the elders know about it. It is not announced to the congregation. This silent censure is not the same as excommunication, but it will lead to it if the brother remains impenitent. A man under discipline cannot partake of the body and blood of Christ (1 Cor. 11:27).

The next step is the first announcement. Reformed churches generally make an announcement in the worship service that there is a member under discipline. The announcement includes the nature of the sin: "a sin against the [...] commandment." But it does not yet include the name of the member, that he may be spared. The congregation is asked to pray for the unnamed individual. The second announcement takes place only after further private admonitions by the elders and the advice of classis. This is necessary because in the second announcement, the brother will be named. Therefore, the consistory must take earnest heed that the case warrants such a public announcement. The brother will also have the opportunity to make an appeal at the meeting of classis. You can see how thorough the process of discipline is. The church does not prematurely reject people without a fair procedure. If classis approves, the consistory will admonish the brother further and, if he still does not repent, the congregation will be informed that the brother (whose name will now be announced) is walking in sin. Following this, a date will be set for the brother's excommunication from the church.

Sadly, few cases of discipline even reach the stage of the second announcement. Many leave the church in an attempt to escape the discipline of the elders. In so doing, they break their membership vow and further increase their guilt.

May God graciously forbid that this should happen with us!

Martyn McGeown

November 19 — Excommunication

> *Deliver such an one unto Satan for the destruction of the flesh.*
> —1 Corinthians 5:5

Excommunication is a word rarely heard today. It is a word which ought to make us shudder. Very few churches practice it. In many churches, there are no elders and no oversight of the life and doctrine of the congregation. In fact, in many churches, there is no official membership list. People come and go, believe what they want, and live as they please without any concern for the law of God. But a true church with discipline, as Christ himself demands it, will not tolerate such sin in her midst. The real Christ is not the affirming, accepting, indulgent Christ who never condemns sinners or their sins. The real Christ is the Christ of Scripture, the holy Son of God, who wills to have a holy church (Eph. 5:26–27; Tit. 2:14). Those who are unholy have no place in the congregation of God's people. In fact, Christ condemns churches that do not practice discipline: "But I have a few things against thee, because thou hast there them that hold the doctrine of Balaam" (Rev. 2:14); "So hast thou also them that hold the doctrine of the Nicolaitans, which thing I hate" (v. 15); "Thou sufferest that woman Jezebel" (v. 20).

We have also seen that there must be no rush to excommunicate. Prior to excommunication—which may God graciously forbid—there is the way of Matthew 18, and the patient, painstaking work of the elders in admonishing, rebuking, and praying for the erring brother. Let no one say that Reformed church elders simply throw a man out of the church!

Only after many warnings and not a few tears (Acts 20:31; Phil. 3:18) do the elders move to actual excommunication. To excommunicate is to remove from the communion of the church, and therefore to place outside the kingdom of Christ. Paul calls this a delivering unto Satan (1 Cor. 5:5; 1 Tim. 1:20). This is the bitter consequence of sin, and a warning to us all. "But every man is tempted, when he is drawn away of his own lust, and enticed. Then when lust hath conceived, it bringeth forth sin: and sin, when it is finished, bringeth forth death" (James 1:14–15). "Wherefore let him that thinketh he standeth take heed lest he fall" (1 Cor. 10:12). Excommunication means that the excommunicated person is no longer a member of the church and, in particular, he is barred from the use of the sacraments. Christ says about such a person that we are to count him as "an heathen man and a publican" (Matt. 18:17). This means that we can no longer have fellowship with him. This will be very painful, especially if the excommunicated person is a family member or friend, and it is very painful for the entire body to lose a member. "And whether one member suffer, all the members suffer with it" (1 Cor. 12:26).

Excommunication takes place in the worship service as a public act. In Reformed churches, a specific form is read. The occasion is solemn as the entire congregation, through the instrumentality of the officebearers, puts away the wicked person from among them. This final step is necessary for the glory of God, the good of the congregation, and even for the salvation of the sinner. Excommunication is the extreme remedy.

Nor must we think that excommunication is the end. In the way of repentance, even after excommunication, there can be restoration. And for that the church prays, even as she excommunicates one of her members at the command of Christ.

Martyn McGeown

Article 33

OF THE SACRAMENTS

We believe that our gracious God, on account of our weakness and infirmities, hath ordained the Sacraments for us, thereby to seal unto us his promises, and to be pledges of the good will and grace of God towards us, and also to nourish and strengthen our faith, which he hath joined to the word of the gospel, the better to present to our senses, both that which he signifies to us by his Word, and that which he works inwardly in our hearts, thereby assuring and confirming in us the salvation which he imparts to us. For they are visible signs and seals of an inward and invisible thing, by means whereof God worketh in us by the power of the Holy Ghost. Therefore the signs are not in vain or insignificant, so as to deceive us. For Jesus Christ is the true object presented by them, without whom they would be of no moment.

Moreover, we are satisfied with the number of Sacraments which Christ our Lord hath instituted, which are two only, namely, the Sacrament of Baptism, and the Holy Supper of our Lord Jesus Christ.

November 20 — **The Sacraments Given for Our Weakness**

Lord, I believe; help thou mine unbelief!
—Mark 9:24

In the preaching of the gospel, which is the chief means of grace, our God declares to us that we have full and free salvation in his Son, our crucified and risen Savior, Jesus Christ. He promises to us who believe that he is our God for the sake of Christ, he pledges himself to be our Father, and he promises us the forgiveness of sins and eternal life. Through believing, we receive that salvation and enjoy covenant fellowship with God.

But our God knows that we are weak. "He [remembers] that we are dust" (Ps. 103:14). The truth of gracious salvation is so astounding, and our sins are so great, that we are tempted in our weakness to doubt and even to tremble in fear. Has God really forgiven my sins, even mine?

With this reality of our weakness, the Belgic Confession begins its treatment of the sacraments: "Our gracious God on account of our weakness and infirmities hath ordained the sacraments for us." The word *sacrament* is not found in the Bible, but that is true for many theological words. It comes from the Latin *sacramentum*, which means an oath or a pledge. A soldier would swear a sacramentum to his superiors, or litigants in a court case would deposit a sacramentum with the judge pending the court's decision. One who gave a sacramentum was promising something. God has given us sacraments to confirm his promises to his church. We notice already that the sacraments are God's gifts. They are not, in the first place, pledges which we make to God, but pledges which he makes to us.

God has already made us exceedingly precious promises. They come to us in the gospel. But because of our weakness he has added sacraments to the gospel promises to confirm them. Perhaps an illustration might help. In marriage, a couple makes promises to love, cherish, and be faithful to one another. But to those promises, they add a wedding ring. The ring is not the marriage, nor is it the promise. When husbands or wives take off their rings—to go swimming, let's say—they are still married. But the ring on the finger is a constant reminder to married people of their marriage, a token of their love. And when an unmarried man looks at a woman's hand and sees a wedding ring, he knows that she is married and that he may not become romantically involved with her.

Thus, it is with the sacraments. They are pledges or tokens of God's faithful friendship. They are not added to the word because the word is insufficient but because our faith is weak and faltering and mixed with much unbelief and doubt. The sacraments are the wedding ring of Christ to his church. The church treasures these sacraments, jealously guards them, and uses them until her Bridegroom returns.

Martyn McGeown

November 21 — Satisfied With Two Sacraments

Howbeit in vain do they worship me,
teaching for doctrines the commandments of men. —Mark 7:7

It is a sad fact of church history that the gift of sacraments—the wedding ring or token of love and friendship that Christ has given to the church—has been an occasion of deep division and bitter dispute among Christians. One of the issues of disagreement between Roman Catholics and the churches of the Reformation is over the number of the sacraments.

Protestant churches believe that Christ has given us only two sacraments—baptism and the Lord's supper. The Roman Catholics have added five more—confirmation, penance, holy orders, matrimony, and extreme unction. Three of these (confirmation, penance, and extreme unction) are not found in the Bible; two (holy orders [ordination of office bearers] and matrimony) are found in the Bible, but they are not sacraments.

A sacrament is not simply any ordinance or ceremony. Foot washing (John 13:14), for example, is not a sacrament; greeting with a holy kiss (2 Cor. 13:12) is not a sacrament. A sacrament must be instituted by Jesus Christ himself. Just as only the husband has the right to give the bride a wedding ring—and no other man is at liberty to give her another wedding ring, nor is she at liberty to make herself a wedding ring—so only the heavenly Bridegroom, Jesus Christ, ordains sacraments. Not even the apostles may ordain new sacraments for the church, much less the pope and his clergy. We have clear teaching that Christ instituted baptism (Matt. 28:19) and the Lord's supper (Luke 22:19; 1 Cor. 11:23–26). But where did Christ institute the five additional "sacraments" of Rome?

Rome's view of salvation requires her to have many sacraments. For Rome, sacraments are the chief way in which God gives grace, which is a kind of spiritual virtue worked in the heart that makes a person righteous. Thus, grace itself is redefined by Rome. Grace in the Bible is unmerited favor, which comes to us by virtue of the finished work of Christ. Grace in Rome is spiritual virtue: the initial grace is unmerited, but further increases of grace are merited through a proper use of the sacraments. The *Catechism of the Catholic Church* states: "No one can merit the initial grace of forgiveness and justification at the beginning of conversion. Moved by the Holy Spirit and by charity, we can then merit for ourselves and others the graces needed for our sanctification, for the increase of grace and charity, and for the attainment of eternal life."*

The Roman Church is like a hospital which has various medicines for the soul. Rome offers a "cradle-to-grave" sacramental salvation plan. Each of the seven sacraments gives a kind of grace: justifying, sanctifying, strengthening grace. But this grace can be resisted and lost. However, Christ has never promised to give grace in these ways. The sacraments do not dispense grace as a doctor dispenses aspirin. The sacraments strengthen faith.

Rome's additional sacraments are unnecessary. Baptism is a sign and seal of the beginning of covenant fellowship with God in Christ. The Lord's supper is a sign and seal of that life which we enjoy within the covenant with God. We are baptized once, and we feed on Christ by faith throughout our lives. We need nothing more. Therefore, with the Belgic Confession we declare: "We are satisfied with the number of sacraments which Christ our Lord hath instituted" (Article 34).

Martyn McGeown

---

* *Catechism of the Catholic Church*, paragraph 2010.

November 22 — **The Seals of God's Promises**

And he received the sign of circumcision, a seal of the righteousness of the faith which he had yet being uncircumcised. —Romans 4:11

Sacraments are seals. We are all familiar with seals. Take some paper money out of your wallet and look at it carefully. It has a seal on it. This is a mark stamped on the money to prove to you that it is real legal tender produced by the government. It is therefore not counterfeit money printed on a criminal's printing press. Or look at an official document—perhaps a letter from a government department, or a diploma issued by an accredited university. There will be a signature and a seal on that document, a stamp of authenticity. By looking at the seal, you know that the document is genuine, not a forgery. Seals were also common in the ancient world. When a king sent a letter, he would take off his signet ring, stamp it into wax, and seal the letter. This would be a guarantee that the letter in question really came from the king, and an unbroken seal indicated that no one had tampered with the letter in transit. The contents of the letter could then be read and believed with confidence.

In Romans 4, we read that circumcision was a seal given to Abraham to strengthen Abraham's faith in God's promises. Before God gave the seal of circumcision, he had already given the promise, which Abraham had believed "yet being uncircumcised" (v. 11). In Genesis 15, two chapters and thirteen years before the institution of circumcision, Abraham "believed in the Lord; and he counted it to him for righteousness" (Gen. 15:6). Therefore, we know that Abraham was not saved through circumcision. He was saved by grace alone, through faith alone, in the righteousness of the coming Messiah. Circumcision was added later—thirteen years later—to confirm God's promise to Abraham and to all God's believing people in the Old Testament.

Circumcision, therefore, was to Abraham what New Testament sacraments are to us.

But we should remember that a seal by itself is meaningless and useless. A seal must seal or authenticate something! It would be absurd to place a stamp of authenticity on a blank piece of paper. That is effectively what is done when we elevate the sacraments above the gospel, when we imagine that we can use sacraments without first believing the gospel, and when we believe that we can replace the gospel with the sacraments. That was the mistake made by many in Christ's day who trusted in circumcision without believing the gospel of grace. Without the gospel promise, circumcision is merely mutilation of the flesh. Without the gospel promise, our sacraments are meaningless rituals. What a wedding ring is without a marriage—a meaningless band of gold—the sacraments are without Jesus Christ and his promises in the covenant. But a wedding ring is precious to a bride because it seals the bridegroom's love to her. Thus we view the sacraments.

Martyn McGeown

November 23 — Pledges of God's Goodwill and Grace

And it shall be a token of the covenant betwixt me and you.
—Genesis 17:11

The sacraments cannot be understood without the covenant. There is much confusion about God's covenant among Christians. Quite simply, God's covenant is a relationship of friendship, a bond of fellowship that God makes with his elect people in Jesus Christ. It is not an agreement that depends on us, but it is a relationship that God brings about, establishes, and preserves by his grace alone. When God makes the covenant, he declares to his people: "I will be your God, and you will be my people." This is the covenant formula common in Scripture. In the covenant, God promises to be a God to us and to our children after us "in their generations for an everlasting covenant" (Gen. 17:7). God promises to love us, to bless us, to forgive our sins, and to bring us into his own fellowship. God's covenant is established by Jesus Christ, who shed his blood to make us the friends of God, and it is realized in time by the Holy Spirit who gives us the life of Christ and sheds God's love abroad in our hearts.

God's covenant—which, remember, is the relationship itself—comes to us with promises. Those promises are rich and gracious. Those promises come to us through the preaching of the gospel. Those promises are for the elect—and their elect children—and are received by faith.

We must understand what a promise is. A promise is a solemn declaration that something will be done by another. God's promise is his solemn declaration to give salvation to his people in Jesus Christ. God's promise is absolutely certain because it is God's promise. Many promises made by men are lies, or they are made with good intentions but for various reasons cannot be fulfilled. A father might promise his daughter that he will take her to the park, but then his car breaks down, it begins to rain, and he is to break his promise. God's promises are not like that, because God is never thwarted by circumstances outside of his control. God's promise does not depend on us: he does not say, "I will give you salvation if you do…" A conditional promise is not certain; God's unconditional promise is.

God desires that his covenant friends know, and are confident of, and therefore enjoy, his promises. Therefore, our merciful Father has, in addition to the preaching, given the sacraments as "pledges of the good will and grace of God towards us" (Article 33). A pledge is a promise, a solemn, binding promise to do something. Think of charity pledges: when a man pledges a sum of money to a charity during fundraising, he promises to pay that sum of money to the charity. The charity can therefore be confident of the goodwill of that person to give. The sacraments are given as pledges. Do you want extra assurance that God is really your God, and that he will really do the things he has promised? Then use the sacraments with faith.

Notice that the sacraments are not pledges of what we will do for God or of what we have done. That is the error of many. Sacraments are the pledges of what God will do for us and of what he has done. The sacraments come to us from our gracious God. How could we then doubt his goodwill and grace toward us?

Martyn McGeown

November 24 — The Sacraments Nourishing Our Faith

And the apostles said unto the Lord, Increase our faith.
—Luke 17:5

What is the relationship between the sacraments and faith? Remember what faith is: God's gift by the Holy Spirit, which he creates in our hearts, and by which we receive for truth everything God has revealed in his word and lean in confidence upon Christ alone for all our salvation. We do not work faith in ourselves. The Spirit does. Therefore, we believe that faith "is the gift of God" (Eph. 2:8; Phil. 1:29). God works that faith in our hearts by the preaching of the gospel. There we hear about Christ, and there we hear the very voice of Christ.

Sacraments, then, do not create faith in the hearts of unbelievers. And for that reason, sacraments are of no spiritual benefit to unbelievers at all. On the contrary, sacraments, which are pledges of God's goodwill and grace to us, only serve to harden unbelievers in their sins, and thus sinners increase their condemnation.

This truth of the Reformed faith is the antithesis of the Roman Catholic view of sacraments. In Rome, the sacraments work more or less automatically. The Latin phrase by which Rome expresses this is *ex opere operato*. These words mean *from the work done*. The idea is that the sacrament is effective by virtue of the performance of the act of administrating it. Therefore, although faith is useful and beneficial, it is not necessary for the sacrament to give grace. Roman Catholics believe that every sacrament gives grace as long as the recipient does not willfully resist God. This view was developed to assure the people that the sacrament does not depend on the holiness or good intention of the priest administering it, but in practice it has come to mean that sacraments dispense automatic grace to all who partake of them, no matter how wicked the partakers might be.

Automatic grace in every sacrament! With this view of sacraments, the preaching of the gospel—by which God works faith in us (Rom. 10:17)—becomes unnecessary. Why have preaching when you can go through a sacramental rite and thus receive grace? Preaching, especially doctrinal preaching which imparts the true knowledge of God, falls by the wayside. But Peter writes: "Grow in grace, and in the knowledge of our Lord and Saviour Jesus Christ" (2 Pet. 3:18). The idea is, grow in grace by growing in knowledge.

Sacraments cannot dispense automatic, easy grace the way a pharmacist dispenses aspirin. Sacraments are for believers who desire to have their faith strengthened and nourished. Unbelievers may not use the sacraments. They must repent and believe, and then join the church and use the sacraments for the increase of faith.

God nourishes our faith through the sacraments, not by directing our faith to the sacraments themselves, but by directing our faith to Christ crucified, who is set forth both in preaching and in the sacraments. Anything that diverts our eyes from Christ is not only not a means to strengthen faith, but it is spiritually harmful.

Let us use the sacraments—but only in faith!

Martyn McGeown

November 25 — Sacraments Joined to the Word

> *Wherein God, willing more abundantly*
> *to shew unto the heirs of promise the immutability of his counsel,*
> *confirmed it by an oath.* —Hebrews 6:17

Yesterday, we looked at the relationship between the sacraments and faith. Faith is closely connected to the word: "faith cometh by hearing, and hearing by the word of God" (Rom. 10:17). But how are sacraments connected to the word? Article 33 explains the relationship thus: God "hath joined [the sacraments] to the word of the gospel, the better to present to our senses."

The word comes by hearing. Although we see the minister while he preaches, the primary way in which we receive the word is through our ears. The sacraments appeal to our other senses, especially to our sight, but also to our sense of taste, touch, and even smell. We see the element of water sprinkled in baptism; we see the elements of bread and wine of the Lord's supper broken and poured out, and we taste and handle these elements of the Lord's supper. These are added to the word as an additional confirmation of what God teaches us in the gospel.

But imagine that a person walks into our worship service near the end just as the minister is sprinkling water on the candidate for baptism or is distributing pieces of bread and the cup of wine. Imagine that that person has never heard of Christianity, has never opened a Bible, and has never heard a sermon in his life. Will he have any inkling of what is going on? In other words, are the sacraments—which are so meaningful and rich to us who have heard and believed the word—not meaningless without the word to explain them? That is why we insist as Reformed churches that the sacraments be administered in the public assemblies of God's people, on the Lord's day, in a worship service, accompanied by preaching. That is why we have the practice of reading a liturgical form—the Form for the Administration of Baptism or the Form for the Administration of the Lord's Supper—when we use the sacraments. These two forms contain a wealth of solid instruction on what the sacraments are.

Moreover, the sacraments do not teach us anything the word does not teach us. It is not that the word teaches us the gospel, and the sacraments give us something extra. Both the word and the sacraments give us Christ, but in different ways. The sacraments are not something mysterious for the hyper-spiritual or the "initiated." Every believer may and should partake of the sacraments.

Finally, the sacraments never teach us anything contrary to the word of the gospel. It is not true, for example, that the gospel teaches us salvation by particular, sovereign, efficacious grace, and then the sacraments contradict that message by teaching us that salvation is by works. There is and must be harmony between the message of the gospel and the sacraments. Thus, we see the close connection between the word and the sacraments as marks of the true church. When the preaching is unfaithful, the administration of the sacraments will be corrupted. But where the true gospel is preached, and the sacraments are faithfully administered according to the same word of God, there God blesses the means of grace to our hearts.

Martyn McGeown

November 26 — **The Sacraments Appealing to Our Senses**

O taste and see that the LORD is good: blessed is the man that trusteth in him. —Psalm 34:8

Some have complained that Reformed Christianity is so centered on the word of God, on hearing the preaching, that we neglect the other senses of the believer. This, of course, is not true. The Lord knows that we are creatures who see, taste, touch, and smell. In the Old Testament, the worship was sensual: that is, it appealed to the senses. The New Testament is less so. The primary organ is the ear. However, God has not neglected our other senses.

This does not mean that we need to invent sensual ways to worship God. We will not, for example, be using images "as books to the laity;"[*] we do not need overhead projectors or PowerPoint presentations to enhance our worship. We will not add drama, sketches, and skits, or puppet shows to teach (or entertain) our congregations; nor do we need elaborately decorated sanctuaries or sweet-smelling incense to improve our experience of salvation.

But, the Lord has given us "visual aids." They are called the sacraments. And since God has ordained them, we know that they are truly visual aids, that is, things we can see (visual) which truly do help (aid) us to understand spiritual realities. God has promised to help our infirmities through these things, not through things we might invent to titillate our senses. God has not promised to strengthen faith through images, dramas, or liturgical dances. In fact, God is offended at human innovations in his worship.

Consider what beautiful aids God has given us. In baptism, we see water being applied to a little baby or to an adult convert. This teaches us that, just as water washes away the filth of the body, so the blood and Spirit of Christ wash away the filth of sin. In the Lord's supper, we see the loaf of bread being broken, and we see the red wine being poured out, and we are immediately reminded of the broken body and shed blood of our Lord Jesus Christ on the cross, which is our very salvation. And then we take the bread, we handle it, we smell it, and we taste it; and we taste, smell, and swallow the wine. These very simple actions teach us a profound truth: just as by eating and drinking bread and wine, we are nourished physically, so by eating and drinking the body and blood of Jesus Christ by faith, we are nourished spiritually unto eternal life.

Let us use these visual aids—and no other—in the church of Jesus Christ.

Martyn McGeown

---

[*] Heidelberg Catechism 98, in Schaff, *Creeds of Christendom*, 3:343.

November 27 — Visible Signs

*Ask thee a sign of the Lord thy God;
ask it either in the depth, or in the height above.* —Isaiah 7:11

The most complete definition of sacraments given in Article 33 is that they are "visible signs and seals of an inward and invisible thing." We have already examined what a seal is—the guarantee of the authenticity of something. With reference to the sacraments, they are seals, because they are God's stamp of authenticity, confirming what he has already promised in his word.

Sacraments are also signs. A sign is some visible object or action that points to a higher reality, which, in the case of the sacraments, is a spiritual, invisible reality. A sign is also a message without words. We have all heard the saying, "A picture is worth a thousand words." A sign (a picture) can communicate a message without using words. Many road signs are like this: they have no words, but every driver instantly recognizes what they mean. Other signs have words but still point to a higher reality. Consider a sign pointing towards the airport. It tells you in which direction the airport is and usually how far away it is. If you follow the sign, you will arrive at your desired destination.

The gospel is a message of invisible, spiritual realities in words. Jesus Christ, the object of our faith, sits at the right hand of the Father; we cannot see the blood of Christ which was shed for our salvation; and the Holy Spirit who applies the blood of Christ to us, thus cleansing us from our sins, is invisible. None of us have ever seen any of those things. The gospel proclaims the truth of our salvation—and especially the forgiveness of sins in the blood of Christ—and the sacraments signify it, or make it known to us by signs.

The Lord has given two signs. The first is baptism, which is the sign of the washing away of our sins. It has other meanings, too, because all of God's signs are rich signs, but washing is its primary meaning. When the water of baptism is applied to a baby or to an adult convert in the public worship service by an ordained man who preaches the word, baptism is a sign of the washing away of sins. We see by faith the washing away of our sins as we contemplate the sacrament. But when you take a shower, that is not a sign of the washing away of your sins. That is not baptism—it has not been designed by God to picture the washing away of your sins and to seal the same by the Holy Spirit who strengthens faith in your heart.

The second is the Lord's supper, which is a sign of Christ feeding our souls by his crucified body and shed blood by faith. Perhaps you eat a large meal at home and are greatly nourished by that. That is not a sacrament—by that, Christ does not feed you with his crucified body and shed blood. Not all washings and not all meals are sacraments.

These signs are designed—as we shall see—to direct our faith away from ourselves to the one sacrifice of Christ accomplished for our salvation on the cross.

Martyn McGeown

November 28 — What Sacraments Signify

Looking unto Jesus the author and finisher of our faith.
—Hebrews 12:2

According to Article 33, the sacraments are signs of mainly two things: "that which [God] signifies to us by his word, and that which he works inwardly in our hearts." Here, again, we see a beautiful harmony between word and sacrament. What the word proclaims, the sacraments signify and seal.

Our salvation is both objective and subjective.

By objective, I mean that which is done outside of us and is done for us. Christ died on the cross for us; he rose again for our justification. This truth of what Christ has done for us is signified and sealed to us in the two sacraments. The sacraments teach us about the whole of our salvation. We see in baptism a beautiful picture of the removal of the guilt, filth, and pollution of our sins. Water washes away dirt; the blood and Spirit of Christ wash away sin. In the Lord's supper, God gives us another picture: as the minister breaks the bread and pours out the wine, we see a picture of the awful sufferings of our Savior on the cross. "This is my body which is broken for you: this do in remembrance of me" (1 Cor. 11:24).

By subjective, I mean that which is done in us, what the Spirit works in our hearts. The sacraments signify and seal unto us that invisible, spiritual life which we have in Christ. Titus 3:5 speaks, for example, of "the washing of regeneration, and renewing of the Holy Ghost." And, in the supper, the Spirit signifies and seals that invisible, spiritual nourishment of our souls as we feed by faith on Jesus Christ. That is, the sacraments teach us about sanctification.

All of these show us that the sacraments are signs and seals of what God does, not of what we do. Baptism is, among other things, a sign of our entering the kingdom of God. We do not enter it by an act of our own, but by the gracious act of God "who hath delivered us from the power of darkness, and hath translated us into the kingdom of his dear Son" (Col. 1:13). It is also a sign of our being buried into Christ and our being raised again with him (Rom. 6:3–4). But we do not bury ourselves into Christ, nor do we raise ourselves from spiritual death. Everything is the gracious work of our God. For this reason, we reject the notions of those who teach that baptism is primarily a testimony to what we do in receiving Jesus as savior. Some have even said that baptism is a visible sign of an invisible decision! Nothing could be further from the truth.

Let us, then, understand what the sacraments signify and receive that by faith.

Martyn McGeown

November 29 — The Spirit's Work in the Sacraments

*But canst not tell whence [the wind] cometh,
and whither it goeth: so is every one that is born of the Spirit.* —John 3:8

The sacraments are real means of grace because the Holy Spirit is pleased to strengthen faith by them. Without the Holy Spirit, the sacraments are and do nothing. Moreover, the preaching and the sacraments are the only means which the Holy Spirit has promised to use. Fanatics and hyper-spirituals despise these means to their own hurt. Those who neglect church membership and a diligent use of means cannot expect to thrive spiritually. We must not expect, therefore, to grow in grace by going for strolls in the forest or gazing at the ocean, "getting close to God through nature." We do expect to grow in grace—and with good reason, because God has promised it—by using the word and sacraments.

How the Spirit works in the sacraments is in many ways mysterious. We can rule out a few errors in this connection. There is no inherent power in the elements of water, bread, and wine to impart any spiritual benefit to us. The sacraments do not work like magic. We reject all forms of sacramental sorcery. The Spirit does not work in the water to give it magical sin-cleansing properties. Nor does he change the bread and wine into something else—the body and blood of Jesus Christ. Moreover, as we have seen, the sacraments do not dispense grace automatically. At the same time, their efficacy does not depend on our faith. God's work never depends on our work. On the contrary, we depend on God for the beginning, strengthening, and continuance of our faith. Christ is "the author and finisher of our faith" (Heb. 12:2).

At the same time, we must resist the temptation to say that the sacraments are mere signs. This was the error of Ulrich Zwingli, one of the earliest Reformers. He overreacted to Rome's errors and stripped the sacraments of their meaning. For Zwingli, the Lord's supper was only a remembrance, and Christ was not present in any sense. The sacraments, then, were not means of grace: they did not nourish and strengthen faith. How could they, if they did not bring Christ? Article 33 warns against an impoverished view of the sacraments: "the signs are not in vain or insignificant, so as to deceive us." Will a man give his bride a wedding ring of fool's gold? How much less will our God give us empty sacraments with no substance?

The Spirit, in a way which surpasses our understanding, takes hold of ordinary water, bread, and wine, and so works in them that by them he strengthens and nourishes our faith by directing us more and more to Jesus Christ. Does he need the sacraments to do this? Not at all. Nevertheless, he is pleased to use them. Let us, then, not be wiser than God by despising these gifts of his grace.

Martyn McGeown

November 30 — The Sacramental Union

*They drank of that spiritual Rock that followed them:
and that Rock was Christ.* —1 Corinthians 10:4

In our treatment of the sacraments, we have seen various relationships. We have examined the relationship between the sacraments and faith: the sacraments strengthen preexisting faith. We have noted the relationship between sacraments and the word: the sacraments are added to the word to confirm its promises and depend upon the word to explain them. We have set forth the relationship between the sacraments and the Holy Spirit: the Holy Spirit is pleased to operate through the sacraments to make them real means of grace. Now, we look at something called the sacramental union. That theological term does not appear in the Belgic Confession, but much confusion in connection with the sacraments will be avoided if we make note of it here.

By *sacramental union*, we mean that there is a definite relationship between the sign (the sacrament) and the thing signified (the reality of covenant salvation in Jesus Christ). The relationship is not one of identity. That would mean that the sign is the thing signified, that the water of baptism is the washing away of sins itself—or even the blood and Spirit of Christ—and that the bread and wine of the Lord's supper are spiritual nourishment—or Christ's actual flesh and blood. If the relationship were one of identity, we would have no sign, only the thing signified. A sign points to something else: it is not that thing to which it points. How foolish would a man be to park his car beside a sign of an airplane and imagine that he had arrived at the airport! Equally foolish are those who imagine that the sacraments are what they signify.

Instead, the sacramental union means that because of the close connection or association between the sign and the thing signified, the one is called after the name of the other. This is rather common in Scripture, but it ought not confuse us. God speaks this way with respect to Old Testament ordinances: "My covenant shall be in your flesh" (Gen. 17:13); "Christ our passover is sacrificed" (1 Cor. 5:7); "That Rock was Christ" (1 Cor. 10:4). Because of the close sacramental union, circumcision is called the covenant, and both the rock and passover are called Christ. The same is true of the New Testament sacraments: "This cup is the new testament in my blood" (Luke 22:20); and "the washing of regeneration" (Tit. 3:5). We know, of course, that neither the cup itself nor the contents of the cup are the testament; and we know that the water of baptism is not regeneration. We do not confuse the sign with the thing signified or the sign with the reality.

Failure to appreciate this language of sacramental union in Scripture leads to the deadly errors of Rome, for, as we shall see, Rome does teach that baptism really washes away sin and that the bread and wine of the Lord's supper become the actual body and blood of Jesus Christ in a kind of magical way. Relationships are important, especially relationships in theology.

Let there be no confusion. Let us use the sacraments without superstition but to our edification and growth in grace.

Martyn McGeown

December 1 — Christ, The True Object of the Sacraments

Let him kiss me with the kisses of his mouth:
for thy love is better than wine. —Song of Solomon 1:2

The sacraments point to Christ and to his perfect work. They are holy pledges of Christ's eternal love to his church—more than once we have called them the wedding ring of the heavenly Bridegroom to the bride, the church. Other theologians have called the sacraments the kiss of Christ. These are all beautiful expressions.

But what bride would be so focused on the wedding ring on her finger as to neglect the bridegroom himself? The wedding ring has no meaning at all without the bridegroom who gives it. Therefore, the sacraments must never be used to draw the devotion of the bride away from Christ but always to deepen the ardent love and passionate longing of the bride for the Bridegroom.

The Bible tells us that as soon as the church was espoused to Christ, the Bridegroom left her to go to heaven. This was not cruel abandonment of the church by Christ. He ascended to heaven to prepare a place for us, and he will be absent from his bride for a short while until everything is ready. Once all the elect are gathered, and all the enemies of our Lord are defeated, then Christ shall return to consummate the marriage, and the eternal "marriage supper of the Lamb" shall take place (Rev. 19:9). In the meantime, the bride of Christ must remain faithful to him. She does this by heeding his voice in the preaching. How the voice of the Bridegroom thrills the heart of the bride! But she also has the sacraments to confirm her, that wedding ring which is a constant reminder to her of that precious relationship with the heavenly Bridegroom. When she meditates upon the promises of Christ by looking at the ring, she says: "I am married. My Lord has promised to return. I will be faithful to him." What comfort and assurance her wedding ring is to her on those long, lonely days when the Bridegroom is absent!

Thus, everything the church does, including the sacraments, must lead her to Christ. Without Christ and our covenant relationship with Christ, the sacraments are meaningless and empty. But the sacraments are not given to us "to deceive us," says Article 33. How so? "Jesus Christ is the true object presented by them, without whom they would be of no moment." The sacraments, in beautiful but mysterious ways, point to Christ and his work on the cross, and in this way, by the power of the Spirit, they strengthen our weak and faltering faith as we wait for our Bridegroom's return.

What a gift God has given us in the sacraments!

Martyn McGeown

Article 34

OF HOLY BAPTISM

We believe and confess that Jesus Christ, who is the end of the law, hath made an end, by the shedding of his blood, of all other sheddings of blood which men could or would make as a propitiation or satisfaction for sin; and that he, having abolished circumcision, which was done with blood, hath instituted the Sacrament of Baptism instead thereof, by which we are received into the Church of God, and separated from all other people and strange religions, that we may wholly belong to him whose ensign and banner we bear, and which serves as a testimony unto us that he will forever be our gracious God and Father. Therefore he has commanded all those who are his to be baptized with pure water, *in the name of the Father, and of the Son, and of the Holy Ghost*: thereby signifying to us, that as water washeth away the filth of the body, when poured upon it, and is seen on the body of the baptized, when sprinkled upon him, so doth the blood of Christ, by the power of the Holy Ghost, internally sprinkle the soul, cleanse it from its sins, and regenerate us from children of wrath unto children of God. Not that this is effected by the external water, but by the sprinkling of the precious blood of the Son of God; who is our Red Sea, through which we must pass to escape the tyranny of Pharaoh, that is, the devil, and to enter into the spiritual land of Canaan. Therefore, the Ministers, on their part, administer the Sacrament, and that which is visible, but our Lord giveth that which is signified by the Sacrament, namely, the gifts and invisible grace; washing, cleansing, and purging our souls of all filth and unrighteousness; renewing our hearts and filling them with all comfort; giving unto us a true assurance of his fatherly goodness; putting on us the new man, and putting off the old man with all his deeds.

Therefore, we believe that every man who is earnestly studious of obtaining life eternal ought to be but once baptized with this only Baptism, without ever repeating the same: since we can not be born twice. Neither doth this Baptism only avail us at the time when the water is poured upon us and received by us, but also through the whole course of our life. Therefore we detest the error of the Anabaptists, who are not content with the one only baptism they have once received, and moreover condemn the baptism of the infants of believers, who, we believe, ought to be baptized and sealed with the sign of the covenant, as the children in Israel formerly were circumcised upon the same promises which are made unto our children. And, indeed, Christ shed his blood no less for the washing of the children of the faithful than for adult persons; and, therefore, they ought to receive the sign and sacrament of that which Christ hath done for them; as the Lord commanded in the law, that they should be made partakers of the sacrament of Christ's suffering and death shortly after they were born, by offering for them a lamb, which was a sacrament of Jesus Christ. Moreover, what Circumcision was to the Jews, that Baptism is to our children. And for this reason Paul calls Baptism the *Circumcision of Christ*.

December 2 — An End of All Other Sheddings of Blood

And almost all things are by the law purged with blood;
and without shedding of blood is no remission. —Hebrews 9:22

In Article 33, we looked at the idea of sacraments in general. Now we consider baptism. Remember two things as we study this important subject. First, we must make a distinction between the sign of baptism (water baptism) and the reality behind the sign (spiritual salvation). Second, sacraments are not only signs, but also seals, or pledges of the goodwill and grace of our God toward us, and therefore are not empty symbols. If we bear these two things in mind, we will avoid many errors.

Article 34 contrasts baptism with circumcision. This is fitting because they have essentially the same meaning. "Jesus Christ," says Article 33, "having abolished circumcision…hath instituted the sacrament of baptism instead thereof."

To understand baptism, therefore, we examine circumcision.

When an Israelite boy was but eight days old, the priest or his father would remove part of that child's flesh in a rite called circumcision. This was done according to God's express commandment. This taught the people that their corrupt flesh had to be cut off, that they had to be cleansed, in order to have fellowship with God. Colossians 2:11 calls circumcision "the putting off the body of the sins of the flesh." What man did with hands, God did spiritually without hands in the heart. Thus, God promised to circumcise the hearts of Israel and of their seed after them (Deut. 30:6).

Circumcision was, therefore, not a sign of Jewishness, of physical descent from Abraham, or of citizenship in the nation of Israel. Circumcision was the sign of the covenant, in which Jehovah was Israel's God and Israel was Jehovah's people "in their generations for an everlasting covenant" (Gen. 17:7, 11). This must be the case because a sign is a visible thing pointing to an invisible, spiritual reality. Neither physical descent from Abraham nor citizenship in Israel are invisible, spiritual realities, but spiritual circumcision of the heart and covenant membership are.

God abolished circumcision in the New Testament and fulfilled it in the better sign of baptism. He did this for at least three reasons. First, only boys were circumcised. In the New Testament, "there is neither male nor female" (Gal. 3:28). Second, circumcision divided Jews from Gentiles. Christ came to unite believing Jews and Gentles "in one body" by his sacrifice on the cross (Eph. 2:13–16). Third, and most importantly, circumcision involved the shedding of blood. In the New Testament, there is no more shedding of blood. By one sacrifice, Jesus Christ has accomplished everything which all shedding of blood in the Old Testament signified and promised. Thus, Article 33 says: "He, having abolished circumcision, which was done with blood, hath instituted the sacrament of baptism instead thereof."

Circumcision was a sacrament. It was a sign and a seal: Abraham "received the sign of circumcision, a seal of righteousness of [the] faith" (Rom. 4:11). In the New Testament, the signs and seals are baptism and the Lord's supper, both bloodless signs and seals of the finished work of our Savior.

Martyn McGeown

December 3 — Baptism: The Sacrament of Initiation

For by one Spirit are we all baptized into one body.
—1 Corinthians 12:13

God has given two sacraments. Both sacraments are bloodless because sacrifices have ceased with the one sacrifice of Christ on the cross, and both sacraments point to (signs) and assure us of (seals) salvation in the finished work of Jesus Christ on the cross. Of the two sacraments, baptism is the sacrament of initiation, for by it "we are received into the church of God" (Article 33).

Remember, again, that the one baptism of Scripture must be distinguished. Real, spiritual baptism (the reality, that which the Spirit performs in the hearts of God's people) is signified and sealed by water baptism (the sacrament). Not all who receive the sign (water baptism) receive the reality (spiritual salvation in the blood of Christ). Not all who are baptized in water are baptized by the Spirit and truly saved. We must never forget that, lest we fall into the errors of those who seek salvation in water baptism.

According to Article 34, water baptism as a sign is an initiatory sign, that is, it is the sign and seal of God bringing us into the covenant, church, and kingdom of God. The Spirit baptizes us into Christ at the beginning of our spiritual lives, so we are baptized with water as a sign of the beginning of our Christian lives.

This explains, too, the use of prepositions in connection with baptism. Prepositions are small but important words in Scripture that describe position or movement. The most common baptismal prepositions are *in* and *into*. Jesus commands that his people be baptized "in [literally *into*] the name of" the triune God (Matt. 28:19). Galatians 3:27 teaches: "For as many of you as have been baptized into Christ have put on Christ." 1 Corinthians 12:13 teaches: "For by one Spirit are we all baptized into one body." And Romans 6:3 teaches: "Know ye not that so many of us as were baptized into Jesus Christ were baptized into his death?" From these passages we conclude that in real spiritual baptism, we are brought into association with Christ; that we are united to him in his death and resurrection; that we come into fellowship with the triune God through Jesus Christ the mediator; and that we are united to Christ's spiritual body, which is the church. All of these glorious benefits (union with Christ and reception of all his benefits) are signified and sealed to us in the sacrament of water baptism.

Again, I issue a caution. Water baptism neither causes nor brings about these things, nor are these things dependent on water baptism. These things are promised to all believers in the gospel, and our confidence that these things are real and are given to us personally is strengthened and confirmed by the use of the sacraments.

Martyn McGeown

December 4 — Baptism: An Ensign and Banner

He brought me to the banqueting house,
and his banner over me was love. —Song of Solomon 2:4

Remember the illustration I used of the sacraments in previous meditations—a wedding ring. The sacraments are the token and pledge of Christ's love to his church, reminding her of his faithfulness and assuring her of his tender affection for her as she awaits his coming. A wedding ring serves another function—it is a mark of ownership. When a man places a wedding ring upon his bride, he says: "You are mine. You belong exclusively to me. You must share your love with no other man." And when a man sees a wedding ring on the finger of a beautiful woman, that ring speaks: "This woman is married. Do not touch her, lest you anger a jealous husband!"

According to Article 34, baptism marks us as belonging to Jesus Christ. This ought not surprise us since we have already learned that baptism signifies and seals our union with Jesus Christ (we are baptized into him). Baptism, therefore, acts as an ensign or banner. That figure, too, is familiar to us. Every organization rallies under a flag of some kind. For Americans, it is the stars and stripes, and for the British, it is the Union Flag. Armies, too, have ensigns and banners under which they gather. The banners are all different, so that one army can be distinguished from another. It would cause utter confusion on the battlefield if soldiers could not identify the banner under which they were fighting.

Spiritually speaking, baptism is the banner under which we rally as soldiers of Jesus Christ. By baptism, Christ marks us as belonging to him. Negatively, baptism separates us "from all other people and strange religions." In the Old Testament, there were the circumcised covenant people of God, and the "uncircumcised Philistines" (Judges 14:3). In the New Testament, there are the baptized people of God (the church) and the non-baptized heathen. Positively, baptism marks us out as Christians: "that we may wholly belong to him whose ensign and banner we bear, and which serves as a testimony to us that he will forever be our gracious God and Father" (Article 34).

This has great implications for how we live. A bride who wears the wedding ring of her husband does not live as if she belonged to herself; a soldier who bears aloft the banner of his commanding officer does not live as he pleases; and a Christian who is baptized does not live as if he belonged to the world. Christian parents who bring their children for baptism, and adult converts who by baptism are received as members of the Christian church, must remember this.

This solemn responsibility comes upon all baptized members, both adults and children: that we live holy lives in devotion to the one in whose name we are baptized. Those who live in ungodliness deny their baptism. Let us live as baptized believers in gratitude to our heavenly Bridegroom, whose love is confirmed to us in the sacrament of baptism!

Martyn McGeown

December 5 — Baptism: A Washing

Arise, and be baptized, and wash away thy sins, calling on the name of the Lord. —Acts 22:16

Water baptism is a washing. This ought to be obvious because of the element of water. In baptism, we do not drink the water, nor do we drown the person in water, but we sprinkle or pour the water on the person who is being baptized. Water is the universal cleansing agent, and it is used both in the Old and New Testament to purify from filth or defilement (Ezek. 36:25; Heb. 10:22).

Even children can understand this very important aspect of baptism. Why do we take showers? Why do we wash our hands? Because we are dirty! Why during the worship service do we bring a person—often a little child—to have water sprinkled upon him? Because in so doing, we confess that we and our children are sinners—spiritually dirty, defiled, and unclean—and we must be washed.

Baptism tells us not only that we need to be washed, but also that we are washed by the blood and Spirit of Jesus Christ. Baptism declares to sinners, guilty and worthy of punishment, shameful and polluted by nature, that God has cleansed and purified us. Baptism takes our eyes off ourselves and directs our attention to the perfect work of Christ. There on the cross, our sins were washed away. And when we see the water of baptism washing the dirt from a baptized person, we are reminded of and strengthened in our faith in the power of Christ's blood to cleanse us from sin.

Thus, water baptism becomes a seal or a guarantee of spiritual salvation. Do you doubt that pure water has the power to wash away the dirt of the body? Then do not doubt that the blood and Spirit of Christ cleanse you from all sin. Of course, we do not believe that water washes away our sins, even the water used in the sacrament of baptism. It is not magical water! But we do believe that the water of baptism is used by God himself to assure us that Christ's blood washes away our sins. This is because the Spirit is pleased to use baptism to strengthen our faith. All this explains the sacramental language of Article 34: "signifying to us, that as water washeth away the filth of body…so doth the blood of Christ, by the power of the Holy Spirit, internally sprinkle the soul…of all filth and unrighteousness."

How foolish, then, to come to water baptism puffed up with notions of one's own righteousness. One who comes to be washed confesses that he is unclean! But what a beautiful picture we have in baptism of our salvation—just as water cleanses the body, so the blood and Spirit of Jesus Christ cleanse us from all sin. Believe that and be comforted!

Martyn McGeown

December 6 — **Christ Our Red Sea**

All our fathers were under the cloud,
and all passed through the sea; and were all baptized unto Moses
in the cloud and in the sea. —1 Corinthians 10:1–2

In the Old Testament, there are two types or pictures pointing ahead to the reality of spiritual baptism, which reality is now signified and sealed to us in the sacrament of water baptism. The first is the flood. Of this, Peter writes: "The like figure whereunto even baptism doth also now save us" (1 Pet. 3:21). The second is the passing through the Red Sea of Exodus 14. Article 34 makes reference to this second picture: "the sprinkling of the precious blood of the Son of God, who is our Red Sea, through which we must pass to escape the tyranny of Pharaoh, that is, the devil, and to enter into the spiritual land of Canaan."

The typology of the passage through the Red Sea is clear. Israel is God's church, loved, chosen, and redeemed by the blood of Christ. Egypt is the world of sin and death, especially its enslaving power, with Pharaoh as the tyrant of that world, the devil. Moses is the mediator of God's people, and therefore a picture of Jesus Christ. Jesus calls us to follow him and promises to bring us safely into the promised land and into fellowship with God there. Canaan is the land where God dwells and is therefore a picture of heaven. And the wilderness wanderings picture the Christian pilgrimage, a life of trials, and a life lived in faith, following Jesus Christ wherever he leads us. The passage through the Red Sea is the means by which God separates his people from sin and death and consecrates them to himself, and the way in which God finally destroys Egypt and the power of sin. Therefore, the crossing of the Red Sea is a type of the cross through which God's people are redeemed. Thus, Article 34 fittingly and beautifully identifies the crucified Christ as "our Red Sea," and the sprinkling of his blood as the way of our salvation. All of these are signified and sealed to us in baptism.

Several other points we notice from this typology. First, not all the Israelites who experienced the type or picture experienced the reality. All the Israelites were baptized (1 Cor. 10:2), but not all were united to Jesus Christ by a living faith. The same is true in the church today: all the members of the church, and all the children of godly parents, are baptized with water, but God gives the reality only to his elect. Second, by baptism unto Moses, Israel was consecrated, or set apart, unto God and his mediator, Moses, who is a picture of Jesus Christ. We saw that already when we considered baptism as an ensign and banner. Third, in both pictures of the Red Sea and the flood, the ungodly were immersed, drowned, and destroyed, while God's people were sprinkled and saved. This has implications for the mode of baptism: Article 34 speaks of sprinkling, not immersion. And, finally, in the passage through the Red Sea, children were baptized. This has importance for the subject of infant baptism in the church today.

What a rich picture God has given us in baptism! Let us use the sacrament believingly and gladly for God's glory and for our own comfort!

Martyn McGeown

December 7 — Not That This is Effected by the External Water

The blood of Jesus Christ his Son cleanseth us from all sin.
—1 John 1:7

Baptism signifies and seals regeneration unto us: "the blood of Christ, by the power of the Holy Spirit, [doth] internally sprinkle the soul, cleanse it from its sins, and regenerate us from children of wrath unto children of God." In addition, baptism signifies and seals unto us: "[God's] gifts and invisible grace; washing, cleansing, and purging our souls of all filth and unrighteousness; renewing our hearts and filling them with all comfort; giving unto us a true assurance of his fatherly goodness; putting on us the new man, and putting off the old man with all his deeds" (Article 34).

As we see the sprinkling of water in the sacrament, we are reminded of these marvelous benefits and assured by the Spirit that these benefits are indeed ours. As water washes us from dirt, so surely and more so do the blood and Spirit of Christ cleanse us from all sin.

But lest we trust superstitiously in the sacrament of water baptism itself, Article 34 adds these words: "Not that this is effected by the external water." These words are necessary to confute the errors of Roman Catholicism. At the time of the Reformation and now, Rome taught and teaches the error of baptismal regeneration. The catechism of the Roman Catholic Church states: "By baptism all *sins* are forgiven, original sin and all personal sins, as well as all punishment for sin."* Earlier, it teaches: "The sacrament is also called *'the washing of regeneration and renewal by the Holy Spirit'* for it signifies and actually brings about the birth of water and the Spirit."** Rome teaches the opposite of the Belgic Confession. Our creed declares: "Not that this is effected by the external water." Rome insists that spiritual salvation is effected by the external water.

Rome's error is simple and deadly. Rome confuses the sign with the reality and thus overthrows the very nature and meaning of sacraments. Sacraments are signs and seals. They are not, and can never be, the reality which they signify. We will see this again when we look at Rome's errors concerning the Lord's supper. Rome fails to understand the sacramental union: that Scripture speaks of the sign in terms of the thing signified because of the close connection between the two (for example, it speaks of "the washing of regeneration" in Titus 3:5).

Wisely, however, Article 34 does not overreact to the errors of Rome. Neither the element of water nor the minister who baptizes can give the reality, but this does not mean that baptism is an empty sign: "our Lord giveth that which is signified by the sacrament, namely, the gifts and invisible grace." We do not seek the reality in water, but neither does God deceive and mock us. God graciously gives the thing signified to us. That's the beauty of our salvation: all of grace!

Martyn McGeown

---

* *Catechism of the Catholic Church*, paragraph 1263.
** *Catechism of the Catholic Church*, paragraph 1215.

December 8 — One Only Baptism

One Lord, one faith, one baptism. —Ephesians 4:5

At the time of the Reformation, the Reformed churches battled against the Roman Catholic Church on the left and against the Anabaptists on the right. Article 34 is harshly critical of Anabaptism: "we detest the error of the Anabaptists." This is the case especially because the civil authorities in Europe wickedly grouped all Protestant "heretics" with the radical Anabaptists. Many of the Anabaptists were violent revolutionaries, some were mystics, others had heretical notions of the person and work of Christ, but all had one thing in common: they rejected infant baptism and insisted on rebaptism for their followers. The name *Anabaptism* means *rebaptism*. The spiritual children of the Anabaptists are especially the Baptists and Charismatics.

Against all Anabaptism, Article 34 insists on one baptism. "Every man who is earnestly studious of obtaining life eternal ought to be but once baptized with this only baptism, without ever repeating the same, since we cannot be born twice."

The Bible is clear: "one baptism" (Eph. 4:5)! The Holy Spirit baptizes all of God's people but once into Christ (Gal. 3:27), but once into Christ's death and resurrection (Rom. 6:3), and but once into Christ's spiritual body (1 Cor. 12:13). Just as we are not born again, and again, and again, so we are not baptized again, and again, and again, either with the reality or with the sign of water. Reformed churches, therefore, refuse to baptize again someone who was properly baptized in another church, as long as his previous baptism was valid—with water, in the name of the triune God, and by an ordained officebearer.

But perhaps someone might object: Should we not be baptized over and over again because we sin over and over again? Not at all: "Neither doth this baptism avail us only at the time when the water is poured upon us and received by us, but also through the whole course of our life." The Spirit engrafts us but once into Christ, but the effects of that spiritual baptism are ongoing. Martin Luther would often take comfort from his baptism. When doubts and temptations assailed him, he would say, "I am baptized." By this, Luther was not trusting in his water baptism but reminding himself of the sign and seal of baptism, that as surely as water washes away the filth of the body, so surely he was washed from his sins in the blood and Spirit of Christ.

An elderly saint can have the same comfort today as he sits in a baptismal service. Many years ago, he was baptized with water. He cannot remember his own baptism, and he certainly does not need to seek another baptism, but every time he sees a baptism, he is reminded of it: "I am baptized. I have—once and for all—the reality which is signified and sealed to me in water baptism. And believing that, I have comfort." So do we!

Martyn McGeown

December 9   **The Baptism of Our Children**

For the promise is unto you, and to your children,
and to all that are afar off, even as many as
the Lord our God shall call. —Acts 2:39

Reformed churches have always practiced infant baptism. We do so, not because we can find an explicit command in the Bible to do so—there is none—but because of God's covenant promise to our children.

Again, Article 34 finds a parallel between baptism and circumcision. In the Old Testament, God's covenant included the children of believers. Therefore, they were marked with the sign of the covenant. Nothing has changed in the New Testament, except the sign itself. In fact, we would be surprised if under the Old Testament times of types and shadows, the children of believers had greater privileges than they do now under the New Testament with the coming of Christ. That would be the case if children were no longer in God's covenant. But, Peter immediately on the day of Pentecost assures the people that God's promise still includes the children of believers: "For the promise is unto you, and to your children" (Acts 2:39).

The argument for infant baptism is surprisingly simple. God promises to give to our children the reality of salvation. Therefore, we give to them the sign of that which God promises. Since God is faithful and keeps his promises, we can be assured as Christian parents that God will save and has already saved our elect seed. That is why we treat the children of believers as the lambs of Christ's flock and the children of God—not the way the Baptists do, as "little vipers," as unsaved, unregenerate children. Thus, Article 34 insists, in opposition to the grievous and distressing error of the Anabaptists: "indeed, Christ shed his blood no less for the washing of the children of the faithful than for adult persons; and therefore they ought to receive the sign and sacrament of that which Christ hath done for them."

First, children of believers are members of the covenant of God. This means that God says about our children: "I will be their God and Father, to love them, care for them, and save them from their sins." In every manifestation of the covenant, God declared to his people that he included the children. Second, children of believers are citizens of Christ's kingdom. Therefore, they are ruled by the word and Spirit of Christ (Mark 10:13–14; Luke 18:16). Third, children of believers are members of the church. Paul addresses them as such (1 Cor. 7:14; Col. 3:20). These promises are not to the children when they grow up, but to the children as they are currently, as children.

If children have the reality—spiritual salvation in Jesus Christ, the forgiveness of their sins, and eternal life—they must be given the sign and seal of the reality. We believe, says Article 34, that they "ought to be baptized and sealed with the sign of the covenant, as the children in Israel formerly were circumcised upon the same promises which are made unto our children." We do not, as the Baptists do, wait until our children are old enough to confess their faith before we baptize them.

What mercy! Christ washes us and our children from sin in his own blood, and he has given us the sign and seal of baptism to assure us of this truth. In this hope, we bring forth and raise children to the glory of his name!

Martyn McGeown

Article 35

OF THE HOLY SUPPER OF OUR LORD JESUS CHRIST

We believe and confess that our Saviour Jesus Christ did ordain and institute the Sacrament of the Holy Supper, to nourish and support those whom he hath already regenerated and incorporated into his family, which is his Church. Now those who are regenerated have in them a twofold life, the one bodily and temporal, which they have from the first birth, and is common to all men; the other spiritual and heavenly, which is given them in their second birth, which is effected by the word of the gospel, in the communion of the body of Christ; and this life is not common, but is peculiar to God's elect. In like manner God hath given us, for the support of the bodily and earthly life, earthly and common bread, which is subservient thereto, and is common to all men, even as life itself. But for the support of the spiritual and heavenly life which believers have, he hath sent a living bread, which descended from heaven, namely, Jesus Christ, who nourishes and strengthens the spiritual life of believers, when they eat him, that is to say, when they apply and receive him by faith, in the Spirit. Christ, that he might represent unto us this spiritual and heavenly bread, hath instituted an earthly and visible bread as a Sacrament of his body, and wine as a Sacrament of his blood, to testify by them unto us, that, as certainly as we receive and hold this Sacrament in our hands, and eat and drink the same with our mouths, by which our life is afterwards nourished, we also do as certainly receive by faith (which is the hand and mouth of our soul) the true body and blood of Christ our only Saviour in our souls, for the support of our spiritual life.

Now, as it is certain and beyond all doubt that Jesus Christ hath not enjoined to us the use of his Sacraments in vain, so he works in us all that he represents to us by these holy signs, though the manner surpasses our understanding, and can not be comprehended by us, as the operations of the Holy Ghost are hidden and incomprehensible. In the mean time we err not when we say that what is eaten and drunk by us is the proper and natural body and the proper blood of Christ. But the manner of our partaking of the same is not by the mouth, but by the Spirit through faith. Thus, then, though Christ always sits at the right hand of his Father in the heavens, yet doth he not, therefore, cease to make us partakers of himself by faith. This feast is a spiritual table, at which Christ communicates himself with all his benefits to us, and gives us there to enjoy both himself and the merits of his sufferings and death, nourishing, strengthening, and comforting our poor comfortless souls, by the eating of his flesh, quickening and refreshing them by the drinking of his blood.

Further, though the Sacraments are connected with the thing signified, nevertheless both are not received by all men: the ungodly indeed receives the Sacrament to his condemnation, but he doth not receive the truth of the Sacrament. As Judas and Simon the sorcerer both, indeed, received the Sacrament, but not Christ, who was signified by it, of whom believers only are made partakers. Lastly, we receive this holy Sacrament in the assembly of the people of God, with humility and reverence, keeping up among us a holy remembrance of the death of Christ our Saviour, with thanksgiving, making there confession of our faith and of the Christian religion. Therefore no one ought to come to this table without having previously rightly examined himself; lest by eating of this bread and drinking of this cup he eat and drink judgment to himself. In a word, we are excited by the use of this holy Sacrament to a fervent love towards God and our neighbor.

Therefore, we reject all mixtures and damnable inventions, which men have added unto and blended with the Sacraments, as profanations of them, and affirm that we ought to rest satisfied with the ordinance which Christ and his Apostles have taught us, and that we must speak of them in the same manner as they have spoken.

December 10 — A Twofold Life, A Twofold Bread

That which is born of the flesh is flesh;
and that which is born of the Spirit is spirit.
Marvel not that I said unto thee,
Ye must be born again. —John 3:6–7

In connection with its teaching on the Lord's supper, Article 35 begins with regeneration. This might be surprising to us, but it is a very fitting approach. There are two kinds of people. First, there is the unregenerate man. God's word uses various terms to describe him: he is "born of the flesh" (John 3:6), "the natural man" (1 Cor. 2:14), and "carnally minded" (Rom. 8:6). The only life of unregenerate people is natural, physical life. Such people do not have spiritual life, eternal life, or everlasting life. They are "dead in trespasses and sins" (Eph. 2:1) and "alienated and enemies in [their] mind by wicked works" (Col. 1:21). Second, there is the regenerate man. He is the opposite of the unregenerate man: he is "born of the Spirit" (John 3:6), "spiritual" (1 Cor. 2:15), and "spiritually minded" (Rom. 8:6). These are God's children, believers, to whom God has given spiritual, eternal, everlasting life.

The difference between unregenerate and regenerate people is God's grace. Graciously, God gives life to some and does not give that life to others. God quickens (or makes alive) some with Jesus Christ; others remain "dead in [their] trespasses and sins" (Eph. 2:1–4). This life, says Article 35, is "peculiar to God's elect." No man can make himself alive. No man can even desire to make himself alive. God quickens or makes alive whom he wills.

Therefore, God's regenerate people have a twofold life, whereas unregenerate unbelievers have only one form of life. One life is corporal and temporal, that is, it pertains to the body and time. It is that biological life that holds body and soul together and ends at physical death. This life—which is common to both believers and unbelievers—is sustained by physical bread, called "earthly and common bread" in Article 35. The other life is called "spiritual and heavenly" by Article 35 because it is worked in us by the Holy Spirit and has its source in heaven. This life is sustained by a different bread, the "living bread…namely, Jesus Christ."

To understand the meaning and benefit of the Lord's supper, we must have this difference clearly before our minds. One who is dead cannot be nourished by bread, even if that bread is placed before him or even placed in his mouth. Bread is for the living, not the dead! One who is spiritually dead (that is, unregenerate) cannot be nourished by the living bread from heaven, who is Jesus Christ, even if that living bread is presented in the preaching of the gospel and in the Lord's supper. The Lord's supper nourishes only the spiritually alive. It cannot nourish those who have no spiritual life because it is not designed to support this "corporal and temporal life."

On the night in which our Lord Jesus Christ was betrayed, he instituted the Lord's supper, a means of grace to his church, by which we partake of the crucified body and shed blood of our savior. By such partaking, the spiritual life of regeneration is nourished and supported. By means of the Lord's supper, God's regenerate, believing people receive the living bread, Jesus Christ. This is a great wonder that we will explain in future meditations.

Martyn McGeown

December 11 — Jesus Christ, the Living Bread

For the bread of God is he which cometh down from heaven,
and giveth life unto the world. —John 6:33

In the synagogue of Capernaum, Jesus Christ proclaimed to a crowd of unbelieving Jews that he is the bread of life.

This caused great offense to the Jews. "How can this man give us his flesh to eat?" they asked (John 6:52). Because the Jews took Jesus' words literally, they could make no sense of them. The law of God forbade the eating of human flesh and the drinking of blood. The very idea was grotesque to a Jew. Later, Jesus says to Jews, albeit believing Jews, to his disciples: "Take, eat; this is my body…Drink ye all of it; for this is my blood" (Matt. 26:26–28). At that time, the disciples, who had been rebuked before for taking Jesus' words too literally (Matt. 16:11–12), showed no sign of alarm.

In John 6 and Matthew 26, Jesus spoke figuratively, but what he said was very significant. First, Jesus makes the bold claim that he—the carpenter from Nazareth—actually came down from heaven. This caused the unbelieving Jews to murmur at the seeming impossibility of it (John 6:33, 41–42). Second, Jesus compares himself to the life-sustaining manna given by God through Moses to God's people in the wilderness (John 6:31–32). Manna was necessary to keep the Israelites physically alive. Without the manna, they would have perished of hunger in the hot, dry, howling wilderness (Deut. 32:10). Jesus Christ is even more necessary for the spiritual life of his people—he is not an optional extra or luxury, but essential to our life. This caused the unbelieving Jews to murmur because they knew Jesus' family in Nazareth and would not believe his words (John 6:42). Third, Jesus shows that his flesh must be broken, and his blood must be shed. Only a crucified and risen Jesus can save us from our sins and impart life: "The bread that I will give is my flesh, which I will give for the life of the world" (John 6:51). Fourth, Jesus shows that a man can only be nourished by the bread of life, which is the flesh and blood of Jesus Christ, by eating and drinking him: "Except ye eat the flesh of the Son of man, and drink his blood, ye have no life in you. Whoso eateth my flesh, and drinketh my blood, hath eternal life…For my flesh is meat indeed, and my blood is drink indeed" (John 6:53–55). These last two points caused the unbelieving Jews to murmur. They knew he was not inviting them to commit cannibalism, but what did Jesus mean?

That Jesus was speaking figuratively here ought to be clear. Thus, Article 35 describes Jesus Christ as one who "nourishes and strengthens the spiritual life of believers when they eat him, that is to say, when they apply and receive him by faith, in the Spirit." This is exactly the explanation which Jesus gives in John 6:35, "I am the bread of life: he that cometh to me shall never hunger; and he that believeth on me shall never thirst."

Christ is the Bread of Life, and we feed on him in the Lord's supper by faith. Only by faith.

Martyn McGeown

December 12 — An Earthly Representative of a Spiritual Bread

Take, eat; this is my body. —Matthew 26:26

The Lord's supper is a sacrament, and we remember that a sacrament is two things: a sign and a seal. That the Lord's supper is a sign of the crucified body and shed blood of Jesus Christ means that the bread and wine of the Lord's supper are visible symbols or representations of something spiritual that we cannot see. The bread and wine are not the things they represent. If they were, they would not be signs, and the Lord's supper would not be a sacrament.

Christ, understanding the weakness of our faith and our incapacity to comprehend spiritual things, has given us an earthly bread to represent a heavenly bread. We know what earthly bread is—the food which we take in with our mouths, digest in our stomachs, and which nourishes our physical life. We have seen what heavenly or spiritual bread is—Jesus Christ, the Son of God, who came in our flesh, was crucified, died, and buried, and who has risen again for us. Therefore, he calls himself the bread of life. He is the vital food for our souls.

What, then, is the relationship between these two "breads"?

To this, several answers have been given. The Belgic Confession does not identify the different views and does not name the controversies swirling around this question at the time of the Reformation, but we can briefly set them forth here. The Roman Catholic Church taught, and still teaches, transubstantiation. The Roman Catholic believes that the bread and wine in the Lord's supper (which Roman Catholics call the mass) have changed. Here are Rome's own words: "in the most blessed sacrament of the Eucharist the body and blood, together with the soul and divinity, of our Lord Jesus Christ, and therefore *the whole Christ, is truly, really, and substantially contained.*"* Rome's view is that the entire substance of the bread and the entire substance of the wine have changed, so that there is no bread and wine, only the body and blood of Christ. Thus, the two "breads" are identical. One bread (the earthly) has changed into the other bread (the heavenly). Lutheranism rejects transubstantiation, but still insists that Christ's physical body is present in the Lord's supper. That view is called consubstantiation, the idea that the body and blood of Christ are "in, with, and under" the bread and wine. Thus, the one bread (the heavenly) coexists with the other bread (the earthly).

We reject both transubstantiation and consubstantiation. Christ's physical body and blood are not present in the Lord's supper. If they were, the sacrament would no longer be a sign. Instead, the one bread (the earthly) is a sign, a representation, of the other bread (the heavenly).

But does that mean, then, that the Lord's supper is merely a sign? Not at all! It is also a seal, as we shall see in our next meditation.

Martyn McGeown

---

* *Catechism of the Catholic Church*, paragraph 1374.

December 13 — He Works in Us All That He Represents to Us

The cup of blessing which we bless, is it not the communion of the blood of Christ? The bread which we break, is it not the communion of the body of Christ? —1 Corinthians 10:16

One of the great dangers in theology is overreacting to the errors of others. This is a great temptation when studying the truth about the sacraments and the Lord's supper in particular. Rome, as we noted yesterday, teaches transubstantiation. Even the Lutherans believe in some kind of physical presence of the body of Christ in the Lord's supper. Should we not distance ourselves from such teaching by insisting that the Lord's supper is merely a symbol with no presence of Christ whatsoever?

That is the view commonly called Zwinglianism, which is advocated by many Evangelicals. For them, any idea of the presence of Christ in the Lord's supper sounds suspiciously like Roman Catholicism. The Reformed—especially John Calvin—resisted the temptation to overreact and taught that Christ's body and blood are really present in the Lord's supper.

In other words, the Lord's supper is not only a sign, but also a seal. A seal is a guarantee of the authenticity of something. It is, as Article 33 explained, a pledge "of the good will and grace of God toward us." If this is the case, the Lord's supper must be more than a mere symbol, a pious remembrance of the death of Christ. To be a seal, the Lord's supper must actually impart Christ to us; we must really partake of him; we must feed upon him; we must have real fellowship with him. And these things are only possible if Christ is really present to feed and nourish us with his own body and blood as he promised. We want to do full justice to the words of the apostle Paul: "The cup of blessing which we bless, is it not the communion of the blood of Christ? The bread which we break, is it not the communion of the body of Christ?" (1 Cor. 10:16). Communion means sharing or partaking!

About this matter, Article 35 is emphatic. It speaks of "the true body and blood of Christ" and even "the proper and natural body and the proper blood of Christ." It insists that Christ has not given us the sacrament "in vain." It reminds us that "he works in us all that he represents to us by these holy signs." This, says the Confession, is "certain and beyond all doubt."

When the Bible says that the bread is the body of Christ, and the wine is the blood of Christ, it speaks sacramentally. It speaks of one in terms of the other, or it speaks of the sign in terms of the thing signified. This is because of the close connection between the two. Thus we read in the Belgic Confession those typical sacramental phrases: "As certainly as we receive and hold this sacrament in our hands…we also do as certainly receive by faith…the true body and blood of Christ our only Savior in our souls, for the support of our spiritual life." We do not doubt that by eating earthly bread, our earthly life is nourished; so we must not doubt that by feeding on Jesus Christ (which we do by a believing partaking of the Lord's supper), our heavenly and spiritual life is nourished.

And, by eating and drinking, we have real communion with our Lord Jesus Christ.

Martyn McGeown

December 14 — The Spiritual Presence of Christ

Whom the heaven must receive until the times of restitution of all things. —Acts 3:21

It is a common misconception that Roman Catholics believe in the real presence of Christ in the Lord's supper and that the Reformed do not. In fact, the Reformed emphatically and vigorously defend the real presence of Christ in the Lord's supper. Consider what Article 35 says: "we err not when we say that what is eaten and drunk by us is the proper and natural body and the proper blood of Christ."

By "proper and natural," we do not mean the physical body and blood of Christ. That is impossible. First, Christ's body and blood, being real human flesh and blood, belong to a real human nature and cannot be in more than one place at once. Certainly, it cannot be at the right hand of God in heaven and also on communion tables in thousands of churches across the world. The real human nature of Christ has the properties of a real human nature. Christ's body, albeit glorified, is not and cannot be omnipresent, or fill heaven and earth. Second, Christ's spatially-limited human nature—with his flesh and blood—is at the right hand of God in heaven. "Christ always sits at the right hand of his Father in the heavens," asserts Article 35. Since that is the location of the body of Christ, it is not on earth.

But this does not mean that Christ is absent when we partake of the Lord's supper. We do partake of him! If we do not partake of him, the Lord's supper cannot be a means of grace to us, and it cannot strengthen and nourish our souls. Christ has to be present in a way which nourishes our souls. Let us imagine, for the sake of argument, that Christ's physical body and blood were present in the supper. What good would that do our souls? Eating flesh and drinking blood, even the flesh and blood of Christ, cannot nourish the soul any more than eating bread and drinking wine can nourish the soul. The eating and drinking of Christ, and therefore the presence of Christ in the Lord's supper, must be spiritual.

At this point, we should allow the careful and modest language of Article 35 to make an impression upon us: "the manner surpasses our understanding, and cannot be comprehended by us, as the operations of the Holy Spirit are hidden and incomprehensible." Can we understand how Christ, who is at God's right hand, makes us "partakers of himself"? Can we fathom how Christ, without physically leaving Heaven, "communicates himself with all his benefits to us"?

To help us understand, and to assure us that it is so, Christ has given us the Lord's supper. We receive the earthly bread as a sign and seal of the heavenly bread, and by receiving the heavenly bread, we are spiritually nourished by Christ, who is spiritually present in the Lord's supper—really present, to feed not our bodies, but our souls!

Martyn McGeown

December 15   Faith, the Hand and Mouth of the Soul

I am the bread of life: he that cometh to me shall never hunger;
and he that believeth on me shall never thirst. —John 6:35

We have seen that in the Lord's supper, Christ is really—spiritually but not physically—present. This is the only way in which the presence of Christ in the Lord's supper could be of benefit to us. If we could eat and drink the physical body and blood of Christ, and we cannot, our souls would not be nourished, and the Lord's supper would be some kind of grotesque cannibalism!

This raises the question—how can our souls eat?

We know how we eat physically. Food is placed before us, and we use our hands or cutlery (knives, forks, and spoons) to put the food into our mouths. But what about our souls? We cannot use our hands or cutlery to put food into our souls. We cannot even take the piece of bread and the cup of wine given to us by the minister in the Lord's supper and place those into our souls. How, then, do we eat spiritually?

Article 35 contains a beautiful answer. We receive Christ by faith, which is "the hand and mouth of our soul." The soul has a hand and mouth by which it partakes of spiritual food—the hand and mouth of faith! Thus, Article 35 underlines this truth: Jesus Christ "nourishes and strengthens the spiritual life of believers when they eat him, that is to say, when they apply and receive him by faith in the Spirit;" "we…receive by faith…the true body and blood of Christ our only Savior in our souls;" "the manner of our partaking of the same is not by the mouth, but by the spirit through faith;" Christ does not "cease to make us partakers of himself by faith."

This, of course, means two things. First, unbelievers do not partake of Christ or feed on him when they sinfully partake of the Lord's supper. An unbeliever is like a man coming to a table laden with good food but who has no hand and no mouth. He cannot feed on Christ. He has no desire to feed on Christ. His soul is without a mouth and a hand! Second, even believers can fail to partake of Christ because they do not come in faith. Again, the figure of faith as the hand and mouth of the soul is helpful. A man could conceivably come to a table laden with good food but refuse to stretch out his hand or open his mouth. Such a man does have a hand and a mouth, but he refuses to use them. He starves! Proverbs 26:15 comes to mind: "The slothful hideth his hand in his bosom; it grieveth him to bring it again to his mouth."

Three things we believe as we come open-mouthed to the supper. First, we believe that we are great sinners, and we are sorry for and humbly confess our sins. Second, we believe that the sacrifice of Jesus Christ on the cross has satisfied the justice of God against our sins, and we trust only in that sacrifice of Christ for our salvation. Third, we resolve to live a new and godly life. In coming to the Lord's supper, we desire our faith to be strengthened.

Thus, we must hear the exhortation: "Open thy mouth wide, and I will fill it" (Ps. 81:10). Come to the preaching and to the sacrament with the hand and mouth of your soul wide open to receive the good things of Jesus Christ. Come, partake of Christ, by faith.

Martyn McGeown

December 16 — Examine Yourself...Then Come

But let a man examine himself, and so let him eat of that bread, and drink of that cup. —1 Corinthians 11:28

Christ calls his people to come to the Lord's table. The holy sacrament is for sinners who are saved by grace, sorry for their sins, and heartily thankful for salvation. The desire of such believing sinners who come to the Lord's supper exercising faith—which is the hand and mouth of the soul—is to be spiritually fed, nourished, and strengthened.

Because the sacrament is holy, those who come to this spiritual feast must come in the proper manner. The bread and wine are holy, not because of any change in their substance, but because by the Spirit they have been separated from common food and drink to be holy symbols of the crucified body and shed blood of Jesus Christ. Those who are too young to understand this, or those who are carnal and unbelieving and who do not consider this, risk eating and drinking judgment to themselves, "not discerning the Lord's body" (1 Cor. 11:29).

Therefore, God demands self-examination of those who would partake of the Lord's supper. We must understand this self-examination because many are confused by it. We do not examine ourselves in order to ask ourselves the question: "Am I a true child of God?" We examine ourselves, already believing that we are true children of God, with these questions: "Am I living as a child of God? Am I walking in the faith of Christ?" By this I mean: "Is there a sinful way in which I am walking?" If so, we ask the Lord to reveal that way to us, so that we might confess our sins and repent of them. We do not torment ourselves with these kinds of questions: "Am I sorry enough for my sins? Is my life holy enough? Is my experience of conversion deep enough? Should I wait until I am holier?" The apostle does not write, "Let a man examine himself, and then let him stay away," but "so let him eat of that bread, and drink of that cup" (1 Cor. 11:28). The Form for the Administration of the Lord's Supper includes this beautiful statement: "But this is not designed (dearly beloved brethren and sisters in the Lord) to deject the contrite hearts of the faithful, as if none might come to the supper of the Lord but those who are without sin."* The Lord's supper is for sinners with weak faith, with a small beginning of the new obedience, for those who hunger and thirst after righteousness.

The Lord's supper, however, is not for unbelievers. An unbeliever cannot piously remember the death of the Lord Jesus on the cross. By his unbelief and other sins he tramples Christ underfoot. Shall he then take the holy signs and seals of Christ's body and blood, when by his life he shows utter contempt for everything Christ did on the cross? God forbid!

The Lord's supper is a fellowship meal. Christ is the gracious host. We are his forgiven friends, and we sit at his table in humility and reverence, marveling that we—who do not even deserve the crumbs under the table—may sit and feast with him and on him by faith!

Martyn McGeown

---

* Form for the Administration of the Lord's Supper, in *The Psalter*, 92.

December 17

Nourishing, Strengthening, Comforting, Quickening, Refreshing Our Poor Comfortless Souls

Blessed are they which do hunger and thirst after righteousness: for they shall be filled. —Matthew 5:6

The Lord's supper is a feast. The table of the Lord is laden with good things. The call goes out to God's believing, penitent people: "Come, hungry and thirsty souls, and be spiritually nourished! Come, empty souls, and be spiritually filled! Come, weary and burdened souls, and be spiritually refreshed! Come, dejected and afflicted souls, and be spiritually comforted!"

We do this, of course, when we come to Jesus Christ himself by faith, as he is set forth in the preaching of the gospel. The preaching (not the sacraments, remember) is the chief means of grace. But we also do this when we come believingly to partake of the Lord's supper—as Article 35 puts it, with "the hand and mouth of our soul" (faith) wide open.

Christ is pleased to give us his crucified body and shed blood in a spiritual manner in the Lord's supper. He is able to make us partake of him, although his physical body and blood are in heaven. Some have objected to the Reformed view because they cannot conceive of how we can eat the flesh and drink the blood of Christ if he remains in heaven and we on earth. But, distance does not prevent Christ imparting his body and blood to his children. Why? Because the exalted Lord Jesus is vitally connected to his body (and to every member) by the Holy Spirit. Thus, all of the benefits of Christ flow to us from Christ. By embracing Christ by faith, we partake of his goodness, just as the branches partake of the sap of the vine, and all parts of the body are supplied by the head (John 15:5; Eph. 4:16; Col. 2:19, etc.).

In moving language, Article 35 describes the spiritual blessings we receive when we partake believingly of the Lord's supper. We do not leave the table empty!

We come with "our poor comfortless souls." In this world of sin and death, we have no source of comfort or life. We are sinners who struggle with the flesh, the devil, and the world, and that struggle makes us weary. We see ourselves in this description of "poor" and "comfortless." But, in the Lord's supper, the Lord Jesus Christ himself comforts, strengthens, nourishes, quickens, and refreshes us. He does that because the Lord's supper, like the preaching and like baptism, directs us to one place: the cross. If any doctrine of the Lord's supper points us anywhere else—to our works—it is of no benefit to us, and it is a dangerous and wicked deception, one of the man-made "mixtures and damnable inventions" against which Article 35 warns.

The Lord's supper reminds us and assures us that as surely as we receive with a believing heart the bread and wine, so surely did Christ give himself on the cross for the salvation of our souls. As the Form for the Administration puts it: "as often as ye eat of this bread and drink of this cup, you shall thereby, as by a sure remembrance and pledge, be admonished and assured of this my hearty love and faithfulness towards you."*

And by bringing us again to the cross where we find all our salvation, in the Lord's supper the Lord Jesus is "nourishing, strengthening, and comforting" and "quickening and refreshing" our poor comfortless souls by making us feed on him, the Living Bread!

Martyn McGeown

---

* Form for the Administration of the Lord's Supper, in *The Psalter*, 93.

Article 36

OF MAGISTRATES

We believe that our gracious God, because of the depravity of mankind, hath appointed kings, princes, and magistrates, willing that the world should be governed by certain laws and policies; to the end that the dissoluteness of men might be restrained, and all things carried on among them with good order and decency. For this purpose he hath invested the magistracy with the sword, *for the punishment of evil doers, and for the praise of them that do well*. And their office is, not only to have regard unto and watch for the welfare of the civil state, but also that they protect the sacred ministry, and thus may remove and prevent all idolatry and false worship;* that the kingdom of antichrist may be thus destroyed, and the kingdom of Christ promoted. They must, therefore, countenance the preaching of the word of the gospel every where, that God may be honored and worshiped by every one, as he commands in his Word.

Moreover, it is the bounden duty of every one, of what state, quality, or condition soever he may be, to subject himself to the magistrates; to pay tribute, to show due honor and respect to them, and to obey them in all things which are not repugnant to the Word of God; to supplicate for them in their prayers, that God may rule and guide them in all their ways, and that we may lead a quiet and peaceable life in all godliness and honesty.

Wherefore we detest the error of the Anabaptists and other seditious people, and in general all those who reject the higher powers and magistrates, and would subvert justice, introduce a community of goods, and confound that decency and good order which God hath established among men.

---

* This phrase, touching the office of the magistracy in its relation to the Church, proceeds on the principle of the Established Church, which was first applied by Constantine and afterwards also in many Protestant countries. History, however, does not support the principle of State domination over the Church, but rather the separation of Church and State. Moreover, it is contrary to the New Dispensation that authority be vested in the State to arbitrarily reform the Church, and to deny the Church the right of independently conducting its own affairs as a distinct territory alongside the State. The New Testament does not subject the Christian Church to the authority of the State that it should be governed and extended by political measures, but to our Lord and King only as an independent territory alongside and altogether independent of the State, that it may be governed and edified by its officebearers and with spiritual weapons only. Practically all Reformed churches have repudiated the idea of the Established Church, and are advocating the autonomy of the churches and personal liberty of conscience in matters pertaining to the service of God.

"The Christian Reformed Church in America, being in full accord with this view, feels constrained to declare that it does not conceive of the office of the magistracy in this sense, that it be in duty bound to also exercise political authority in the sphere of religion, by establishing and maintaining a State Church, advancing and supporting the same as the only true Church, and to oppose, to persecute and to destroy by means of the sword all the other churches as being false religions; and to also declare that it does positively hold that, within its own secular sphere, the magistracy has a divine duty towards the first table of the Law as well as towards the second; and furthermore that both State and Church as institutions of God and Christ have mutual rights and duties appointed them from on high, and therefore have a very sacred reciprocal obligation to meet through the Holy Spirit, who proceeds from the Father and Son. They may not, however, encroach upon each other's territory. The Church has rights of sovereignty in its own sphere as well as the State" (Acts of Synod, 1910).

December 18 — Magistrates Appointed Because of Man's Depravity

But if thou do that which is evil, be afraid;
for he beareth not the sword in vain. —Romans 13:4

Article 36 deals with the subject of the civil magistrate or the state. This subject is immensely practical for all Christians because all of us live as citizens under an earthly government of one kind or another. The Bible has a lot to say on the role of the civil government and even more to say on the Christian's obligation to government. God is a God of order, and he has ordained authorities in various spheres: the family, the church, and the civil government.

This article begins by explaining the reason—indeed, the necessity—of civil government. There are, and always have been, anarchists who desire to overthrow all civil government. They desire liberty from all forms of human government because they fear tyranny. Nevertheless, the Bible does not support an absolutely libertarian view of government. In fact, the Bible does not even mandate what form government should take—whether absolute dictatorship, totalitarian and despotic states, kingdoms, empires, or the various forms of democracy known to many of us today. Democracy, as such, was unheard of in the days in which the Bible was written. In the Old Testament, there was either the theocratic state of Israel—God was king in Israel, and he ruled through his officebearers the kings, especially the Davidic kings—or various forms of tyrannical government, such as Pharaoh's Egypt, Nebuchadnezzar's Babylon, or Cyrus' Persia. In the New Testament era, the dominant form of government was the Roman Empire. Believers in the Old and New Testaments recognized and honored the leaders placed over them. Paul summarizes this in Romans 13:1, "The powers that be [that is, the powers that exist] are ordained of God."

The reason God has ordained government ("kings, princes, and magistrates," as Article 36 explains it) is "because of the depravity of mankind" and "to the end that the dissoluteness of men might be restrained." Dissoluteness is unbridled wickedness. The French word used in the original version of the Belgic Confession means *overflowing*, the idea being that man's sin will flow unchecked without civil government.

Those who advocate the overthrow of government (such as the Anabaptists) often have a poor understanding of sin. Without civil government, man's sin will not be restrained. Imagine how many more murders, thefts, and other crimes there would be if there were no police force, if there were no prisons, and if—in some cases—there were no penalties inflicted upon offenders! A corrupt government is better than civil unrest and anarchy. But we must not make the mistake of thinking that civil government restrains man in such a way that he becomes better morally. Civil government does not improve man—he is still totally depraved. Civil government restrains a man the way a muzzle restrains a violent dog.

"Our gracious God…hath appointed kings" (Article 36). He has done so for the good of his church, which is called to live in the midst of a sinful world. This, too, is part of his care for us.

Martyn McGeown

December 19 — The Sword Power of the Magistracy

For the punishment of evildoers,
and for the praise of them that do well.
—1 Peter 2:14

There are many theories about the role of the state. Political opinions vary between the left and the right, between totalitarianism and limited government. Some men favor capitalism, and others socialism or even communism. The Bible does not contain detailed instructions on the role of the government. In fact, the government really has one function, and this can be summed up in one short phrase: sword power.

God "hath invested the magistracy with the sword," says Article 36, following Paul's instruction in Romans 13. "He [the civil power] beareth not the sword in vain: for he is the minister of God, a revenger to execute wrath upon him that doeth evil" (v. 4). The sword in Scripture is symbolic of the power and authority to coerce, force, and punish the wicked, and to promote virtue in society, so that the wickedness of man might be restrained and good order maintained. Modern governments do not use the steel sword. They use a well-trained army with modern weaponry, a police force with various government agencies, a justice department, and a network of prisons. Some still inflict the death penalty, but death by beheading by the sword is extremely rare. Modern governments also concern themselves with other aspects of the lives of their citizens—education, employment, social welfare, finance, etc.—but these are not the state's function according to Scripture.

We noticed in Articles 30–32 that the church does not have sword power. She has much greater power—the power to open and close the kingdom of heaven with the keys, the power of spiritual weapons, and the power of the sword of the Spirit (Matt. 16:18; 18:18–19; 2 Cor. 10:3–5; Eph. 6:17). In fact, the church may not use the sword. The magistrate, however, whose kingdom is not spiritual, must use the sword. God wills it! The magistrate who allows criminals to escape unpunished and the magistrate who punishes the innocent will be judged by God.

How must we view the power of the sword? First, we must not envy it. The church has a greater spiritual power than the magistrate could ever dream about! Second, we must fear it. Writing to Christians, Paul warns: "If thou do that which is evil, be afraid" (Rom. 13:4). Christians are not exempt from arrest, prosecution, and punishment if—and may God graciously forbid—they transgress the civil law. Peter, again writing to Christians, warns: "But let none of you suffer as a murderer, or as a thief, or an evildoer" (1 Pet. 4:15). A Christian who commits a crime will go to prison, let's say, even if he is repentant and is forgiven by the church. Third, we must be thankful for it. Let us be thankful that God has ordained that there be prisons for thieves who might break in and steal our property, that there is the death penalty for murderers, rapists, and other violent offenders, and so on. Let us be thankful for the police, the judges, and the soldiers, whose job is to protect us and to maintain law and order.

No government is perfect. Many governments are overly intrusive, rapacious in their taxation, or wasteful in their spending of taxpayers' money. Many governments are tyrannical—increasingly so, as the end approaches—and corrupt, failing to punish the wicked and refusing to reward the good. That was the case in Paul's day also. Paul wrote Romans 13 in the context of the Caesars of Rome, hardly a power friendly to the Christian church!

But for all that, Paul wrote: "The powers that be [whether a Roman Emperor such as Nero or the president, prime minister, or king of your country] are ordained of God. Whosoever therefore resisteth the power, resisteth the ordinance of God" (Rom. 13:1–2).

Martyn McGeown

December 20 — **The Relationship Between Church and State**

*The church of the living God, the pillar
and ground of the truth.* —1 Timothy 3:15

Article 36 is the only one with an explanatory footnote. This is because the Reformed churches have debated the relationship between the church and state and have concluded that the Belgic Confession—while reflecting what the Reformers believed and taught—is not in line with Scripture and needs to be corrected. No church may take the revision of her creeds lightly, but at the same time, no creed is infallible.

The article in its original form mandated the magistrate to promote the true church and to suppress heresy with the power of the sword. That this was the prevalent view throughout the Middle Ages and in Reformation days, no scholar denies. The Reformers, especially Calvin, as well as the Roman Catholics, believed that the magistrate had the role to enforce the law of God. A Latin phrase, *cuius regio eius religio*, sums up the principle. It means, "Whose the realm, his the religion." In Europe, there were Reformed areas, Lutheran areas, and Roman Catholic areas, and this could change with a change of leadership. In England, for example, the rule swung from Protestant to Roman Catholic and back to Protestant again, depending on who occupied the throne. There were also varying degrees of religious freedom, as well as examples of intolerance and persecution. In some European countries, even today, there are established churches officially recognized by the state. This recognition comes at a high price—interference by the state into the affairs of the church. Often, the state would determine the officebearers of the church, call or forbid ecclesiastical assemblies, determine worship practices, and pay for the upkeep of property and the salaries of ministers. He who pays the piper calls the tune!

The Reformers, who argued that the role of the magistracy was to "protect the sacred ministry and thus [to] remove and prevent all idolatry and false worship" (Article 36), appealed to the Old Testament examples of godly, reformatory kings such as Josiah and Hezekiah. These men put idolaters to death, purged the temple, and promoted the worship of the true God. However, upon reflection, we have come to understand that this appeal was mistaken. The Old Testament Israel was a state religion, but in the New Testament, the church (and not the state) is the spiritual, "holy nation" of God (1 Pet. 2:9) without an earthly king. Christ's "kingdom is not of this world"—it is not a political power (John 18:36). It is wholly separate and distinct from the civil state.

The civil government has neither the calling nor the competency to "remove and prevent all idolatry and false worship" (Article 36). How could the civil government determine what is true and false worship? And besides this, the civil government does not have the calling to enforce the ten commandments of God's law. The law of God is not an external moral code, but it is "holy, and just, and good" (Rom. 7:12), a law which governs the sinner's heart. The civil magistrate can punish murderers, but can it mandate love for the neighbor from the heart? The civil government can punish theft, but can it forbid and punish envy, discontent, and covetousness?

We—with the footnote to our beloved Belgic Confession—reject the establishment principle and teach a separation of church and state. The state must promote true religion only in this sense: the state must preserve order so that the church can worship in peace, and the state must not persecute or interfere with the true church as she does her work of preaching the gospel. When the state oversteps her bounds, the state sins. But the church does not rebel: she suffers patiently, waiting for the coming of her Lord.

Martyn McGeown

December 21 — Our Duty to Submit to Magistrates

Put them in mind to be subject to principalities and powers, to obey magistrates. —Titus 3:1

The calling of the Christian with respect to the civil government is to submit. Submission is the deliberate, conscious placing of oneself under the authority of another. Submission is not exactly the same as obedience, although in most instances, a submissive person is also an obedient person.

A submissive Christian recognizes several truths.

First, he understands that God is sovereign and that God in his providence has given power to rulers. This is the case whether the person occupying the office—whether king, queen, judge, police officer, president, prime minister, senator, congressman, etc.—is good or evil, a believer or an unbeliever. God's word is clear: "the powers that be [and not the powers as we would like them to be, or as they are according to some idealistic, political ideology] are ordained of God" (Rom. 13:1). This truth is taught everywhere. To despotic King Nebuchadnezzar, Daniel declares: "Thou, O king, art a king of kings: for the God of heaven hath given thee a kingdom, power, and strength, and glory" (Dan. 2:37). Later, he adds: "The most High ruleth in the kingdom of men, and giveth it to whomsoever he will, and setteth up over it the basest of men" (Dan. 4:17). The same is true in the New Testament: God ordained that Nero be emperor when Paul was writing the book of Romans. God ordained your civil leaders, whether you like them or not. And a righteous civil ruler is rare in this world.

Second, the Christian understands the fifth commandment. He interprets this commandment in a comprehensive way: it includes the command to obey parents, the civil magistrate, one's employer, and ecclesiastical officebearers. Peter writes: "Submit yourselves to every ordinance of man for the Lord's sake; whether it be to the king, as supreme; or unto governors, as unto them that are sent by him" (1 Pet. 2:13–14). We "obey [our] parents in the Lord" (Eph. 6:1), we obey our masters "as to the Lord" (Col. 3:22–23), and we submit to rulers "for the Lord's sake" (1 Pet. 2:14).

Third, the Christian understands that this requirement is valid even when the leaders are ungodly, as they often are. A Christian wife's submission is not conditional on her husband's love for her; a Christian employee's submission is not conditional on his employer's equitable treatment of him; and a Christian citizen's submission is not conditional on the government's righteous treatment of him or on the government's establishment of godly laws and ordinances (1 Pet. 2:18; 3:1). The calling of the government is "not [to be] a terror to good works, but to the evil" (Rom. 13:3), but its legitimacy does not depend on its doing this.

Some Christians object that we are not required to submit to an unjust government, but this objection does not fit with Scripture. If we are not required to pay taxes to, obey the laws of, and recognize the legitimacy of a wicked government today, how could the apostles have required these things of Christians in their day (see Rom. 13:6–7; 1 Pet. 2:13–15)?

Our calling is clear—and difficult for the flesh. We must submit to the government, obey her laws, pay our taxes, and suffer wrong, if that becomes necessary. If we have legitimate avenues of appeal, we may use them, but in all things, we must be loyal, obedient citizens, and indeed, the best citizens, of the nation in which we sojourn.

All to the glory of God.

Martyn McGeown

December 22 — We Must Obey Except...

We ought to obey God rather than men. —Acts 5:29

Earlier, we underlined the truth that the Christian must submit to the government, no matter what kind, and even when the government fails to do God's calling to punish evildoers and reward the good. However, this does not mean that the Christian obeys the government at all times.

Submission is to place oneself under the authority of another. Obedience is to do what a superior says. Even when a Christian may not in good conscience obey, he must be submissive. We might say that he must disobey submissively. A wonderful example of this is found in Daniel's three friends. Notice how they address the king—respectfully, politely, humbly, and submissively: "O, Nebuchadnezzar, we are not careful to answer thee in this matter…be it known unto thee, O king, that we will not serve thy gods" (Dan. 3:16, 18). But for all that, they disobey. Paul is respectful and submissive to authorities, even to authorities which mistreat him (Acts 21:37; 23:5; 24:10; 26:2, 25). We must, therefore, not speak evil of our leaders, slander them, make fun of them, or teach our children to disrespect them.

Nevertheless, we do not obey our leaders when they command us to disobey God. Then, we follow the principle of Acts 5:29, "We ought to obey God rather than men." Those occasions where we are called to disobey God are rare. Is it disobedience to God to pay taxes to a government that uses those taxes to fund immoral practices? No. We are called to pay our taxes (Rom. 13:7). Did Rome's taxes not fund her military, her oppression of the people of God, her gladiatorial shows, her idolatry, and the emperor's excesses? Paul did not exempt Christians from paying taxes for those reasons. Is it disobedience to God to curb one's speed on the highway or to comply with the multiplicity of regulations imposed by politicians today? No. Peter says we must "submit [ourselves] to every ordinance of man for the Lord's sake" (1 Pet. 2:13). You might find man's ordinances illogical, foolish, and inconvenient, but unless obeying man means disobeying God, you must obey. An example given in Acts is when the apostles, who were commanded to preach Christ Jesus, were told not to do so by the Sanhedrin. The apostles rightly answered that they must obey God rather than men. But in everything else, the apostles obeyed the laws of the magistrates as submissive citizens of the state.

In modern democracies, of course, the Christian has more options. The Christian can criticize the government. John the Baptist did this. The Christian can appeal to or petition the government to change its laws for the better. The Christian can even run for public office—this is an avenue open to the individual believer, although politics are not the calling of the church institute.

But what the Christian may never do is to rebel against the government. That is sin.

Martyn McGeown

December 23 — Detesting the Sedition of the Anabaptists

They that resist shall receive to themselves damnation.
—Romans 13:2

The Belgic Confession was written against the backdrop of severe persecution of the Reformed churches by the civil magistrate, Philip II of Spain, who at that time ruled the Netherlands. This violent persecution occurred at the behest of the Roman Catholic Church, which viewed the Reformed as heretics to be exterminated. But despite the injustice of the state, the Reformed did not advocate rebellion. In fact, in church history, when the Reformed rebelled, the end has always been disastrous.

Part of the justification which the Roman Catholics gave for the persecution of the Reformed was that they were seditious. This was slander. There were seditious persons at the time of the Reformation. There were men and women who sought to overthrow rightful, God-ordained authority. There were men and women who rejected civil magistrates and who said that the church must establish a godly kingdom on earth by overturning existing rulers. These were the Anabaptists. Their teachings are condemned more than once in the Belgic Confession. The most radical Anabaptist leader was Thomas Müntzer, who was put to death in 1525 for his part in the Peasants' Revolt. Not all Anabaptists were radical. Some, like Menno Simons, were strict pacifists. The Belgic Confession was written to distance the Reformed from the Anabaptists. The authorities found it convenient to lump all heretics together, but this was unjust. In 1562, a copy of the Belgic Confession was sent to Philip II. In it, the Reformed declared themselves ready to obey the government in all lawful things, although they would "offer their backs to stripes, their tongues to knives, their mouths to gags, and their whole bodies to fire, rather than deny the truth of God's word."* Thousands of godly, Reformed Christians were put to death by the authorities, a fate they patiently endured for the sake of Christ.

Godly Christians throughout history have been loyal citizens, ready and willing to submit to God-ordained authority. It has been the radicals and the fanatics who have sought to overthrow law and order. "We detest the Anabaptists," declares Article 36, "and other seditious people, and in general all those who reject the higher powers and magistrates." Jesus gives this principle: "Put up again thy sword into his place: for all they that take the sword shall perish with the sword" (Matt. 26:52). He that takes up arms against the government will perish, and deservedly so. "They that resist shall receive to themselves damnation" (Rom. 13:2). Consider the Jewish zealots of the first century AD. They were fanatical Jews who sought to overthrow the Roman oppressor by force. One of Jesus' disciples had been a zealot (Luke 6:15; Acts 1:13), and Barabbas and the thieves crucified with Jesus were undoubtedly zealots (Luke 23:18–19, 32–33, 40–41). The Roman government was illegitimate in its views, its laws were ungodly, its taxes were unfair and oppressive, it did not reward the good and punish the evil. But none of that justified rebellion.

The calling of the Christian is to suffer patiently when he is unjustly treated. No Christian or instituted church may ever rebel against the government. All such rebellion is sin.

Martyn McGeown

---

* Quoted in Schaff, *Creeds of Christendom*, 1:505.

December 24 — Praying for Civil Rulers

I exhort therefore, that, first of all, supplications, prayers, intercessions and giving of thanks, be made for all men; for kings, and for all that are in authority. —1 Timothy 2:1–2

How often do you pray for the civil magistrate? Do you pray for the government as much or as often as you complain about it? Do you imagine that praying for the government would be a waste of your time? Perhaps those thoughts crossed Timothy's mind when he received Paul's epistle. In 1 Timothy 2, Paul begins to give instruction on public worship and "how [Timothy ought] to behave [himself] in the house of God, which is the church of the living God" (3:15). The first thing Paul mentions is the need to pray for all men. The context shows us that Paul does not mean all men head for head—how could anyone ever do that?—but all kinds of men. Timothy might imagine that it would be fitting to pray for old and young, rich and poor, male and female. But then Paul adds "for kings, and for all that are in authority" (2:2).

Does that surprise you? It may have surprised Timothy. Pray for "kings"—for men like Herod and Nero—and for "all that are in authority"—for men like Felix, Festus, and Pilate! Perhaps you can think of rulers today you would rather not mention in your prayers—unscrupulous politicians, corrupt judges, arrogant and ungodly men and women. Perhaps the church in Ephesus could think of persecutors of the church by name. Should we pray for them? Jesus commanded: "Pray for them which despitefully use you, and persecute you" (Matt. 5:44).

Article 36 reminds us of this calling, too: "It is the bounden duty of every one…to supplicate for them in their prayers, that God may rule and guide them."

Scripture gives several reasons for this. First, God will answer our prayers in such a way that "we may lead a quiet and peaceable life in all godliness and honesty" (1 Tim. 2:2). God guides civil rulers so that the right atmosphere will prevail in which the church can worship and live as Christians. If anarchy prevails in society, public worship becomes impossible, and the work of the church in preaching the gospel is greatly hindered. Second, God wills that we pray for civil rulers—as part of the "all men" of 1 Timothy 2:1—because God wills the salvation of all men, and he has sent Christ to be a ransom for all men. This does not mean that God desires the salvation of every human person without exception. The context demands that "all men" in verses one, four, and six be understood as "all kinds of men." This is also how the words are used in everyday speech. If I greet a group of people with, "Good evening, all" nobody understands it to mean that I am greeting anyone except the immediate group to whom I am speaking. If I say to that group, "Everyone needs to be finished by 3 o'clock," it is obvious that I have a specific number of "ones" in mind. The extent of "all" must always be determined by the context.

God wills even the salvation of some kings and other civil rulers. Although "not many mighty, not many noble, are called" (1 Cor. 1:26), God is pleased to save some such. Remember Elector Frederick, who commissioned the Heidelberg Catechism, or King Edward VI of England, who was called the English Josiah by his grateful subjects, or, of course, the godly kings in the Old Testament (David, Josiah, Hezekiah, etc.).

Let us then pray for and be thankful for our civil rulers, under whose hand our gracious God is pleased to govern us.

Martyn McGeown

Article 37

OF THE LAST JUDGMENT

Finally, we believe, according to the Word of God, when the time appointed by the Lord (which is unknown to all creatures) is come, and the number of the elect complete, that our Lord Jesus Christ will come from heaven, corporally and visibly, as he ascended with great glory and majesty, to declare himself Judge of the quick and the dead, burning this old world with fire and flame to cleanse it. And then all men will personally appear before this great Judge, both men and women and children, that have been from the beginning of the world to the end thereof, being summoned by the voice of the archangel, and by the sound of the trumpet of God. For all the dead shall be raised out of the earth, and their souls joined and united with their proper bodies in which they formerly lived. As for those who shall then be living, they shall not die as the others, but be changed in the twinkling of an eye, and from corruptible become incorruptible.

Then the books (that is to say, the consciences) shall be opened, and the dead judged according to what they shall have done in this world, whether it be good or evil. Nay, all men shall give an account of every idle word they have spoken, which the world only counts amusement and jest; and then the secrets and hypocrisy of men shall be disclosed and laid open before all.

And, therefore, the consideration of this judgment is justly terrible and dreadful to the wicked and ungodly, but most desirable and comfortable to the righteous and the elect; because then their full deliverance shall be perfected, and there they shall receive the fruits of their labor and trouble which they have borne. Their innocence shall be known to all, and they shall see the terrible vengeance which God shall execute on the wicked, who most cruelly persecuted, oppressed, and tormented them in this world; and who shall be convicted by the testimony of their own consciences, and, being immortal, shall be tormented in that everlasting fire which is prepared for the devil and his angels.

But on the contrary, the faithful and elect shall be crowned with glory and honor; and the Son of God will confess their names before God his Father, and his elect angels; all tears shall be wiped from their eyes; and theii cause, which is now condemned by many judges and magistrates as heretical and impious, will then be known to be the cause of the Son of God. And, for a gracious reward, the Lord will cause them to possess such a glory as never entered into the heart of man to conceive.

Therefore we expect that great day with a most ardent desire, to the end that we may fully enjoy the promises of God in Christ Jesus our Lord. Amen.

"Even so, come, Lord Jesus." —Revelation 22:20

December 25 — **The Time Appointed by the Lord**

For a thousand years in thy sight are but as yesterday when it is past, and as a watch in the night. —Psalm 90:4

In our day, men and women are interested in eschatology, or the doctrine of the last things. Surprisingly, the Belgic Confession devotes only one article—the last—to this subject. This is because, apart from the error of purgatory, there was little difference among the Reformed, Lutherans, and Roman Catholics on the last things. There was also very little doctrinal development in the area of eschatology.

The Apostles' Creed was concise: "From thence he [Christ] shall come to judge the quick [living] and the dead." All of Christendom believed in a future, personal, visible, glorious coming of Jesus Christ to resurrect and then judge all the living and the dead. However, we shall see why on one hand, the Reformed derived great comfort from the coming of Christ as judge, whereas on the other, the medieval Roman Catholics were terrified by the prospect. What a comfort the gospel is! What a difference the gospel makes!

Although the Belgic Confession devotes only one article to the second coming, what it teaches us is significant and beautiful. The Reformed understand the second coming of Christ as the glorious day which will bring history and all of God's purposes with this present creation to a close. Just as history and creation had a beginning in God's counsel, so they have a determined ending. That ending is known only to God, and its exact moment is hidden from all creatures—even from Christ himself according to his limited human soul (Mark 13:32). If the Son of God himself according to the flesh did not know, we can be sure that God has not revealed that day to any creature—not even foolish doomsday preachers such as Harold Camping!

It must be of great comfort to us as we see the unfolding of history around us—a history which is often chaotic, confused, and frightening—that the future is not in the hands of men and nations, or even in the hands of the devil. The future is in the hands of God. "Known unto God are all his works from the foundation of the world" (Acts 15:18). Therefore, history can neither end one moment before God has determined nor continue one moment longer than he has planned. Article 37 calls this "the time appointed by the Lord."

We might wonder why history must last so long. Why has the church had to wait for some two thousand years since the ascension of Christ? Peter answered that question in his second epistle. Scoffers arise who question this: "Where is the promise of his coming?" (2 Pet 3:4). The answer is that God "is longsuffering to us-ward, not willing that any should perish, but that all should come to repentance" (v. 9). This does not mean that God desires the salvation of all humans. That would not give a reason for the seeming delay in Christ's return. It does not mean that God is giving as many as possible a chance to be saved. It means that God is longsuffering (which "is salvation," v. 15) to us (not to everyone, but to us) because he is not willing that any (of us) should perish, but that all (of us) should come to repentance.

In other words, Christ shall come when "the number of the elect [is] complete" (Article 37).

Will you be among that number? If you are a believer, you must know that you will be.

Martyn McGeown

December 26 — Christ's One Future Visible Coming

*For the Lord himself shall descend from heaven
with a shout, with the voice of the archangel,
and with the trump of God.* —1 Thessalonians 4:16

According to Article 37, "our Lord Jesus Christ will come from heaven, corporally and visibly, as he ascended, with great glory and majesty." It is important to remember that the Reformed do not accept the teaching of premillennial dispensationalism that the Lord will come twice in the future, once secretly in a rapture and then later visibly in a revelation. These meditations are not the place to examine premillennial dispensationalism in any detail, but we should contrast briefly what Article 37 says over against this popular doctrine.

Those who believe in the doctrine of the rapture often appeal to 1 Thessalonians 4. They believe that at any moment the Lord will secretly snatch away all faithful Christians from the earth. This will cause great consternation because suddenly millions of people will disappear without trace! After the rapture, history will continue, and God will pour out his wrath upon the world of those left behind—unbelievers and unfaithful Christians. After seven years of awful tribulation (mostly for the nation of Israel), Christ shall return visibly and destroy his enemies to set up an earthly kingdom for one thousand years in Jerusalem. After the period of one thousand years is complete, the Lord will crush one final rebellion of Satan. History will then end with Christ's judgment of the wicked.

Article 37 contradicts that scheme in several ways. First, when Christ returns, the wicked will be oppressing the church—there is no indication that the church will have been removed from the earth. Second, "all the dead" shall be resurrected and "all men will personally appear before this great Judge" on the same day—there is no indication that the resurrection of the wicked and the just (and their judgments) will be separated by a number of years. Third, the one, future, visible coming will be "with great glory and majesty"—there is no indication that he will come secretly.

1 Thessalonians teaches the very opposite of a secret, silent, invisible coming of Christ to take away his church. On the contrary, Christ shall descend "with a shout, with the voice of the archangel, and with the trump of God"—an event so loud that it shall summon the dead to judgment (4:16)! Moreover, when Paul writes that "the dead in Christ shall rise first" (v. 16), he does not mean they shall rise some one thousand years before the wicked, but that the dead in Christ shall rise before those who are alive at Christ's coming. Paul's concern was to comfort the Thessalonians concerning their dead, believing relatives—would they miss out since they had died before the second coming? Absolutely not!

The hope of the saints is not that they be snatched away secretly, but that they—whether dead or alive at his coming—partake in his glory which is publicly to be revealed.

Is that your hope?

Martyn McGeown

December 27 — Christ Coming with Great Glory and Majesty

And they shall see the Son of man coming in the clouds of heaven with power and great glory. —Matthew 24:30

The most glorious and awe-inspiring day of history is in the future. It will be the last day, the culmination of all things, the bringing to an end of the purpose of God with this present creation. It will be the second coming of our Lord Jesus Christ.

Article 37 speaks of Christ coming "with great glory and majesty, to declare himself Judge." Many passages of Scripture describe that day, both as a warning for the wicked and as a comfort for the godly. Let us examine some of the aspects of that day.

First, Christ himself shall come personally. Christ comes in other senses in Scriptures—he comes to the believer at death to take him to himself, and he came at Pentecost in the outpouring of the Spirit—but the second coming will be a personal coming. 1 Thessalonians 4:16 says: "the Lord himself shall descend from heaven." Article 37 uses the word *corporally*, which means *bodily*.

Second, Christ's coming will be visible—not an invisible rapture, not a mystical, spiritual coming, but a coming which all men shall see. "All the tribes of the earth...shall see the Son of man coming" (Matt. 24:30). "Every eye shall see him" (Rev. 1:7). This means that the Lord Jesus Christ—who presently is at God's right hand in heaven and whom no mortal eye can see—will suddenly be revealed for who he is. Heaven will be opened, and he shall come forth, and everything which veils him from our view shall be removed. Christ describes his coming in terms of lightning flashing across the sky. None will be able to miss it or to ignore it. "For as the lightning cometh out of the east, and shineth even unto the west; so shall also the coming of the Son of man be" (Matt. 24:27).

Third, Christ's coming will be audible. He will not come sneaking on tiptoe into this world, but with "a shout" (1 Thess. 4:16) and "with a great sound of a trumpet" (Matt. 24:31). Article 37 speaks of all men, women, and children "being summoned by the voice of the archangel, and by the sound of the trumpet of God." A trumpet makes a long, sharp, loud blast which no one can miss. The trumpet was God's instrument for gathering his people to attention—Christ's trumpet will arrest the attention of all mankind. This is the final call of God to all men: stand to attention, my Son is here. Look up, church, and see your salvation; look up, wicked, and behold your doom!

Fourth, Christ will come with great glory and with the trappings of deity. "They shall see the Son of man coming in the clouds of heaven with power and great glory" (Matt. 24:30). These clouds are not fluffy, white clouds on a cool summer's day. These clouds are thick, dark, awesome, billowing thunderclouds. In the Bible, Jehovah rides on the clouds (Ps. 104:3)—so does Christ!

That awesome day will be the end of the world. "The sun [shall] be darkened, and the moon shall not give her light" (Matt. 24:29). "The heavens shall pass away with a great noise, and the elements shall melt with fervent heat, the earth also and the works that are therein shall be burned up" (2 Pet. 3:10).

But we who believe in Jesus Christ and who watch for his coming will rejoice in that day. For us, it will be the beginning of something unutterably wonderful.

Martyn McGeown

December 28 — All the Dead Shall Be Raised out of the Earth

Marvel not at this: for the hour is coming in which all that are in the graves shall hear his voice. —John 5:28

The coming of Christ is connected to three main events. Article 37 describes them. First, "all the dead shall be raised out of the earth." Second, "the books…shall be opened, and the dead judged." Third, Christ shall "[burn] this old world with fire and flame to cleanse it."

When we die, our souls are separated from our bodies. The souls of believers ascend into heaven into the presence of Christ, while the souls of the wicked descend into hell to be punished (Luke 16:22–24). The bodies of believers and unbelievers alike decay and perish, returning to the dust from which God made them. The Bible speaks of Christians sleeping in Jesus because, although they enjoy conscious fellowship in the soul with Christ after death, their bodies sleep in the ground until the day of their resurrection. This separation of body and soul at death is temporary—and those who are alive at the second coming will not experience such a separation because they will not experience physical death. It is God's promise to us that we will be saved both in soul and body. Therefore, our bodies must also be resurrected and partake of the glory of Christ. "We look for the Saviour, the Lord Jesus Christ: who shall change our vile body, that it may be fashioned like unto his glorious body, according as he is able even to subdue all things unto himself" (Phil. 3:20–21).

Article 37, reflecting Scripture's teaching, explains this marvelous truth: "For all the dead shall be raised out of the earth, and their souls joined and united with their proper bodies in which they formerly lived. As for those who shall then be living, they shall not die as the others, but be changed in the twinkling of an eye."

Several aspects of this truth are highlighted by our Confession here. First, there is a certain continuity between the body we have now and the one we will have in the resurrection. It is the same body ("proper bodies in which they formerly lived"). Christ will not make us brand-new bodies which in no way resemble our human bodies. This is necessary because of the justice and mercy of God. It would be unjust for God to punish another man's tongue for one man's swearing, another man's hand for stealing, another man's eye for lusting; and it would not be a gracious reward to reward another man's tongue for praising and another man's hand for ministering to the saints. This is also necessary for redemption—Christ redeemed me (body and soul). Therefore, I will have my body on the last day! Second, there is a radical difference between our bodies as they are now and our bodies as they shall be. Quoting from 1 Corinthians 15:51–52, Article 37 reminds us that we shall "be changed in the twinkling of an eye." Perhaps you do not like your body, but the main reason we should be (in a holy manner) dissatisfied with our present body is that we cannot serve God as we want. These bodies—even the healthiest and most beautiful specimens—are affected by sin. In our renewed resurrection bodies, we will be able to serve God in a higher, freer, and better way than ever before.

Paul uses a beautiful figure of the sowing of a seed (1 Cor. 15:37, 42–44). When you plant an apple seed, you do not expect it to remain an apple seed, but at the same time, you do not expect a thorn bush! You expect an apple tree—more glorious than an apple seed, but essentially the same.

Thus shall our resurrection bodies be: bodies glorified, fitted for heaven!

Martyn McGeown

December 29 — And the Dead Shall Be Judged

And the dead were judged out of those things which were written in the books, according to their works. —Revelation 20:12

One of the reasons for the resurrection of the dead is that they will be summoned to judgment. Christ will not judge disembodied souls, but all men, women, and children will be judged in their bodies. This is fitting because human beings consist of body and soul, and because human beings commit good or bad deeds in the body as well as in the soul.

This is a summons that no man will be able to ignore. Perhaps when a bailiff comes with the summons from an earthly judge, a man might be able to flee, escape, or pretend not to be at home, but the power of Christ will draw every man, woman, and child who has ever lived to his judgment seat. Revelation 20 describes the awesome scene: "And the sea gave up the dead which were in it; and death and hell delivered up the dead which were in them: and they were judged every man according to their works" (v. 13). Revelation 6 describes the terrified cries of the wicked when they see the judge coming: they "hid themselves in the dens and in the rocks of the mountains; and said to the mountains and rocks, Fall on us, and hide us from the face of him that sitteth on the throne, and from the wrath of the Lamb: for the great day of his wrath is come; and who shall be able to stand?" (vv. 15–17).

Scripture makes clear that the final judgment will be a glorious occasion for Christ. He will be the judge! In the courtroom, the judge has a certain august presence. He is addressed with "Your Honor." To Christ, the triune God has committed all judgment. What glory, honor, and majesty for Christ! Those who once judged him will themselves be judged. Those who escaped judgment in this world and whose crimes were never uncovered will face a far more strict and exacting—and yet, perfectly righteous—judgment at Christ's judgment seat. Matthew 25:31–32 describes the scene: "When the Son of man shall come in his glory, and all the holy angels with him, then shall he sit upon the throne of his glory: and before him shall be gathered all nations." Paul speaks of that day "when the Lord Jesus shall be revealed from heaven with his mighty angels, in flaming fire taking vengeance…when he shall come to be glorified in his saints, and to be admired in all them that believe" (2 Thess. 1:7–8, 10).

The judgment of mankind will happen on one day—the wicked and the righteous together. It will be a public judgment, so that everyone shall see the outcome and justice will not only be done, but will be seen to be done with respect to all men. Article 37 underlines the public nature of the judgment in these words: "All men shall give an account of every idle word they have spoken, which the world only counts amusement and jest; and then the secrets and hypocrisy of men shall be disclosed and laid open before all."

There are many aspects of the judgment day that remain unknown. How will God make known all the works performed by all men? The Bible says that the "books shall be opened"—which Article 37 interprets as "consciences." How is it possible to judge every man who has ever lived in the space of one day? How long will that take? These things might cause unbelievers to mock the idea of a judgment, but we believe what is written.

Judgment is coming—is the Judge also your Savior?

Martyn McGeown

December 30 — Justly Terrible and Dreadful to the Wicked

Then shall all the tribes of the earth mourn,
and they shall see the Son of man coming in the clouds of heaven
with power and great glory. —Matthew 24:30

A guilty man fears the judge. A criminal fears the police who come to arrest him on the order of the judge. The guilty naturally flee from judgment because they know that they will be punished for their crimes. If that is true with earthly judges who have the power to cast into prison or even to put a criminal to death, how much more is it true with respect to the judge of all men, Jesus Christ? The day of judgment, the last day of human history, will be a day of unspeakable horror for all the wicked.

Consider the wicked who will be alive at that day. One moment they will be living carelessly, foolishly, and in disobedience to God; the next moment they will look up, see, and hear the coming of Jesus Christ—the coming of the one in whom they have not believed, whose word and gospel they have spurned; the one whom they have disobeyed, mocked, and blasphemed, and have hated. Jesus says that when he comes, the people shall mourn (Matt. 24:30). That word does not mean that the wicked shall repent—the wicked are too stubbornly wedded to sin to repent—but that they shall wail inconsolably with great and intense anguish. The word *mourn* means *to beat upon one's breast*. Despair will fill their souls because they will know that there is no escape from the one they hated! Naked they will stand in their sins before Christ, trembling to hear the awful verdict that shall send them away into everlasting punishment.

The Belgic Confession, written during severe persecution, describes the punishment of the wicked. God's people "shall see the terrible vengeance which God shall execute on the wicked, who most cruelly persecuted, oppressed, and tormented them in this world." Later, Article 37 speaks of Christianity "which is now condemned by many judges and magistrates as heretical and impious." Imagine the consternation of a man like Nero (d. AD 62), the Emperor of Rome, who crucified, burned alive, and tortured Christians, when he stands before Christ to be judged. Imagine the wailing of a man like the Duke of Alva (d. AD 1582), who persecuted the Dutch believers at the time of the writing of the Belgic Confession, when Christ summons him to give account for his wickedness. Imagine the anguish of Mary I of England (dubbed "Bloody Mary," d. AD 1558), under whose reign many Reformed believers were burned at the stake, when she must answer for her crimes. Or consider some of the wicked persecutors of the Old Testament: Antiochus Epiphanes IV (d. 164 BC) or Nebuchadnezzar (d. 562 BC). All these—and many others whose persecution of the church is less well-known—will have to stand before Christ to be judged. For them, there will be no escape.

And the day of judgment will be only the beginning of a misery that will last forever. Article 37 describes it: "[they] shall be convicted by the testimony of their own consciences, and, being immortal, shall be tormented in that everlasting fire which is prepared for the devil and his angels" (see also Matt. 25:46).

There is only one way to avoid this awful, eternal punishment—in Jesus Christ, and him alone. Are you found in Jesus Christ by faith, clothed in his righteousness? Then rejoice. This doom will not be yours. Are you unbelieving and impenitent? Flee from the wrath to come, to Jesus the only savior!

Martyn McGeown

December 31 — Expecting That Day with a Most Ardent Desire

Come, ye blessed of my Father, inherit the kingdom prepared for you from the foundation of the world. —Matthew 25:34

The day of judgment sometimes troubles believers. Will we really be judged as well as the wicked? Should that not make us fear the day of judgment—will that not make that day less desirable for us?

These fears are based on a misconception that judgment is not the same as condemnation. The wicked shall be judged with a view to their public condemnation. We will be judged as well, but with a view to our public acquittal and justification. The Bible makes it clear that both the elect and reprobate, the righteous and wicked, shall be present in the judgment. In Matthew 25, Christ has all nations stand before him, and he separates them as a shepherd separates the sheep from the goats. In Romans 14:10–11, 2 Corinthians 5:10, and Revelation 20:12, we learn that all shall stand before the judgment seat. But there is a world of difference between a man who stands before a judge as guilty and a man who stands before a judge as acquitted!

Moreover, our sins—even our most secret—will be exposed on the day of judgment, as well as all of the deeds we performed that were unrewarded and unnoticed by men. This must not frighten us either, because we will not experience guilt, shame, or embarrassment before the judgment seat of our savior. This aspect of the judgment is necessary for two reasons. First, the whole world must see how unworthy we are of salvation, so that our God is seen to be the gracious God who freely forgives. Second, we must see how terrible our sins are, so that we understand with unmistakable clarity that our salvation is all of grace, and so that we praise God for his mercy. Besides, our sins will be displayed as forgiven sins, sins not held against us, sins not imputed to us, sins for which Christ has made atonement, and sins which he has washed in his own blood. What a surprise this will be to the wicked: that Christian whom they mocked for refusing to join in their sins, that Christian whom they condemned as heretical and impious, will be declared innocent. And what a joy it will be for us, who will hear the verdict from the Judge: "This one is my son, my daughter. I have loved him; I have loved her. See, my righteousness covers his sins, her iniquities." The Belgic Confession describes that day thus: "Their full deliverance shall be perfected, and there they shall receive the fruits of their labor and trouble which they have borne. Their innocence shall be known to all…the faithful and elect shall be crowned with glory and honor, and the Son of God will confess their names before God his Father and his elect angels" (Article 37).

No wonder, therefore, that the Belgic Confession encourages us to look forward to that day—the day of our public acquittal, the day of our glorification, the day of the fullness of our salvation! No wonder Paul calls it "that blessed hope and the glorious appearing of the great God" (Tit. 2:13). That day, says our Confession, is "most desirable and comfortable to the righteous and elect" and "we expect that great day with a most ardent desire."

Does your soul burn in passion within you? Will you look forward to your vacations and not to that great day? Come, Lord Jesus, yea, come quickly!

Martyn McGeown

I Belong
Heidelberg Catechism Question and Answer One for Children
by Joyce Holstege

It's comforting to belong to God because you know he will care for you. The Bible tells you that when you pass through the deep waters and when you walk through the fire, God will be with you.

I Belong is a picture book for ages four to seven that explains each comforting phrase of Heidelberg Catechism Question and Answer 1 to young children, in language that they understand. Colorful illustrations of a diverse group of children will capture readers' imaginations as they learn what it means to belong to their faithful Savior.

This book can be used as a short book of devotions for families with younger children or can be read by older children on their own.

Reformed Spirituality set
Peace for the Trouble Heart, Communion with God, All Glory to the Only Good God
by Herman Hoeksema

These poetic, experiential, and sound meditations are for every believer who desires to be edified and encouraged along the Christian pilgrimage with all its trials and triumphs. Though deep, Hoeksema's writing is clear and the chapters are short, which makes these books ideal devotional material.

I Believe
Sermons on the Apostles' Creed
by Herman Hoeksema

"As God's people we embrace the teachings of the Apostles' Creed. We embrace these teachings because we believe them. However, we believers can easily fall into the practice of treating the Creed as only a simple statement, a statement which we do not think about too deeply. We do not seek to understand the depths of its riches. Consequently, we do not grow in our faith. This fine volume on the Apostles' Creed, replete with many Scripture references, will cause our faith and understanding of biblical truth to grow."

—Rev. Jerome Julien,
emeritus minister in the United Reformed Churches in North America

All books available at **rfpa.org**,
or by calling the Reformed Free Publishing Association
at **616-457-5970** or emailing **mail@rfpa.org**.

Our Mission

To glorify God by making accessible to the broadest possible audience material that testifies to the truth of Scripture as understood and developed in the Reformed tradition.

Reformed Free Publishing Association
1894 Georgetown Center Drive
Jenison, MI 49428-7137
Website: rfpa.org
E-mail: mail@rfpa.org
Phone: 616-457-5970

www.ingramcontent.com/pod-product-compliance
Lightning Source LLC
Chambersburg PA
CBHW052230230426
43666CB00035B/2597